Beginning
ActionScript 2.0

C0-ATU-099

Beginning
ActionScript 2.0

Nathan Derksen and Jeff Berg

WILEY

Wiley Publishing, Inc.

Beginning ActionScript 2.0

Published by
Wiley Publishing, Inc.
10475 Crosspoint Boulevard
Indianapolis, IN 46256
www.wiley.com

Copyright © 2006 by Wiley Publishing, Inc., Indianapolis, Indiana

Published simultaneously in Canada

ISBN-13: 978-0-7645-7768-0
ISBN-10: 0-7645-7768-9

Manufactured in the United States of America

10 9 8 7 6 5 4 3 2 1

1MA/QT/QU/QW/IN

Library of Congress Cataloging-in-Publication Data:
Derksen, Nathan, 1974-
  Beginning ActionScript 2.0 / Nathan Derksen and Jeff Berg.
      p. cm.
  "Wiley Technology Publishing."
  Includes index.
  ISBN-13: 978-0-7645-7768-0 (paper/website)
  ISBN-10: 0-7645-7768-9 (paper/website)
  1. Computer animation. 2. Flash (Computer file) 3. Web sites--Design. 4. ActionScript (Computer program language) I.
Berg, Jeff, 1975- II. Title.
  TR897.7.D493 2006
  006.6'96 — dc22

No part of this publication may be reproduced, stored in a retrieval system or transmitted in any form or by any means,
electronic, mechanical, photocopying, recording, scanning or otherwise, except as permitted under Sections 107 or 108 of
the 1976 United States Copyright Act, without either the prior written permission of the Publisher, or authorization
through payment of the appropriate per-copy fee to the Copyright Clearance Center, 222 Rosewood Drive, Danvers, MA
01923, (978) 750-8400, fax (978) 646-8600. Requests to the Publisher for permission should be addressed to the Legal
Department, Wiley Publishing, Inc., 10475 Crosspoint Blvd., Indianapolis, IN 46256, (317) 572-3447, fax (317) 572-4355, or
online at http://www.wiley.com/go/permissions.

LIMIT OF LIABILITY/DISCLAIMER OF WARRANTY: THE PUBLISHER AND THE AUTHOR MAKE NO REPRESEN-
TATIONS OR WARRANTIES WITH RESPECT TO THE ACCURACY OR COMPLETENESS OF THE CONTENTS OF
THIS WORK AND SPECIFICALLY DISCLAIM ALL WARRANTIES, INCLUDING WITHOUT LIMITATION WAR-
RANTIES OF FITNESS FOR A PARTICULAR PURPOSE. NO WARRANTY MAY BE CREATED OR EXTENDED BY
SALES OR PROMOTIONAL MATERIALS. THE ADVICE AND STRATEGIES CONTAINED HEREIN MAY NOT BE
SUITABLE FOR EVERY SITUATION. THIS WORK IS SOLD WITH THE UNDERSTANDING THAT THE PUBLISHER IS
NOT ENGAGED IN RENDERING LEGAL, ACCOUNTING, OR OTHER PROFESSIONAL SERVICES. IF PROFES-
SIONAL ASSISTANCE IS REQUIRED, THE SERVICES OF A COMPETENT PROFESSIONAL PERSON SHOULD BE
SOUGHT. NEITHER THE PUBLISHER NOR THE AUTHOR SHALL BE LIABLE FOR DAMAGES ARISING HERE-
FROM. THE FACT THAT AN ORGANIZATION OR WEBSITE IS REFERRED TO IN THIS WORK AS A CITATION
AND/OR A POTENTIAL SOURCE OF FURTHER INFORMATION DOES NOT MEAN THAT THE AUTHOR OR THE
PUBLISHER ENDORSES THE INFORMATION THE ORGANIZATION OR WEBSITE MAY PROVIDE OR RECOM-
MENDATIONS IT MAY MAKE. FURTHER, READERS SHOULD BE AWARE THAT INTERNET WEBSITES LISTED IN
THIS WORK MAY HAVE CHANGED OR DISAPPEARED BETWEEN WHEN THIS WORK WAS WRITTEN AND
WHEN IT IS READ.

For general information on our other products and services please contact our Customer Care Department within the
United States at (800) 762-2974, outside the United States at (317) 572-3993 or fax (317) 572-4002.

Trademarks: Wiley, the Wiley logo, Wrox, the Wrox logo, Programmer to Programmer, and related trade dress are trademarks or registered trademarks of John Wiley & Sons, Inc. and/or its affiliates, in the United States and other countries,
and may not be used without written permission. Macromedia Flash 8 copyright © 1995-2003. Macromedia, Inc., 600
Townsend Street, San Francisco, CA 94103 USA. All Rights Reserved. Macromedia Flash are trademarks or registered
trademarks of Macromedia, Inc. in the United States and/or other countries. All other trademarks are the property of their
respective owners. Wiley Publishing, Inc., is not associated with any product or vendor mentioned in this book.

Wiley also publishes its books in a variety of electronic formats. Some content that appears in print may not be available
in electronic books.

About the Authors

Nathan Derksen

Nathan Derksen is a Web media architect working in IBM's Global Services division. Nathan has more than 6 years of experience with IBM, and 9 years' experience in the field of Web development. Mr. Derksen was the technical editor for the book *Animation and Effects with Macromedia Flash MX 2004* (Jen DeHaan, Macromedia Press), and is a moderator on the Macromedia Flash forum at www.flash8forums.com. Nathan can be reached through his personal site at www.nathanderksen.com.

Jeff Berg

Jeff Berg is a patent-winning digital media designer and Flash developer. He leads the development of user interfaces for rich Internet applications. Jeff leverages a fine arts degree to approach interface design and programming with problem-solving creativity. His user-centric approach includes self-imposed standards for user experience, usability, and information design. Jeff's visual background provides a unique position to work on projects with visual design concerns while maintaining concepts of design patterns and object-oriented programming. Jeff currently is focusing on museum and public space projects utilizing pervasive devices in handheld kiosk solutions. He lives in Chicago with his wife Kara and children Cary and Evie. Jeff maintains a web site at www.memoryprojector.com.

For the love of my life, Renée.
For my parents and my brother.
For my dear grandpa, Otto.

—*Nathan Derksen*

To my wife Kara, my son Cary, and my daughter Evie.
Thank you.

—*Jeff Berg*

Credits

Executive Editor
Chris Webb

Development Editors
Kelly Henthorne
Maryann Steinhart

Technical Editor
Sean Christmann

Production Editor
Pamela Hanley

Copy Editor
Kim Cofer

Editorial Manager
Mary Beth Wakefield

Production Manager
Tim Tate

Vice President and Executive Group Publisher
Richard Swadley

Vice President and Publisher
Joseph B. Wikert

Project Coordinator
Ryan Steffen

Graphics and Production Specialists
Denny Hager
Jennifer Heleine
Alicia B. South

Quality Control Technician
Laura Albert

Media Development Project Supervisor
Shannon Walters

Media Development Specialist
Angela Denny

Media Development Coordinator
Laura Atkinson

Proofreading and Indexing
Techbooks

Acknowledgments

There are too many people to count who have given me support and well wishes as I have worked away on this book. I would first like to acknowledge my parents for their constant love and support. They have helped to make me who I am. They also inspired me to pursue computing science as a career, for which I am eternally grateful. I would also like to acknowledge my fiancée, Renée. She has been supremely caring, supportive, and patient, has given me encouragement when I needed it. Through her actions she has been brought even closer to me than I could have imagined.

I would also like to acknowledge Jen DeHaan (`www.deseloper.com`), who gave me the generous gift of the opportunity to write this book, as well as providing me with a forum to help the Flash developer community. I am very grateful for her generosity. I am also grateful for the whole support team at Wiley, including my editor, Maryann Steinhart, for her tireless efforts to make this book happen, and my technical editor, Sean Christmann, who helped me with many valuable suggestions for improvements throughout the book.

There is no way I could undertake the effort of writing this book on my own. A big thank-you goes to Jeff Berg, who took on the daunting task of writing half of this book. He has been a great person to work with, both with the book and at IBM: Jeff has always been available to bounce ideas off of, is very creative with his solutions, and loves playing with the technology. He has also been a support on a personal level and a friend.

Thank you to Greg Charbonneau for making the time to take my photo for the cover. It was through the camera I initially bought from him that I earnestly started photography as a hobby. Thank you to all my friends and co-workers who regularly asked me about my book, and to my manager Elvyna who supported my writing efforts. Finally, thank you also for all those in the Flash Lounge who have been my champions, and who have been chomping at the bit to get an autographed copy of the book. At last it is ready!

—Nathan Derksen

I want to thank my co-author, Nathan Derksen, for his support and guidance. Nathan, your attitude, knowledge, and dedication are an inspiration. Also wish to thank Jack Blanchard. Jack, you taught me what an `if` statement was so many years ago, and you continue to guide me to new discoveries.

I could not have completed this project without the patient support of my wife Kara, the inspiration from my son Cary, and joy from my daughter Evie.

—Jeff Berg

Contents

Contents

Contents

Contents

Contents

Contents

Contents

Contents

Contents

Contents

Contents

Contents

Contents

Introduction

Macromedia Flash began as a vector animation tool, designed to help put a bit more punch into otherwise motionless web pages. At the time, web pages were simple and data-driven sites were few, so animation was one way to differentiate your pages from the rest of the crowd. Many people still hold the perception that Flash is only a tool for animation, in part due to the preponderance of Flash-based site intros and a very visible presence in banner and pop-up ads. While it remains a very good tool for animation, it has grown into a powerful means to do much more.

Macromedia Flash is a full-fledged application development environment. The real focus on using Flash for coding came with version 6, which introduced a new coding and event model leading to a cleaner, more flexible coding style. That version was the first major step in giving the developer power to create many interesting and useful applications. Flash 7 added a major scripting update, resulting in ActionScript 2.0. It provides a more structured, flexible, and maintainable programming style. Finally, Macromedia Flash 8 has expanded the offering, adding bitmap support, filters, and blending modes, file upload and download capabilities, an interface for communicating with the browser, and much more. All of the add-ons can be manipulated with script, not just with visual tools within the development environment.

The mature capabilities of Macromedia Flash 8 have the potential to redefine user interactions and usability on the Web. Flash enables you to develop full-fledged applications that either run in a web browser or run standalone as an executable.

Regardless of whether you are just interested in dabbling with scripting, or you want to develop applications with thousands of lines of code, ActionScript is for you. Want to build a major e-business application, to create a personal portfolio, to create a game, or to work with media? This book will help you out. If you've done any work with any other scripting language such as JavaScript or programming language such as Java or Perl, you are already halfway there. Even if you've never touched a line of code, you still can learn to apply ActionScript to Macromedia Flash projects through the many examples shown in the successful Wrox "Try It Out" format.

Who This Book Is For

The Macromedia Flash development environment is useful for a wide range of tasks, from creating marketing pieces, to creating a personal portfolio, to creating enterprise-level e-commerce applications, to creating games. As such, the diverse group of people who use it have different backgrounds, different mixes of technical and artistic skills, and different goals. This book assumes no prior programming or Macromedia Flash development experience. If you do have basic knowledge of ActionScript, there is plenty of content about how to work with different aspects of Macromedia Flash with script. This book includes techniques for animating using only code, working with audio, video, and graphics, interacting with the user, communicating with a server, and much more. This book also includes a primer on object-oriented programming, and the last chapter shows you how to create your own custom classes, a very valuable skill to acquire.

Regardless of what you want to get out of Macromedia Flash, this book is a good starting point to get you to where you want to go.

How This Book Is Structured

Beginning ActionScript 2.0 teaches by example, using small, well-chosen programming examples, presented in the Wrox trademark "Try It Out" format. By typing each example, running it, and examining the results, you gain experience with the entire process of coding, running, and debugging Macromedia Flash projects. Experience has shown that a hands-on approach is one of the most effective ways to learn. In addition to the code samples, each example provides you with detailed descriptions of exactly what the code does, and why it was done that particular way. Where appropriate, the example overview also talks about some of the implications of developing code in that particular way, and with a mind toward other ways of performing the same task.

Here's a breakdown of what this book provides:

In Chapter 1, you learn the aspects of the development environment, including how to create, work with, and publish a Macromedia Flash project. You create your first scripted project, put it in an HTML wrapper, and make your project viewable on the Web.

Chapters 2–4 take you right into the guts of the language. You learn all the aspects of ActionScript, including variables, data types, conditionals, loops, events, and errors. By the time you get through these chapters, you will have a good understanding of how to use the core aspects of the language.

Chapters 5 and 6 get you up and running with ActionScript, explaining such things as where to place your code and how to structure your Macromedia Flash project. You learn simple coding conventions that will help you create projects that are easier to read and to update. You see different ways to structure your project, learn the benefits and issues with each, and find out about some techniques that will help you through the debugging process.

In Chapters 7 and 8, you start using ActionScript to work with a core Macromedia Flash technology: components. You find out all about components—how to apply them to your project, have them communicate with each other, and customize their look on-the-fly through component styles. When you've finished these chapters, you'll be well on your way to building form-based applications.

Chapters 9–11 show you how to work with the core container: the movie clip. You explore how to create blank movie clips and how to draw in them on-the-fly, how to work with movie clips in the library, and how to load external movie clips. You learn how to change variables and content in one movie clip from another and how to implement a movie pre-loader. You also study different ways to structure movie clips within a project. After you have completed this chapter, you will have a good understanding of many aspects the Macromedia Flash core building block.

Chapter 12 teaches you some techniques for debugging code. You learn some of the methodology that makes debugging less of a hit-or-miss scenario, how to use the debugger, and how to use the output panel to get a better sense of what is going on with your code.

Chapters 13–15 teach you how to work with drawing and to apply effects with ActionScript. You learn how to use the drawing API, how to apply filters and blending modes, and how to work with the new Bitmap class to manipulate individual pixels.

You extend your knowledge of the movie clip in Chapters 16 and 17. You learn the concepts of time-based and frame-based animation, and how to animate with ActionScript. That knowledge is extended by adding basic physics to your animations, and is topped off by using the Tween class to simplify some types of animations. After finishing these chapters, you'll know how to create scripted animations.

In Chapter 18, you learn the intricacies of working with text, including the different types of text fields, issues related to embedding fonts into your project, and how to apply visual styles to text. Because text handling is one of the largest sources of problems with new Macromedia Flash developers, this chapter is replete with annotated examples illustrating how to deal with this subject.

Chapters 19 and 20 show you how to integrate images, sound, video, and live camera feeds into your project. You learn to work with features such as loading, streaming, and embedding media. Through this chapter, you get a good grasp of the various media management issues, and learn ways to deal with issues specific to working with different media types.

Chapters 21 and 22 explain how to get your project to pass data between the web browser and a server. You learn the details of communicating with a server using a number of different communication techniques, including LoadVars and XML. Security issues are reviewed and solutions are presented for dealing with many of those issues.

Chapters 23–25 provide techniques for communication between a movie and the browser, and between separate movies. You learn to use new classes for communicating between the browser and the Macromedia Flash plug-in, for starting up movies on-the-fly with JavaScript, and for saving information long-term on the user's computer. Cross-platform communication issues are addressed, so you can ensure that your project will work in different browsers on different platforms.

Chapter 26 examines the capabilities and limitations of working with the user's operating system. You learn to retrieve information about the user's operating environment through the System object. You learn to launch programs, open windows, and make your own system calls from a standalone projector. You also see examples of using third-party tools to greatly expand the capabilities of the projector. Basically, this chapter teaches you how to interact with the operating system from within the Macromedia Flash plug-in.

Chapter 27 shows you how to create custom ActionScript classes, how to think in a more object-oriented way, and some techniques for working with your own classes.

Each chapter ends with exercises for you to work on your own, and Appendix A provides solutions to those exercises.

What You Need to Use This Book

This book targets Flash 8, but because ActionScript 2.0 made its debut in Macromedia Flash MX 2004 and because the language has not substantially changed in Flash 8, much of this book is also relevant to those using Macromedia Flash MX 2004. A few features require Flash 8, and that's noted as they're used. You can use either Macromedia Flash MX 2004 or Flash 8 development environments, although this book assumes that you are using the professional version. You can download a fully functioning 30-day demo of Flash 8 from www.macromedia.com/downloads. Flash player version 7 does exist for Linux, although version 8 is not yet available for Linux. Macromedia does not provide a Linux development environment. As a result, you need to use either at least Mac OS X 10.3 or at least Windows 2000 to run the Flash development environment.

Although the script editor in the Flash development environment is quite suitable, you may want to use a separate text editor, preferably one that supports syntax highlighting for ActionScript 2.0. Chapter 1 offers a number of suggestions for text editors that you may want to use.

Conventions

To help you get the most from the text, a number of conventions are used throughout the book.

Asides to the current discussion are offset and placed in italics like this.

Information of importance outside of the regular text looks like this.

As for styles used in the text:

❑   Important words are *highlighted* when introduced.

❑   Keyboard combination strokes are presented like this: Ctrl+A.

❑   Filenames, URLs, and code within the text appears in a special monofont typeface, like this: `System.capabilities`.

Code blocks and examples appear in two different ways:

```
In code examples, new code has a gray background.
```

```
The gray background is not used for code that is less important in the present
context or that has been shown before.
```

And in some instances, parts of a code example may be boldface to make it easier for you to spot a change from earlier code.

Occasionally a code line won't fit on one line in the book. In those instances, a code continuation character (`@@ta`) at the end of a line indicates that the next line is actually a continuation of it.

Source Code

As you work through the examples in this book, you can choose either to type in all the code manually, or use the source code files that accompany this book. All of the source code used in this book is available for download at `www.wrox.com`. Once at the site, simply locate the book's title (either by using the Search box or by using one of the title lists) and click the Download Code link on the book's detail page to obtain all the source code for the book.

Because many books have similar titles, you may find it easiest to search by ISBN; for this book, the ISBN is 0-7645-7768-9.

After you download the code, just decompress it with your favorite decompression tool.

Errata

Every effort is made to ensure that there are no errors in the text or in the code. However, no one is perfect and mistakes do occur. If you find an error in one of our books, like a spelling mistake or a faulty piece of code, we would be very grateful for your feedback. By sending in errata you may save another reader hours of frustration; at the same time, you are helping us provide higher quality information.

To find the errata page for this book, go to www.wrox.com, and locate the title using the Search box or one of the title lists. Then, on the Book Search Results page, click the Errata link in the About This Book bar. On this page, you can view all errata that has been submitted for this book and posted by Wrox editors. If you don't spot "your" error on the book's Errata page, click the Errata Form link and complete the form there to send us the error you have found. We'll check the information and, if appropriate, post a message to the book's errata page and fix the problem in subsequent editions of the book.

Getting Started with Macromedia Flash

Flash is a term used to refer to both the vector-based animation format (Flash movies) as well as the authoring tool that is commonly used to create the aforementioned content. Flash Player is the program that is capable of playing back Flash content. ActionScript is the scripting language that is encoded into Flash content and interpreted by Flash Player when that content is played back. You can use the Flash authoring tool to add ActionScript code to Flash content. As such, it's particularly useful to learn how to use the Flash authoring tool for that purpose as a first step when learning about ActionScript. In this chapter you learn about how to work with the Flash authoring tool for the purposes of writing ActionScript.

Introducing the Development Environment

Flash utilizes a panel system to organize specific functionalities available within the program. The panels can be docked and undocked as well as moved outside of the application area. This enables you to efficiently use and customize your working environment. You can find panels and layout options in the Window menu in the main navigation. Many of the descriptions in this chapter assume that you are working with the default panel layout. For example, when a panel is described as appearing in the upper left of the workspace, it means that the panel appears in that location in the default layout. You can open the default layout by selecting Window⇨Workspace Layout⇨Default.

By default, Flash 8 opens to a start page (see Figure 1-1) that enables you to launch projects quickly. You can specify whether Flash should display the start page. If you click the Don't Show Again checkbox at the bottom of the start page, it will not display by default. You can always edit the start page preferences from the Preferences dialog (Edit⇨Preferences) by selecting the appropriate option from the On launch menu.

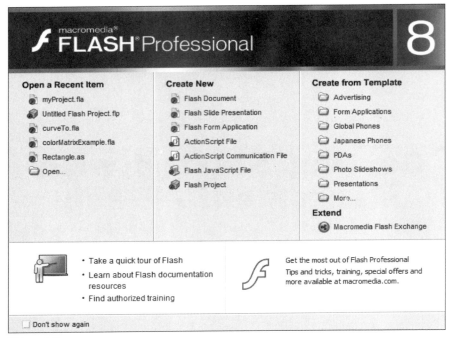

Figure 1-1

The following sections briefly explore other features of the Flash authoring program, which is frequently called the Flash IDE (Integrated Development Environment).

Tools Panel

On the left of the IDE is the Tools panel (see Figure 1-2), which contains the drawing tools that enable you to add vector content and edit existing vector content. This is where you select drawing tools, set tool attributes, and specify drawing tool options. The drawing tool attributes are expanded in the Properties panel, which is often called the Property inspector. This panel can be found at the bottom of the IDE. If you cannot see it, select Window⇨Properties⇨Properties.

Properties Panel

The Properties panel (also shown in Figure 1-2) presents the options for the item in focus on the stage or the selected tool. It is clearly contextual in that it changes depending on what object is selected (or if no objects are selected) or what tool is selected. For example, if you have nothing selected on the stage and choose the Selection tool, the Properties panel enables you to adjust document-wide settings such as stage dimensions and frame rate. However, if you select the Line tool, you'll see that the Properties panel enables you to adjust the settings for the Line tool such as line thickness and style. If you use the Selection tool to select a line on the stage, you are presented with the same set of options as when using the Line tool. But when you change the properties for a selected line, the line immediately reflects those changes.

Timeline

The Flash Timeline (see Figure 1-2) appears below the main navigation. The timeline enables you to add content that changes over time in a visual manner. The timeline is a clear indicator of Flash's origins as an animation tool.

Tools panel

Timeline

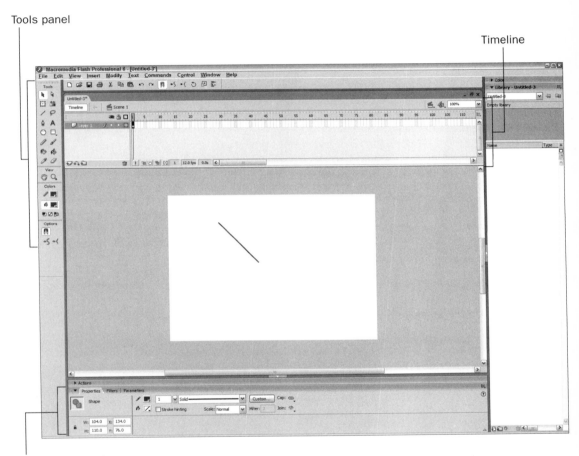

Properties panel

Figure 1-2

Keyframes and Animation

Timelines enable you to add frames to animate content over time. By default a timeline has just one frame at frame 1. You can add frames by selecting Insert⇨Timeline⇨Frame or by pressing F5. Where Flash adds the new frame or frames depends on what frame is currently selected on the timeline. If you select an existing frame in the timeline, Flash inserts the new frame immediately following the selected frame, and it moves subsequent frames to the right by one. If you select a frame placeholder after any existing frames, Flash adds the new frame at that location. If necessary, Flash also adds frames for all the frames between the new frame and previously existing frames. For example, if the timeline has one frame and you select the frame placeholder at frame 5 and press F5, Flash adds four new frames — one at frame 5 and three in the frames between the existing frame and the new frame.

Flash also has keyframes, which are special frames to which you can add content. Regular frames simply add time between keyframes. Keyframes are the only frames to which you can add artwork, text, and so on. The default frame in a timeline is always a keyframe. You can add new keyframes by selecting Insert⇨ Timeline⇨Keyframe or by pressing F6. When you select an existing keyframe and add a new keyframe, the new one is added immediately following the selected frame. If the following frame is an existing regular frame, it is converted to a keyframe. If the following frame is a keyframe, no change is made. If there is no frame following the selected frame, a new keyframe is appended. If you add a keyframe by selecting a placeholder where no frame yet exists, Flash adds the keyframe and regular frames to all frames between the last existing frame and the new keyframe. If you select an existing frame and add a keyframe, Flash converts the existing frame to a keyframe.

Keyframes are denoted by circles on the timeline. When a keyframe has no content, the circle is an outline. When content is added to the keyframe the circle appears as a solid black dot. Regular frames following a keyframe appear white when the keyframe has no content. When the keyframe has content, the subsequent regular frames are gray.

At the document level, there is always at least one timeline. This default, top-level timeline is often referred to as the main timeline or the root timeline. In ActionScript, the main timeline has two names: _root and _level0. Many types of library symbols also have timelines. For example, movie clip symbols have timelines. A common error for novice and expert Flash developers alike is to edit the wrong timeline by mistake. You can determine what timeline you are editing by looking to the right of the Timeline toggle button. Flash displays the name of the timeline you are currently editing. By default, the name Flash displays for the main timeline is Scene 1. If you edit a symbol, the name of the symbol appears to the right of Scene 1. You are always editing the timeline that appears the farthest to the right of Scene 1, and you can always return to the main timeline by clicking Scene 1.

About the Library and Symbols

Flash content is composed of elements such as text, vector artwork, bitmaps, sounds, and video. To most effectively manage content, it is frequently placed within symbols. Flash has many symbol types, including Button, Graphic, Movie Clip, Bitmap, Font, Sound, and Video. Of the types, three (Button, Graphic, and Movie Clip) allow you to group together content from the stage, and place it into a reusable symbol. The symbols are then stored in the Library. The Library appears on the right side of the IDE in the default layout. You can toggle the visibility of the panel by selecting Window⇨Library.

You can make a new Button, Graphic, or Movie Clip symbol in one of several ways. You can draw content on the stage, select it, and convert it to a symbol by selecting Modify⇨Convert to Symbol or by pressing F8. Optionally, you can select Insert⇨New Symbol, press Ctrl+F8 on Windows or Cmd+F8 on a Mac, or select New Symbol from the Library panel menu to add a new symbol that doesn't initially contain any content. In either case — whether converting to a symbol or adding a new empty symbol — you're presented with a dialog that prompts you for a symbol name and type.

The name of a symbol is arbitrary — there are no naming rules you must follow. The name you assign a symbol is the name that appears next to the symbol in the Library. It's advisable to select a name that accurately reflects the content of the symbol. For example, if you create a symbol containing a drawing of a cloud, it would be appropriate to name the symbol cloud.

The type you select for a symbol is important. The three options — Movie Clip, Button, and Graphic — behave very differently, and each ought to be used appropriately. Graphic symbols are useful for grouping artwork and/or animation sequences. However, you cannot control Graphic symbols or instances of those symbols with ActionScript, so they are not discussed in this book. Button symbols are symbols with very specialized timelines. Button symbol timelines have four keyframes labeled Up, Over, Down, and Hit. When you place an instance of a Button symbol on the stage and export the movie, Flash automatically jumps to the keyframes that correspond to the mouse state. For example, when the user moves the mouse over a Button instance, Flash jumps to the Over frame. You can read more about Button symbols in the following section, "Working with Buttons." Button symbols are useful for making clickable objects. Movie Clip symbols, however, are the powerhouse of symbols in the context of ActionScript. Using ActionScript, you can add instances of Movie Clip symbols and you can control those instances. You can read more about Movie Clip symbols in the "Working with Movie Clips" section a little later in this chapter.

Once you've added a Graphic, Button, or Movie Clip symbol to the Library, you have a repository of reusable templates. You can think of symbols as blueprints. You can then add one or more instances of a symbol to the stage. Generally, you add instances by dragging the symbol from the library to the stage. Each instance is based on the same template — the symbol. However, each instance is unique and independent of any other instances that may happen to be based on the same symbol. Deleting a symbol from the Library also deletes all the instances.

Working with Buttons

Button symbols have four states available: Up, Over, Down, and Hit. The Button symbol timeline is instantly recognizable because it has four frames labeled to correspond to the states. You can add Movie Clip instances, Graphic instances, ActionScript code, sounds, and so on to the frames just as you would any other timeline.

By default Button timelines have just one frame defined — the Up state. If you add content to the Up state, add an instance of the Button symbol to the stage, and test the movie, you'll notice that the mouse cursor changes when you move the mouse over the instance. If you define a keyframe on the Over frame, add content to the frame that differentiates it from the Up state, test the movie, and move the mouse over the instance, you'll notice that this time the content of the Button instance automatically changes to the Over state. As you move the mouse off of the instance, the content changes back to the Up state. Likewise, if you add a keyframe and unique content to the Down state, Flash automatically changes to that frame when the user clicks the button. The Hit state is never visible when testing the movie; it defines the region that activates the Over and Down states. For example, if the content for the Up state consists of text, the user will have to move the mouse directly over the font outline to activate the Over or Down states. If the mouse is not directly over the font outline, it will not activate. However, if you define a Hit state, moving the mouse anywhere over the Hit state will activate the Button.

Chapter 1

Try It Out   **Working with Button Symbols**

In this exercise you create a simple interactive button. Here's what to do:

1. Create a new Macromedia Flash document by selecting File⇨New and choosing Flash Document from the New Document panel. Save it as `symbolExample.fla`.

2. If the Library is not open, select Window⇨Library from the main navigation.

3. Select Insert⇨New Symbol.

4. The New Symbol dialog opens. Name the symbol `myButton` and be sure the Button option is selected. Don't worry about the other options. Click OK.

5. The button's stage and timeline appear in the IDE's main view area. Select the first frame, which is named Up.

6. In the Tools panel on the left side of the IDE, select the Rectangle tool.

7. The Tools panel contains two color swatches. The upper color is for lines, and the lower color is for fills. Click the upper swatch and select a dark gray or black for the line color. Click the Fill swatch and select a dark red.

8. Draw a rectangle on the stage by clicking the stage and dragging until the desired shape of a rectangle is achieved. Don't worry about centering the rectangle perfectly within the symbol. The rectangle should look something like the one shown in Figure 1-3.

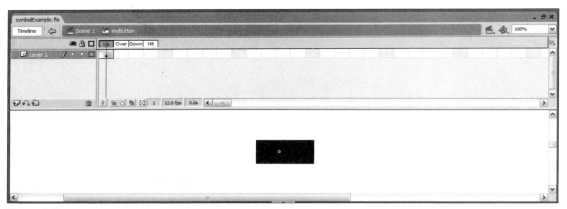

Figure 1-3

9. Click the Selection tool (small black arrow) in the Tools panel. Use it to select the rectangle on the stage by double-clicking the rectangle's fill area.

10. The Properties panel at the bottom of the IDE reflects the properties of the selected rectangle. In it, change the height to 30 and the width to 120 and set the x and y values to 0.

11. Select the Over, Down, and Hit frames in the timeline. To do this, click the empty frame named Hit, and drag the mouse to the left until all three frames are selected.

12. With the three frames selected, right-click (option+click) the Over frame. Select Convert to Keyframes from the context menu. The new keyframes contain copies of the content from the first keyframe. In this case, each keyframe now has a copy of the rectangle.

13. Select the Over frame. Select the Rectangle by clicking it with the Selection tool. Change the fill color to pink.

14. Select the Down frame, and then select the Rectangle by clicking it with the Selection tool and change the Fill color to white.

15. Create a new timeline layer by clicking the Insert Layer icon at the bottom left of the Timeline panel. (The icon looks like a sheet of paper with a plus sign (+) on it.)

16. Select the first frame of layer 2, and choose the Text tool (capital A) in the Tools panel.

17. Click anywhere on the stage to produce a text field. Enter the word `Play` in the field.

18. Choose the Selection tool from the Tools panel and click the text field you just created. (If you lose the location of the text field because it is the same color as the stage, click the first frame in layer 2 again.) The Properties panel populates with the attributes of the text field. Click the color swatch and change the color to a light gray.

19. Align the text to the center of the rectangle.

20. In the Timeline panel select the words `Scene 1`. Your button disappears from view and is in the Library. Open the Library, select the button, and drag it to the stage to create a new instance.

21. Test your application by selecting Control⇨Test Movie.

22. Test your button by mousing over it and clicking it.

How It Works

In this exercise, you used basic vector graphics tools, the Library, and the icons and options within the Timeline to quickly produce an interactive button that reacts to mouse events. You also resized and realigned your button.

Later in this book you see how to import image files into your button symbols for each button state. You can use your favorite image editing program to create `.jpeg`, `.gif`, and `.png` files to give the button states a slick look.

Save your Flash document; you'll use it in the next Try It Out.

Working with Movie Clips

Movie Clip symbols have their own timelines that can play back independently of any other timeline in the Flash movie, and you can control instance of Movie Clip symbols programmatically with a sophisticated assortment of functionality. These things make Movie Clip symbols the most common symbol type for use with ActionScript. Movie Clip symbols are of such importance to Flash movies that they require an entire chapter to discuss. You can read more about Movie Clip symbols in Chapter 7.

About Layers, Depth, and Levels

Timelines enable you to add layers. If you place content on unique layers, you can then sort the layer order to affect which content appears in front and which appears behind. You can change the order of layers by dragging them up or down within the timeline.

Layers are an authoring time convention. Flash Player doesn't know anything about layers. Instead, when a Flash movie is exported, it converts all content on layers to depths. Conceptually, depths are similar to layers, but they are accessible programmatically. Flash allows only one object per depth. If you add content to a depth that already contains content, the existing content is deleted.

ActionScript enables you to add content programmatically. Because programmatic content is added at runtime, you must use depths and not layers. Methods such as `attachMovie()` and `createTextField()` that add content programmatically require that you specify depths. Depths are integer values. The higher the number, the further in front an object appears. For example, an object with a depth of 2 appears in front of an object with a depth of 1. Content added at authoring time (on layers on the timeline) are placed at depths starting at –13683. That means that authoring time content appears behind content added programmatically, assuming you use positive depths when you add that content.

Every movie clip encapsulates its own set of depths. For example, if you have two Movie Clip instances, A and B, and each contains nested Movie Clip instances, the depths of A and B affect how the contents of each movie clip appear relative to one another. If A has a higher depth, then all the contents of A appear in front of all the contents of B, even if the contents of B have higher depths than the contents of A. That also means that you can add content to A at depth 1 and content to B at depth 1 without one overwriting the other.

Flash also uses a concept called levels. By default there is just one level in a Flash movie. It has the name `_level0`. You can only add levels by loading content using MovieClipLoader or the older global function `loadMovieNum()`. In general it's not advantageous to work with levels; levels are primarily a legacy concept going back to a time when Flash didn't have programmatic depths.

Setting Up Your Scripting Environment

In this book you use the Flash IDE for writing the majority of the code examples. When you are writing ActionScript in Flash you'll likely appreciate the capability to customize how the code is formatted and how Flash assists you in adding code. In the next sections you read about the Actions panel and the options available for customizing it.

Introducing the Actions Panel

When you want to add ActionScript within a Flash document, you'll need to use the Actions panel. You can open the Actions panel by selecting Window⇨Actions or by pressing F9. From the Actions panel you can add ActionScript to a keyframe or a symbol instance. Flash will add the script to a keyframe if you've selected the keyframe from the timeline and it will add the script to a symbol instance if you've selected the instance on the stage. Adding code to symbol instances is no longer advisable. Prior to Flash MX it was the only way to add certain types of code. However, adding code to symbol instances has disadvantages in that it generally requires much more code, it doesn't scale well, and it can be difficult to keep track of where you've placed code. For those reasons it's recommended that when you add code to a Flash document, you always add it to a keyframe. A common mistake made by novices and experts alike is to accidentally add code to a symbol instance when intending to add it to a keyframe. Before you attempt to add any code to the Actions panel, always make sure it says Actions – Frame in the title bar of the panel.

On the left side of the panel is the Actions toolbox and Script navigator. Both are seldom necessary or useful for anyone wanting to learn ActionScript beyond a very basic level. On the right is the Script pane where you can directly add ActionScript code. The Script pane is essentially a text editor.

Exploring ActionScript Preferences

Next you see how to customize the Actions panel. You can open the Preferences dialog by selecting Edit⇨Preferences (see Figure 1-4).

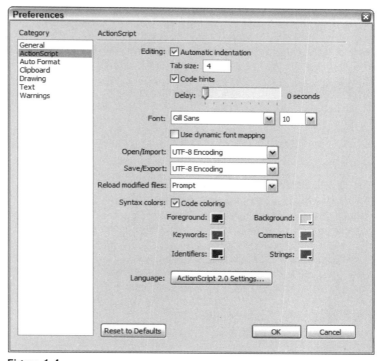

Figure 1-4

The following sections introduce you to some of the ActionScript preferences (select ActionScript from the Category list on the left side of the Preferences dialog).

Automatic Indentation

By convention code blocks are indented for readability. Code blocks are denoted by curly braces ({ and }). When you add a left curly brace ({) and a newline, Flash can automatically indent the next line. The Automatic indentation option is selected by default. If you don't want Flash to automatically indent your code, deselect the option.

Tab Size

The default tab size is the equivalent of four spaces. You can change the value if you want to indent more or less when pressing the Tab key.

Code Hints

Code hints are a way that Flash can help you by providing a list of likely options based on what code you've provided so far. For example, if you type the name of a variable that Flash recognizes as a movie clip, it can automatically display a list of functionality associated with movie clips.

Code hints can be triggered manually by using suffixes after an underscore in the variable name. For example, type the following code into the ActionScript panel:

```
example_array.
```

After you type the dot a drop-down menu of available array methods is presented. You can read a list of suffixes Flash uses in a document entitled "About Using Suffixes To Trigger Code Hints" in the Help panel.

Although suffixes work, they are no longer the preferred method of triggering code hints. With ActionScript 2.0, you can use strict typing to control code hints. Strict typing tells Flash what type of data a variable points to. That, in turn, allows Flash to display code hints regardless of whether you use suffixes in the variable name. For example, type the following code into the ActionScript panel:

```
var example:Array;
example.
```

The drop-down list of available methods for an array is presented as before. However, this time you aren't required to use a specific suffix as part of the variable name. You learn more about ActionScript syntax, variable declaration, and strict typing in the following chapters.

You can also specify how long a delay Flash should use before displaying code hints. The delay is between the trigger (usually a dot following a variable name) and the display of the code hints. A short delay could mean that code hints might appear even if you don't want them to appear. If the delay is too long, you'll have to wait for the code hints to appear. The default value is 0 seconds, which means the code hints appear immediately after the trigger.

Font

Although font is generally a matter of personal taste, some fonts are not advisable for coding. Georgia, for example, is a font in which the lowercase o is identical to its zero. This can make debugging and reading code extremely difficult. You want to avoid fonts that cause this type of problem.

Serif fonts are generally better for distinguishing letters from numbers and they better define individual words. Monospace fonts are generally better for code as well. For that reason the default ActionScript font that Flash uses is a monospace serif font such as Courier or Courier New.

You'll want to experiment. If you have colors and a font you like in another editor, carry them over. You'll be glad you did. If you don't yet have a preference, take the time to try some out. A scripting environment that suits you specifically is more welcoming, easier to work with, and more conducive to your way of working.

Color

One of the basic Actions panel enhancements you can make is color — color of the background, keywords, strings, comments, and so on. You can reduce eyestrain by changing the colors to those that suit you. For example, I generally don't like to code on a stark white background because after many hours of coding, I can no longer look at the screen without squinting. To alleviate this, I give the Background color a newsprint shade, somewhere near #E0DBC7.

Because there are generally few keywords in code, I set them apart from the rest of the code by assigning the Keywords color setting to #0066CC, which is a blue.

Identifier words are the names of classes and data types you use to declare variables. As such, they appear very frequently in code. I want to be able to quickly scan the code for identifiers, so I set the Identifiers color to a red, #990000.

Foreground color applies to the text, which is the meat and potatoes of the code, including functions that you create and methods that aren't tied to specific objects (`clear()` rather than `this.clear()`, for instance). The default color is black, but I prefer a lower contrast, so I generally choose #333333, which is on the gray side of black.

Comments are like road signs in code. They can often warn you of certain code peculiarities, as well as show you how the code is used or fits within the larger project. I usually set the Comments color to orange (#CC6600) so that I can easily see alerts and comments placed in the code.

Strings are a special case. It is important to be able to scan the code quickly and see the difference between `this.n.clear()` and `this.n = "clear";`. I use #009900, a primary green, for my Strings color; it's easy to discern among other colors.

Of course, you'll want to choose your own colors, and you can always return to the Preferences dialog and change them.

ActionScript 2.0 Settings

The Language section at the bottom of the ActionScript preferences dialog has a button that leads you to ActionScript 2.0 settings. A new dialog box opens (see Figure 1-5) that enables you to assign values for the classpath.

The classpath is a list of locations where Flash can locate code in class files when compiling. A class package can reside anywhere, as long as you have a classpath specified so that the compiler can find it. That means you can build libraries of code that you can use in many projects.

The list of classpaths should contain a default classpath, which targets the classes that ship with Flash. Do not remove the default classpath. You will also see a classpath that is simply a period (.). It specifies that Flash also looks in the same folder as the Flash document for any classes that are referenced by your code.

Flash searches for classes in the order in which you list the directories in the classpath. Flash uses the first instance of a class it encounters to compile. You can add a new directory to the classpath by clicking the plus sign (+), and you can remove an existing directory from the classpath by selecting it from the list and clicking the minus sign (–). You can reorder the directories with the arrow buttons.

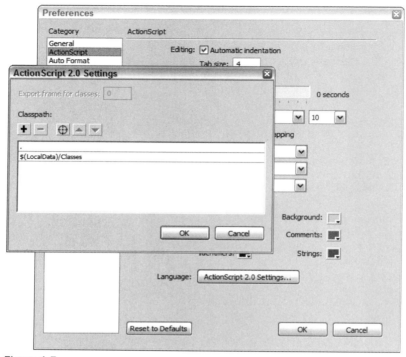

Figure 1-5

Exploring Auto Format Preferences

The Actions panel adds and indents characters when the Auto Format button is clicked. You can specify a few of those behaviors by first selecting Auto Format in the Preferences dialog box to display the appropriate page (see Figure 1-6).

The first two settings determine where Flash inserts the curly brace. If you check these options, the curly brace remains on the same line. If you leave these options unchecked, the curly brace is placed on the following line. If you've never used ActionScript before, you probably have no idea what this is about, but rest assured that you'll find out when you begin looking at functions and statements.

Just keep the Preferences dialog in mind for now because you'll probably want to come back to these settings once you start coding with ActionScript and become more familiar with how you prefer to work. Code examples in this book generally are formatted with none of the Auto Format options checked. The default settings are easy to read, though, and don't contain any surprises for fellow coders.

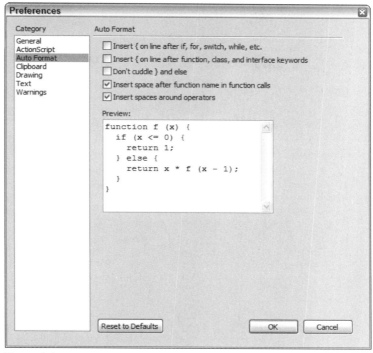

Figure 1-6

Publishing a Project

Once you've authored your Flash project you'll want to publish it so that you can deploy it. Flash has a Publish command that enables you to export to a variety of formats such as SWF, Quicktime, and even standalone executables. The Publish Settings dialog gives you the capability to select the formats to which you want to publish. It also enables you to customize the settings for each format. The Publish Settings dialog lets you automate the construction of JavaScript Flash Player detection as well as replacement images or HTML when a Flash player is not detected. The Publish Settings panel can help you target special Flash players such as Flash Lite and the Pocket PC player.

The Publish Settings dialog (see Figure 1-7) enables you to save and preserve profiles. This is handy for sharing the proper publish settings among developers or for storing a specific default profile you'd like to start with for all projects.

In the Publish Settings dialog you can select which formats you want to publish. By default the Flash and HTML formats are selected. When you select the Publish command (File⇨Publish), Flash exports those formats that are checked in the Publish Settings dialog. You can use default paths to publish your assets. Alternatively, you can specify unique paths for each format. The Publish Settings are saved when you save your Flash document.

Figure 1-7

A new tab appears for each format you select (except the Projector formats, which don't have any special settings). By default, therefore, the Publish Settings dialog has three tabs — Formats, Flash, and HTML.

The Flash Tab

The Flash tab in the Publish Settings panel specifies the options for the SWF file. The version setting determines which players will be able to display your application. You should target a Flash version that best suits your audience and what you'd like your application to do. For example, if your Flash application takes advantage of Flash 8 text rendering because you require text to display at its best, you'll need to require Flash 8. However, if you're building a simple animation and interaction you may only need Flash 5. When you publish the FLA to SWF, the IDE will warn you if the code within the Flash document will not work in the targeted player specified in the Publish Settings panel.

Load order specifies how the first frame of the application should initially render. On slower machines this draw is more visible, so you should consider how you would like it to look. The default top to bottom, however, is sufficient.

The ActionScript version should match the ActionScript type you plan to use in your application. Although you can use ActionScript 2 output and use no version 2 code constructs, you should change this setting to at the very least alert future developers who might open your Flash document about the syntax used. The setting affects the compiler and compiler directives as well as error checking and strict type compliance.

The next group of options enables you to set attributes in the resulting SWF application. If you select Protect From Import as an attribute to include in your SWF, you are given the option of allowing the SWF to be accessed via a password. This can help protect your SWF file should anyone find it and attempt to load it into a new FLA or larger application.

Debugging allows the debugger to access the SWF file. Be careful to not have this setting selected on your actual deployment SWF application. This is just a faux pas, and wouldn't affect the application for regular users.

Compress Your Movie is a handy setting that enables you to save 10, 20, or even 30% of your SWF file size. The SWF player has a built-in decompressor to decompress the file when it's loaded into the player. This attribute is very handy for rich applications with a lot of skin attributes, ActionScript, and embedded content, but less so for fully dynamic SWF files, which import almost everything at runtime.

JPEG Quality is an often overlooked setting that can help cut down on overall SWF size. This setting affects any bitmap that does not have an individual quality setting applied to it. Open the Properties panel for each bitmap in the Library to specify the quality attribute for individual images.

The two Audio settings affect only audio that has been placed directly upon a timeline from the Library.

The HTML Tab

When publishing an SWF file it is often advantageous to define an HTML wrapper for it. Although most browsers will open the Flash plug-in and play SWF content as is, it is difficult to know if the Flash version installed on the user system is new enough for your SWF content. The HTML wrapper can include JavaScript and object tag plug-in version checking to automate the process of checking for the correct version of Flash.

The HTML you choose can also be specific to a device or target browser. For example, mobile devices have their own markup for inserting plug-in objects upon a page. Just as the Flash Player version is carefully considered, so too should the target HTML be considered for compliance with end user systems. You can use the drop-down menu to select the HTML wrapper for your target system. The next section covers some simple JavaScript detection of the Flash Player version.

In the HTML Publish Settings panel (see Figure 1-8), you can select playback states and attributes to be placed in the object and embed tags automatically. You can, of course, create your own HTML, and change the attributes any way you like.

As with any Publish Settings selection, you should test each decision to see how it affects performance and cross-browser compatibility.

It is possible to create custom HTML templates.

The Image Tabs

If you return to the Publish Settings Formats panel, you see the three types of images that can be created when the SWF file is compiled. Each of these file types has options for setting image attributes when the images are created. The attributes include size, quality, smoothing, and more. As with all publish settings, trial and error is the best way to understand how the settings affect the image output. The goal in publishing images is to create the highest quality image with the lowest possible file size. This is always a compromise and dependent upon the complexity of the content within the image.

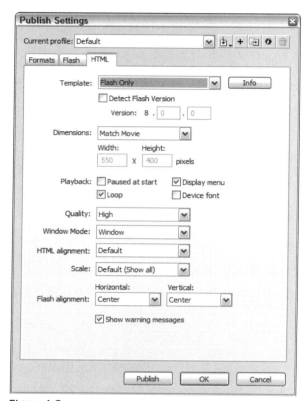

Figure 1-8

For example, Figure 1-9 shows the PNG tab in Publish Settings panel.

Options for Detecting the Flash Player

Once you have created the SWF file you'll want to be sure that all that hard work can be viewed on as many systems as possible. You have several options to choose from. The most robust, and easiest to use, is the Flash Detection Kit. Flash 8 integrates the kit into the HTML Publish dialog. The kit is also available as download. The downloadable kit can help implement the kit within servlet pages, as well as legacy HTML pages that require the detection update.

The default Flash Only HTML template provided by the Publish dialog can display your content when a Flash player is known to exist on a system. This template is fine for testing your SWF locally. However, using no detection leaves the plug-in issue resolution to the browser. Internet Explorer utilizes an alert message to ask the user if he would like to install or update the Flash player. It then automatically begins the install process using a simple certificate-based installation. Due to malware and other concerns, many users simply reject a certificate when presented. On all other browsers, however, a plug-in issue is often a simple message with no resolution or a link about where to go to get help about plug-ins. This is hardly acceptable, or user friendly.

Figure 1-9

The detection kit exports a JavaScript-based SWF wrapper within an HTML page. After the kit has detected that Flash exists and the Version Is passes `true`, the JavaScript uses the `document.write` method to print the actual object and embed tags.

In the event that the Flash player is too old to play your SWF file, an alternative method is called that writes an image tag and specifies a `.gif` image.

If the browser does not have JavaScript enabled, the kit has a third and final method, which uses the noscript html tag to write an image tag and specify a `.gif` image.

Generally, I allow Flash to publish the kit in this way and then edit the output HTML file to behave the way I want. In some cases, replacing SWF content with GIF is acceptable, but generally not for SWF applications. In these cases it is better to use the `document.write` method to print HTML with instructions on how to resolve a plug-in update. This enables users to update their systems, and understand why the SWF application may not have worked on their first visit.

For any plug-in detection, it is better to display what you can right away and seamlessly integrate each level of compliance into your page design. Then gracefully deal with updates without alarming warnings and zero content displays.

Summary

This chapter serves as a brief introduction to the IDE. The IDE has many facets that you will discover and use. You might wonder why these weren't covered, but this book focuses on ActionScript and it is the intention of this chapter to introduce you to the IDE so that you can begin and complete the exercises throughout the book. In each example you'll see small shortcuts and work flows that weren't covered here. Keyboard shortcuts can speed your work a great deal, and each operating system has slightly different keyboard shortcuts. If a shortcut encountered in the book doesn't seem to be working, try using the manual menu system to find the action. In most cases, the keyboard shortcut is listed right next to the action in the menu system. Additionally, Appendix B is all about keyboard shortcuts.

The Flash IDE is extremely malleable. You may find that the work flows presented here are completely foreign to your method of working. Because the IDE is so flexible, I encourage you to deviate when possible and explore the IDE to see what it is capable of. The IDE also runs on basic settings files found in the application settings folder on your operating system. Sometimes if you wish you had a particular option, or could remove or simplify an aspect of the IDE, it isn't difficult to go poking around the Application Settings to see what you can find.

Exercises

1. Create a new FLA (Macromedia Flash document) by selecting File⇨New and choosing Flash Document from the New Document panel. Create a Layer, and place a vector drawing or image object onto the stage. Place a simple `Hello World` ActionScript on the frame. Rename the layer `test` and save your FLA. Open a new FLA. Return to your original FLA, right-click (option+click) the frame with the `Hello World` ActionScript, and select Copy. Paste the frame into your new SWF. Examine the results.

2. Open a new FLA and open the Library. Add a symbol using the panel's context menu. Add a button or Movie Clip. Double-click the instance you just created and create some graphics within it. Open a new FLA file. Open the new FLA file's library. Return to the original FLA file's library and drag the object instance you created to the new FLA. Notice that the symbol now resides in both libraries.

3. Open multiple FLA files. Move between the FLA files by using the tab system at the top of the IDE. Minimize or un-maximize one of the FLA files. Note how the IDE enters a collapsible window mode.

Getting Started with ActionScript 2.0

Computers are dumb; they cannot think for themselves — they can only follow instructions. Computers are also very precise, so they must be told in exact terms what needs to be done. The purpose of a programming language is to provide you with a means of clearly and accurately telling the computer what you want it to do. ActionScript provides this structure in a way that you also can read and understand.

This chapter gets you started learning ActionScript syntax and structure by introducing the statement and the variable. Do not worry about memorizing each fact and concept that's covered in this chapter. The more actual examples you try for yourself, the more comfortable you will become with ActionScript 2.0.

Understanding Statements

When you write a letter or an email message, you create sentences and string them together to form paragraphs. Each sentence is structured of verbs, nouns, adjectives, and other elements of the English language, and each sentence expresses one discrete message. Similarly, writing code is a process of creating individual statements that communicate to Flash one discrete task that you want it to perform. A sequence of statements spells out how to perform a larger task in detail, much like sentences are strung together into paragraphs to explain a larger idea.

Using Simple Statements

The building block of ActionScript coding is the simple statement, generally just referred to as a statement. Each statement represents one distinct operation that is to be performed. Sequences of statements are executed one after another in the order that they appear.

A statement is generally represented by a single line of code. It consists of a combination of keywords, variables, and operators, and terminates with a semicolon (;). Don't worry about the details of what's on each line right now; just take the high-level view of them.

One statement might perform a mathematical calculation and save the result for future use:

```
position = 350 / 2;
```

Another might move an onscreen element to a new position:

```
helicopterClip._x = 25;
```

Yet another might open a Web page in a new browser window:

```
getURL("http://www.apple.com/ipod/", "externalWindow");
```

Usually a statement cannot run until the previous one has completely finished. In the following example, the first statement calculates a value and saves it temporarily, and then the second statement makes use of that value to position an onscreen element:

```
position = 350 / 2;
helicopterClip._x = position;
```

> **Generally, no statement runs until the previous one is completely finished. The exception to this is loading external media, where calls to load an external file pass to the next statement before the external file has loaded. You learn more about this beginning in Chapter 7.**

Using Compound Statements

Compound statements are composed of multiple statements. Curly braces surround everything that is part of the compound statement. Here's an example:

```
if (position < 500)
{
    position = position + 10;
    helicopterClip._x = position;
}
```

Without worrying too much about the details, both of the statements or neither of the statements between the brackets will run, depending on the outcome of the if statement.

Understanding Operators

Each statement consists of a certain amount of code grammar that defines what that statement does. Relating back to the sentence analogy, a simple sentence might consist of two nouns, or targets of an action, and a verb, or action. The sentence "Marie is given a ball" basically consists of two nouns (Marie and ball) and a verb that describes the interaction (is given). An *operator* is akin to a verb in that it describes an action, an interaction, or a relationship. Here's an example:

```
mariesToy = "ball";
```

This line contains two "items" that can interact. The first, `mariesToy`, is a container for data (called a variable) and the second, `"ball"`, is data that can be placed within that container. The = symbol is the equals operator, which invokes the action of assigning whatever is to the right of the = symbol to the variable on the left of the symbol.

Multiple operators can be used in the same statement. For instance, the following line adds a value to whatever value is already in the `numToys` variable:

```
numToys = numToys + 1;
```

If you are a mathematician, your head might be spinning because this is not a correct math formula. But it isn't a math formula, and if you think in terms of the operators that are at work, you see that this works just fine. The first operator that is evaluated is the +. It grabs the number to its right, retrieves the value contained of `numToys`, and adds the two. Next, the = operator is evaluated; it assigns the result of the addition back to `numToys`. If `numToys` initially held the number 1, it now holds the number 2.

Not all operators require items on both sides of the operator. The increment operator (++), for example, is shorthand for adding 1 to a container, and it only needs a container on its left:

```
numToys++;
```

This operator retrieves the number held by `numToys`, adds one to that number, and then assigns the new number back to the `numToys` container. If `numToys` holds the value 3 before this line executes, it holds the value 4 afterward.

You can use a number of mathematical operators, including addition (+), subtraction (-), multiplication (*), division (/), and remainder/modulo (%). Take a look at the following example:

```
a = 6;
b = 4;
c = 2;
calculationResult = a + b - c; //  calculationResult contains 8
calculationResult = a / b; // calculationResult contains 1.5
calculationResult = a % b; // calculationResult contains 2
```

The first three lines assign numbers to variables, which are discussed later in this chapter. The next three lines use mathematical operators to calculate new values and to assign those values to another variable.

The modulo (%) operator returns the remainder of a division. In this example, 4 divides into 6 once, with a remainder of 2, so the modulo operator returns 2.

A series of calculate-and-assign operators act as shorthand for some common mathematical operations. The following two lines of code, for example, are equivalent:

```
a = a + 2;
```

```
a += 2;
```

The first line adds the value already stored in variable a and the number 2, and then assigns the new value back to a. If a stored the value 7 before this line runs, it stores 9 afterward. The second line does the same thing, but performs the addition and the assignment in one step. The same convention applies with the subtract and assign (-=), multiply and assign (*=), divide and assign (/=), and modulo and assign (%=) operators. In general, these shortcut operators provide a convenient notation for simple calculate-and-assign operations, but there's nothing holding you back from using the a = a + 2; syntax if you prefer.

Not all operators perform assignments or calculations. For instance, the round bracket operators — () — are used to clarify a statement and to force the order in which the operators are evaluated. The following two statements, for example, return different results:

```
result =  6 + 4 * 2; // result contains 12

result = (6 + 4) * 2 // result contains 20
```

In the first line, the * operator takes precedence over the + operator, so 4 * 2 is calculated first, and the result of that is added to 6. In the second line, the brackets create a higher priority, forcing 6 + 4 to be calculated first, and that result is then multiplied by 2.

This last example brings up the issue of figuring out which operator is evaluated first, because they apparently are not evaluated from left to right. Which operators take priority?

Using Operator Precedence

If you are wondering why the + operator in the numToys = numToys + 1; statement is evaluated before the = operator, or why a multiplication operator is evaluated before an addition operator, just know that there is an order to the chaos. Each operator is assigned an *operator precedence*, which is basically a ranking. The operator with the higher precedence is always evaluated before the operator with lower precedence. This ranking has been worked out by the people who write compiler specifications so that operations flow in a way that produces behavior that works properly and predictably.

When it comes to mathematical operators, the field of mathematics defines its own rules about what calculations are performed first: multiplication and division take place before addition and subtraction, and round brackets take overall precedence. These rules are reflected in the ActionScript operator precedence ranking.

The ranking is shown in the upcoming "Understanding the Common Operators" section.

Exploring Operator Associativity

An operator can act on code that is to its right and can act on code to its left. Which does it do first? That's where operator associativity comes in. The associativity of an operator means that it either first looks to the left or it first looks to the right. If an operator first looks to the left, it has left-to-right associativity; otherwise it has right-to-left associativity. In an earlier example, you saw the = operator look first to the right for a value to assign, and then assign it to the container on its left, so the = operator uses right-to-left associativity. In the numToys++ statement, the ++ operator started by getting the value on its left. It didn't actually do anything with the right, but the associativity that it uses is still called left-to-right. The table in the following section includes the associativity for the common operators.

For the most part, you don't need to care about this too much because the associativity for the different operators has been chosen to make them just work the way you would expect; still, it's a good idea for you to know the concept to understand how operators work.

Understanding the Common Operators

The following table lists some common operators. They are ranked from the highest operator precedence to the lowest. You learn more about these operators in this and the next few chapters.

Operator	Name	Associativity	Description
++	Increment	Left to right	Adds 1 to a number and assigns the new number back to the variable.
--	Decrement	Left to right	Subtracts 1 from a number and assigns the new number back to the variable.
[ ]	Array element	Left to right	Accesses an individual element from a collection of data.
( )	Parentheses	Left to right	Forces the operators within the parentheses to be evaluated before any operators outside the parentheses.
-	Negation	Left to right	Inverts the sign on a number. The negation operator is different from the subtraction operator only by the context in which it sits.
!	Logical NOT	Right to left	Converts a `false` value to `true` or a `true` value to `false`.
*	Multiply	Left to right	Multiplies two values.
/	Divide	Left to right	Divides the value to the right of the operator from the value to the left of the operator.
%	Modulo	Left to right	Returns the remainder of a division of two whole numbers.
+	Plus	Right to left	Adds two values.
-	Minus	Right to left	Subtracts the value on the right from the value on the left.
<	Less than	Left to right	Returns `true` if the value on the left is less than the value on the right; otherwise it returns `false`.
<=	Less than or equal to	Left to right	Returns `true` if the value on the left is less than or equal to the value on the right; otherwise it returns `false`.
>	Greater than	Left to right	Returns `true` if the value on the left is greater than the value on the right, otherwise it returns `false`.

Table continued on following page

Operator	Name	Associativity	Description
>=	Greater than or equal to	Left to right	Returns `true` if the value on the left is greater than or equal to the value on the right; otherwise it returns `false`.
==	Equal	Left to right	Returns `true` if the value on the left is equal to the value on the right; otherwise it returns `false`.
!=	Not equal	Left to right	Returns `true` if the value on the left is not equal to the value on the right; otherwise it returns `false`.
&&	Logical AND	Left to right	Returns `true` only if both the value on the left of the operator and the value on the right of the operator are `true`; otherwise it returns `false`.
||	Logical OR	Left to right	Returns `true` if either the value on the left of the operator or the value on the right of the operator is `true`; otherwise it returns `false`.
=	Assignment	Right to left	Assigns the value on the right of the operator to the variable on the left of the operator.
*=	Multiply and assign	Right to left	Multiplies the variable on the left by the number to the right, and then assigns the new number to the variable.
/=	Divide and assign	Right to left	Divides the variable on the left by the number to the right, and assigns the new number to the variable.
%=	Modulus and assign	Right to left	Retrieves the modulus from the division of the value on the left by the value on the right, and assigns the new number to the variable.
+=	Add and assign	Right to left	Adds the number on the right and the variable on the left and assigns the new number to the variable.
-=	Subtract and assign	Right to left	Subtracts the number on the right from the variable on the left and assigns the new number to the variable.
,	Comma	Left to right	Delimits repeating items, such as elements in an array.

Using White Space

The Flash compiler ignores all the white space in your code. This means that the spaces, tabs, and returns in your code have no impact on the compiler. That's great news because it enables you to adopt a coding style that works well for you, and that is easy to read, just by changing how you use white space in your code.

The following three statements all work, despite the differences in white space:

```
getURL("http://www.apple.com/ipod/","externalWindow");

getURL( "http://www.apple.com/ipod/", "externalWindow" );

    getURL ( "http://www.apple.com/ipod/" ,
            "externalWindow" ) ;
```

Similarly, compound statements can be formatted in numerous ways:

```
if (position < 500)
{
    position = position + 10;
    helicopterClip._x = position;
}


if (position < 500) {
    position = position + 10;
    helicopterClip._x = position;
}
```

Short compound statements might fit on one line, although we do not favor that format:

```
if (position < 500) { helicopterClip._x = position; }
```

As you learn ActionScript, you will start using compound statements within compound statements. Indenting by using tabs makes that code more readable:

```
if (position < 500)
{
    if (isEnabled == true)
    {
        position = position + 10;
        helicopterClip._x = position;
    }
}
```

Whatever style you use, use it consistently.

Many code editors, such as the one built into Flash, have commands for auto-formatting code. Look for the Auto-format button (see Figure 2-1) at the top of the Actions panel or the script file editor.

Figure 2-1

Using Comments

Not every line in your script needs to be executable code. You can place comments throughout your code to either annotate your code or prevent lines of code from being compiled without actually deleting the code. Two types of comments exist: inline and block.

An inline comment is designated by two leading slashes (//). The compiler ignores everything after the second slash until the line break. Inline comments are great for adding short annotations, such as the following:

```
// TODO: Get rid of the hard-coded string
getURL("http://www.apple.com/ipod/","externalWindow");

helicopterClip._x = 25; // Position of the landing pad.
```

When you need larger comments, you can use the block comment, which begins with a slash and asterisk (/*) and ends with an asterisk and slash (*/). Everything between /* and */ is ignored by the compiler.

```
/* Author:        Nathan Derksen
 * Creation Date: June 3, 2006
 * Change log:    June 4, 2006 - Added easing effect to animation
 */
```

This is not recommended, though. It's preferable to use the double-slash syntax at the start of each comment line, and to use the block syntax for "commenting out" sections of code (that is, preventing those sections from being run). If you think about it for a minute, you'll understand why. The compiler ignores everything after one /* until it reaches a */. If there's a multiline comment included in that code block, the compiler ignores its opening /* and then begins to try to run the code that follows the comment (the first */ it comes to). If that doesn't throw an error, one will certainly be thrown when the compiler runs into the second */ — the one at the end of the code block, which, to the compiler, has no starting /* and is therefore out of place. Here's an example:

```
/*
if (position < 500)
{
    /* TODO: Implement animation of the helicopter
       Needs to be done before rest of project can proceed. */
    position = position + 10;
    helicopterClip._x = position;
}
*/
```

Here the compiler ignores the `if` statement and the comment up to the `*/`, and then tries to run the `position =` statement, and if it gets to the `*/` at the end of the code block, it throws a syntax error for an out-of-place `*/`. Here's commented code that works as intended:

```
/*
if (position < 500)
{
    // TODO: Implement animation of the helicopter
    // Needs to be done before rest of project can proceed.
    position = position + 10;
    helicopterClip._x = position;
}
*/
```

The following will work as intended.

Here's an example that shows a block of code that's been commented out, preventing all the statements between the `/*` and `*/` markers from being run. This usage can be a real boon to debugging because it enables you to isolate code blocks to pin down errors.

```
/*
if (position < 500)
{
    position = position + 10;
    helicopterClip._x = position;
}
*/
```

You learn more about good commenting practices in Chapter 5.

Introducing Variables

A *variable* is simply a way of storing some piece of data for later use. A single variable stores a single chunk of data, with no limit to the size of that chunk. To make space for your data, you *declare* a variable. The process of declaring a variable does several things:

1. Requests that space be set aside in main memory (RAM) for some data.
2. Links that reserved space with a variable name of your choice.
3. Optionally assigns some initial data to that reserved space.

Declaring a variable is as simple as this:

```
var myTitle:String;
```

The keyword `var` indicates that what is to follow is a variable declaration. The variable name (`myTitle`, in this example) comes next. The variable name that you choose provides the means of accessing any data stored within the variable from later statements.

The data type (`String`) comes next, separated from the variable name by a colon (`:`). The data type declaration tells the compiler the kind of data — a chunk of text, a numerical value, or a date — can be stored in the variable. The data type is optional; if no data type is to be declared, there should be no colon after the variable name. Although declaring a data type is optional, it's a good practice to follow, as you see shortly. Finally, a semicolon indicates the end of the statement.

Assigning Data to a Variable

For a variable to be truly useful, it needs to be assigned some data. One way to do this is by assigning an initial value during the variable declaration:

```
var myTitle:String = "Programmer";
```

The equals sign is an assignment operator that says to assign the data that follows — in this example, the literal string `Programmer` — to the referenced variable. The literal string is surrounded by quotation marks to distinguish it as text data instead of code to execute.

Data can also be assigned to a variable in a separate statement, like this:

```
var myTitle:String;
myTitle = "Programmer";
```

The first statement declares the variable `myTitle`, but leaves it empty. The second statement assigns the string literal `Programmer` to the variable.

Viewing the Contents of a Variable

To find out what data a variable contains, the contents need to be read and then output to the screen. A built-in function called `trace()` enables you to see the contents of a variable. When you place the variable name between the function's round brackets, `trace()` reads the contents of the variable and displays it in the Output panel. Here's an example that declares a variable, assigns a String value to it, and then runs `trace` on the variable. The variable's content, the string `Programmer`, is output to the screen.

```
var myTitle:String;
myTitle = "Programmer";
trace(myTitle);
// Outputs: Programmer
```

You see the `trace()` statement in the examples throughout this book. To better read the output, use the string concatenation operator (+) to add a description to the output, like this:

```
var myTitle:String;
myTitle = "Programmer";
trace("My title is: " + myTitle);
// Outputs: My title is: Programmer
```

If the variable passed into the `trace()` *function is not of type String, Flash converts the data to a string the best way it knows how.*

Two keywords represent the absence of data in a variable: `null` and `undefined`. Retrieving the contents of a variable that has been declared but has not yet had data assigned to it results in the `null` value being returned. Attempting to test the contents of a variable that has not been declared results in the `undefined` value being returned. Here are examples:

```
var myEmptyVar:String;
trace(myEmptyVar);
// Outputs: null

trace(myUndefinedVar);
// Outputs: undefined
```

Passing Data from Variable to Variable

Data can also be passed from one variable to another in the same way that a literal string value is assigned to a variable:

```
var myTitle:String;
var yourTitle:String;

myTitle = "Programmer";
yourTitle = myTitle;

trace(yourTitle);
// Outputs: Programmer
```

The data contained by the `myTitle` variable is assigned to the `yourTitle` variable. Both variables end up containing the string `Programmer`.

Naming Variables

Variable names can be named pretty much anything you want, with the restrictions that they can only include letters, numbers, and the underscore characters, and cannot start with a number. In addition, they cannot consist of any of the words that are reserved by the ActionScript compiler. The easiest way to tell if there is a conflict is if your variable name turns blue in the editor. The compiler warns you if you use any core language keywords, such as `default`, `if`, `while`, `new`, `Key`, or `Date`. Chapter 5 includes a list of keywords in its discussion of best practices. You can find a complete list at `http://livedocs .macromedia.com/flash/8/main/wwhelp/wwhimpl/common/html/wwhelp.htm?context= LiveDocs_Parts&file=00001236.html`.

Variables are case sensitive, so `myVariable` and `myvariable` are two different variables. Having variable names differ only by case is, as you can imagine, not a good practice and can cause quite a bit of confusion down the road.

One common variable naming convention is camelBack notation, which consists of multiple words strung together with a capitalized first letter for each, beginning with the second word: `myLong VariableName`. Whatever naming convention you use, make sure the names make it quickly obvious what each variable is used for and what kind of data it stores.

Here are a few bad examples of variable naming:

```
var fp:Boolean;    // Not explicit
var users:Number;  // Does not describe the nature of the data
var scores:Array;  // Give no clue about the kind of data the variable contains
var sound:Sound;   // Uses only case to differentiate from a reserved keyword
```

Better names for these variables would be

```
var isFirstPass:Boolean;
var numRegisteredUsers:Number;
var highScoreArray:Array;
var backgroundSoundLoop:Sound;
```

It is common for programmers to choose the shortest variable names they can under the misconception that it will save time typing. Whatever time might be saved typing will be lost several-fold in debugging. A worthy goal of programming is to write self-documenting code, where the variable names that you choose contribute to quickly understanding what your code does.

Introducing Constants

A close companion of the variable is the constant. The constant holds some piece of data, but that is defined only when the constant is declared, and is not changed from that point on. This is very useful for referring to values that are referenced in multiple places in the code. These values may need to be changed in future versions of a project, but do not change during the execution of the application. When the value of a constant is to be changed, that change is made only where the constant is defined, and every place in the code that uses the constant automatically uses the new value. Constants are declared in the same way as variables, but use a naming convention of all uppercase letters with underscore characters separating words. Constants are restricted by convention to storing only Boolean, String, and Number values. Here are some examples:

```
var APP_NAME:String = "Yet Another Test Application";
var ROOT_SERVER_PATH:String = "/Applications/YATA/";
var BASE_FILE_NAME:String = "YATA.swf";
trace("Loading " + APP_NAME + " from " + ROOT_SERVER_PATH + BASE_FILE_NAME);
// Outputs: Loading Yet Another Test Application from /Applications/YATA/YATA.swf
```

Technically, there is nothing to prevent you from assigning a new value to a constant during the execution of the program, but it should never be done. The naming convention of using all uppercase letters is used as a reminder during coding that you should treat the constant data as read-only.

Using Strong Variable Typing

Variables can store different *types* of data, such as a string, a number, or a date. The type of data used has an impact on how you can work with it. Consider the following code:

```
var numCars = 1;
var numTrucks = "2";
trace(numCars + numTrucks);
// Outputs: 12
```

This example shows what happens when care is not taken with data types. The variable `numCars` contains a number, whereas the variable `numTrucks` contains a string. The + operator has two possible meanings depending on the type of data on either side of the operator. Only if the values on both sides are Numbers does the operator perform a mathematical addition; otherwise it converts non-String data to a String and then joins the two Strings together. This is an example of *weak typing*.

Making use of *strong typing* lets the compiler help you with data type issues. Strong typing includes the variable type information with the variable declaration. The compiler then remembers the data type for each subsequent use of that variable, and each time new data is to be assigned to a variable, it checks that the data being assigned is of the same type as the variable being assigned the new data. Any time that the compiler sees a potential data type incompatibility, it reports the error and refuses to finish the compile. Modifying the preceding example to take advantage of strong typing, you get the following code:

```
var numCars:Number = 1;
var numTrucks:Number = "2";
trace(numCars + numTrucks);
// Outputs: **Error** Scene=Scene 1, layer=Layer 1, frame=1:Line 2: Type ⟳
    mismatch in assignment statement: found String where Number is required.
```

The compiler correctly flags that there is a String in a place on line 2 where a Number has been specified, and prevents the compile from succeeding until the error is fixed.

The practice of using strong typing is a huge time-saver for debugging because the compiler shows you errors that could otherwise take hours to find. For strong typing to be most effective, you must be consistent in using it every time you declare a new variable. Strong typing also helps prevent Flash from changing the type of a variable on-the-fly, a capability ActionScript 2.0 inherited from ActionScript 1.0 to maintain backward compatibility. Variables that are created without a type in their declarations are sometimes referred to as *variants* because their types can vary during execution of the code through automatic type conversions. Variants are generally looked down upon because they can introduce hard-to-find errors into your programs.

The following Try It Out illustrates how strong typing can help prevent data type errors such as those brought on by variants.

In keeping with this best practice, all examples in this book declare variable types any time a variable is created.

Try It Out   ## Using Strong Typing to Find Errors Faster

The following steps show some of the impact of using strong typing to find errors that would otherwise be difficult to trace.

1. Create a new Macromedia Flash document by selecting File⇨New and choosing Flash Document from the New Document panel.

2. Click the first frame in the timeline, open the Actions panel (Window⇨Actions), and type in the following ActionScript code:

```
var isFirstTime;
isFirstTime = "false";
if (isFirstTime == false)
```

```
{
    trace("isFirstTime is false");
}
```

3. Select Control⇨Test Movie and take a look at the contents of the output panel.

4. Modify the code to look like this:

```
var isFirstTime:Boolean;
isFirstTime = "false";
if (isFirstTime == false)
{
    trace("isFirstTime is false");
}
```

5. Select Control⇨Test Movie and take a look at the contents of the output panel.

6. Fix the error by removing the quotes from around `false`:

```
var isFirstTime:Boolean;
isFirstTime = false;
if (isFirstTime == false)
{
    trace("isFirstTime is false");
}
```

7. Select Control⇨Test Movie and take a look at the contents of the output panel.

8. Add the following code to the end of the listing:

```
var numRecords;
numRecords = "23";
for (var i:Number = 0; i < numRecords + 1; i++){
    trace("Parsing row " + i);
}
```

9. Select Control⇨Test Movie and take a look at the contents of the output panel.

10. Modify the added code to look like this:

```
var numRecords:Number;
numRecords = "23";
for (var i:Number = 0; i < numRecords + 1; i++){
    trace("Parsing row " + i);
}
```

11. Select Control⇨Test Movie and take a look at the contents of the output panel.

12. Fix the error by removing the quotes from around `23`:

```
var numRecords:Number;
numRecords = 23;
for (var i:Number = 0; i < numRecords + 1; i++){
    trace("Parsing row " + i);
}
```

13. Select Control⇨Test Movie and take a look at the contents of the output panel.

How It Works

A `Boolean` data type is very simple, given that it can hold only a `true` or a `false` value, yet it is a common source for errors. One error is to surround the keywords `true` and `false` with quotes, which turns them into String values instead of Boolean values. The first line assigns a String value to what should be a Boolean variable. The next line does a check to see if the variable `isFirstTime` contains the Boolean value `false`, but because `isFirstTime` contains the String value `"false"`, the `trace()` statement does not run.

When the first line is changed to read `var isFirstTime:Boolean;`, the compiler gives the following warning and does not complete the compilation:

```
**Error** Scene=Scene 1, layer=Layer 1, frame=1:Line 1: Type mismatch in assignment
statement: found String where Boolean is required.
    isFirstTime = "false";

Total ActionScript Errors: 1    Reported Errors: 1
```

This error is a good thing because it reports a potential problem that could otherwise go initially undetected and be difficult to debug. The error reports which line of the source code is at issue, prints out the line, and describes the problem. In this example, the line number is preceded by a description of the timeline that holds the line of code in question, which is generally the first layer of the first frame in the main timeline. If the code is from an external file, the name of the file containing the problematic code is shown instead. Here a type mismatch is reported, where the type of `"false"`, which is a string, does not match the declared type of `isFirstTime`, which is a Boolean. Removing the quotes from around `"false"` is enough to fix the problem.

The example using the `numRecords` variable is a bit nefarious because Flash actually changes the type of the variable on-the-fly. First there's the variable declaration where `numRecords` is assigned the String `"23"`. This is distinct from the number 23, which would not be surrounded by quotes.

```
var numRecords = "23";
```

Loops are discussed later in this book, so don't worry about the details of the loop itself right now. What you should note is that the code between the curly brackets is supposed to run 23 + 1 = 24 times. Instead, it runs 231 times! What happens is that `numRecords` contains a String, and the operation `"23" + 1` causes the + operator to be used for concatenating strings instead of mathematical addition. The number 1 is converted to a string and joined with `"23"`, resulting in the string `"231"`. Unfortunately, the loop then uses the string `"231"` to determine when to stop. Seeing that it looks like a number, it converts the string on-the-fly and happily loops through 231 times.

When you add the strong typing to declare `numRecords` as a Number, the compiler catches the problem and spits out a type mismatch error. Once again, removing the quotes fixes the problem.

Exploring Data Types

Variables can store many different types of data. To see what data types are all available, open a new Macromedia Flash document, open the Actions panel (Window⇨Development Panels⇨Actions Panel), and type `var myData:`. After typing the colon, the auto-complete feature shows you a drop-down of all the data types from which you can choose. The built-in data types include the following:

Chapter 2

❑   Array — Stores a collection of data.

❑   Boolean — Stores either the value true or the value false.

❑   Date — Stores dates and times.

❑   MovieClip — Stores a data structure that defines an onstage movie clip.

❑   Number — Stores an integer or a decimal value.

❑   Object — The base type from which the other types are derived.

❑   String — Stores text.

❑   TextField — Allows access to an onscreen text field.

The data types Boolean, Number, and String are referred to as *primitive data types* because they cannot be broken down into anything simpler. Other types, such as Date, MovieClip, and TextField, place some sort of structure on the data stored within. These are referred to as *composite data types*. The Date type consists of a numerical representation of the date, plus methods that enable you to retrieve just a portion of the date, such as the month, the day, or the hour of the day. The MovieClip type is a complex representation of all the elements contained within a movie clip, plus additional information regarding position, transparency, attached variables, and much more. The TextField type stores information about text placed onscreen, such as the actual string to display, the position onscreen, the font in which to display it, and the font size. Another composite data type, the Array, is a structured collection of data of any type. (Arrays are discussed in detail later in this chapter.) In general, composite data types internally consist of a collection of data types, plus they provide code that enables you interact with the data in a controlled way.

Data types exist to represent many entities within Macromedia Flash, including components. (Components are examined in detail in Chapters 9–11.) When working with components, you may from time to time see notation like the following:

```
var saveButton:mx.controls.Button;
```

A component definition is treated as a data type. A special dotted data type notation indicates that the definition for the Button component is organized in a hierarchy, similar to the way in which you organize your computer files into folders. This example declaration of myButton tells the compiler to look for the definition for the particular data type in a specific location, namely the file Button.as in <Flash Application Root>/First Run/Classes/mx/controls/.

Distinguishing Primitive and Composite Data Types

The reason for classifying data types into two categories is that their data is stored differently (see Figure 2-2) in main memory, and as a result, the variables behave differently. There's only one value to store for primitive data types, and that can fit directly in the variable's assigned memory space. There are multiple data elements to store for composite data types, and they require additional structure to be stored in main memory.

Composite data is too large to store directly in the variable, so it's stored elsewhere in main memory and the variable holds only a numerical address describing where to find the actual data. This address is sometimes referred to as a *pointer* because it points to where in memory the actual data can be found. You never see this address, nor will you work with it directly. You need to know about it only because it affects the way you work with passing variables.

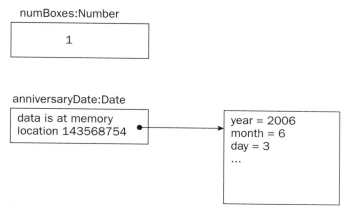

numBoxes:Number

1

anniversaryDate:Date

data is at memory
location 143568754

year = 2006
month = 6
day = 3
...

Figure 2-2

Passing by Value Versus Pass by Reference

When primitive data types are passed from one variable to another, the data is *passed by value*, which means that a complete duplicate of the data is made and passed along to the receiving variable.

Composite data types behave differently, in that assigning a composite data type from one variable to another does not make a copy of the data, but only of the numerical address describing where the data is located. This behavior is called *passing by reference*.

Here's an example that shows what happens when you use variable assignment to copy a date. Many people try to make a copy of a date by assigning a variable holding a date to another variable, but as you've learned, copying the contents of a variable containing composite data does not work as expected.

```
var anniversaryDate:Date = new Date(2006, 5, 3); // Create a new date
var nextAnniversaryDate:Date = anniversaryDate;  // Assign the date to
                                                 // nextAnniversaryDate
nextAnniversaryDate.setYear(2007);  // Change the year to 2007
trace("anniversaryDate: " + anniversaryDate);
trace("nextAnniversaryDate: " + nextAnniversaryDate);
```

Line 1 creates a new Date. A Date is a composite data type, so `anniversaryDate` does not store the actual date; it only stores the reference to where the date data is located. Line 2 assigns the contents of `anniversaryDate` to `nextAnniversaryDate`. It is easy to think that this makes a copy of the date, but it does not. Instead, just the reference to the date data is copied from `anniversaryDate` to `nextAnniversaryDate`, so that they point to the same date data, as shown in Figure 2-3. In line 3, the year is changed to 2007. In the last two lines, the `trace()` statements retrieve the data held by `anniversaryDate` and by `nextAnniversaryDate`, and reveal that they hold the same value.

Basically, you just can't use variable assignment to duplicate anything other than Number, Boolean, and String values. But that doesn't mean you can't duplicate the data of other data types.

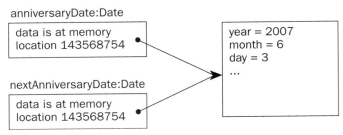

anniversaryDate:Date

data is at memory
location 143568754

nextAnniversaryDate:Date

data is at memory
location 143568754

year = 2007
month = 6
day = 3
...

Figure 2-3

Duplicating Data for Composite Types

Given that assigning a variable containing a composite data type to another variable does not actually copy the data, how is a copy made? In general, the data to be duplicated needs to either be copied manually, or it needs to provide the capability to clone itself. In the previous section, you saw how trying to make a copy of the Date class did not quite work as expected. This class does not support the capability to clone itself, so you have to create a second copy manually:

```
var anniversaryDate:Date = new Date(2006, 6, 3); // Create a new date
var nextAnniversaryDate:Date = new Date(2007, 6, 3); // Create a second date
                                               //manually
```

The MovieClip class provides a means of cloning itself. To duplicate a movie clip, use the duplicate() method that the class makes available. To see how this works, first put a movie clip on the stage:

```
var ball1Clip:MovieClip;
ball1Clip = _level0.createEmptyMovieClip("ball1_mc", 1);
ball1Clip._x = 100;
trace(ball1._x); // Outputs: 100;
```

This code creates a single empty movie clip on level 0, which is the bottom-most level in any Flash movie. It then moves the movie clip to an x coordinate of 100, which places it 100 pixels from the left edge of the movie. If you try this, you won't actually see anything because there is nothing in the movie clip. The trace() statement indicates, though, that the movie clip has moved to its starting position. Now make a copy of the movie clip:

```
var ball1Clip:MovieClip;
ball1Clip = _level0.createEmptyMovieClip("ball1_mc", 1);
var ball2Clip:MovieClip = myMC1.duplicateMovieClip("ball2_mc", 2);
ball1Clip._x = 100;
ball2Clip._x = 200;
trace(ball1Clip._x); // Outputs: 100;
trace(ball2Clip._x); // Outputs: 200;
```

In the third line, duplicateMovieClip() makes a complete copy of the movie clip referenced by ball1Clip, and assigns a handle to the new movie clip to ball2Clip. When the _x properties for each of the two variables are assigned, it's apparent that the two variables now point to two separate movie clips because they report two different _x coordinates.

As you saw with the Date class, not all data types have convenient methods for making copies, and there is no consistency between data types in how copies are made. This is not unusual, and is not as much of a limitation as you might think. Each data type works in a way that is appropriate for the nature of the data contained within, and that means that making a complete copy of the data is not always the best way to duplicate it.

Now that you have an understanding of variables and data types, you're ready to see what you can actually do with the different types of data. But first, you need to take a look at one more concept: dot syntax.

Using Dot Syntax

ActionScript is an object-oriented language, which means that it combines data with the code that works on the data into a single entity. Say you have a variable containing an important date. The variable contains not only the date, but also provides you access to some ways of working with the data that make up the date, such as advancing the year or getting the day of the week. You access the code that can work with data through what is called *dot syntax*.

Every type of data that you work with is represented a *class*. A class provides the definition for what you can do with data of that type. It defines the nature of the data, the code that acts on the data (called methods), and the properties that describe the data. Dot syntax is used to call a class method or to refer to a class property. (You learn more about classes, objects, methods, and properties as you work your way through this book.)

In dot syntax, the variable is followed by a dot, which is followed the name of a code routine (a method) or of a data descriptor (a property). The general formats for using the dot syntax are

```
variable.method();
```

```
variable.property;
```

To see listings of all the properties and methods for the standard ActionScript classes, open the Help panel within the authoring environment, and then select ActionScript 2.0 Language Reference⇨ ActionScript Classes. Clicking a class brings up a synopsis of all the properties and methods that you can use with that class.

To illustrate the syntax, take a look at how to call properties and methods with the Date class. First, create a new Date instance (you can create the Date instance at the same time you declare the variable, for brevity):

```
var specialDate:Date = new Date(2006, 5, 3);
```

This creates a new date on June 3, 2006. (The month is 0-based — month 0 is January — so 5 represents June, not May.) Want to find out which day of the week this date falls on? Checking the language reference for the Date class within the Flash help panel (ActionScript 2.0 Reference⇨ActionScript Classes⇨ Date) turns up a method called getDay() , which gives you that information:

```
var specialDate:Date = new Date(2006, 5, 3);
trace(currentDate.getDay()); // Returns 6, which is Saturday
```

A method is always followed by a pair of round brackets, which contain any parameters that the method accepts. In this instance, the `getDay` method takes no parameters, so the brackets remain empty:

```
var specialDate:Date = new Date(2006, 5, 3);
specialDate.setYear(2007);
trace(specialDate.getDay()); // Returns 0, which is Sunday
```

The Date class consists only of methods; to see a property in action, convert the date to a string, and assign it to a text field:

```
var specialDate:Date = new Date(2006, 5, 3);
this.createTextField("specialDateField", 1, 0, 0, 200, 20);
this.specialDateField.text = currentDate.toString();
```

A few things are going on in this code. Starting on the second line, `this` is a special movie clip reference that points to the current timeline. One of the methods available to all movie clips is `createTextField()`. (You can find more details about the movie clip class within the Flash help panel under ActionScript 2.0 Reference⇨ActionScript Classes⇨MovieClip.) `createTextField()` assigns the new text field to `_level0`, which is made into a property that can be accessed through dot notation as `_level0.specialDateField`. (Don't worry about the other parameters for now.)

According to the TextField class documentation, the `text` property enables you to set the contents of the text field. The last line takes a string representation of the date and assigns it to the `text` property for the text field. The last line also shows how dot notation can be used to chain together properties and methods. The `specialDateField` property is made available from `_level0`, and the `text` property is in turn made available from `specialDateField`.

There's really no limit to the number of methods and properties that can be chained together, although as you can imagine, as the number increases, it becomes more and more difficult to read the code. Chaining is very useful for accessing nested movie clips, something you see more of in Chapter 4.

Discerning Special Variables and Keywords

A number of special variables are built into the Flash player. Of particular note are `_level0`, `_root`, `_global`, and `this`. The first three should be avoided, but you should know what they are and why to avoid them. The last one, `this`, is a very useful keyword that's important to understand. The following sections discuss each of these.

_root

Flash uses the concept of movie clips, where each movie clip is a container that can contain other content, such as images, graphics, or other movie clips. When you start with a completely empty slate, there is still one special movie clip that makes up the main stage that you see. That starting movie clip always exists; it is called the root timeline, and it can be accessed from any script in any timeline through the `_root` keyword. For example, if you drag a button component onto the stage from the Components panel, and change the instance name to `saveButton`, you can refer to that button from any other timeline by accessing `_root.saveButton`. To reposition the button, for instance, you could do the following:

```
_root.saveButton._x = 20;
_root.saveButton._y = 10;
```

You should avoid using the _root keyword because it prevents your code from being reusable in anything other than a project with the same movie clip structure as yours, which is not very likely. If you were to load your movie into another movie, the _root references would then refer to that parent movie, and your code would fail completely. The alternative is to use relative addressing using _parent and this keywords. You learn more about this in later chapters.

_level0

Flash is organized so that content can be layered in different ways, with separate layerings for depths and for levels. Each movie clip uses the concept of depth, in that each item placed within a movie clip is placed on a different depth number. If any two separate units of content within the same movie clip overlap, the content in the higher depth shows over the content with the lower depth number. This behavior is seen within the visual development environment when creating two layers within the time-line and placing content in each of those layers assigns the content to two different depths. It also can be seen with the movie clip method createEmptyMovieClip(<name>, <depth>), which requires that a depth number that is unique within the parent movie clip be assigned to the new movie clip.

Levels are similar to depths, however they exist only at the top of a movie, and they are managed differently. At least one depth is always in use, which is referred to by the keyword _level0. This keyword works in exactly the same way as the _root keyword, and in fact _level0 and _root are synonyms — both can be called from any timeline to refer to the base of the movie. The same issue about using _root also applies to _level0, so you are discouraged from using it. This book does not cover the use of levels because that is a legacy feature better served by loading content into movie clips, which is discussed later in the book.

_global

_global is a special keyword that enables you to access a variable from any code anywhere. By simply assigning data to any global variable you create, you can access that data from anywhere. For example, if you create a global variable called currentScore:

```
_global.currentScore = 200;
```

You can refer to it variable from anywhere as

```
trace(_global.currentScore);
```

Although this may be convenient, it is discouraged for a few reasons:

❏   You cannot strongly type a global variable, so type-related errors are harder to debug.

❏   It encourages sloppy programming, especially when you start working with functions.

❏   It is harder to find all the places where the global variable is being manipulated.

You spend more time with global variables in Chapter 5.

this

The this keyword refers to the parent of whatever code is making the reference. When the reference is made in code that sits in a movie clip, it refers to the movie clip holding the code. Here's a trace statement called from the root timeline:

```
trace(this); // Outputs: _level0
```

If the same `trace` statement were made in another nested movie clip, it would show the path to that movie clip.

If you drag a button component onto the stage from the Components panel and change the instance name to `saveButton`, you can refer to that button from the same timeline by accessing `this.saveButton`, like this:

```
this.saveButton._x = 20;
this.saveButton._y = 10;
```

The `this` keyword is often implied, so you could refer to `saveButton` on its own to achieve the same result.

You see more of `this` in action in Chapter 7.

Working with Collections of Data

So far you've looked at variables that contain only one thing at a time. Now take a look at some types of variables that can store multiple things, namely arrays and associative arrays.

Understanding Arrays

An *array* is a container that can hold any number of individual pieces of data. Each piece of data within a particular array needs to be of the same data type, so one array could potentially store a sequence of strings, and another array could store just `true` and `false` values. In general, each item stored in the array is somehow related and used in a similar fashion to every other item. For example, an array might be used to store a list of high scores, or perhaps a list of logged-in users.

Arrays are always indexed by sequential integers, starting with 0. In an array of 50 elements, for example, the last element is found at index number 49. It might seem a little odd to represent the first array element by the number 0, but it is a convention adopted from the C language where it makes for faster array access, and is used in C++, Java, and most other modern programming languages.

Arrays are created through the following syntax:

```
var loggedInUsers:Array = new Array();
```

The first part of the syntax, `var loggedInUsers:Array`, should look familiar by now; here, though, it uses a new data type: Array. `new` is a special keyword that makes a copy of whatever follows it, and `Array()` can be thought of as a template that the `new` keyword copies from and assigns to the `loggedInUsers` variable. The end result is that once this line is invoked, `loggedInUsers` contains an empty data structure that is then used to actually hold your data.

Arrays can also be created and simultaneously pre-populated with data, as the following example shows:

```
var loggedInUsers:Array = new Array("johndoe", "janedoe");
```

Here the `loggedInUsers` array is declared and populated with two elements, `"johndoe"` and `"janedoe"`. There is also an alternate syntax:

```
var loggedInUsers:Array = [];
var loggedInUsers:Array = ["johndoe", "janedoe"];
```

The syntax used is largely personal preference; however, the first version is more explicit and is used throughout this book.

To set or retrieve any particular element in an array, use the square bracket syntax for the index number of the element to access:

```
var loggedInUsers:Array = new Array("johndoe", "janedoe");
trace(loggedInUsers[0]);
// Outputs: johndoe
trace(loggedInUsers[1]);
// Outputs: janedoe
```

Do not worry about having to know which piece of data corresponds to which index. The purpose of an array is to provide an easy mechanism to search through data. You use indexes in Chapter 3 when you explore loops, which enable you to go through each element in an array and do something useful with it. The main purpose at this point for the indexes is to provide an ordering to the data, so that element zero is stored before element one, which is stored before element two, and so on.

You can add data to an array in two ways: by using the `push()` method or by assigning a value to a particular array element. The `push()` method is convenient because it does not need to know how many elements are already defined: it automatically appends the data after the last defined array element. The following example shows the creation and population of the `loggedInUsers` array, and then the use of `push()` to add another element to the array:

```
var loggedInUsers = new Array();
loggedInUsers[0] = "johndoe";
trace(loggedInUsers);
// Outputs: johndoe

loggedInUsers.push("janedoe");
trace(loggedInUsers);
// Outputs: johndoe,janedoe
```

Macromedia Flash does not force elements to be assigned values starting at position 0 in the array. Assigning a value to a particular non-zero element before assigning values to elements earlier in the array, however, causes the earlier elements to be listed as `undefined`, as the following example shows:

```
var loggedInUsers = new Array();
loggedInUsers[3] = "johndoe";
trace(loggedInUsers);
// Outputs: undefined,undefined,undefined,johndoe
```

This is generally not a recommended approach to assigning data to an array.

An array's length property is determined solely on the position of the last element. If element 3 is the last element containing data, the length of the array is 4. If an array contains no defined elements, its length is 0.

> The keywords `null` and `undefined` have special meanings in ActionScript. A variable that has been declared with the `var` keyword but contains no data is represented by the `null` value, whereas a variable that has not been declared at all is represented by the `undefined` value.

Once an array has been populated with data, numerous methods are available to manipulate it, including the following:

Method	Description
concat()	Combines two arrays into one single array, or adds any number of elements to the end of one array.
join()	Joins each array element into a single string value.
push()	Adds a new element to the end of an array.
reverse()	Reverses the order of an array.
shift()	Removes the first element of an array, and returns that element.
slice()	Extracts a range of elements from an array.
sort()	Changes the ordering of elements in an array.
sortOn()	Changes the ordering of elements in a multidimensional array based on a specific field.
splice()	Adds and removes elements in an array.
toString()	Outputs a string representation of an array.
unshift()	Adds elements to the beginning of an array.

The following sections explore some of the more common array methods.

concat()

The concatenation method — `concat()` — takes two arrays and combines them, or takes one array and adds elements to the end. The method does not directly manipulate the source array(s); instead, it concatenates the array values together and returns a new array. Here are some examples:

```
// Join two arrays together, then assign the new joined array back to
// the variable firstArray.
var loggedInUsers:Array = new Array("johndoe", "janedoe", "rahibdoe");
var recentUsers:Array = new Array("ngt", "loc");

loggedInUsers = loggedInUsers.concat(recentUsers);
trace(loggedInUsers);
// Outputs: johndoe,janedoe,rahibdoe,ngt,loc

// Add elements to the end of an array
var newlyAddedUsers:Array = new Array("ngt", "loc");
```

```
newlyAddedUsers = newlyAddedUsers.concat("schin", "bchan");
trace(newlyAddedUsers);
// Outputs: ngt,loc,schin,bchan
```

join()

The `join()` method is used to output a string representation of an array. The method converts each array element to a string, and then places each of those strings together into one large string, separated by a delimiter character. The delimiter character that is passed to `join()` can be anything you want, and it can actually be more than one character in length. If no delimiter is specified, a comma is used. The `join()` method does not touch the original array; instead, the new string is passed as a return value that can then be assigned to another variable or passed as a parameter to another method. Here's an example:

```
// Concatenate each of the array elements together.
var loggedInUsers:Array = new Array("johndoe", "janedoe", "rahibdoe");
trace(loggedInUsers.join(":"));
// Outputs: johndoe:janedoe:rahibdoe
```

The counterpart to the `join()` method is the `split()` method, which chunks up a string into an array. There are some very powerful ways of doing string manipulation by chaining together `join()` and `split()` methods. See Chapter 18 for more on using these methods together.

push()

As you saw earlier, the `push()` method is an easy way to add elements to an array. Without it, adding an element to the end of an existing array would look like this:

```
loggedInUsers[loggedInUsers.length-1] = "johndoe";
```

`push()` makes it simpler:

```
loggedInUsers.push("johndoe");
```

This syntax is more readable, is easier to understand, and results in comparable performance.

sort()

Thankfully, ActionScript arrays come with built-in methods to perform various sorting tasks. The built-in documentation for the `sort()` method makes it look a little intimidating, but it is in fact very simple to use.

To sort an array in ascending alphabetical order (from a to z), use `sort()` with no additional options specified:

```
var birdsArray:Array = new Array("robin", "hummingbird", "parakeet", "crane");
birdsArray.sort();
trace(birdsArray);
// Outputs: crane,hummingbird,parakeet,robin
```

To sort an array in descending order (from z to a), add the DESCENDING parameter to `sort()`:

```
var birdsArray:Array = new Array("robin", "hummingbird", "parakeet", "crane");
birdsArray.sort(Array.DESCENDING);
trace(birdsArray);
// Outputs: robin,parakeet,hummingbird,crane
```

A number of other options can be passed to `sort()`, including the following:

❑ `Array.CASEINSENSITIVE` — Letter case is ignored when determining sort order.

❑ `Array.UNIQUESORT` — Specifies that any particular value cannot appear more than once in an array. The sort stops early if it finds that this is the case.

❑ `Array.RETURNINDEXEDARRAY` — Leaves the original array unchanged, and returns a sorted copy of the array.

❑ `Array.NUMERIC` — The array is sorted by number rather than by string, allowing 3 to come before 15 in the sort order.

Multiple options can be passed if each is separated by the | symbol.

When sorting strings, it is a good idea to use the case-insensitive search; otherwise you might not get what you expect in the results. For example:

```
var birdsArray:Array = new Array("robin", "Woody Woodpecker", "crane", "parakeet");
birdsArray.sort();
trace(birdsArray);
// Outputs: Woody Woodpecker,crane,crane,parakeet,robin
```

A standard sort — `sort()` — lists uppercase elements before listing lowercase ones. Now if you sort the same array using the `Array.CASEINSENSITIVE` option, all of the elements are output in alphabetical order, which is probably the result you want:

```
birdsArray.sort(Array.CASEINSENSITIVE);
trace(birdsArray);
// Outputs: crane,crane,parakeet,robin,Woody Woodpecker
```

To sort a numerical array, use the `Array.NUMERIC` option. Here's why:

```
// Perform sort on an array of numbers
var fileSizes:Array = new Array(15, 3, 260, 22, 43);
fileSizes.sort();
trace(fileSizes);
// Outputs: 15,22,260,3,43
```

The standard `sort()` outputs the elements in the order of the *first* digit (the 1 in 15, the 2 in 22 and 260, and so on). The `Array.NUMERIC` option considers the entire element in its sort:

```
fileSizes.sort(Array.NUMERIC);
trace(fileSizes);
// Outputs: 3,15,22,43,260
```

Here's an example of combining options, resulting in a reverse numerical output (two options, separated by a |):

```
fileSizes.sort(Array.NUMERIC | Array.DESCENDING);
trace(fileSizes);
// Outputs: 260,43,22,15,3
```

splice()

The `splice()` method enables you to add and delete the array in one call. The general splice syntax is as follows:

```
myArray.splice(index, numDelete, addedElements);
```

You delete elements by setting the index from which to start deletion, and passing in the number of elements to delete:

```
var birdsArray:Array = new Array("robin", "crane", "parakeet");
// Delete two elements, starting from array index 1.
birdsArray.splice(1, 2);
trace(birdsArray);
// Outputs: robin
```

Replacing elements is a combination of adding and removing elements at the same time. First, elements are deleted starting from the index number provided in the first parameter, and then elements are inserted, also starting from the index number provided:

```
var birdsArray:Array = new Array("robin", "crane", "parakeet");
// Delete one element at index 1, then insert
// elements "blue jay" and "finch" at index 1.
birdsArray.splice(1, 1, "blue jay", "finch");
trace(birdsArray);
// Outputs: robin,blue jay,finch,parakeet
```

One element at index 1, `"crane"`, is deleted, and then `"blue jay"` and `"finch"` are inserted at index 1, pushing anything currently at position one and later further to the right.

If you want to add elements at one index and remove elements at another index, you need to use two separate `splice()` calls specifying two different indexes, like this:

```
var birdsArray:Array = new Array("robin", "crane", "parakeet");
// Delete "robin" at index 0
birdsArray.splice(0, 1);
// Insert "blue jay" element at index 1
birdsArray.splice(1, 0, "blue jay");
trace(birdsArray);
// Outputs: crane,blue jay,parakeet
```

Here, element 0 — `"robin"` — is deleted, and then `"blue jay"` is inserted at element 1.

Exploring Associative Arrays and Objects

An *associative array* is very similar to the indexed array, but instead of defining an order (index) to pieces of data, it defines *relationships* among data pairs. For example, say the following pieces of data are to be stored:

❏   User nderksen is a guest.

❏   User jberg is an administrator.

❏   User msmithe is a moderator.

These three pairs of related data are represented by the following associative array:

```
var userAccountsArray:Object = new Object();
userAccountsArray["nderksen"] = "guest";
userAccountsArray["jberg"] = "administrator";
userAccountsArray["msmithe"] = "moderator";
trace(userAccountsArray["nderksen"]);
// Outputs: guest
```

With the data stored in this manner, doing a lookup requires no looping through data to find a value. A quick single `trace` line does the trick.

The general form for an associative array is as follows:

```
var myAssociativeArray:Object = new Object();
myAssociativeArray[<key>] = <value>;
```

An associative array behaves differently from a regular array in several important ways:

❑   Associative arrays are indexed by string, not by number.

❑   The ordering of elements in an associative array is not guaranteed. Element order can change as the associative array is manipulated.

❑   Array methods and properties, such as `push()`, `splice()`, and `length`, do not apply to associative arrays.

An associative array is not created by making a new instance of the Array class, as indexed arrays are. Instead, it is created through a new instance of the Object class. Before you learn why this is the case, you should understand the Object class.

An associative array can be created from an array instance, but none of the Array class's properties or methods will work on the array. Historically, associative arrays were frequently implemented this way; however, the proper technique is to create them by instantiating the Object class.

Viewing the Object Class as a Container

The Object class is the base class from which all other ActionScript classes are derived. Through the mechanism of inheritance, all classes have access to the methods and properties that the Object class provides. In addition, the Object class acts as a container that can store related pairs of data.

Two ways exist to create a new copy of the Object class. The first uses the `new` keyword to generate the Object instance and then assigns values to properties that you make up:

```
var userData:Object = new Object();
userData.firstName = "Nathan";
userData.lastName = "Derksen";
trace(userData.firstName);
// Outputs: Nathan
trace(userData.lastName);
// Outputs: Derksen
```

Most classes don't let you just make up arbitrary properties on-the-fly, but the Object class does. As a result, it makes a great container for data.

The second approach uses a shorthand notation that creates the object and assigns the properties in one step:

```
var userData:Object = {firstName:"Nathan", lastName:"Derksen"};
trace(userData.firstName);
// Outputs: Nathan
trace(userData.lastName);
// Outputs: Derksen
```

Once an Object container contains data, two ways exist to retrieve that data. The first accesses the property directly through dot notation, as you just saw with `userData.firstName`. Here's an example of the second:

```
var userData:Object = {firstName:"Nathan", lastName:"Derksen"};
trace(userData["firstName"]);
// Outputs: Nathan
trace(userData["lastName"]);
// Outputs: Derksen
```

Are you thinking, "Didn't I just see this a moment ago?" Indeed you did! This syntax is identical to the syntax for accessing associative array elements. It turns out that associative arrays are just another front to the Object class, and the two syntaxes are completely interchangeable.

The following example shows how values are set with the associative array notation and retrieved with the dot notation:

```
var userData:Object = new Object();
userData["firstName"] = "Nathan";
userData["lastName"] = "Derksen";
trace(userData.firstName);
// Outputs: Nathan
trace(userData.lastName);
// Outputs: Derksen
```

Revisiting the Associative Array

Although the associative array and the Object are really the same thing, it is still useful to conceptually separate the two. By combining an associative array with a collection of objects, you can store much more complex sets of data. Here's some example data to illustrate how that's done:

❑   User nderksen is a guest; has been a forum member since April 1, 2005; and has made 24 posts.

❑   User jberg is an administrator; has been a forum member since February 18, 2003; and has made 1,824 posts.

❑   User msmithe is a moderator; has been a forum member since September 9, 2004; and has made 943 posts.

The information can be easily stored and accessed using a combination of associative array and Object syntax:

```
var userAccountsArray:Object = new Object();
userAccountsArray["nderksen"] = {group:"guest", joined:"2005/04/01", posts:24};
userAccountsArray["jberg"] = {group:"administrator", joined:"2003/02/18", ⤷
    posts:1824};
```

```
userAccountsArray["msmithe"] = {group:"moderator", joined:"2004/09/09", posts:943};

trace(userAccountsArray["nderksen"].group);
// Outputs: guest

trace(userAccountsArray["jberg"].joined);
// Outputs: 2003/02/18

trace(userAccountsArray["msmithe"].posts);
// Outputs: 943
```

This code creates a lookup table, indexed by username, where any attribute for any username can be accessed with a single line of code.

Similarly, a regular indexed array can be used to store objects:

```
var highScoresList:Array = new Array();
highScoresList.push({score:2030045, name:"Jeffrey Berg"});
highScoresList.push({score:1980320, name:"Mary Smithe"});
highScoresList.push({score:10034, name:"Nathan Derksen"});

trace(highScoresList[0].name);
// Outputs: Jeffrey Berg

trace(highScoresList[0].score);
// Outputs: 2030045
```

It's a very practical construct that can be used any time records of data need to be kept in memory.

Because objects and associative arrays are interchangeable, and because all ActionScript classes inherit from the Object class, it follows that this syntax can be used elsewhere as well, such as with the MovieClip class. The normal syntax for creating a new text field in a movie clip is as follows:

```
this.createTextField("myTextField", 1, 0, 0, 200, 50);
this.myTextField.text = "The quick brown fox";
// Outputs: The quick brown fox
```

The associative array syntax is quite similar:

```
this.createTextField("myTextField", 1, 0, 0, 200, 50);
this["myTextField"].text = "The quick brown fox";
// Outputs: The quick brown fox
```

The keyword this points to the main timeline, and the createTextField() method adds a property to the base movie clip that points to the text field. The associative array syntax for movie clips becomes very useful when creating an arbitrary number of text fields or movie clips on the timeline, as the following example shows:

```
for (var i:Number = 0; i < 5; i++)
{
    this.createTextField("myTextField" + i, i, 0, i*20, 200, 50);
    this["myTextField" + i].text = "Text field number " + i;
}
```

This code creates five text fields on the timeline, each separated by 20 pixels vertically, and each containing the text Text field number: <n>, where <n> is the number indicating the order in which the field was created.

Without the associative array syntax, the more involved eval() *method would be needed to create these fields.* eval() *is a means of accessing variables whose names are constructed on-the-fly. This book doesn't cover* eval() *functionality, which is fairly complex, because the associative array syntax is much less confusing.*

Try It Out   **Storing Data for a Photo Viewer**

Creating structures to store data is central to many Macromedia Flash applications. Imagine a photo viewer for showing your photos to friends: You would need to store a filename for the image, perhaps a file size to show onscreen, and a description of the photo.

Here's how you can work with such a data structure:

1. Create a new Macromedia Flash document by selecting File⇨New and choosing Flash Document from the New Document panel.

2. Click the first frame in the timeline, open the Actions panel (Window⇨Development Panels⇨ Actions), and type in the following ActionScript code:

```
#include "tryItOut_trackData.as"
```

3. Select File⇨Save As, name the file tryItOut_trackData.fla, choose an appropriate directory, and save it.

4. Create a new script file by selecting File⇨New and choosing ActionScript File from the New Document panel.

5. Select File⇨Save As and ensure it is showing the directory containing the Flash project file. Give the file the name tryItOut_trackData.as and save it.

6. Enter the following code into the new ActionScript file:

```
var photoArray:Object = new Object();

photoArray["weddingPhoto1"] = new Object();
photoArray["weddingPhoto1"].fileName = "weddingPhoto1.jpg";
photoArray["weddingPhoto1"].fileSize = 150;
photoArray["weddingPhoto1"].description = "Exchanging of the rings.";

photoArray["westIndiesVacation1"] = new Object();
photoArray["westIndiesVacation1"].fileName = "vacation1.jpg";
photoArray["westIndiesVacation1"].fileSize = 64;
photoArray["westIndiesVacation1"].description = "Arriving at the airport ⤶
    in sweltering heat.";

trace(photoArray["weddingPhoto1"].fileName);
trace(photoArray["weddingPhoto1"].fileSize);
trace(photoArray["westIndiesVacation1"].description);
```

7. Save the file (File⇨Save), return to the Flash project file, and select Control⇨Test Movie.

How It Works

You use an associative array to store the details of each photo. Each photo is given an ID that is used for all future access to its data. The first line sets up the associative array. The second line sets up the object that is going to store the details for the first photo. The third, fourth, and fifth lines assign data to the object for the first photo. The process in lines 2–5 is repeated for each photo to be placed in the photo album.

The `trace()` statements show how to access individual elements within the associative array. The `photoArray["weddingPhoto1"]` reference stores an object that holds all of the properties for the photo with the id `weddingPhoto1`. Each property can be accessed through dot notation.

In the next chapter, you see how you can do useful work with this data structure by looping through each element.

The output from this code should look like the following:

```
trace(photoArray["weddingPhoto1"].fileName);
// Outputs: weddingPhoto1.jpg

trace(photoArray["weddingPhoto1"].fileSize);
// Outputs: 150

trace(photoArray["westIndiesVacation1"].description);
// Outputs: Arriving at the airport in sweltering heat
```

Summary

This chapter introduced you to the ActionScript language. Of course, you'll be learning a lot more about it as you work through the book. Points to remember from this chapter, though, include the following:

❑ Variables are the basic means of holding data. The type of data held in the variable determines what kinds of things can be done with that data.

❑ You can make use of white space to help make your code more readable.

❑ Strong typing helps you find type-related errors quickly. All variables should include a type definition when they are first declared.

❑ Dot syntax enables you to call methods and properties from an object. Commands can be chained together by "connecting the dots."

❑ An array holds a sequential list of data.

❑ An associative array is not really an array, but an unordered list key/value pairs.

❑ An object can be used to store arbitrary data as property/value pairs.

❑ An associative array can store a list of objects as a convenient way of storing data records.

Exercises

1. Determine which of the following variable declarations are not valid and why.

    a. `var my_var:Number = 0;`

    b. `var someOtherVar:Integer = 0;`

    c. `myString:String;`

    d. `var 1stPlaceFinisher:String;`

    e. `var _width:Number = 25;`

    f. `var isFinished:Boolean = "false";`

2. Work through the order in which the operators are evaluated in the following statement:

    ```
    totalAmount = (numItemsPickedUp - numItemsPrepaid) * perItemCost + handlingFee;
    ```

3. If the values for the preceding statement are `numItemsPickedUp`, 10; `numItemsPrepaid`, 5; `perItemCost`, 20; and `handlingFee`, 30, determine — without running the code — what value would be assigned to `totalAmount`.

    ```
    totalAmount = (numItemsPickedUp - numItemsPrepaid) * perItemCost + handlingFee;
    ```

4. Predict the outcome of the following:

    ```
    var birdsArray:Array = new Array("finch", "blue jay");
    birdsArray.push("warbler");
    birdsArray.splice(2, 0, "crow");
    birdsArray.splice(0, 1);
    trace(birdsArray.join("-"));
    ```

Understanding ActionScript Expressions and Loops

So far you've learned about the basic structure of the ActionScript language and the core data element, the variable, but you've seen only scenarios in which every line of code executes exactly once. In this chapter, you add a very important set of tools, including the capability to use the contents of variables to make decisions about which lines of code to execute and the capability to loop repeatedly through blocks of code.

The concepts of decision making and looping through code are referred to as *flow control*. A program's flow is the sequence in which lines of code are executed. Through some of the statements that ActionScript provides, you can control that flow.

This chapter starts by exploring the capability to make decisions in code.

Making Decisions

Throughout the course of your day, you make decisions about what to do. When you wake up, do you drink one cup of coffee or two? Which pair of shoes will you wear? Do you drive or walk to your morning destination? Your entire day is composed of many decisions all performed in sequence.

In the same way, a program is composed of logic used to make many decisions, except you have to provide the guidelines needed to make those decisions. These guidelines are called *conditionals* and are simple logical rules that spell out those guidelines in an unambiguous way. Conditionals are composed of three elements:

❑ Expressions — An expression is a precise specification of the decision to be made. Each decision requires one expression to describe it.

❑ Operators — An operator is used within an expression to impose conditions on the decision, such as to make a comparison, or to specify that there are multiple parts to a decision. One expression can consist of any number of operators.

❏ Statements — A statement is code that executes if the expression evaluation results in a `true` (yes) decision. A conditional can contain any number of statements grouped inside a pair of curly brackets.

The overall makeup of a conditional is as follows:

```
if (numPhotos == 0)
{
    trace("There are no photos");
}
```

In this example, the expression is `numPhotos == 0`, where you test whether the contents of the `numPhotos` variable equals the number zero. The two = symbols together form the "is equal to" conditional operator, and the line with the `trace()` code is a statement that is executed only if the expression `numPhotos == 0` evaluates to `true`.

> The = operator and the == operator are completely different and frequently get mixed up. The = operator assigns the contents of one variable to another variable, whereas the == operator compares two variables to see if they contain the same data. If you use the = operator within an `if` statement by accident, the expression always returns `true`.

Expressions

An expression is the means to formally describe a decision. In the real world, a decision can be at least yes, no, or maybe. For a computer, a decision can consist only of yes (`true`) or no (`false`). An expression always results in a single value of `true` or `false`. With the expression `myHair == "brown"`, for example, the value stored in the variable `myHair` is retrieved first and then compared with the string value `"brown"` to see if they are equal. Depending on the result of the comparison, a `true` or `false` value is returned.

Putting together a single decision comparing two values at once is pretty straightforward, but when two, three, or more decisions are placed into a single expression, things can quickly get complex. (Don't worry, though — shortly you learn techniques for dealing with complex expressions.)

The ultimate output of an expression is a single `true` or `false` value and nothing else. If the whole expression evaluates to `true`, all the statements are executed; if it evaluates to `false`, none of the statements is executed and the next line of code after the closing curly bracket is executed.

Consider the following examples. First, two string values are compared:

```
var typeOfPants:String = "jeans";
if (typeOfPants == "dress pants")
{
    trace("Wearing dress pants");
}
```

This expression compares the contents of the `typeOfPants` variable with the string value `"dress pants"`. The variable contains the value `"jeans"`, so the expression becomes `"jeans" == "dress` pants". Because the values on either side of the equal-to operator are different, the result of the comparison is the value `false`, and the statement between the curly brackets is skipped.

Here's an example that compares two numbers:

```
var numPhotos:Number = 2;
if (numPhotos > 1)
{
    trace("There is more than one photo");
}
```

The expression compares the contents of the `numPhotos` variable, 2, with the number 1. The operator used is > (greater than), which returns `true` if the value on the left is larger than the value on the right. The 2 is indeed greater than 1, so the expression returns `true` and the `trace()` statement is executed.

The greater than (>) and less than (<) operators are frequently confused. The open part of the symbol always faces the larger value, and the pointed end points to the smaller value.

The next example compares two Boolean values:

```
var isDaytime:Boolean = true;
if (isDaytime == false)
{
    trace("It is not daytime");
}
```

This example compares the contents of the `isDaytime` variable (`true`) with the value `false`. (Remember, == is the equal operator; = is the assignment operator.) `true` does not equal `false`, so the comparison operator returns an overall value of `false`, and the `trace()` statement is skipped.

Building Expressions

Just as there are no limits to the kinds of decisions you can make throughout your day, there are no limits to the numbers of different expressions you can build. You can use expressions to make mathematical comparisons or determine whether one number falls within a range of numbers, to evaluate what to do based on user input, and to evaluate several criteria at once.

Take a look at a couple of examples:

```
var weaponType1:String = "pen";
var weaponType2:String = "sword";
trace(weaponType1.length > weaponType2.length);
// Outputs: false
```

This expression returns `true` only if the number of characters in the word `pen` is greater than the number of characters in the word `sword`.

```
var numSitups:Number = 5;
trace(numSitups >= 0 && numSitups <= 10);
// Outputs: true
```

The expression returns `true` if the value held in `numSitups` is from the number `0` to the number `10`, inclusive. This is the standard way of checking to see if the value of a variable falls between a specific range of numbers.

The expression involves several operators, so pay attention to the order in which operators are evaluated. According to the operator listing earlier in this chapter, the `>=` (greater than or equal to) and `<=` (less than or equal to) operators have higher priority than the `&&` (logical AND) operator, so those are evaluated first. The variable `numSitups` contains the value 5, so the comparison `numSitups >= 0` becomes `5 >= 0`, which is `true` because 5 is greater than or equal to 0. The comparison `numSitups <= 10` becomes `5 <= 10`, which is `true` because 5 is less than or equal to 10. The results of these two comparisons are used by the `&&` (logical AND) operator, reducing the expression to `true && true`. The `&&` operator returns `true` only if the values on both sides are `true`, as is the case in this example.

The process that the Flash player uses to evaluate your expressions involves simplifying until only a `true` or `false` value remains. Here's how it works:

1. The starting expression:

   ```
   numSitups >= 0 && numSitups <= 10
   ```

2. Replace the variables with the values that they hold:

   ```
   5 >= 0 && 5 <= 10
   ```

3. Evaluate the highest priority operators:

   ```
   true && true
   ```

4. Evaluate the remaining operator:

   ```
   true
   ```

   Chapter 2 introduced operators in ActionScript code and included a table that described them in the order in which they are evaluated in expressions

That was a lot of detail for a single evaluation, but it's important that you understand what happens when an expression is evaluated.

The following example incorporates a mathematical operator in the form of a subtraction:

```
var currentRecord:Number = 10;
var numRecords:Number = 11;
trace(currentRecord <= numRecords - 1);
// Outputs: true
```

This expression involves a computation and then a comparison. First, the mathematical operation takes place, where 1 is subtracted from the contents of `numRecords` (11), returning a value of 10. The result of the computation is compared to the contents of `currentRecord` (10) using the `<=` (less than or equal to) operator — `10 <= 10` — which evaluates to `true`.

Expressions can be used to modify program behavior based on the result of user actions, as the following example shows:

```
var lastClickTime:Number = 235246;
var thisClickTime:Number = 235370;
var shiftPressed:Boolean = false;
trace(thisClickTime - lastClickTime < 1500 && shiftPressed == true);
// Outputs: false
```

This expression evaluates two things and requires that they both be `true` for the whole expression to be true.

1. The starting expression:

```
thisClickTime - lastClickTime < 1500 && shiftPressed == true
```

2. Replace the variables with the values that they hold:

```
235370 - 235246 < 1500 && false == true
```

3. Evaluate the highest priority operator(s) — in this case, subtraction:

```
126 < 1500 && false == true
```

4. Evaluate the next highest operators (the less than and the equals operators). The `==` operator returns `true` only if the values on both sides are the same.

```
true && false
```

5. Evaluate the last operator (`&&`). The `&&` operator returns `true` only if the values on both sides are true.

```
false
```

When multiple comparisons are used, it may help to use round brackets (parentheses) to clarify the order in which the comparisons are to be performed. Comparisons within brackets are always evaluated first. Compare the following two variations of the same expression:

```
var recordNum1:Number = 5;
var recordNum2:Number = 10;
var skipCheck:Boolean = true;
```

```
trace(recordNum1 == 5 || recordNum2 == 9 && skipCheck == false);
// Output: true
```

```
trace((recordNum1 == 5 || recordnum2 == 9) && skipCheck == false);
// Output: false
```

The order in which the comparisons are made in the first `trace()` is not obvious. It is unclear whether the `||` (OR) operation is performed before the `&&` (AND) operation, or vice versa. It turns out that the `&&` operator is evaluated before the `||` operator. The first expression is evaluated in the following order:

1. The starting expression:

```
recordNum1 == 5 || recordNum2 == 9 && skipCheck == false
```

2. Replace the variables with the values that they hold:

```
5 == 5      ||      10 == 9      &&      true == false
```

3. Evaluate the highest priority operations (==):

```
true      ||      false      &&      false
```

4. Evaluate the next highest priority operation (&&):

```
true      ||                  false
```

5. Evaluate the last operator (||):

```
true
```

|| *evaluates to* true *if the value on at least one side of the operator is* true.

In the second trace, brackets have been added to make the order in which the operators are evaluated more explicit, and to force the || operator to take precedence over the && operator:

1. The starting expression:

```
(myNum1 == 5 || myNum2 == 9) && myBoolean == false
```

2. Replace the variables with the values that they hold:

```
(   5 == 5   ||   10 == 9   ) &&   true == false
```

3. Evaluate the highest operators (==) within the brackets:

```
(   true   ||   false   ) &&   true == false
```

4. Evaluate the next highest operator (||) within the brackets:

```
(           true           ) &&   true == false
```

5. With the operations within the brackets concluded, their result is now part of the simpler expression, and the highest remaining operator (==) is evaluated:

```
true           &&      false
```

6. Evaluate the final operator (&&): which gives the value true only if both of the values next to the operator are true.

```
false
```

&& *evaluates to* true *only if the values on both sides of it are* true.

Although the two expressions are essentially identical, changing the order in which the operators are evaluated results in different outcomes. If you are ever unsure about the order in which an operator is evaluated, just add brackets to enforce the order you want used. The operators within round brackets are always evaluated before operators outside the brackets.

Macromedia Flash allows any data to be compared to any other data, but comparing anything other than numbers, strings, and Booleans leads to unpredictable results. Take the example of comparing two Date objects representing the same date as follows:

```
var date1:Date = new Date(2010, 1, 1);
var date2:Date = new Date(2010, 1, 1);
trace(date1 == date2);
// Outputs: false
```

The issue is that the variables date1 and date2 do not contain actual dates; they simply contain a number representing where each Date object is located in memory. Two separate Date objects cannot exist at exactly the same point in memory, so the comparison between date1 and date2 will always be false. To compare the actual dates, use a string or a numerical representation of the dates:

```
var date1:Date = new Date(2010, 1, 1);
var date2:Date = new Date(2010, 1, 1);
trace(date1.getTime() == date2.getTime());
// Outputs: true
```

Calling getTime() on a Date object outputs a number that can be compared (see Figure 3-1).

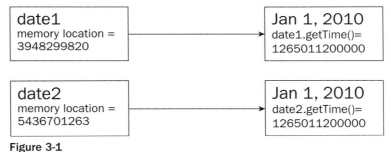

Figure 3-1

The following sections look at some standard conditional statements.

Using if..then..else

The main conditional statement used in any program is if..then..else (*if* an expression is true, *then* statement x is called; otherwise (*else*), statement y is called):

```
if (expression)
{
     // Statements to be called if the expression is true
}
else
{
     // Statements to be called if the expression is false
}
```

If the expression evaluates to `true`, all the statements in the first set of braces are run, otherwise all the statements in the second set of braces are run. The `else` portion of the statement is optional. If it is only important to act on a `true` statement, only the first set of braces needs to be included:

```
if (expression)
{
    // Statements to be called if the expression is true
}
```

`if..then..else` statements may be nested within each other. The inner statement executes only if the expression in the outer statement evaluates to `true`:

```
if (myAge >= 18)
{
    if (haveLicense == true)
    {
        // Statements to be called if myAge >= 18 and haveLicense == true
    }
}
```

There are different ways to write the same set of conditions. The preceding example can be re-written to remove the nesting:

```
if (myAge >= 18 && haveLicense == true)
{
    // Statements to be called if myAge >= 18 and haveLicense == true
}
```

Numerous reasons exist for why you would or would not use nesting. Non-nested statements, for instance, provide a slight performance advantage because there's only one expression to evaluate. The code is also more compact. Nesting makes complex expressions more readable by breaking them into smaller statements.

Overall, how you structure your `if` statements is more a matter of personal preference and style. Some situations lend themselves to one style over another, but there are always multiple ways to structure the same set of decisions. Recognizing when to use one style over the other simply takes practice.

Using switch..case

Many cities have a recycling program where people can place items destined for recycling in specially provided bins and bags. The blue bin hold cans and containers, the blue bag holds newsprint, and the yellow bag holds glossy paper products, for example. For each item to be tossed, a decision is made regarding what to do with it. Glass bottles and milk cartons go in the blue bin, newspapers go in the blue bag, magazines go in the yellow bag, and oil-soaked pizza boxes go to the trash. This scenario could be coded using the following `if` statements:

```
if (garbagePiece == "glass bottle")
{
    trace("Put in blue bin");
}
```

```
    else if (garbagePiece == "newspaper")
    {
        trace("Put in blue bag");
    }
    else if (garbagePiece == "magazine")
    {
        trace("Put in yellow bag");
    }
    else if (garbagePiece == "milk carton"
    {
        trace("Put in blue bin");
    }
    else if (garbagePiece == "pizza box")
    {
        trace("Put in garbage bin");
    }
```

The switch..case statement makes multiple simple comparisons with one piece of data, but without a whole mess of if statements to do it. The switch..case syntax gives the following code:

```
switch (garbagePiece)
{
    case "glass bottle":
        trace("Put in blue bin");
        break;
    case "newspaper":
        trace("Put in blue bag");
        break;
    case "magazine":
        trace("Put in yellow bag");
        break;
    case "milk carton":
        trace("Put in blue bin");
        break;
    case "pizza box":
        trace("Put in garbage bin");
}
```

As you can see, switch..case statements are more readable and more efficient. The general syntax is as follows:

```
switch (variable)
{
    case "value1":
        //Statements for value 1
        break;
    case "value2":
        //Statements for value 2
        break;
    default:
        // Default statements
}
```

The variable can contain only a string or a numerical value, and each possible value to test for starts with the `case "value":` statement and ends with the `break;` statement. An optional `default` block contains statements that are run only if the data contained by the variable is not matched by any of the case statements.

The `break` statement indicates that there are no further statements for that case and breaks out of that particular `switch` statement entirely. If `break` is not included after every `case` statement, program flow continues to the next statement, even if it is part of the next case block. This might seem a bit strange, but there's good reason for it. By omitting `break` statements in strategic locations, multiple values can be compared against the variable and each match can execute the same code, as the following example shows:

```
switch (garbagePiece)
{
    case "plastic pop bottle":
        trace("Crush pop bottle");
    case "glass bottle":
    case "aluminum cans":
    case "milk carton":
        trace("Put in blue bin");
        break;
    case "newspaper":
    case "non glossy flyer":
        trace("Put in blue bag");
        break;
    case "magazine":
    case "glossy flyer":
        trace("Put in yellow bag");
        break;
    default:
        trace("Put in garbage bin");
}
```

Here, glass bottles, plastic pop bottles, aluminum cans, and milk cartons go in the blue bin, newspapers and non-glossy flyers go in the blue bag, magazines and glossy flyers go in the yellow bag, and everything else, including pizza boxes, goes into the garbage bin. In addition, plastic pop bottles are crushed before being put into the blue bin.

Figure 3-2 steps through a `switch..case` statement for `plastic pop bottle`.

```
var garbagePiece:String = "plastic pop bottle";
switch (garbagePiece)
{
    case "plastic pop bottle"
        trace("Crush pop bottle")
    case "glass bottle":
    case "aluminum cans":
    case "milk carton":
        trace("Put in blue box");
        break;
    case "newspaper":
    case "non glossy flyer":
        trace("Put in blue bag");
        break;
    case "magazine":
    case "glossy flyer":
        trace("Put in yellow bag");
        break;
    default:
        trace("Put in garbage bin");
}
// Next statement
```

Figure 3-2

First, each case statement is stepped through until a match is found. Once found, lines of code continue to be run until a break statement is reached, at which point the switch statement ends. In this case, the output is

```
Crush pop bottle
Put in blue bin
```

In Figure 3-3, each case statement is compared to the string banana peel.

```
var garbagePiece:String = "banana peel";
switch (garbagePiece)
{
    case "plastic pop bottle"
            trace("Crush pop bottle")
    case "glass bottle":
    case "aluminum cans":
    case "milk carton":
            trace("Put in blue box");
            break;
    case "newspaper":
    case "non glossy flyer":
            trace("Put in blue bag");
            break;
    case "magazine":
    case "glossy flyer":
            trace("Put in yellow bag");
            break;
    default:
            trace("Put in garbage bin");
}
// Next statement
```

Figure 3-3

This time no match is found, so once the `default:` statement is reached, all subsequent code is executed until the closing switch brace. The output from this code segment is simply

```
Put in garbage bin
```

Try It Out   **Handling Keystrokes in a Game**

If you want to use Macromedia Flash to develop games, one of the things you need to be able to do is map key presses to an action to perform. The `switch..case` statement is perfectly suited for this. Follow these steps to see how simple it is to set up:

1.   Create a new Macromedia Flash document by selecting File⇨New and choosing Flash Document from the New Document panel.

2.   Click the first frame in the timeline, open the Actions panel (Window⇨Development Panels⇨ Actions), and type in the following ActionScript code:

```
#include "tryItOut_decisions.as"
```

3. Select File⇨Save As, name the file `tryItOut_decisions.fla`, choose an appropriate directory, and save it.

4. Create a new script file by selecting File⇨New and choosing ActionScript File from the New Document panel.

5. Select File⇨Save As and ensure it is showing the directory containing the `.fla` file. Name the new file `tryItOut_decisions.as` and save it.

6. Enter the following code into the new ActionScript file:

```
var keyListener:Object = new Object();
keyListener.onKeyDown = function()
{
    var pressedKeyCode:Number = Key.getCode();
    trace("Pressed key number: " + pressedKeyCode);
    switch (pressedKeyCode)
    {
        case Key.LEFT: // left arrow
            movePlayerLeft();
            trace("moving left");
            break;
        case Key.UP: // up arrow
            movePlayerUp();
            trace("moving up");
            break;
        case Key.RIGHT: // right arrow
            movePlayerRight();
            trace("moving right");
            break;
        case Key.DOWN: // down arrow
            movePlayerDown();
            trace("moving down");
            break;
        case Key.ENTER:
        case Key.SHIFT:
        case Key.CONTROL:
        case Key.SPACE:
            fire();
            trace("firing");
            break;
        case Key.TAB:
            switchWeapons();
            trace("switching weapons");
            break;
        case Key.ESCAPE:
            pauseGame();
            trace("pausing game");
            break;
    }
};
Key.addListener(keyListener);
```

7. Save the file (File⇨Save), return to the Flash project file, and select Control⇨Test Movie.

> The Macromedia Flash test environment blocks some of the keystrokes used here, preventing all of the conditions from working. To enable your code to successfully receive notification of every key press while in the test movie mode, select Control⇨Disable Keyboard Shortcuts before running the movie. (You need to do this only in the test environment.) This issue does not come up when interacting with a movie running in a browser or as a standalone executable.

How It Works

This code uses an event listener to capture events generated by the keyboard. A *listener* is simply a chunk of code that "listens" for a particular event to occur, and then acts on that event. (Listeners are discussed in greater detail in the "Handling Events" section in the next chapter.) The first line creates a generic object to act as a listener. The second line creates an event handler for a specific event — in this case, the onKeyDown event. The last line assigns the listener to the Key() object, which is built into the Flash player and which broadcasts key press events to all interested listeners.

In the event handler code, the first line captures the code associated with the pressed key, and the switch..case statement decides what action should be taken based on the key that's pressed. Notice that while the top-most trace() statement gives a numerical value for each key, none of the case statements seem to refer to an actual number. The named references to the keys are called static constants, and they contain the key code numbers for non-character keys on the keyboard. For instance, Key.ENTER returns the number 13, and Key.ESCAPE returns the number 27. Using these static constants makes code more readable and means that you do not have to remember obscure character codes.

Press the Enter, Shift, Ctrl, and space keys while the movie is running and you will see the output "firing" every time. The case statements that test for ENTER, SHIFT, and CONTROL have no break statement, so if one of those three conditions is matched, the flow of execution falls through, executing all statements until the next break statement is reached.

The optional default statement isn't used here because there's no concern about what happens when any other keys are pressed. As a result, any keys pressed that don't match one of the case conditions are simply ignored by the switch statement.

Understanding Loops

Good programmers are lazy by nature. That doesn't mean that they do not get things done; it means that they get things done in the most efficient way possible. If a task needs to be done repeatedly, they will find a way to automate it. The *loop* is the programmatic means to automate a task, and is fundamental to working with arrays and searching through data. Macromedia Flash provides four loop statements that you can work with: for, for..in, while, and do..while.

The for Loop

The workhorse of the loop statements is the for statement, and it's the one that you will no doubt become very familiar with. Its primary use is for iterating through indexed arrays, which is likely what you will be doing the most. The basic structure of the for statement is as follows:

```
for (init; condition; iterator)
{
    // Statements
}
```

The `init` portion contains the initializing code that runs once before the loop begins. The condition is an expression that is evaluated before every iteration of the loop that tests to see whether it should continue looping or break out of the loop completely. The iterator causes the variable(s) used in the condition to change, and is executed for every iteration. The statements contained between the braces run for every pass of the loop.

Here's an example of a classic `for` loop:

```
var fruitArray:Array = new Array("Apple", "Orange", "Pear");
var numFruit:Number = fruitArray.length;
for (var i:Number = 0; i < numFruit; i++)
{
    trace(i + ": " + fruitArray[i]);
}

// Outputs:
// 0: Apple
// 1: Orange
// 2: Pear
```

The execution of this loop is broken down as follows:

1. The initialization code `var i:Number = 0;` is run, setting the contents of the variable i to zero.

2. Comparison between i and `numFruit` is performed. With i = 0 and `numFruit` = 3, then 0 < 3 is true, and execution of the loop proceeds.

3. The `trace()` function displays 0: `Apple`.

4. The iterator is executed, and the variable i now contains the value 1.

5. Comparison between i and `numFruit` is performed. With i = 1 and `numFruit` = 3, then 1 < 3 is true, and execution of the loop proceeds.

6. The `trace()` function displays 1: `Orange`.

7. The iterator is run, and the variable i now contains the value 2.

8. Comparison between i and `numFruit` is performed. With i = 2 and `numFruit` = 3, then 2 < 3 is true, and execution of the loop proceeds.

9. The `trace()` function displays 2: `Pear`.

10. The iterator is run, and the variable i now contains the value 3.

11. Comparison between i and `numFruit` is performed. With i = 3 and `numFruit` = 3, then 3 < 3 is false, and execution of the loop stops.

The convention for naming variables used for loop indices is to use the letters i through n.

It is worth mentioning that the loop could have checked the length of the array directly each time:

```
for (var i:Number = 0; i < fruitArray.length; i++)
```

Instead, the length of the array was saved to a temporary local variable, and that variable was used in the stop-loop test. Local variables are implemented in the player using features of the computer's processor that speed up access to the variables. The difference is not noticeable for small numbers of loops, but for intensive looping operations, it helps measurably.

A `for` loop can be applied for purposes other than managing arrays. The Fibonacci sequence, for example, is a mathematical sequence of numbers that follow a pattern. Each number is the sum of the two preceding numbers, where the first two numbers in the series are defined as 0 and 1. This sequence yields a pattern that has many important applications in both nature and in pure mathematics. To get the value for any particular number in the series, a number of additions need to be done beforehand. This is a perfect task for the `for` loop:

```
var sequenceLength:Number = 10;
var number1:Number = 0;
var number2:Number = 1;
var currentNumber:Number;

for (var i:Number = 3; i <= sequenceLength; i++)
{
    currentNumber = number1 + number2;
    number1 = number2;
    number2 = currentNumber;
    trace("Fibonacci #" + i + ": " + currentNumber);
}

// Outputs:
// Fibonacci #3: 1
// Fibonacci #4: 2
// Fibonacci #5: 3
// Fibonacci #6: 5
// Fibonacci #7: 8
// Fibonacci #8: 13
// Fibonacci #9: 21
// Fibonacci #10: 34
```

This loop does not start at zero, as most other for loops do. The first two terms (0 and 1) are given, not calculated, so it is only necessary to start calculating for the third term. Also, you're not working with an array, which always starts at index 0 as the first element. As a result, when i = 3, you actually do have the third term in the sequence. When i = sequenceLength, the loop should proceed with that last iteration rather than stopping, as opposed to an array where you want to stop at the index arrayLength - 1.

Another useful application of the `for` loop is for creating and initializing multiple movie clips. The following example creates 10 movie clips, positions them, and draws a square inside each one:

```
var movieClipHandle:MovieClip;
var baseMovieClip:MovieClip = _level0;
var numMovieClips:Number = 10;
for (var i:Number=0; i < numMovieClips; i++)
{
    baseMovieClip.createEmptyMovieClip("movieClip" + i, i);
```

```
        movieClipHandle = baseMovieClip["movieClip" + i];
        movieClipHandle._x = i * 20;
        movieClipHandle._y = 0;
        movieClipHandle.lineStyle(1, 0x000000, 100);
        movieClipHandle.moveTo(0, 0);
        movieClipHandle.lineTo(0, 10);
        movieClipHandle.lineTo(10, 10);
        movieClipHandle.lineTo(10, 0);
        movieClipHandle.lineTo(0, 0);
    }
    // Output:
    // Creates ten empty movie clips, places them 20 pixels apart along the top of
    // the stage, and draws a 10x10-pixel square inside each one.
```

The first line creates a variable used to temporarily hold each movie clip, the second one creates a temporary handle to the root movie clip that contains each movie clip being created, and the third sets how many movie clips you want to create. For each iteration of the loop, it creates an empty movie clip, saves a temporary handle to that clip, moves the clip 20 pixels to the right of the previous clip, and draws four lines inside it to make the square.

The for..in Loop

The `for` loop may be the programmer's workhorse, but the `for..in` loop is a little more specialized although still extremely useful. This loop is the companion to the associative array and the object collection. Most arrays are indexed numerically, so `myArray[0]` gets the first chunk of data, `myArray[1]` gets the second, and so on. Associative arrays, you recall, allow data to be indexed by strings instead of by numbers and are used to store relationships between pieces of data. Objects group a set of properties and corresponding values together into property/value pairs. (Associative arrays and object collections are examined in the "Working with Collections of Data" section earlier in this chapter.) The base syntax for the `for..in` loop is as follows:

```
for (var iterator:String in collectionObject)
{
    // Statements
}
```

The `collectionObject` variable can be any associative array or object collection. The iterator variable is a temporary variable used just within the `for` loop. With each time through, the iterator holds the name portion of each name/value pair, which is used to retrieve the corresponding value. Here's an example:

```
var labelArray = new Array();
labelArray["car"] = "Voiture";
labelArray["truck"] = "Camion";
labelArray["motorcycle"] = "Motocyclette";
labelArray["bicycle"] = "Bicyclette";

for (var labelId:String in labelArray)
{
  trace("id: " + labelId + " translation: " + labelArray[labelId]);
```

```
      }

      // Outputs:
      //id: bicycle translation: Bicyclette
      //id: motorcycle translation: Motocyclette
      //id: truck translation: Camion
      //id: car translation: Voiture
```

Notice that the order of the output in this example is reversed from the order in which the associative array elements were assigned. Do not rely on associative arrays for maintaining any specific order.

Associative arrays are also very useful for maintaining a simple database of records. The for..in loop can be used to loop through records, looking for ones with specific characteristics:

```
      var photoListing = new Object();
      photoListing["whiteLanding"] = {title:"White Landing", width:1024, ⤶
          height:768, size:123};
      photoListing["texture1"] = {title:"Study in Texture 1", width:1024, ⤶
          height:768, size:186};
      photoListing["texture2"] = {title:"Study in Texture 2", width:1280, ⤶
          height:1024, size:195};
      photoListing["kitsSunset"] = {title:"Sunset on Kits Beach", width:1280, ⤶
          height:1024, size:325};
      photoListing["studyInGrey"] = {title:"Study in Grey", width:1024, ⤶
          height:768, size:144};

      for (var photoId:String in photoListing)
      {
          if (photoListing[photoId].size < 200 && photoListing[photoId].width <= 1024)
          {
              trace("Photo matches criteria: " + photoId);
          }
      }

      // Outputs:
      // Photo matches criteria: studyInGrey
      // Photo matches criteria: texture1
      // Photo matches criteria: whiteLanding
```

This example loops through an associative array looking for records with specific criteria (size less than 200 and width less than or equal to 1024). It outputs the ID of each matching record it finds. Code could easily be added to do a more involved task, such as add a thumbnail of the associated photo into a search results area.

The while Loop

Like the for loop, the while loop keeps iterating through a series of statements until a specific condition is met. However, the while loop is better suited for situations where the termination condition relies on something more complex than the value of a single integer variable.

The basic syntax of the `while` loop is as follows:

```
while (condition)
{
    //statements
}
```

The execution of the loop is very simple. As long as the condition evaluates to `true`, the statements continue to execute. Here's the order of the loop's execution:

1. The condition is evaluated.

2. If the condition evaluates to `true`, the statement block is executed. (If the condition evaluates to `false`, the loop halts, and the next line of code outside of the closing bracket is executed.)

3. Return to step 1.

The `while` loop can be used to exactly duplicate the behavior of the `for` loop:

```
var fruitArray:Array = new Array("Apple", "Orange", "Pear");
var i:Number = 0;

while (i < fruitArray.length)
{
    trace(fruitArray[i]);
    i++;
}

// Outputs:
// Apple
// Orange
// Pear
```

This code is not quite as compact as the `for` loop, and is a little more prone to simple programming errors. If the `i++;` statement is left out by accident, for instance, an infinite loop results, and would require a forceful closing of the movie to terminate. You cannot get into that circumstance with the `for` loop because the compiler displays a warning about the missing iterator and prevents the compilation from even happening.

A better example of the `while` loop is where the termination condition is more complex, and where it is not known in advance how many times the loop should run:

```
var stopCharacter:String = ".";
var paragraphText:String = "The quick brown fox. Jumped over the lazy dog.";
var sentenceText:String = "";
var i:Number = 0;

while (i < paragraphText.length && paragraphText.charAt(i) != stopCharacter)
{
    sentenceText += paragraphText.charAt(i);
    i++;
}
```

```
        trace("Sentence: " + sentenceText);

    // Outputs:
    // Sentence: The quick brown fox
```

This `while` loop is designed to extract the first sentence from a string of text. It compares each character in the string, looking for a period. When it finds one, it stops execution and outputs the text leading up to the period. If the loop finds no periods in the text, it stops when it runs out of letters to compare and returns the whole string.

The `while` loop is quite powerful, but it is not as commonly used as the `for` loop: It is more complex, more prone to runtime errors, and often unnecessary. Before implementing a `while` loop, consider whether a `for` loop would better serve the purpose.

The do..while Loop

The `do..while` loop is almost identical to the `while` loop, in that it continues to loop until a specific condition has been met. It is different only in the order that the loop evaluation happens. A `while` loop evaluates the condition *before* executing the statements in the loop block; a `do..while` loop evaluates the condition *after* executing the statements. One of the side effects of this behavior is that the statement block is guaranteed to execute at least once.

The basic syntax for the `do..while` loop is as follows:

```
do
{
    //statements
}
while (condition)
```

Here's the order in which a `do..while` loop runs:

1. The statement block is executed.

2. The condition is evaluated.

3. If the condition evaluates to `false`, the loop halts, and the next statement after the `while` statement is executed. If the condition evaluates to `true`, the loop returns to step 1.

The example `while` loop can be reworked a little bit to make it into a `do..while` loop:

```
var stopCharacter:String = ".";
var paragraphText:String = "The quick brown fox. Jumped over the lazy dog.";
var sentenceText:String = "";
var i:Number = 0;

do
{
    sentenceText += paragraphText.charAt(i);
    i++;
}
while (i < paragraphText.length && paragraphText.charAt(i) != stopCharacter)
```

```
trace("Sentence: " + sentenceText);

// Outputs:
// Sentence: The quick brown fox
```

This is almost identical to the previous example. The difference is that it examines the first character before testing the termination condition. This alternate syntax really is not very helpful, especially because if the string is empty, it still tries to access the first (non-existing) character. In practice, this loop is used very rarely. You are always better off using a `while` loop instead.

Try It Out   Using Arrays to Track Data

In this project, you work with indexed arrays, associative arrays, and objects, as well as loops and conditional logic.

1. Create a new Macromedia Flash document by selecting File⇨New and choosing Flash Document from the New Document panel.

2. Click the first frame in the timeline, open the Actions panel (Window⇨Development Panels⇨ Actions), and type in the following ActionScript code:

```
#include "tryItOut_trackData2.as"
```

3. Select File⇨Save As, name the file `tryItOut_trackData2.fla`, choose an appropriate directory, and save it.

4. Create a new script file by selecting File⇨New and choosing ActionScript File from the New Document panel.

5. Select File⇨Save As and ensure it is showing the same directory containing the `.fla` file. Name the file `tryItOut_trackData2.as` and save it.

6. Enter the following code into the new ActionScript file:

```
// Set up array for tracking numbers and total weight for each type of vehicle
var vehicleTotals:Array = new Object();
vehicleTotals["car"] = { totalCategoryNumbers:0, totalCategoryWeight:0 };
vehicleTotals["pickup"] = { totalCategoryNumbers:0, totalCategoryWeight:0 };
vehicleTotals["semi"] = { totalCategoryNumbers:0, totalCategoryWeight:0 };

// Track total weight of all vehicles
var totalWeight:Number = 0;

// Set up array holding information about each vehicle
var vehicleArray:Array = new Array();
vehicleArray.push( { id:"345", type:"car", weight:1218 } );
vehicleArray.push( { id:"730", type:"pickup", weight:1684 } );
vehicleArray.push( { id:"312", type:"semi", weight:14456, cargo:11023 } );
vehicleArray.push( { id:"943", type:"car", weight:1306 } );
vehicleArray.push( { id:"109", type:"car", weight:16349 } );

// Save total number of vehicles to a variable for use in loop.
var numVehicles:Number = vehicleArray.length;

// A temporary variable for convenience
```

73

```
var currentVehicleType:String;

// Iterate through each vehicle
for (var i:Number = 0; i < numVehicles; i++)
{
  // Get the type of this vehicle, and save it to a temporary
  // variable to help make the code more readable
  currentVehicleType = vehicleArray[i].type;

    // Add weight of this vehicle to total weight.
    totalWeight += vehicleArray[i].weight;

    // Add one to the number tracking this type of vehicle.
    vehicleTotals[currentVehicleType].totalCategoryNumbers += 1;
    // Add this vehicle weight to the number tracking total weight.
    // of this type of vehicle.
    vehicleTotals[currentVehicleType].totalCategoryWeight += ⤸
        vehicleArray[i].weight;
    // If the vehicle is a semi, add the weight of its cargo
    if (currentVehicleType == "semi")
    {
        totalWeight += vehicleArray[i].cargo;
        vehicleTotals[currentVehicleType].totalCategoryWeight += ⤸
            vehicleArray[i].cargo;
    }
}

// Iterate through each type of vehicle
for (vehicleType in vehicleTotals)
{
    trace("Number of " + vehicleType + "s: " + ⤸
        vehicleTotals[vehicleType].totalCategoryNumbers);
    trace("Total weight of " + vehicleType + "s: " + ⤸
        vehicleTotals[vehicleType].totalCategoryWeight);
}

trace("Sum of vehicle weights: " + totalWeight);
```

7. Save the file (File⇨Save), return to the Flash project file, and select Control⇨Test Movie.

How It Works

This program creates two arrays, one to hold data about each vehicle, and one to hold calculated data about each group of vehicles. It begins by creating an associative array to store data about the different types of vehicles and then creates an object for each vehicle type, initializing each object property to zero:

```
var vehicleTotals:Array = new Object();
vehicleTotals["car"] = { totalCategoryNumbers:0, totalCategoryWeight:0 };
vehicleTotals["pickup"] = { totalCategoryNumbers:0, totalCategoryWeight:0 };
vehicleTotals["semi"] = { totalCategoryNumbers:0, totalCategoryWeight:0 };
```

The program initializes a counter to track the total vehicle weight and total number of vehicles, and it sets up the data for each individual vehicle using an indexed array of objects. Each row contains information about one specific vehicle. In cases where an array stores a series of records, each row usually has a unique ID. In this instance, the ID is not used anywhere, but it would normally be used to allow a search for information on a specific vehicle, or to relate the record to some other data, such as data on a server.

```
var vehicleArray:Array = new Array();
vehicleArray.push( { id:"345", type:"car", weight:1218 } );
vehicleArray.push( { id:"730", type:"pickup", weight:1684 } );
vehicleArray.push( { id:"312", type:"semi", weight:14456, cargo:11023 } );
vehicleArray.push( { id:"943", type:"car", weight:1306 } );
vehicleArray.push( { id:"109", type:"car", weight:16349 } );
```

It then loops through each vehicle, updating the variables' tracking numbers and weight accordingly. First it stores the type of the current vehicle being checked in a variable, just to make subsequent lines a bit cleaner:

```
currentVehicleType = vehicleArray[i].type;
```

It adds the weight of the vehicle to the variable tracking the total weight:

```
totalWeight += vehicleArray[i].weight;
```

And it then updates the tallies for the appropriate vehicle type:

```
vehicleTotals[currentVehicleType].totalCategoryNumbers += 1;
vehicleTotals[currentVehicleType].totalCategoryWeight += vehicleArray[i].weight;
```

Semis have an additional cargo weight property, so that value is added to the total as well:

```
if (currentVehicleType == "semi")
{
    totalWeight += vehicleArray[i].cargo;
    vehicleTotals[currentVehicleType].totalCategoryWeight += ⊃
        vehicleArray[i].cargo;
}
```

Finally, it iterates through each vehicle type, reports their stats, and reports the overall total weight:

```
// Iterate through each type of vehicle
for (vehicleType in vehicleTotals)
{
    trace("Number of " + vehicleType + "s: " + ⊃
        vehicleTotals[vehicleType].totalCategoryNumbers);
    trace("Total weight of " + vehicleType + "s: " + ⊃
        vehicleTotals[vehicleType].totalCategoryWeight);
}

trace("Sum of vehicle weights: " + totalWeight);
```

The results in the output panel should look something like the following:

```
Number of semis: 1
Total weight of semis: 25479
Number of pickups: 1
Total weight of pickups: 1684
Number of cars: 3
Total weight of cars: 18873
Sum of vehicle weights: 46036
```

Dealing with Loop Errors

As much as you'd like each of your loops to work the first time, you will likely face a number of problems. Some won't be apparent unless you actually carefully examine your program's output, whereas others will cause your program to grind to a halt and stop responding completely. Developing debugging strategies is important to finding and fixing these problems, and both the trace statement and the debugger panel are instrumental in troubleshooting. (Chapter 27 includes tips for effective debugging.) The following sections examine off-by-one errors and infinite loops, providing some strategies for dealing with these errors.

Off-by-One Errors

Remember, almost all of your loops will start at zero, not at one. All indexed arrays are zero-based, which means that the first element is at position 0, the second element is at position 1, and so on until the last element, which will be at position arrayLength – 1. If the wrong expression is used for the condition, the loop goes out of the bounds of the array. Here's an example:

```
var fruitArray:Array = new Array("Apple", "Orange", "Pear");
var numFruit:Number = fruitArray.length;
for (var i:Number = 0; i <= numFruit; i++)
{
    trace(i + ": " + fruitArray[i]);
}

// Outputs:
// 0: Apple
// 1: Orange
// 2: Pear
// 3: undefined
```

In this traced code, you see that there are only three elements in the array, but the loop has tried to access the array four times. The first three iterations work fine, but when i reaches 3, the condition 3 <= 3 returns true and allows the loop to continue for a fourth iteration. The trace() statement then attempts to access position 3 within the array, which is really element 4, and because that exceeds the bounds of the array, the attempt to access the element returns the keyword undefined. Using the wrong loop termination operator is a common mistake and is frequently referred to as an *off-by-one* error. To guard against this, use trace() statements to test whether you are getting the expected results both at the beginning and at the end of your loops. If you stick to the tried-and-true format of for (var i:Number = 0; i < arrayLength; i++), you should rarely go wrong.

Infinite Loops

The bane of developers is the *infinite loop* — the loop's termination condition never evaluates to `false`, so the loop never stops running. The result is that code statements that should be executed do not, yet the processor is pushed to the limit. Macromedia Flash Player and the Macromedia Flash development environment help mitigate the effects of an infinite loop enough so that you can escape from a stuck project. If a loop continues for a given period of time, usually around 20 seconds, the player shows a warning (see Figure 3-4) and gives you an opportunity to shut down the movie. Unfortunately, the mechanism to abort an infinite loop does not always work, and sometimes the only option is to force-quit the browser or the development environment.

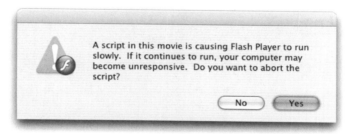

A script in this movie is causing Flash Player to run slowly. If it continues to run, your computer may become unresponsive. Do you want to abort the script?

No   Yes

Figure 3-4

Infinite loops occur most frequently in `while` loops. Take a look at the following loop:

```
var i:Number = 0;
var numIterations:Number = 100;

while (i < numIterations)
{
    trace(i);
}
```

This simple example results in an infinite loop because the iterator variable `i` never changes, so `i<numIterations` never evaluates to `false` and the `trace()` statement continuously outputs zero. All that's needed to fix this is the addition of a single line that increments the iterator `i`:

```
var i:Number = 0;
var numIterations:Number = 100;

while (i < numIterations)
{
    i++;
    trace(i);
}
```

A slightly more complex example is more difficult to debug:

```
var stopCharacter:String = ".";
var paragraphText:String = "The quick brown fox";
var sentenceText:String = "";
```

77

```
var i:Number = 0;

while (paragraphText.charAt(i) != stopCharacter)
{
    sentenceText += paragraphText.charAt(i);
    i++;
}
trace("Sentence: " + sentenceText);
```

To understand what is causing an infinite loop here requires some knowledge of the data and of the logic flow. This code goes through each character in the input string looking for a period. Once it finds a period, it quits. The problem is that the data has no periods, and the code does not test to see if it has run out of data to check. Inserting a `trace()` statement may not work, because the first trace statements (the ones you need to see) will likely scroll out of the output area.

If you can't see what is causing the problem, you might need to step into the debugger. Here's how:

1. Create a new Macromedia Flash document by selecting File⇨New and choosing Flash Document from the New Document panel.

2. Click the first frame in the timeline, open the Actions panel (Window⇨Development Panels⇨ Actions), and type in the preceding ActionScript code.

3. Right-click the line with the `while` statement and select Set Breakpoint, or click the line number. A red dot should appear on the left (see Figure 3-5).

Figure 3-5

4. Select Control⇨Test Movie. The debugger panel appears.

5. Click `_level0` in the top-left pane of the debugger panel.

6. Click the variables tab in the middle-left pane of the debugger panel (see Figure 3-6).

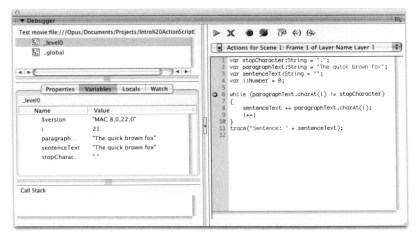

Figure 3-6

7. Click the green arrow at the top of the main debugger panel. Click a few more times while watching the values in the variables section change.

One of the things you will see is that i constantly increases in value, even after the last letter has been examined.

The solution to this is to be more careful about dealing with different data conditions. Doing an additional check to see if the end of the array has been reached would resolve this issue:

```
var stopCharacter:String = ".";
var paragraphText:String = "The quick brown fox";
var sentenceText:String = "";
var i:Number = 0;

while (i < paragraphText.length && paragraphText.charAt(i) != stopCharacter)
{
    sentenceText += paragraphText.charAt(i);
    i++;
}
trace("Sentence: " + sentenceText);

// Outputs:
// Sentence: The quick brown fox
```

Summary

You are now getting into the thick of learning the core ActionScript language. Some points to remember include the following:

❑ Decisions in code are made through working with the `if..then..else` and the `switch..case` conditionals.

❑ A conditional is a combination of an expression made up of one or more operators, plus a block of one or more statements that are executed if the result of the decision is `true`.

❑ The `for`, `for..in`, `while`, and `do..while` loops enable you to work with repeating data.

❑ The `for` loop is perfect for working with indexed arrays.

❑ The `for..in` loop works for iterating through data in an associative array.

❑ The `while` loop is used when you do not initially know how many times that the loop should iterate. It stops when a condition or a set of conditions has been met.

❑ Off-by-one errors involve situations in which there is a miscount in the number of times a loop should iterate. This error can be avoided in the for loop by sticking to the syntax `for (var i:Number = 0; i < arrayLength; i++)`.

❑ Infinite loops result when the condition that is supposed to stop the loop never takes place. The debugger is frequently helpful in figuring out what is happening in an errant loop.

Exercises

1. With the following shopping cart data, create an array that stores the data, and then create a loop that traces out each piece of data and prints out a total dollar amount.

❑ Purchased one MP3 music player, model number ip300, priced at $299.

❑ Purchased one player case, model number ip300c, priced at $49.

❑ Purchased two sets of earbuds, model number eb100, priced at $29 each.

❑ Purchased a car charger kit, model number cc250, priced at $69.

2. Convert the following `if..then` statement to a `switch..case` statement:

```
var vehicleType:String = "semi";
var spareCabin:Boolean = false;
var numDoors:Number;

if (vehicleType == "sedan")
{
    numDoors = 4;
}
else if (vehicleType == "sportscar")
{
    numDoors = 3;
}
else if (vehicleType == "semi" && spareCabin == true)
```

```
{
    numDoors = 3;
}
else if (vehicleType == "semi" && spareCabin == false)
{
    numDoors = 2;
}
else
{
    numDoors = 2
}
trace(numDoors);
```

3. Convert the following `while` statement to a `for` statement:

```
var fruitArray:Array = new Array("banana", "pear", "strawberry", "grape");
var numFruit:Number = fruitArray.length;
var currentFruit:Number = 0;
var foundFruit:Number = 0;
var numLetters:Number = 6;

while (currentFruit < numFruit)
{
    if (fruitArray[currentFruit].length >= numLetters)
    {
        trace(fruitArray[currentFruit]);
        foundFruit++;
    }
    currentFruit++;
}

trace("found " + foundFruit + " fruits with 6 or more letters in the name");
```

Exploring ActionScript Functions and Scope

Several critical aspects of programming include reusability, organization, and understandability. Reusability enables you to take a section of code and to apply it in numerous places within your program and within other programs. Organization allows code to be found easily, and to have different sections of code relate in ways that make sense. Understandability means that your code still makes sense when you return to it after several weeks.

This chapter introduces you to ways of organizing your code so that it is logically structured, easy to read, and easy to reuse.

Functions

The code snippets used in this book so far have been quite short, and have been written in sort of a stream-of-thought style. As programs get larger, code reusability, organization, and understandability become essential.

The first step toward this goal is the proper use of *functions*. A function is a reusable grouping of code that performs a single task. A function may require data to be passed in as *arguments*, and a function may *return* data as a result of some computation.

Say that you need to write some code that includes formatting an email address, and that several places within the code need such formatting. Rather than duplicating the code that is responsible for the formatting, you write it once in a function. Wherever an email address needs to be formatted in your program, the function is called to handle it. The function acts as a reusable container that saves you effort, and in this case allows for any later changes in the formatting routine to be done in one place rather than in several places.

The general form for declaring a function is as follows:

```
function functionName(inputValue:DataType):ReturnType
{
    // Statements
    return <value>;
}
```

First, the `function` keyword indicates that what follows is a function definition. It's followed by the name of the function, which is something that you make up, and should reflect the function's intended purpose. A function name can consist of any combination of letters, numbers, and the underscore character, but it cannot start with a number, and it cannot be the same as a reserved word. Function names are case sensitive, so `emailformat()` and `emailFormat()` are two different functions.

A pair of round brackets immediately follows the function name. Any input parameters that the function should accept go inside the brackets. A function can define as many input variables as are needed. If none is needed, the round brackets are empty; otherwise they contain a comma-separated list of variable names and variable data types. The variable names can be anything: they are just placeholders to refer to within the function. The data type reflects the kind of data that the variable will contain, such as Boolean, Number, or String. The compiler uses this data type information to ensure that when the function is called, the data that is passed in is consistent with the data types that have been defined (if it isn't, the compiler halts and gives an error).

At the end of the first line, the return type defines the kind of data the function sends back, if any. If a return type is defined, there must always be at least one `return` statement. The `return` statement immediately stops the function and sends back a value. If the function is not to return any data, you set the return type to the keyword `Void`.

Finally, a pair of curly brackets follows the function declaration. Any code placed between the brackets executes when the function is called.

To call a function, the general syntax is as follows:

```
var returnVar:ReturnType = functionName(inputValue);
```

Or if no data is to be returned from the function:

```
functionName(inputValue);
```

Here, `inputValue` is a variable representing data that needs to be passed to the function, which in turn sends the result of the call back to the variable `returnVar`.

Here's an example that illustrates how functions are used:

```
function formatEmailAddress(userName:String, domainName:String):String
{
    return userName + "@" + domainName;
}
var email1:String = createEmailAddress("jsmith", "somedomain.com");
trace(email1);
```

```
// Outputs: jsmith@somedomain.com

var email2:String = createEmailAddress("bhill", "somedomain.com");
trace(email2);
// Outputs: bhill@somedomain.com
```

This function declaration defines input parameters for a username and a domain name. The two input parameters are combined into a properly formatted email address, which is then sent back as a `return` value. The function is called twice, with different usernames, and each result is assigned to its own variable. The `trace()` statements show that those two variables contain the formatted email addresses.

Here's a more complicated example. One task that you might need in any number of projects is to get the current time in a particular format, such as with just hours and minutes. This function takes care of the formatting, so that you only have to call the function whenever you need the current time:

```
function getCurrentTime():String
{
    var currentTime:Date = new Date();
    var currentTimeString:String = "";

    currentTimeString = String(currentTime.getHours()) + ":";

    if (currentTime.getMinutes() < 10)
    {
        currentTimeString += "0" + String(currentTime.getMinutes());
    }
    else
    {
        currentTimeString += String(currentTime.getMinutes());
    }

    return currentTimeString;
}

var currentTime:String = getCurrentTime();
trace(currentTime);
// Outputs 14:34
```

The `getCurrentTime()` function takes no parameters; it just gets the current time and returns the hours and minutes as a string formatted in the international 24-hour time format. If the data type in `currentTime:String` were to be changed to something else, such as `currentTime:Number`, the compiler would give an error:

```
**Error** Scene=Scene 1, layer=Layer 1, frame=1:Line 149: Type mismatch in
assignment statement: found String where Number is required.

Total ActionScript Errors: 1     Reported Errors: 1
```

The compiler is reporting that `getCurrentTime()` returns a String, but the variable assigned to the return data expects a Number. This error message is actually a very good thing! The compiler is telling you right off the bat that you're working with incompatible data types. Without this validation, data errors could show up later on, and would likely require significant time to track down and fix.

Functions in Action

Say you want to create a small application that enables someone to schedule a Web conference online. The user might be presented with a text field for the email addresses of all invitees, and two text fields into which she could type a start time and an end time. One of the things that the application would need to do is to check that the dates are valid before saving the reservation and sending out the invitations. Without the use of a function, the code might look something like this:

```
var fromTime_str:String = "12:00";
var toTime_str:String = "100";
var isFromValid:Boolean = false;
var isToValid:Boolean = false;

// Validate the first time
if (fromTime_str.length == 4 && fromTime_str.indexOf(":") == 1)
{
    // The time has four characters, and the second character is a ":"
    isFromValid = true;
}
else if (fromTime_str.length == 5 && fromTime_str.indexOf(":") == 2)
{
    // The time has five characters, and the third character is a ":"
    isFromValid = true;
}

// Validate the second time
if (toTime_str.length == 4 && toTime_str.indexOf(":") == 1)
{
    // The time has four characters, and the second character is a ":"
    isToValid = true;
}
else if (toTime_str.length == 5 && toTime_str.indexOf(":") == 2)
{
    // The time has five characters, and the third character is a ":"
    isToValid = true;
}

// Check if both times are valid
if (isFromValid && isToValid)
{
    trace("Both fields contain valid times.");
}
else
{
    trace("There is an error in one of the fields.");
}
```

The code goes through the text that comes from two text fields, looking to see if the strings are the right length and the " : " characters are in the right place. You no doubt noticed that the code doing the validation has been duplicated: The code checking the "from" time and the code checking the "to" time is identical except for the different variable names. Placing the validation code within a function helps clean things up:

```
function isTimeValid(inputTime_str:String):Boolean
{
    var isTimeValid:Boolean = false;

    if (inputTime_str.length == 4 && inputTime_str.indexOf(":") == 1)
    {
        // The time has four characters, and the second character is a ":"
        isTimeValid = true;
    }
    else if (inputTime_str.length == 5 && inputTime_str.indexOf(":") == 2)
    {
        // The time has five characters, and the third character is a ":"
        isTimeValid = true;
    }

    return isTimeValid;
}

var fromTime_str:String = "12:00";
var toTime_str:String = "100";

if (isTimeValid(fromTime_str) && isTimeValid(toTime_str))
{
    trace("Both fields contain valid times.");
}
else
{
    trace("There is an error in one of the fields.");
}
```

The validation code can now be easily reused. Even better, the code in the function can readily be extended to do something new, such as checking to see if the hour portion is less than 24 and the minute portion is less than 60. Any changes made to this function take effect wherever this function is called. A few things to note about this new program are that it is shorter, it uses fewer variables, and it groups related logic together. With this one modification, the reusability, organization, and understandability of the code are improved.

An Alternate Syntax

There is another way to define a function in which you create what is sometimes called an anonymous function, and assign that nameless function to a variable of type Function. The alternate syntax looks like this:

```
var functionName:Function = function(inputValue:DataType):ReturnType
{
    // Statements
    return <value>;
}
```

Compare it to the first function syntax:

```
function functionName(inputValue:DataType):ReturnType
{
    // Statements
    return <value>;
}
```

You can see that the alternate syntax actually creates a variable with a data type of `Function`. It is designed for situations in which the function is only going to be used in one place. Clearly this goes against what a function is normally used for, but anonymous functions are useful in situations where code needs to be called in response to a specific user action. For instance, say that you have a movie clip on the stage that you want to respond with some action when it is clicked. The following example enables you to invoke some code when a movie clip with the instance name `continueButton` is clicked:

```
continueButton.onRelease = function()
{
    trace("Pressed the continue button");
}
```

This code assigns an anonymous function to the movie clip's `onRelease` handler, which is a special property of all movie clips. Any function that has been assigned to this property is invoked when the user clicks the contents of the movie clip. In this case, the `trace()` statement executes every time the user clicks and releases the mouse button over the `continueButton` movie clip.

Don't worry if you try this out and have difficulties getting it to work; it's just a preview of what is to follow. You see much more of this type of function and about working with movie clips in general in Chapter 7.

Passing Functions as Arguments

Anonymous functions are interesting because they reveal something that would otherwise not be apparent, which is that functions are actually just another type of variable. Take a look at the following example:

```
var openBrowserWindow:Function;
openBrowserWindow = function(url:String):Void
{
    getURL(url, "externalWindow");
}

openBrowserWindow("http://www.apple.com/ipod");
```

In this code, a variable of type `Function` is created. That variable is then assigned an anonymous function. Once the anonymous function is assigned to the variable, the variable behaves exactly like a function, because it is! This example shows that functions can be assigned to a variable just like a string or a number can be assigned to a variable. Similarly, functions can be passed to other functions, as you see next.

In some situations a function takes another function as an argument. Generally, this occurs when something is to happen after a delay, or in response to a user action such as a mouse click. When the action occurs, the function that you supply responds to the action. A good example of working with a delayed action is the global `setInterval()` function, which is built into the Flash player. It takes two arguments: a function that you provide, and the number of milliseconds to wait until that function is called:

```
function moveShip():Void
{
    spaceshipClip._x += 10;
    updateAfterEvent();
}

setInterval(moveShip, 30);
```

Here, the `setInterval()` function accepts a function called `moveShip`, and an interval value of 30 ms (milliseconds). Every 30 ms, the `moveShip()` function is called, causing a movie clip with the instance name `spaceshipClip` to move 10 pixels to the right.

Notice that when the `moveShip()` function is passed to `setInterval()`, the round brackets are omitted, which means that the function does not actually execute and can be passed to another function. When the brackets are included after a function name, the function is called and any return values are passed back. Consider what would happen if you included the round brackets when passing `moveShip()` to `setInterval()`:

```
setInterval(moveShip(), 30);
```

Instead of passing the `moveShip()` function, this line executes that function. `moveShip()` defines a return type of `Void`, so it does not return any value, and `setInterval()` ends up with its first parameter being `undefined`.

One frequent error is to put quotes around the name of the function that's being passed in, like this:

```
setInterval("moveShip", 30);
```

Quotes indicate string data, and a string doesn't work for `setInterval()` because it does not contain the reference to the actual function code.

Try It Out   Executing a Function Passed as an Argument

In this project, you work with passing functions as arguments. Here are the steps to follow:

1. Create a new Macromedia Flash document by selecting File⇨New and choosing Flash Document from the New Document panel.

2. Click the first frame in the timeline, open the Actions panel (Window⇨Development Panels⇨ Actions), and type in the following ActionScript code:

```
#include "tryItOut_passingFunctions.as"
```

3. Make sure that the library panel is open. (If it isn't, select Window⇨Library.)

4. Make sure that the components panel is open. (If it isn't, select Window⇨Components.)

5. Open the components panel's UI Components section and locate the Button component. Drag that component to the library panel.

6. Select File⇨Save As, name the file `tryItOut_passingFunctions.fla`, choose an appropriate directory, and save it.

7. Create a new script file by selecting File⇨New and choosing ActionScript File from the New Document panel.

8. Name the file `tryItOut_passingFunctions.as` and save it in the directory containing the `.fla` file.

9. Type the following code into the new ActionScript file:

```
// Create a button using the standard Flash button component.
function createButton(callbackFunction:Function, buttonText:String, ⤵
    x:Number, y:Number):Void
{
    var currentDepth:Number = this.getNextHighestDepth();
    var newButton:mx.controls.Button;

  createClassObject(mx.controls.Button, "button"+currentDepth, currentDepth);

    newButton = _level0["button" + currentDepth];
    newButton.label = buttonText;
    newButton._x = x;
    newButton._y = y;
    newButton.addEventListener("click", callbackFunction);
}

// Function to be called when the start button is clicked
function handleStart():Void
{
    trace("Start button clicked");
}

// Function to be called when the stop button is clicked
function handleStop():Void
{
    trace("Stop button clicked");
}

// Create the start and stop buttons
createButton(handleStart, "Start", 10, 10);
createButton(handleStop, "Stop", 130, 10);
```

10. Save the file, return to the Flash project file, and select Control⇨Test Movie. Two buttons should be on the screen. Clicking them generates messages in the output panel.

How It Works

This program demonstrates the use of a function to simplify a repeating task, and passing functions as arguments to other functions.

The program first defines a function to place a button on the screen:

```
// Create a button using the standard Flash button component.
function createButton(callbackFunction:Function, buttonText:String, ⤵
```

```
        x:Number, y:Number):Void
{
    // ...
}
```

For a button to react to a click, it needs to be passed a function. This example's first line, which is the function declaration, does this by requiring a function to be passed as the first argument. It also requires a text label to place inside the button, as well as x and y coordinates for button placement.

createButton() places a Button component on the stage (you get to components a little later in this book) and lets the button know to call your function when it is clicked.

Two variables are created in the createButton() function, one to get the next available depth number and one to temporarily hold the new button:

```
var currentDepth:Number = this.getNextHighestDepth();
var newButton:mx.controls.Button;
```

Next, the button is created:

```
createClassObject(mx.controls.Button, "button"+currentDepth, currentDepth);
```

createClassObject() is a special function that's used to place copies of components to the stage on-the-fly. It creates a button using the class called mx.controls.Button as a template and assigns a name to the new button. The name is combined with the depth number assigned to the component to ensure a unique name so that there are no naming conflicts.

Now you have a button (with a name that's something like button1), but you need a way to work with it. The following line saves a handle to the new button, grabbing it by name from this, the current timeline:

```
newButton = this["button" + currentDepth];
```

The button is given a label, and moved to a particular x and y coordinate:

```
newButton.label = buttonText;
newButton._x = x;
newButton._y = y;
```

Finally, the function that you provided is assigned to the button so that it is called when the button is clicked. You learn more about how this works in the Chapter 9 about Components. The important thing to note here is that the callbackFunction variable represents the function that you passed to createButton():

```
newButton.addEventListener("click", callbackFunction);
```

The next two functions, which you pass to createButton(), are created to react to the user clicking either of the buttons:

```
// Function to be called when the start button is clicked
function handleStart():Void
{
```

```
        trace("Start button clicked");
    }

    // Function to be called when the stop button is clicked
    function handleStop():Void
    {
        trace("Stop button clicked");
    }
```

Finally, two calls are made to createButton(), one passing in a handle to the handleStart() function, and one passing in a handle to the handleStop() button:

```
    // Create the start and stop buttons
    createButton(handleStart, "Start", 10, 10);
    createButton(handleStop, "Stop", 130, 10);
```

At this point, the buttons are placed on the stage, and are ready to respond to being clicked.

Variable Scope

When a variable is created using the var keyword, it may be visible to some lines of code, but not visible to others. The visibility of a variable to other parts of a program is called *variable scope* and the path that the Macromedia Flash player searches to find a variable is called the *scope chain*. Until functions were discussed, variable scope was not an issue because the variables created were visible throughout the timeline. Now that you are working with functions. . .

When a variable is declared inside a function, it cannot be seen outside of that function. This is called being local in scope, and the variables are referred to as *local variables*. When the function terminates, variables declared within it are automatically destroyed.

When a variable is created on the main timeline, it is not immediately visible from another movie clip's timeline. Likewise, a variable created within a nested movie clip is not immediately visible from the main timeline. These are called *timeline variables*. When a movie clip containing timeline variables is destroyed, so are the timeline variables.

When a variable is prepended with the keyword _global, the variable is made visible to every piece of code throughout the project. Such variables are called *global variables* and persist as long as the movie plays, or until explicitly deleted.

Figure 4-1 shows a simplified representation of how the scope chain is organized. Code within a function has access to its own local function variables, as well as to timeline variables and global variables. Code on the timeline has access to its own timeline variables and to global variables, but has no access to any function's local variables.

> *Code always works in the context of a timeline, so code placed on a movie clip's timeline always has direct access to both global variables and variables defined within the same timeline.*

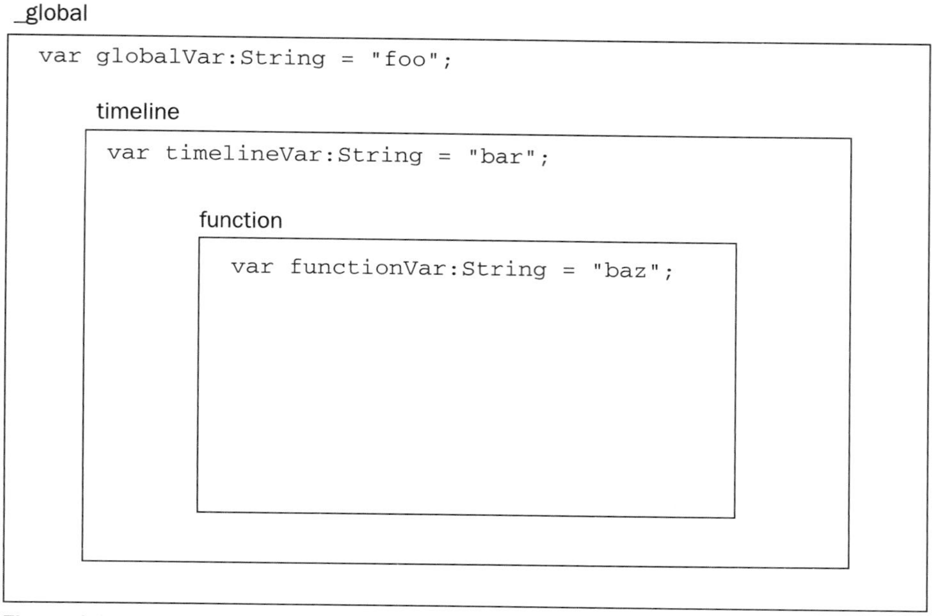

_global

```
var globalVar:String = "foo";
```

timeline

```
var timelineVar:String = "bar";
```

function

```
var functionVar:String = "baz";
```

Figure 4-1

Here's an example that demonstrates variable scope in action:

```
_global.myGlobalVar = "foo";
var myTimelineVar:String = "bar";

function myFunction1():Void
{
    var myFunctionVar1:String = "baz";
    trace("myFunction1->myGlobalVar: " + _global.myGlobalVar);
    trace("myFunction1->myTimelineVar: " + myTimelineVar);
    trace("myFunction1->myFunctionVar1: " + myFunctionVar1);
    trace("myFunction1->myFunctionVar2: " + myFunctionVar2);
    myFunction2();
}

function myFunction2():Void
{
    var myFunctionVar2:String = "qux";
    trace("myFunction1->myFunction2->myGlobalVar: " + _global.myGlobalVar);
    trace("myFunction1->myFunction2->myTimelineVar: " + myTimelineVar);
    trace("myFunction1->myFunction2->myFunctionVar1: " + myFunctionVar1);
    trace("myFunction1->myFunction2->myFunctionVar2: " + myFunctionVar2);
}

myFunction1();

trace("myGlobalVar: " + _global.myGlobalVar);
```

```
trace("myTimelineVar: " + myTimelineVar);
trace("myFunctionVar1: " + myFunctionVar1);
trace("myFunctionVar2: " + myFunctionVar2);

// Outputs:
// myFunction2->myGlobalVar: foo
// myFunction2->myTimelineVar: bar
// myFunction2->myFunctionVar1: undefined
// myFunction2->myFunctionVar2: qux

// myFunction1->myGlobalVar: foo
// myFunction1->myTimelineVar: bar
// myFunction1->myFunctionVar1: baz
// myFunction1->myFunctionVar2: undefined

// myGlobalVar: foo
// myTimelineVar: bar
// myFunctionVar1: undefined
// myFunctionVar2: undefined
```

The last four lines of output show that code on the timeline can see timeline variables and global variables, but not the local variable in either of the two functions. The middle four lines of output show that code within myFunction1() can see its own local variable as well as timeline variables and global variables, but not the local variable in myFunction2(). The top four lines of output show that myFunction2() can see its own local variable as well as timeline variables and global variables, but not the local variable in myFunction1(). This last case is actually a bit different than in some other programming languages, where a function that is called by another function has access to the calling function's local variables.

There is a slight change in scope when it comes to a function defined within another function. In the preceding example, you saw that the local variable in myFunction1() was not visible from within myFunction2() and vice versa. When an anonymous function is created within another function, the anonymous function does have access to the parent function's local variables, as the following example shows:

```
function myFunction1():Void
{
    var myFunctionVar1:String = "foo";
    var myFunction2:Function = function():Void
    {
        var myFunctionVar2:String = "bar";
        trace("myFunction2->myFunctionVar1: " + myFunctionVar1);
        trace("myFunction2->myFunctionVar2: " + myFunctionVar2);
    }
    myFunction2();

    trace("myFunction1->myFunctionVar1: " + myFunctionVar1);
    trace("myFunction1->myFunctionVar2: " + myFunctionVar2);
}

myFunction1();

// Outputs:
```

```
// myFunction2->myFunctionVar1: foo
// myFunction2->myFunctionVar2: bar

// myFunction1->myFunctionVar1: foo
// myFunction1->myFunctionVar2: undefined
```

In this example, code within `myFunction2()` has access to the local variables for `myFunction1()`! That only happens for anonymous functions defined within another function, and is extremely handy when you deal with event handlers, which are discussed in Chapter 10.

Managing Variable Scope

Managing variable scope in an application is important in making code behavior predictable and helping track down problems. The axiom to follow is

> **Keep variable scope as narrow as possible.**

Countless hours can be wasted trying to track down and fix problems with variables that are too visible to other parts of a project. This means thinking twice before creating a timeline variable, and thinking three times before creating a global variable.

Several reasons exist for minimizing the use of global variables in particular:

❑   They persist through the duration of the project's execution, taking up memory.

❑   They increase the impact of a code change. The effect of changing global data isn't always immediately visible, and is harder to debug.

❑   They reduce code reusability. Functions that reference global variables cannot be copied and pasted into another project without also implementing the global variables in the same way.

Instead of using global variables, use function arguments to pass data that is needed for any particular function.

The use of timeline variables should be minimized for the same reasons as for global variables, although you will likely need to use at least some timeline variables. As you become a more experienced ActionScript programmer, you may want to learn to create your own custom classes to manage your data and to organize the structure of your code. Chapter 5 introduces you to how object-oriented programming can help you better organize your code, and Chapter 27 gets you started working with custom classes.

Try It Out   Accessing Variables Declared in Different Places

In this project, you pass functions as arguments.

1.   Create a new Macromedia Flash document.

2.   Click the first frame in the timeline, open the Actions panel, and type in the following ActionScript code:

```
#include "tryItOut_variableScope.as"
```

3. Save the file as `tryItOut_variableScope.fla` in an appropriate directory.

4. Create a new script file.

5. Save the file as `tryItOut_variableScope.as` in the directory in which you saved the `.fla` file.

6. Type the following code into the new ActionScript file:

```
_global.someVar = 0;
var someVar:Number = 1;

function someFunction():Void
{
    var someVar:Number = 2;
    trace(someVar);
}
someFunction();
trace(someVar);
delete someVar;
trace(someVar);
```

7. Save the file, return to the `.fla`, and select Control⇨Test Movie.

How It Works

Using the same variable name for multiple variables exposes how the scope chain works. The variable within the function takes precedence over the timeline variable and the global variable, so the trace prints out the value 2. Outside the function, the timeline variable is next in the scope chain, so the trace prints out the value 1. When the timeline variable is deleted, the trace prints out the value 0, which is the variable within the function.

This example also shows why it is not a good idea to have variable naming matches between local, timeline, and global variables.

Side Effects

When a function manipulates data through a means other than a `return` statement, it is said to have *side effects*. The goal of good programming is to reduce a function's side effects because they tend to make code harder to debug and fix. A side effect of a function might be the changing of a global variable, the modification of data in one of its input arguments, or the sending of data to a server. Here's an example of a function with a side effect:

```
var numCars:Number = 10;

function incrementNumber(incAmount:Number):Number
{
    numCars = numCars + incAmount;
}

trace(numCars);
```

```
// Outputs: 10

incrementNumber(5);
trace(numCars);
// Outputs: 15
```

The side effect for the function `incrementNumber()` is to directly modify a timeline variable. This would be better done as follows:

```
var numCars:Number = 10;

function incrementNumber(startingNumber:Number, incAmount:Number):Number
{
    return startingNumber + incAmount;
}

trace(numCars);
// Outputs: 10

numCars = incrementNumber(numCars, 5);

trace(numCars);
// Outputs: 15

incrementNumber(numCars, 5);

trace(numCars);
// Outputs: 15
```

This version is cleaner because it is explicit about what the function does. The variable `numCars` does not get modified unless it is explicitly assigned the incremented value. Looking through the first two `trace()` statements, it does get incremented, but only because it is assigned the output of the `incrementNumber()` function. The third trace shows that calling `incrementNumber()` without assigning the return value to `numCars` has no effect on `numCars`.

It is possible for a function to modify one or more arguments that have been passed in. Recall from the discussion on variables at the beginning of this chapter that when a primitive data type is assigned to another variable, a copy is made. When a composite data type is assigned to another variable, the variable is not copied. Instead, the new variable points to the same data in the same location in memory as the source variable. This is the same behavior that takes place when a variable is passed into a function, and it is through this sharing of memory that it is possible for a function to manipulate the contents of an argument variable. Here's an example:

```
var currentDate:Date = new Date();

function getDateNextWeek(inputDate:Date):Date
{
    inputDate.setTime(inputDate.getTime() + 7 * 24 * 60 * 60 * 1000);
    return inputDate;
}

trace(currentDate);
```

```
// Outputs: Thu Jul 14 21:24:08 GMT-0700 2005

trace(getDateNextWeek(currentDate));
// Outputs: Thu Jul 21 21:24:08 GMT-0700 2005

trace(currentDate);
// Outputs: Thu Jul 21 21:24:08 GMT-0700 2005
```

The variable `currentDate` is passed to `getDateNextWeek()` as a parameter. The function adds seven days to the date passed in and then returns the new date. Unfortunately, the Date data type is a composite data type, so the function actually changes the original value in doing its calculation. To keep this from happening, a new Date instance needs to be created within the function:

```
var currentDate:Date = new Date();

function getDateNextWeek(inputDate:Date):Date
{
    var tempDate = new Date();
    tempDate.setTime(inputDate.getTime());
    tempDate.setTime(tempDate.getTime() + 7 * 24 * 60 * 60 * 1000);
    return tempDate;
}

trace(currentDate);
// Outputs: Thu Jul 14 21:38:59 GMT-0700 2005

trace(getDateNextWeek(currentDate));
// Outputs: Thu Jul 21 21:38:59 GMT-0700 2005

trace(currentDate);
// Outputs: Thu Jul 14 21:38:59 GMT-0700 2005
```

This time the argument isn't changed, so there are no longer any side effects.

Side effects are not always terrible, and many functions are written specifically for their side effects, such as to send data to a server through the LoadVars or the XML class. You see examples of these classes in use later in this book. Side effects are bad primarily when it is not immediately obvious what kind of side effect a function has. Clear, explicit naming of functions and variables goes a long way in making it easier to work with and to debug functions that use side effects. For instance, a function called `getFormFields()` grabs the contents of several text fields and drop-down boxes, and sends that data to the server; but it isn't obvious from its name that the function is actually responsible for sending data to a server. If the function were named `sendFormDataToServer()` or even just `sendFormData()`, the side effect would be more apparent.

Summary

This chapter finishes up the introduction to the core ActionScript language. Some points to remember include the following:

❑   A function is the core container for integrating chunks of code into a single command that can be reused.

❑ Different variables have different visibility, depending on where and how they are declared. The three types of variable scope are local, timeline, and global.

❑ Be careful about introducing side effects to a function. A function should not modify outside data unless it is clear from the function's name that that is the function's intended purpose.

Exercises

1. Create a function that takes two string arguments and returns the one that alphabetically comes first. (Hint: Check out the behavior of the comparison operators.)

2. Modify the following function so that it does not directly access the timeline variable from within the function, nor modify the original array:

```
var fruitArray:Array = new Array("kumquat", "apple", "pear", "strawberry",
"banana");
trace(fruitArray);

function sortArray():Void
{
    fruitArray.sort();
}
sortArray();
trace(fruitArray);
```

3. Modify the `convertToButton()` function so that it also works with rollover and rollout events. Choose a new color to use for the mouseover state.

```
function drawRectangle(targetMC:MovieClip, rectWidth:Number, rectHeight:Number,
bgColor:Number):Void
{
    targetMC.moveTo(0, 0);
    targetMC.lineStyle(1, 0x000000);
    targetMC.beginFill(bgColor, 100);
    targetMC.lineTo(rectWidth, 0);
    targetMC.lineTo(rectWidth, rectHeight);
    targetMC.lineTo(0, rectHeight);
    targetMC.lineTo(0, 0);
}

function buttonClickHandler():Void
{
    trace("Button pressed");
}

function convertToButton(targetMC:MovieClip, callbackFunction:Function):Void
{
    drawRectangle(targetMC, 100, 30, 0x333399);

    targetMC.onPress = function()
    {
        this.clear();
        drawRectangle(this, 100, 30, 0x3333CC);
```

```
    }

    targetMC.onRelease = function()
    {
        this.clear();
        drawRectangle(this, 100, 30, 0x333399);
        callbackFunction();
    }
}

this.createEmptyMovieClip("testButton", 1);
convertToButton(testButton, buttonClickHandler);
```

Getting Started with Coding

With an understanding of the mechanics of programming with ActionScript, it is time to apply some structure to that knowledge. Part of developing programming skills is to learn some larger constructs that help you move from the realm of a coder to the realm of a developer. Even if you are learning ActionScript purely as a personal hobby, you will benefit from these constructs.

This chapter begins by presenting a primer on object-oriented programming (OOP) principles. You learn some of the key object-oriented terminology and why the principles behind object-oriented programming are important. Then the bulk of the chapter teaches you about some programming best practices, and finally you learn some techniques for creating your own functions. You've got a lot ahead of you, so let's get started.

Introduction to Object-Oriented Programming

The concept of object-oriented programming is core to how many modern programming and scripting languages operate. By learning about OOP principles, you'll have a better understanding of why ActionScript works the way it does, and if you decide to proceed to making your own custom classes, the knowledge will help you to better grasp that process, too.

Defining Object-Oriented Programming

Numerous definitions of object-oriented programming exist, and there can be many debates about some of the finer details, but the basic premise boils down to the concept of an *object*, which is

> A single entity that holds data and code that acts on that data.

The use of objects as units of organization is different from the older procedural model where code is basically seen as a list of instructions given to the computer. Technically all programs are just a list of instructions, but object-oriented programming practitioners work at applying a particular organization to those instructions. Various programming languages include features that help in this effort, such as the dot syntax used in ActionScript, JavaScript, and Java.

The package of code and data consists of three things: the data, the methods that act on the data, and the properties that describe the data (see Figure 5-1). The methods that act on the data are really functions, just with a different name. Properties are basically variables, again just with a different name.

```
Object

Data
"the quick brown fox"

Methods (Functions)
indexOf()
substring()
toLowerCase()
toUpperCase()
...

Properties (Variables)
length
...
```

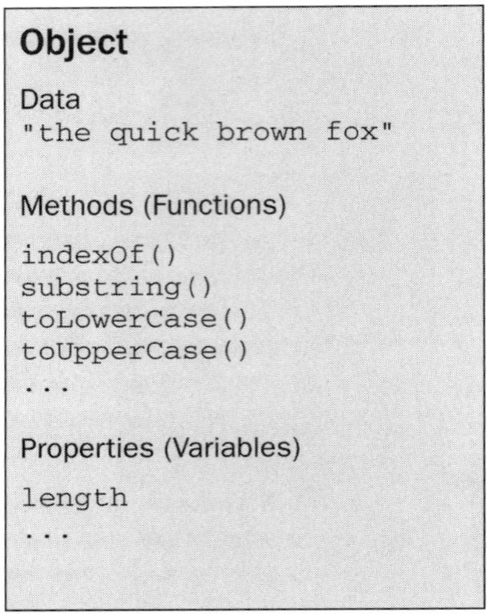

Figure 5-1

The dot syntax is used to access methods and properties from an object. In the following example, some text is assigned to a variable called stringObject:

```
var stringObject:String = "the quick brown fox";

trace(stringObject.length);
// Outputs: 19

trace(stringObject.toUpperCase());
// Outputs: THE QUICK BROWN FOX
```

This variable now contains a String object, which contains the data "the quick brown fox" as well as different properties and methods that you can use on that data. For instance, the length property reports on the number of characters in the string, and the toUpperCase() method returns a copy of the string with all letters in the string converted to capitals.

It is definitely convenient to have all the functionality that could possibly apply to a particular data type attached directly to that data. There are no libraries to import, no associations to create, and by knowing the data type, a quick search through its documentation reveals all the properties and methods that can be accessed.

Classes Versus Objects

A class is a definition or a template from which an object is derived. There is only one copy of any single class definition in memory at any time. The class includes all the code needed by an object, but does not include the data. An object stores the actual data that the class code is to work on, and each object has its own independent data store. Even though you hear the terms object and class used interchangeably, they are not the same thing.

Figure 5-2 illustrates a basic class that is built into the Flash player: the String class.

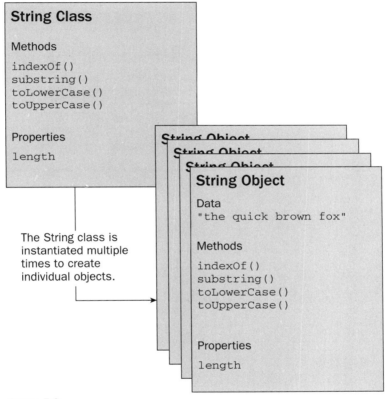

Figure 5-2

There is always exactly one String class, but there can be any number of String objects. Any time that data is assigned to a variable of type String, a String object is created. The following code shows that the properties and methods apply equally well to a String literal as they do to a variable containing a String object:

```
trace("the quick brown fox".length);
// Outputs: 19

trace("the quick brown fox".toUpperCase());
// Outputs: THE QUICK BROWN FOX
```

The term for a single String object is an *instance*, and the process of creating an instance is called *instantiation*. Because no real work is needed to create an instance of the String class, it is called *implicit instantiation*.

Figure 5-2 shows that with each object, all the methods and properties defined by the class are available in the object. Although it looks like all the code is duplicated for each object, this is not the case. Figure 5-3 gives a more accurate picture of what happens.

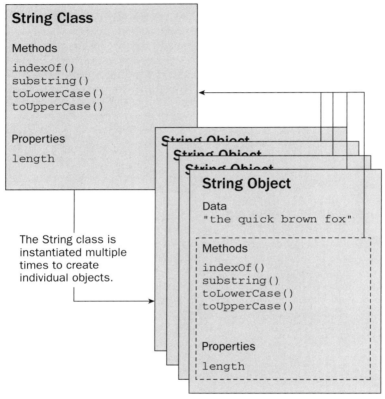

Figure 5-3

Duplicating the code for all the properties and methods would take up too much memory, so each object simply points to the code within the class.

The same relationships exist in the Sound class (see Figure 5-4), a more complex data type.

The process for instantiating a new Sound object from the Sound class is a little bit different than the String class's process. The new operator is used to indicate which class is to be instantiated. The following code snippet creates a new Sound instance:

```
var introSound:Sound = new Sound();
```

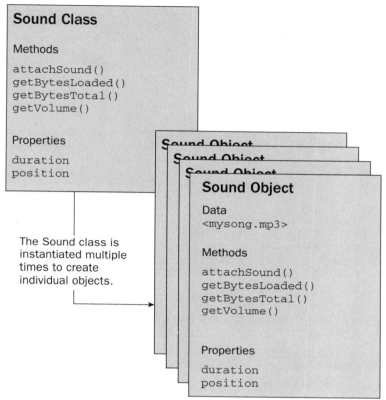

Sound Class

Methods

```
attachSound()
getBytesLoaded()
getBytesTotal()
getVolume()
```

Properties

```
duration
position
```

The Sound class is instantiated multiple times to create individual objects.

Sound Object
Sound Object
Sound Object

Sound Object

Data
`<mysong.mp3>`

Methods

```
attachSound()
getBytesLoaded()
getBytesTotal()
getVolume()
```

Properties

```
duration
position
```

Figure 5-4

The new operator creates objects explicitly, and therefore the process is called *explicit instantiation*. Once instantiated, the object needs to be assigned to a variable so that it can be accessed. The variable to hold the new object is declared to be of the same data type as the class being instantiated.

> **New instances of the primitive data types — String, Number, and Boolean — are created through implicit instantiation, although explicit instantiation is also possible through the** new **operator. New instances for all other data types are explicitly created through the** new **operator.**

The following code snippet loads a sound file into the Sound object and starts the playback once the sound file has completely loaded:

```
var introSound:Sound = new Sound();
introSound.onLoad = function()
{
    this.start();
}
introSound.loadSound("myFirstArrangement.mp3");
```

There is a naming convention for classes and objects as well. Class names all start with a capital letter, whereas the names of variables holding object instances, which really encompasses all variables, start with a lowercase letter.

Class Inheritance

The concept of inheritance is also part of object-oriented programming. A good OOP technique is to manage relationships between different classes. Where relationships exist, inheritance allows one class, and thus all objects created from that class, to *inherit* properties and methods from another class. Inheritance starts from a *base class*, which defines core methods and properties. Classes can *extend* (add on to) the base class. Classes that extend a class inherit all of that class's properties and methods, and can add their own or modify existing ones. Creating your own custom classes is a more advanced topic that is fully explained in Chapter 27.

A good example of inheritance at work in real life is the components that come with the Macromedia Flash development environment. Open the Flash Help panel, navigate to Components Language Reference⇨ComboBox Component⇨ComboBox Class, and you see a number of tables listing the properties, methods, and events available to use with the ComboBox component. Headings include "Method summary for the ComboBox class," "Methods inherited from the UIObject class," and "Methods inherited from the UIComponent class." The UIObject and UIComponent classes are inherited by all components, automatically providing functionality without having to redefine each method, property, and event for each component. For instance, the ComboBox component inherits the setSize() method from the UIObject class. To resize a ComboBox on the stage with the instance name chooseColorCombo, you'd use the following line of code:

```
chooseColorCombo.setSize(200, 22);
```

The setSize() method is automatically included with each component that inherits from the UIObject class, without any additional effort by you.

Inheritance allows common code to be implemented once, rather than duplicated in similar classes, and applies a common set of methods to similar classes. This results in consistent usage of the classes and helps keep code clean and focused.

Goals of Object-Oriented Programming

Although a number of goals for object-oriented programming exist, the overriding one is to make code easier to work with, whether you're part of a group project or on your own. Stemming from this one are the other OOP goals:

❑ **Keep code focused.** Focused code performs a small number of closely related tasks, rather than a large number of loosely related tasks. Methods within a class are there specifically to support the goal of the class, so classes tend to be fairly focused by design.

❑ **Promote code re-use.** Being able to reuse and share code brings significant benefits to the programming process, such as simplifying the code, and saving time from not having to re-implement the same task. Smaller elements often work best. If one class has multiple roles, for example, it may work better to break the class into several single-role classes. Those smaller classes can be more readily reused in other parts of the project, or in different projects completely.

❏ **Reduce impact of change.** It is common for changes to be required either in the middle of development or after all primary development has wrapped up. Even in personal undertakings, it isn't unusual to alter a project's goal in mid-development. These changes can be more readily accommodated by code that is easily adapted to different needs — self-contained and focused code.

❏ **Keep code understandable.** Be organized, use good variable and function naming conventions, and make use of white space. Keep functions small, focused, and well defined. Object-oriented programming helps give code a structure that is easy to follow.

Coding Best Practices

The term *best practice* is common in the business world. It refers to the process of discovering which organizations excel in a given field, analyzing how they execute their projects, and then looking for common traits in the execution of each of those projects. Those common traits are called the best practices for that field and are used as a model for others to follow. Best practices change over time as technologies change and as new ideas take hold. These practices are not divine gospel, but are an opportunity to learn from the experience of others, and to apply to and expand with your own development work.

A number of best practices taken from other ActionScript programmers will help you in getting started with ActionScript. The following sections explore those practices in the following topics:

❏ Variable naming

❏ Variable typing

❏ Commenting

❏ Formatting code

❏ Variable scope

❏ Accessing variables in another timeline

❏ Creating your own functions

Understanding Variable Naming

How variables are named contributes to how understandable the code is. Developing good variable naming habits will save hours of frustration during debugging and during later development. Here are a few strategies to follow for naming variables.

Making Variable Names Readable

One common variable formatting style is called camelBack. It consists of separating multiple words in a variable name by capitalizing the first letter of each word beginning with the second word. Here are some examples of variables named in the camelBack style:

```
var applicationName:String;
var isFirstPass:Boolean;
var highScoresArray:Array;
```

An alternative is to use a separator, such as an underscore, between words. The camelBack syntax allows English-like variable names to be used and easily read without the addition of separators, which take up more screen space.

Variable names should be descriptive, but should not be sentences. Use the shortest name that is still meaningful.

The only time a variable name should consist of only one letter is when it's used as an iterator within a `for` loop. The convention is to use the letters i through n as iterators, starting at i and using subsequent letters as loops are nested inside of each other. Here's an example in which the variable j is in a `for` loop nested in a `for` loop that includes the variable i:

```
for (var i=0; i < someNum; i+)
{
    // Outer loop
    for (var j=0; j < someDifferentNum; j++)
    {
        //Inner loop
    }
}
```

Making Boolean Variables into Questions

Boolean variable names should be written in such a way that it is immediately obvious what `true` and `false` signify. One approach is to write the variable name in the form of a question, usually starting with the word *is*. Here are some examples:

```
var isFirstPass:Boolean;
var isDone:Boolean;
var isOpen:Boolean;
var isPendingApproval:Boolean;
```

The names should always be phrased as a positive statement. The following should not be used:

```
var isNotDone:Boolean = false;
var isNotApproved:Boolean = true;
var isNotOpen:Boolean = true;
```

They would be better written as:

```
var isDone:Boolean = true;
var isApproved:Boolean = false;
var isClosed:Boolean = true; // or
var isOpen:Boolean = false;
```

Avoiding Reserved Words

ActionScript reserves a number of words for its own use, and you must avoid using them in your code. Two main groups of reserved words exist: keywords (core statements) and words that are reserved for future use. The compiler usually spits out an error and stops the compilation when a reserved keyword is used for a variable name. Variables named the same as common methods or properties still work, but they may obscure access to the method or the property. The rule of thumb is that when the Macromedia Flash editor highlights a variable name in blue, there is a reserved keyword or a built-in method or property with the same name, and you should change your variable's name.

Following is a list of reserved keywords:

Reserved Keywords			
add	Extends	interface	set
and	finally	intrinsic	static
break	for	le	switch
case	function	lt	tellTarget
catch	ge	ne	this
class	get	new	throw
continue	gt	not	try
default	if	on	typeof
delete	ifFrameLoaded	onClipEvent	var
do	implements	or	void
dynamic	import	private	while
else	in	public	width
eq	instanceof	return	

Here are the keywords that ActionScript has reserved for future use:

Keywords Reserved for Future Use			
abstract	double	goto	synchronized
byte	enum	long	throws
char	export	protected	transient
debugger	float	short	volatile

There is also a list of class names and component names that should not be used for variable names. Though the compiler is case sensitive and allows a variable name such as object or string, it is bad practice to have a variable name that differs from a keyword only by case. Here's the list:

Reserved Class and Component Names			
Accessibility	Date	Microphone	StyleManager
Accordion	DateChooser	Mouse	System
Alert	DateField	MovieClip	TextArea
Array	Delta	MovieClipLoader	TextFormat
Binding	DeltaItem	NetConnection	TextInput
Boolean	DeltaPacket	NetStream	TextSnapshot
Button	DepthManager	Number	TransferObject
Camera	EndPoint	NumericStepper	Tree
CellRenderer	Error	Object	TreeDataProvider
CheckBox	FocusManager	PendingCall	TypedValue
Collection	Form	PopUpManager	UIComponent
Color	Function	PrintJob	UIEventDispatcher
ComboBox	Iterator	ProgressBar	UIObject
ComponentMixins	Key	RadioButton	Video
ContextMenu	Label	RDBMSResolver	WebService
ContextMenuItem	List	Screen	WebServiceConnector
CustomActions	Loader	ScrollPane	Window
CustomFormatter	LoadVars	Selection	XML
CustomValidator	LocalConnection	SharedObject	XMLConnector
DataGrid	Log	Slide	XUpdateResolver
DataHolder	Math	SOAPCall	
DataProvider	Media	Sound	
DataSet	Menu	Stage	
DataType	MenuBar	String	

Distinguishing Variable Names from Class Names

Variable and function names should always start with a lowercase letter. Names that start with an uppercase letter are used only for classes and data types.

Variable Typing

As you learned in Chapter 2, variable typing allows explicit declaration of what kind of data each variable should hold. Here are a number of reasons why this is a good practice:

❑   It catches numerous errors at compile time, errors which would otherwise require significant time to track down at run time.

❑   It allows the development environment to provide code hinting for variables.

❑   It helps you write better code by ensuring all functions and methods properly declare their input and output types.

❑   It causes no performance slow-downs whatsoever; it is used only at compile time.

ActionScript 1.0 provided code hinting but required that variables be named in a specific manner to take advantage of the hinting. Each variable needed to end with _code where code was a specific set of letters that needed to be remembered. Here are some examples:

```
var submit_btn;
var username_array;
var base_mc;
var currentScore_txt;
```

This is still a good practice to follow, although with strong typing, you are no longer tied to specific character codes. The following versions of these variables are equally if not more understandable, even though they result in longer variable names:

```
var submitButton:Button;
var usernameArray:Array;
var baseMovieClip:MovieClip;
var currentScoreTextField:TextField;
```

Whatever naming convention you decide to use, it should be apparent from the variable name what kind of data the variable contains, and the naming convention should be used consistently through your projects.

Following are suggested variable name suffixes you might consider:

Data Type	Version 1	Version 2
Array	*_array	*Array
Button	*_btn	*Button
Camera	*_camera	*Camera
Color	*_color	*Color
ContextMenu	*_cm	*ContextMenu
ContextMenuItem	*_cmi	*ContextMenuItem
Date	*_date	*Date
Error	*_err	*Error
LoadVars	*_lv	*LoadVars
LocalConnection	*_lc	*LocalConnection
Microphone	*_mic	*Microphone
MovieClip	*_mc	*MovieClip
MovieClipLoader	*_mcl	*MovieClipLoader
NetConnection	*_nc	*NetConnection
NetStream	*_ns	*NetStream
PrintJob	*_pj	*PrintJob
SharedObject	*_so	*SharedObject
Sound	*_sound	*Sound
String	*_str	*String
TextField	*_txt	*TextField
TextFormat	*_fmt	*TextFormat
Video	*_video	*Video
XML	*_xml	*XML
XMLNode	*_xmlnode	*XMLNode
XMLSocket	*_xmlsocket	*XMLSocket

Type Casting

Whenever you assign one variable to another, and the variables are of different types, Macromedia Flash attempts to convert the type of the source variable to the type of the destination variable. This is a process called *type casting*. It generally works only when the target variable is a primitive data type (String, Number, or Boolean).

The difficulty with automatic type casting is that you do not know about it when it happens, so you might get behavior that is inconsistent with your expectations. The solution is to manually cast your variables whenever there is a discrepancy in type between two variables. The following code shows examples of casting.

```
// Cast a number to a string
var currentDay:Number = 23;
currentDayTextField.text = String(currentDay);

// Cast a string to a number
var currentDay:Number = Number(currentDayTextField.text);

// Cast a string to a Boolean
var isBackgroundShown:Boolean = Boolean("true");

// Cast a number to a Boolean
var isBackgroundShown:Boolean = Boolean(1);
```

Try It Out   Creating Understandable Code

This example presents before and after looks at how using strong typing and good variable naming conventions helps make code easier to work with. In addition, the first code listing includes a bug that strong typing will quickly find.

1. Create a new Macromedia Flash document by selecting File⇨New and choosing Flash Document from the New Document panel.

2. Click the first frame in the timeline, open the Actions panel (Window⇨Development Panels⇨ Actions), and type in the following ActionScript code:

```
#include "tryItOut_understandableCode.as"
```

3. Select File⇨Save As, name the file tryItOut_understandableCode.fla, choose an appropriate directory, and save it.

4. Create a new Macromedia Flash document and save it as tryItOut_understandableCode.as in the same directory as your .fla file.

5. Enter the following code into the new ActionScript file:

```
var hasBackground;
var date = new Date();
var month = date.getMonth();
var startingDay;
var x;
var y;
var base;

date.setDate(1);
startingDay = date.getDay();
hasBackground = "true";
base = _level0;

while (date.getMonth() == month)
{
```

```
    x = date.getDay() * 20 + 2;
    y = Math.floor( ( startingDay + date.getDate() - 1) / 7 ) * 20 + 2;

    base.createTextField("dateField"+date.getDate(), ⤵
        this.getNextHighestDepth(), x, y, 17, 17);
    base["dateField" + date.getDate()].text = date.getDate();

    if (hasBackground == true)
    {
        base.moveTo(x-3, y-3);
        base.beginFill(0xAAAAAA);
        base.lineStyle(1, 0x333333);
        base.lineTo(x-3, y+17);
        base.lineTo(x+17, y+17);
        base.lineTo(x+17, y-3);
        base.lineTo(x-3, y-3);
    }
    date.setDate(date.getDate() + 1);
}
```

6. Save the file, return to the Macromedia Flash project file, and select Control⇨Test Movie.

7. Create a new Macromedia Flash document, name it `tryItOut_understandableCode2.as`, and save it in the same directory as the `.fla` file.

8. Enter the following code into the new ActionScript file:

```
var hasBackground:Boolean;
var currentDate:Date;
var currentMonthNumber:Number;
var startingDayNumber:Number;
var textFieldX:Number;
var textFieldY:Number;
var baseMovieClip:MovieClip;

currentDate = new Date();
currentDate.setDate(1);
startingDayNumber = currentDate.getDay();
hasBackground = true;
currentMonthNumber = currentDate.getMonth();
baseMovieClip = _level0;

while (currentDate.getMonth() == currentMonthNumber)
{
    textFieldX = currentDate.getDay() * 20 + 2;
    textFieldY = Math.floor((startingDayNumber + currentDate.getDate() - 1) ⤵
        / 7) * 20 + 2;

    baseMovieClip.createTextField("dateField"+currentDate.getDate(),⤵
        this.getNextHighestDepth(), textFieldX, textFieldY, 17, 17);
    baseMovieClip["dateField" + currentDate.getDate()].text = ⤵
        String(currentDate.getDate());

    if (hasBackground == true)
    {
```

```
        baseMovieClip.moveTo(textFieldX-3, textFieldY-3);
        baseMovieClip.beginFill(0xAAAAAA);
        baseMovieClip.lineStyle(1, 0x333333);
        baseMovieClip.lineTo(textFieldX-3, textFieldY+17);
        baseMovieClip.lineTo(textFieldX+17, textFieldY+17);
        baseMovieClip.lineTo(textFieldX+17, textFieldY-3);
        baseMovieClip.lineTo(textFieldX-3, textFieldY-3);
    }
    currentDate.setDate(currentDate.getDate() + 1);
}
```

9. Click the first frame in the timeline, open the Actions panel (Window⇨Development Panels⇨ Actions), and modify the following ActionScript code to point to the new ActionScript file:

```
#include "tryItOut_understandableCode2.as"
```

10. Save the file, return to the Flash project file, and select Control⇨Test Movie.

How It Works

The difference between the first and second code listings is that variable names are changed and strong typing is added. Numerous issues exist with the variable declarations and variable assignments in the first listing:

```
var hasBackground;
var date = new Date();
var month = date.getMonth();
var startingDay;
var x;
var y;
var base;

startingDay = date.getDay() + 2;
hasBackground = "true";
base = _level0;
```

First of all, it is a bit neater to have variable assignments all happening together. Line 2 shows the variable date that differs from the data type Date by only its case, which is not a good practice. The variable month gives no indication on its own whether it contains a numeric or string value. The x and y variables do not indicate what coordinates they hold. The variable base gives no indication of the kind of data it should hold. Finally, the variable assignment for hasBackground assigns a string to a variable of type Boolean, which causes the if statement a bit later on to always evaluate to false. With strong typing, this error is caught by the compiler.

The equivalent code from the second code listing resolves all of those issues:

```
var hasBackground:Boolean;
var currentDate:Date;
var currentMonthNumber:Number;
var startingDayNumber:Number;
var textFieldX:Number;
var textFieldY:Number;
var baseMovieClip:MovieClip;
```

115

```
currentDate = new Date();
startingDayNumber = currentDate.getDay() + 2;
hasBackground = true;
currentMonthNumber = currentDate.getMonth();
baseMovieClip = _level0;
```

Also of note is the following line from the first listing:

```
base["dateField" + date.getDate()].text = date.getDate();
```

This line assigns the date as a label to a text field. Two different data types are actually being used here. The text field expects a string label, but `date.getDate()` returns a number. Macromedia Flash automatically converts the data types, but it is more explicit to do it through a type casting:

```
baseMovieClip["dateField" + currentDate.getDate()].text = ⮒
    String(currentDate.getDate());
```

The `String()` typecast makes it clear that the data type to be passed to the `.text` property is a string.

Sometimes it's fine to let Flash automatically cast one data type to another. For instance, the preceding example shows `"dateField" + currentDate.getDate()`, *where the number returned by* `currentDate.getDate()` *is automatically cast to a string and appended to* `"dateField"`. *In such cases, you could manually cast it using* `"dateField" + String(currentDate.getDate())`, *but when appending a string and another data type together, manual casting is not strictly needed because it's fairly clear that the result will be a string.*

Commenting

Annotating (commenting) code to make it understandable is an important part of coding. Chapter 2 introduced you to comments. Now you'll explore how to make the best use them.

Comments in code take three forms:

❑   Self-documenting code

❑   Comments to explain particular issues with the code

❑   Commented-out code

The best type of commenting to do is to make the code easily readable in the first place. That's what's called writing *self-documenting* code. It involves using variable and function names that are clear and English-like, and that readily indicate what their purpose is. If you write code that is self-documenting, you lessen the need for added comments.

> **Comments are not a replacement for writing clear, well-structured, easy-to-understand code. Think of comments as additional guidance to help with maintenance.**

Relatively few people really know how to comment properly. Comments are not needed for every line or couple of lines, nor are they needed to explain obvious chunks of code. Instead, comments should be used to help someone through the hard parts of your code, and to document the purpose and usage for each function. Single-line comments in code always begin with two slashes: //. A few places where comments come in handy include the following, with examples:

❑ Within complex if statements to give an English-like description of the statement:

```
if ((currentDay == 0 || currentDay == 6) &&  ⟳
    (currentMonth == 1 || currentYear == 2006)) {
// Look for weekends in February for any year and look for any weekend in 2006
```

❑ Next to tricky chunks of code that someone may not want to touch unless he really knows the code:

```
// ******************
// *** TRICKY: Impacts client stability
// ******************
```

❑ Next to a spot where a particularly hackish technique has been used:

```
// ******************
// *** HACK: Does not work without following line of code. I don't know why.
// ******************
```

❑ At the start of a function:

```
// ******************
// Name:      createCalendar
// Purpose:   Creates a visual calendar for the given month. Clicking on any of
//            the days will call a function and pass the date to that function.
// Inputs:    yearNum (Number): The year to show.
//            monthNum (Number): The month to show. Starts at 0 for January.
//            callbackFunction (Function): A function to call when a date button has
//            been clicked on. A date object containing the selected date will
//            be passed to the callback function.
// Example:   function calendarCallback(selectedDate:Date):Void
//            {
//                trace(selectedDate);
//            }
//
//            createCalendar(2005, 11, calendarCallback);
// ******************
```

Comments are also invaluable as a debugging tool. The single-line comment can be used to remove small numbers of lines of code to test how the application behaves without them. The /* */ syntax can be used to block out larger chunks of code, including entire functions or groups of functions. (Remember to use // for comments inside a code block that you're commenting out.)

The previous examples all used the single-line comment syntax (//). Here's an example of how you'd comment out a block of code:

```
/*
if (hasBackground == true)
{
    baseMovieClip.moveTo(textFieldX-3, textFieldY-3);
    baseMovieClip.beginFill(0xAAAAAA);
    baseMovieClip.lineStyle(1, 0x333333);
    baseMovieClip.lineTo(textFieldX-3, textFieldY+17);
    baseMovieClip.lineTo(textFieldX+17, textFieldY+17);
    baseMovieClip.lineTo(textFieldX+17, textFieldY-3);
    baseMovieClip.lineTo(textFieldX-3, textFieldY-3);
}
*/
```

Formatting Code

Many styles for formatting code exist, and choosing is usually a matter of personal preference, yet some coding styles are definitely more readable than others. The most important attribute about formatting code is to use white space. Code crammed together to take as little space as possible makes reading and understanding it difficult. Placing blank lines between sections of code allows related sections of code to be distinguishable, much like paragraphs of text, and inserting spaces before and after operators helps split up a line into word-like chunks.

The following styles have been found by the authors to be effective ways of formatting code:

❑   Put start and end braces on their own lines. This applies to functions, if statements, for statements, and all other statements that use braces. The extra line between the top statement and the brace body makes it clear where the statement body begins:

```
function myFunction()
{
    // Function code goes here
}

if (something == true)
{
    // If statement code goes here
}
else
{
    // Else statement code goes here
}

for (var i=0; i < 20; i++)
{
    // Loop content goes here
}
```

You can configure Flash to auto-format braces to this style by selecting Flash⇨Preferences (Macintosh) or Edit⇨Preferences (Windows), choosing the Auto Format item, and then checking the first three checkboxes: Insert { On Line After If, For, Switch, While, Etc.; Insert { On Line After Function, Class, And Interface Keywords; and Don't Cuddle } And Else. These settings apply any time you select Tools⇨Auto Format while editing an ActionScript file or when you click the auto-format button in the Actions panel.

❑ Use spaces between operators and operands:

```
// Without spaces
var totalCroutonWeight:Number=numCroutons*(croutonWeight-crumbleFactor);

// With spaces
var totalCroutonWeight:Number = numCroutons * (croutonWeight - crumbleFactor);
```

❑ Avoid the shorthand `if..then..else` notation, which can quickly lead to some grotesque, impossible-to-read code lines. In the following code example, you can see that the second version is much clearer, even though it takes up more lines of code:

```
var inputValue = "";
var localValue;

// Avoid:
localValue = (inputValue == "") ? "defaultValue" : inputValue;

// Use instead:
if (inputValue == "")
{
    localValue = "defaultValue";
}
else
{
    localValue = inputValue;
}
```

Understanding Variable Scope

Every variable takes up some amount of memory and exists for a particular length of time. Variables that are declared within a function—and are therefore local in scope—last only for the duration of the function. As a result, the impact of local variables on the overall memory footprint of the project is relatively small. Timeline variables and global variables last longer. If the project runs all code in a single frame, the timeline variables last for the duration of the project, and an accumulation of timeline and global variables increases the memory footprint of the application.

Memory usage is important, but more significant is the impact of timeline and global variables on your ability to find and fix problems. Every global variable used in a function works against the principle of having well-defined input and output for each function. There's certainly a need for global and timeline variables, but there are some strategies for limiting their impact on your code, which the following sections explain.

Declaring All Global and Timeline Variables in One Place

Do not scatter global and timeline variable declarations throughout your code. Reserve a specific section at the beginning for variables. Definitely don't declare global variables from within a function, although it is a good idea to create a startup function that can assign starting values to global variables, such as the following example shows:

```
// Declare timeline variables
var currentScore:Number;
var startingNumLives:Number;
```

```
var numLives:Number;
var shieldLevel:Number;
var ammoLeft:Number;

// Initialize application
init();

function init():Void
{
    currentScore = 0;
    startingNumLives = 9;
    numLives = 9;
    shieldLevel = 50;
    ammoLeft = 200;
}
```

Creating an Object Just for Data

Instead of having several variables on the timeline, it may make sense to group variables into a container object. This lessens the chance of having those variables conflict with properties from built-in classes, and it also helps organize related variables into a single grouping. The disadvantage of doing this is that you cannot use strong typing for the object properties of the container object. The following code shows how startup code is grouped into a function called init(), which is the only function actually called from the main script file. It can call additional functions as needed for more complex projects.

```
// Declare timeline variables
var playerStats:Object;

// Initialize application
init();

function init():Void
{
    playerStats = new Object();
    playerStats.currentScore = 0;
    playerStats.startingNumLives = 9;
    playerStats.numLives = 9;
    playerStats.shieldLevel = 50;
    playerStats.ammoLeft = 200;
}
```

Creating Access Functions

In general, global and timeline variables should not be accessed directly. If the global data implementation changes, then every function that accesses or changes the data needs to be modified as well. Instead, make the changes through intermediary access functions that are responsible for manipulating global or timeline variables. The following code shows how the currentScore, numLives, and shieldLevel properties in the playerStats timeline variable are accessed through the addToScore(), decrementNumLives(), and powerUpShield() functions:

```
// Declare timeline variables
var playerStats:Object;

// Initialize application
```

```
init();

function init():Void
{
    playerStats = new Object();
    playerStats.currentScore = 0;
    playerStats.startingNumLives = 9;
    playerStats.numLives = 9;
    playerStats.shieldLevel = 50;
    playerStats.ammoLeft = 200;
}

function addToScore(addAmount:Number):Void
{
    playerStats.currentScore += addAmount;
}

function decrementNumLives():Void
{
    playerStats.numLives -= 1;
}

function powerUpShield(addAmount:Number):Void
{
    playerStats.shieldLevel += amount;
}

// etc...
```

Using access functions instead of directly changing global or timeline variables provides the additional benefit of being able to respond to changes in variables that may need to be reflected by the screen state.

An even better way of manipulating important global and timeline variables is through the creation of custom classes.

Managing Data with Custom Classes

The best way to deal with global data is through the creation of one or more custom classes. The process of creating a custom class is explored in Chapter 27, so here it's just discussed at a high level.

A custom class is the object-oriented approach to managing global data. You recall from the object-oriented programming introduction that an object is the combination of data and the methods that work with that data. Placing the access functions within the custom class along with the data, instead of placing them directly on the timeline, means that the only global reference that's needed is the one to the object itself. Here's an example that shows how the player stats can be manipulated through methods called from the custom playerStatsClass instead of through functions sitting on the main timeline:

```
// Declare timeline variables
var playerStats:PlayerStatsClass = new PlayerStatsClass();

// Data can now be modified through object methods and properties
playerStats.addToScore(50);
playerStats.powerUpShield(20);
trace(playerStats.getScore());
```

The `addToScore()`, `powerUpShield()`, and `getScore()` methods provide ways to read from and write to the variables stored internally by the class.

In this example none of the player stats is directly accessed; the implementation of the data is hidden, so it can easily be changed without affecting other code. (Creating a second instance of `PlayerStatsClass` easily accommodates a two-player scenario.)

Accessing Variables in Another Timeline

It is generally not a good idea to scatter code or variables throughout the timeline, yet there are times when variables need to be set in individual movie clips. You can easily do this without actually having to click a movie clip on the stage and setting the variable in the Actions panel. The following line of code placed on the main timeline creates a variable called `screenId` within a movie clip on the main timeline called `screenHolder`, and it assigns the string value `"intro1"` to that variable:

```
screenHolder.screenId = "intro1";
```

Retrieving the variable is done similarly:

```
trace(screenHolder.screenId);
```

To set a variable within a nested movie clip, use the dot syntax to traverse the path of nested clips and set the variable:

```
applicationHolder.screenHolder.screenId = "intro1";
trace(applicationHolder.screenHolder.screenId);
```

Two ways exist for code placed directly within a movie clip to access variables within the parent. The first is to use the `_parent` property:

```
// Retrieve value of screenId in screenHolder from within
// a movie clip nested inside screenHolder
_parent.screenId = "intro1";
trace(_parent.screenId);
// Outputs: intro1
```

The second is to use an absolute reference, starting from the base of the project and traversing through each nested movie clip:

```
// Retrieve value of screenId in screenHolder from anywhere
_level0.applicationHolder.screenHolder.screenId = "intro1";
trace(_level0.applicationHolder.screenHolder);
// Outputs: intro1
```

Using the `_parent` syntax is generally preferred because it means that a group of movie clips can be moved around and the references will be preserved. It also means that if the project is later loaded into another project, the references will still work.

Try It Out   **Access Timeline Variable from Another Movie Clip**

In this exercise you access variables located in different movie clips from other movie clips.

1.   Create a new Macromedia Flash document by selecting File⇨New and choosing Flash Document from the New Document panel.

2.   Rename the current timeline layer to `Scripts`. Click the first frame in the timeline, open the Actions panel (Window⇨Development Panels⇨Actions), and type in the following ActionScript code:

```
var baseClipTestVar:String = "base clip data";
movieClip1.movieClip1TestVar = "clip 1 data";
movieClip1.movieClip2.movieClip2TestVar = "clip 2 data";

trace("***************");
trace("Accessing variables from base:");
trace("movieClip1.movieClip1TestVar: " + movieClip1.movieClip1TestVar);
trace("movieClip1.movieClip2.movieClip2TestVar: " +
movieClip1.movieClip2.movieClip2TestVar);
```

3.   Select File⇨Save As and name the file `tryItOut_accessTimelineVars.fla`, choose an appropriate directory, and save it.

4.   Create a new layer using the Create Layer button in the toolbar underneath the timeline. Name the layer `Movie Clip 1`.

5.   Use the rectangle tool to draw a rectangle onscreen. Choose the Selection tool (filled arrow icon in the toolbar) and drag across the shape to select the whole shape.

6.   With the shape selected, choose Modify⇨Convert To Symbol. Give the symbol a name, such as `Movie Clip 1`, make sure that the Movie Clip radio button is selected, and click OK.

7.   With the shape still selected, go to the Properties panel (Window⇨Properties) and type **movieClip1** into the text field on the top-left (see Figure 5-5).

8.   Double-click the shape to go into edit mode for the new movie clip.

9.   Rename the only layer in the timeline to `Shape`. Add two more layers, name them `Script` and `Movie Clip 2`, and drag them so that they are on top of the Shape layer.

10.   Click the empty frame in the timeline on the Script layer, and type the following code into the Actions panel:

```
trace("***************");
trace("Accessing variables from movieClip1:");
trace("_parent.baseClipTestVar: " + _parent.baseClipTestVar);
trace("_level0.baseClipTestVar: " + _level0.baseClipTestVar);
trace("movieClip2.movieClip2TestVar: " + movieClip2.movieClip2TestVar);
```

11.   Click the empty frame in the timeline on the Movie Clip 1 layer. Select the rectangle tool, and choose any different color from the Color Picker in the toolbar. Draw a new rectangle within the first rectangle.

12.   Choose the Selection tool and drag across the shape to select the whole shape.

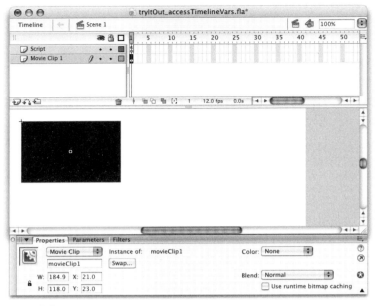

Figure 5-5

13. With the shape selected, choose Modify⇨Convert To Symbol. Give the symbol a name, such as Movie Clip 2, make sure that the Movie Clip radio button is selected, and click OK.

14. With the shape still selected, go to the Properties panel (Window⇨Properties) and type **movieClip2** into the text field on the top-left (see Figure 5-6).

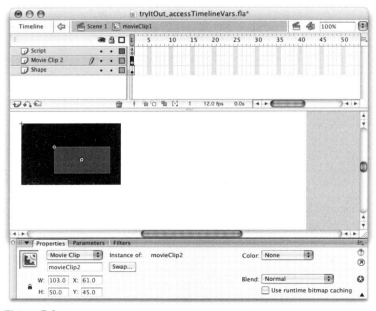

Figure 5-6

15. Double-click the shape to go into edit mode for the new movie clip.

16. Rename the only layer in the timeline to `Shape`. Add one more layer called `Script`.

17. Click the empty frame in the timeline on the Script layer, and type the following code into the Actions panel:

```
trace("***************");
trace("Accessing variables from movieClip2:");
trace("_parent._parent.baseClipTestVar: " + _parent._parent.baseClipTestVar);
trace("_parent.movieClip1TestVar: " + _parent.movieClip1TestVar);
trace("_level0.baseClipTestVar: " + _level0.baseClipTestVar);
trace("_level0.movieClip1.movieClip1TestVar: " +
    _level0.movieClip1.movieClip1TestVar);
```

18. Save the file and select Control⇨Test Movie.

How It Works

The nested movie clips created in this example query the variables from other movie clips using both relative and absolute references.

The first segment of code on the base timeline does the actual setting of data to the root timeline, to the first movie clip, and to the nested movie clip:

```
var baseClipTestVar:String = "base clip data";
movieClip1.movieClip1TestVar = "clip 1 data";
movieClip1.movieClip2.movieClip2TestVar = "clip 2 data";
```

The second segment of code accesses the variables relative to the base timeline:

```
trace("***************");
trace("Accessing variables from base:");
trace("movieClip1.movieClip1TestVar: " + movieClip1.movieClip1TestVar);
trace("movieClip1.movieClip2.movieClip2TestVar: " +
    movieClip1.movieClip2.movieClip2TestVar);
```

Within the script for the first movie clip, the code accesses the variable at the base timeline by using the relative _parent property, and then by using the absolute _level0 property. It then accesses the variable in the nested movie clip through dot syntax relative to movieClip1:

```
trace("***************");
trace("Accessing variables from movieClip1:");
trace("_parent.baseClipTestVar: " + _parent.baseClipTestVar);
trace("_level0.baseClipTestVar: " + _level0.baseClipTestVar);
trace("movieClip2.movieClip2TestVar: " + movieClip2.movieClip2TestVar);
```

Within the script for the second movie clip, the variable on the root timeline and the variable on the parent movie clip are both accessed through relative paths. Finally, those same two variables are accessed through absolute paths:

```
trace("***************");
trace("Accessing variables from movieClip2:");
trace("_parent._parent.baseClipTestVar: " + _parent._parent.baseClipTestVar);
trace("_parent.movieClip1TestVar: " + _parent.movieClip1TestVar);
```

```
trace("_level0.baseClipTestVar: " + _level0.baseClipTestVar);
trace("_level0.movieClip1.movieClip1TestVar: " + ⤶
    _level0.movieClip1.movieClip1TestVar);
```

The output for this example should look like the following:

```
* * * * * * * * * * * * * *
Accessing variables from base:
movieClip1.movieClip1TestVar: clip 1 data
movieClip1.movieClip2.movieClip2TestVar: clip 2 data
* * * * * * * * * * * * * *
Accessing variables from movieClip1:
_parent.baseClipTestVar: base clip data
_level0.baseClipTestVar: base clip data
movieClip2.movieClip2TestVar: clip 2 data
* * * * * * * * * * * * * *
Accessing variables from movieClip2:
_parent._parent.baseClipTestVar: base clip data
_parent.movieClip1TestVar: clip 1 data
_level0.baseClipTestVar: base clip data
_level0.movieClip1.movieClip1TestVar: clip 1 data
```

One of the reasons why you might want to dynamically assign a variable to a movie clip is because you have a number of almost identical buttons that each need to be distinguished from one another when they call a single common click handler. You may come across this scenario when creating clickable image thumbnails, a custom calendar with clickable dates, or a custom menu. The next Try It Out exercise explores how to handle clicks on different buttons with a single button handler function.

Try It Out　　**Assign an ID to a Dynamically Created Movie Clip**

This example shows how to dynamically assign an ID to a number of dynamic movie clips, and to then reference that ID when a button is clicked.

1. Create a new Macromedia Flash document by selecting File⇨New and choosing Flash Document from the New Document panel.

2. Click the first frame in the timeline, open the Actions panel (Window⇨Development Panels⇨ Actions), and type in the following ActionScript code:

```
#include "tryItOut_assignID.as"
```

3. Select File⇨Save As, name the file tryItOut_assignID.fla, choose an appropriate directory, and click Save.

4. Create a new script file by selecting File⇨New and choosing ActionScript File from the New Document panel.

5. Select File⇨Save As and ensure it is showing the same directory containing the .fla file. Name the file tryItOut_assignID.as and click Save.

6. Type the following code into the new ActionScript file:

```
var baseMovieClip:MovieClip = _level0;
var tempMovieClipHolder:MovieClip;

for (var i:Number = 0; i < 5; i++)
{
    // Create a movie clip
    baseMovieClip.createEmptyMovieClip("buttonClip" + i, ⤵
        baseMovieClip.getNextHighestDepth());
    tempMovieClipHolder = baseMovieClip["buttonClip" + i];

    // Assign an ID to a timeline variable tied to the button
    tempMovieClipHolder.buttonID = i;

    // Draw something inside the button so it can be seen and clicked on
    tempMovieClipHolder.lineStyle(1, 0x333333);
    tempMovieClipHolder.beginFill(0x6666AA);
    tempMovieClipHolder.moveTo(0, 0);
    tempMovieClipHolder.lineTo(50, 0);
    tempMovieClipHolder.lineTo(50, 25);
    tempMovieClipHolder.lineTo(0, 25);
    tempMovieClipHolder.lineTo(0, 0);

    // Position the button
    tempMovieClipHolder._y = 10;
    tempMovieClipHolder._x = i * 60 + 10;

    // Make the button clickable. Pass along the ID that was assigned
    // to the button's timeline
    tempMovieClipHolder.onRelease = function()
    {
        handleButtonClick(this.buttonID);
    }
}

function handleButtonClick(buttonID:Number)
{
    trace("Clicked on button number: " + buttonID);
}
```

7. Save the file, return to the `.fla`, and select Control⇨Test Movie.

How It Works

When a number of buttons are dynamically created onscreen, and each performs a similar function, something must be embedded in each button to allow it to be uniquely identified. The actual process of doing this is very simple, and most of the code in this example is there just to create, fill, and position the buttons.

First, a couple of timeline variables are declared:

```
var baseMovieClip:MovieClip = _level0;
var tempMovieClipHolder:MovieClip;
```

The first step performed within the `for` loop is to create empty movie clips:

```
// Create a movie clip
baseMovieClip.createEmptyMovieClip("buttonClip" + i, ↩
    baseMovieClip.getNextHighestDepth());
tempMovieClipHolder = baseMovieClip["buttonClip" + i];
```

Next, an ID is assigned to the movie clip. The ID can take any form, but it's convenient to use the iterator i:

```
// Assign an ID to a timeline variable tied to the button
tempMovieClipHolder.buttonID = i;
```

The movie clip is then filled with something so that it is visible:

```
// Draw something inside the button so it can be seen and clicked on
tempMovieClipHolder.lineStyle(1, 0x333333);
tempMovieClipHolder.beginFill(0x6666AA);
tempMovieClipHolder.moveTo(0, 0);
tempMovieClipHolder.lineTo(50, 0);
tempMovieClipHolder.lineTo(50, 25);
tempMovieClipHolder.lineTo(0, 25);
tempMovieClipHolder.lineTo(0,  0);

// Position the button
tempMovieClipHolder._y = 10;
tempMovieClipHolder._x = i * 60 + 10;
```

The clickable area depends on the contents of the clip, so an empty button is un-clickable.

The final step in the loop is to create a click handler for the movie clip. An anonymous function is created to retrieve the variable assigned to the movie clip and pass it along to a handler function:

```
// Make the button clickable. Pass along the ID assigned to the
// button's timeline
tempMovieClipHolder.onRelease = function()
{
    handleButtonClick(this.buttonID);
}
```

The `this` keyword refers to the parent object, which is the movie clip holding this particular `onRelease` handler. You could have assigned the handler function directly to the `onRelease` event property, but it isn't possible to retrieve the ID from within that function:

```
tempMovieClipHolder.onRelease = handleButtonClick;
function handleButtonClick()
{
    trace("Clicked on button number: "+this.buttonID);
}
```

Finally, the handler function is declared:

```
function handleButtonClick(buttonID:Number)
{
    trace("Clicked on button number: " + buttonID);
}
```

Creating Your Own Functions

Here are a number of best practices to keep in mind when you create custom functions (as you will in Chapter 27):

- ❑ Strongly type function arguments.
- ❑ Avoid hard-coded movie clip references.
- ❑ Declare return values.
- ❑ Avoid oversized functions.
- ❑ Avoid entanglement.
- ❑ Avoid duplication.

These guiding principles are examined in the following sections.

Strongly Typing Function Arguments

Chapter 2 discussed the advantages of strong typing, and those advantages apply to function arguments as well as to the variables that you declare. In fact, for strong typing to really be useful, all variables, including function arguments, should be strongly typed. This guideline is easy to adhere to, but needs to be followed consistently to take advantage of compile-time type checking and code completion. The following code shows a function with strongly typed arguments:

```
function createButton(baseMovieClip:MovieClip, labelText:String):Void
{
    // Function contents
}
```

On rare occasions, you might not know exactly what data type will be passed in. If that's the case, declare the type as Object rather than omitting the type declaration. Here's an example:

```
function deleteObject(objectToDelete:Object):Void
{
    if (typeof(objectToDelete) == "movieclip")
    {
        objectToDelete.stop();
        objectToDelete.removeMovieClip();
    }
    else
    {
```

```
                delete objectToDelete;
        }
    }
```

Avoiding Hard-Coded Movie Clip References

Avoid hard-coding movie clip references to function code. If a function contains hard-coded movie clip references, it becomes harder to reuse the function elsewhere. Pass a base movie clip reference as a parameter. The following snippet shows a function with a hard-coded movie clip reference:

```
function createButton(instanceName:String):Void
{
    _level0.baseMovieClip.createEmptyMovieClip(instanceName, ⤴
        _level0.baseMovieClip.getNextHighestDepth());
}
createButton("button1", "Button One");
```

This code can be reworked a bit to make it more generic and therefore easier to reuse:

```
function createButton(baseClip:MovieClip, instanceName:String):Void
{
    baseClip.createEmptyMovieClip(instanceName, baseClip.getNextHighestDepth());
}
createButton(_level0.baseMovieClip, "button1", "Button One");
```

Declaring Return Values

When declaring a function that should return a value, make sure that the return type is declared. If no value is to be returned, declare the special type Void. Here's an example:

```
function setName(nameString:String):Void
{
    myName = nameString;
}

function getName():String
{
    return myName;
}
```

Make sure that a function that is to return a value will return something every time, including in error cases. The following example shows you both non-returning and returning code:

```
// This function will not always return a value
function getCameraMake(cameraModel:String):String
{
    if (cameraModel == "D70")
    {
        return "Nikon";
    }
    else if (cameraModel == "10D")
    {
        return "Canon";
```

```
        }
    }

    // This function contains a default statement
    function getCameraMake(cameraModel:String):String
    {
        if (cameraModel == "D70")
        {
            return "Nikon";
        }
        else if (cameraModel == "10D")
        {
            return "Canon";
        }
        return "<Unknown>";
    }
```

Remember that execution of a function terminates as soon as a return statement is reached. By putting a default return statement on the last line of the function, you're assured that if the function manages to get as far as the last line, some value will be returned.

Avoiding Oversized Functions

Large functions generally mean that they're doing too many things. A function should generally have a single focus to it, and a task should take no more than 20 to 30 lines of code. If your functions are consistently more than one or two screens, take a closer look to see if chunks of code can be pulled into their own functions.

Avoiding Entanglement

To entangle is to twist together into a confusing mass. There is nothing better to describe the worst case of code entanglement. When that definition is applied to code, it refers to the mixing together of code with different purposes. Consider an action game in which the code needs to respond to the keyboard. Here's an example of a key detect function:

```
var keyListener:Object = new Object();
keyListener.onKeyDown = function()
{
    switch (Key.getCode())
    {
        case Key.SPACE :
            gunSound.start();
            spaceship.fireEffect.gotoAndPlay(1);
            ammoLeft -= 10;
            spaceshipVelocity -= 2;
            break;
        case Key.LEFT :
            // Code to move ship left
            break;
        case Key.UP :
            // Code to move ship up
            break;
        case Key.RIGHT :
            // Code to move ship right
```

Chapter 5

```
            break;
        case Key.DOWN :
            // Code to move ship down
            break;
    }
};
Key.addListener(keyListener);
```

Two main entanglement issues exist within this routine. First, it contains code that has nothing to do with key detection. Second, within the code to detect the pressing of the space bar, there is direct access to other elements of the project. The effect of these issues is that if you want something else to trigger this code, say through the addition of a joystick, the code would have to be duplicated. It also means that if one element of the game is to change, there is no single place where you can make the changes. The following version is less entangled:

```
var keyListener:Object = new Object();
keyListener.onKeyDown = function()
{
    switch (Key.getCode())
    {
        case Key.SPACE:
            handleFireKey();
            break;
        case Key.LEFT:
            handleMove("left");
            break;
        case Key.UP:
            handleMove("up");
            break;
        case Key.RIGHT:
            handleMove("right");
            break;
        case Key.DOWN:
            handleMove("down");
            break;
    }
};
Key.addListener(keyListener);

function handleFireKey():Void
{
    playSound("gun");
    triggerFireAnimation();
    adjustVelocity(-2);
    adjustAmmo(-10);
}

function handleMove(moveDirection:String):Void
{
    // Move code goes here
}
```

The process of adapting functions is called *refactoring*, and involves the rewriting of code while retaining existing functionality.

Avoiding Duplication

Functions are good at making repetitive tasks easier. If you go through your code, and see a number of places where the same code appears, it's a good idea to place that code in its own function. If the functionality needs to change later on, it can be modified in one place to take effect throughout the project.

Refactor Problematic Code

This example shows you a bit of the process of reworking code to improve its style and organization. You split code into functions, and then rework those functions to improve their versatility and organization.

1. Create a new Macromedia Flash document by selecting File⇨New and choosing Flash Document from the New Document panel.

2. Click the first frame in the timeline, open the Actions panel (Window⇨Development Panels⇨ Actions), and type in the following ActionScript code:

```
#include "tryItOut_refactor.as"
```

3. Select File⇨Save As, name the file `tryItOut_refactor.fla`, choose an appropriate directory, and save it.

4. Create a new script file by selecting File⇨New and choosing ActionScript File from the New Document panel.

5. Select File⇨Save As and ensure it is showing the same directory containing the Flash project file. Give the file the name `tryItOut_refactor.as` and save it.

6. Enter the following code into the new ActionScript file:

```
// Create play button
_level0.createEmptyMovieClip("playButton", 1);
playButton.onRelease = function()
{
    trace("Pressed play");
    presentationArea.play();
}
playButton._x = 10;
playButton._y = 10;
playButton.beginFill(0xAAAAFF);
playButton.lineStyle(1, 0x333333);
playButton.moveTo(0, 0);
playButton.lineTo(50, 0);
playButton.lineTo(50, 20);
playButton.lineTo(0, 20);
playButton.lineTo(0, 0);
playButton.createTextField("labelField", 1, 4, 4, 50, 15);
playButton.labelField.text = "Play";

// Create stop button
_level0.createEmptyMovieClip("stopButton", 2);
stopButton.onRelease = function()
{
    trace("Pressed stop");
    presentationArea.stop();
```

```
}
stopButton._x = 70;
stopButton._y = 10;
stopButton.beginFill(0xAAAAFF);
stopButton.lineStyle(1, 0x333333);
stopButton.moveTo(0, 0);
stopButton.lineTo(50, 0);
stopButton.lineTo(50, 20);
stopButton.lineTo(0, 20);
stopButton.lineTo(0, 0);
stopButton.createTextField("labelField", 1, 4, 4, 50, 15);
stopButton.labelField.text = "Stop";

// Create presentation area, and load a movie clip into it
_level0.createEmptyMovieClip("presentationArea", 3);
presentationArea._x = 10;
presentationArea._y = 40;
presentationArea.loadMovie("http://www.nathanderksen.com/book/⤵
    tryItOut_refactorAnimation.swf");
```

7. Save the file (File⇨Save), return to the project file, and select Control⇨Test Movie.

8. Remove the contents of each `onRelease` event handler, and place it into their own functions, called `invokePlay()` and `invokeStop()`. Place a call to both of these functions from within the respective `onRelease` event handler:

```
function invokePlay():Void
{
    trace("Pressed play");
    presentationArea.play();
}

function invokeStop():Void
{
    trace("Pressed stop");
    presentationArea.stop();
}

playButton.onRelease = function()
{
    invokePlay();
}

stopButton.onRelease = function()
{
    invokeStop();
}
```

9. Create a new function called `setupMovie()`, and move the last four lines of code inside the function:

```
function setupMovie():Void
{
    // Create presentation area, and load a movie clip into it
    _level0.createEmptyMovieClip("presentationArea", 3);
```

```
       presentationArea._x = 10;
       presentationArea._y = 40;
       presentationArea.loadMovie("http://www.nathanderksen.com/book/↩
           tryItOut_refactorAnimation.swf");
}
```

10. Create a new function called `createButton()`. Give it five input arguments: `buttonName` of type String, `buttonLabel` of type String, `xPos` of type Number, `yPos` of type Number, and `callback` of type Function.

11. Copy the code from the `// Create play button` comment until just before the `// Create stop button` comment, and paste it in the `createButton()` function.

12. Modify the contents of `createButton()` to look like the following code:

```
function createButton(buttonName:String, buttonLabel:String, ↩
    xPos:Number, yPos:Number, callback:Function):Void
{
    var buttonHandle:MovieClip;
    _level0.createEmptyMovieClip(buttonName, _level0.getNextHighestDepth());
    buttonHandle = _level0[buttonName];
    buttonHandle.onRelease = function()
    {
        callback();
    }
    buttonHandle._x = xPos;
    buttonHandle._y = yPos;
    buttonHandle.beginFill(0xAAAAFF);
    buttonHandle.lineStyle(1, 0x333333);
    buttonHandle.moveTo(0, 0);
    buttonHandle.lineTo(50, 0);
    buttonHandle.lineTo(50, 20);
    buttonHandle.lineTo(0, 20);
    buttonHandle.lineTo(0, 0);
    buttonHandle.createTextField("labelField", 1, 4, 4, 50, 15);
    buttonHandle.labelField.text = buttonLabel;
}
```

13. Remove the code that creates the play button and the pause button from the top of the code listing.

14. Add two calls to the create button function, and one call to `setupMovie()`:

```
createButton("playButton", "Play", 10, 10, invokePlay);
createButton("stopButton", "Stop", 70, 10, invokeStop);
setupMovie();
```

15. Your code should now look something like this:

```
function invokePlay():Void
{
    trace("Pressed play");
    presentationArea.play();
}

function invokeStop():Void
{
```

```
        trace("Pressed stop");
        presentationArea.stop();
}

function setupMovie():Void
{
    // Create presentation area, and load a movie clip into it
    _level0.createEmptyMovieClip("presentationArea", 3);
    presentationArea._x = 10;
    presentationArea._y = 40;
    presentationArea.loadMovie("http://www.nathanderksen.com/book/↩
        tryItOut_refactorAnimation.swf");
}

function createButton(buttonName:String, buttonLabel:String, ↩
    xPos:Number, yPos:Number, callback:Function):Void
{
    var buttonHandle:MovieClip;
    _level0.createEmptyMovieClip(buttonName, _level0.getNextHighestDepth());
    buttonHandle = _level0[buttonName];
    buttonHandle.onRelease = function()
    {
        callback();
    }
    buttonHandle._x = xPos;
    buttonHandle._y = yPos;
    buttonHandle.beginFill(0xAAAAFF);
    buttonHandle.lineStyle(1, 0x333333);
    buttonHandle.moveTo(0, 0);
    buttonHandle.lineTo(50, 0);
    buttonHandle.lineTo(50, 20);
    buttonHandle.lineTo(0, 20);
    buttonHandle.lineTo(0, 0);
    buttonHandle.createTextField("labelField", 1, 4, 4, 50, 15);
    buttonHandle.labelField.text = buttonLabel;
}

createButton("playButton", "Play", 10, 10, invokePlay);
createButton("stopButton", "Stop", 70, 10, invokeStop);
setupMovie();
```

16. Save the file, return to the Flash project file, and select Control⇨Test Movie. The project should work identically as before.

17. You've done a significant amount of refactoring, and it's a definite improvement. You can still do better, though. Create a new function called `drawBox()` and give it five arguments: `targetMovieClip` of type MovieClip, as well as `boxWidth`, `boxHeight`, `boxColor`, and `lineColor`, each of type Number. Copy the code in the `createButton()` function from the line calling `beginFill()` to the last `lineTo()` call, and paste it into the `drawBox()` function. Modify the code to match the following:

```
function drawBox(targetMovieClip:MovieClip, boxWidth:Number, ↩
    boxHeight:Number, boxColor:Number, lineColor:Number):Void
{
```

```
        targetMovieClip.beginFill(boxColor);
        targetMovieClip.lineStyle(1, lineColor);
        targetMovieClip.moveTo(0, 0);
        targetMovieClip.lineTo(boxWidth, 0);
        targetMovieClip.lineTo(boxWidth, boxHeight);
        targetMovieClip.lineTo(0, boxHeight);
        targetMovieClip.lineTo(0, 0);
}
```

18. Replace the code in the `createButton()` function from the line calling `beginFill()` to the last `lineTo()` call with the following line:

```
drawBox(buttonHandle, 50, 20, 0xAAAAFF, 0x333333);
```

19. The final code listing should look like this:

```
function invokePlay():Void
{
    trace("Pressed play");
    presentationArea.play();
}

function invokeStop():Void
{
    trace("Pressed stop");
    presentationArea.stop();
}

function setupMovie():Void
{
    // Create presentation area, and load a movie clip into it
    _level0.createEmptyMovieClip("presentationArea", 3);
    presentationArea._x = 10;
    presentationArea._y = 40;
    presentationArea.loadMovie("http://www.nathanderksen.com/book/⤶
        tryItOut_refactorAnimation.swf");
}

function createButton(buttonName:String, buttonLabel:String, ⤶
    xPos:Number, yPos:Number, callback:Function):Void
{
    var buttonHandle:MovieClip;
    _level0.createEmptyMovieClip(buttonName, _level0.getNextHighestDepth());
    buttonHandle = _level0[buttonName];
    buttonHandle.onRelease = function()
    {
        callback();
    }
    buttonHandle._x = xPos;
    buttonHandle._y = yPos;
    drawBox(buttonHandle, 50, 20, 0xAAAAFF, 0x333333);
    buttonHandle.createTextField("labelField", 1, 4, 4, 50, 15);
    buttonHandle.labelField.text = buttonLabel;
}
```

```
function drawBox(targetMovieClip:MovieClip, boxWidth:Number, ⤴
    boxHeight:Number, boxColor:Number, lineColor:Number):Void
{
    targetMovieClip.beginFill(boxColor);
    targetMovieClip.lineStyle(1, lineColor);
    targetMovieClip.moveTo(0, 0);
    targetMovieClip.lineTo(boxWidth, 0);
    targetMovieClip.lineTo(boxWidth, boxHeight);
    targetMovieClip.lineTo(0, boxHeight);
    targetMovieClip.lineTo(0, 0);
}

createButton("playButton", "Play", 10, 10, invokePlay);
createButton("stopButton", "Stop", 70, 10, invokeStop);
setupMovie();
```

20. Save the file, return to the Flash project file, and select Control⇨Test Movie. The project should work identically as before.

How It Works

The issues in the code at the beginning of this example include entanglement of drawing routines with button creation code, entanglement of animation control code with the button handlers, duplication of code, hard-coded movie clip references, and code that is inflexible overall. You fixed some of these problems through refactoring.

The first issue is that the button handlers contain code that directly starts and stops the animation. Even though each contains only one line of code, it should still be externalized into its own function (without this, later refactoring steps won't work):

```
function invokePlay():Void
{
    trace("Pressed play");
    presentationArea.play();
}

function invokeStop():Void
{
    trace("Pressed stop");
    presentationArea.stop();
}

playButton.onRelease = function()
{
    invokePlay();
}

stopButton.onRelease = function()
{
    invokeStop();
}
```

Next, the code that sets up and loads an external animation should be grouped in its own function:

```
function setupMovie():Void
{
    // Create presentation area, and load a movie clip into it
    _level0.createEmptyMovieClip("presentationArea", 3);
    presentationArea._x = 10;
    presentationArea._y = 40;
    presentationArea.loadMovie("http://www.nathanderksen.com/book/⤸
        tryItOut_refactorAnimation.swf");
}
```

There is very clearly duplicated code, which calls for creating a function that can convert the duplicated code into a single command to be called whenever needed:

```
function createButton(buttonName:String, buttonLabel:String, ⤸
    xPos:Number, yPos:Number, callback:Function):Void
{
    var buttonHandle:MovieClip;
    _level0.createEmptyMovieClip(buttonName, _level0.getNextHighestDepth());
    buttonHandle = _level0[buttonName];
    buttonHandle.onRelease = function()
    {
        callback();
    }
    buttonHandle._x = xPos;
    buttonHandle._y = yPos;
    buttonHandle.beginFill(0xAAAAFF);
    buttonHandle.lineStyle(1, 0x333333);
    buttonHandle.moveTo(0, 0);
    buttonHandle.lineTo(50, 0);
    buttonHandle.lineTo(50, 20);
    buttonHandle.lineTo(0, 20);
    buttonHandle.lineTo(0, 0);
    buttonHandle.createTextField("labelField", 1, 4, 4, 50, 15);
    buttonHandle.labelField.text = buttonLabel;
}
```

Next, drawing routines are entangled within the createButton() function. These can easily be removed and placed in their own function that can potentially be reused elsewhere:

```
function createButton(buttonName:String, buttonLabel:String, ⤸
    xPos:Number, yPos:Number, callback:Function):Void
{
    var buttonHandle:MovieClip;
    _level0.createEmptyMovieClip(buttonName, _level0.getNextHighestDepth());
    buttonHandle = _level0[buttonName];
    buttonHandle.onRelease = function()
    {
        callback();
    }
    buttonHandle._x = xPos;
    buttonHandle._y = yPos;
```

```
        drawBox(buttonHandle, 50, 20, 0xAAAAFF, 0x333333);
        buttonHandle.createTextField("labelField", 1, 4, 4, 50, 15);
        buttonHandle.labelField.text = buttonLabel;
    }

    function drawBox(targetMovieClip:MovieClip, boxWidth:Number, ⤵
        boxHeight:Number, boxColor:Number, lineColor:Number):Void
    {
        targetMovieClip.beginFill(boxColor);
        targetMovieClip.lineStyle(1, lineColor);
        targetMovieClip.moveTo(0, 0);
        targetMovieClip.lineTo(boxWidth, 0);
        targetMovieClip.lineTo(boxWidth, boxHeight);
        targetMovieClip.lineTo(0, boxHeight);
        targetMovieClip.lineTo(0, 0);
    }
```

At this point, significant improvements have been made to the quality of this code. A couple issues still exist, such as a hard-coded level reference within createButton(), and although the drawing routine can now support variable-sized backgrounds, the button cannot. An exercise at the end of this chapter gives you a chance to fix these issues.

Summary

This chapter explored the principles of OOP (object-oriented programming) and examined what's meant by best practices in coding. Here are some of the points about OOP that you'll want to remember:

❑   OOP involves packaging data and the code that acts on that data into a single entity.

❑   The OOP term for a function is a method, and the term for a variable is a property.

❑   A class is a template for an object. Objects are copies derived from a class through the process of instantiation.

❑   Class inheritance allows a sub-class to acquire methods and properties from a parent class.

❑   Goals of OOP include keeping code focused, promoting re-use, reducing impact of change, and keeping code understandable.

You also learned a number of things about coding best practices. Some of the key points include the following:

❑   Variable names should be readable, reflect the kind of data contained in the variable, and not be a reserved word.

❑   Variable types should be declared along with the variable.

❑   Strong typing helps to make code clearer and easier to debug.

❑   Comments should supplement code, but clean, easy-to-read variables and syntax are essential to understanding the code.

❑   A variable's scope refers to its visibility to other parts of the project. The three types of scope are local, timeline, and global.

❑ Variables should be scoped as narrowly as possible. Avoid global and timeline variables whenever possible.

❑ Do not directly modify global variables. Create accessor functions that are responsible for modifying global variables.

❑ The best way to store global data is through the use of a custom class.

❑ Variables can be set and retrieved in other movie clips using dot syntax.

❑ All function input parameters and return values should be strongly typed.

❑ Functions should be small, well-defined units of code. Function code that becomes too large, too complicated, too repetitive, or too entangled should be refactored.

In the next chapter, you continue to learn about project setup, including some best practices for organizing the library, working with screens, and placement of code. Before proceeding to the next chapter, work through the following exercises to help solidify the material that you just learned.

Exercises

1. Which of the following are valid, correct statements? For the ones that are not valid or correct, explain why.

   a. `var myString:String = new String("the quick brown fox");`

   b. `var myNextString:String = "the quick brown fox";`

   c. `var myDate:Date = new Date("2005/05/12");`

   d. `var myNextDate:Date = Date(2005, 05, 12);`

   e. `var myObject:Object = {property1:"foo", property2:"bar"};`

   f. `var myNextObject:Object = new Object();`

   g. `var myArray = new Array();`

   h. `var myNumber:Number = "20";`

2. Without running the code, determine what the output of each trace statement in the following code snippet would be.

```
var myString:String = "baz";
var mySecondString:String = "foo";
_global.mySecondString = "bar";

function testFunction():Void
{
    var myString:String = "qux";
    trace("testFunction->myString: " + myString);              //a.
    trace("testFunction->mySecondString: " + mySecondString);  //b.
}

testFunction();
trace("myString: " + myString);                                //c.
trace("mySecondString: " + mySecondString);                    //d.
```

Chapter 5

```
delete mySecondString;
trace("mySecondString: " + mySecondString);                    //e.
```

3. Which of the following function declarations are valid?

a.

```
function myFunction1():Void
{
    // Function contents
}
```

b.

```
var myFunction2:Function = function():Void
{
    // Function contents
}
```

c.

```
var myFunction3:Function = new function():String
{
    // Function contents
}
```

d.

```
function myFunction4(inputString:String):String
{
    // Function contents
    return true;
}
```

e.

```
var myFunction5():Void
{
    // Function contents
}
```

f.

```
function myFunction6(inputString, inputNumber)
{
    // Function contents
}
```

4. Modify the final code for the "Refactor Problematic Code" Try It Out to allow the following:

   ❑ Modify the createButton() function so that a width and height parameter can be sent in to create a variable-sized button. The function should automatically assign dimensions if the input width and height values are 0, null, or undefined.

   ❑ Modify any statements within createButton() that refer directly to _level0 so that they instead refer to a movie clip that is passed in through an additional function argument.

142

Setting Up Flash Projects

ActionScript programming involves more than just coding. Working on a Macromedia Flash project includes organizing timelines, structuring symbols in the library, structuring elements on state, working with media, and creating a structured movie clip environment that can be controlled with code. As you've seen, a number of guidelines help you to make the most of your project.

In this chapter, you learn to set up your library, work with bitmap images, and use movie clips and frames.

Setting Up the Library

In even a medium-sized project, the number of items that accumulate in the library can become quite large, so it's a good idea to organize library folders before placing anything in the project. Figure 6-1 shows a suggested system for organizing the library.

At the base, two folders are created, one (global) for content that is not specific to any particular screen, and one (screens) for content that belongs to a specific screen. The screens folder shows one subfolder for each screen in the project: home, photography, and tutorials. Within each of the screen folders and the global folder exist five subfolders:

❑   bitmaps — Stores bitmap images that have been imported into the project.

❑   buttons — Holds complete button clips.

❑   graphics — Contains artwork that is just illustrative in nature.

❑   movie clips — Stores clips containing animation or holding other clips or media.

❑   tweens — Holds clips that are automatically created whenever tweens are created on the timeline.

Figure 6-1

The _buttons folder within the bitmaps folder is for bitmaps to be used in buttons. It is prepended with the underscore character to force the folder to the top of the sort order. You can use this technique any time you want a folder to come before any other folders or movie clips on the same folder level.

Try out this system, and modify it as you learn what works best for you.

Working with Bitmap Images

Different situations call for different treatment of bitmap images. Sometimes you'll find it preferable to load them dynamically with ActionScript, whereas at other times it's preferable to have them in the library. Following are several reasons why it might be better to embed images into the library rather than to load them on-the-fly:

❑ Images are easier to implement, and no separate preloading is needed.

❑ Macromedia Flash player version 8 supports loading of JPG, GIF, and PNG images, although versions 6 and 7 support only dynamic loading of JPG images. To take advantage of images that make use of transparency effects and to target player versions earlier than 8, the images need to be in the library.

❏   Images that are embedded in the library can be used more easily in tweened animations.

The following sections examine a few things to keep in mind when handling bitmap images.

Keep Images Organized on the Desktop

Maintain one folder within the project directory that is dedicated to holding images. This keeps the project folder neat and the images easily accessible for making changes.

Use a standard naming convention for each image, preferably so that when they are sorted by name, they are grouped by function or by screen. Also, keep a directory structure within the library to organize the images.

Figure 6-2 shows a possible organizational system where an images folder has been placed next to the Flash project file. Within the images folder, the global folder holds images that are global in nature, such as for common navigation. The screens folder contains one subfolder per screen for all images specific to that screen.

Figure 6-2

Keep Images Organized in the Library

The library is arranged in a similar manner to the desktop images folder. A global folder holds media that is common to the project, and individual screen folders hold media specific to each screen.

Figure 6-3 shows the library panel for `portfolio.fla`.

Embed Images into Movie Clips

It is generally not a good idea to place bitmap images directly on the timeline. If the image is placed in several places within the project, and it later becomes necessary to swap the image with another, it will be necessary to find and replace each image individually.

Effects, animation, and scripting cannot be done directly on a bitmap image; you can deal with both of those by always nesting bitmap images within a movie clip. Then, rather than dragging the bitmap to the stage whenever it is needed, drag the movie clip containing the bitmap to the stage. Once done, effects can be applied to the movie clip, the movie clip can be easily tweened, and updating a bitmap image involves just updating the contents of the one movie clip.

In the next Try It Out you work with symbols in the library, and begin putting together a multi-screen project.

Figure 6-3

Try It Out   Working with Bitmap Images

Follow these steps to get acquainted with the process of working with bitmap images:

1. Open `portfolio.fla` from the book's source files at <source file directory>/Chapter 6/ portfolio v1/.

2. Select File⇨Import⇨Import to Library and choose `headerImage.png` from the folder portfolio v1/images/global.

3. Select File⇨Import⇨Import to Library and choose `featuredPhoto.png` from the folder portfolio v1/images/screens/home.

4. Open the library (Window⇨Library) and drag `headerImage.png` from the base of the library into the folder global/bitmaps.

5. Drag `featuredPhoto.png` from the base of the library into the folder screens/home/bitmaps.

6. Double-click anywhere on the gray part of the header bar on the top of the stage. You should be put into editing mode for the headerBackground movie clip.

7. Click the empty keyframe for the layer named Background Image. From the library, drag `headerImage.png` onto the stage so that it is aligned top-right within the movie clip.

8. Click the image on the stage to select it. Take a look at the options currently available in the properties panel (Window⇨Properties).

9. With the image still selected, right-click and select Convert to Symbol, or choose Modify⇨Convert to Symbol. Name the symbol `headerImage`, and ensure that the Movie Clip radio button has been selected. Click OK.

10. Take another glance at the properties panel. It now shows the text field on the top left for entering an instance ID, and it also provides a drop-down menu for color selection.

11. Drag the `headerImage` movie clip at the root of the library into the global/graphics library folder.

12. Return to the main stage by clicking the Scene 1 button just above the timeline. Open the Home layer set, and select the keyframe in the Featured Photo layer.

13. Drag `featuredPhoto.png` from the library's screens/home/bitmaps folder onto the stage, just below the featured photo heading.

14. Click the image to select it. Right-click and select Convert to Symbol or select Modify⇨Convert to Symbol. Name the symbol `featuredPhoto` and ensure that the Movie Clip radio button has been selected. Click OK.

15. Drag the featuredPhoto movie clip at the root of the library into the screens/home/graphics library folder.

16. Click the featuredPhoto movie clip on the stage to select it again. Right-click and select Convert to Symbol, or choose Modify⇨Convert to Symbol. Name the symbol `featuredPhotoButton` and ensure that the Button radio button has been selected. Click OK.

17. With the symbol still selected on the stage, go to the properties panel and type `featuredPhoto_btn` in the top-left text field.

18. Double-click the thumbnail image, which is now a button, to go into editing mode for the button clip.

19. Click the Down keyframe in the timeline. Select Insert⇨Timeline⇨Keyframe.

20. Click the thumbnail image on the stage. In the properties panel, select Brightness from the Color drop-down menu and choose a negative value, such as −10%.

21. Return to the main stage by clicking the Scene 1 button just above the timeline. Drag the featuredPhotoButton movie clip at the root of the library into the screens/home/buttons library folder. Your stage and library should now look something like Figure 6-3.

22. Save the file and select Control⇨Test Movie. Clicking the featured photo image should cause the button color effect to show when the mouse button is down.

How It Works

This example acquainted you with importing images, preparing them for the stage, and keeping them organized.

The header image was imported, placed on the stage, and then placed in its own movie clip. There was no particular need to place it in a clip now, but part of setting up a project is to plan for possible changes. By placing the bitmap image in a movie clip rather than just placing it directly on the stage, it allows the possibility for it to be animated in the future.

You looked at the properties panel for the bitmap image and for the image once placed within a movie clip. Two of the differences in properties were the instance name text field and the color drop-down. The instance name text field enables an instance name to be given to the clip so that ActionScript can be used to manipulate the clip. The color drop-down allows color and transparency effects to be applied. If you are working with the Macromedia Flash 8 development environment, you will also see a blend drop-down menu that enables you to set how the movie clip blends with the content behind the clip. (You find more about blending modes in later in the book.)

The featured photo bitmap was placed within a movie clip, which was then placed within a button. A button movie clip allows graphics for up, over, and down button states to be included in the button. You applied a simple color effect to the down state, which was possible because the image was wrapped in its own movie clip. In addition, whenever a new featured photo is to be shown, the bitmap needs only to be swapped within the one movie clip and all button states will get the new image.

Nesting Sections within a Movie Clip

In the preceding Try It Out, the home screen had all of its content directly on the main timeline. This is generally not a good idea because it makes managing the site increasingly difficult as more screens are needed and more layers are added to the main timeline. To simplify management of each screen, group related content together in one movie clip. A single container movie clip can be more easily manipulated than a spread-out group of movie clips can. Here are several reasons why using a container movie clip is a good thing:

❑   Moving a screen involves moving just a single movie clip.

❑   Manipulating an entire screen programmatically involves manipulating a single movie clip using ActionScript.

❑   The base timeline contains fewer layers, and becomes easier to work with.

Try It Out   Using a Movie Clip as a Base

In this exercise, you take a group of content on the main timeline and place it in its own movie clip.

1.   Open the completed `portfolio.fla` file from the preceding Try It Out, or open `portfolio.fla` from the book's source files at <source file directory>/Chapter 6/portfolio v2/.

2. Make sure that you are looking at the main stage and are not in edit mode for any movie clips. (You can return to the main stage by clicking the Scene 1 button just above the timeline.)

3. Open the Home layer set. Select the keyframes for all the layers within the Home layer set by dragging across them. You can also click the keyframe for the first layer, and then hold down the Shift key and click the keyframe for the last layer.

4. Select Edit⇨Timeline⇨Cut Frames.

5. Open the library (Window⇨Library). Select New Symbol from the tools menu on the top right of the library panel. Give the new symbol the name `screen_home`, and make sure that the Movie Clip radio button is selected. Click the Yes button.

6. Drag the screen_home movie clip from the library to the screens/home folder.

7. Click the only empty keyframe on the timeline. Select Edit⇨Timeline⇨Paste Frames.

8. With all of the content still selected, open the properties panel (Window⇨Properties) and set the x position to 25 and the y position to 50.

9. Return to the main stage. Click the Home layer set to select it, and then click the delete icon just below the timeline. Click OK.

10. Create a new layer, and drag it between the Header layer set and the Script layer. Name the new layer `Home Screen`.

11. Click the empty keyframe on the Home Screen layer, and then drag the screen_home movie clip from the library to the stage. Use the two stage guides to help align the movie clip in the top-left corner. You should end up with an arrow right underneath the Home button in the main menu.

12. Save the file.

How It Works

In previous Try It Out exercises, new movie clips were created using the Convert to Symbol command. You could have done this here as well, but you would have lost the layer setup. The organization that the layers give you is retained when frames are copied from the main timeline and pasted into the new movie clip instead.

Using Keyframes to Manage Application State

One technique to manage application state is to use keyframes as a way to navigate to individual screens. The content for each screen is fit into a frame, with one frame corresponding to one screen. Each frame is assigned a label, and the playhead is moved from one screen to another simply by calling `gotoAndStop("framelabel")`. The `gotoAndStop()` method could just reference the frame number for the screen you want to display, but if another screen is inserted before this one, the wrong screen would show. Using labels ensures that if a screen is moved, the link is not lost. It also is more meaningful to look at a text label in the code rather than a frame number.

Figure 6-4 shows the timeline for a project that uses keyframes to manage screen state.

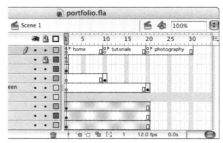

Figure 6-4

Next, explore how to use keyframes on the main timeline to navigate between screens.

Managing Screen State with Frames

In this exercise you use separate frames to hold different screens.

1. Open the completed `portfolio.fla` file from the preceding Try It Out, or open `portfolio.fla` from the book's source files at <source file directory>/Chapter 6/portfolio v3/.

2. Make sure that you are looking at the main stage and are not in edit mode for any movie clips.

3. Create three new layers and change the names to `Labels`, `Tutorial Screen`, and `Photography Screen`. Place the Labels layer on top, and place the other two underneath the Home Screen layer.

4. Click frame 10 of the Labels layer and select Insert⇨Timeline⇨Keyframe. Do the same on frames 20 and 30.

5. Click the keyframe on frame 1 of the Labels layer. Open the properties panel (Window⇨ Properties) and type `home` into the frame label field. Click frame 10 of the Labels layer and label it `tutorials`. Click frame 20 of the Labels layer and label it `photography`.

6. Click the keyframe on frame 1 of the Labels layer. Open the Actions panel (Window⇨Actions) and type `stop();` into the panel. Repeat for frames 10 and 20.

7. Click the keyframe on frame 1 of the Scripts layer. Enter the following script into the Actions panel:

```
// Set up code to respond to main menu buttons
home_btn.onRelease = function()
{
    gotoAndStop("home");
}

tutorials_btn.onRelease = function()
{
    gotoAndStop("tutorials");
}

photography_btn.onRelease = function()
{
    gotoAndStop("photography");
}
```

8. Click frame 10 of the Tutorial Screen layer and select Insert⇨Timeline⇨Keyframe.

9. Open the library, locate the movie clip called tutorials_screen in the folder screens/tutorials, and drag the clip to the stage. Use the guides to help you position the movie clip.

10. Click frame 20 of the Tutorial Screen layer and select Insert⇨Timeline⇨Keyframe.

11. Open the library, locate the movie clip called photography_screen in the folder screens/photography, and drag the clip to the stage. Use the guides to help you position the movie clip.

12. Save the file and test the movie. Clicking the home, tutorials, and photography buttons should switch between screens.

How It Works

To use frames to switch between screens, you first set up a system of labels and keyframes. For each screen to be displayed, you need one keyframe and one keyframe label. The keyframes can be in adjacent frames, or they can be separated by other frames. Using a number of frames between the frames for each screen makes it easier to see the separation and to read the frame labels on the timeline. Additional frames are added to the right of the rightmost keyframe so that the label photography is visible in the timeline.

The code placed within the Actions panel responds to user clicks on the main navigation buttons. The names of each button used in the code (namely home_btn, tutorials_btn, and photography_btn) correspond with instance names given to each of those buttons. Click any of those buttons and look in the properties panel; you will see the same ID in the instance name text field.

Each screen is contained within its own movie clip. As a result, each movie clip holding a screen can be easily assigned to an individual keyframe. Compare this setup with the earlier one in which the home screen was spread across layers in the main timeline and it is readily apparent that containing each screen within a movie clip is considerably cleaner.

Keeping Code in External Files

In general, it is not a good idea to place any significant amount of code directly on the timeline. Some reasons for this include the following:

❏ If the .fla file becomes corrupted and you have to revert to a previous version, any code changes made in between those two versions will also be lost.

❏ Having code scattered throughout different timelines makes the code hard to find.

❏ You can use any text editor to edit code in an external file; you must use the editor in the Macromedia Flash development environment if the code is in a timeline.

The #include directive allows external files to hold ActionScript code. Adding the following line to the timeline does the equivalent of placing all the code from the text file into that same spot in the timeline:

```
#include "<filename>.as"
```

Note that there is no semicolon at the end of the line. `#include` is called a pre-processor statement, in that it is executed before any other code runs. When a project is compiled, the compiler does a pass through all the code looking for pre-processor statements. When an `#include` statement is found, the compiler replaces the directive with all the code from that external file. The compiler then parses all included code as if it were typed directly in the Actions panel.

As the amount of script gets large, it can help to further break the code out into separate files. Simply create as many script files as are needed, and then place the `#include` statements one after another in the Actions panel.

It is a common error to keep the `.as` files used for compilation next to the compiled `.swf` file when deploying the project to a server. The `.swf` contains the compiled version of the code from the included script file(s), so it is not necessary to place your script files on the web server with the `.swf` files. It is not a good practice, either, because others might then find the source code.

Try It Out   Attaching Code to a Project

In this exercise, you remove code embedded in the `.fla` and place it in an external text file. You also make some changes to improve the style of the code.

1. Open the completed `portfolio.fla` file from the preceding Try It Out, or open the `portfolio` `.fla` file from the book's source files at <source file directory>/Chapter 6/portfolio v4/.

2. Make sure that you are looking at the main stage and are not in edit mode for any movie clips.

3. Click the keyframe on the Script layer, open the Actions panel (Window⇨Actions), and copy all the code within the panel.

4. Create a new Macromedia Flash document by selecting File⇨New and choosing ActionScript File from the New Document panel.

5. Name the file `portfolio.as` and save it in the directory containing the `.fla` file.

6. Paste the script into the new file and save it.

7. Click the keyframe on the Script layer, return to the Actions panel, and delete all the code.

8. Type the following line of code into the Actions Panel:

```
#include "portfolio.as"
```

9. Save the file and select Control⇨Test Movie. Clicking the home, tutorials, and photography buttons should still switch between screens.

10. Add the following function to the end of the `portfolio.as` file:

```
function gotoScreen(screenName:String):Void
{
    gotoAndStop(screenName);
}
```

11. Update the three `gotoAndStop()` calls to use the `gotoScreen()` function:

```
home_btn.onRelease = function()
{
    gotoScreen("home");
}

tutorials_btn.onRelease = function()
{
    gotoScreen("tutorials");
}

photography_btn.onRelease = function()
{
    gotoScreen("photography");
}
```

12. Save the file and select Control⇨Test Movie. Clicking the home, tutorials, and photography buttons should still switch between screens.

How It Works

Taking code out from the Actions panel and putting it into a separate text field is a fairly simple matter, but an important step to take for any scripting project. The `#include` directive is all that is needed.

The small bit of cleanup is related to the issue of code entanglement. Even though the code to switch screens is very simple, it is still not a good practice to put that code in the button handler. Instead, a function is created to perform this task. If the implementation of the screens needs to change, only the switch screen function needs to be updated.

Using Script to Manage Application State

ActionScript enables you to place items on the stage at runtime rather than having to place them in advance. The `attachMovie()` method allows any movie clip in the library to be attached to the stage. The attachment process copies the symbol in the library. As a result, a single movie clip can be attached to the stage multiple times. Here's the syntax for the `attachMovie()` method:

```
baseMovieClip.attachMovie(id:String, name:String, depth:Number, initObject:Object);
```

The `id` parameter corresponds to a linkage ID given to a movie clip within the library. The `name` parameter is the instance name to be given to the new clip, `depth` is a Number that must be incremented for each attached movie, and the optional `initObject` allows startup parameters to be given to the new clip.

Linkage IDs must be unique within the library. To set a linkage ID, select the desired movie clip in the library and open the properties pane by right-clicking the library symbol and selecting Properties. If only the topmost properties in Figure 6-5 are visible, click the Advanced button. Select the Export for ActionScript checkbox, type in a linkage ID in the Identifier field, and click OK. The movie clip can now be attached using `attachMovie()`.

Once a movie clip has been attached to the stage, its visibility can be easily controlled with its `_visible` property, which shows (`true`) or hides (`false`) the clip.

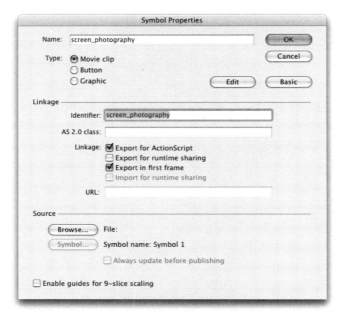

Figure 6-5

The techniques of attaching movie clips dynamically and showing and hiding movie clips on-the-fly give you an alternative to using frames to manage screen state. Entire applications can be built with only a single frame of the main timeline being used. This provides the greatest amount of control over the project, while increasing project complexity by only a nominal amount. Screens are swapped by making movie clips visible or invisible instead of swapping frames.

This method also offers the best opportunity for expansion. Adding another screen is simply a matter of creating that screen, and inserting a reference to it within the code.

Try It Out   Creating a Single Frame Application

In this exercise, you work with an application that is entirely controlled with ActionScript.

1. Open the completed `portfolio.fla` file from the preceding Try It Out, or open the `portfolio .fla` file from the book's source files at <source file directory>/Chapter 6/portfolio v5/.

2. Make sure that you are looking at the main stage and are not in edit mode for any movie clips.

3. Delete the Labels, Home Screen, Tutorial Screen, and Photography Screen layers.

4. Select all the frames from frame 2 onward. In the Background layer, either click and drag from frame 2 of the Buttons layer to frame 20, or click frame 2 of the Buttons layer and, while holding down the Shift key, click frame 20. Select Edit➪Timeline➪Delete Frames.

5. Open the library panel (Window⇨Library). Find the symbol called screen_home in the screens/home folder. Right-click the symbol and select Properties. (If you see only one text field, one set of radio buttons, and a few buttons, click the Advanced button.) Click the Export for ActionScript checkbox to select it. Leave the Export in First Frame checkbox selected. Ensure that the contents of the Identifier text field read `screen_home`.

6. Repeat step 5 for symbols screens/tutorials/screen_tutorial and screens/photography/screen_photography.

7. Create a new function called `init()` at the bottom of the file, and give it the code to attach the movie clips to the stage:

```
function init():Void
{
    var screenHolderHandle:MovieClip;

    _level0.createEmptyMovieClip("screenHolder", ⊃
        _level0.getNextHighestDepth());
    screenHolderHandle = _level0["screenHolder"];
    screenHolderHandle.attachMovie("screen_home", "home", ⊃
        screenHolderHandle.getNextHighestDepth());
    screenHolderHandle.attachMovie("screen_tutorials", "tutorials", ⊃
        screenHolderHandle.getNextHighestDepth());
    screenHolderHandle.attachMovie("screen_photography", "photography", ⊃
        screenHolderHandle.getNextHighestDepth());
    gotoScreen("home");
}
```

8. Return to the `portfolio.as` script file, and update the `gotoScreen()` function so that it looks like the following:

```
function gotoScreen(screenName:String):Void
{
    var screenHolderHandle:MovieClip;
    screenHolderHandle = _level0["screenHolder"];

    // Hide all screens within the screen holder movie clip
    for (screen in screenHolderHandle)
    {
        screenHolderHandle[screen]._visible = false;
    }
    // Show the selected screen
    screenHolderHandle[screenName]._visible = true;

}
```

9. Add the following call to the `init()` function at the bottom of the file:

```
init();
```

10. Save the file, return to `portfolio.fla`, and select Control⇨Test Movie. Clicking the home, tutorials, and photography buttons should still switch between screens.

How It Works

In steps 5 and 6, linkage IDs are assigned to movie clips for three screens in the library. These IDs allow the library symbols to be linked up with the code to place copies of the library symbols on stage. The init() function then creates a base movie clip to hold all of the screens, and it attaches the three scenes to it:

```
function init():Void
{
    var screenHolderHandle:MovieClip;

    _level0.createEmptyMovieClip("screenHolder", _level0.getNextHighestDepth());
    screenHolderHandle = _level0["screenHolder"];
    screenHolderHandle.attachMovie("screen_home", "home", ↩
        screenHolderHandle.getNextHighestDepth());
    screenHolderHandle.attachMovie("screen_tutorials", "tutorials", ↩
        screenHolderHandle.getNextHighestDepth());
    screenHolderHandle.attachMovie("screen_photography", "photography", ↩
        screenHolderHandle.getNextHighestDepth());
    gotoScreen("home");
}
```

Using a base clip to hold the screens prevents possible naming conflicts with other movie clips on the stage and gives some organization to the project. The three movie clips that are attached to the base movie clip are copies of the library symbol. At the end of the init() function is a call to the gotoScreen() function, which hides all the screens, and then shows just the home screen. The _visible properties for each screen can be directly set as they are attached, but using gotoScreen() gives a single change point if the choice of which start screen to use changes. Adding a feature to remember where the user left off and to resume at the same place when he returns could be more easily accomplished with the gotoScreen() function.

Next, the gotoScreen() function is updated to handle the new method of switching screens:

```
function gotoScreen(screenName:String):Void
{
    var screenHolderHandle:MovieClip;
    screenHolderHandle = _level0["screenHolder"];

    // Hide all screens within the screen holder movie clip
    for (screen in screenHolderHandle)
    {
        screenHolderHandle[screen]._visible = false;
    }
    // Show the selected screen
    screenHolderHandle[screenName]._visible = true;
}
```

The extra step taken to pull the screen switch code into its own function in the preceding Try It Out pays off because now only one function needs to be changed to handle the new means of switching screens. Using the for..in loop, gotoScreen() goes through all the movie clips within the screen holder clip and makes them invisible. The function then makes the clip visible for the screen to be shown.

Finally, the last line of code makes the actual call to the init() function:

```
init();
```

Summary

This chapter covered a number of techniques for setting up a Flash project. Some points to remember include the following:

❑ Giving order to the images directory and to the library helps with finding library symbols as the project size grows.

❑ Bitmaps should be placed within their own movie clip.

❑ Individual screens should have a single movie clip holding all screen content.

❑ Code should be kept within an external text file instead of placed directly within the Actions panel.

❑ Screens can be managed both by navigating through frames on the timeline and by using script to attach and show each screen.

In the next chapter, you start learning about components, reusable assets that can be used to build full-fledged applications. Before proceeding to the next chapter, go through the following exercise to help solidify the material that you just learned.

Exercise

Modify the final Try It Out project as follows:

❑ Remove the photo buttons in the photography section movie clip from the stage.

❑ Dynamically attach the photo buttons to the photography section movie clip with ActionScript, and add `onRelease` event handlers to each button.

Tip: Create an array listing each image ID, namely aStudyInTexture, buntzenWinter, flowerInDetail, and galianoSunset. Loop through that array to attach each image from the library and to assign an `onRelease` *event handler.*

❑ Add a function to be called by each button's `onRelease` handler that will load the selected image into the movie clip holding the large image. The library contains the three additional images that are needed for this.

Tip: When attaching the button to the stage, also add an ID property to the button and assign it the ID from the array. Use this in the button handler to construct a path for `loadMovie()`.

Controlling Movie Clips

Macromedia Flash gives you an incredible number of creative opportunities, and the movie clip is the digital canvas for your ideas. Regardless of whether you are interested in creating animations that treat the senses, games that entertain, or applications that help with productivity, mastering the movie clip is the key to exercising your creativity.

With Macromedia Flash, you can create your projects by manually piecing them together in the timeline, by creating a project entirely from script, or through a mixture of code and manual assembly on the timeline. There is no one right way to do it, just the way that best fits your needs.

This chapter teaches you a number of techniques to get you well on your way to mastering movie clips. You learn how to create movie clips on-the-fly, how to load external content, how to pull content to the stage from different sources, and how to manipulate content once it is there. You also take a look at how to use movie clips as masks, and learn about some performance issues surrounding movie clips.

The Movie Clip Revealed

You have already learned the three types of symbols that you can work with: graphic, button, and movie clip. The graphic symbol is used for holding media that does not require its own timeline. It cannot be controlled with ActionScript, so its usefulness for coding is very limited. The button clip can be controlled with script, but it is primarily just a source for events, and can be controlled only in limited ways. The movie clip can be completely controlled with ActionScript, and has many methods available to use. These methods are introduced shortly.

You have also already learned that Macromedia Flash works on the principle of a timeline. Each movie clip has its own timeline, so each movie clip can independently position, size, and otherwise control all of its own content. The timeline is split up into frames. If the frame rate for the project is set to 15 frames per second, then every 1/15th of a second each movie clip has an opportunity to make a change to any of its content, either through tweens or through script.

Many methods, properties, and events are available for you to use in controlling a movie clip through script. Some of these are defined in the following sections.

MovieClip Class Methods

The movie clip comes with its own set of tools in the form of methods. Methods such as `attachMovie()`, `createEmptyMovieClip()`, and `duplicateMovieClip()` enable you to create movie clip containers, either empty or already populated with content. Drawing methods such as `moveTo()`, `lineTo()`, `curveTo()`, `beginFill()`, and `endFill()` enable you to create script-generated shapes within a movie clip. The following table describes many of the methods that the movie clip makes available to you:

Method	Returns	Description
attachBitmap	Nothing	Attaches a bitmap object to an empty movie clip. (*Flash Player 8 only*)
attachMovie	Movie clip	Makes a copy of a movie clip from the library and places the copy inside the specified movie clip on the stage.
beginFill	Nothing	Indicates that the shape to be drawn using the movie clip drawing methods should be filled in.
clear	Void	Clears a movie clip of all shapes drawn inside using the movie clip drawing methods.
createEmpty MovieClip	Movie clip	Creates a new empty movie clip inside another movie clip.
createTextField	Text field	Creates a new text field inside a movie clip.
duplicate MovieClip	Movie clip	Makes a copy of an existing movie clip.
endFill	Nothing	Indicates that subsequent lines drawn using the movie clip drawing methods should not add to the filled-in shape.
getBytesLoaded	Number	Gets the number of bytes loaded of an externally loaded movie clip.
getBytesTotal	Number	Gets the total number of bytes of an externally loaded movie clip.
getURL	Nothing	Calls a browser window to load content from the specified URL.
gotoAndPlay	Nothing	Moves the playhead for the specified movie clip to a specific frame and then continues playing.
hitTest	Boolean	Determines whether two movie clips overlap each other.
lineStyle	Nothing	Sets visual characteristics of subsequent lines drawn using the movie clip drawing methods.
lineTo	Nothing	Draws a line from the current position to the specified x and y coordinates.

Method	Returns	Description
loadMovie	Nothing	Loads external content into the designated movie clip.
moveTo	Nothing	Moves the drawing marker to the specified x and y coordinates without drawing a line.
play	Nothing	Starts playback of the specified movie clip from where the playhead last stopped.
removeMovieClip	Nothing	Removes a movie clip that has been added to the stage using attachMovie(), createEmptyMovieClip(), or duplicateMovieClip().
setMask	Nothing	Uses a second movie clip to designate which parts of the specified movie clip are visible.
startDrag	Nothing	Enables the user to drag a movie clip around the screen.
stop	Nothing	Stops playback for the specified movie clip.
stopDrag	Nothing	Stops a draggable movie clip from being dragged.
swapDepths	Nothing	Swaps the stacking order of two movie clips, or moves a movie clip to a specific depth.
unloadMovie	Nothing	Unloads the contents of a movie clip that has been populated through loadMovie().

The following sections illustrate how to use the methods and provide each method's *prototype*. A prototype is an example of a method that shows all the possible input values along with their data types, as well as the data type of any return value. Any parameters that are in square brackets are optional and can be omitted from the method call, if desired.

attachBitmap()

The Bitmap object, which is new to Flash Player version 8, allows pixels to be individually manipulated. It gives great power for controlling animation, but requires more code to do it. A Bitmap object is not visible until it is linked up to a movie clip. The attachBitmap() method performs this linkage, making the bitmap visible within the designated movie clip.

The attachBitmap() method takes between two and four parameters. The first is a handle to a Bitmap instance. The second is a movie clip depth to use for the bitmap. The third, which is optional, sets whether the pixels in the bitmap object automatically snap to the nearest screen pixel location. Possible values are auto (the default), always, and never. The final parameter, also optional, sets whether the bitmap should be smoothed when scaled. The default value is true. The following prototype shows the basic form of the attachBitmap() method:

```
baseMovie.attachBitmap(bmpData:BitmapData, depth:Number, [pixelSnapping:String],
    [smoothing:Boolean]) : Void
```

Here's an example of using `attachBitmap()`:

```
import flash.display.*;

this.createEmptyMovieClip("bitmapHolder", this.getNextHighestDepth());
var bmpData:BitmapData = new BitmapData(100, 100, false, 0x000066);
bitmapHolder.attachBitmap(bmpData, bitmapHolder.getNextHighestDepth());
```

Updates to bitmaps take effect immediately. The player does not wait for the next frame to be processed before updating the display.

attachMovie()

The `attachMovie()` method is used for making copies of library symbols and placing them onstage. It takes either three or four parameters. The first is the linkage ID for the library symbol to be attached. The linkage ID for a symbol is set in the symbol's library properties. The second parameter is an instance name to give the new movie clip instance. The third is a movie clip depth to use for the new instance. The fourth parameter, which is optional, allows initialization properties to be passed to the new instance. The following prototype shows the basic form of the `attachMovie()` method:

```
baseMovie.attachMovie(id:String, name:String, depth:Number, ⊃
    [initObject:Object]) : MovieClip
```

Here's an example of using `attachMovie()` to create a copy of the movie clip with linkage ID `"templateClip"`. It gives the new copy the name `"newClip"`, sets the depth to be the next highest one available in the current timeline, and sets the _x and _y properties to 20:

```
this.attachMovie("templateClip", "newClip", this.getNextHighestDepth(), ⊃
    {_x:20, _y:20});
```

beginFill()

`beginFill()` works in combination with `moveTo()`, `lineTo()`, and `endFill()` and defines an area in which to draw a solid shape. It takes two parameters: the first is the fill color to use, and the second is the transparency of the fill, with 100 being fully opaque. The following prototype shows the basic form of the `beginFill()` method:

```
baseMovie.beginFill(color:Number, alpha:Number) : Void
```

Here's an example of using `beginFill()`, showing the creation a blue triangle:

```
this.createEmptyMovieClip("triangleClip", this.getNextHighestDepth());
triangleClip.moveTo(50, 0);
triangleClip.beginFill(0x000066, 100);
triangleClip.lineTo(0, 100);
triangleClip.lineTo(100, 100);
triangleClip.lineTo(50, 0);
triangleClip.endFill();
```

If the starting and ending points are not the same, a line automatically connects them and the resulting shape is filled.

clear()

Over time, repeated use of the drawing methods to draw inside a movie clip that stays on the stage all the time induces additional processor and memory overhead. Even if drawing one shape completely obscures another shape, the original shape still takes up memory and is part of the drawing routine. The `clear()` method removes all shapes from the drawing cycle and should be used periodically for heavy drawing routines to keep the movie running quickly.

This method takes no parameters. Here's its prototype:

```
myMovieClip.clear() : Void
```

This method does not touch shapes manually created in the movie clip from the development environment's drawing tools, nor does it remove nested movie clips.

createEmptyMovieClip()

The `createEmptyMovieClip()` method is very important to drawing out screen content with ActionScript. It is used for creating containers for other content, such as drawn-out shapes, loaded content, and components.

It takes two parameters. The first is a string representing the instance name of the new movie clip, and the second is a depth to place the new clip. This is one of the core methods used to build content at runtime. Here is its prototype:

```
baseMovie.createEmptyMovieClip(name:String, depth:Number) : MovieClip
```

createTextField()

The `createTextField()` method is the equivalent of creating a dynamic text field on the stage with the text tool, and is one of the core methods for building content at runtime.

This method takes six parameters. The first is a string representing the instance name of the new movie clip, and the second is a depth to place the new text field. The next two are x and y coordinates for placing the text field, and the last two set the width and the height. The following method prototype shows the basic form of `createTextField()`:

```
baseMovie.createTextField(name:String, depth:Number, x:Number, y:Number, ⤴
    width:Number, height:Number) : TextField
```

duplicateMovieClip()

The `duplicateMovieClip()` method is used for duplicating existing content on the stage. Its use has diminished since the addition of the `attachMovie()` method.

Two forms of `duplicateMovieClip()` exist. The first takes either two or three parameters: a string representing the instance name of the new movie clip, a depth to place the new movie clip, and, optionally, an Object instance containing properties to pass to the new movie clip. Here's the method prototype for `duplicateMovieClip()`:

```
baseMovie.duplicateMovieClip(name:String, depth:Number, ⤴
    [initObject:Object]) : MovieClip
```

The following example creates an empty movie clip, draws a triangle in that clip, duplicates the movie clip, and moves the new clip to a different location on the screen. This results in two triangles being shown on the screen:

```
this.createEmptyMovieClip("triangleClip", this.getNextHighestDepth());
triangleClip.moveTo(50, 0);
triangleClip.beginFill(0x000066, 100);
triangleClip.lineTo(0, 100);
triangleClip.lineTo(100, 100);
triangleClip.lineTo(50, 0);
triangleClip.endFill();
  triangleClip.duplicateMovieClip("newClip", this.getNextHighestDepth(), ⤵
    {_x:50, _y:50});
```

The second form of this method is actually a global function, not a movie clip method. The following prototype shows the basic form of the duplicateMovieClip() global function:

```
duplicateMovieClip(target:MovieClip, name:String, depth:Number) : Void
```

This function was commonly used in version 4 of the Flash plug-in; before the attachMovie() method was introduced, it was the only way to duplicate movie clips programmatically. In general, it's better either to use attachMovie() to create new movie clip instances from the library, or to use the first form of duplicateMovieClip().

endFill()

endFill() works in combination with the beginFill(), moveTo(), and lineTo() methods and defines an area in which to draw a solid shape. This method takes no arguments. The following prototype shows the basic form of endFill():

```
baseClip.endFill() : Void
```

Here's an example that draws a blue triangle on the screen:

```
this.createEmptyMovieClip("triangleClip", this.getNextHighestDepth());
triangleClip.moveTo(50, 0);
triangleClip.beginFill(0x000066, 100);
triangleClip.lineTo(0, 100);
triangleClip.lineTo(100, 100);
triangleClip.lineTo(50, 0);
triangleClip.endFill();
```

As a matter of interest, this method does not perform any fill operation. The fill is actually drawn in every time the lineTo() method is called. The endFill() method tells future lineTo() calls not to continue to add to the filled-in shape.

getBytesLoaded()

The getBytesLoaded() method is used in conjunction with getBytesTotal() for movie clip preloader code. A repeated call to check the bytes loaded is made, and when the bytes loaded and the total bytes are the same, the loaded movie can be played. This method takes no arguments. Here's the prototype of its basic form:

```
baseClip.getBytesLoaded() : Number
```

The following example shows `getBytesLoaded()` used as part of a pre-loader:

```
var intervalId:Number;
this.createEmptyMovieClip("loadedMovie", this.getNextHighestDepth());
this.createTextField("percentLoadedField", this.getNextHighestDepth(), 10, 10, ⮌
    100, 20);

function checkLoadProgress()
{
    if (loadedMovie.getBytesTotal() > 0)
    {
        loadedMovie.stop();
        percentLoadedField.text = String(Math.ceil(loadedMovie.getBytesLoaded() ⮌
            / loadedMovie.getBytesTotal() * 100)) + "%";
        if (loadedMovie.getBytesTotal() - loadedMovie.getBytesLoaded() == 0)
        {
            clearInterval(intervalId);
            loadedMovie.play();
        }
    }
}

loadedMovie.loadMovie("http://www.nathanderksen.com/book/sampleAnimation.swf");
intervalId = setInterval(checkLoadProgress, 100);
```

Chapter 8 covers this topic in greater detail.

There is a brief period of time at the beginning of the load process where getting a percentage loaded value by dividing the results of the `getBytesLoaded()` *call by the results of* `getBytesTotal()` *returns an undefined number. During this time, subtracting* `getBytesLoaded()` *from* `getBytesTotal()` *returns 0 in the same way that it does when the movie has loaded completely. Check that* `getBytesTotal()` *returns a non-zero value before using both of these methods to calculate progress.*

getBytesTotal()

`getBytesTotal()` is used in conjunction with the `getBytesLoaded()` method for movie clip pre-loader code. It returns zero bytes until it can find out the size of the file to download. This method takes no arguments. The following prototype shows its basic form:

```
baseClip.getBytesTotal() : Number
```

A sample implementation of this method used as part of a pre-loader might look like this:

```
var intervalId:Number;
this.createEmptyMovieClip("loadedMovie", this.getNextHighestDepth());
this.createTextField("percentLoadedField", this.getNextHighestDepth(), 10, 10, ⮌
    100, 20);

function checkLoadProgress()
{
```

```
    if (loadedMovie.getBytesTotal() > 0)
    {
        loadedMovie.stop();
        percentLoadedField.text = String(Math.ceil(loadedMovie.getBytesLoaded() ⤵
            / loadedMovie.getBytesTotal() * 100)) + "%";
        if (loadedMovie.getBytesTotal() - loadedMovie.getBytesLoaded() == 0)
        {
            clearInterval(intervalId);
            loadedMovie.play();
        }
    }
}

loadedMovie.loadMovie("http://www.nathanderksen.com/book/sampleAnimation.swf");
intervalId = setInterval(checkLoadProgress, 100);
```

Chapter 8 covers this topic in greater detail.

getURL()

The getURL() method is used to replace the Web page containing the Flash movie with a new page, to open a Web page in another window, or to communicate with the browser using JavaScript.

Both movie clip method and global function versions of this call exist. The movie clip method takes between one and three parameters. The first parameter is a URL for a resource to load in the browser window containing the Macromedia Flash movie. The optional second parameter is a string designating the name of a different target browser window. The optional third parameter sets a method for submitting variables to a target server-side script, with possible values being GET or POST. The following prototype shows getURL()'s basic form:

```
baseClip.getURL(url:String, [windowName:String], [method:String]) : Void
```

Here's an example implementation:

```
myMC.getURL("http://www.apple.com/", "_blank"); // Load Web page into a new window
myMC.getURL("newPage.html"); // Load Web page into the current window
getURL("javascript:alert('The quick brown fox');"); // Call a JavaScript function
```

Both versions of getURL() *can be used to call any URL that could potentially be typed in the browser address bar, not just web pages.*

The global function version of this method takes between one and three parameters. The first is a URL for a resource to load in the browser window containing the Macromedia Flash movie. The optional second parameter is a string designating the name of a different target browser window. The optional third parameter is a string holding name/value pairs to send to the server in the form of &var1=value1&var2=value2. Here's the prototype of the basic getURL() global function:

```
getURL(url:String, windowName:String, [variables:String]) : Void
```

The LoadVars and the XML classes are preferred ways to send data to a server.

The global function version of `getURL()` is preferred over the method version. The method version does not actually depend on the movie clip it is called from unless it is being used to send variables to the server.

gotoAndPlay()

`gotoAndPlay()` has both movie clip method and global function versions. The movie clip method takes one parameter, which is either the number of or a string label for the label of the frame from which to start playing. This method controls the playhead within the specified movie clip. Here's its prototype:

```
baseClip.gotoAndPlay(frame:Object) : Void
```

Following are examples of a call made with each parameter:

```
myMC.gotoAndPlay(20);
```

```
myMC.gotoAndPlay("photographyScreen");
```

Using frame labels rather than frame numbers is preferred, but frame labels can be applied only in the Flash development environment and can't be set at runtime.

The global function version of `gotoAndPlay()` takes two parameters. The first, the name of a scene to target, is optional. The second parameter is either the number or string label of the frame from which to start playing. This function controls the playhead on the base timeline. Here's the prototype of its basic form:

```
gotoAndPlay(frame:Object) : Void
```

It is highly recommended that you avoid using scenes, especially for ActionScript programming. They result in more complicated code, and numerous issues are associated with accessing scenes with ActionScript.

hitTest()

The `hitTest()` method is used to detect whether two movie clips are overlapping each other. It can be used for collision detection in games, but it is limited in that it uses a rectangle around both movie clips to test for overlapping. If the contents of the movie clips are not rectangular, the method may return `true` even if the contents of the two clips are not actually visibly overlapping.

`hitTest()` takes a single parameter, which is a handle to the movie clip to compare with. The following prototype shows the method's basic form:

```
baseClip.hitTest(targetMovie:MovieClip) : Boolean
```

The following example shows the method in use. Two movie clips containing triangles are created, and the first one is made draggable. When it is dragged over the second triangle and the mouse is released, a trace statement indicates that the movie clips overlap:

```
this.createEmptyMovieClip("triangle1Clip", this.getNextHighestDepth());
triangle1Clip.moveTo(50, 0);
triangle1Clip.beginFill(0x000066, 100);
triangle1Clip.lineTo(0, 100);
```

```
trianglelClip.lineTo(100, 100);
trianglelClip.lineTo(50, 0);
trianglelClip.endFill();
trianglelClip.duplicateMovieClip("triangle2Clip", this.getNextHighestDepth(), ⤴
    {_x:50, _y:50});

trianglelClip.onPress = function()
{
    this.startDrag();
};

trianglelClip.onRelease = function()
{
    this.stopDrag();
    if (this.hitTest(triangle2Clip) == true)
    {
        trace("shapes are overlapping");
    }
};
```

If one triangle is within the rectangle that bounds the other triangle, the hit test returns `true` even though the triangles themselves may not actually be touching. This limits the usefulness of the `hitTest()` method for irregular shapes. For more information about using ActionScript to detect collisions, go to www.moock.org/webdesign/flash/actionscript/collision/.

lineStyle()

The `lineStyle()` method defines the characteristics of a line to draw for any `lineTo()` method calls. If it isn't called before a `lineTo()`, no line is drawn.

This method takes between one and eight parameters:

1. `thickness`. A Number indicating the thickness of the line.

2. `color`. A Number representing the color to use.

3. `alpha`. A Number representing the transparency to use, with `100` being fully opaque.

The `thickness`, `color`, and `alpha` (opacity) parameters work in Flash Player 6, but the remaining parameters require at least Flash Player 8:

4. `pixelHinting`. A Boolean indicating whether to use pixel hinting, where strokes are made to end on a full pixel.

5. `noScale`. A String indicating how to scale the line if the parent movie clip scales. Possible values are `normal`, `none`, `vertical`, and `horizontal`.

6. `capsStyle`. A String indicating how to cap off the ends of lines. Possible values are `round`, `square`, and `none`.

7. `jointStyle`. A String indicating how line segment joints are to be displayed. Possible values are `round`, `miter`, and `none`.

8. `miterLimit`. A Number that controls how large mitered corners are allowed to get before being cut off.

The following prototype shows the basic form of `lineStyle()`:

```
baseClip.lineStyle(thickness:Number, [color:Number], [alpha:Number],
    [pixelHinting:Boolean], [noScale:String], [capsStyle:String],
    [jointStyle:String], [miterLimit:Number]) : Void
```

The method is used in this example, which draws two connected lines:

```
this.createEmptyMovieClip("shapeClip", this.getNextHighestDepth());
shapeClip.lineStyle(5, 0x000000, 100, true, "normal", "square", "miter", 3);
shapeClip.moveTo(100, 50);
shapeClip.lineTo(50, 150);
shapeClip.lineTo(150, 150);
```

Multiple calls to this method can be made through the course of drawing to the movie clip. A line style applies to all drawing commands until the next line style call is made, after which all subsequent drawing commands take on the new line style.

You cannot change just one style attribute with a subsequent `lineStyle()` call. All styles left unspecified in the method revert to their default values.

lineTo()

The `lineTo()` method is used to draw a line, and also to designate the bounds for a filled shape.

This method takes just the x and the y coordinates for the new coordinate. The line is drawn from the previous `lineTo()` coordinates or from the previous `moveTo()` coordinates and extends to the specified x and y values. `lineTo()` is used in conjunction with the `lineStyle()` and `moveTo()` methods, and is very useful for dynamically drawing buttons, backgrounds, or code-generated animation. The following prototype shows the method's basic form:

```
baseClip.lineTo(x:Number, y:Number) : Void
```

Here's an example of using `lineTo()`:

```
this.createEmptyMovieClip("shapeClip", this.getNextHighestDepth());
shapeClip.lineStyle(1, 0x000000);
shapeClip.moveTo(100, 50);
shapeClip.lineTo(50, 150);
shapeClip.lineTo(150, 150);
```

loadMovie()

`loadMovie()` is a core method for loading external content. It takes either one or two parameters. The first is the URL for the content to load into the movie clip. The second is an optional parameter for sending or loading variables, with possible values GET and POST. This method can load `.jpg` and `.swf` files, and, as of version 8 of the player, it can also load `.gif` and `.png` files. The following prototype shows the method's basic form:

```
baseClip.loadMovie(url:String, [method:String]) : Void
```

Here's a sample implementation of the method:

```
this.createEmptyMovieClip("animationHolder", this.getNextHighestDepth());
animationHolder.loadMovie("http://www.nathanderksen.com/book/sampleAnimation.swf");
```

When loading external content, many methods will not work on that movie clip until it has at least begun to download from the server. A pre-loader is needed to delay these methods' execution until the movie clip is ready. Pre-loaders are covered in detail in Chapter 8.

moveTo()

The moveTo() method moves the drawing pen to a starting position before anything is actually drawn. It takes two parameters: the x and y coordinates to go to. The following prototype shows its basic form:

```
baseClip.moveTo(x:Number, y:Number) : Void
```

Here's an example showing its use:

```
this.createEmptyMovieClip("shapeClip", this.getNextHighestDepth());
shapeClip.lineStyle(1, 0x000000);
shapeClip.moveTo(100, 50);
shapeClip.lineTo(50, 150);
shapeClip.lineTo(150, 150);
```

play()

play() has both movie clip method and global function versions. The movie clip method takes no parameters, and it resumes playback of the specified movie clip from the current playhead position. Here's the prototype of its basic form:

```
baseClip.play() : Void
```

The global function version takes no parameters, and it resumes playback of the timeline holding the code from the current playhead position. The following prototype shows its basic form:

```
play() : Void
```

removeMovieClip()

The removeMovieClip() method removes a movie clip that has been dynamically placed on the stage through the attachMovie(), duplicateMovieClip(), or createEmptyMovieClip() methods. It takes no parameters. The following prototype shows the method's basic form:

```
baseClip.removeMovieClip() : Void
```

removeMovieClip() is not used to remove movie clips that have been placed on the stage with the authoring tool. These clips are all assigned negative depth values. One work-around is to use swapDepths() to move the movie clip to a positive depth, and then to delete the clip. Another option, which is actually preferable, is to dynamically place all movie clips on the stage so that they can all be dynamically removed.

setMask()

`setMask()` uses the shape of one movie clip to define what is visible on another movie clip. It is useful for numerous visual effects and to define a cropping area for a clip that may be scrolled. This method takes a single parameter, which is a movie clip to use for the mask. The following prototype shows the basic form of `setMask()`:

```
baseClip.setMask(maskClip:Object) : Void
```

Here's an example implementation of the method:

```
this.createEmptyMovieClip("shapeClip", this.getNextHighestDepth());
shapeClip.beginFill(0x000066);
shapeClip.moveTo(150, 50);
shapeClip.lineTo(50, 250);
shapeClip.lineTo(250, 250);
shapeClip.lineTo(150, 50);
shapeClip.endFill();

this.createEmptyMovieClip("maskClip", this.getNextHighestDepth());
maskClip.beginFill(0x660000);
maskClip.moveTo(100, 100);
maskClip.lineTo(200, 100);
maskClip.lineTo(200, 300);
maskClip.lineTo(100, 300);
maskClip.lineTo(100, 100);
maskClip.endFill();

shapeClip.setMask(maskClip);
```

Only the shape of the mask is used to determine which parts of the main movie clip are to be visible. Semi-transparent areas of the mask have no impact on the transparency of the main movie clip: they just add to the overall shape of the mask.

startDrag()

The `startDrag()` method is used to indicate that if a user clicks and drags over the movie clip, the clip should follow the cursor. It takes between zero and five parameters. The first parameter is a Boolean that, when `true`, centers the movie clip under the mouse cursor when the drag operation starts. The next four parameters delimit the left, top, right, and bottom edges of a rectangle that restricts the range of the drag motion. The following prototype shows the method's basic form:

```
baseClip.startDrag([lockCenter:Boolean], [left:Number], [top:Number], ⤶
    [right:Number], [bottom:Number}) : Void
```

Setting `left` and `right` to the same value restricts the drag to only vertical movement, whereas setting `top` and `bottom` to the same value restricts the drag to only horizontal movement. This method is generally called when the mouse button is pressed, and its corresponding method, `stopDrag()`, is generally called when the mouse button is released. The following example creates a movie clip, draws a shape inside the movie clip, and then sets the movie clip to be draggable when the mouse button has been pressed:

```
this.createEmptyMovieClip("shapeClip", this.getNextHighestDepth());
shapeClip.beginFill(0x000066);
shapeClip.moveTo(150, 50);
shapeClip.lineTo(50, 250);
shapeClip.lineTo(250, 250);
shapeClip.lineTo(150, 50);
shapeClip.endFill();

shapeClip.onPress = function()
{
    this.startDrag();
};

shapeClip.onRelease = function()
{
    this.stopDrag();
};
```

stop()

The `stop()` method has both movie clip method and global function versions. The movie clip method takes no parameters, and it stops playback of the specified movie clip. The following prototype shows its basic form:

```
baseClip.stop() : Void
```

The global function version takes no parameters, and it stops playback of the timeline holding the code. Here's the prototype of its basic form:

```
stop() : Void
```

stopDrag()

The `stopDrag()` method is used to stop a dragging operation, and it is generally called when the mouse button has been released. It takes no parameters. The following prototype shows its basic form:

```
baseClip.stopDrag() : Void
```

Here's an example implementation:

```
this.createEmptyMovieClip("shapeClip", this.getNextHighestDepth());
shapeClip.beginFill(0x000066);
shapeClip.moveTo(150, 50);
shapeClip.lineTo(50, 250);
shapeClip.lineTo(250, 250);
shapeClip.lineTo(150, 50);
shapeClip.endFill();

shapeClip.onPress = function()
{
    this.startDrag();
};
```

```
    shapeClip.onRelease = function()
    {
        this.stopDrag();
    };
```

swapDepths()

swapDepths() is useful for changing the movie clip stacking order. It takes one parameter, which is either a handle to a movie clip or a depth number. Here's the prototype of the method's basic form:

```
    baseClip.swapDepths(secondClip:MovieClip) : Void
```

If a movie clip handle is passed, the two movie clips swap depths. If a number is passed, the movie clip switches to that depth number. The following example demonstrates the behavior by swapping the two movie clips when the square is clicked:

```
    this.createEmptyMovieClip("triangleClip", this.getNextHighestDepth());
    triangleClip.beginFill(0x000066);
    triangleClip.moveTo(150, 50);
    triangleClip.lineTo(50, 250);
    triangleClip.lineTo(250, 250);
    triangleClip.lineTo(150, 50);
    triangleClip.endFill();

    this.createEmptyMovieClip("squareClip", this.getNextHighestDepth());
    squareClip.beginFill(0x660000);
    squareClip.moveTo(25, 25);
    squareClip.lineTo(25, 150);
    squareClip.lineTo(150, 150);
    squareClip.lineTo(150, 25);
    squareClip.lineTo(25, 25);
    squareClip.endFill();

    squareClip.onRelease = function()
    {
        this.swapDepths(triangleClip);
    };
```

For two movie clips to swap depths, they must have the same parent movie clip.

unloadMovie()

The unloadMovie() method is used when removing external content that has been loaded using the loadMovie() method. It takes no parameters. Here's its basic form:

```
    baseClip.unloadMovie() : Void
```

The following code example loads an external movie, waits three seconds, and then unloads the movie:

```
    var intervalId:Number;
    this.createEmptyMovieClip("mediaClip", this.getNextHighestDepth());
    mediaClip.loadMovie("http://www.nathanderksen.com/book/sampleAnimation.swf");
```

```
intervalId = setInterval(unloadContent, 3000);

function unloadContent()
{
    mediaClip.unloadMovie();
    clearInterval(intervalId);
}
```

You need to try this from a server for it to work.

There is an apparent bug in version 8 of the Flash player that mistakenly identifies a remote file as try-ing to manipulate a local file and prevents the action, when it is actually the other way around.

MovieClip Class Properties

The MovieClip class comes with some properties that describe a number of aspects of the movie clip. For instance, the _x, _y, _width, _height, _xscale, and _yscale properties enable you to specify the position and the size of any movie clip. You use the _alpha property to set how transparent a movie clip is, and the _visible property indicates whether a movie clip is being rendered to the stage. Any prop-erty that starts with an underscore character is a core movie clip property that has for the most part been available in the Flash Player since version 5. In version 6, some of the new properties used the under-score convention, and some did not. In version 7 and later, the convention was to not use the underscore as a part of property names.

The following table describes the core properties available for your use:

Property	Type	Description
_alpha	Number	The movie clip transparency.
_currentframe	Number	The frame number where the playhead is currently posi-tioned. (Read only.)
_droptarget	String	The path to the movie clip that a draggable clip was dropped on. (Read only.)
_focusrect	Boolean	Indicates whether the movie clip currently has keyboard focus.
_framesloaded	Number	The number of frames of an externally loaded movie clip that have loaded so far. (Read only.)
_height	Number	The height of the movie clip.
_lockroot	Boolean	Designates the specified movie clip as the target for all refer-ences to _root that occur in code within that movie clip.
_name	String	The instance name of the movie clip.
_parent	Movie Clip	The handle to the movie clip that contains the specified clip.
_quality	String	Sets the rendering quality used to display movie clip content. Can be low, medium, high, or best.

Property	Type	Description
`_rotation`	Number	Sets the number of degrees to rotate the movie clip.
`_target`	String	Gets the path to the movie clip relative to the main timeline in slash notation. (Read only.)
`_totalframes`	Number	Gets the total number of frames used by the movie clip. (Read only.)
`_url`	String	Gets the address from which an SWF, JPG, GIF, or PNG file was loaded into the movie clip. (Read only.)
`_visible`	Boolean	The visibility of the movie clip.
`_width`	Number	The width of the movie clip.
`_x`	Number	The x coordinate of the movie clip relative to the parent movie clip.
`_xmouse`	Number	The x coordinate of the mouse pointer relative to the main timeline. (Read only.)
`_xscale`	Number	The percentage horizontal scaling of the clip. A value of 100 designates normal width.
`_y`	Number	The y coordinate of the movie clip relative to the parent movie clip.
`_ymouse`	Number	The y coordinate of the mouse pointer relative to the main timeline. (Read only.)
`_yscale`	Number	The percentage vertical scaling of the clip. A value of 100 designates normal height.

Properties such as `blendMode` and `filters` provide the capability to create unique effects, and `scale9grid` and `transform` are powerful new tools to manipulate movie clips. The following properties supplement the core movie clip properties:

Property	Type	Description
`blendMode`	Object	The type of blending that the movie clip uses with content behind it. Possible values are `normal`, `layer`, `multiply`, `screen`, `lighten`, `darken`, `difference`, `add`, `subtract`, `invert`, `alpha`, `erase`, `overlay`, and `hardlight`. (Flash Player 8 only.)
`cacheAsBitmap`	Boolean	Sets whether the player will store a bitmap representation of the movie clip for faster rendering. (Flash Player 8 only.)
`enabled`	Boolean	If set to `false`, blocks event handlers from being called by the movie clip.

Table continued on following page

Property	Type	Description
filters	Object	Stores an array of filters that have been applied to the movie clip. (Flash Player 8 only.)
focusEnabled	Boolean	Allows a movie clip to receive focus, even if it is not a button.
hitArea	Object	Allows the clickable area of a movie clip used as a button to be defined by the shape of another movie clip.
menu	Object	Associates a contextual menu object with the movie clip.
opaque Background	Number	Sets the transparent portions of the movie clip to the selected color. (Flash Player 8 only.)
scale9Grid	Rectangle	Allows a movie clip to be scaled so that some areas stretch while other areas maintain their dimensions. (Flash Player 8 only.)
scrollRect	Rectangle	Defines a cropping rectangle for movie clip content. Content that falls outside that area is hidden until scrolled to. (Flash Player 8 only.)
tabChildren	Boolean	Determines which child movie clips are included in the automatic tab ordering.
tabEnabled	Boolean	Determines whether the movie clip is to be included in the automatic tab ordering.
tabIndex	Number	Determines the position of the movie clip in the tab ordering.
trackAsMenu	Boolean	When set to true, changes the button click behavior so that clicking down on one button, dragging onto another button, and then releasing the mouse will engage the second button.
transform	Transform	Holds an object that records details of the movie clip's transformation matrix, color transform details, and pixel bounds. (Flash Player 8 only.)
useHandCursor	Boolean	Changes the cursor to a hand when hovering over the movie clip.

MovieClip Class Events

Movie clips provide a means to follow up with your own action when certain actions take place, such as when the user mouses over or clicks a movie clip. When such actions take place, the movie clip generates an event, which is a signal that something of note has happened. You can write code that responds by assigning a function to that event. The following example shows that assigning a function to the onRelease event causes the code within the function to be executed every time the movie clip is clicked:

```
this.createEmptyMovieClip("triangleClip", this.getNextHighestDepth());
triangleClip.beginFill(0x000066);
triangleClip.moveTo(150, 50);
triangleClip.lineTo(50, 250);
```

```
triangleClip.lineTo(250, 250);
triangleClip.lineTo(150, 50);
triangleClip.endFill();

triangleClip.onRelease = function()
{
    trace("Clicked on triangle");
};
```

The following movie clip events are available for you to use:

Event	Type	Description
onDragOut	Function	Fires when the mouse button has been pressed and the mouse leaves the bounds of the movie clip.
onDragOver	Function	Fires when the mouse button has been pressed and the mouse leaves and re-enters the bounds of the movie clip.
onEnterFrame	Function	Fires every time the playhead moves to the next frame.
onKeyDown	Function	Fires when the movie clip has input focus and a key on the keyboard is pressed.
onKeyUp	Function	Fires when the movie clip has input focus and a key on the keyboard is released.
onKillFocus	Function	Fires when the movie clip loses keyboard focus.
onLoad	Function	Fires when a new movie clip instance appears on the timeline. Does not fire when external content is loaded into an existing movie clip.
onMouseDown	Function	Fires when the mouse button has been pressed.
onMouseMove	Function	Fires when the position of the mouse changes from the previous time the event fired.
onMouseUp	Function	Fires when the mouse button has been released.
onPress	Function	Fires when the mouse button has been pressed while over the movie clip.
onRelease	Function	Fires when the mouse button has been released while over the movie clip.
onRelease Outside	Function	Fires when the mouse button has been pressed while over the movie clip, moved, and then released outside the movie clip.
onRollOut	Function	Fires when the mouse leaves the bounds of the movie clip.
onRollOver	Function	Fires when the mouse enters the bounds of the movie clip.
onSetFocus	Function	Fires when the movie clip gains keyboard focus.
onUnload	Function	Fires after the movie clip is removed from the timeline.

Creating Movie Clips On-the-Fly

Now you're ready to apply some of the MovieClip class methods. The first task for working with movie clips is to place them on the stage. You can create a new movie clip in two ways:

❑ Create a new movie clip symbol in the library, drag it to the desired location on the stage, and give it an instance name in the properties panel. The limitation of this approach is that if the implementation of this particular clip is to change later on, it will likely need to be changed both within the project file and within the ActionScript code.

❑ Use the `createEmptyMovieClip()` method. This technique enables complete programmatic control over how a project is structured.

`createEmptyMovieClip()` is fundamental to building interfaces using ActionScript. With this method, it is possible to create an entire project with code that is script-generated and that sits on just one frame in the main timeline.

Each movie clip must have a parent movie clip. If no movie clips are on the stage yet, use the base timeline as the parent movie clip. The following line creates a movie clip on the main timeline:

```
_level0.createEmptyMovieClip("firstClip", 1);
```

The `_level0` reference is an *absolute reference*. The problem with using it is that if you were to later load your project into a movie clip in a different project, the `_level0` reference would have to be changed to refer to the location of the new movie clip. In the context of movie clips, the `this` keyword is a *relative reference* that refers to the timeline holding the code. In this case, it would refer to the timeline at `_level0`. If it is later loaded into a movie clip in a different project, the reference resolves to the new parent movie clip and doesn't have to be changed. Here's how to create a movie clip on the current timeline using a relative reference:

```
this.createEmptyMovieClip("firstClip", 1);
```

The instance name parameter provides a way to access the new movie clip once it has been created. You can refer to the new movie clip in three ways:

❑ Through the reference that the method returns on completion. This is a handy way to hold onto a movie clip reference when creating multiple clips with a loop, especially when that clip needs to be referenced many times in a single iteration. Here's an example that assigns the new movie clip to a variable handle, and then uses that handle to manipulate the position of the movie clip:

```
var movieClipHandle:MovieClip = this.createEmptyMovieClip("firstClip", 1);
movieClipHandle._x = 20;
```

❑ By referencing the variable created on the timeline. This is good to use when creating one movie clip at a time. The following code demonstrates that once you create a movie clip, it automatically creates a variable on the timeline that you can use to access the new movie clip:

```
this.createEmptyMovieClip("firstClip", 1);
this.firstClip._x = 20; // or
firstClip._x = 20; // 'this' is implied
```

❑   Through the associative array syntax. Recall from Chapter 2 that object properties can be accessed either through dot notation or through associative array notation. A movie clip is itself a property of its parent movie clip, and it is thus also available through the associative array syntax. Like the first technique, this is handy when creating multiple movie clips within a loop. The following example shows how the associative array syntax is used:

```
this.createEmptyMovieClip("firstClip", 1);
this["firstClip"]._x = 20;
```

When assigning a depth parameter for the new movie clip, the depth number must be unique within the parent movie clip. No two movie clips with the same parent can share the same depth. If a new movie clip is assigned a depth that is already in use, the item that already occupies that depth is removed from the stage. In the following example, a movie clip is created on depth number 1, and then a second movie clip is created on the same depth. Once the second movie clip has been created, the first one is destroyed.

```
this.createEmptyMovieClip("firstClip", 1);
trace(firstClip);
// Outputs: _level0.firstClip

this.createEmptyMovieClip("secondClip", 1);
trace(firstClip);
// Outputs: undefined
trace(secondClip);
// Outputs: _level0.secondClip
```

The best practice for assigning depths to movie clips is to use the `getNextHighestDepth()` method. It works in version 7 of the player and later, and it prevents depths from conflicting. The following code shows that when you use this method, you don't have to worry about accidentally destroying another movie clip by allocating a depth number that's already been assigned:

```
this.createEmptyMovieClip("firstClip", this.getNextHighestDepth());
trace(firstClip);
// Outputs: _level0.firstClip

this.createEmptyMovieClip("secondClip", this.getNextHighestDepth());
trace(firstClip);
// Outputs: _level0.firstClip
trace(secondClip);
// Outputs: _level0.secondClip
```

Try It Out   Create a Simple Button

Creating a new movie clip only requires a single line of code; working with it can be as complex as you want it to be. This exercise demonstrates a function that creates a new movie clip, draws inside of it, gives it a label, and makes it clickable.

1.   Create a new Macromedia Flash document by selecting File⇨New and choosing Flash Document from the New Document panel.

2.   Click the first frame in the timeline, open the Actions panel (Window⇨Development Panels⇨ Actions), and type in the following ActionScript code:

```
#include "tryItOut_createButton.as"
```

3. Select File⇨Save As, name the file `tryItOut_createButton.fla`, choose an appropriate directory, and save it.

4. Create a new Macromedia Flash document by selecting File⇨New and choosing ActionScript File from the New Document panel.

5. Select File⇨Save As, ensure it is showing the same directory containing the Flash project file, name the file `tryItOut_createButton.as`, and save it.

6. Type the following code into the new ActionScript file:

```
function createButton(buttonName:String, buttonLabel:String, ↩
    parentClip:MovieClip, xPos:Number, yPos:Number) : Void
{
    var newClip:MovieClip = this.createEmptyMovieClip(buttonName, ↩
        parentClip.getNextHighestDepth());

    newClip._x = xPos;
    newClip._y = yPos;

    newClip.moveTo(0, 0);
    newClip.lineStyle(1, 0x000000);
    newClip.beginFill(0xCCCCCC, 100);
    newClip.lineTo(100, 0);
    newClip.lineTo(100, 20);
    newClip.lineTo(0, 20);
    newClip.lineTo(0, 0);
    newClip.endFill();

    newClip.createTextField("labelField", newClip.getNextHighestDepth(), ↩
        5, 3, 100, 20);
    newClip.labelField.text = buttonLabel;

    newClip.onRelease = function()
    {
        trace("Pressed button: " + this._name);
    }
}

createButton("button1", "Button One", this, 20, 20);
```

7. Save the file, return to the Macromedia Flash project file, and select Control⇨Test Movie.

How It Works

The first line of code in the function creates a movie clip and assigns a reference to it to a local variable:

```
var newClip:MovieClip = this.createEmptyMovieClip(buttonName, ↩
    parentClip.getNextHighestDepth());
```

Next, the clip is positioned:

```
newClip._x = xPos;
newClip._y = yPos;
```

A background and an outline are drawn:

```
newClip.moveTo(0, 0);
newClip.lineStyle(1, 0x000000);
newClip.beginFill(0xCCCCCC, 100);
newClip.lineTo(100, 0);
newClip.lineTo(100, 20);
newClip.lineTo(0, 20);
newClip.lineTo(0, 0);
newClip.endFill();
```

Note that this code could have used the associative array syntax instead. For example, the following code is also valid:

```
this.createEmptyMovieClip(buttonName, parentClip.getNextHighestDepth());

parentClip[buttonName]._x = xPos;
parentClip[buttonName]._y = yPos;

parentClip[buttonName].moveTo(0, 0);
parentClip[buttonName].lineStyle(1, 0x000000);
parentClip[buttonName].beginFill(0xCCCCCC, 100);
// etc...
```

As you can see, when there are frequent references to the same movie clip, it is neater to assign to a short temporary variable and to use that variable throughout.

Next, a new text field is created, and a label is assigned:

```
newClip.createTextField("labelField", newClip.getNextHighestDepth(), ⏎
    5, 3, 100, 20);
newClip.labelField.text = buttonLabel;
```

The movie clip is then made to behave like a button by defining an onRelease event handler:

```
newClip.onRelease = function()
{
    trace("Pressed button: " + this._name);
}
```

Finally, outside of the function, the createButton() function is called:

```
createButton("button1", "Button One", this, 20, 20);
```

Attaching Movie Clips from the Library

Creating a new movie clip and then defining the clip content using code can be a fair bit of work, especially if the content involves curves, complex shapes, or many layers. In some cases, it may be simpler to create the content with the authoring tool, and then pull that content from the library and attach it to the stage programmatically. The mechanism that makes this possible is the attachMovie() method.

Two major differences exist between the parameters accepted by `attachMovie()` and those accepted by `createEmptyMovieClip()`:

❑ `attachMovie()` requires an ID that corresponds to the linkage ID of the library symbol. You can set a linkage ID for any movie clip in the library by going to the symbol's library properties window, ensuring the advanced properties are showing, selecting the Export for ActionScript checkbox, and assigning an identifier.

Any library symbol that is set to export for ActionScript will be included in the published `.swf` *file, even if it is not referenced in any code or anywhere on the stage.*

❑ `attachMovie()` accepts an Object parameter that allows for a number of parameters to be sent to the new movie clip instance. This is a handy way to set button properties. The following code snippet shows that the _x and _y properties are given initial values that result in the new movie clip being positioned to an x coordinate of 10 and a y coordinate of 20:

```
this.attachMovie("buttonTemplate", "button1", 1, {_x:10, _y:20});
trace(button1._x);
// Outputs: 10
trace(button1._y);
// Outputs: 20
```

Now try this method out for yourself.

Try It Out   Create a Simple Button, Version 2

In this example you perform the same task as in the previous Try It Out, but you use the `attachMovie()` method and draw out parts of the button with the authoring tool instead of with script.

1. Create a new Macromedia Flash document.

2. Click the first frame in the timeline, open the Actions panel, and type in the following ActionScript code:

```
#include "tryItOut_attachMovie.as"
```

3. Open the library (Window⇨Library) and from the menu on the top-right of the library palette, choose New Symbol. The Symbol Properties dialog box opens (see Figure 7-1).

4. Name the symbol `buttonTemplate`, and make sure that the Movie Clip radio button is selected. Select the Export for ActionScript checkbox, and make sure that the identifier field also contains the text `buttonTemplate`. Click the OK button. (If you do not see these options, click the Advanced button to reveal them.)

5. Rename the only layer in the timeline `Background`. Create a new layer in the timeline called `Label`.

6. Select the keyframe on the Background layer. Choose the rectangle tool from the Tools palette (Window⇨Tools) and draw on the stage a rectangle that is approximately 100 pixels wide by 25 pixels high.

7. Select the only keyframe on the `Label` layer. Choose the text tool from the Tools palette and drag from the top left to the bottom right of the rectangle to create a text field that is slightly smaller than the rectangle. Use the resize handle on the text field while still in text field edit mode to adjust the size.

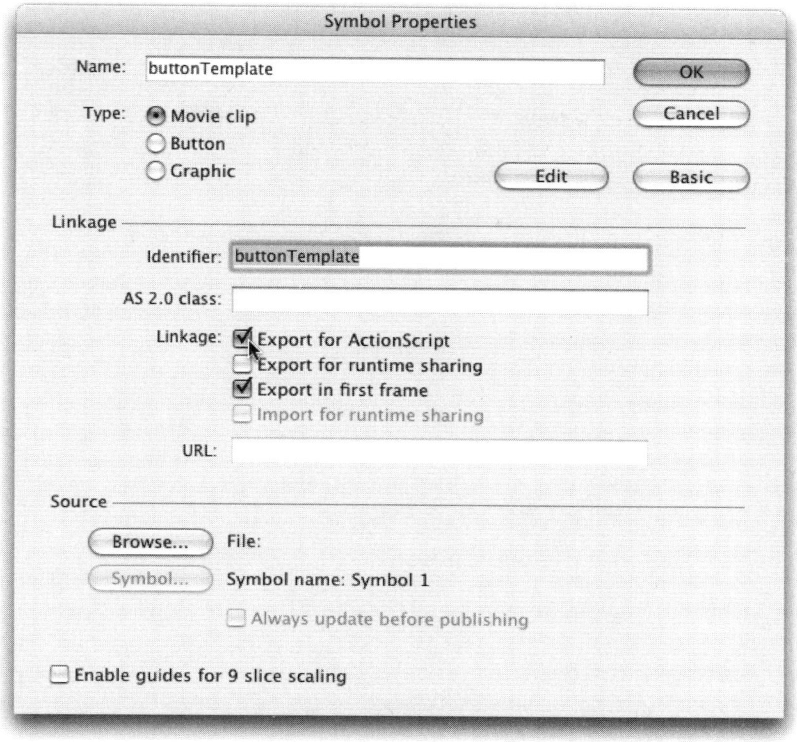

Figure 7-1

8. With the text field still selected, go to the properties panel (Window⇨Properties) and make sure that the drop-down on the top left of the panel shows `Dynamic Text` and the text field just below it reads `labelField`.

9. Select File⇨Save As, name the file `tryItOut_attachMovie.fla`, choose an appropriate directory, and save it.

10. Create a new Macromedia Flash document. Name it `tryItOut_attachMovie.as`, and save it in the directory containing the Flash project file.

11. Enter the following code into the new ActionScript file:

```
function createButton(buttonName:String, buttonLabel:String, ⊃
    parentClip:MovieClip, xPos:Number, yPos:Number) : Void
{
    var newClip:MovieClip = this.attachMovie("buttonTemplate", buttonName, ⊃
        parentClip.getNextHighestDepth(), {_x:xPos, _y:yPos});

    newClip.labelField.text = buttonLabel;

    newClip.onRelease = function()
    {
        trace("Pressed button: " + this._name);
```

```
        }
    }

    createButton("button1", "Button One", this, 20, 20);
```

12. Save the file, return to the Macromedia Flash project file, and select Control⇨Test Movie. Clicking the button should produce a trace statement in the output panel.

How It Works

The first line of code makes a copy of the library symbol with the instance ID `buttonTemplate` and places it on the stage. It also sets the _x and _y positions for the new movie clip by sending the properties to the method via the initialize properties object:

```
var newClip:MovieClip = this.attachMovie("buttonTemplate", buttonName, ⊃
    parentClip.getNextHighestDepth(), {_x:xPos, _y:yPos});
```

Next, the label is set. Although the text field was created manually in the authoring tool, you interact with it as if it were created with code:

```
newClip.labelField.text = buttonLabel;
```

The movie clip is made to behave like a button by defining an `onRelease` event handler:

```
newClip.onRelease = function()
{
    trace("Pressed button: " + this._name);
}
```

This automatically causes the cursor to change to a hand when the mouse hovers over the movie clip. Finally, the `createButton()` function is called:

```
createButton("button1", "Button One", this, 20, 20);
```

Loading External Movies

Until this point, you've been working with content that exists within the same project file. What if you want to load other movies or images? Fortunately, this is pretty straightforward, and once again the movie clip is the container that makes it possible. The media types that can be loaded at runtime include .swf and .jpg files. With version 8 of the Flash player, .gif and .png files also can be loaded at runtime.

Two primary ways to load an external media file exist: by loading it into its own level, and by loading it into a movie clip container.

Loading Movies into Levels

As you know from Chapter 1, levels are basically stacked movie clips with a special identifier for accessing each clip. Every project has at least one level, and the base level is accessed with the global handle _level0.

Technically, you can load images into a level. Practically, levels should be restricted for loading only `.swf` files. The means to load a `.swf` file into a level is done through the global function `loadMovieNum()`. Here's the general form for that function:

```
loadMovieNum(url:String, level:Number, [method:String]) : Void
```

To place a movie into level 10, for example, simply call

```
loadMovieNum("http://www.nathanderksen.com/book/sampleAnimation.swf", 10);
```

Once loaded, the reference `_level10` allows access to this content.

There is, unfortunately, a complication. When loading content into a level, the handle to the level is not created right away. The player first checks to see if the file exists, and if it does exist, the player finds out the size of the media. Only after that process is complete is the handle to the level available, and because it involves a potential trip across a network to a server, there is no way to know for sure when that will be. In the following code snippet, the `trace()` function shows that the `_level10` reference is not yet defined although the request to load a file to level 10 has been made:

```
loadMovieNum("http://www.nathanderksen.com/book/sampleAnimation.swf", 10);
trace(_level10);
// Outputs: undefined
```

A delay is needed until the handle is available for accessing the level. The `setInterval()` function allows for a repeated test to find out when the level is ready to access. In the following example, `setInterval()` calls the `repositionMedia()` function every 200 ms to check whether the `_level10` reference is defined. Once it is, the whole level is moved 100 pixels to the right and the `setInterval()` call is halted:

```
loadMovieNum("http://www.nathanderksen.com/book/sampleAnimation.swf", 10);
var intervalID:Number = setInterval(repositionMedia, 200);

function repositionMedia()
{
    trace(_level10);
    if (_level10 != undefined)
    {
        _level10._x = 100;
        clearInterval(intervalID);
    }
}
// Outputs:
// undefined
//_level1
```

Several ways exist to determine when movie clip content is ready to use; Chapter 8 gets into the details.

Loading Media into Existing Movie Clips

Although loading content into a level is simple, there are some limitations. For instance, levels cannot be swapped, level numbers have to be manually tracked, and levels cannot be nested within other content.

Using movie clips as containers for loaded content offers greater flexibility than using levels: there is no delay between when a movie clip is created and when the handle is available, there is a mechanism to manage movie clip depths, and movie clips can easily be created and deleted anywhere. Movie clips are also more appropriate for images and can generate a large variety of events based on user interactions.

Loading content into a movie clip is as simple as this:

```
this.createEmptyMovieClip("swfHolder", this.getNextHighestDepth());
swfHolder.loadMovie("http://www.nathanderksen.com/book/sampleAnimation.swf");

this.createEmptyMovieClip("jpgHolder", this.getNextHighestDepth());
jpgHolder.loadMovie("http://www.nathanderksen.com/book/afternoonShower.jpg");
```

If you target Macromedia Flash Player version 8, you can also load .gif and .png files. If you use the transparency feature of these image formats, the Flash 8 player properly makes those areas transparent. The following code shows what happens when a .png image with a transparent area is viewed over other content, such as another copy of the same image:

```
this.createEmptyMovieClip("pngHolder", this.getNextHighestDepth());
pngHolder.loadMovie("http://www.nathanderksen.com/book/flowerInDetail.png");

this.createEmptyMovieClip("pngHolder2", this.getNextHighestDepth());
pngHolder2.loadMovie("http://www.nathanderksen.com/book/flowerInDetail.png");
pngHolder2._x = 60;
pngHolder2._y = 60;
```

Unlike with levels, the content does not need to start loading before the container movie clip is manipulated. The following code shows scaling take effect immediately, even before the image is displayed:

```
this.createEmptyMovieClip("jpgHolder", this.getNextHighestDepth());
jpgHolder._xscale = 50;
jpgHolder.loadMovie("http://www.nathanderksen.com/book/afternoonShower.jpg");
```

There is still one complication that needs to be dealt with. When images are loaded into a clip, the dimensions cannot be known until the image has completely loaded. In this case, a pre-loader is needed so that any code that relies on this information is called right after the image has finished loading. Pre-loaders are covered in detail in the next chapter.

Fully Qualified, Absolute, and Relative URLs

When passing a URL, you have the choice of three addresses to use:

❑ **A fully qualified address.** It loads media from any URL regardless of whether it is on the same server as the main Flash movie, or whether it is on the same server but in a different directory. It begins with a declaration of the name of the server hosting the file in the form of http:// <servername>/ and includes the full path to where the file to be loaded is located on the specified server. The following are examples of fully qualified addresses:

```
http://www.nathanderksen.com/book/sampleAnimation.swf
http://images.apple.com/ipod/gallery/images/ipodgalleryfamily20051011.jpg
```

❑ **An absolute address.** It loads media from anywhere on the same server. It always starts with a leading slash, and includes the full path to where the file to be loaded is located on the same server. The following are examples of absolute addresses:

```
/book/sampleAnimation.swf
/ipod/gallery/images/ipodgalleryfamily20051011.jpg
```

❑ **A relative address.** It assumes that the media to be loaded is in a fixed spot relative to where the main .swf file is located. The following are examples of relative addresses:

```
sampleAnimation.swf
images/ipodgalleryfamily20051011.jpg
```

Which address to use is generally up to you. Here are some things to consider in your decision:

❑ If the media you are loading is on a different server, you have no choice but to use a fully qualified address.

❑ It is preferable to use relative URLs because they are the same in your local development environment as they will be on a server. This means you can move the whole project to any location, and the links will all work.

❑ Absolute URLs may be appropriate if the media you are loading is to be on the same server as your main movie, but is outside of your control. If you move your files to a new location, the references will not break.

<hr>

Try It Out   **Creating Thumbnail Buttons**

This example extends the chapter's first Try It Out example, adding the capability to place externally loaded images in the buttons.

1. Create a new Macromedia Flash document.

2. Click the first frame in the timeline, open the Actions panel, and type in the following ActionScript code:

```
#include "tryItOut_thumbnailButtons.as"
```

3. Select File⇨Save As, name the file tryItOut_thumbnailButtons.fla, choose an appropriate directory, and save it.

4. Create a new Macromedia Flash document.

5. Name the file tryItOut_thumbnailButtons.as and save it in the directory containing the Flash project file.

6. Find the thumbnails folder in the Chapter 7 folder of the book source files and copy it to the same directory holding the .as and .fla files.

7. Type the following code into the new ActionScript file:

```
function createButton(buttonName:String, buttonLabel:String, ↩
buttonImage:String, parentClip:MovieClip, xPos:Number, yPos:Number) : Void
{
    var newClip:MovieClip = this.createEmptyMovieClip(buttonName, ↩
```

```
                parentClip.getNextHighestDepth());
        var thumbnailClip:MovieClip = ⤸
            newClip.createEmptyMovieClip("thumbnailClip", ⤸
            newClip.getNextHighestDepth());

        thumbnailClip.loadMovie(buttonImage);
        thumbnailClip._x = 5;
        thumbnailClip._y = 5;

        newClip._x = xPos;
        newClip._y = yPos;

        newClip.moveTo(0, 0);
        newClip.lineStyle(1, 0x666666);
        newClip.beginFill(0xFFFFFF, 100);
        newClip.lineTo(170, 0);
        newClip.lineTo(170, 60);
        newClip.lineTo(0, 60);
        newClip.lineTo(0, 0);
        newClip.endFill();

        newClip.createTextField("labelField", newClip.getNextHighestDepth(), ⤸
            60, 25, 100, 20);
        newClip.labelField.text = buttonLabel;

        newClip.onRelease = function()
        {
            trace("Pressed button: " + this._name);
        }
    }

    var ROOT_PATH:String = "thumbnails/";

    createButton("image1", "A Study In Texture", ⤸
        ROOT_PATH + "aStudyInTexture_off.jpg", this, 20, 20);
    createButton("image2", "Buntzen Winter", ⤸
        ROOT_PATH + "buntzenWinter_off.jpg", this, 20, 90);
    createButton("image3", "Flower In Detail", ⤸
        ROOT_PATH + "flowerInDetail_off.jpg", this, 20, 160);
    createButton("image4", "Galiano Sunset", ⤸
        ROOT_PATH + "galianoSunset_off.jpg", this, 20, 230);
```

8.   Save the file, return to the Macromedia Flash project file, and select Control⇨Test Movie.
     Clicking each of the buttons should produce a trace statement in the output panel.

How It Works

The function call has been modified to allow an additional parameter (shown in bold) to provide a path
to an image:

```
function createButton(buttonName:String, buttonLabel:String, ⤸
    buttonImage:String, parentClip:MovieClip, xPos:Number, yPos:Number) : Void
```

Within the function, two movie clips are created:

```
var newClip:MovieClip = this.createEmptyMovieClip(buttonName, ⏎
    parentClip.getNextHighestDepth());
var thumbnailClip:MovieClip = newClip.createEmptyMovieClip("thumbnailClip", ⏎
    newClip.getNextHighestDepth());
```

The first movie clip is an overall button container; the second is created within the first and is used to hold the image. The two nested clips are needed because loading external content removes event handlers and properties assigned to the movie clip, and controlling external content is easier when it sits within a dedicated movie clip.

Next the thumbnail image and the button container clips are loaded and positioned:

```
thumbnailClip.loadMovie(buttonImage);
thumbnailClip._x = 5;
thumbnailClip._y = 5;

newClip._x = xPos;
newClip._y = yPos;
```

A background color and an outline are drawn:

```
newClip.moveTo(0, 0);
newClip.lineStyle(1, 0x666666);
newClip.beginFill(0xFFFFFF, 100);
newClip.lineTo(170, 0);
newClip.lineTo(170, 60);
newClip.lineTo(0, 60);
newClip.lineTo(0, 0);
newClip.endFill();
```

Drawing a background serves more than just an aesthetic purpose; it also provides a larger area for the user to click on. Without the background, the user can activate the button by clicking the icon and the label, but the user cannot click the button just outside of those boundaries. Figure 7-2 illustrates the difference.

Figure 7-2

If you want to define a larger clickable area, but don't want a visible background, draw a background with the alpha set to 0 and with no line style. The shape still adds to the button's clickable area, but it isn't visible. The bold line in the following example shows how to create an invisible background by setting the alpha parameter of the beginFill() method to 0:

```
newClip.moveTo(0, 0);
newClip.beginFill(0xFFFFFF, 0);
newClip.lineTo(170, 0);
newClip.lineTo(170, 60);
```

```
newClip.lineTo(0, 60);
newClip.lineTo(0, 0);
newClip.endFill();
```

Next, the text field is created and a label is assigned:

```
newClip.createTextField("labelField", newClip.getNextHighestDepth(), ⊃
    60, 25, 100, 20);
newClip.labelField.text = buttonLabel;
```

The movie clip is made into a clickable button:

```
newClip.onRelease = function()
{
    trace("Pressed button: " + this._name);
}
```

Finally, four buttons are placed on the stage:

```
var ROOT_PATH:String = "http://www.nathanderksen.com/book/thumbnails/";

createButton("image1", "A Study In Texture", ⊃
    ROOT_PATH + "aStudyInTexture_off.jpg", this, 20, 20);
createButton("image2", "Buntzen Winter", ⊃
    ROOT_PATH + "buntzenWinter_off.jpg", this, 20, 90);
createButton("image3", "Flower In Detail", ⊃
    ROOT_PATH + "flowerInDetail_off.jpg", this, 20, 160);
createButton("image4", "Galiano Sunset", ⊃
    ROOT_PATH + "galianoSunset_off.jpg", this, 20, 230);
```

The `rootPath` constant is there to keep each `createButton()` call a bit shorter, and also so that if the location were to change, it would need to be updated in only one place.

Using Movie Clips as Masks

One of the cool things that you can do with movie clips is to mask them. *Masking* involves using the shape of one movie clip to indicate to another movie clip which parts should be visible. Figure 7-3 shows an example of using one shape to mask another.

  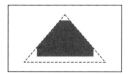

Shape   Mask   Masked Shape

Figure 7-3

This feature can be used for a number of things, such as ensuring that content does not fall outside a given area, creating transitions, and creating cursor reveal effects.

The basic form for applying a mask is as follows:

```
baseClip.setMask(maskClip:MovieClip) : Void
```

Only the shape of the mask is considered when it is applied to a movie clip. Any filters or blending modes that are applied do not have an impact on the masked shape. Also, one of the limitations of masks is that alpha transparency effects do not apply, so even if a mask symbol has an alpha value of zero, it still contributes to the overall mask shape.

In the following example two movie clips are created; a triangle is drawn in the content clip and a rectangle is drawn in the mask clip. Any part of the triangle that falls outside of the bounding box is not shown.

```
this.createEmptyMovieClip("contentClip", this.getNextHighestDepth());
this.createEmptyMovieClip("maskClip", this.getNextHighestDepth());

contentClip.beginFill(0x000066, 100);
contentClip.moveTo(200, 0);
contentClip.lineTo(400, 300);
contentClip.lineTo(0, 300);
contentClip.lineTo(200, 0);

maskClip.beginFill(0x000000, 100);
maskClip.moveTo(50, 50);
maskClip.lineTo(300, 50);
maskClip.lineTo(300, 250);
maskClip.lineTo(50, 250);
maskClip.lineTo(50, 50);

contentClip.setMask(maskClip);
```

Next, use a mask to create a camera-shutter transition effect.

Try It Out **Creating an Animated Masking Effect**

In this exercise you use an animated mask to achieve a transition effect: revealing an image by opening an animated camera iris.

1. Grab the file called `tryItOut_shutterMask.swf` from the Chapter 7 folder in the downloadable source folder and place the file in a convenient location.

2. Create a new Macromedia Flash document.

3. Click the first frame in the timeline, open the Actions panel, and type in the following ActionScript code:

```
#include "tryItOut_maskEffect.as"
```

4. Select File⇨Save As, name the file `tryItOut_maskEffect.fla`, choose the directory where you placed the shutter effect file in step 1, and save it.

5. Create a new Macromedia Flash document.

6. Select File⇨Save As and ensure it is showing the directory containing the Flash project file. Name the file `tryItOut_maskEffect.as` and save it.

7. Enter the following code into the new ActionScript file:

```
this.createEmptyMovieClip("imageHolderClip", this.getNextHighestDepth());
this.createEmptyMovieClip("maskClip", this.getNextHighestDepth());

var loadListener:Object = new Object();
loadListener.onLoadStart = function(contentHolder:MovieClip)
{
    contentHolder._visible = false;
    maskClip._visible = false;
}

loadListener.onLoadInit = function(contentHolder:MovieClip)
{
    if (contentHolder._name == "imageHolderClip")
    {
        contentHolder._x = Stage.width / 2 - contentHolder._width / 2;
        contentHolder._y = Stage.height / 2 - contentHolder._height / 2;
        contentLoader.loadClip("tryItOut_shutterMask.swf", maskClip);
    }
    else
    {
        imageHolderClip._visible = true;
        maskClip._xscale = 120;
        maskClip._yscale = 120;
        maskClip._x = -10;
        maskClip._y = -50;
        imageHolderClip.setMask(maskClip);
        maskClip.play();
    }
};

var contentLoader:MovieClipLoader = new MovieClipLoader();
contentLoader.addListener(loadListener);
contentLoader.loadClip("http://www.nathanderksen.com/book/afternoonShower.jpg", ⤴
    imageHolderClip);
```

8. Save the file, return to the Macromedia Flash project file, and select Control⇨Test Movie.

How It Works

Most of the code in this example is for handling the timing of loading two external movie clips. You want to make sure that the animation does not start until both the loaded image and the mask clip are ready, otherwise either the mask animation will start before the image is on the screen, or the mask may not be applied and a red shape will animate instead.

First, placeholder movie clips are created:

```
this.createEmptyMovieClip("imageHolderClip", this.getNextHighestDepth());
this.createEmptyMovieClip("maskClip", this.getNextHighestDepth());
```

Next, the pre-loader event handlers are defined:

```
var loadListener:Object = new Object();
loadListener.onLoadStart = function(contentHolder:MovieClip)
{
    contentHolder._visible = false;
    maskClip._visible = false;
}
```

The `onLoadStart` handler ensures that the movie clip holding the image does not show until the mask has been applied, otherwise there will be a short flicker where the full image is visible.

The `onLoadInit` handler is called when the image and the mask clip are both loaded and rendered onscreen, ready to be used:

```
loadListener.onLoadInit = function(contentHolder:MovieClip)
{
    if (contentHolder._name == "imageHolderClip")
    {
        contentHolder._x = Stage.width / 2 - contentHolder._width / 2;
        contentHolder._y = Stage.height / 2 - contentHolder._height / 2;
        contentLoader.loadClip("tryItOut_shutterMask.swf", maskClip);
    }
    else
    {
        imageHolderClip._visible = true;
        maskClip._xscale = 120;
        maskClip._yscale = 120;
        maskClip._x = -10;
        maskClip._y = -50;
        imageHolderClip.setMask(maskClip);
        maskClip.play();
    }
};
```

Because the same pre-loader is used for loading both the image and the mask, a check is done to see which clip has been loaded. If it is the image holder that has just finished loading, the image is centered onscreen, and then the mask is loaded. If it is the mask holder that has loaded, the mask is sized, positioned, and applied to the image holder movie clip. Take a look at the `tryItOut_shutterEffect.fla` file; you'll see that the movie clip used for the mask is in fact a multi-frame animation. As the animation plays, it changes which part of the image is masked, creating the iris effect.

Finally, the pre-loader class is set up, and the loading of the image is triggered:

```
var contentLoader:MovieClipLoader = new MovieClipLoader();
contentLoader.addListener(loadListener);
contentLoader.loadClip("http://www.nathanderksen.com/book/afternoonShower.jpg", ↩
    imageHolderClip);
```

Next, you take masking a step further.

Try It Out   **Creating a Mouse-Driven Masking Effect**

In this exercise you create a masking effect that follows the position of the cursor.

1. Create a new Macromedia Flash document.

2. Click the first frame in the timeline, open the Actions panel, and type in the following ActionScript code:

```
#include "tryItOut_maskEffect2.as"
```

3. Select File⇨Save As, name the file `tryItOut_maskEffect2.fla`, choose the directory where you placed the shutter effect file in step 1, and save it.

4. Create a new Macromedia Flash document.

5. Select File⇨Save As and ensure it is showing the directory containing the Flash project file. Name the file `tryItOut_maskEffect2.as` and save it.

6. Enter the following code into the new ActionScript file:

```
function drawCircle(movieClipHandle:MovieClip, x:Number, y:Number, ⤸
    radius:Number) : Void
{
    var c1 = radius * (Math.SQRT2 - 1);
    var c2 = radius * Math.SQRT2 / 2;

    movieClipHandle.beginFill(0x000000, 100);
    movieClipHandle.moveTo(x + radius, y);
    movieClipHandle.curveTo(x + radius, y + c1, x + c2, y + c2);
    movieClipHandle.curveTo(x + c1, y + radius, x, y + radius);
    movieClipHandle.curveTo(x - c1, y + radius, x - c2, y + c2);
    movieClipHandle.curveTo(x - radius, y + c1, x - radius, y);
    movieClipHandle.curveTo(x - radius, y - c1, x - c2, y - c2);
    movieClipHandle.curveTo(x - c1, y - radius, x, y - radius);
    movieClipHandle.curveTo(x + c1, y - radius, x + c2, y - c2);
    movieClipHandle.curveTo(x + radius, y - c1, x + radius, y);
}

this.createEmptyMovieClip("contentClip", this.getNextHighestDepth());
this.createEmptyMovieClip("maskClip", this.getNextHighestDepth());

contentClip.beginFill(0x000066, 100);
contentClip.moveTo(200, 0);
contentClip.lineTo(400, 300);
contentClip.lineTo(0, 300);
contentClip.lineTo(200, 0);

drawCircle(maskClip, 0, 0, 30);

contentClip.setMask(maskClip);

var mouseListener:Object = new Object();
```

```
mouseListener.onMouseMove = function()
{
    maskClip._x = _xmouse;
    maskClip._y = _ymouse;
}
Mouse.addListener(mouseListener);
```

7. Save the file, return to the Macromedia Flash project file, and select Control⇨Test Movie.

How It Works

This example uses a circular mask, so a function called `drawCircle()` handles the complexity of drawing the circle:

```
function drawCircle(movieClipHandle:MovieClip, x:Number, y:Number, ↪
    radius:Number) : Void
{
    // ...
}
```

Two movie clips are created — one for the main content and one for the mask:

```
this.createEmptyMovieClip("contentClip", this.getNextHighestDepth());
this.createEmptyMovieClip("maskClip", this.getNextHighestDepth());
```

A triangle is drawn to the main content movie clip:

```
contentClip.beginFill(0x000066, 100);
contentClip.moveTo(200, 0);
contentClip.lineTo(400, 300);
contentClip.lineTo(0, 300);
contentClip.lineTo(200, 0);
```

A circle is then drawn in the movie clip to be used for the mask:

```
drawCircle(maskClip, 0, 0, 30);
```

The event handler causes the position of the mask to be updated every time the mouse cursor moves:

```
var mouseListener:Object = new Object();
mouseListener.onMouseMove = function()
{
    maskClip._x = _xmouse;
    maskClip._y = _ymouse;
}
Mouse.addListener(mouseListener);
```

You see more about using event handlers in Chapter 9.

Improving Movie Clip Performance

Unfortunately, there is a limit as to how much complexity can be added before visible lags in animation playback occur. You can do a few things to reduce the impact of animation on the user's computer:

❑ Make use of bitmap caching for Flash 8 movies.

❑ Watch your use of transparency.

❑ Make use of the _visible property when targetting Flash Player version 7 and earlier.

❑ Moderate your use of filters and blending modes.

❑ Refrain from using full-screen movies.

Keep in mind that many people do not have machines as capable as yours.

Bitmap Caching

Macromedia Flash player version 8 includes a new feature designed to improve playback performance. All movie clips in Macromedia Flash take processing power to render for every frame, even if the contents within the movie clip do not animate. Any movie clip whose contents will not be animated can benefit from being marked for bitmap caching. At runtime, Flash goes through each movie clip so marked, renders it once as a bitmap, and then uses that bitmap instead of the movie clip for all future rendering purposes. Bitmaps are significantly faster to render than vector shapes, so the whole movie benefits from a speed boost.

Bitmap caching can be enabled from the visual development environment and also programmatically through ActionScript. Figure 7-4 shows the Properties panel checkbox to select to mark a movie clip for bitmap caching.

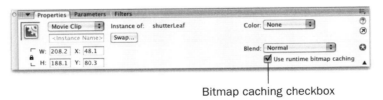

Bitmap caching checkbox

Figure 7-4

The same thing can be easily done with ActionScript:

```
movieClipInstance.cacheAsBitmap = true;
```

This property needs to be set for each movie clip instance to be cached.

Transparency

The transparency of a movie clip is the degree to which you can see content behind a movie clip. The degree of transparency of a movie clip is called its alpha value. An alpha value of 100 means that you cannot see through the movie clip, and an alpha value of 0 means that you cannot see the movie clip content, just the content behind the movie clip.

Transparency is one of the biggest causes of processor slowdown. The greater the number of movie clips that have an alpha value of 1 to 99, the bigger the processor drag is. If you have a complex animation within a movie clip and set the base movie clip to anything other than 100 alpha, each child of the movie clip needs to be involved in the alpha calculations as well.

The rule of thumb is that the greater the number of movie clips that have alpha effects applied to them and the greater the pixel dimensions of those clips, the slower the movie becomes.

Additionally, with Flash Player version 7 and earlier, movie clips that have an alpha value of 0 also take part in the rendering cycle. In version 8 of the player, an optimization was added to exclude movie clips with the _alpha property set to 0 from the rendering cycle. If you are targeting Flash Player version 7 or earlier and if you don't need a movie clip temporarily, set the _visible property of the clip to false instead of setting the _alpha property to 0. This prevents the renderer from trying to draw the clip and saves processor cycles. If you no longer need a movie clip at all, delete it from the stage using the removeMovieClip() method.

Filters and Blending Modes

Filters and blending modes are great additions to Flash 8, but they do require significant processing power from users' computers. In particular, filters can take a huge amount of processor power to render. If you are working with content that is not animated, there is no problem with applying both filters and blending modes. Performance primarily becomes an issue when you start adding filters and blending modes to animated content.

Be careful about applying filters and blending modes to animated content, and be especially careful about applying multiple filters to the same animated content simultaneously. Always remember that many people who view your work do not have as powerful a computer as you do.

Full Screen

Many people enjoy expanding their Flash presentations to take up the full screen. Unfortunately, the greater the pixel dimensions of the stage being used, the slower the animation. If you resist the temptation to present a full-screen site, the performance will be better, and your users will likely also appreciate having more screen real estate available for their other applications.

Summary

This chapter went into significant detail on using the movie clip. Some of the things you learned include the following:

❑ The movie clip is one of three primary symbol types. The other two types are the graphic symbol and the button symbol. Only the movie clip is suitable for most ActionScript programming tasks.

❑ New movie clips can be placed on the stage with the createEmptyMovieClip() method.

- Library content can be placed on the stage by assigning a linkage ID and then using the `attachMovie()` method.

- External content can be loaded by using the movie clip `loadMovie()` method, or by using the global `loadMovieNum()` function. Using `loadMovie()` is the preferred way to load external content.

- Movie clips can be used as masks, which allow some underlying content to show through and other content to remain hidden.

- Some strategies for improving playback performance include using bitmap caching; minimizing the use of transparency, filter, and blending mode effects; hiding content using the `_visible` property; and refraining from making projects full screen.

Exercises

1. Create a one-week calendar using `createEmptyMovieClip()`, `createNewTextField()`, and the movie clip drawing methods to draw it out. The calendar should consist of seven movie clips, each containing a text field and each outlined with a square. The calendar should also have next week and previous week buttons that call functions to go forward and back by one week, plus there should be a label for the current month. Consult with the Date object in the Flash help panel for the date methods to help you out. Hint: `var todaysDate:Date = new Date();` gets today's date.

2. Create two movie clips on the main timeline. Draw a square in the first clip and a triangle in the second clip by using the movie clip drawing methods. Apply the second movie clip as a mask over the first clip, and then switch them and apply the first movie clip as a mask over the second movie clip.

3. Extend exercise 2 to make the triangle clip move to follow the mouse. The code for responding to mouse movement is as follows:

```
var mouseListener:Object = new Object();
mouseListener.onMouseMove = function ()
{
    // Code to respond to mouse motion goes here
};
Mouse.addListener(mouseListener);
```

Pre-Loading Movies

When loading external content, situations frequently occur in which you need to wait until the content has completely loaded before you can work with that content. You also may have some external content that is quite large, and you just want to provide some feedback on the load progress.

Pre-loaders are useful any time content needs to be loaded, such as when the main movie is initially loaded, when movies are requested on demand, when images are loaded, or even when large amounts of XML data need to be transferred from a server. A pre-loader ensures that the content has completely loaded before allowing it to run. Once the content starts to download, it is periodically polled to see how many bytes have been loaded. When the number of bytes loaded is the same as the total number of bytes, the movie can proceed with the next step.

This chapter looks at a number of different pre-loading approaches. You go into the guts of creating one yourself so that you can see how a pre-loader actually works, explore the MovieClipLoader class, and learn to use the Loader and ProgressBar components. Finally you examine pre-loaders in the context of two project architectures. The first is the monolithic movie approach where all content is contained in a single `.swf` file. The second is the split-up movie approach, where a smaller shell is initially loaded, and subsequent content is loaded on demand.

Using a Custom Pre-Loader

The main tools you need to create a pre-loader from scratch are the `getBytesLoaded()` and `getBytesTotal()` methods, plus a timing mechanism. Here's what a first stab at it might look like:

Each of these code snippets is available in the downloadable content for this book. Feel free to experiment with each snippet.

```
var intervalID:Number;

this.createEmptyMovieClip("myMovie", this.getNextHighestDepth());
myMovie.loadMovie("http://www.nathanderksen.com/book/trailer.swf");
```

```
intervalID = setInterval(monitorProgress, 100);

function monitorProgress() : Void
{
    var percentDone:Number;
    percentDone = myMovie.getBytesLoaded() / myMovie.getBytesTotal() * 100;
    trace("percentDone: " + percentDone);
    if (myMovie.getBytesTotal() == myMovie.getBytesLoaded())
    {
        clearInterval(intervalID);
        trace("Content has finished loading.");
    }
}
```

This code creates a new movie clip to hold the content, starts the load process, and polls every 100 milliseconds to see how far the download has gotten. The timing mechanism takes the form of the setInterval() function, which is designed to call a designated function at predefined intervals, independent of whatever else is going on. The monitorProgress() function calculates the percent complete, and tests to see whether the movie has finished loading.

This is a good start, but the trace output that is generated when the code is run shows the following:

```
percentDone: NaN
Content has finished loading.
```

The problem is that it takes a little while for the player to contact the server to find out the size of the file. In the meantime, it returns zero, so when the percent done value is calculated, it suffers from a divide-by-zero error. (The value NaN that is returned stands for Not a Number, and commonly indicates a divide-by-zero error.) Adding a check for a zero value fixes this:

```
var intervalID:Number;

this.createEmptyMovieClip("myMovie", this.getNextHighestDepth());
myMovie.loadMovie("http://www.nathanderksen.com/book/trailer.swf");
intervalID = setInterval(monitorProgress, 100);

function monitorProgress() : Void
{
    var percentDone:Number;
    if (myMovie.getBytesLoaded() > 0)
    {
        percentDone = myMovie.getBytesLoaded() / myMovie.getBytesTotal() * 100;
        trace("percentDone: " + percentDone);
        if (myMovie.getBytesTotal() == myMovie.getBytesLoaded())
        {
            clearInterval(intervalID);
            trace("Content has finished loading.");
        }
    }
}
```

That's definitely better. Now, nothing is done until it is known how large the loaded content is. Unfortunately, the movie starts playing as soon as the first bit of content loads, and you want to delay when the movie starts playing. One solution is to stop the playhead and hide the clip as soon as the movie starts to load. When the movie has finished loading, playback is allowed to start and the clip is displayed:

```
var intervalID:Number;

this.createEmptyMovieClip("myMovie", this.getNextHighestDepth());
myMovie.loadMovie("http://www.nathanderksen.com/book/trailer.swf");
intervalID = setInterval(monitorProgress, 100);

function monitorProgress() : Void
{
    var percentDone:Number;
    myMovie.stop();
    myMovie._visible = false;
    if (myMovie.getBytesLoaded() > 0)
    {
        percentDone = myMovie.getBytesLoaded() / myMovie.getBytesTotal() * 100;
        trace("percentDone: " + percentDone);
        if (myMovie.getBytesTotal() == myMovie.getBytesLoaded())
        {
            clearInterval(intervalID);
            myMovie.play();
            myMovie._visible = true;
            trace("Content has finished loading.");
        }
    }
}
```

The only drawback is that there's no way for the person viewing the content to know the progress of the content loading. Create a function that draws out a progress bar and call it from the monitorProgress() function:

```
var intervalID:Number;

this.createEmptyMovieClip("myMovie", this.getNextHighestDepth());
this.createEmptyMovieClip("progressMovie", this.getNextHighestDepth());
progressMovie._x = 60;
progressMovie._y = 120;
progressMovie.createTextField("percentDoneLabel", ⟳
    progressMovie.getNextHighestDepth(), 40, 0, 100, 20);

myMovie.loadMovie("http://www.nathanderksen.com/book/trailer.swf");
intervalID = setInterval(monitorProgress, 100);

function monitorProgress() : Void
{
    var percentDone:Number;
    myMovie.stop();
    myMovie._visible = false;
    if (myMovie.getBytesLoaded() > 0)
```

```
        {
            percentDone = myMovie.getBytesLoaded() / myMovie.getBytesTotal() * 100;
            showProgress(percentDone);
            trace("percentDone: " + percentDone);
            if (myMovie.getBytesTotal() == myMovie.getBytesLoaded())
            {
                clearInterval(intervalID);
                myMovie.play();
                myMovie._visible = true;
                progressMovie._visible = false;
                trace("Content has finished loading.");
            }
        }
    }
}

function showProgress(percentDone:Number) : Void
{
    var barWidth:Number = percentDone;
    progressMovie.percentDoneLabel.text = String(Math.ceil(percentDone)) + " %";
    progressMovie.clear();

    // Draw a border
    progressMovie.moveTo(0, 20);
    progressMovie.lineStyle(1, 0x666666);
    progressMovie.lineTo(100, 20);
    progressMovie.lineTo(100, 30);
    progressMovie.lineTo(0, 30);
    progressMovie.lineTo(0, 20);

    // Draw the bar
    progressMovie.moveTo(0, 20);
    progressMovie.beginFill(0xCCCCCC, 100);
    progressMovie.lineTo(barWidth, 20);
    progressMovie.lineTo(barWidth, 30);
    progressMovie.lineTo(0, 30);
    progressMovie.lineTo(0, 20);
    progressMovie.endFill();
}
```

First, a movie clip is created to hold the loading animation. Every time checkProgress() is called, the showProgress() function is also called. When loading is complete, the pre-loader animation is hidden.

You now have a pre-loader that provides control over the loaded content and provides feedback to the user, yet the implementation could be cleaned up a bit. The hitch is that this code is very specific to the project, with movie clip references embedded right in the checkProgress() function. It would help if you could pass a couple of parameters instead of hard-coding the references, like this:

```
var intervalID:Number;

this.createEmptyMovieClip("myMovie", this.getNextHighestDepth());
this.createEmptyMovieClip("progressMovie", this.getNextHighestDepth());
progressMovie._x = 60;
progressMovie._y = 120;
```

```
progressMovie.createTextField("percentDoneLabel",
progressMovie.getNextHighestDepth(), 40, 0, 100, 20);

myMovie.loadMovie("http://www.nathanderksen.com/book/trailer.swf");
intervalID = setInterval(monitorProgress, 100, progressMovie, showProgress);

function monitorProgress(progressBarHolder:MovieClip, ⤶
    progressUpdater:Function) : Void
{
    var percentDone:Number;
    myMovie.stop();
    myMovie._visible = false;
    if (myMovie.getBytesLoaded() > 0)
    {
        percentDone = myMovie.getBytesLoaded() / myMovie.getBytesTotal() * 100;
        progressUpdater(percentDone, progressBarHolder);
        trace("percentDone: " + percentDone);
        if (myMovie.getBytesTotal() == myMovie.getBytesLoaded())
        {
            clearInterval(intervalID);
            myMovie.play();
            myMovie._visible = true;
            progressBarHolder._visible = false;
            trace("Content has finished loading.");
        }
    }
}

function showProgress(percentDone:Number, progressBarHolder:MovieClip) : Void
{
    var barWidth:Number = percentDone;

    progressBarHolder._visible = true;
    progressBarHolder.percentDoneLabel.text = String(Math.ceil(percentDone))+" %";
    progressBarHolder.clear();

    // Draw a border
    progressBarHolder.moveTo(0, 20);
    progressBarHolder.lineStyle(1, 0x666666);
    progressBarHolder.lineTo(100, 20);
    progressBarHolder.lineTo(100, 30);
    progressBarHolder.lineTo(0, 30);
    progressBarHolder.lineTo(0, 20);

    // Draw the bar
    progressBarHolder.moveTo(0, 20);
    progressBarHolder.beginFill(0xCCCCCC, 100);
    progressBarHolder.lineTo(barWidth, 20);
    progressBarHolder.lineTo(barWidth, 30);
    progressBarHolder.lineTo(0, 30);
    progressBarHolder.lineTo(0, 20);
    progressBarHolder.endFill();
}
```

This code is now easier to re-use because the hard-coded references to the progress bar holder and to showProgress() have been changed to parameters that can be passed in instead.

Polling with onEnterFrame() Versus setInterval()

There is a variation of the preceding technique to poll for the number of bytes loaded. `setInterval()` was last used to call a function at predetermined intervals, but there's another timing mechanism that can be used as well: the `onEnterFrame()` event handler. Every time the playhead advances to another frame, an `onEnterFrame()` event handler is called by the player. You can make use of this to call your polling code. Here's an example of how:

```
var intervalID:Number;

this.createEmptyMovieClip("myMovie", this.getNextHighestDepth());
this.createEmptyMovieClip("progressMovie", this.getNextHighestDepth());
progressMovie._x = 60;
progressMovie._y = 120;
progressMovie.createTextField("percentDoneLabel",
progressMovie.getNextHighestDepth(), 40, 0, 100, 20);

myMovie.loadMovie("http://www.nathanderksen.com/book/trailer.swf");
this.onEnterFrame = function()
{
    monitorProgress(this, progressMovie, showProgress);
}

function monitorProgress(contentHolder:MovieClip, progressBarHolder:MovieClip, ⤶
    progressUpdater:Function) : Void
{
    var percentDone:Number;
    myMovie.stop();
    myMovie._visible = false;
    if (myMovie.getBytesLoaded() > 0)
    {
        percentDone = myMovie.getBytesLoaded() / myMovie.getBytesTotal() * 100;
        progressUpdater(percentDone, progressBarHolder);
        trace("percentDone: " + percentDone);
        if (myMovie.getBytesTotal() == myMovie.getBytesLoaded())
        {
            clearInterval(intervalID);
            myMovie.play();
            myMovie._visible = true;
            progressBarHolder._visible = false;
            delete contentHolder.onEnterFrame;
            trace("Content has finished loading.");
        }
    }
}

function showProgress(percentDone:Number, progressBarHolder:MovieClip) : Void
{
    var barWidth:Number = percentDone;

    progressBarHolder._visible = true;
```

```
progressBarHolder.percentDoneLabel.text = String(Math.ceil(percentDone))+" %";
progressBarHolder.clear();

// Draw a border
progressBarHolder.moveTo(0, 20);
progressBarHolder.lineStyle(1, 0x666666);
progressBarHolder.lineTo(100, 20);
progressBarHolder.lineTo(100, 30);
progressBarHolder.lineTo(0, 30);
progressBarHolder.lineTo(0, 20);

// Draw the bar
progressBarHolder.moveTo(0, 20);
progressBarHolder.beginFill(0xCCCCCC, 100);
progressBarHolder.lineTo(barWidth, 20);
progressBarHolder.lineTo(barWidth, 30);
progressBarHolder.lineTo(0, 30);
progressBarHolder.lineTo(0, 20);
progressBarHolder.endFill();
}
```

In this code, the `onEnterFrame()` event from the base timeline is captured and used. You could have captured the event from the `myMovie` clip; however, the act of loading content into that movie clip removes the handle to your custom `onEnterFrame()` event handler after the first time through. An additional parameter is sent through to the `monitorProgress()` function so that when the clip has finished loading, the custom event handler can be removed.

The reason why one technique might be used over another is largely personal. Some find `onEnterFrame()` easier to work with, and are accustomed to using it for animation. Others prefer the `setInterval()` technique because it is kinder on the main processor for slower machines and allows flexibility with how frequently the progress bar is to be updated. Although we generally prefer the `setInterval()` technique, you should use whichever one is more comfortable for you.

Understanding the MovieClipLoader Class

Now that you have created a full-fledged pre-loader, take a look at another option, the MovieClipLoader class. The advantage of this class is that it takes care of a lot of these details for you and it gives fine control over what code gets called at which stage in the load process. Following are the events and methods that are available with the MovieClipLoader class.

MovieClipLoader Class Events

The MovieClipLoader class provides a number of events that fire at different points through the process of loading a movie clip or image. These events allow you to customize how your code interacts with externally loaded media throughout the loading process. You see examples of these events in use along with the introduction of the MovieClipLoader class methods. The following table describes the events of the MovieClipLoader class:

Event	Type	Description
onLoadComplete	Listener	Fires when the all the content has been downloaded.
onLoadError	Listener	Fires when the content load process fails.
onLoadInit	Listener	Fires when the first frame of the loaded content has been run. For images, this happens after onLoadComplete. For movie clips, this happens before onLoadComplete.
onLoadProgress	Listener	Fires every time content is written to disc.
onLoadStart	Listener	Fires when the content has successfully begun to download.

MovieClipLoader Class Methods

Four class methods are available for you to use to load and unload media, to get the load progress, and to work with events. The following table delineates the methods of the MovieClipLoader class:

Method	Return	Description
addListener	Boolean	Binds the loader instance to an object that defines the event handlers.
getProgress	Object	Provides access to the bytes loaded and total bytes for the currently loading movie clip.
loadClip	Boolean	Starts the loading of a movie clip. Used instead of the movie clip loadMovie() method.
unloadClip	Boolean	Removes the movie clip that was loaded with loadClip().

The following sections demonstrate how to use these methods.

addListener()

The addListener() method binds the loader to an object holding the event handlers. It takes a single parameter, which is a handle to an object holding the event handler code. The following prototype shows the basic form of the addListener() method:

```
loaderObject.addListener(listener:Object) : Boolean
```

Here's an example implementation that loads an external movie clip called section1.swf into a movie clip called sectionHolder. The example demonstrates how to create an event listener, and to link the listener with the loader. By creating a custom method with the listener object that has the same name as the name of the event to be handled, the method is automatically called when the event takes place.

```
this.createEmptyMovieClip("sectionHolder", this.getNextHighestDepth());

var loadListener:Object = new Object();
```

```
loadListener.onLoadComplete = function(contentHolder:MovieClip)
{
    trace("Content has been loaded");
};

var contentLoader:MovieClipLoader = new MovieClipLoader();
contentLoader.addListener(loadListener);
contentLoader.loadClip("section1.swf", sectionHolder);
```

getProgress()

The `getProgress()` method is used to manually get the progress of the loaded content. Normally, the `onLoadProgress` event provides this information.

This method takes a single parameter, which is a handle to the movie clip container. It is a way of explicitly getting the bytes loaded and bytes total values for the movie clip being loaded. The return object contains two parameters, `bytesLoaded` and `bytesTotal`. The following prototype shows the basic form of the `getProgress()` method:

```
loaderObject.getProgress(targetClip:MovieClip) : Object
```

The method returns an anonymous object with two properties, `bytesLoaded` and `bytesTotal`. Here's an example:

```
var contentLoader:MovieClipLoader = new MovieClipLoader();

this.createEmptyMovieClip("sectionHolder", this.getNextHighestDepth());

function checkProgress()
{
    var statusObject:Object = contentLoader.getProgress(contentHolder);
    trace("bytes loaded: " + statusObject.bytesLoaded);
    trace("bytes total: " + statusObject.bytesTotal);
}

setInterval(checkProgress, 50);
contentLoader.loadClip("section1.swf", sectionHolder);
```

loadClip()

The `loadClip()` method triggers the actual loading of the media and is used instead of the movie clip `loadMovie()` method. The `MovieClip.loadMovie()` method also works for loading external media, however it does not allow you to work with load events as easily as the MovieClipLoader class does. The `loadClip()` method takes two parameters: the URL for the movie clip to load and a handle to the movie clip container that is to receive the content. The following prototype shows the basic form of the `loadClip()` method:

```
loaderObject.loadClip(url:String, target:Object) : Boolean
```

Here's an example implementation that loads an external movie clip called `section1.swf` into a movie clip called `sectionHolder`:

```
this.createEmptyMovieClip("sectionHolder", this.getNextHighestDepth());

var loadListener:Object = new Object();
loadListener.onLoadComplete = function(contentHolder:MovieClip)
{
    trace("Content has been loaded");
};

var contentLoader:MovieClipLoader = new MovieClipLoader();
contentLoader.addListener(loadListener);
contentLoader.loadClip("section1.swf", sectionHolder);
```

removeListener()

The `removeListener()` method is used to break the binding between the event handlers and the pre-loader. It takes one parameter, which is the handle to the listener object that was initially passed in to the `addListener()` method. The following prototype shows the basic form of the `removeListener()` method:

```
loaderObject.removeListener(listener:Object) : Boolean
```

If, for example, you want to hold up playback until enough of the movie has downloaded to ensure that playback is not impeded by network delays, you could handle it like the following example, which removes the listener and starts playback after 50% of the movie has downloaded:

```
this.createEmptyMovieClip("sectionHolder", this.getNextHighestDepth());

var loadListener:Object = new Object();
loadListener.onLoadProgress = function(contentHolder:MovieClip, ⤸
    bytesLoaded:Number, bytesTotal:Number)
{
    var percentDone:Number = bytesLoaded / bytesTotal * 100;
    if (percentDone > 50)
    {
        contentHolder.play();
        contentLoader.removeListener(this);
    }
};

var contentLoader:MovieClipLoader = new MovieClipLoader();
contentLoader.addListener(loadListener);
contentLoader.loadClip("section1.swf", sectionHolder);
```

unloadClip()

Media should be properly unloaded from the movie clip before another clip is loaded. The `unloadClip()` method takes one parameter, which is a handle to the movie clip containing the loaded media. The following prototype shows the basic form of the `unloadClip()` method:

```
loaderObject.unloadClip(target:Object) : Boolean
```

The following example shows how you can unload a movie clip:

```
this.createEmptyMovieClip("sectionHolder", this.getNextHighestDepth());

var contentLoader:MovieClipLoader = new MovieClipLoader();
contentLoader.loadClip("section1.swf", sectionHolder);

cancelButton.onRelease = function()
{
    contentLoader.unloadClip(sectionHolder);
};
```

Implementing the MovieClipLoader Class

With an understanding of the MovieClipLoader class, you're ready to put it into action. First, put together a shell for the event handlers and tie that in to a new loader instance:

```
this.createEmptyMovieClip("sectionHolder", this.getNextHighestDepth());

var loadListener:Object = new Object();
loadListener.onLoadStart = function(contentHolder:MovieClip)
{
};

loadListener.onLoadProgress = function(contentHolder:MovieClip, ⊃
    bytesLoaded:Number, bytesTotal:Number)
{
};

loadListener.onLoadComplete = function(contentHolder:MovieClip)
{
};

var contentLoader:MovieClipLoader = new MovieClipLoader();
contentLoader.addListener(loadListener);
contentLoader.loadClip("http://www.nathanderksen.com/book/trailer.swf", ⊃
    sectionHolder);
```

Here, an empty object is created, and one method is added for each event to be handled. Not all events have to be handled, just the ones that you need. A new instance of the loader class is created and is bound to this object. Finally, the clip is loaded into the container movie clip. At this point you have a working pre-loader; it just does not call anything yet before, during, or after loading.

Each of these code snippets is available in the downloadable content for this book. Feel free to experiment with each snippet.

Like the custom loader created previously, you still need to provide visual feedback for the user. Add the shell code for this:

```
this.createEmptyMovieClip("sectionHolder", this.getNextHighestDepth());
this.createEmptyMovieClip("progressMovie", this.getNextHighestDepth());
progressMovie._x = 60;
progressMovie._y = 120;
```

```
progressMovie.createTextField("percentDoneLabel",
progressMovie.getNextHighestDepth(), 40, 0, 100, 20);

var loadListener:Object = new Object();
loadListener.onLoadStart = function(contentHolder:MovieClip)
{
};

loadListener.onLoadProgress = function(contentHolder:MovieClip, ⤸
    bytesLoaded:Number, bytesTotal:Number)
{
};

loadListener.onLoadComplete = function(contentHolder:MovieClip)
{
};

var contentLoader:MovieClipLoader = new MovieClipLoader();
contentLoader.addListener(loadListener);
contentLoader.loadClip("http://www.nathanderksen.com/book/trailer.swf", ⤸
    sectionHolder);
```

```
function showProgress(percentDone:Number, progressBarHolder:MovieClip) : Void
{
    var barWidth:Number = percentDone;
    progressBarHolder.percentDoneLabel.text = String(Math.ceil(percentDone))+" %";
    progressBarHolder.clear();

    // Draw a border
    progressBarHolder.moveTo(0, 20);
    progressBarHolder.lineStyle(1, 0x666666);
    progressBarHolder.lineTo(100, 20);
    progressBarHolder.lineTo(100, 30);
    progressBarHolder.lineTo(0, 30);
    progressBarHolder.lineTo(0, 20);

    // Draw the bar
    progressBarHolder.moveTo(0, 20);
    progressBarHolder.beginFill(0xCCCCCC, 100);
    progressBarHolder.lineTo(barWidth, 20);
    progressBarHolder.lineTo(barWidth, 30);
    progressBarHolder.lineTo(0, 30);
    progressBarHolder.lineTo(0, 20);
    progressBarHolder.endFill();
}
```

As before, a movie clip holds the progress bar and the percent progress text field, and the
showProgress() function draws the progress bar and updates the percent progress value.

Finally, you need to fill out the event handlers:

```
this.createEmptyMovieClip("sectionHolder", this.getNextHighestDepth());
this.createEmptyMovieClip("progressMovie", this.getNextHighestDepth());
progressMovie._x = 60;
```

```
progressMovie._y = 120;
progressMovie.createTextField("percentDoneLabel",
progressMovie.getNextHighestDepth(), 40, 0, 100, 20);

var loadListener:Object = new Object();
loadListener.onLoadStart = function(contentHolder:MovieClip)
{
    progressMovie._visible = true;
    contentHolder._visible = false;
    contentHolder.stop();
};

loadListener.onLoadProgress = function(contentHolder:MovieClip, ⤴
    bytesLoaded:Number, bytesTotal:Number)
{
    var percentDone:Number = bytesLoaded / bytesTotal * 100;
    showProgress(percentDone, progressMovie);
};

loadListener.onLoadComplete = function(contentHolder:MovieClip)
{
    progressMovie._visible = false;
    contentHolder._visible = true;
    contentHolder.play();
};

var contentLoader:MovieClipLoader = new MovieClipLoader();
contentLoader.addListener(loadListener);
contentLoader.loadClip("http://www.nathanderksen.com/book/trailer.swf", ⤴
    sectionHolder);

function showProgress(percentDone:Number, progressBarHolder:MovieClip) : Void
{
    var barWidth:Number = percentDone;
    progressBarHolder.percentDoneLabel.text = String(Math.ceil(percentDone))+" %";
    progressBarHolder.clear();

    // Draw a border
    progressBarHolder.moveTo(0, 20);
    progressBarHolder.lineStyle(1, 0x666666);
    progressBarHolder.lineTo(100, 20);
    progressBarHolder.lineTo(100, 30);
    progressBarHolder.lineTo(0, 30);
    progressBarHolder.lineTo(0, 20);

    // Draw the bar
    progressBarHolder.moveTo(0, 20);
    progressBarHolder.beginFill(0xCCCCCC, 100);
    progressBarHolder.lineTo(barWidth, 20);
    progressBarHolder.lineTo(barWidth, 30);
    progressBarHolder.lineTo(0, 30);
    progressBarHolder.lineTo(0, 20);
    progressBarHolder.endFill();
}
```

The custom loader created earlier had no designated spot to put initialization code and required a manual test to see if the bytesLoaded() method returned zero. The MovieClipLoader class gives you an onLoadStart event that is a good place for initialization code, and the class deals with some of the intricacies of load startup so that you do not have to.

A good thing to add to this code is an onLoadError event handler. This handler provides a graceful response to an incorrect URL or an interrupted transfer. You have an opportunity to add this event handler in an end-of-chapter exercise.

Examining the Loader and ProgressBar Components

One of the tradeoffs with using a pre-existing component versus one created from scratch is that there is a balance between complexity and control. Your homemade pre-loader is definitely the most flexible, but also requires the most work. The MovieClipLoader class takes control over how the polling process works during the load, but it makes up for it in reusability. The Loader and ProgressBar components do the most to take over the work of implementing loader code and implementing visual feedback drawing code, but using them restricts you to the features provided by the components.

One drawback to the Loader and ProgressBar components is that they cause Flash to compile the whole component framework into the movie you are creating. The framework together with the two components results in around 32 kilobytes of additional file size that needs to be loaded. This makes these components unsuitable for the initial loading of content, because it takes a while before the progress status makes it to the screen. Instead, these components work better for situations where you need to load chunks of content in a piecemeal fashion after the main content has loaded.

Before going into how to implement the Loader and ProgressBar components, take a look at their properties, methods, and events.

Loader Component Method, Properties, and Events

The Loader component is a container to load content into, and it can hold either an .swf file or a .jpg file. With version 8 of the Flash player, it also supports .gif and .png files, including those with transparency. Whereas the MovieClipLoader class requires a movie clip to be provided, the Loader component comes with its own movie clip.

There's only one Loader method, load(), which triggers the start of the load process. It takes either no argument or one single argument. If no argument is given, the contentPath property must have been specified beforehand. If one argument is given, it is a string representing the path to the content to be loaded. load() returns nothing. The following prototype shows the basic form of the load() method:

```
loaderInstance.load([contentPath:String]) : Void
```

If the autoLoad property is set to true, then setting the contentPath property automatically triggers the load, making the load() method unnecessary.

Following is a delineation of the component's properties:

Property	Type	Description
autoLoad	Boolean	If true, content loads immediately upon setting the content Path property. If false, the loader waits for a load() call.
bytesLoaded	Number	The total number of bytes loaded. (Read only.)
bytesTotal	Number	The total number of bytes for the content. (Read only.)
content	MovieClip	A handle to the movie clip holding the content. (Read only.)
contentPath	String	The path to the loaded content.
percentLoaded	Number	The percentage of the content already loaded. (Read only.)
scaleContent	Boolean	If true, content scales to fit the size of the loader. If false, content is not scaled and the loader size adjusts to fit.

The Loader component has two events, described in the following table.

Event	Type	Description
complete	Listener	Fires when the content has finished loading.
progress	Listener	Fires repeatedly during the load process.

ProgressBar Component Method, Properties, and Events

The ProgressBar component works alongside the Loader component to provide visual feedback of the media load progress. This component has only one method: setProgress(). The setProgress() method is for setting the progress values manually, and works only when the mode property is set to manual. It takes two arguments: first, a value for the total amount loaded and, second, a value for the total to load. The following prototype shows the basic form of the setProgress() method:

```
progressBarInstance.setProgress(completed:Number, total:Number) : Void
```

You can use the progress bar in manual mode for purposes other than recording bytes loaded. It can, for example, show a progression of number of files loaded where completed *represents the number of files loaded and* total *indicates the total number of files to load.*

The ProgressBar component's properties are described in the following table.

Property	Type	Description
conversion	Number	Conversion factor for converting bytes loaded into another unit for display purposes. Using a value of 1024 converts bytes loaded into kilobytes loaded.
direction	String	The direction that the progress bar advances. Values available are left and right.
indeterminate	Boolean	If true, an animated striped fill is used instead of a solid fill. Used when loading content of unknown size. If false, the progress bar advances normally.
label	String	The text to use to indicate loading progress. The text can include the key strings %1, %2, %3, and %%. The first is a placeholder for bytes loaded, the second is for total bytes, the third is for percent loaded, and the final is to show a percent symbol. A sample label is %1 out of %2 bytes loaded, %3%% complete.
labelPlacement	String	Sets the position of the label relative to the progress bar. Possible values are left, right, top, bottom, and center.
maximum	Number	Holds the largest progress value for when the mode property is set to manual.
minimum	Number	Holds the smallest progress value for when the mode property is set to manual.
mode	String	Controls how progress deals with loaded content. Possible values are event, polled, and manual. The value event is for working with the Loader component, polled is for working with movie clips, and manual is for manual setting the progress.
percentComplete	Number	Indicates the percentage of the content that has been loaded. (Read only.)
source	Object	A source of progress information. Can be a Loader component or a movie clip.
value	Number	Indicates the progress that has been made between the minimum and maximum properties when the mode property is set to manual.

The following table delineates the ProgressBar component's two events:

Event	Type	Description
complete	Listener	Fires when the content has finished loading.
progress	Listener	Fires repeatedly during the load process.

Implementing the Loader and ProgressBar Components

Unlike a class, which is either available directly from the player or is compiled into the .swf by design, components are not automatically included in the compile. You can call the code to create a new instance on the stage, but if the component isn't in the library, it won't appear on the stage. You have two ways to place a copy of a component in the library:

❑ Drag one of each component needed from the Components panel onto the stage and then delete each one from the stage. Dragging a component to the stage automatically places the component in the library. This is the standard approach in the Flash MX 2004 authoring environment.

❑ In the Flash 8 authoring environment, drag each component needed from the Components panel onto the Library panel.

With that done, you can create instances of the two components:

```
this.createClassObject(mx.controls.Loader, "loaderComponent", ↵
    this.getNextHighestDepth());
this.createClassObject(mx.controls.ProgressBar, "progressComponent", ↵
    this.getNextHighestDepth());
progressComponent._x = 50;
progressComponent._y = 100;
```

This code creates an instance of the Loader component and of the ProgressBar component and places them on the stage with the instance IDs loaderComponent and progressComponent. It also positions the progress bar so that it will show in the middle of the loader component. The createClassObject() method enables you to place any component on the stage programmatically instead of having to manually place each instance on the stage. This method is described in more detail in Chapter 9.

Next, you place the code to actually work with these components. By setting the source property of the progress bar to point to loaderComponent, the two are linked and the progress bar automatically reflects the status of the loader component:

```
this.createClassObject(mx.controls.Loader, "loaderComponent", ↵
    this.getNextHighestDepth());
this.createClassObject(mx.controls.ProgressBar, "progressComponent", ↵
    this.getNextHighestDepth());
progressComponent._x = 50;
progressComponent._y = 100;

progressComponent.source = loaderComponent;
loaderComponent.scaleContent = false;
loaderComponent.load("http://www.nathanderksen.com/book/trailer.swf");
```

Now you have a working progress bar. The source property links up the loader as a source of progress information for the bar to use. The scaleContent property makes sure that the content does not scale to the size of the Loader component; instead, the component resizes itself to accommodate whatever dimensions the content ends up having.

A couple of issues remain. First, the content starts playing before loading is done, and second, the progress bar stays around after loading is complete. These can be dealt with by adding a couple of event listeners:

```
this.createClassObject(mx.controls.Loader, "loaderComponent", ⤵
    this.getNextHighestDepth());
this.createClassObject(mx.controls.ProgressBar, "progressComponent", ⤵
    this.getNextHighestDepth());
progressComponent._x = 50;
progressComponent._y = 100;
```

```
var loadHandler:Object = new Object();
loadHandler.progress = function(eventObject:Object)
{
    loaderComponent.content.stop();
}


loadHandler.complete = function(eventObject:Object)
{
    loaderComponent.content.play();
    progressComponent._visible = false;
}
```

```
progressComponent.source = loaderComponent;
loaderComponent.scaleContent = false;
loaderComponent.addEventListener("progress", loadHandler);
loaderComponent.addEventListener("complete", loadHandler);
loaderComponent.load("http://www.nathanderksen.com/book/trailer.swf");
```

Here, two events are defined and then bound to the Loader instance. Unfortunately the Loader component only provides a `progress` event and a `complete` event. As a result, the initialization code to stop the playback of the loaded movie clip until it is complete has to go into the `progress` event handler. This means that the initialization code is called many times when it only needs to be called once, but that's not enough to hamper performance.

Note the amount of code that is needed to implement the Loader and ProgressBar components versus the MovieClipLoader class and versus our homegrown loader. The homegrown loader code took around 43 lines of code to implement, the MovieClipLoader class took roughly 38 lines of code, and the component implementation took about 15 lines of code. Most of this savings in code from using the components comes from replacing the drawing function with two lines of code to use the ProgressBar component. This component can also work with the MovieClipLoader class, as you see in the exercises at the end of this chapter.

One frequent question that developers ask is how to customize the appearance of the Loader component. The `setStyle()` method that is available for any component provides a capability to customize aspects of component appearance. The following snippet shows how the text color, text size, and progress bar color properties can be changed:

```
progressComponent.setStyle("color", 0x0000CC);
progressComponent.setStyle("fontSize", 14);
progressComponent.setStyle("themeColor", 0xCC0000);
```

The styles that can be changed for the Loader component are described in the following table.

Style	Type	Description
themeColor	String or Number	Color to use for component accents, in this case the color for the progress bar itself. Possible values are haloGreen, haloBlue, haloOrange, or a numerical color value.
color	Number	Color for label text.
disabledColor	Number	Color for label text when the component is disabled.
embedFonts	Boolean	Set to true if the font specified in the fontFamily style is an embedded font, set to false otherwise.
fontFamily	String	The name of the font to use for the label.
fontSize	Number	The pixel size of the font to display for the label.
fontStyle	String	The style of the label text. Possible values are normal and italic.
fontWeight	Number	The weight of the label text. Possible values are bold and none.
textDecoration	Boolean	Indicates whether the label text should be underlined. Possible values are underline and none.
barColor	Number	The color of the progress bar. Has no effect with the default Halo theme.
trackColor	Number	The color of the progress track. Has no effect with the default Halo theme.

Strategies for Using Pre-Loaders

The structure of your main project determines in part how you implement a loader. Two approaches to consider are the monolithic movie approach and the split-up movie approach.

The Monolithic Movie Approach

If having a very responsive interface is important, or if you are just looking for a simple project structure and straightforward implementation, the monolithic movie approach is likely the one you will want to use. This approach suffers from a longer initial load time but benefits from quicker response once the movie has loaded. Many ways of implementing a pre-loader for a monolithic movie exist, only one of which we will talk about, which is the loader shim technique. This technique actually makes use of two movies. The first movie is the loader movie, sometimes referred to as a loader *shim*, which, because of its small size, loads to the user's browser very quickly. Once loaded, the shim loads the primary .swf. This technique is very easy to implement. Just develop your project as you normally would, and then at the end create the loader shim and give it the path to your main movie.

Try It Out   Using the Monolithic Approach

In Chapter 6, you completed a number of Try It Out exercises that worked with a portfolio project. Now you extend that project to incorporate a pre-loader.

1. Open the file <downloaded files>/Chapter 8/portfolio v6/portfolio.as.

2. Go through the file looking for all instances of _level0 and change them to the this keyword. For example, _level0.createEmptyMovieClip should be this.createEmptyMovieClip and _level0["screenHolder"] should be this["screenHolder"]. Four changes are needed.

3. Save the file and close it.

4. Go to <downloaded files>/Chapter 8/portfolio v6, and open the file portfolio.fla.

5. Publish the movie (File⇨Publish), and then close the file.

6. Create a new Macromedia Flash document by selecting File⇨New and choosing Flash Document from the New Document panel.

7. Click the first frame in the timeline, open the Actions panel (Window⇨Development Panels⇨Actions), and type in the following ActionScript code:

```
#include "loaderShim.as"
```

8. Open up the components panel (Window⇨Components) and in the User Interface section, open the library panel (Window⇨Library). Drag the Loader and the ProgressBar components to the middle of the library panel. If you are using Flash MX 2004, drag the two components onto the stage and then delete them from the stage.

9. Select Modify⇨Document, and set the dimensions to 800 wide by 600 high.

10. Select File⇨Save As, name the file loaderShim.fla, and save it in the same directory as portfolio.fla.

11. Create a new Macromedia Flash document by selecting File⇨New and choosing ActionScript File from the New Document panel.

12. Name it loaderShim.as and save it in the directory containing the Flash project file.

13. Enter the following code into the new ActionScript file:

```
this.createEmptyMovieClip("myContent", this.getNextHighestDepth());
this.createEmptyMovieClip("progressMovie", this.getNextHighestDepth());
progressMovie._x = 60;
progressMovie._y = 120;
progressMovie.createTextField("percentDoneLabel", ⤶
    progressMovie.getNextHighestDepth(), 40, 0, 100, 20);

var loadListener:Object = new Object();
loadListener.onLoadStart = function(contentHolder:MovieClip)
{
    progressMovie._visible = true;
    contentHolder._visible = false;
    contentHolder.stop();
```

```
    };

    loadListener.onLoadProgress = function(contentHolder:MovieClip, ⤵
        bytesLoaded:Number, bytesTotal:Number)
    {
        var percentDone:Number = bytesLoaded / bytesTotal * 100;
        showProgress(percentDone, progressMovie);
    };

    loadListener.onLoadComplete = function(contentHolder:MovieClip)
    {
        progressMovie._visible = false;
        contentHolder._visible = true;
        contentHolder.play();
    };

    var contentLoader:MovieClipLoader = new MovieClipLoader();
    contentLoader.addListener(loadListener);
    contentLoader.loadClip("portfolio.swf", myContent);

    function showProgress(percentDone:Number, progressBarHolder:MovieClip) : Void
    {
        var barWidth:Number = percentDone;
        progressBarHolder.percentDoneLabel.text = String(Math.ceil(percentDone))+" %";
        progressBarHolder.clear();

        // Draw a border
        progressBarHolder.moveTo(0, 20);
        progressBarHolder.lineStyle(1, 0x666666);
        progressBarHolder.lineTo(100, 20);
        progressBarHolder.lineTo(100, 30);
        progressBarHolder.lineTo(0, 30);
        progressBarHolder.lineTo(0, 20);

        // Draw the bar
        progressBarHolder.moveTo(0, 20);
        progressBarHolder.beginFill(0xCCCCCC, 100);
        progressBarHolder.lineTo(barWidth, 20);
        progressBarHolder.lineTo(barWidth, 30);
        progressBarHolder.lineTo(0, 30);
        progressBarHolder.lineTo(0, 20);
        progressBarHolder.endFill();
    }
```

14. Save the file (File⇨Save), return to the Macromedia Flash project file, and select Control⇨ Test Movie. The loader should show up briefly and then the portfolio interface should take its place.

How It Works

This exercise makes use of the MovieClipLoader class instead of the Loader and ProgressBar components because using the MovieClipLoader class keeps the loader shim very small, on the order of 1 KB versus 32 KB.

The first part involves changing a few references from _level0 to the this keyword. The _level0 keyword is an absolute reference that always refers to the base timeline. Unfortunately, because the pre-loader loads the content into its own nested movie clip rather than onto the main timeline, the content no longer sits directly on _level0. The this reference in the context of movie clips is a relative reference to whatever movie clip the code happens to sit inside. If you had tried to load the content through the pre-loader, the content would be visible but none of the buttons would work. Clearly, using the relative this reference instead of the absolute _level0 reference makes content portable.

Within the loaderShim.as file, the first few lines shown in the following code set up the movie clips. First, a movie clip is created into which the main content will be loaded. Next, a second movie clip is created to hold the progress bar graphics. That movie clip is positioned, and a text field inserted:

```
this.createEmptyMovieClip("myContent", this.getNextHighestDepth());
this.createEmptyMovieClip("progressMovie", this.getNextHighestDepth());
progressMovie._x = 60;
progressMovie._y = 120;
progressMovie.createTextField("percentDoneLabel", ⤸
    progressMovie.getNextHighestDepth(), 40, 0, 100, 20);
```

An event listener is then created. The content clip is hidden and the progress bar is revealed once the load has begun:

```
var loadListener:Object = new Object();
loadListener.onLoadStart = function(contentHolder:MovieClip)
{
    progressMovie._visible = true;
    contentHolder._visible = false;
    contentHolder.stop();
};
```

The following code updates the progress bar every time a chunk of content is downloaded:

```
loadListener.onLoadProgress = function(contentHolder:MovieClip, bytesLoaded:Number,
bytesTotal:Number)
{
    var percentDone:Number = bytesLoaded / bytesTotal * 100;
    showProgress(percentDone, progressMovie);
};
```

Once all the content has been downloaded, the progress bar is hidden, the content is displayed, and playback begins in case the content consists of more than one frame:

```
loadListener.onLoadComplete = function(contentHolder:MovieClip)
{
    progressMovie._visible = false;
    contentHolder._visible = true;
    contentHolder.play();
};
```

The movie clip loader is created, is linked with the event listener, and the load process is initiated:

```
var contentLoader:MovieClipLoader = new MovieClipLoader();
contentLoader.addListener(loadListener);
contentLoader.loadClip("portfolio.swf", myContent);
```

The `showProgress()` function redraws the progress bar and updates the text field to reflect how much content has downloaded:

```
function showProgress(percentDone:Number, progressBarHolder:MovieClip) : Void
{
    var barWidth:Number = percentDone;
    progressBarHolder.percentDoneLabel.text = String(Math.ceil(percentDone))+" %";
    progressBarHolder.clear();

    // Draw a border
    progressBarHolder.moveTo(0, 20);
    progressBarHolder.lineStyle(1, 0x666666);
    progressBarHolder.lineTo(100, 20);
    progressBarHolder.lineTo(100, 30);
    progressBarHolder.lineTo(0, 30);
    progressBarHolder.lineTo(0, 20);

    // Draw the bar
    progressBarHolder.moveTo(0, 20);
    progressBarHolder.beginFill(0xCCCCCC, 100);
    progressBarHolder.lineTo(barWidth, 20);
    progressBarHolder.lineTo(barWidth, 30);
    progressBarHolder.lineTo(0, 30);
    progressBarHolder.lineTo(0, 20);
    progressBarHolder.endFill();
}
```

When you try this out, the loader only shows up for a moment, largely because loading local content is very fast and also because the file is still fairly small. Placing the .swf files on a server is a better way of seeing the effect. As more content is placed into the portfolio, the larger it will get and the longer the progress bar will stay up.

The Split-Up Movie Approach

You might not want to use the monolithic movie approach for a couple of reasons. As project size gets large, initial load time can become quite significant. Also, changes and additions to the project must be made directly to the main Flash project file. It is generally easier to maintain projects that are split up into smaller chunks. Splitting a movie into chunks also lowers initial load time and saves bandwidth. The split-up movie is generally implemented in an on-demand fashion, where content for a specific section loads only once the user elects to visit that section. If a section goes unvisited by the user, the content for that section does not load.

The cost of the split-up movie approach is, of course, a slight increase in complexity. The following Try It Out shows how to use this approach.

Try It Out   Using the Split-Up Movie Approach

This exercise builds on the previous Try It Out. You learn to separate content from the main project, and then call individual screens as needed.

1. Open the completed `portfolio.fla` and `portfolio.as` files from the previous Try It Out, or open up the source `.fla` and `.as` files from the book's source files at <downloaded files>/ Chapter 8/portfolio v7/portfolio.fla and <downloaded files>/Chapter 8/ portfolio v7/portfolio.as.

2. Select the `portfolio.fla` document, open the Library panel (Window⇨Library), and look for the movie clip symbol at /screens/home/screen_home. Double-click the symbol to take it into edit mode.

3. Drag across all the keyframes to select them. Alternatively, click the keyframe on the Menu Marker layer, and then shift+click the keyframe on the Featured Photo layer. Select Edit⇨ Timeline⇨Copy Frames.

4. Create a new Macromedia Flash document.

5. Select the empty keyframe in the new document's timeline. Select Edit⇨Timeline⇨ Paste Frames.

6. Open the properties panel (Window⇨Properties) and select Edit⇨Select All. Enter an x value of 25 and a y value of 50.

7. Select Modify⇨Document, and set the dimensions to 800 wide and 600 high.

8. Save the document and name it `home.fla`.

9. Select File⇨Publish to create a `.swf` file.

10. Repeat steps 2 to 11 for the library symbols at /screens/tutorials/screen_tutorial and at /screens/photography/screen_photography. Save the new files as `tutorials.fla` and `photography.fla`.

11. Return to `portfolio.fla`, and delete all library elements in the screens folder.

12. In `portfolio.fla`, open the User Interface section of the components panel. Open the Library panel (Window⇨Library), and drag the Loader and the ProgressBar components to the middle of the Library panel. If you are using Flash MX 2004, drag the two components onto the stage and then delete them from the stage. Save `portfolio.fla` to make sure you do not lose your changes.

13. Go to the `portfolio.as` ActionScript file. Make sure the contents of that file look like the following code. The bold lines indicate new or modified code:

```
// Set up code to respond to main menu buttons
home_btn.onRelease = function()
{
    gotoScreen("home");
}

tutorials_btn.onRelease = function()
{
    gotoScreen("tutorials");
}

photography_btn.onRelease = function()
{
```

```
        gotoScreen("photography");
}


function gotoScreen(screenName:String):Void
{
    loaderComponent.unload();
    loaderComponent.load(screenName + ".swf");
}

function init():Void
{
    var screenHolderHandle:MovieClip;
    var loadHandler:Object = new Object();

    this.createClassObject(mx.controls.Loader, "loaderComponent", ⤸
        this.getNextHighestDepth());
    this.createClassObject(mx.controls.ProgressBar, "progressComponent", ⤸
        this.getNextHighestDepth());

    progressComponent._x = Stage.width / 2 - progressComponent._width / 2;
    progressComponent._y = Stage.height / 2 - progressComponent._height / 2;

    progressComponent.source = loaderComponent;
    progressComponent.setStyle("color", 0x888888);
    progressComponent.setStyle("fontSize", 12);
    progressComponent.setStyle("themeColor", 0x888888);

    loadHandler.progress = function(eventObject:Object)
    {
        loaderComponent.content.stop();
        progressComponent._visible = true;
    }

    loadHandler.complete = function(eventObject:Object)
    {
        loaderComponent.content.play();
        progressComponent._visible = false;
    }

    loaderComponent.scaleContent = false;
    loaderComponent.addEventListener("progress", loadHandler);
    loaderComponent.addEventListener("complete", loadHandler);

    gotoScreen("home");
}

init();
```

14. Save the file, return to `portfolio.fla`, and select Edit⇨Publish.

15. Open the file `loaderShim.fla` and select Control⇨Test Movie. There should be two initial flashes of the progress bar, and clicking each menu item should result in a short flash of the progress bar. You may not see the initial flash of the progress bar until you try uploading the files to a server and view the project through a browser.

How It Works

When you previously worked on this project, each screen was a movie clip in the library that was attached to the screen through the `attachMovie()` method. In this exercise, each of those movie clips was placed in its own .fla file and published. Because the screens in the portfolio.fla library have linkage IDs, they are still included in the published file. You no longer need any of the screens, so it is easiest just to delete them from the library.

Note that in this project you can choose whether to use the initial loader shim. The size of the parent movie is smaller than before, but it is still a good idea to use the shim.

The button handler code has not changed at all from last time:

```
// Set up code to respond to main menu buttons
home_btn.onRelease = function()
{
    gotoScreen("home");
}

tutorials_btn.onRelease = function()
{
    gotoScreen("tutorials");
}

photography_btn.onRelease = function()
{
    gotoScreen("photography");
}
```

A small change to the `gotoScreen()` method lets you use the Loader component to unload the previous screen and load the next screen:

```
function gotoScreen(screenName:String):Void
{
    loaderComponent.unload();
    loaderComponent.load(screenName + ".swf");
}
```

Finally, the `init()` function is changed to set up the components:

```
function init():Void
{
    var screenHolderHandle:MovieClip;
    var loadHandler:Object = new Object();

    this.createClassObject(mx.controls.Loader, "loaderComponent", ⤴
        this.getNextHighestDepth());
    this.createClassObject(mx.controls.ProgressBar, "progressComponent", ⤴
        this.getNextHighestDepth());

    progressComponent._x = Stage.width / 2 - progressComponent._width / 2;
    progressComponent._y = Stage.height / 2 - progressComponent._height / 2;

    progressComponent.source = loaderComponent;
    progressComponent.setStyle("color", 0x888888);
```

```
    progressComponent.setStyle("fontSize", 12);
    progressComponent.setStyle("themeColor", 0x888888);

    loadHandler.progress = function(eventObject:Object)
    {
        loaderComponent.content.stop();
        progressComponent._visible = true;
    }

    loadHandler.complete = function(eventObject:Object)
    {
        loaderComponent.content.play();
        progressComponent._visible = false;
    }

    loaderComponent.scaleContent = false;
    loaderComponent.addEventListener("progress", loadHandler);
    loaderComponent.addEventListener("complete", loadHandler);

    gotoScreen("home");
}

init();
```

The implementation of the pre-loader is very similar to the load shim created in the previous Try It Out exercise. One thing to note here is that the re-factoring that you did in the Chapter 6 exercises paid off; the code was organized in a cleaner way. As a result, even though you just completely re-did how screens are loaded, you only had to make relatively minor changes to two functions.

Summary

This chapter covered pre-loaders at great length. Some of the key points include the following:

❑ Pre-loaders provide feedback for long loads. They also provide a way for follow-up code to run right after a load has finished.

❑ The two main pre-loaders available are the MovieClipLoader class and the combination of the Loader and ProgressBar components. Additional control can be obtained by creating your own pre-loader.

❑ The Loader and ProgressBar components result in an additional 32 KB being added to your project. As a result, they are not appropriate for the initial download of the main content. They are better suited for loading additional content on demand once the main content has downloaded.

❑ Two approaches to structuring a site are the monolithic movie approach and the split-up movie approach. The first sacrifices longer initial load time for greater response time, and is simple to implement. The second approach lowers initial load time and makes for easier-to-expand projects, but adds some complexity to the project.

Exercises

1. Modify the following code to add an `onLoadError` event handler that alerts the user when an error occurs. It should deal separately with an incorrect URL error and a download timeout error. Refer to the built-in Flash help panel under ActionScript 2.0 Language Reference⇨ ActionScript Classes⇨MovieClipLoader Class for details on the `onLoadError` event.

Here's a hint: upload the file `exercise1Trailer.swf`, *available in the Chapter 8 folder of the downloadable source code, to a remote server. Change the URL in the* `loadClip()` *method to point to the file on your server.*

```
this.createEmptyMovieClip("movieHolder", this.getNextHighestDepth());
this.createEmptyMovieClip("progressMovie", this.getNextHighestDepth());
progressMovie._x = 60;
progressMovie._y = 120;
progressMovie.createTextField("percentDoneLabel",
progressMovie.getNextHighestDepth(), 40, 0, 100, 20);

var loadListener:Object = new Object();
loadListener.onLoadStart = function(contentHolder:MovieClip)
{
    progressMovie._visible = true;
    contentHolder._visible = false;
    contentHolder.stop();
};

loadListener.onLoadProgress = function(contentHolder:MovieClip, ⊃
    bytesLoaded:Number, bytesTotal:Number)
{
    var percentDone:Number = bytesLoaded / bytesTotal * 100;
    showProgress(percentDone, progressMovie);
};

loadListener.onLoadComplete = function(contentHolder:MovieClip)
{
    progressMovie._visible = false;
    contentHolder._visible = true;
    contentHolder.play();
};

var contentLoader:MovieClipLoader = new MovieClipLoader();
contentLoader.addListener(loadListener);
contentLoader.loadClip("exercise1Trailer.swf", movieHolder);

function showProgress(percentDone:Number, progressBarHolder:MovieClip) : Void
{
    var barWidth:Number = percentDone;
    progressBarHolder.percentDoneLabel.text = String(Math.ceil(percentDone))+" %";
    progressBarHolder.clear();

    // Draw a border
    progressBarHolder.moveTo(0, 20);
```

```
        progressBarHolder.lineStyle(1, 0x666666);
        progressBarHolder.lineTo(100, 20);
        progressBarHolder.lineTo(100, 30);
        progressBarHolder.lineTo(0, 30);
        progressBarHolder.lineTo(0, 20);

        // Draw the bar
        progressBarHolder.moveTo(0, 20);
        progressBarHolder.beginFill(0xCCCCCC, 100);
        progressBarHolder.lineTo(barWidth, 20);
        progressBarHolder.lineTo(barWidth, 30);
        progressBarHolder.lineTo(0, 30);
        progressBarHolder.lineTo(0, 20);
        progressBarHolder.endFill();
    }
```

2.   Modify exercise 1 to use the ProgressBar component instead of using the `showProgress()` function.

Working with Components

Imagine what it would be like if you had to build everything that you work with during the day from scratch! It sounds silly, but in the "old" days that's what developers had to do with their code. Many developers continue to do so, although it's redundant and adds to the workload.

Since MX 2004 (version 7), Flash has had a complete component architecture that lends itself to drag-and-drop authoring and to re-use between developers. Components can be bundled into individual extensions, and the extension manager is responsible for putting the pieces of each component in all the right places. The component architecture makes use of the class development mechanism to simplify component creation, and the idea of the compiled clip allows components to be completely self-contained into clips that could not be tinkered with except through defined mechanisms.

Thankfully, you do not need to re-create user interface controls every time they are needed. There is a growing body of components out there that anyone can use to extend their projects. Take a look at Macromedia's component exchange at `http://www.macromedia.com/exchange/` for a large collection of components.

New to Version 2.0

Version 1.0 of the component architecture was introduced with Flash MX, which corresponds to the introduction of version 6 of the Flash player. Version 2.0 was introduced with Flash MX 2004 (version 7) and continues mostly unchanged in Flash 8. The version 2.0 component architecture includes many new features over version 1.0:

❑   The version 2.0 components are written using ActionScript 2.0 instead of ActionScript 1.0.

❑   A fresh appearance makes components look more professional.

❑   Creating a new skin can change the global look of all components.

❑   Updating styles can modify many appearance traits. Styles can be applied for a single component instance, for all instances of a component, or globally across all v2 components.

Chapter 9

❑   A focus manager handles keyboard access of components.

❑   A more flexible event model is used.

There are other benefits as well, such as for component creators. You examine the creation of a sample component in Chapter 27.

Unfortunately, not everything that is new is good. The main drawback to version 2 components over version 1 components is the amount that they add to the size of the .swf files that contain them. The first component used adds a total of approximately 40 KB to the size of the published file because the entire component framework needs to be included in the file. Subsequent components add less, but it can still add up quickly.

> **Even though version 2.0 of the component architecture was introduced with version 7 of the Flash player, it works in movies that target version 6.0.79 and later. They require only that the movie be published to target ActionScript 2.0. This should not be a concern, because movies that target ActionScript 2.0 can still run ActionScript 1.0 code.**

Exploring Components

First, take a look at Flash's Components panel (see Figure 9-1) and the default component groupings.

Figure 9-1

The following sections explore the components available in each grouping.

Data Components

Data components specialize in managing data. They communicate with each other through a data-binding mechanism, which is a structured way of passing data from one component to another. The Name column of the following table provides the component name and its fully qualified class name used for placing the component on the stage with code. Here are descriptions of the various data components:

Name	Description

DataHolder
`mx.data.components`
`.DataHolder`
	A repository for data that generates events when the data has changed. Allows for the storing of arbitrary data.

DataSet
`mx.data.components`
`.DataSet`
	A repository for a collection of data records. Provides methods for iterating, sorting, and broadcasting events.

RDBMSResolver
`mx.data.components`
`.RDBMSResolver`
	An interface between the DataSet component and a server-side database. Provides a synchronization of data between the two data stores.

WebServiceConnector
`mx.data.components`
`.WebServiceConnector`
	An interface that allows access to web services through the standard SOAP protocol.

XMLConnector
`mx.data.components`
`.XMLConnector`
	A means to send and receive data packaged into an XML document.

XUpdateResolver
`mx.data.components`
`.XUpdateResolver`
	An interface between the DataSet component and a server-side XML database. Uses the XUpdate language specification to synchronize data between the two data stores.

FLV Playback and FLV Playback Custom UI Components

The FLV Playback component enables you to play video content through a user interface that is already set up to allow the user to control playback and volume. Although this component enables you to choose from a number of pre-made designs through the `skin` parameter in the Parameters panel, you may want to customize the look further. Along with the FLV Playback component, Macromedia now provides a number of custom UI components that you can incorporate into your own design. If you want to create your own custom control layout, take the following steps:

1. Drag an FLV Playback component to the stage and click the component to select it.

2. Open the Properties panel (Window⇨Properties) and give the component an instance name, such as `videoPlayer`.

3. Open the Parameters panel (Window⇨Parameters) and select `None` from the skin drop-down.

4. Drag any number of the custom UI components listed in the following table and arrange them on the stage in the way that you want. Give each of the components you place on the state an instance name using the Properties panel.

5. For each custom UI component that you have placed on the stage, add a line of ActionScript code to the main timeline to link the component to the video player. If your video player has the instance name `videoPlayer`, and you are adding a button that automatically switches between pause and play with the instance name `newPausePlayButton`, use

```
videoPlayer.pausePlayButton = newPausePlay;
```

The following table describes the FLV Playback component, and gives the linkage information for each custom component:

Name	Description
FLVPlayback `mx.video.FLVPlayback`	A video player component that provides basic play, pause, scrub, and mute controls, plus a huge number of properties and methods that can be called to modify the component's behavior. [Flash Player version 8]
BackButton	An add-on button that sends a back message to the video player. Use the `backButton` property of the FLV Player component to link a BackButton component to the player.
BufferingBar	An add-on interface element that shows when a streaming video is being buffered. Use the `bufferingBar` property of the FLV Player component to link a BufferingBar component to the player.
ForwardButton	An add-on button that sends a forward message to the video player. Use the `forwardButton` property of the FLV Player component to link a ForwardButton component to the player.
MuteButton	An add-on mute button for the video player. Use the `muteButton` property of the FLV Player component to link a MuteButton component to the player.
PauseButton	An add-on button that sends a pause message to the video player. Use the `pauseButton` property of the FLV Player component to link a PauseButton component to the player.
PlayButton	An add-on button that sends a play message to the video player. Use the `playButton` property of the FLV Player component to link a PlayButton component to the player.
PlayPauseButton	An add-on button that toggles between sending a pause and a play message to the video player. The button switches between showing a pause symbol or a play symbol, according to playback state. Use the `playPauseButton` property of the FLV Player component to link a PlayPauseButton component to the player.
SeekBar	An add-on interface element that allows the user to scrub through the video. Use the `seekBar` property of the FLV Player component to link a SeekBar component to the player.
StopButton	An add-on button that sends a stop message to the video player. Use the `stopButton` property of the FLV Player component to link a StopButton component to the player.
VolumeBar	An add-on control that sends a volume set message to the video player. Use the `volumeBar` property of the FLV Player component to link a VolumeBar component to the player.

Media Components for Flash Players 6 and 7

The media components are recommended only if you need to support version 6 or 7 of the Flash plug-in. The component's name and its fully qualified class name (used for placing the component on the stage with code) are included in the first column of the following table, which describes these components:

Name	Description
MediaController mx.controls.MediaController	A video controller, providing interface controls for controlling video playback.
MediaDisplay mx.controls.MediaDisplay	A canvas area for displaying video.
MediaPlayback mx.controls.MediaPlayback	A combination of the MediaController and MediaDisplay components.

User Interface Components

User interface (UI) components are available for building interfaces to interact with the user. The following table describes these components. Below each name is the package name, needed for placing components with script:

Name	Description
Accordion mx.containers.Accordion	A holder for controls for a multi-step process. As the user finishes one process, the container holding controls for the next step slides into view. A user can easily navigate back to previous steps.
Alert mx.controls.Alert	A modal window that displays a message, and a combination of OK, Cancel, Yes, and No buttons.
Button mx.controls.Button	A standard push button.
CheckBox mx.controls.CheckBox	A standard checkbox form element.
ComboBox mx.controls.ComboBox	A drop-down selection list.
DataGrid mx.controls.DataGrid	A way of presenting multi-row tabular data. Provides ways to select rows, place custom controls within each row, and, through data binding, load data from an external data source.
DateChooser mx.controls.DateChooser	A monthly calendar that allows the user to select a date.
DateField mx.controls.DateField	A text field with a clickable date chooser icon.

Table continued on following page

Name	Description
Label mx.controls.Label	A single line of text to show to the user. Similar to a dynamic text field, only it is set up to better enable accessibility.
List mx.controls.List	A scrollable list box. It allows for single- and multi-selections, and it can link up with an external data provider.
Loader mx.controls.Loader	A container for externally loaded images and movies. It allows for automatic scaling of images, and can work together with the progress bar to provide progress status.
Menu mx.controls.Menu	A pop-up menu. Can be triggered from a menu bar, or from a contextual menu event.
MenuBar mx.controls.MenuBar	A menu holder that behaves like a standard application menu bar.
NumericStepper mx.controls.NumericStepper	A container for a number that provides up and down buttons for progressively increasing or decreasing the number.
ProgressBar mx.controls.ProgressBar	A mechanism for showing loading progress. It can be used to show how much is left to load, or if the load amount is not known, it can just show that an activity is in progress.
RadioButton mx.controls.RadioButton	A standard radio button.
ScrollPane mx.containers.ScrollPane	A scrollable area for externally loaded image or movie content.
TextArea mx.controls.TextArea	A scrollable area for allowing the user to enter a large amount of text.
TextInput mx.controls.TextInput	A standard text input field.
Tree mx.controls.Tree	A means of showing hierarchical data, such as directory structures.
UIScrollBar mx.controls.UIScrollBar	A scroll bar that can be added to a standard text field.
Window mx.containers.Window	A component that behaves like a standard window. It can be either modal or non-modal.

The rest of the chapter shows you how to use components.

Placing Components Manually

You can place components on the stage in two ways: manually and with ActionScript. To place a component manually, simply drag it to the stage (see Figure 9-2).

Figure 9-2

That's the easiest way to place components, and it is also the most appropriate for using Flash as a rapid application prototyping tool.

Once the component is on the stage, you have two ways to customize its startup parameters. The first is to set the parameters in the Properties panel (see Figure 9-3).

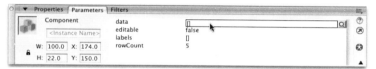

Figure 9-3

The second is to give the component an instance name and set the parameters with script:

```
var comboBoxArray:Array = new Array();
comboBoxArray.push({data:1, label:"Selection 1"});
comboBoxArray.push({data:2, label:"Selection 2"});
comboBoxArray.push({data:3, label:"Selection 3"});
comboBoxArray.push({data:4, label:"Selection 4"});
comboBoxArray.push({data:5, label:"Selection 5"});


myComboBox.dataProvider = comboBoxArray;
```

You use both the manual and ActionScript methods of putting components on the screen as you progress through this chapter.

Try It Out   **Placing Components on the Stage**

This example demonstrates how to place components on the stage, how to set properties with the authoring environment, and the effect of components on the size of the published file. Figure 9-4 shows the result of this exercise.

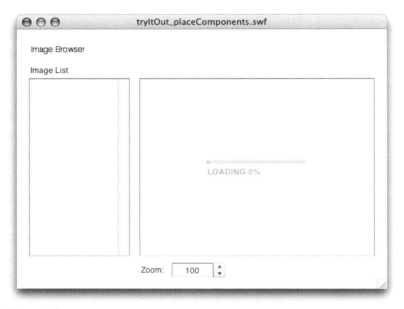

Figure 9-4

1.   Create a new Macromedia Flash document by selecting File⇨New and choosing Flash Document from the New Document panel.

2.   Select File⇨Save As, name the file tryItOut_scriptingComponents.fla, choose an appropriate directory, and save it.

3.   Open the Components panel (Window⇨Components), open the UI Components section, and then drag the List component to the stage.

4.   With the new List component selected, go to the Properties panel (Window⇨Properties) and set the x position to 18, the y position to 75, the width to 150, and the height to 275. Give it the instance name imageList.

5.   Select File⇨Publish to create the SWF file. Open a file browser with your operating system, and locate the file tryItOut_scriptingComponents.swf. Take a look at its properties, noting the file size.

6.   Return to the Flash project file. Add a ScrollPane component by dragging it onto the stage from the Components panel. Give it an x position of 182, a y position of 75, a width of 350, a height of 275, and an instance name of imageViewerPane.

7.   Drag a ProgressBar component onto the stage from the Components panel. Give it x position 280 and y position 200. Give it the instance name imageViewerProgress.

8. Drag a NumericStepper component onto the stage from the Components panel. Give it x position 230 and y position 360. Make the instance name zoomStepper.

9. With the new NumericStepper still selected, choose the Parameters tab within the Properties panel. Set the maximum value to 200, minimum to 25, stepSize to 25, and value to 100.

10. Drag a Label component onto the stage from the Components panel. Set the x position to 18 and the y position to 53. In the Properties panel, set the text property to Image List.

11. Drag a second Label component to the stage. Set the x position to 182 and the y position to 381. Within the Properties panel, set the text property to Zoom:.

12. Drag a third Label component to the stage. Set the x and y positions to 18. In the Properties panel, set the text property to Image Browser:.

13. Save the file and select Control⇨Test Movie. Open a file browser with your operating system, and locate the file tryItOut_scriptingComponents.swf. Take a look at its properties, noting the file size.

How It Works

Placing a component on the stage automatically adds the component to the library. When you publish the project, the file size of the generated SWF file is quite big, likely on the order of 48 KB for a single component. After adding four different components and publishing the project, the published file is larger only by about 16 KB.

When any one of the built-in components is included in a project, it automatically pulls in a large set of support classes. Those classes are part of the overall version 2.0 component framework, and are shared among all of the components. As a result, adding a second, third, or fourth component only increases the size of the published file by a small amount.

In this example, you set some of the parameters for the NumericStepper and Label components in the Parameters panel. If you interact with the NumericStepper instance in the test movie environment, clicking the up and down arrows raises and lowers the value by 25 each time. The stepper should limit the range to a minimum value of 25, a maximum value of 200, and a starting value of 100, as specified in the Parameters panel. The panel is specific to components, and it allows certain startup values to be set without requiring code. Because coding is what you're learning here, the next exercise shows you how to perform the same tasks with ActionScript.

Placing Components on the Stage with Script

It's possible to place every user interface component on the stage with script instead of manually dragging it to the stage. Using script to place components on the stage gives maximum control over all aspects of your user interface, and it means that you can create an entire application with code in only one frame and with nothing on the timeline. It isn't the Holy Grail of development that some make it out to be because issues exist with this type of development as well, including the following:

❑ You cannot see the results of what you are developing until you compile and test the movie.

❑ It is harder to do rapid application development because small changes in layout result in needing to calculate how many pixels to adjust each component's position and size, making the adjustment, and then compiling to see whether your calculations were correct.

❑ Some things are just quicker and easier to do on the timeline, especially when it involves complex animations.

That said, creating an entire Flash project out of ActionScript is a very powerful approach, and is pretty cool, too!

The method used to attach a component to the stage is `createClassObject()`, which is a method of the UIObject class. It is defined as follows:

```
UIObject.createClassObject(className:Object, instanceName:String,
    depth:Number, [initObject:Object]) : UIObject
```

Here's an example:

```
this.createClassObject(mx.controls.List, "imageList", this.getNextHighestDepth());
```

In this example, a List component is placed on the current timeline with default properties set and with the instance name `imageList`. Once the component instance is on the stage, it can be manipulated with ActionScript in the same way as if it were placed on the stage by hand.

Despite the implication of its name, the `className` parameter is not a string; it is actually a package reference. A package is a container of classes that are placed within a particular structure to keep them organized and to make sure that if another developer creates a component with the same name, the two component names do not conflict. Think of a package as being like a directory structure. The first directory here is called `mx`, and within it is another directory called `controls`, which holds the class definition file for the List component. In fact, that's exactly how packages are organized. In most operating systems, a single directory cannot hold two files with the same name, but two different files with the same name can co-exist nicely in two different directories. In the same way, a component with the package name com.nathanderksen.ui.List will not conflict with the component mx.controls.List that Macromedia provides.

When working with packaged components, the last portion of the package reference is referred to as the component name, and everything before it is the package name. In mx.controls.List, List is the component name, and mx.controls is the package name.

Using the `import` statement can save a little space when referring to a packaged class. Once a package has been imported, from that point on you can refer just to the component name and can leave out the package name. The following code shows how the `createClassObject()` method can now refer just to `List`, and Flash will automatically associate it with mx.controls.List:

```
import mx.controls.List;
this.createClassObject(List, "imageList", this.getNextHighestDepth());
```

Once a packaged class has been imported, further references to the class can omit the package name, making the code a bit more compact. It is also possible to import a whole set of classes through a wildcard. The following code shows that the wildcard asterisk (*) character has been used with the `import` statement to import all the classes directly within the mx.controls package. The List component, plus any other components in the same package, can then be referred to without the package name.

```
import mx.controls.*;
this.createClassObject(List, "imageList", this.getNextHighestDepth());
```

Only classes that are actually used are compiled into the `.swf`, and it's recommended that you import only the classes that you need and refrain from using the wildcard. Having a list of packaged classes at the top of your code tells you what all of your dependencies are, and because avoiding wildcards prevents components that you do not use and may know about from entering your name space, there is less of a chance of two components with the same name entering your name space at the same time and conflicting.

The `createClassObject()`, which is modeled on the `attachMovie()` method, enables you to set component properties on creation, as the following example shows:

```
import mx.controls.List;
this.createClassObject(List, "imageList", this.getNextHighestDepth(), ⟳
    {_x:18, _y:50});
```

Although that's convenient, it also makes the code line long enough that you can't see the properties on the screen without scrolling. Setting the properties on separate lines makes the code a little easier to read:

```
import mx.controls.List;
this.createClassObject(List, "imageList", this.getNextHighestDepth());
imageList._x = 18;
imageList._y = 50;
```

You do this in the following Try It Out.

Try It Out   Placing Components on the Stage with Script

In this exercise you create the same screen as the preceding Try It Out, but this time you do it all with code. (Don't worry; you'll be reusing your precise layout from the previous exercise, so your work won't go to waste.)

1. Create a new Macromedia Flash document by selecting File⇨New and choosing Flash Document from the New Document panel.

2. Click the first frame in the timeline, open the Actions panel (Window⇨Development Panels⇨ Actions), and type in the following ActionScript code:

```
#include "tryItOut_attachWithScript.as"
```

3. Open the Components panel (Window⇨Components) and open the User Interface section. Open the library panel (Window⇨Library), and then drag the Label, List, NumericStepper, and ScrollPane components to the middle of the library panel. If you are using Flash MX 2004, drag the four components onto the stage and then delete them from the stage instead.

4. Select File⇨Save As, name the file `tryItOut_attachWithScript.fla`, choose an appropriate directory, and save it.

5. Create a new Macromedia Flash document by selecting File⇨New and choosing ActionScript File from the New Document panel.

6. Name the file `tryItOut_attachWithScript.as` and save it in the same directory as the Flash project file.

7. Type the following code into the new ActionScript file:

```
import mx.controls.List;
import mx.controls.NumericStepper;
import mx.controls.Label;
import mx.containers.ScrollPane;

function drawScreen():Void
{
    this.createClassObject(Label, "titleLabel", this.getNextHighestDepth());
    titleLabel._x = 18;
    titleLabel._y = 18;
    titleLabel.text = "Image Browser";

    this.createClassObject(List, "imageList", this.getNextHighestDepth());
    imageList.setSize(150, 275);
    imageList._x = 18;
    imageList._y = 75;

    this.createClassObject(ScrollPane, "imageViewerPane", ⤵
        this.getNextHighestDepth());
    imageViewerPane.setSize(350, 275);
    imageViewerPane._x = 182;
    imageViewerPane._y = 75;

    this.createClassObject(NumericStepper, "zoomStepper", ⤵
        this.getNextHighestDepth());
    zoomStepper._x = 230;
    zoomStepper._y = 360;

    this.createClassObject(Label, "imageListLabel", ⤵
        this.getNextHighestDepth());
    imageListLabel._x = 18;
    imageListLabel._y = 53;
    imageListLabel.text = "Image List";

    this.createClassObject(Label, "zoomLabel", this.getNextHighestDepth());
    zoomLabel._x = 182;
    zoomLabel._y = 361;
    zoomLabel.text = "Zoom:";
}

drawScreen();
```

8. Save the file, return to the Macromedia Flash project file, and select Control⇨Test Movie.

How It Works

Before you can attach components to the stage with script, the components need to be dragged to the library. If the components are not in the library, Flash cannot link them in. This is different from classes where just referring to a class causes the code to be linked in.

Importing the component packages is always the first thing to do in code:

```
import mx.controls.List;
import mx.controls.NumericStepper;
```

```
import mx.controls.Label;
import mx.containers.ScrollPane;
```

The `drawScreen()` function contains the code to place all the components and labels on the screen. First a label is created for the title of the application:

```
this.createClassObject(Label, "titleLabel", this.getNextHighestDepth());
titleLabel._x = 18;
titleLabel._y = 18;
titleLabel.text = "Image Browser";
```

At the moment, it doesn't look like much, but later in the chapter you apply styles to components, including this label to make it stand out more.

Next, the list box is created, positioned, and sized:

```
this.createClassObject(List, "imageList", this.getNextHighestDepth());
imageList.setSize(150, 275);
imageList._x = 18;
imageList._y = 75;
```

Notice that `setSize()` is used to resize the component. Setting the `_width` and `_height` properties do not work the way you expect because everything scales in proportion, including lines and text. `setSize()` calls the component's redraw method to make sure that it resizes in the proper way.

The image viewer pane is created:

```
this.createClassObject(ScrollPane, "imageViewerPane", ⤸
    this.getNextHighestDepth());
imageViewerPane.setSize(350, 275);
imageViewerPane._x = 182;
imageViewerPane._y = 75;
```

The zoom stepper is created:

```
this.createClassObject(NumericStepper, "zoomStepper", ⤸
    this.getNextHighestDepth());
zoomStepper._x = 230;
zoomStepper._y = 360;
```

Finally, two labels are created, and the label values are assigned.

```
this.createClassObject(Label, "imageListLabel", this.getNextHighestDepth());
imageListLabel._x = 18;
imageListLabel._y = 53;
imageListLabel.text = "Image List";

this.createClassObject(Label, "zoomLabel", this.getNextHighestDepth());
zoomLabel._x = 182;
zoomLabel._y = 361;
zoomLabel.text = "Zoom:";
```

Scripting Components

Each component has a set of methods, properties, and events that are available for you to use. To find out what these are and how to use them, open the Help panel, go to the Components Language Reference section, and open the section for the component in which you're interested. Figure 9-5 shows an overview of the ComboBox component in the Help panel.

Figure 9-5

In the component documentation you find sections in the overall class definition that mention the methods, properties, and events that are inherited from the UIObject and the UIComponent classes. These two classes are part of the overall component framework, and the methods, properties, and events that they expose are accessible to all version 2.0 components.

The documentation for the NumericStepper class shows that it has some properties with the same name as some of the ones you just saw in the Properties panel, as well as numerous other properties, methods, and events. These are collectively known as an application programming interface (API). To take full advantage of a component, the Properties panel is not enough. You must make use of the component's API.

To interact with a component, give it an instance name (see Figure 9-6), and then refer to that instance name within the code.

Instance name

Figure 9-6

Once an instance name is assigned, the general form for working with the component instance is simple:

```
instanceName.propertyName = "foo";
instanceName.methodName();
```

The code for setting the same properties that were set in the Parameters panel for the preceding Try It Out exercise looks like this:

```
zoomStepper.maximum = 200;
zoomStepper.minimum = 25;
zoomStepper.stepSize = 25;
zoomStepper.value = 100;
```

The following Try It Out extends the first one in this chapter by using code to do the work of the Parameters panel. At this point, for space reasons, we will no longer make use of the example code that places the components onscreen with ActionScript.

Try It Out   Scripting Components

In this exercise, you start working with the API for several components.

1. Open the completed `tryItOut_scriptingComponents.fla` file from the first Try It Out exercise, or open `tryItOut_scriptingComponents.fla` from the book's source files at <source file directory>/Chapter 9/tryItOut_scriptingComponents_v1/.

2. Create a new layer on the main timeline; name it Script. Move it so that it is the top layer. Click in the keyframe for the layer, open the Actions panel (Window➪Actions), and type in the following ActionScript code:

```
#include "tryItOut_scriptingComponents.as"
```

3. Save the file.

4. Create a new Macromedia Flash document by selecting File➪New and choosing ActionScript File from the New Document panel.

5. Name the file `tryItOut_scriptingComponents.as` and save it in the directory containing the Flash project file.

6. Place the following code into the new ActionScript file:

```
function init() : Void
{
    // Send data to the image list component
    var imageArray:Array = new Array();
    imageArray.push({data:"images/aStudyInTexture.jpg", label:"A Study In
Texture"});
    imageArray.push({data:"images/buntzenWinter.jpg", label:"Buntzen Winter"});
    imageArray.push({data:"images/flowerInDetail.jpg", label:"Flower In Detail"});
    imageArray.push({data:"images/galianoSunset.jpg", label:"Galiano Sunset"});
    imageList.dataProvider = imageArray;

    // Setup for the progress bar component
    imageViewerProgress.mode = "manual";
```

```
        imageViewerProgress._visible = false;

        // Setup for the scrollable image viewer component
        imageViewerPane.scrollDrag = true;

        // Setup for the zoom stepper component
        zoomStepper.maximum = 400;
        zoomStepper.minimum = 25;
        zoomStepper.stepSize = 25;
        zoomStepper.value = 100;
    }

    init();
```

7. Save the file, return to the Macromedia Flash project file, and select Control➪Test Movie.

How It Works

The exercise begins with initializing the components, giving them startup data, and changing some of their properties. The first few lines of the init() function set up a data provider for the image list component. (A data provider is an array of objects containing properties.) In this case each object contains a data property that provides a unique internal identifier and a label property to show the user. The following code shows the creation of the data provider, with the name of the photo as the label, and the URL as the data for each row:

```
// Send data to the image list component
var imageArray:Array = new Array();
imageArray.push({data:"images/aStudyInTexture.jpg", label:"A Study In Texture"});
imageArray.push({data:"images/buntzenWinter.jpg", label:"Buntzen Winter"});
imageArray.push({data:"images/flowerInDetail.jpg", label:"Flower In Detail"});
imageArray.push({data:"images/galianoSunset.jpg", label:"Galiano Sunset"});
imageList.dataProvider = imageArray;
```

The progress bar is set up:

```
// Setup for the progress bar component
imageViewerProgress.mode = "manual";
imageViewerProgress._visible = false;
```

mode is set to manual, which means that you have to give it a progress value yourself.

The scrollDrag property of the ScrollPane allows the user to grab the image and drag to reposition it:

```
// Setup for the scrollable image viewer component
imageViewerPane.scrollDrag = true;
```

Finally, the numeric stepper component is given initial parameters (which correspond with the values that you set earlier in the Parameters pane):

```
// Setup for the zoom stepper component
zoomStepper.maximum = 400;
zoomStepper.minimum = 25;
zoomStepper.stepSize = 25;
zoomStepper.value = 100;
```

In the next chapter, you look at coding some user interactions into your components.

Summary

This chapter explored many different aspects of components. Some points to remember include the following:

❑ Macromedia Flash comes with a variety of components that enable drag-and-drop reusability. Additional components can be added from component repositories such as Macromedia's Exchange site.

❑ Components can be either placed on the stage manually or added with script. When a component is dragged to the stage, a copy of it is placed in the Library automatically. A component must be manually placed in the Library before it can be added to the stage with script.

❑ Parameters can be set either through the Parameters tab or by setting properties with script.

❑ Each component has an API, a set of properties, methods, and events that can be set or captured with script. You can explore APIs in detail by going to the built-in Help panel and opening the Components Language Reference.

Exercises

1. Create the beginning of a note taker application. Place a DataGrid, two Buttons, three Labels, a TextInput and a TextArea component on the stage with script. Label and arrange them as per Figure 9-7.

Figure 9-7

2. Add code that populates the Notes data grid with some data. It should get three properties from an array of objects: `title`, `size`, and `text`. Only `title` and `size` will be shown in the data grid; the other is for data storage purposes. Make the `size` property a calculated value representing the length of the `text` string.

Interacting with the User

The whole point of using Flash to create web applications is to interact with the user. The richness of the interface depends on having a good selection of events that various components can generate. It's all well if clicking is the only thing that is recognized, but how about mouse-overs, dragging, tabbing, or key presses? These all add to the set of tools for the developer to enhance the user experience.

Most people initially consider only user-generated events such as the ones just mentioned as being important, but there is also the class of system-generated events that occur as a result of either data changes or network communications. You may have asked the server for new data, or perhaps a value changed in response to a user interaction, and that new value needs to be broadcasted to other components. Though you may wonder how this falls under "interacting with the user," keep in mind that the data generally feeds what the user sees in some way or another. Changes to background data often require updating elements of the user interface.

Handling Events

Any time an event is generated, you need a way to act on that event. When a button is clicked, specific code needs to run. When an entry is selected in a drop-down menu, you need to know that a change has happened, and you need to find out which element is chosen. The code that you write to respond to an event is called an event handler. Event handlers keep you from having to manually query your interface every frame to see if something's changed. You just assign a block of code to a component, telling it which event to respond to, and the component automatically calls that code every time the event takes place.

Creating a Listener Object

Components use an event handler called a *listener*. As the name implies, the role of a listener is exclusively to listen for when an event takes place. A listener is an object that is assigned a method for each event for which it will listen. The process of creating a listener is as follows:

1. A custom object is created:

```
var imageListListener:Object = new Object();
```

2. A method with the same name as the name of the event is assigned to the object:

```
var imageListListener:Object = new Object();
imageListListener.change = function(eventObject:Object)
{
    // Handler code goes here
}
```

3. The listener is registered to a component:

```
var imageListListener:Object = new Object();
imageListListener.change = function(eventObject:Object)
{
    // Handler code goes here
}
imageList.addEventListener("change", imageListListener);
```

Every time the `imageList` component generates a change event from the user's selecting a different value, the listener code runs. To handle multiple events from the same component, you add additional methods to the event listener object, and then make additional calls to `addEventListener()`:

```
var imageListListener:Object = new Object();
imageListListener.change = function(eventObject:Object)
{
    // Handler code goes here
}
imageListListener.itemRollOver = function(eventObject:Object)
{
    // Handler code goes here
}
imageListListener.itemRollOout = function(eventObject:Object)
{
    // Handler code goes here
}
imageList.addEventListener("change", imageListListener);
imageList.addEventListener("itemRollOver", imageListListener);
imageList.addEventListener("itemRollOut", imageListListener);
```

Every time an event listener is called, it is passed a handle to an event object. The event object contains two properties:

❑ `type` — Gives the name of the event that was generated.

❑ `target` — Holds a reference to the component that generated the event.

The `target` property is indispensable because it provides the information that you need about the state of the calling component. The following code shows how you use the target property to access the value (the visible label) and the data property for the row that the user clicked:

```
var imageListListener:Object = new Object();
imageListListener.change = function(eventObject:Object)
{
    trace(eventObject.target.selectedItem.value);
    trace(eventObject.target.selectedItem.data);
}
imageList.addEventListener("change", imageListListener);
```

The code gets a handle to the target (a List component) from the event object. From that handle, any List component properties or methods can be used. The List component property used here is `selectedItem`, which holds a reference to the last selected row. Each row is a custom object that consists of two properties:

- ❑ `value` — Holds the label that is shown to the user.

- ❑ `data` — Holds a non-viewable piece of data associated with the selected row.

Different components provide different ways of getting to the information about the event from within the handler. The List component is a common way of doing it. The Menu component is different. Instead of exposing a `target` property, it exposes a `menuBar`, a `menu`, and a `menuItem` property. The `menuItem` property is generally the one to use because it holds the data used to generate that menu item. The following example shows how the label for the selected menu item can be retrieved:

```
var menuListener:Object = new Object();
menuListener.change = function (eventObject:Object)
{
    trace("Selected menu item: " + eventObject.menuItem.attributes.label);
}
```

It isn't possible to remember all of the ways to access event data for each component, but there is an easy way to get to that information. Open in turn the built-in Help panel (F1), the Components Language Reference section, and the subsection for the component with which you're working. In the documentation for the component is a page called "<Component Name> Class" that outlines each of the applicable properties, methods, and events. Look for the name of the event that you want to work with, and then look for the page with the same name in that section. It provides the details on how to access the event data for the component.

Try It Out   Creating a Listener Object

In this exercise you create an event listener. Just follow these steps:

1. Create a new Macromedia Flash document by selecting File⇨New and choosing Flash Document from the New Document panel.

2. Rename the existing layer in the timeline to `Script`. Create a new layer, `Components`, below the Script layer.

3. Click the keyframe on the Components layer to select it. Open the Components panel (Window⇨Components) and then open its User Interface section. Drag one Button component to the stage.

4. Open the Properties panel (Window⇨Properties), click the button on the stage, and set the instance ID in the text field at the top left of the panel to `myButton`.

5. The code for this example is very small, so enter it in the Actions panel instead of creating a separate `.as` file. Click the first frame in the timeline, open the Actions panel (Window⇨ Development Panels⇨Actions), and type in the following ActionScript code:

```
var buttonListener:Object = new Object();
buttonListener.click = function(eventObject:Object)
{
```

```
        trace("Button clicked");
    }
    myButton.addEventListener("click", buttonListener);
```

6.   Select File➪Save As, name the file tryItOut_listenerObject_1.fla, choose an appropriate directory, and save it. Select Control➪Test Movie.

How It Works

This example shows how to use an event listener object to capture an event. The listener object is created, a custom method with the same name as the event to be captured is created, and the listener object is registered with the component.

The previous example showed only a simple situation. Now you're ready for something a bit more complex.

Try It Out   A More Involved Listener Object Setup

This exercise expands on how to work with event listener objects. Figure 10-1 shows the result.

Figure 10-1

1.   Create a new Macromedia Flash document by selecting File➪New and choosing Flash Document from the New Document panel.

2.   Click the first frame in the timeline, open the Actions panel (Window➪Development Panels➪ Actions), and type in the following ActionScript code:

```
#include "tryItOut_listenerObject_2.as"
```

3.   Rename the existing layer in the timeline to Script. Create a new layer, Components, below it.

4.   Open the Components panel (Window➪Components), and then open its User Interface section. Drag one Button component, three CheckBox components, and three RadioButton components to the stage. Arrange them as shown in Figure 10-1.

5.   Open the Properties panel (Window➪Properties), click each component in turn, and set an instance ID in the text field at the top left of the panel. Name the checkboxes dinnerOption1, dinnerOption2, and dinnerOption3. Name the radio buttons dessertOption1, dessertOption2, and dessertOption3. Name the button orderButton.

6. Select the Parameters tab in the Properties panel. Click the checkboxes to set their label components: `Curried Lamb`, `Samosa`, and `Garden Salad`.

7. Click the radio button components and set the following values:

Data	Label	Group Name
chocolateMousse	Chocolate Mousse	dessertOptions
applePie	Apple Pie	dessertOptions
tiramisu	Tiramisu	dessertOptions

8. Select File⇨Save As, name the file `tryItOut_listenerObject_2.fla`, choose an appropriate directory, and save it.

9. Create a new Macromedia Flash document, name it `tryItOut_listenerObject_2.as`, and save it in the directory containing the Flash project file.

10. Enter the following code in the new ActionScript file:

```
// Handle the selection of one of the dinner checkboxes
var dinnerOptionListener:Object = new Object();
dinnerOptionListener.click = function(eventObject:Object)
{
    var checkBoxLabel:String = eventObject.target.label;
    var isCheckBoxSelected:Boolean = eventObject.target.selected;
    if (isCheckBoxSelected == true)
    {
        trace("Selected: " + checkBoxLabel);
    }
    else
    {
        trace("Deselected: " + checkBoxLabel);
    }
}
dinnerOption0.addEventListener("click", dinnerOptionListener);
dinnerOption1.addEventListener("click", dinnerOptionListener);
dinnerOption2.addEventListener("click", dinnerOptionListener);

// Handle the selection of one of the dessert radio buttons
var dessertOptionListener:Object = new Object();
dessertOptionListener.click = function(eventObject:Object)
{
    var radioButtonLabel:String = eventObject.target.selection.data;
    trace("Selected: " + radioButtonLabel);
}
dessertOptions.addEventListener("click", dessertOptionListener);

// Handle the clicking of the order button
var parentTimeline:MovieClip = this;
var orderButtonListener:Object = new Object();
orderButtonListener.click = function(eventObject:Object)
{
```

```
    var myOrder:String = "Ordering: ";
    var tempCheckBoxHandle:mx.controls.CheckBox;

    // Find out which dinner options were checked
    for (var i:Number = 0; i < 3; i++)
    {
        tempCheckBoxHandle = parentTimeline["dinnerOption" + i];
        if (tempCheckBoxHandle.selected == true)
        {
            myOrder += tempCheckBoxHandle.label + ", ";
        }
    }

    // Find out which dessert was selected
    if (dessertOptions.selection != undefined)
    {
        myOrder += dessertOptions.selection.label;
    }

    trace(myOrder);
}
orderButton.addEventListener("click", orderButtonListener);
```

11. Save the file, return to the Macromedia Flash project file, and select Control➪Test Movie.

How It Works

Three sets of components each generate a click event, so three sets of listener objects are created. The first listener handles the clicking of any of the checkboxes. First, an associative array is created to keep track of what was selected for later reference:

```
var dinnerOrderArray:Array = new Object();
```

Then the listener object is created, and a method is added to the object with the same name as the event to be captured:

```
var dinnerOptionListener:Object = new Object();
dinnerOptionListener.click = function(eventObject:Object)
{
    // ...
}
```

A handle to the component that generated the event is obtained from the event object. With this, you can find out the text label for the component, as well as whether it was checked:

```
var checkBoxLabel:String = eventObject.target.label;
var isCheckBoxSelected:Boolean = eventObject.target.selected;
if (isCheckBoxSelected == true)
{
    trace("Selected: " + checkBoxLabel);
}
else
{
    trace("Deselected: " + checkBoxLabel);
}
```

The event listener object is then assigned to each of the checkboxes:

```
dinnerOption1.addEventListener("click", dinnerOptionListener);
dinnerOption2.addEventListener("click", dinnerOptionListener);
dinnerOption3.addEventListener("click", dinnerOptionListener);
```

The same process is performed for the radio buttons:

```
// Handle the selection of one of the dessert radio buttons
var dessertOptionListener:Object = new Object();
dessertOptionListener.click = function(eventObject:Object)
{
    var radioButtonLabel:String = eventObject.target.selection.data;
    trace("Selected: " + radioButtonLabel);
}
dessertOptions.addEventListener("click", dessertOptionListener);
```

The process for adding listener objects to radio buttons is a bit different, in that radio buttons actually have a parent component called RadioButtonGroup that tracks the last selected radio button. Setting the groupName parameter on the Parameters tab automatically creates the group and associates the radio button with that group. As a result, the event listener needs to be assigned only once to the radio button group instead of three times to each radio button.

A reference to the timeline is kept for use in the button handler code, where this refers to the base timeline, _level0:

```
var parentTimeline:MovieClip = this;
```

Next, the listener for the order button is created:

```
// Handle the clicking of the order button
var orderButtonListener:Object = new Object();
orderButtonListener.click = function(eventObject:Object)
{
  // ...
}
orderButton.addEventListener("click", orderButtonListener);
```

The code loops through all the checkboxes, looking for ones that are checked. When it finds one, the label of the selected checkbox is added to an output string that lists everything that has been ordered:

```
var myOrder:String = "Ordering: ";
var tempCheckBoxHandle:mx.controls.CheckBox;

// Find out which dinner options were checked
for (var i:Number = 0; i < 3; i++)
{
    tempCheckBoxHandle = parentTimeline["dinnerOption" + i];
    if (tempCheckBoxHandle.selected == true)
    {
        myOrder += tempCheckBoxHandle.label + ", ";
    }
}
```

The associative array syntax in the loop is used to get the selected state and label of each checkbox. You can do this without the loop:

```
var myOrder:String = "Ordering: ";

// Find out which dinner options were checked
if (dinnerOption0.selected == true)
{
    myOrder += dinnerOption0.label + ", ";
}
if (dinnerOption1.selected == true)
{
    myOrder += dinnerOption1.label + ", ";
}
if (dinnerOption2.selected == true)
{
    myOrder += dinnerOption2.label + ", ";
}
```

But, obviously, this would get quite unwieldy with any more than a few checkboxes.

The radio button group is checked, and the label for the selected radio button is added to the order list:

```
// Find out which dessert was selected
if (dessertOptions.selection != undefined)
{
    myOrder += dessertOptions.selection.label;
}
```

Finally, the order is made:

```
trace(myOrder);
```

Variation of Creating a Listener Object

A variation of the technique just discussed is a little cleaner for some applications. The general idea is that instead of creating a new listener object to hold the event handlers, you use an existing object such as the main timeline:

```
change = function(eventObject:Object)
{
    // Handler code goes here
}
imageList.addEventListener("change", this);
```

This is sometimes convenient for simple cases with only one listener object. Because it can support only one listener object, though, its usage is discouraged in favor of the original listener object technique.

Try It Out   **Using the Stage as a Listener**

In this exercise you use the stage to hold an event listener.

1.   Create a new Macromedia Flash document.

2.   Rename the existing layer in the timeline to `Script`. Create a new layer below it called `Components`.

3.   Click the keyframe on the Components layer to select it. Open the Components panel (Window⇨Components) and then open its User Interface section. Drag one Button component to the stage.

4.   Open the Properties panel (Window⇨Properties), click the button on the stage, and set the instance ID in the text field at the top left of the panel to `myButton`.

5.   The code for this example is small, so enter it in the Actions panel instead of creating a separate ActionScript file. Click the first frame in the timeline, open the Actions panel (Window⇨ Development Panels⇨Actions), and type in the following ActionScript code:

```
click = function(eventObject:Object)
{
    trace("Button clicked");
}
myButton.addEventListener("click", this);
```

6.   Select File⇨Save As, name the file `tryItOut_stageListener.fla`, choose an appropriate directory, and save it. Select Control⇨Test Movie.

How It Works

This example shows how you would use the timeline as an event listener object. The timeline is a child of the Object class, making it a candidate to hold custom methods.

Creating a Listener Function

Another variation of the listener involves using a regular function instead of an object:

```
function myChangeHandler(eventObject:Object)
{
    // Handler code goes here
}
imageList.addEventListener("change", myChangeHandler);
```

This is more in line with how events are handled outside components, where functions are assigned to a property representing the event. One of the differences between a listener function and a listener object is that of variable scope. Consider what happens when using the `this` keyword in a listener object and a listener function. First, the listener object:

```
imageListListener.change = function(eventObject:Object)
{
    trace(this);
```

```
    }
    imageList.addEventListener("change", this);
    // Outputs: [object Object]
```

Next, the listener function:

```
    function myChangeHandler(eventObject:Object)
    {
        trace(this);
    }
    imageList.addEventListener("change", myChangeHandler);
    // Outputs: _level0.imageList
```

Recall that `this` refers to the containing object for any code that calls it. When called from code placed directly on the main timeline, it refers to the timeline. When called from a class or a function called by a class, it refers to the class instance. In the case of the listener object, `this` refers to the listener object itself. In the case of the listener function, `this` refers to the calling component. As a result of this listener function characteristic, you can access all of the component's properties and methods without having to access the event object. The following code shows that the List component properties `rowCount` and `selectedItem` can be directly accessed from within the listener function:

```
    function myChangeHandler(eventObject:Object):Void
    {
        trace("num rows: " + this.rowCount);
        trace("row data: " + this.selectedItem.data);
    }
    imageList.addEventListener("change", myChangeHandler);
    // Outputs:
    // num rows: 4
    // row data: http://www.nathanderksen.com/book/fullsize/aStudyInTexture.jpg
```

As a result, the handle to the event object is not needed in this case.

Try It Out   Using a Listener Function

In this exercise you learn how to use a listener function. Just follow these steps:

1. Create a new Macromedia Flash document by selecting File⇨New and choosing Flash Document from the New Document panel.

2. Rename the existing layer in the timeline to `Script`. Create a new layer below the script layer called `Components`.

3. Click the keyframe on the Components layer to select it. Open the User Interface section of the Components panel. Drag two Button components to the stage.

4. Open the Properties panel (Window⇨Properties), select the first button on the stage, and set the instance ID in the text field at the top left of the panel to `playButton`. Select the second button on the stage and set the instance ID to `pauseButton`.

5. The code for this example is small, so enter it in the Actions panel instead of creating a separate ActionScript file. Click the first frame in the timeline, open the Actions panel (Window⇨ Development Panels⇨Actions), and type in the following ActionScript code:

```
function buttonHandler(eventObject:Object):Void
{
    switch(this._name)
    {
        case "playButton":
            trace("Pressed play button");
            break;
        case "pauseButton":
            trace("Pressed pause button");
            break;
    }}
playButton.addEventListener("click", buttonHandler);
pauseButton.addEventListener("click", buttonHandler);
```

6. Name the file `tryItOut_listenerFunction.fla`, and save it in an appropriate directory. Select Control⇨Test Movie.

How It Works

In this example you created a single listener function that handles events from multiple Button components. The function has access to the name of the button, which it uses to decide how to respond.

Which Listener Technique Should You Use?

Basically, you should use the listener technique with which you're most comfortable. The listener object technique is the one in most widespread use, and almost all documentation shows it within the examples. The code for the variation that uses the stage as a listener object looks a bit cleaner and is fine for very simple projects, but it loses the versatility that the listener is supposed to provide. The listener function technique is very rarely seen in the wild, possibly because few people know about it; however, its structural similarity to older event-handling techniques makes it a bit easier to understand and work with, while its broadcast qualities give the same advantages that listener objects provide.

Try It Out   **Adding Event Handlers to Your Image Viewer**

In this exercise you add listener event handlers to the picture viewer to respond to user interactions. You also put into place the remaining code needed to make this a functional example. Here are the steps to follow:

1. Open the completed `tryItOut_scriptingComponents.fla` file from the preceding Try It Out exercise, or open `tryItOut_scriptingComponents.fla` from the book's source files at <source file directory>/Chapter 10/tryItOut_scriptingComponents_v2/.

2. Open the completed `tryItOut_scriptingComponents.as` file from the preceding Try It Out exercise, or open `tryItOut_scriptingComponents.as` from the book's source files at <source file directory>/Chapter 10/tryItOut_scriptingComponents_v2/.

3. Copy the <source file directory>/Chapter 10/tryItOut_scriptingComponents_v2/images directory (not just the directory contents) into the directory containing your `.fla` and `.as` files.

4. Update the ActionScript file to contain the following code:

```
var imageListListener:Object = new Object();
imageListListener.change = function(eventObject:Object)
{
    loadImage(eventObject.target.selectedItem.data);
}

var zoomListener:Object = new Object();
zoomListener.change = function(eventObject:Object)
{
    setZoom(eventObject.target.value);
}

var imageViewerListener:Object = new Object();
imageViewerListener.progress = function(eventObject:Object)
{
    var bytesLoaded:Number = eventObject.target.getBytesLoaded();
    var bytesTotal:Number = eventObject.target.getBytesTotal();
    trace("Image Viewer Progress: "+bytesLoaded+"/"+bytesTotal);
    if(bytesLoaded == -1)
    {
        loadImageError();
    }
    else
    {
        imageViewerProgress.setProgress(bytesLoaded, bytesTotal);
    }
}

imageViewerListener.complete = function(eventObject:Object)
{
    trace("Image Viewer Complete");
    imageViewerProgress._visible = false;
    setZoom(zoomStepper.value);
}

function init() : Void
{
    // Send data to the image list component
    var imageArray:Array = new Array();
    imageArray.push({data:"images/aStudyInTexture.jpg", label:"A Study In
Texture"});
    imageArray.push({data:"images/buntzenWinter.jpg", label:"Buntzen Winter"});
    imageArray.push({data:"images/flowerInDetail.jpg", label:"Flower In Detail"});
    imageArray.push({data:"images/galianoSunset.jpg", label:"Galiano Sunset"});
    imageList.dataProvider = imageArray;
    imageList.addEventListener("change", imageListListener);

    // Setup for the progress bar component
    imageViewerProgress.mode = "manual";
    imageViewerProgress._visible = false;

    // Setup for the scrollable image viewer component
    imageViewerPane.scrollDrag = true;
```

```
        imageViewerPane.addEventListener("progress", imageViewerListener);
        imageViewerPane.addEventListener("complete", imageViewerListener);

        // Setup for the zoom stepper component
        zoomStepper.maximum = 400;
        zoomStepper.minimum = 25;
        zoomStepper.stepSize = 25;
        zoomStepper.value = 100;
        zoomStepper.addEventListener("change", zoomListener);
    }

    function loadImage(imagePath:String) : Void
    {
        trace("loading: " + imagePath);
        if (imagePath != "" && imagePath != undefined)
        {
            imageViewerPane.contentPath = "";
            imageViewerPane.contentPath = imagePath;
            imageViewerProgress._visible = true;
            imageViewerProgress.setProgress(0, 100);
        }
    }

    function loadImageError() : Void
    {
        imageViewerProgress._visible = false;
        imageList.selectedIndex = null;
        imageViewerPane.contentPath = "";
    }

    function setZoom(zoomValue:Number) : Void
    {
        imageViewerPane.content._xscale = zoomValue;
        imageViewerPane.content._yscale = zoomValue;
        imageViewerPane.invalidate();
    }

    init();
```

5.   Save the file, return to the Macromedia Flash project file, and select Control⇨Test Movie.

How It Works

You first create the event listener objects, beginning with one for the image list component:

```
var imageListListener:Object = new Object();
imageListListener.change = function(eventObject:Object)
{
    loadImage(eventObject.target.selectedItem.data);
}
```

The listener defines a handler for the change event, which fires every time the user clicks a different list row. The event listener gets the image URL from the selected row's data property and passes that to the loadImage() function.

The listener is created for the zoom stepper component:

```
var zoomListener:Object = new Object();
zoomListener.change = function(eventObject:Object)
{
    setZoom(eventObject.target.value);
}
```

Once again, a change event handler is defined, which fires every time a new zoom value is selected from the NumericStepper component, either from clicking the up or down arrows, or by typing in a new value and pressing Enter.

Notice that the code in these two event handlers is minimal. Part of the best practices for development is to make code as generic as possible. Rather than writing code directly in the event handlers to load and to zoom the image, that code is placed within the functions. This provides greater flexibility in working with events.

The image viewer listener object is created, and a progress listener is constructed to check to see how much of the image has loaded and whether there was an error in finding the image (this code is taken from the pre-loader examples earlier in the book):

```
var imageViewerListener:Object = new Object();
imageViewerListener.progress = function(eventObject:Object)
{
    var bytesLoaded:Number = eventObject.target.getBytesLoaded();
    var bytesTotal:Number = eventObject.target.getBytesTotal();
    trace("Image Viewer Progress: "+bytesLoaded+"/"+bytesTotal);
    if(bytesLoaded == -1)
    {
        loadImageError();
    }
    else
    {
        imageViewerProgress.setProgress(bytesLoaded, bytesTotal);
    }
}
```

Once the image is loaded, some maintenance needs to be performed. The complete listener fires at the end of the image load, hiding the progress bar and scaling the image to match the scaling set in the zoom stepper component:

```
imageViewerListener.complete = function(eventObject:Object)
{
    trace("Image Viewer Complete");
    imageViewerProgress._visible = false;
    setZoom(zoomStepper.value);
}
```

Next, the init() function is defined. For the most part this is the same function as in the preceding Try It Out exercise. The only code that has been added is to assign event listeners to the imageList and zoomStepper components:

```
function init() : Void
{
    // Send data to the image list component
    var imageArray:Array = new Array();
    imageArray.push({data:"images/aStudyInTexture.jpg", label:"A Study In
Texture"});
    imageArray.push({data:"images/buntzenWinter.jpg", label:"Buntzen Winter"});
    imageArray.push({data:"images/flowerInDetail.jpg", label:"Flower In Detail"});
    imageArray.push({data:"images", label:"Galiano Sunset"});
    imageList.dataProvider = imageArray;
    imageList.addEventListener("change", imageListListener);

    // Setup for the progress bar component
    imageViewerProgress.mode = "manual";
    imageViewerProgress._visible = false;

    // Setup for the scrollable image viewer component
    imageViewerPane.scrollDrag = true;

    // Setup for the zoom stepper component
    zoomStepper.maximum = 400;
    zoomStepper.minimum = 25;
    zoomStepper.stepSize = 25;
    zoomStepper.value = 100;
    zoomStepper.addEventListener("change", zoomListener);
}
```

That's all that is needed to actually implement the event listeners. The remaining code provides the actual functionality behind the application:

```
function loadImage(imagePath:String) : Void
{
    trace("loading: " + imagePath);
    if (imagePath != "" && imagePath != undefined)
    {
        imageViewerPane.contentPath = "";
        imageViewerPane.contentPath = imagePath;
        imageViewerProgress._visible = true;
        imageViewerProgress.setProgress(0, 100);

        clearInterval(intervalID);
        intervalID = setInterval(checkProgress, 200);
    }
}
```

The loadImage() function makes sure that the string passed in with the path to the image is not blank, starts loading the image, and sets up the progress bar. The two calls to contentPath are there so that any image already shown in the image viewer pane is cleared out first. The call to setInterval() starts a polling process to monitor the progress of the image loading. The call to clearInterval() makes sure that if this is interrupting a previous load, the previous polling process is stopped.

If the image could not be found, some cleanup is performed. The selected row in the image list is deselected, the progress bar is hidden, and the image viewer pane is reset:

```
function loadImageError() : Void
{
    imageViewerProgress._visible = false;
    imageList.selectedIndex = null;
    imageViewerPane.contentPath = "";
}
```

The `setZoom()` function does the actual scaling of the image based on the percent scale value passed in, and the `invalidate()` call tells the component to redraw itself because the scroll bars need to be updated to properly reflect the new size of the re-sized image:

```
function setZoom(zoomValue:Number) : Void
{
    imageViewerPane.content._xscale = zoomValue;
    imageViewerPane.content._yscale = zoomValue;
    imageViewerPane.invalidate();
}
```

Finally, the startup function is called:

```
init();
```

Attaching Multiple Listeners to Multiple Components

So far, all of the event handling you've seen uses a one-to-one mapping between the listener object and the component. Although the preceding example does show how one listener could be assigned to multiple checkboxes, it misses the real advantage of using listeners: Not only can you assign a listener to multiple components, you can assign multiple listeners to a single component.

Listeners work by a system of publishing and subscribing. In much the same way as many people can subscribe to a magazine, multiple objects can subscribe to the same event on the same component. Each time the `addEventListener()` method is called on a component, a new subscriber is added to that component's subscriber list. Every time the component generates an event, it notifies each of its subscribers.

Figure 10-2 shows some additional functionality in the ongoing image viewer project. A second list component is added on the left to list basic video content. It gives you another source of events for your listeners.

As you add functionality to a project, you may find that the listener setup becomes more complex and harder to work with. Once (or preferably before) this happens, it's a good idea to step back and take a look at whether you can better organize the listeners.

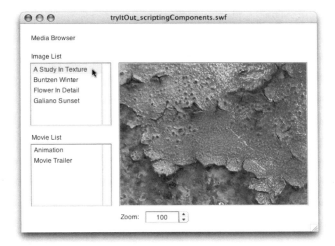

Figure 10-2

Organizing the Listeners

As you add functionality to an interface, you have to structure the code to best handle that functionality. You need to know how to best apply your listener objects to handle user input.

One possibility is to have one listener object for each component on the screen, giving you four listeners for the image viewer project. That works, and many people do it that way. But instead of thinking in terms of the components on the screen, consider the functionality you have, and then map that to the components that provide the functionality. In Figure 10-2, for example, you can divide the interface into two functional groupings: the media list menus (the two list boxes) and the media viewer area (the scroll pane and zoom box).

Take a look at what the listener structure for that setup might look like:

```
var mediaListListener:Object = new Object();
mediaListListener.change = function(eventObject:Object)
{
    // Handler code
}
imageList.addEventListener("change", mediaListListener);
movieList.addEventListener("change", mediaListListener);

var mediaViewerListener:Object = new Object();
mediaViewerListener.change = function(eventObject:Object)
{
    // Handler code
}
imageList.addEventListener("change", mediaViewerListener);
movieList.addEventListener("change", mediaViewerListener);
zoomStepper.addEventListener("change", mediaViewerListener);
```

This has two listener objects: one for managing the menu and one for managing the media viewer area. Both objects subscribe to the change event of both list components. It looks like there's not much separation between the two functional areas, but consider what the event handlers need to do. The menu handler's job is basically to ensure that when something from one list is selected, the other list has nothing selected. That's it.

The media viewer listener subscribes to the image list and the movie list components because it needs to know when to load new content. Once it gets that event, it operates as a self-contained unit that loads, zooms, and unloads content.

Handling Events from Multiple Sources

The functional listener structure could work, but there's a small problem. The event that is of interest in all of the components is change. You have just one click handler in each listener object, so how do you know which component generated the event?

Fortunately, there is an easy way to deal with that. It is not listed within the component documentation, but every object in Flash that has an instance name also has a _name property that you can use to retrieve the instance name. You have a handle to the calling component via the event target property, so the following gets the name of the component generating the event:

```
var mediaListListener:Object = new Object();
mediaListListener.change = function(eventObject:Object)
{
    trace("Instance name: " + eventObject.target._name);
}
imageList.addEventListener("change", mediaListListener);
movieList.addEventListener("change", mediaListListener);
```

You can use the same listener now to handle events from both an image list component and a movie list component:

```
var mediaListListener:Object = new Object();
mediaListListener.change = function(eventObject:Object)
{
    if (eventObject.target._name == "imageList")
    {
        // Deselect anything selected in movieList
    }
    else if (eventObject.target._name == "movieList")
    {
        // Deselect anything selected in imageList
    }
}
imageList.addEventListener("change", mediaListListener);
movieList.addEventListener("change", mediaListListener);
```

Similarly, you can create a media viewer listener that can listen for events from an image list component, a movie list component, and the zoom stepper:

```
var mediaViewerListener:Object = new Object();
mediaViewerListener.change = function(eventObject:Object)
{
    if (eventObject.target._name == "imageList")
    {
        // Load an image
    }
    else if (eventObject.target._name == "movieList")
    {
        // Load a movie
    }
    else if (eventObject.target._name == "zoomStepper")
    {
        // Set the content area scaling
    }
}
imageList.addEventListener("change", mediaViewerListener);
movieList.addEventListener("change", mediaViewerListener);
zoomStepper.addEventListener("change", mediaViewerListener);
```

You now have a blueprint for how to manage each component's events. Try this out on the image viewer application.

Try It Out   Organizing Events for the Image Viewer Project

In this exercise, you add a list component to the interface. You also modify the event listener objects so that they better separate units of functionality. Here are the steps:

1. Open the completed `tryItOut_scriptingComponents.fla` file from the first Try It Out exercise, or open `tryItOut_scriptingComponents.fla` from the book's source files at <source file directory>/Chapter 10/tryItOut_scriptingComponents_v3/.

2. Copy the <source file directory>/Chapter 10/tryItOut_scriptingComponents_v3/movies directory (not just the directory contents) into the directory containing your `.fla` and `.as` files.

3. Click the image list component on the stage to select it. Open the Properties panel and change the height to `120` pixels.

4. Open the Components panel's User Interface section and drag a new List component to the stage. Change its properties to x: `18`, y: `30`, width: `150`, and height: `120`.

5. Drag a new Label component to the stage. Set its x and y values to `18` and `208` pixels, respectively. Switch to the Parameters tab in the Properties panel and set the text parameter to `Movie List`.

6. Save the file.

7. Open the completed `tryItOut_scriptingComponents.as` file from the first Try It Out exercise, or open `tryItOut_scriptingComponents.as` from the book's source files at <root TBD>/Chapter 5/tryItOut_scriptingComponents_v3/.

8. Update the ActionScript file so that it looks like this:

```
// Handle the appearance of the list components
var mediaListListener:Object = new Object();
mediaListListener.change = function(eventObject:Object)
{
    if (eventObject.target._name == "imageList")
    {
        movieList.selectedIndex = null;
    }
    else if (eventObject.target._name == "movieList")
    {
        imageList.selectedIndex = null;
    }
}

// Zoom listener removed

// Handle changes to the main content area
var mediaViewerListener:Object = new Object();
mediaViewerListener.change = function(eventObject:Object)
{
    if (eventObject.target._name == "imageList")
    {
        loadMedia(eventObject.target.selectedItem.data, "image");
    }
    else if (eventObject.target._name == "movieList")
    {
        loadMedia(eventObject.target.selectedItem.data, "video");
    }
    else if (eventObject.target._name == "zoomStepper")
    {
        setZoom(eventObject.target.value);
    }
}

mediaViewerListener.progress = function(eventObject:Object)
{
    var bytesLoaded:Number = eventObject.target.getBytesLoaded();
    var bytesTotal:Number = eventObject.target.getBytesTotal();
    trace("Image Viewer Progress: "+bytesLoaded+"/"+bytesTotal);
    if(bytesLoaded == -1)
    {
        loadImageError();
    }
    else
    {
```

```
            mediaViewerProgress.setProgress(bytesLoaded, bytesTotal);
    }
}


mediaViewerListener.complete = function(eventObject:Object)
{
    trace("Image Viewer Complete");
    mediaViewerProgress._visible = false;
    setZoom(zoomStepper.value);
}

function init() : Void
{
    // Send data to the image list component
    var imageArray:Array = new Array();
    imageArray.push({data:"images/aStudyInTexture.jpg", label:"A Study In
Texture"});
    imageArray.push({data:"images/buntzenWinter.jpg", label:"Buntzen Winter"});
    imageArray.push({data:"images/flowerInDetail.jpg", label:"Flower In Detail"});
    imageArray.push({data:"images/galianoSunset.jpg", label:"Galiano Sunset"});
    imageList.dataProvider = imageArray;
    imageList.addEventListener("change", mediaListListener);
    imageList.addEventListener("change", mediaViewerListener);

    // Send data to the movie list component
    var movieArray:Array = new Array();
    movieArray.push({data:"movies/animation.swf", label:"Animation"});
    movieArray.push({data:"movies/snowStorm.swf", label:"Snow Storm"});
    movieList.dataProvider = movieArray;
    movieList.addEventListener("change", mediaListListener);
    movieList.addEventListener("change", mediaViewerListener);

    // Setup for the progress bar component
    mediaViewerProgress.mode = "manual";
    mediaViewerProgress._visible = false;

    // Setup for the scrollable media viewer component
    mediaViewerPane.scrollDrag = true;
    mediaViewerPane.addEventListener("progress", mediaViewerListener);
    mediaViewerPane.addEventListener("complete", mediaViewerListener);

    // Setup for the zoom stepper component
    zoomStepper.maximum = 400;
    zoomStepper.minimum = 25;
    zoomStepper.stepSize = 25;
    zoomStepper.value = 100;
    zoomStepper.addEventListener("change", mediaViewerListener);
}

function loadMedia(mediaPath:String, type:String) : Void
{
    trace("loading: " + mediaPath);
    if (mediaPath != "" && mediaPath != undefined)
    {
        mediaViewerPane.contentPath = "";
```

```
        mediaViewerPane.contentPath = mediaPath;
        mediaViewerProgress._visible = true;
        mediaViewerProgress.setProgress(0, 100);
    }
}

function loadMediaError() : Void
{
    trace("loadMediaError");
    mediaViewerProgress._visible = false;
    imageList.selectedIndex = null;
    videoList.selectedIndex = null;
    mediaViewerPane.contentPath = "";
}

function setZoom(zoomValue:Number) : Void
{
    mediaViewerPane.content._xscale = zoomValue;
    mediaViewerPane.content._yscale = zoomValue;
    mediaViewerPane.invalidate();
}

init();
```

9. Save the file, return to the Macromedia Flash project file, and select Control⇨Test Movie.

How It Works

First, listener objects are created to handle functionality from different parts of the application. The media list listener deals only with handling the interaction between the two list components:

```
var mediaListListener:Object = new Object();
mediaListListener.change = function(eventObject:Object)
{
    if (eventObject.target._name == "imageList")
    {
        movieList.selectedIndex = null;
    }
    else if (eventObject.target._name == "movieList")
    {
        imageList.selectedIndex = null;
    }
}
```

The listener checks to see which list component generated the event. If the image list component generated the event, the listener deselects anything that might be selected in the movie list component, and vice versa. This code does not deal with any aspects of loading the media, just with managing the menu. If you were to add additional functionality — say, for example, thumbnail image buttons for selecting images — only this listener would need to be updated to accommodate it.

The media viewer listener manages the loading and presentation of the media in the scroll pane component:

```
var mediaViewerListener:Object = new Object();
mediaViewerListener.change = function(eventObject:Object)
```

```
    {
        if (eventObject.target._name == "imageList")
        {
            loadMedia(eventObject.target.selectedItem.data, "image");
        }
        else if (eventObject.target._name == "movieList")
        {
            loadMedia(eventObject.target.selectedItem.data, "video");
        }
        else if (eventObject.target._name == "zoomStepper")
        {
            setZoom(eventObject.target.value);
        }
    }
}
```

Once again, the listener checks to see which component generated the event. If it is one of the list components, it loads the selected media clip into the scroll pane; if the event originates from the zoom box, it adjusts the scaling of the content.

The two `loadMedia()` functions pass along a parameter selecting the media type. This is not actually used here, but it could handle different media presentation implementations based on the media type. For instance, the video could be placed inside a movie clip instead of the scroll pane because movies generally should not scroll. If this change were to be made, only the media viewer listener would need to change. The media list listener would not need to be touched.

Next, the initialization function is defined. The image list component is loaded with data, and both listeners are registered with this component:

```
var imageArray:Array = new Array();
imageArray.push({data:"images/aStudyInTexture.jpg", label:"A Study In Texture"});
imageArray.push({data:"images/buntzenWinter.jpg", label:"Buntzen Winter"});
imageArray.push({data:"images/flowerInDetail.jpg", label:"Flower In Detail"});
imageArray.push({data:"images/galianoSunset.jpg", label:"Galiano Sunset"});
imageList.dataProvider = imageArray;
imageList.addEventListener("change", mediaListListener);
imageList.addEventListener("change", mediaViewerListener);
```

The movie list component is loaded with data, and both listeners are registered with this component:

```
// Send data to the video list component
var movieArray:Array = new Array();
movieArray.push({data:"images/animation.swf", label:"Animation"});
movieArray.push({data:"movies/snowStorm.swf", label:"Snow Storm"});
movieList.dataProvider = movieArray;
movieList.addEventListener("change", mediaListListener);
movieList.addEventListener("change", mediaViewerListener);
```

The zoom stepper is initialized, and the media viewer listener is registered with this component. The listener call takes the place of the separate zoom stepper listener:

```
// Setup for the zoom stepper component
zoomStepper.maximum = 400;
```

```
zoomStepper.minimum = 25;
zoomStepper.stepSize = 25;
zoomStepper.value = 100;
zoomStepper.addEventListener("change", mediaViewerListener);
```

The remaining code deals with the actual implementation of the loading and resizing, and is not changed significantly from the previous exercise with this project.

Manually Invoking Events in a Component

So far, it's been assumed that component events are always triggered by a user action. That is not always the case; sometimes you may want to manually trigger an event, just so you do not have to write code to do something that's already been handled. Say you have a list component, and you want to pre-select the first item in the list. You would do this with

```
componentHandle.selectedIndex = 0;
```

The problem is that the `change` event is generated only when a change is initiated by the user, so setting the selected row doesn't affect the rest of your interface. You could manually call the same code that the event handler calls, but that is a waste. Instead, manually trigger the event using the `dispatchEvent()` method as follows, and any interested listeners also will be triggered:

```
componentHandle.dispatchEvent({type:"change"});
```

Try it out in the following exercise.

Try It Out   **Manually Trigger an Event**

In this exercise you manually trigger an event that otherwise would require a user action.

1. Create a new Macromedia Flash document.

2. Rename the existing layer in the timeline to `Script`. Create a new layer below it called `Components`.

3. Click the keyframe on the Components layer to select it. Open the Components panel's User Interface section. Drag one List component to the stage.

4. Open the Properties panel, click the button on the stage, and set the instance ID to `myList`.

5. The code for this example is small, so enter it in the Actions panel instead of creating a separate ActionScript file. Click the first frame in the timeline, open the Actions panel, and type in the following ActionScript code:

```
var listListener:Object = new Object();
listListener.change = function(eventObject:Object)
{
    trace("Selected item: " + eventObject.target.selectedItem.data);
```

```
    }

    var listArray:Array = new Array();
    listArray.push({data:"value1", label:"Label 1"});
    listArray.push({data:"value2", label:"Label 2"});
    listArray.push({data:"value3", label:"Label 3"});
    myList.dataProvider = listArray;
    myList.addEventListener("change", listListener);

    myList.selectedIndex = 0;
```

6. Name the file `tryItOut_manualEvent.fla`, choose an appropriate directory, and save it. Select Control⇨Test Movie.

7. Add the following line to the end of the code listing and then test the movie again:

```
    myList.dispatchEvent({type:"change"});
```

How It Works

When you run this program without the `dispatchEvent()` call, the change event is not dispatched so nothing's sent to the output panel even though the first item is selected. By adding the `dispatchEvent()` method, the listener's `change` event is triggered, and the output panel shows a line giving the value of the selected row.

Summary

This chapter explored the process of working with component events. Some points to remember include the following:

❑ Events are used for user interaction. They are captured through the use of listeners that are invoked whenever an event is broadcasted from a component.

❑ Listeners work on a subscription model where a component builds a list of all the listeners interested in a particular event from that component, and it notifies them all when that event takes place.

❑ Listeners can be structured so that there's good separation between different areas of functionality. Listeners do not need to be created to provide a one-to-one mapping to component instances.

❑ The stage is itself an object, and functions on the stage can be used as listeners for some simple setups.

❑ Listener functions can be used in place of listener objects. Which you use is largely a matter of personal preference, but listener objects are more commonly used and better documented.

Exercise

1. Extend exercise 2 from Chapter 9 by adding two event listener objects to respond to the click events of each of the three buttons and to the change event of the data grid. The first event listener is to manage adding, removing, and updating rows in the data grid when any of the three buttons are clicked. The second event listener manages what to show in the title and the text fields when any of the buttons are clicked or a new row is selected in the data grid. The interface should behave as follows:

❏ The Add, Save, and Delete buttons are disabled by default.

❏ Making changes to the Title or Text fields enables the Add and Save buttons.

❏ Clicking a row populates the Title and the Text fields, and enables the Delete button.

❏ Clicking Delete removes the selected row, and automatically selects the next row in the list. If there are no rows left, the Delete button is disabled.

❏ Clicking the Add button creates a new row based on the contents of the Title and the Text fields, and automatically highlights the new row in the list.

❏ Clicking the Save button updates the values for the currently selected row to reflect any changes to the Title and the Text fields.

Controlling Components

Macromedia Flash has, since MX 2004, the capability for components to pass data between each other automatically. This is done through the concept of *data binding*, in which component inputs and outputs are linked to each other. You can set up data bindings either through the Component Inspector panel or by using the set of bindings classes. This book introduces how to set up bindings only through the Component Inspector panel because using the bindings classes is a complicated process that would almost require its own book.

Introducing the Component Inspector Panel

The Component Inspector panel (Window⇨Component Inspector) contains a tabbed interface as shown in Figure 11-1.

The Parameters tab, open in Figure 11-1, is a duplicate of the Parameters tab in the Properties panel. It contains basic startup information such as the URL for the XML file to load for the XMLConnector component.

The Bindings tab (see Figure 11-2) provides the means to link components together. One component can bind to multiple properties on multiple different components.

The Schema tab, open in Figure 11-3, shows the properties that are available for binding with other components. For the XMLConnector component, you can link specific tags in your XML file to different components by adding information about the XML data. You can also define custom properties that can send and receive data.

Figure 11-1

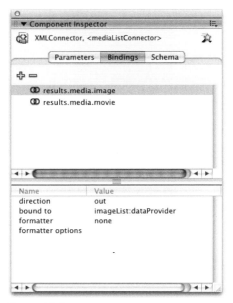

Figure 11-2

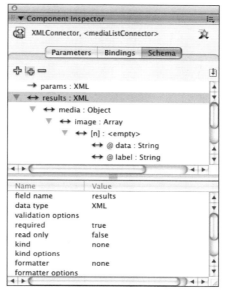

Figure 11-3

Through these three panels, nearly every exposed property on any of the pre-installed components can be linked to any other exposed property on any other component.

Creating Data Bindings between Components Using the Bindings Tab

The process of creating a binding between two components basically involves selecting a source component, choosing the parameter on the source component to use as data, and then selecting a target component and a data parameter for the target. An example is the easiest way to demonstrate how this works.

Try It Out **Setting Up a Binding**

In this exercise you link together two bindable properties on two different components. Here's what to do:

1. Create a new Macromedia Flash document.

2. Open the User Interface section of the Components panel. Drag one DateChooser component and one Label component to the stage.

3. Click the DateChooser component to select it. Open the Properties panel and give the component the instance name myDateChooser.

4. Select the Label component and give it the instance name myLabel. Go to the Parameters tab of the Properties panel and set the autoSize parameter to left.

5. Click the DateChooser component again. Open the Component Inspector panel (Window⇨ Component Inspector) and select the Bindings tab.

6. Click the + icon under the tab names. In the dialog box that opens, choose the selectedDate option and click OK.

7. In the binding details area at the bottom of the panel, change the `direction` to `out`. Double-click the data area next to the bound to label. In the dialog box that opens, select `myLabel`, make sure the `text` property is highlighted, and click OK. The panel should now look like Figure 11-4.

Figure 11-4

8. Select File⇨Save As, name the file `tryItOut_bindingComponents.fla`, choose an appropriate directory, and save it. Select Control⇨Test Movie, and select a date from the date chooser.

9. Close the movie test window and return to the Flash file. Return to the Bindings tab for the date chooser, and select the Date option from the drop-down menu next to the formatter label. Double-click the data area next to the formatter options field, enter MM/DD/YYYY into the prompt that appears, and click OK.

10. Click the Label component on the stage and observe that it shows a binding as well, but from the opposite direction of the data flow.

11. Save the Flash file and select Control⇨Test Movie. Select a date from the date chooser.

How It Works

In this exercise, you create a simple binding between the `selectedDate` property in the `myDateChooser` component and the `text` property of the `myLabel` component. The binding is created from the perspective of the date chooser component, where data is flowing out of the component. Once you set up the data binding, the Flash binding framework automatically deals with the flow of data between the components. In this case, any time the calendar component's `selectedDate` property changes, the binding framework automatically broadcasts that change to all interested listeners. The only interested listener here is a label component, whose `text` property is assigned the value of the calendar's `selectedDate` property.

The binding could also have been created the other way around, by selecting the label component, linking its `text` property to the `selectedDate` property of the date chooser, and setting the data direction to `in` instead of `out`. Figure 11-5 shows what the settings look like when viewing from the perspective of the label instead of the date chooser.

Figure 11-5

Setting up a binding for simple components is a straightforward process, although there are a couple of issues to keep in mind. First, you are restricted to the properties that are designated as bindable. For instance, the `selected` property of a checkbox cannot be linked to the `enabled` property of another component, because no components expose a bindable `enabled` property even though all components have that property.

The other issue is that as the number of components increase, the number of connections can potentially increase significantly as well. It also means that dependencies can form where there is not a clear separation in functionality between one part of the interface and another.

As a result of these issues, I recommend avoiding component binding for anything other than low to medium complexity interfaces.

Using an XML File as a Data Source

A fairly natural extension of list-type components — ComboBox, DataGrid, List, and Tree — is to be able to populate them from an external data source. (Chapter 21 covers XML in depth, so we skip many of those details here when using XML with data bindings to populate components.)

The steps for using an XML file as a data source are similar to those used in the previous data binding example, except that you need to add an XML *schema*. A schema is a model for data. Although many components already have a pre-built schema that provides a list of bindable properties, there is no way that the Flash authoring environment can know the data makeup of your XML file without actually seeing it. Once the schema of your XML file is known, you can start binding XML data to other components.

The first step in setting up an XML connector is to give it a sample XML file that represents the data that you will be using. There's an icon on the top right of the Schema tab in the Component Inspector panel that enables you to select an XML file. Here's an example file:

```
<?xml version="1.0"?>
<media>
    <image data="some data" label="some label" />
    <image data="some data" label="some label" />
    <movie data="some data" label="some label" />
    <movie data="some data" label="some label" />
</media>
```

Generally, you just use the same XML file that is to be loaded during runtime. The Schema mechanism gets two things out of this file: how the data is organized, and which elements are repeating. Any elements that repeat are candidates to bind with a list view. In this case, there's one root element, the <media> element (all XML files must have exactly one root element). Within that, there are two repeating nested elements, <image> and <movie>.

Figure 11-6 shows the schema for the XML connector before and after importing a sample XML file. The circled button is the one to use to initiate the import of the sample XML file.

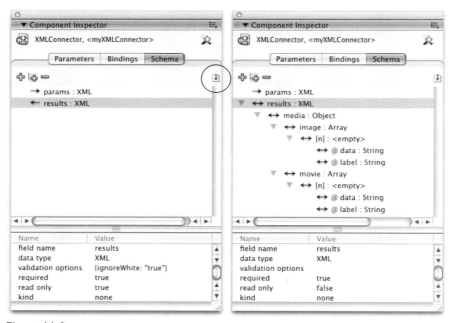

Figure 11-6

Once the schema is set up, you handle the binding much like you did in the preceding Try It Out. The following exercise takes you through the process step-by-step.

Try It Out   Adding an XML Connector to Your Image Viewer

In this exercise, you connect two list components to data fed in from an XML connector.

1. Using your preferred text editor, create a text file called `mediaList.xml` and save it to the same folder that you will use for the rest of this exercise. Enter the following XML markup into this file:

```
<?xml version="1.0"?>
<media>
    <image data="http://www.nathanderksen.com/book/↩
        fullsize/aStudyInTexture.jpg" label="A Study In Texture" />
    <image data="http://www.nathanderksen.com/book/↩
        fullsize/buntzenWinter.jpg" label="Buntzen Winter" />
    <image data="http://www.nathanderksen.com/book/↩
        fullsize/flowerInDetail.jpg" label="Flower In Detail" />
    <image data="http://www.nathanderksen.com/book/↩
        fullsize/galianoSunset.jpg" label="Galiano Sunset" />
    <movie data="http://www.nathanderksen.com/book/movieClipOverview.swf" ↩
        label="Animation" />
    <movie data="http://www.nathanderksen.com/book/trailer.swf" ↩
        label="Movie Trailer" />
</media>
```

2. Open the completed `tryItOut_scriptingComponents.fla` file from the first Try It Out exercise, or open `tryItOut_scriptingComponents.fla` from the book's source files at <source file directory>/Chapter 11/tryItOut_scriptingComponents_v4/.

3. Open the Components panel (Window⇨Components) and drag a new XMLConnector component from the Data section to the stage. Place it anywhere; it won't show up when published.

4. Open the Properties panel (Window⇨Properties) and give the component an instance name of `mediaListXMLConnector` by typing this name into the top-left text box in the panel.

5. Open the Component Inspector panel and select the Schema tab. Click the results row to select it. Click the small document icon (highlighted in Figure 11-6) with a down-pointing arrow located at the top right of the panel, just under the tab. In the dialog box that opens, locate and select the XML file that you created step 1.

6. Select the Bindings tab in the Component Inspector. Click the + button to add a binding. Select the row labeled `image:Array` and click the OK button.

7. With the new binding selected in the bindings list, change the `direction` option to `out`. Double-click the empty cell to the right of the bound to label. In the dialog box that pops up, select the component with the ID `imageList`, make sure that `dataProvider` is selected, and click the OK button.

8. Click the + button to add another binding. Select the row labeled `movie:Array` and click the OK button.

9. With the new binding selected in the bindings list, change the direction option to `out`. Double-click the empty cell to the right of the `bound to` label. In the dialog box that pops up, select the component with the ID `movieList`, make sure that `dataProvider` is selected, and click the OK button. Your Bindings tab should now look like Figure 11-7.

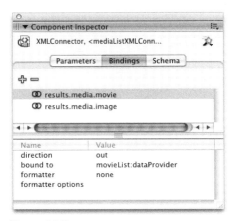

Figure 11-7

10. Open the completed `tryItOut_scriptingComponents.as` file from the first Try It Out exercise, or open `tryItOut_scriptingComponents.as` from the book's source files at <source file directory>/Chapter 11/tryItOut_scriptingComponents_v4/.

11. Update the `init()` function in the ActionScript file so that it looks like this:

```
function init() : Void
{
    // Send data to the image list and movie list components
    mediaListXMLConnector.direction = "receive";
    mediaListXMLConnector.URL = "mediaList.xml";
    mediaListXMLConnector.trigger();

    imageList.addEventListener("change", mediaListListener);
    imageList.addEventListener("change", mediaViewerListener);

    movieList.addEventListener("change", mediaListListener);
    movieList.addEventListener("change", mediaViewerListener);

    // Setup for the zoom stepper component
    zoomStepper.maximum = 400;
    zoomStepper.minimum = 25;
    zoomStepper.stepSize = 25;
    zoomStepper.value = 100;
    zoomStepper.addEventListener("change", mediaViewerListener);

    // Setup for the progress bar component
    mediaViewerProgress.mode = "manual";
    mediaViewerProgress._visible = false;

    // Setup for the scrollable media viewer component
    mediaViewerPane.scrollDrag = true;
}
```

12. Save the file, return to the Macromedia Flash project file, and select Control⇨Test Movie.

How It Works

The first thing this exercise needs is some sample XML. Generally, you can just use the same XML file that is loaded at runtime. When the XML file is chosen for the schema, the Flash development environment parses through that file and guesses at what the data structure is supposed to represent. If you try taking one of the <movie> elements out of the XML file so that there is only one left, then try creating the schema based on that file, you will get a substantially different schema because the parser will no longer see <movie> as a repeating element.

If you have trouble getting this exercise to work, make sure that when you define your schema, you have the results row selected, not the params row. That is a common error because the params row is selected by default.

Now that the schema is set up, you have a way of binding individual data elements to a component. Flash recognizes that there are two different elements nested at the same level within the XML file, and it enables you to treat the two separately. Here, the <image> elements are bound to the dataProvider parameter of the imageList component, and the <movie> elements are bound to the dataProvider parameter of the movieList component.

With those changes made, all that remains are a few changes to the init() function. First, a couple of parameters are set with the XML connector, and the load is started by calling the trigger() method:

```
mediaListXMLConnector.direction = "receive";
mediaListXMLConnector.URL = "mediaList.xml";
mediaListXMLConnector.trigger();
```

The code to create two arrays and assign them to the components' dataProvider properties has been removed. Instead of the arrays, the bindings now deal with assigning data to the dataProvider properties.

The remaining code in the init function is the same as for the previous image viewer exercise, performing component setup and listener registration tasks.

Controlling Component Appearance

Although the visual appearance of the version 2.0 components is definitely an improvement over the version 1.0 components, there is still the need to be able to customize the look of the components to better fit in with the design of your site. Two ways exist to customize components:

❑   Styles — Styles enable you to change characteristics such as font properties, highlights, and colors.

❑   Skinning — Skinning allows the entire look of a component to be completely changed.

You explore both ways in the following sections.

Using setStyle() to Change Component Styles

The main mechanism for setting component styles is through the `setStyle()` method. Every component has this method available to call because it's inherited from the UIObject class upon which all components are based. In addition, there are ways to use this method to set styles to classes of components, to components of the same component type, and to all components globally. The general form of the `setStyle()` method is as follows:

```
componentInstance.setStyle(styleName:String, styleValue:Object);
```

For instance, the following code sets the text color, weight, font, and text size for an instance of the Button component:

```
this.createClassObject(mx.controls.Button, "myButton", this.getNextHighestDepth());
myButton.label = "My Button";
myButton.setStyle("color", 0x666666);
myButton.setStyle("fontWeight", "bold");
myButton.setStyle("fontFamily", "Arial");
myButton.setStyle("fontSize", 14);
```

Here's an example that sets alternating background colors for the rows, a solid border with no shadow, a light blue header, and black text:

```
var testArray:Array = new Array();
testArray.push({col1:"foo", col2:"bar"});
testArray.push({col1:"foo", col2:"bar"});

this.createClassObject(mx.controls.DataGrid, "myDataGrid", ⊃
    this.getNextHighestDepth());
myDataGrid.dataProvider = testArray;
myDataGrid.setStyle("alternatingRowColors", [0xFFFFFF, 0xCCCCCC]);
myDataGrid.setStyle("borderStyle", "solid");
myDataGrid.setStyle("headerColor", 0x9999CC);
myDataGrid.setStyle("color", 0x000000);
```

Setting Styles Globally

A global variable called `_global.style` is used for setting global styles. Any style set on this variable applies to any component that uses that style.

The following example sets the font face, size, and color for all component text labels:

```
_global.style.setStyle("fontFamily", "Arial");
_global.style.setStyle("fontSize", 10);
_global.style.setStyle("color", 0x666666);
```

Here's an example that sets all borders in components that support this style to be solid, and tells all list-based components to use alternating colors:

```
_global.style.setStyle("borderStyle", "solid");
_global.style.setStyle("alternatingRowColors", [0xFFFFFF, 0xCCCCCC]);
```

Setting Styles for a Component Type

In addition to the `_global.style` variable, there is also a `_global.styles` variable. This variable refers to classes of styles. Each component has a reserved class name already registered with `_global.styles` and can be accessed by referring to `_global.styles.<componentName>`. One example of this in use is

```
if (_global.styles.Label == undefined)
{
    _global.styles.Label = new mx.styles.CSSStyleDeclaration();
}
_global.styles.Label.setStyle("color", 0x003399);
```

Note the `if` statement here. Before a style class can be used, it must be assigned a new `CSSStyleDeclaration` instance. The CSSStyleDeclaration class is used throughout to store style settings. Individual component instances already have an instance of this class as part of their makeup, but style classes do not. If you make a `setStyle()` call on a component class that has not been initialized yet, it has no effect.

Setting Styles Using Custom Classes

Another way to control how styles are applied to components is to define custom classes and to set styles on each custom class. Whenever a custom class is assigned to a component instance, the instance acquires each of the styles set on the custom class.

The process for setting styles for a custom class is very similar to the process of setting styles for a component type. A CSSStyleDeclaration class is instantiated, styles are applied to the instance, and then the class is assigned to individual component instances, as the following example shows:

```
_global.styles.listStyle = new mx.styles.CSSStyleDeclaration();
_global.styles.listStyle.setStyle("color", 0xCC3333);
_global.styles.listStyle.setStyle("fontWeight", "bold");
_global.styles.listStyle.setStyle("fontSize", 12);

myList.setStyle("styleName", "listStyle");
```

To keep the lines a bit shorter, the styles can first be applied to a temporary variable before being assigned to the `styles` variable. Also, it's a good idea to import the CSSStyleDeclaration class for easier reference:

```
import mx.styles.CSSStyleDeclaration;

var tempStyle:Object = new CSSStyleDeclaration();
tempStyle.setStyle("color", 0xCC3333);
tempStyle.setStyle("fontWeight", "bold");
tempStyle.setStyle("fontSize", 12);
_global.styles.listStyle = tempStyle;

myList.setStyle("styleName", "listStyle");
```

Style Search Order

Flash component styles have an order of precedence. The search order used to see which particular style setting takes precedence is as follows:

1. Styles applied directly to a component instance
2. Styles applied via a custom style declaration
3. Styles applied to all components of a specific type
4. Styles applied globally

With the following two style declarations and a List component called `myList`, the color for `myList` ends up being `0x00FF00`:

```
// Set style globally
_global.style.setStyle("color", 0xFF0000);
// Set style to all List component instances
_global.styles.List = new mx.styles.CSSStyleDeclaration();
_global.styles.List.setStyle("color", 0x00FF00);
```

With the following three style declarations and a List component called `myList`, the color for `myList` ends up being `0x0000FF`:

```
// Set style globally
_global.style.setStyle("color", 0xFF0000);
// Set style to all List component instances
_global.styles.List = new mx.styles.CSSStyleDeclaration();
_global.styles.List.setStyle("color", 0x00FF00);
// Set style to all component instances assigned the style "myListStyle"
_global.styles.myListStyle = new mx.styles.CSSStyleDeclaration();
_global.styles.myListStyle.setStyle("color", 0x0000FF);
myList.setStyle("styleName", "myListStyle");
```

With the following four style declarations and a List component called `myList`, the color for `myList` ends up as `0xFFFF00`:

```
// Set style globally
_global.style.setStyle("color", 0xFF0000);
// Set style to all List component instances
_global.styles.List = new mx.styles.CSSStyleDeclaration();
_global.styles.List.setStyle("color", 0x00FF00);
// Set style to all component instances assigned the style "myListStyle"
_global.styles.myListStyle = new mx.styles.CSSStyleDeclaration();
_global.styles.myListStyle.setStyle("color", 0x0000FF);
myList.setStyle("styleName", "myListStyle");
// Set style directly to component instance
myList.setStyle("color", 0xFFFF00);
```

Available Styles

The following table describes some of the more common styles that are available for you to use. You can find the complete set of styles for any particular component in the Help panel under Components Language Reference⇨<Component Name>⇨Customizing the <Component Name> Component. Not all of these styles can be used everywhere, or for every theme.

Style	Description	Applies To
alternatingRowColors	Sets both colors used for alternating rows. Overrides the backgroundColor style.	Example: setStyle("alternating RowColors", [0xFFFFFF, 0xCCCCCC]); DataGrid, List, Menu
backgroundColor	Sets the component background color. The default is white.	Button (not Halo), ComboBox, DataGrid, DateChooser, DateField, List, Menu, TextArea, TextInput, Tree, Window
borderStyle	Sets the kind of border to use. Can be none, inset, outset, or solid. The inset and outset options give a drop-shadow effect either inside the border or outside the border.	Accordion, Alert, Button (not Halo), ComboBox, DataGrid, Loader, Menu, ScrollPane, TextArea, Tree, Window
color	Sets the text color.	All components
disabledColor	Sets the text color for when the component is disabled.	All components
embedFonts	Sets whether the font specified in the fontFamily style is embedded into the library. To refer to an embedded font, fontFamily should be set to the linkage ID of a font added to the library.	All components
fontFamily	Sets the name of the font to use for all text within the component. The default font is _sans. The name should correspond to the name of a font on the end-user's computer, or to the linkage ID of a font added to the library. Labels using embedded fonts need to have the embedFonts style set to true for the text to be visible.	All components
fontSize	Sets the pixel size to use for text. The default is 10 pixels.	All components
fontStyle	Sets the text style to use, either normal or italic.	All components

Table continued on following page

Style	Description	Applies To
fontWeight	Sets the weight of the text, either bold or none.	All components
rollOverColor	Sets the color of an element when it is rolled over with the mouse. The default value is 0xE3FFD6.	DateChooser, DateField, List, Menu, Tree
selectionColor	Sets the color of an element when it has been selected. The default value is 0xCDFFC1.	DateChooser, DateField, List, Menu, Tree
selectionDisabledColor	Sets the color of a row when the component is disabled. The default value is 0xDDDDDD.	List, Tree
textAlign	Sets the alignment of text in each cell. Can be left, right, or center.	DataGrid, Menu, NumericStepper, TextArea, TextInput, Window
textDecoration	Sets whether to underline the text. Can be either underline or none.	All components
textRollOverColor	Sets the color of the text when the cursor is over the row. The default value is 0x2B333C.	List, Menu, Tree
textSelectedColor	Sets the color of the text in the selected row. The default value is 0x005F33.	List, Menu, Tree
themeColor	Sets the color scheme for component highlights. Options are haloGreen, haloBlue, haloOrange, or a specific color value. Applies only to the Halo theme.	All components

Alert Style Names

The Alert component has a way of applying styles to the components embedded inside by applying styles directly to one of three static properties, which you use as follows:

❑   buttonStyleDeclaration — Set the style of the response button(s) in the Alert component.

❑   messageStyleDeclaration — Set the style of the alert message text.

❑   titleStyleDeclaration — Set the style of the title bar.

The following code shows how to customize the Alert component by creating style declarations and assigning them to the component's static style properties:

```
import mx.controls.Alert;
import mx.styles.CSSStyleDeclaration;

var messageStyle = new CSSStyleDeclaration();

messageStyle.setStyle("fontWeight", "bold");
messageStyle.setStyle("fontSize", 14);
messageStyle.setStyle("color", 0x990000);
Alert.messageStyleDeclaration = messageStyle;

var titleStyle = new CSSStyleDeclaration();
titleStyle.setStyle("fontWeight", "normal");
titleStyle.setStyle("fontSize", 12);
titleStyle.setStyle("color", 0x000000);
Alert.titleStyleDeclaration = titleStyle;

Alert.show("The credit card number entered is not valid.", "Validation Error");
```

> **As of this writing, there was a problem with the custom style properties for the Alert component. The buttonStyleDeclaration would be overridden by the messageStyleDeclaration, even if the messageStyleDeclaration was not specified.**

Custom Date Classes

The DateChooser and DateField components define three custom classes that can be used to style parts of the calendar:

- ❑ `HeaderDateText` — This declaration enables you to set styles for the month name label.
- ❑ `WeekDayStyle` — Use this declaration to set styles for the days of the week labels.
- ❑ `TodayStyle` — Set styles for the label for today's date.

These style declarations work exactly the way other custom style declarations do, except that the CSSStyleDeclaration class is already instantiated for you. The general form for using these declarations is as follows:

```
_global.styles.WeekDayStyle.setStyle("color", 0x003399);
```

Try It Out   **Using setStyle() to Change Component Appearance**

Now you use what you've learned to apply styles to your image viewer application. At the end of the exercise, the application should look something like Figure 11-8.

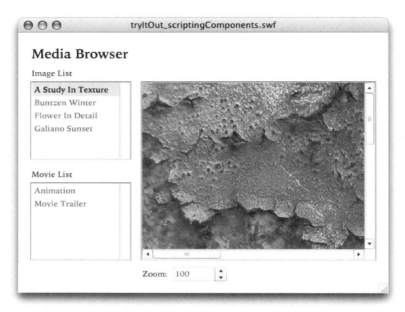

Figure 11-8

1. Open the completed `tryItOut_scriptingComponents.fla` file from the previous Try It Out exercise, or open `tryItOut_scriptingComponents.fla` from the book's source files at <source file directory>/Chapter 11/tryItOut_scriptingComponents_v5/.

2. Open the Library panel, and from the menu on the top right, select New Font.

3. In the New Font panel, enter the name `alternateFont` and from the drop-down list, select a font that you would like to apply to the interface. Click OK.

4. Click the new font in the library to select it. From the menu at the top right of the panel, select Linkage, and in the dialog box that opens, check the Export for ActionScript checkbox. Click the OK button.

5. Open the completed `tryItOut_scriptingComponents.as` file from the first Try It Out exercise, or open `tryItOut_scriptingComponents.as` from the book's source files at <source file directory>/Chapter 11/tryItOut_scriptingComponents_v5/.

6. Update the `init()` function in the ActionScript file so that it looks like this:

```
function init() : Void
{
    // Send data to the image list and movie list components
    mediaListXMLConnector.direction = "receive";
    mediaListXMLConnector.URL = "mediaList.xml";
    mediaListXMLConnector.trigger();

    imageList.addEventListener("change", mediaListListener);
    imageList.addEventListener("change", mediaViewerListener);

    movieList.addEventListener("change", mediaListListener);
```

```
movieList.addEventListener("change", mediaViewerListener);

// Setup for the zoom stepper component
zoomStepper.maximum = 400;
zoomStepper.minimum = 25;
zoomStepper.stepSize = 25;
zoomStepper.value = 100;
zoomStepper.addEventListener("change", mediaViewerListener);

// Setup for the progress bar component
mediaViewerProgress.mode = "manual";
mediaViewerProgress._visible = false;

// Setup for the scrollable media viewer component
mediaViewerPane.scrollDrag = true;
mediaViewerPane.addEventListener("progress", mediaViewerListener);
mediaViewerPane.addEventListener("complete", mediaViewerListener);

// Set styles for application

// Set global styles
_global.style.setStyle("borderStyle", "solid");
_global.style.setStyle("fontFamily", "alternateFont");
_global.style.setStyle("fontSize", 12);
_global.style.setStyle("embedFonts", true);
_global.style.setStyle("color", 0x666666);
_global.style.setStyle("themeColor", 0xDDDDFF);
_global.style.setStyle("textSelectedColor", 0x000000);

// Set styles for all Label components
if (_global.styles.Label == undefined)
{
    _global.styles.Label = new mx.styles.CSSStyleDeclaration();
}
_global.styles.Label.setStyle("color", 0x003399);
_global.styles.Label.setStyle("fontWeight", "bold");

// Set title style
var appTitleStyle:Object = new mx.styles.CSSStyleDeclaration();
_global.styles.appTitle = appTitleStyle;
appTitleStyle.setStyle("fontSize", 20);
appTitleStyle.setStyle("fontWeight", "bold");
appTitleStyle.setStyle("color", 0x000000);
appTitleLabel.setStyle("styleName", "appTitle");

// Set component instance styes
zoomStepper.setStyle("textAlign", "left");
}
```

7. Save the file, return to the Macromedia Flash project file, and select Control⇨Test Movie.

How It Works

The first chunk of code within the init() function is the same as the previous exercise's, so start by looking at the code that actually applies the styles.

First, the global styles are applied:

```
_global.style.setStyle("borderStyle", "solid");
_global.style.setStyle("fontFamily", "alternateFont");
_global.style.setStyle("fontSize", 12);
_global.style.setStyle("embedFonts", true);
_global.style.setStyle("color", 0x666666);
_global.style.setStyle("themeColor", 0xDDDDFF);
_global.style.setStyle("textSelectedColor", 0x000000);
```

All components will override their default styles with these, unless category, class, or individual styles override the global ones.

Next, styles are applied to the category of Label components:

```
if (_global.styles.Label == undefined)
{
    _global.styles.Label = new mx.styles.CSSStyleDeclaration();
}
_global.styles.Label.setStyle("color", 0x003399);
_global.styles.Label.setStyle("fontWeight", "bold");
```

It isn't actually necessary to apply the `if` statement here because you know that no code has already created a CSSStyleDeclaration for this style category. You could have just done the following:

```
_global.styles.Label = new mx.styles.CSSStyleDeclaration();
_global.styles.Label.setStyle("color", 0x003399);
_global.styles.Label.setStyle("fontWeight", "bold");
```

Next, a custom style class is created and is assigned to the `appTitleLabel` component:

```
var appTitleStyle:Object = new mx.styles.CSSStyleDeclaration();
_global.styles.appTitle = appTitleStyle;
appTitleStyle.setStyle("fontSize", 20);
appTitleStyle.setStyle("fontWeight", "bold");
appTitleStyle.setStyle("color", 0x000000);
appTitleLabel.setStyle("styleName", "appTitle");
```

Finally, a style is applied directly to the `zoomStepper` component:

```
zoomStepper.setStyle("textAlign", "left");
```

Skinning Components

The component styles that you set with `setStyle()` give you one method of changing component appearance. For the most part, `setStyle()` is used to manipulate the overall color scheme and the font styles. What `setStyle()` does not give you is the capability to affect the whole component look and feel. For instance, you might want to change the shape of the scroll buttons or remove the gradients used within the scroll thumb. These kinds of style elements are individually called *skin properties*, the collection of skin properties for all components is referred to as a *skin*, and the process of changing the component skin properties is called *skinning*. In addition to using styles to change the appearance of components, Macromedia Flash also provides the capability to re-skin them, where you can completely change the appearance of each component's visual features. Skinning is not hard to learn, but is a bit tricky to master.

Flash comes with two skins, called *themes*. A theme is a file containing a set of pre-skinned library symbols that can be dropped into the library for any `.fla` file. Halo is the default theme that all components automatically start with. Generally, you won't use the Halo theme as a starting point for your skinning efforts because of the more complicated nature of the skin. The Sample theme is considerably simpler to work with, and should be the basis for any skins that you may want to create.

The process of skinning does not actually involve scripting, but it's a process that Flash coders and designers often ask how to do, so it's included here.

Here's how to switch to a new theme:

1. Open the `.fla` file to which you want to apply the theme.

2. Open the Flash file `SampleTheme.fla` at <application root>/Configuration/ComponentFLA/. The application root is generally at /Applications/Macromedia Flash 8 for Mac OS or /Program Files/Macromedia/Flash 8 for Windows.

3. Open the Library panel (Window⇨Library) and select the movie clip `SampleTheme` from the Flash UI Components 2 folder. From the menu at the top right of the Library panel, select Copy.

4. Switch to the Flash file that you opened in step 1. From the menu at the top right of the Library panel for that Flash file, select Paste.

5. Test the project (Controls⇨Test Movie).

When you copy this movie clip over, it automatically brings with it all of the additional movie clips needed to set the appearance of all the components. Double-click the SampleTheme movie clip and you see groupings of all the component skins on the state. Open the Themes folder that has been added to the Library to see groupings of theme elements. This folder does not actually list each component. Some, like the List component, are actually a collection of other components. Although not all components show up in the list, they are all represented. Changing the ScrollBar component, for instance, affects the scroll bar in the List component.

The next exercise gives you an opportunity to work with skin elements.

Try It Out   Re-Skinning Components

This exercise demonstrates how to add the sample skin to the image viewer project, and how to edit individual skin elements. Figure 11-9 shows the end result. You won't actually redraw individual component elements, but you will see how a skin is broken up so that you can try it for yourself.

Figure 11-9

1. Open the completed `tryItOut_scriptingComponents.fla` file from the previous Try It Out exercise, or open `tryItOut_scriptingComponents.fla` from the book's source files at <source file directory>/Chapter 11/tryItOut_scriptingComponents_v6/.

2. Open `SampleTheme.fla` in <application root>/Configuration/ComponentFLA/. (The application root is generally at /Applications/Macromedia Flash 8 for Mac OS or /Program Files/Macromedia/Flash 8 for Windows.)

3. Open the library and select the movie clip `SampleTheme` from the Flash UI Components 2 folder. From the menu at the top right of the Library panel, select Copy.

4. Switch to `tryItOut_scriptingComponents.fla`. From the menu at the top right of the Library panel for that project, select Paste.

5. Close `SampleTheme.fla`. You no longer need it for this exercise.

6. Open the Library folder at Themes⇨MMDefault⇨ScrollBar Assets. Double-click the HScroll BarAssets movie clip.

7. Double-click the arrow icon on the top left to edit the scroll up arrow skin element. You should see the name of the symbol, `ScrollUpArrowUp`, in the timeline bar at the top of the Flash document.

   Figure 11-10 shows the six regions for which you'll be setting the indicated colors.

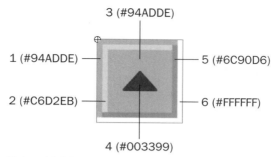

Figure 11-10

8. Select View⇨Magnification⇨800% and scroll the stage region to center the button in the window.

9. Double-click region 1, the top-left portion of the button. Click in the middle of the square to select the shape. Open the Properties panel (Window⇨Properties). Click the shape fill swatch in the Properties panel, type #94ADDE in the color picker text field, and press Enter.

10. Click the ScrollUpArrowUp button above the timeline to return to the main arrow symbol. Double-click region 2, the top-left button highlight. Click in the middle of the square to select the shape. Click the shape fill swatch in the Properties panel, type #C6D2EB in the color picker text field, and press Enter.

If you are having problems selecting individual parts of the button, make sure that any previous selection has been deselected by clicking anywhere outside the button. Also, try further enlarging the view by selecting View⇨Zoom In.

11. Click the ScrollUpArrowUp button above the timeline to return to the main arrow symbol. Click once on region 3, the background color of the button. Click the shape fill swatch next to the Color drop-down in the Properties panel, type #94ADDE in the color picker text field, and press Enter.

Important: This step changes the color effect applied to the movie clip instead of the color of the shape inside the movie clip. Changing the color of the shape affects the outside border color because they are linked.

12. Double-click region 4, the button arrow icon. Click in the middle of the square to select the shape. Click the shape fill swatch in the Properties panel, type #003399 in the color picker text field, and press Enter.

13. Click the ScrollUpArrowUp button above the timeline to return to the main arrow symbol. Double-click region 5, the bottom-right button shadow. Click in the middle of the square to select the shape. Click the shape fill swatch in the Properties panel, type #6C90D6 in the color picker text field, and press Enter.

14. Click the ScrollUpArrowUp button above the timeline to return to the main arrow symbol. Double-click region 6, the bottom-right button border. Click in the middle of the square to select the shape. Click the shape fill swatch in the Properties panel, type #FFFFFF in the color picker text field, and press Enter.

15. Click the HScrollBarAssets button above the timeline to return to the scroll bar assets clip. Double-click the scroll down arrow button at the bottom left of the clip.

The following steps apply to the scroll down arrow button, ScrollDownArrowUp.

16. Click once on region 3, the background color of the scroll down button. Click the shape fill swatch next to the Color drop-down in the Properties panel, type #94ADDE in the color picker text field, and press Enter.

17. Double-click region 4, the button arrow icon. Click in the middle of the square to select the shape. Click the shape fill swatch in the Properties panel, type #003399 in the color picker text field, and press Enter.

18. Click the HScrollBarAssets button above the timeline to return to the scroll bar assets clip. Double-click the scroll track clip at the top right of the movie clip. Double-click the symbol again. Click once on the gray shape to select it. Click the shape fill swatch in the Properties panel, type #C6D2EB in the color picker text field, and press Enter.

19. Click the HScrollBarAssets button above the timeline to return to the scroll bar assets clip. Double-click the disabled scroll track clip at the bottom right of the movie clip. Click the gray shape to select it. Click the shape fill swatch in the Properties panel to open the color picker, type #C6D2EB in the color picker text field, and press Enter.

20. Open the mediaList.xml file in the same folder as the Flash project file in your favorite text editor. Duplicate a few of the <image> entries so that there are at least 8 <image> tags to ensure that the scroll bar will appear in the top list view.

21. Test the project (Controls➪Test Movie).

How It Works

Each skin symbol is divided up into multiple symbols that can be independently edited. You will notice that by changing the symbol colors in one place, it takes effect in other places. This has a benefit and a drawback. The benefit is that the sharing of movie clips keeps you from having to make changes to every component clip to change an effect throughout. For instance, notice that the zoom stepper component instance has adopted the new skin style without your needing to change the stepper itself. The disadvantage is that if you want to change the shape of the component feature completely, the different clips can make it difficult to figure out how your changes are going to take effect elsewhere. In that case, you may want to just delete the contents of the symbol that you want to change and redraw each one by hand.

Summary

This chapter explored many different aspects of components. Some points to remember include the following:

❏ Component bindings provide a semi-automated way of passing data between components.

❏ Bindings are fine for simple interfaces, however as the interface gets more complex, more work has to be done to manage and work around the bindings' implementation.

❏ Component appearance can be customized through the use of styles and skins.

❏ A theme is a file containing skinned library elements that you can copy to any Flash project file to change the appearance of components within that file.

❏ The setStyle() method is the mechanism for changing style attributes.

Exercises

1. Take the results of what you created for Chapter 10 exercise 1 and update the application styles so that all text fields use an embedded font of your choice. Change the font size and color to values of your liking. Set the DataGrid component instance to remove any vertical lines, and change the color of the header bar. Change the label color of the Delete button to red.

2. Create a skin of your liking for the application.

Debugging Debugged

When you write code, you can expect problems to creep in. No matter how hard you try, there is always something that just doesn't work. Fortunately, strategies exist for reducing, finding, and fixing these bugs. This chapter brings you up to speed on the kinds of bugs you'll be facing.

Types of Bugs

Numerous types of bugs exist that, for the most part, fall into two categories: compile-time bugs and logic bugs. Compile-time bugs are problems that are detected by the compiler and usually involve code syntax or structure errors. Logic bugs involve code that successfully runs, but that does not operate the way that you intend. They are the bugs that you will be mostly concerned with, and that will require the most attention.

Compile-Time Bugs

Compile bugs are the easiest to deal with. As the Flash compiler creates an SWF file, it goes through all of your code and makes sure that it conforms to the required syntax. If any code is invalid, such as an opening brace not having a matching closing brace, or a `for` statement that does not have the correct usage, it aborts the compile. Additionally, it lets you know where the error is and gives you a description of what is wrong.

The compiler also tests to make sure that all variable, function, and class usage conforms to the rules in their respective definitions. That means that if you declare a variable of type Boolean, and you assign it to a variable of type Number, the compiler will flag the mismatch. You'll also appreciate the compile-time class checking once you get into creating your own classes.

Compiler bugs are very good for development. The more errors that can be caught at compile time, the less debugging you have to do. You can help this process by consistently using strongly typed variables throughout your code.

The Flash compiler is pretty good at giving you feedback on where a syntax or usage error is located, although sometimes it gives you huge lists of errors. Don't worry too much about this because often one little error has put a whole bunch of things out of whack. Fixing the top two or three errors in a long list usually removes most or all of the remaining problems when you next try to compile.

Logic Bugs

Once your program successfully compiles, there is still a host of potential errors. The most common of these are described in the following sections along with some strategies for dealing with them.

If Statement Logic Errors

Working with `if` statements is an exercise in precision. It's easy for these decision statements to get complex and out of control. They need not be difficult to debug, and a few strategies exist for both avoiding and debugging `if` statements.

Use Brackets

If you are ever unsure about how an `if` statement is going to be evaluated, make it clear through the use of round brackets. Anything inside a set of brackets is evaluated before anything outside of the brackets. The following example is ambiguous as to whether the and (`&&`) or the or (`||`) operator is evaluated first:

```
if (variable1 == "foo" || variable2 == "bar" && variable3 == "baz") { }
```

Adding a pair of brackets around the term that you want to be evaluated first clarifies your intention and forces that order of operations:

```
if ( (variable1 == "foo" || variable2 == "bar") && variable3 == "baz") { }
```

Here the `&&` operator takes precedence and is evaluated first, so without the extra brackets, the outcome of the expression would be different than intended.

Add Additional Nesting

A key aspect of debugging is your ability to read and understand the code. One way to clarify how an expression is to be evaluated is to separate it into more than one expression through nested `if` statements. Any spot in the expression where there is an `&&` operator is a candidate for nesting the statements. Take the previous expression:

```
if ( (variable1 == "foo" || variable2 == "bar") && variable3 == "baz") { }
```

You can separate it into two nested expressions, with the expression for the outside statement taken from the left of the `&&` operator and the expression for the inside statement taken from the right of the `&&` operator:

```
if (variable1 == "foo" || variable2 == "bar")
{
    if (variable3 == "baz")
    {
        // Statements
    }
}
```

Those who are concerned about performance may complain that this will be slower than the single expression version. Although this is true, it is so negligible that the only time it is of concern at all is within intensive loops, such as those responsible for scripted animation. In that case, optimizing the code may take precedence over code readability.

Use Trace Statements

One way to debug your logic is by placing `trace()` statements throughout the statement blocks. Some are just to indicate where the logic flow is going; others are to give an idea of what is happening to the variables used in the decisions. When you look at the entries in the output panel, you should have enough information to evaluate the problem. The following code places a `trace()` statement in each of three `if` statement blocks. When the code runs, you can tell which block executed by examining the output panel for the relevant output statement. For instance, if you see `"Breakpoint 1"` in the output panel and you expected to see `"Breakpoint 2"`, you can add a `trace()` statement before the initial `if` statement and run the code again to determine the values of the variables being tested:

```
trace("variable 1: " + variable1 " variable2: " + variable2 + ⏎
    " variable3: " + variable3);
if (variable1 == "foo" || variable2 == "bar")
{
    trace("Breakpoint 1");
    // Statements ...
}
else if (variable3 == "baz")
{
    trace("Breakpoint 2");
    // Statements ...
}
else
{
    trace("Breakpoint 3");
    // Statements ...
}
```

Make sure that you remove the `trace()` statements once you have found the problem to avoid confusing them with `trace()` statements you use later.

Uninitialized Variables

Working with uninitialized data can result in hard-to-trace errors. The issue is that when you declare a variable, it is not given any start value until you assign it one. When you declare a variable without assigning a value, you get the following behavior:

```
var myBoolean:Boolean;
trace(myBoolean);
// Outputs: undefined
```

If you try to use that variable for something, you do not get the results you want:

```
var myBoolean:Boolean;
if (myBoolean == true)
{
    trace("myBoolean: true");
```

```
}
if (myBoolean == false)
{
    trace("myBoolean: false");
}
// Outputs: nothing
```

Another common error involves trying to assign data to an array, like this:

```
var myArray:Array;
myArray.push("foo");
trace("Array length:  " + myArray.length");
// Outputs: Array length: undefined
```

The solution is to make sure that unless you know that a variable is going to be assigned data right away, give it an initial value when you declare it:

```
var myArray:Array = new Array();
myArray.push("foo");
trace("Array length:  " + myArray.length");
// Outputs: Array length: 1
```

The same principle applies to data types other than arrays. The following code shows common initialization values for the core data types:

```
var myBoolean:Boolean = false;
var myNum:Number = 0;
var myString:String = "";
var myArray:Array = new Array();
var myObject:Object = new Object();
```

It's common to dedicate a function to initializing your project. The initialization function is responsible for setting initial values for all your global and timeline variables. This gives you only one place to look for any initialization issues, making it easier to find and fix problems related to uninitialized variables. The following code illustrates an initialization function:

```
var myBoolean:Boolean;
var myNum:Number;
var myString:String;
var myArray:Array;
var myObject:Object;

function init():Void
{
    myBoolean:Boolean = false;
    myNum:Number = 0;
    myString:String = "";
    myArray:Array = new Array();
    myObject:Object = new Object();

    // ...}
init();
```

Both solutions are fine. The first option is generally more compact, whereas the second one promotes grouping initialization code into a dedicated function, which is good for code organization.

Off-by-One Errors

An off-by-one error is a loop that miscounts how many times it needs to iterate, either one less or one greater than the needed number. One source of this error is forgetting that arrays start at element 0, not element 1, as in this example:

```
var fruitArray:Array = new Array("apple", "orange", "pear");
for (var i:Number = 1; i < fruitArray.length; i++)
{
    trace("Element " + i + ": " + fruitArray[i]);
}
// Outputs:
// Element 1: orange
// Element 2: pear
```

The output fails to show element 0, "apple", because the assigned start was 1. The simple solution to this is to make sure that all loops that iterate through an array start at element 0.

Another source of this error involves using the wrong termination condition, such as using a <= operator instead of a < operator, which results in the loop trying to access an element of the array that does not exist:

```
var fruitArray:Array = new Array("apple", "orange", "pear");
for (var i:Number = 0; i <= fruitArray.length; i++)
{
    trace("Element " + i + ": " + fruitArray[i]);
}
// Outputs:
// Element 0: apple
// Element 1: orange
// Element 2: pear
// Element 3: undefined
```

All arrays start at 0, but array length counts actual elements, so that an array length of 3 contains elements 0, 1, and 2. The last element of any array is at fruitArray.length – 1. A loop should not proceed if the iterator variable i is equal to the array length because there's no element at that point.

Fence Post Errors

A variation of the off-by-one error is the fence post error. Consider a fence with three sections. How many fence posts does it have? You might say that there are three — one for each section of fence. But there's a post on each end of the fence, so in reality a three-section fence has four posts.

Where this comes into play with programming is when calculating ranges of numbers. Say you need to work with array elements 12 through 18 with a while loop, and you need to calculate how many times to run the loop. Most people would calculate 18 – 12 = 6, but that would be incorrect. Twelve through 18 is seven numbers: 12, 13, 14, 15, 16, 17, and 18. The correct calculation is 18 – 12 + 1 = 7. In general, when calculating a range of numbers from m to n, the formula to follow is n – m + 1 = total.

Infinite Loops

The extreme case of a looping error is the infinite loop. You'll usually notice this one right away because your movie will grind to a halt, eventually prompting an error from the Flash player, giving you an option to terminate the movie. Usually this error occurs as a result of forgetting to increment an iterator variable. The following `while` loop will never terminate because it contains no code to increment `i`:

```
var i:Number = 0;
while (i < 20)
{
    // i++;
    // Remaining code ...
}
```

Make sure that within any `while` loop, there is always a way for the loop to end.

For the most part, `for` loops are not prone to infinite loops, although they're still possible. In the following code, an item is being continually added to the array, so that the length of the array increases by one for each loop — and `i` can never catch up:

```
var fruitArray:Array = new Array("apple");
for (var i:Number = 0; i < fruitArray.length; i++)
{
    fruitArray.push("pear" + i);
}
```

It's better idea to create a variable for holding the length and to use that variable for the array. That works well from a performance standpoint, too. Here's an example:

```
var fruitArray:Array = new Array("apple");
var numFruit:Number = fruitArray.length;
for (var i:Number = 0; i < numFruit; i++)
{
    fruitArray.push("pear" + i);
}
```

The best tool for debugging infinite loops is the Flash debug panel, to be discussed shortly.

Numerical Precision Errors

It may surprise you to learn that computers actually are fairly limited in their mathematical precision and, under certain conditions, can provide wildly inaccurate results. The issue arises when the computer attempts to store a floating-point number in its native number format. Some floating-point numbers cannot be accurately represented in a binary format, and so must be approximated. Try the following to see this in operation:

```
trace(1 - 0.9 - 0.1);
```

The result of the calculation should be 0, but the computer's answer is a very small fractional amount of 0.0000000000000000277558. The following code illustrates how numerical precision errors can affect a `while` loop:

```
var currentPosition:Number = 0;
var endPosition:Number = 100;
while (currentPosition < 100)
{
    currentPosition += (endPosition - currentPosition) * 0.1;
    trace(currentPosition);
}
```

The condition checking to see if currentVal is less than 100 will never return true. If you try this, wait until the error message comes up warning you about the script running too slowly, and abort it. You should see a row of 99.99999999999 trace statements in the output window. The currentVal variable never reaches exactly 100 because of limitations in computer numeric precision. The most reliable way of dealing with this problem is to just accommodate for the imprecision:

```
var currentPosition:Number = 0;
var endPosition:Number = 100;
while (currentPosition < 99.9)
{
    currentPosition += (endPosition - currentPosition) * 0.1;
    trace(currentPosition);
}
```

while *loops like this one are commonly used in animation to make a moving movie clip decelerate. You learn more about how to use code for animation in Chapter 16.*

Develop to Debug

Debugging involves more than searching for errors. How you develop your code has a major impact on how easy it is to debug. You make the process so much easier for yourself and for anyone who needs to look at your code if you consistently follow some good basic development practices:

- ❑ Make your code readable.
- ❑ Develop in small chunks.
- ❑ Use small functions.

Make Your Code Readable

The most important aspect of debugging is to be able to understand the code that you wrote. Many people write what takes the least time to type. Here's an example:

```
function plot(i:Number, line:Boolean)
{
    base["layer" + cl].lineStyle(1, lc, 100);
    base["layer" + cl].moveTo(x[i], y[i]);
    px[i] = (Math.cos(pd[i]) * ps[i]);
    py[i] = (Math.sin(pd[i]) * ps[i]);
```

```
        if (line == true)
        {
            base["layer" + cl].lineTo(px[i], py[i]);
        }
    }
```

This code is nice and compact, but can you tell me what the difference is between lc and cl, or between pd and ps? The easiest kind of code to debug is that which is self-documenting. That is, code that you or someone working with your code can understand without having to refer to documentation. You will find it much easier to work with your code if you make variable and function names understandable and if you put thought into making sure their names reflect what they contain. Here's a much better version of the example:

```
function plotLine(i:Number, drawLine:Boolean)
{
    pBaseTimeline["layer" + pCurrentLayer].lineStyle(1, pLineColour, 100);
    pBaseTimeline["layer" + pCurrentLayer].moveTo(pPointX[i], pPointY[i]);
    pPointX[i] = (Math.cos(pPointDegree[i]) * pPointScale[i]);
    pPointY[i] = (Math.sin(pPointDegree[i]) * pPointScale[i]);
    if (drawLine == true)
    {
        pBaseTimeline["layer" + pCurrentLayer].lineTo(pPointX[i], pPointY[i]);
    }
}
```

This code is much more explicit, and will make more sense when you have to pick it up in a few months or when placing code snippets on an online forum for someone to help you debug a problem.

Develop in Small Chunks

You will find it easier to locate problems if you keep the number of code changes down from the last time you got the code working. Do not write a whole application at once and then try to get all of that code working. Instead, break up your development process into chunks and get one chunk of code completely working before moving to the next chunk. In this way, you can build a project a piece at a time, comfortable in the knowledge that most of the problems you will find will be in the code you just wrote, rather than the code you wrote right at the beginning.

One caveat is that you should avoid the other extreme as well: don't write the code one line at a time, testing each line as you go. That's a very slow approach, and removes the focus from what you need to do to implement a particular feature. It works best if you focus on writing code for one self-contained feature and, when you've finished, verify that the feature works before going on to the next one.

Use Small Functions

To support the idea of developing code in pieces, use functions to allow for self-contained pieces of functionality that are easy to debug. A function has a defined set of inputs and outputs and should behave in an easy-to-predict way. It is much easier to debug a single function than a screen full of code. Functions should be small and focused, ideally between 10 and 30 lines of code. If a function becomes longer than 50 lines of code, consider how you might pull out some of its code into a second function.

The Science of Debugging

In the field of science, every study and experiment uses the scientific process:

1. Develop a theory to test.

2. Run an experiment that tests that theory.

3. Analyze the result to see if the experiment validates the theory.

4. If the results do not validate the theory, revise the theory.

The process of debugging can be thought of in terms of this scientific process, where every time you compile and run your project, you run an experiment. The scientific process can be tweaked to take debugging in mind:

1. Develop a theory about why the program is behaving the way it is.

2. Run an experiment in which you change the parameters, add/remove functionality, or add debug information, and then run the program to test the theory.

3. Analyze the execution of the program and the contents of the output panel to see if the experiment validates your theory.

4. If the results do not validate the theory, revise the theory.

The following sections examine this process.

Develop a Theory

The most important part of an experiment is to establish a theory to be tested. That theory then forms the basis for the experiment and revolves around trying to determine the reason why some code failed.

Take a look at some code that does not work, and develop a theory to help establish how to fix it.

Try It Out **Develop a Theory**

In this exercise, you look at some code that is supposed to load a thumbnail image and then position a text field just to the right of the thumbnail. You can see how the code fails for yourself, and from that, you can form a theory as to why it fails.

1. Find any available photo or image in the JPG format; use your favorite image editor to crop the image so that it is 50 pixels wide by 50 pixels high. Save the image somewhere convenient and call it `thumbnail.jpg`. If you do not have one handy, you can use `thumbnail.jpg` in <source file directory>/Chapter 12/tryItOut_debug/.

2. Create a new Macromedia Flash document.

3. Click the first frame in the timeline, open the Actions panel (Window➪Development Panels➪ Actions), and enter in the following ActionScript code:

```
init();

function init():Void
```

```
{
    this.createEmptyMovieClip("imageHolder", 1);
    imageHolder.loadMovie("thumbnail.jpg");
    handleLoad();
}

function handleLoad():Void
{
    imageHolder._x = 10;
    imageHolder._y = 10;

    this.createTextField("description1Field", 1, 70, 25, 100, 20);
    description1Field.text = "Description 1";
}
```

4.   Select File⇨Save As, name the file `tryItOut_debug.fla`, and save it in the same directory as the `thumbnail.jpg` image.

5.   Select Control⇨Test Movie to try it out.

6.   From looking at the code and trying it out, what is your theory about what went wrong?

How It Works

If the program worked as designed, an image appears on the screen with a text field located 10 pixels to the right of the image. Instead, there is a text field but no image.

If the problem was that the image being loaded could not be found, Flash would output an error message in the output panel stating this. There is no such error, so the problem must be with something else. One possibility is that the movie clip created right at the beginning was not successfully created, or was created but not where you expected. Proceed with the theory that it was not created in the first place.

Run an Experiment

Now that you have a theory, you need to test it. You have a few ways to do so: using the built-in debugger, using `trace()` statements, and commenting out code.

Using the Built-In Debugger

The built-in debugger is a great tool for getting to the root of a problem. Figure 12-1 introduces you to the Debugger panel.

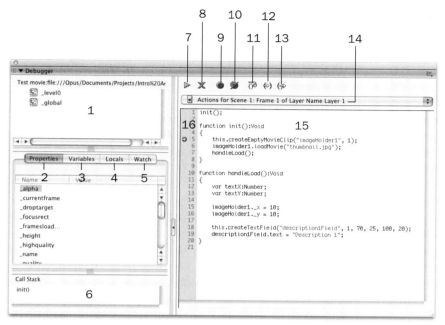

Figure 12-1

Following are descriptions of the panel's main parts:

1. **Movie clip browser:** Shows all the movie clips in the project. Movie clips nested within other movie clips are indented to show the hierarchy. Clicking any of the movie clips enables you to view its properties and variables.

2. **Properties tab:** Reveals all the properties for the movie clip selected in the movie clip browser.

3. **Variables tab:** Reveals all the variables assigned to the movie clip selected in the movie clip browser.

4. **Locals tab:** Reveals all the local variables available within the currently executing function, including any arguments passed to the function.

5. **Watch tab:** Reveals all the timeline and local variables that you have indicated you want to monitor. Designate a variable as a watched variable by right-clicking the variable and selecting Watch.

6. **Call Stack:** Shows the hierarchy of function calls currently being executed. (One function can call another function, which can call another function. The first function continues to run until all the functions it calls complete.)

7. **Play button:** Starts execution of the project and resumes execution after it has stopped at a breakpoint.

8. **Cancel button:** Terminates the project. It is equivalent to clicking the close button of the running SWF file.

9. **Set Breakpoint button:** Sets a breakpoint at the current point of execution.

10. **Clear All Breakpoints button:** Clears all breakpoints that have been set in the entire project, not just for the code currently shown in the code preview pane.

11. **Step Over button:** Causes the function currently highlighted by the progress arrow to run, and then advances the progress arrow to the next line of code. It does not cause the progress arrow to enter that function.

12. **Step In button:** Causes the progress arrow to proceed into any custom function currently highlighted by the progress arrow, starting at the first line of code for that function. If you want to examine each line of code in each function and nested function, simply click this button repeatedly.

13. **Step Out button:** Causes the progress arrow to continue to the next line of code in the calling function, skipping any remaining code in the current function.

14. **Code Selector:** If code is located in multiple places on the timeline, or within multiple included files, this drop-down enables you to navigate between the different timelines or files.

15. **Code Preview pane:** Shows the currently running code in its context. It does not allow you to edit any code at runtime.

16. **Breakpoint and progress area:** The gray area on the left is used for setting or removing breakpoints, and for showing the line to be executed next. The Set Breakpoint button (number 9 in this list) sets a breakpoint only for the currently running line. This area allows breakpoints to be set and removed for any line of code by clicking to the left of the number of the code line of interest. Breakpoints cannot be set for lines containing function declarations, opening or closing brackets for a function, or blank lines. The gray area on the left is also used to show the progress of code execution. A yellow arrow appears to the left of the line number for the line of code that will be executed next.

Ready to try out the debugger?

Try It Out   Working with the Debugger

This exercise gives you some practice with using the debugger.

1. Create a new Macromedia Flash document.

2. Select Modify⇨Document and change the stage dimensions to be 400 pixels wide by 400 pixels high.

3. Click the first frame in the timeline, open the Actions panel (Window⇨Actions), and enter in the following ActionScript code:

```
init();

function init()
{
    var stageSize:Number = Stage.height;
    var squareSize:Number = stageSize / 8;
    var currentX:Number;
```

```
    var currentY:Number;

    this.createEmptyMovieClip("checkerBoardClip", this.getNextHighestDepth());

    for (var i:Number = 0; i < 8; i++)
    {
        currentY = i * squareSize;
        for (var j:Number = 0; j < 8; j++)
        {
            currentX = j * squareSize;
            if ((i + j) % 2 == 0)
            {
                drawSquare(checkerBoardClip, currentX, currentY, ⤵
                    squareSize, 0x000000);
            }
        }
    }
}

function drawSquare(sourceClip:MovieClip, x:Number, y:Number, ⤵
    size:Number, color:Number):Void
{
    sourceClip.beginFill(color, 100);
    sourceClip.moveTo(x, y);
    sourceClip.lineTo(x, y + size);
    sourceClip.lineTo(x + size, y + size);
    sourceClip.lineTo(x + size, y);
    sourceClip.lineTo(x, y);
}
```

4. Select File⇨Save As, name the file tryItOut_debuggerPractice.fla, and save it in an appropriate directory.

5. Click just to the left of the line number of the first line in the init() function to set a breakpoint. The breakpoint marked should appear next to the first bold line in the preceding code.

6. Click just to the left of the line number of the first line in the drawSquare() function to set a breakpoint. The breakpoint marked should appear next to the second bold line in the preceding code.

7. Choose Control⇨Debug Movie.

8. Click the Locals tab. Click the Play button in the debug panel.

9. Click the Step Over button repeatedly, observing the changes in the local variables.

10. Click the Step Into button repeatedly, making a couple of passes through the entire code. Observe the changes in the local variables and the call stack. Also observe the drawing on the screen as it steps through the drawSquare() function.

11. Select the checkerBoardClip movie clip in the movie clip browser. Select the Properties tab. Click the Play button repeatedly, watching the periodic change in the _height property.

12. If the progress arrow is not already within the drawSquare() function, click the Play button so that the arrow is shown on top of the second breakpoint icon. Click the Step Out button to continue to the next line of code in the calling function.

13. Close the debug panel.

How It Works

Breakpoints are used to stop execution when the marked line of code is about to be executed. The Step Over, Step In, and Step Out buttons are used to offer fine control over the progress of code execution. The Play button is used to continue execution until the next breakpoint. The Step Over button runs the line of code with the progress arrow next to it, but does not attempt to stop at any of the lines of code within that function. The Step In button proceeds to the first line of code within the function marked by the progress arrow, if possible. The Step Out button proceeds to the line of code in the parent function that immediately follows the currently running function. It is important to note that as the progress arrow moves around, it is not preventing lines of code from running. Each line of code is run in sequence; the navigation buttons control only which line of code to pause at next.

The local variables indicate the state of the function that is currently in scope, and updates with each change of the variable. The movie clip `_height` property increases as each row of squares begins to be added.

Closing the debug panel terminates the debug session, but allows the movie to keep playing from where it was last paused.

Try It Out   **Debugging the Experiment**

This exercise uses the debugger to track down the problem with the image loader code.

1. Open the completed `tryItOut_debug.fla` file, or open `tryItOut_debug.fla` from the book's source files at <source file directory>/Chapter 12/tryItOut_debug/.

2. Click to the left of line number for the first line within the `init()` function. A red breakpoint marker should appear.

3. Choose Control⇨Debug Movie.

4. Click the Step Into button once, and note the state of the movie clip explorer.

5. Continue to click the Step Into button until the end of execution is reached, noting the state of the movie explorer as you go.

How It Works

By using the debugger, you should have noticed that the imageHolder movie clip was, in fact, created. While the experiment disproved the theory, it proved something else. What appears to have happened is that creating the text field deleted the movie clip from the stage. At this point, you would take a closer look at the data being passed into the `createTextField()` method and notice that both the movie clip and the text field share the same depth. Changing the `depth` argument for the `createTextField()` method to 2 fixes the problem. Even better would be to pass in `this.getNextHighestDepth()` to both methods instead of the actual number because it manages depths for you.

Using the Trace Statement

One debugging technique that is low-tech but useful is the `trace()` statement. You have seen it used many times throughout this book. Although it isn't very sophisticated, it is about the most useful and reliable debugging tool there is.

Two things that `trace()` statements are good for are to get a sense of the flow of your code and the state of your project. For instance, `trace()` can tell you whether and when a function is being executed and what data is being passed to the function. The following example shows a `trace()` statement at the beginning of a function. When the output from the `trace()` statement shows up in the output panel, you know that the function has been called, and by the data that is added to the `trace()` output, you know what data was passed to the function:

```
function animateText(inputString:String):Void
{
    trace("animateText() - inputString: " + inputString);
    // Function code ...
}
```

If you are unsure about how an `if` statement is executing, placing `trace()` statements in each `if` statement block will tell you exactly how the logic affects the execution of the program. In the following code, `trace()` statements are used to show the values of the variables being tested in the `if` statements and also to show which of the `if` statement blocks are executed:

```
trace("variable1: " + variable1);
trace("variable2: " + variable2);
trace("variable3: " + variable3);
if (variable1 == "foo" || variable2 == "bar")
{
    trace("Breakpoint 1");
    // Statements ...
}
else if (variable 3 == "baz")
{
    trace("Breakpoint 2");
    // Statements ...
}
else
{
    trace("Breakpoint 3");
    // Statements ...
}
```

Now debug the image loader code time using `trace()` statements.

Try It Out   Debugging with the Trace() Statement

This exercise uses `trace()` statements to track down the problem with the image loading code.

1. Open the completed `tryItOut_debug.fla` file, or open `tryItOut_debug.fla` from the book's source files at <source file directory>/Chapter 12/tryItOut_debug/.

2. Click the first frame in the timeline, open the Actions panel (Window⇨Development Panels⇨ Actions), and add the following `trace()` statements (shown in bold):

```
init();

function init():Void
{
    this.createEmptyMovieClip("imageHolder", 1);
    trace("imageHolder test 1: " + imageHolder);
    imageHolder.loadMovie("thumbnail.jpg");
    trace("imageHolder test 2: " + imageHolder);
    handleLoad();
}

function handleLoad():Void
{
    imageHolder._x = 10;
    imageHolder._y = 10;

    trace("imageHolder test 3: " + imageHolder);
    this.createTextField("description1Field", 1, 70, 25, 100, 20);
    trace("imageHolder test 4: " + imageHolder);
    description1Field.text = "Description 1";
}
```

3. Choose Control⇨Test Movie.

How It Works

Of course, from trying this with the debugger, you already know where the problem lies, but just pretend for a moment that you do not have that knowledge. The theory being tested by this experiment is that the `imageHolder` movie clip is not being created. The first `trace()` statement tests that out by showing whether the `imageHolder` reference returns a value or returns `undefined`. It returns a value, disproving the theory. The next theory might be that loading the image could be causing the containing movie clip to disappear, perhaps through a load error. The second `trace()` statement shows that the movie clip is still there right after the `loadMovie()` method call, disproving that theory. The next theory might be that the text field is causing the problem. Bracketing the field with `trace()` statements tests this, and shows that, yes, that is the case.

Commenting Out Code

Commenting out code is another technique for testing a theory. The goal is to comment out the code to a point where the functionality works, and then uncomment code progressively until it stops working. This process can be refined to a point where an individual line can be isolated as the source of the problem.

This technique does not work for every type of problem, nor is it necessarily recommended as a standard debugging technique. Resist using this technique blindly with a constant change-compile process instead of using it to test an actual theory. It is truly helpful for very complex or difficult-to-understand code where it's simply too complicated to work more precisely.

Remember, you can comment out single lines of code by prefacing each line with // (double slash), and you comment out a code block with /* before the first line to be commented out and */ after the last line to be commented out.

Try It Out   **Debugging by Commenting Out**

In this exercise you comment out code to track down the problem with the image loading code.

1. Open the completed `tryItOut_debug.fla` file, or open `tryItOut_debug.fla` from the book's source files at <source file directory>/Chapter 12/tryItOut_debug/.

2. Click the first frame in the timeline, open the Actions panel (Window⇨Development Panels⇨ Actions), and comment out the `handleLoad()` function, as shown in the bold code here:

```
function init():Void
{
    this.createEmptyMovieClip("imageHolder", 1);
    imageHolder.loadMovie("thumbnail.jpg");
//    handleLoad();
}
```

3. Choose Control⇨Test Movie.

4. Uncomment the `handleLoad()` call, and comment out the line with the `createTextField()` method.

5. Choose Control⇨Test Movie.

How It Works

The goal of using the comment-out method is to start with something that works, and then comment out code until it stops working. By commenting out the `handleLoad()` method, you test whether the code works without that function. Because it does, the theory that `imageHolder` is not being created is disproved. You then uncomment the function and you then comment out the most likely source of the problem within the `handleLoad()` method. By commenting out only that suspect line, you establish a baseline for when you try running it with that line re-enabled. If it stops working again after commenting out that one line, you know that the theory is wrong and that you should look elsewhere. Because the code worked, you know that the commented-out line is the source of the problem.

Analyze the Results

Once the experiment has been run, it's time to analyze the results. In the "Debugging the Experiment" Try It Out earlier in the chapter, you used the debugger to test a theory about why the image did not load, and proved that the theory was wrong. You then revised your theory and tested that.

Analyzing the results is generally an ongoing process as you test your theories and as each piece of debug information is revealed to you. Sometimes you come across an a-ha! moment when you suddenly realize what the problem is. When that happens, you think through how to best fix it, make the correction, and perform the test again to ensure that your revision actually works. Other times, you may need to perform the test multiple times, each time adding more `trace()` information or commenting out more code to get enough information to analyze whether your theory is correct. And occasionally you may not get enough information even after numerous attempts. This may mean that it is time to put your testing aside for a few minutes and take a break. Performing some research online to see whether other people have encountered the same problem may help, and getting the opinion of an experienced Flash developer may also help.

If the results of your testing indicate that your theory is wrong, it's time to revise the theory and start testing anew. You might make a list of all the possible errors you can think of. For example, if the problem that you are debugging involves an image not loading, some possibilities include the following:

❑ The image is missing from the server.

❑ There is an error in the URL given to load the image.

❑ The code to load the image is not being called.

❑ The movie clip to hold the image is off-screen, or has its `_visible` attribute set to `false`.

❑ The movie clip to hold the image does not exist.

Experience will help you to quickly come up with theories that are closer to the mark. If you consistently follow the methodology of developing a theory, testing your theory, and analyzing the results, you should be able to debug even the toughest code.

Summary

This chapter laid the groundwork for debugging code. Some points to remember include the following:

❑ Compile-time bugs result in the aborting of the compile process and are generally the easiest to debug.

❑ Make consistent use of strong typing to cause as many bugs as possible to be flagged at compile time.

❑ Logic bugs take more effort to fix. They include `if` statement errors, uninitialized variables, off-by-one and fence post errors, infinite loops, and numerical precision errors.

❑ Follow development best practices such as making code readable, developing in small chunks, and keeping functions small.

❑ The debugging process should closely follow the scientific process of developing a theory, testing that theory, analyzing the results of the test, and revising the theory if needed.

❑ Debugging techniques that are available to use include the use of the built-in debugger, the use of `trace()` statements, and use of the comment-out technique.

Exercises

1. Split the following `if` statement into two nested statements to make it easier to see how the statement works:

```
if ((shipType == "hospital" || shipConfiguration == "peacetime") && ⤶
    (shipDirection == "east" || shipDirection == "west"))
{
    // do stuff
}
```

2. Use one or more `trace()` statements to find out why the second `if` block is not being evaluated, and fix the problem. (Hint: you may want to review the Date class documentation in the Flash Help panel.)

```
var tempDate:Date = new Date(2006, 11, 20);

if (tempDate.getMonth() > 5 && tempDate.getMonth() < 11)
{
    // Stuff goes here
}
else if (tempDate.getYear() == 2006 && tempDate.getMonth() == 11)
{
    trace("You should see this text");
    // Stuff goes here
}
else
{
    // Stuff goes here
}
```

3. The following code should create three squares on the screen, but it only creates a single bow-tie shape. Use the debugger to step through the code to see where the problems lie.

```
var movieClipHandle:MovieClip;
var baseMovieClip:MovieClip = _level0;
var numMovieClips:Number = 3;

for (var i:Number = 0; i < numMovieClips; i++)
{
    baseMovieClip.createEmptyMovieClip("movieClip" + i, 0);
    movieClipHandle = baseMovieClip["movieClip" + i];
    movieClipHandle._x = i * 30 + 20;
    movieClipHandle._y = 20;
    movieClipHandle.lineStyle(1, 0x000000, 100);
    movieClipHandle.moveTo(0, 0);
    movieClipHandle.lineTo(20, 20);
    movieClipHandle.lineTo(0, 20);
    movieClipHandle.lineTo(20, 0);
    movieClipHandle.lineTo(0, 0);
}
```

4. The following code should extract the sentences from the input string and place them into an array. Instead, the code gets caught in an infinite loop and the array containing the sentences ends up containing no information. Use debug methods of your choice to uncover the issues.

```
var stopCharacter:String = ".";
var paragraphText:String = "The quick brown fox. Jumped over the lazy dog. ⊃
 Again. And again.";
var sentenceText:String = "";
var sentenceArray:Array;
var i:Number = 0;

while (i < paragraphText.length)
{
```

```
        if (paragraphText.charAt(i) == stopCharacter)
        {
            sentenceArray.push(sentenceText);
            sentenceText = "";
        }
        else
        {
            sentenceText += paragraphText.charAt(i);
            i++;
        }
    }

    // Trace out the array
    for (var i = 0; i < sentenceArray.length; i++)
    {
        trace(i + ": " + sentenceArray[i]);
    }
```

5. The following code should create two buttons on the screen, one with the label Play, one with the label Stop. They should have a colored background, and the play and stop `trace()` statements should show up only when the proper button is clicked. Debug this code so that it behaves in the way described.

```
function invokePlay():Void
{
    trace("Pressed play");
    presentationArea.play();
}

function invokeStop():Void
{
    trace("Pressed stop");
    presentationArea.stop();
}

function createButton(parentMovieClip:MovieClip, buttonName:String, ⤸
    buttonLabel:String, xPos:Number, yPos:Number, buttonWidth:Number, ⤸
    buttonHeight:Number, callback:Function):Void
{
    var buttonHandle:MovieClip;
    parentMovieClip.createEmptyMovieClip(buttonName, ⤸
        parentMovieClip.getNextHighestDepth());
    buttonHandle = parentMovieClip[buttonName];
    buttonHandle.onMouseUp = function()
    {
        callback();
    }
    buttonHandle._x = xPos;
    buttonHandle._y = yPos;
    drawBox(buttonHandle, buttonWidth, buttonHeight, AAAAFF, 333333);
    buttonHandle.createTextField("labelField", 1, 4, 4, 50, 15);
    buttonHandle.labelField.label = buttonLabel;
}

function drawBox(targetMovieClip:MovieClip, boxWidth:Number, ⤸
```

```
        boxHeight:Number, boxColor:Number, lineColor:Number):Void
{
    targetMovieClip.beginFill(boxColor);
    targetMovieClip.lineStyle(1, lineColor);
    targetMovieClip.moveTo(0, 0);
    targetMovieClip.lineTo(boxWidth, 0);
    targetMovieClip.lineTo(boxWidth, boxHeight);
    targetMovieClip.lineTo(0, boxHeight);
    targetMovieClip.lineTo(0, 0);
}
createButton(this, "playButton", "Play", 10, 10, 70, 20, invokePlay);
createButton(this, "stopButton", "Stop", 90, 10, 35, 20, invokeStop);
```

Working with Vector Graphics

Flash 8 provides unprecedented control over every pixel on the stage. In previous versions of Flash you had the drawing API coupled with tricks and techniques to accomplish drawing tasks that required pixel-level precision. Pixel-level control had not been one of Flash's strong points. But all that's changed in Flash 8, which provides a drawing API that encompasses a wide range of graphic control including color matrices and gradients.

One of the most important Flash 8 pixel-control objects is the Bitmap object. It allows specific pixel examination and modification. With methods such as `getPixel`, `setPixel`, and others, most detail-oriented developers will be thrilled with the Bitmap object.

Flash 8 also provides a good selection of blending modes, including Luminosity, Lighten, Darken, and Multiply. Blending modes enable you to composite one layer of a movie clip into the next clip by displaying only those pixels that are, for example, darker than the underlying layers. You may be familiar with blending modes used in popular image editing programs. They permit a wider range of movie clip effects than ever before.

The capability to apply real-time filters to pixel data on the stage is also new. These filters, which are similar to those found in image editing programs, include drop shadows, blurring, gradients, bevels, and more.

Flash 8 also enables robust video integration, and not only on a user interface level — using filters, color, and blending modes, you can integrate video so well that the video rectangle is a thing of the past.

In this chapter you explore the Flash 8 drawing API as it has changed in Flash 8 and find out how to work with filters.

Using the Drawing API

The drawing API (application programming interface) enables you to use ActionScript to draw vector shapes directly to the stage.

For beginners, it is easy to draw an object on the stage using the IDE tools, wrap the object in a movie clip, and call it onto the stage when needed from the library. That's certainly an avenue you can choose, but many situations call for dynamic graphics and user interface elements that are much more easily managed using reusable code blocks that create graphics very quickly, while keeping initial SWF file load size down.

You should keep a couple of things in mind if you've used the drawing API in past versions of Flash. You must take into consideration your target player version and publish for that version. If you attempt to use Flash 8 syntax and compile to Flash 7, some of the drawing methods may not act as expected. Also, if you use Flash 6 or 7 syntax and publish for Flash 8, you may see unexpected results.

The Flash 8 drawing API provides bitmap fills, line gradients, and color matrixes. The Matrix is not just a movie, it is an object that is used to transform and manipulate the behavior of bitmap and vector pixels.

Tools for Drawing Vectors with ActionScript

The drawing methods of the MovieClip object are very simple and follow conventions found in other languages that are capable of the same task:

- ❏ lineStyle()
- ❏ beginFill()
- ❏ beginBitmapFill()
- ❏ beginGradientFill()
- ❏ endFill()
- ❏ moveTo()
- ❏ lineTo()
- ❏ curveTo()
- ❏ clear()

That might not seem to be very many methods, but in combination and with the Matrix object, there's almost nothing you can do with IDE tools that you can't do with ActionScript. ActionScript enables a few features not seen in the IDE, whereas the IDE offers only one or two capabilities not found in ActionScript. You'll notice these as you read through the methods.

The following sections explore ActionScript's drawing methods.

lineStyle()

The lineStyle() method is used to set specific properties about the behavior of a line when one is drawn. Each time you need a new type of line, this method must be called.

lineStyle() has eight parameters (five more than it had in Flash 6 and 7). Following are their descriptions:

Parameter	Description
thickness:Number	thickness specifies in pixels the width of the line along its axis. A higher number creates a fatter line. When these lines are scaled up, they appear thicker and thicker, unless you use the noScale parameter. thickness can also be used to specify a zero-width line, which produces a one-pixel-wide line that, when scaled, does not change thickness regardless of the noScale parameter value.
rgb:Number	rgb is the hexadecimal value of the color of the line. The RGB value accepts a number with the format 0xRRGGBB. The 0x is simply a hexadecimal designator that tells Flash how to handle the number values to convert to red, green, and blue values.
alpha:Number	A numeric value of 0–100 that sets the alpha value (transparency) of the line. It is not an RGBA value. Values between –255 and 255 do not affect this value. Numbers below 0 are ignored and are rendered as 0. Numbers higher than 100 also are ignored; they're rendered as 100.
pixelHinting:Boolean	Pixel hinting is a means of smoothing the look of the line. This parameter is a Boolean. A true value renders the line with interpolated pixels along its edges so it blends more smoothly with the pixels surrounding it. The default value is false.
noScale:Boolean	The noScale parameter's default is a Boolean false. Setting it to true preserves the thickness of the line on its axis regardless of length changed during scaling. (To see how this works, create an example line and scale the clip, setting this value to false, and then to true.)
capsStyle:String	This parameter is a String that defaults to round. In the past, all lines ended with a rounded tip. When creating corners, this caused a square to look somewhat less sharp than what might have been needed. Flash 8 makes line tip control much more precise. The three string values available are round, square, and none. square gives you a squared-off line end, producing an extremely sharp line. round makes a line that has a much softer appearance at its tip. This might sound not as desirable, but round-tipped lines easily create simple circles and large rounded corners on squares. A value of none creates a line tip similar to the square value, although the line ends abruptly at whatever control point is specified. It can be used when specific height values are required, such as for absolutely square line joints, or lines used to show precise values in information graphics.
jointStyle:String	The jointStyle parameter is also a String. It is similar to capStyle, except it defines how lines connect to one another when lineTo is called consecutively. The values are miter, round, and beveled. A miter joint produces a very sharp point, and a round joint produces a rounded joint, giving a softer look. The beveled joint is a squared-off joint that does not come to a sharp point, but each line ends abruptly in a style similar to capStyle:none.

Table continued on following page

Parameter	Description
miterLimit:Number	miterLimit is a Number value from 0 to 255 that stipulates how many pixels a corner should be allowed to extend beyond the control point when using a miter joint. There are, of course, limits to this value depending upon the angle of the two lines being joined. If two lines join at an acute angle, for example, the miter corner can only extend so far before it becomes a sharp point.

beginFill()

beginFill() remains unchanged and works as it did in Flash 6 and 7. It defines the color that should fill the space created by lineTo. This method fills a space with color regardless of whether lineTo closes a final gap. An open gap is ignored and the fill uses the shortest distance between the last lineTo and the previous lineTo method calls to close the shape. Using fragmented shapes can lead to undesired behavior. Always be sure to close your shapes with the appropriate lineTo set. beginFill() accepts the following two parameters:

Parameter	Description
rgb:Number	rgb is the hexadecimal value of the fill color, a number in the format 0xRRGGBB.
alpha:Number	The alpha value is a Number from 0 to 100. It is not an RGBA alpha value, and it does not accept a value below 0 or above 100.

beginBitmapFill()

beginBitmapFill() is similar to the beginFill() method, except that it fills a shape with the contents of a bitmap instead of a single specified color. You choose how the bitmap fills the shape: repeating or nonrepeating. A repeating image tiles until the entire bitmap is filled; a nonrepeating image does not tile. Methods also exist that determine how the bitmap is smoothed. You can specify any Bitmap object to occupy the target shape and use all of the bitmap methods available to manipulate the bitmap.

beginBitmap() takes the following four parameters:

Parameter	Description
source:BitmapData	The source parameter defines the source bitmap to fill the shape. You can modify the bitmap any way you want before defining this parameter. If you make changes to your bitmap you will need to call the beginBitmapFill() method again to reflect changes.

Parameter	Description
`matrixObject:Matrix`	This parameter is a Matrix object, which is found in the Flash.geom object. It defines transformations to apply on the bitmap at the time it is drawn within the shape. Subsequent transformations must be called again by `beginBitmapFill()` to reflect changes. You may transform your bitmap before calling this method. The bitmap transforms from the state it is received in. Here's an example matrix: `var myMatrix = new flash.geom.Matrix();` `myMatrix.scale(.5,.5);` In it, the bitmap is scaled to half its original size. Many properties associated with the Matrix object enable you to manipulate the Bitmap object.
`repeat:Boolean`	The `repeat` parameter takes a Boolean value. If `true`, the image is repeated until it fills the entire shape. If `false` (the default), the edges of the image are extruded until they reach the edge of the bitmap. `repeat` can produce some interesting fill effects. Use it in conjunction with a Matrix object to create complex fill transformations.
`smooth:Boolean`	The `smooth` parameter is a Boolean. If `true`, the pixels in the bitmap are rendered with a smoothing method. Smoothing can absorb CPU time, and cause complex transformations to slow down. Consider the activities currently using CPU cycles in your SWF before employing smoothing in large or complex bitmaps. The default value is `false`.

beginGradientFill()

`beginGradientFill()` fills a shape with a gradient. In Flash 8 it enables complex transformations and effects. The method accepts seven parameters, as described here:

Parameter	Description
type:*String*	`type`'s values are `linear` or `radial`. A linear gradient fades from the beginning index to an ending index without bending or wrapping. A radial gradient begins from a specified focal point and fades outward. Both can be modified using a matrix.
colors:*Array*	`colors` is an Array object of hexadecimal color values. The fill uses the value to create the gradient.
alphas:*Array*	`alphas` is an array of 0–100 alpha values associated with each value in the colors array. If an alpha array is defined, it must be the same length as the color array.

Table continued on following page

Parameter	Description
ratios:*Array*	`ratios` is an of array of 0–255 values. The value defines the percentage of width the corresponding color in the colors array may occupy across the full width of the fill. This array must be the same length as the colors array.
matrix:*Object*	The Matrix object has a `createGradientBox` method to conveniently manipulate a gradient fill. `beginGradientFill()` expects the values in the matrix created by the `createGradientBox`.`matrix` may fail if not all expected values are present. `createGradientBox` is explained in "The Matrix Object" section later in this chapter.
spreadMethod:*String*	`spreadMethod` accepts String values of `pad`, `reflect`, or `repeat`. `pad`, the default value, begins a gradient fill at the index specified and takes it to the end point specified. If space within the shape exists beyond the end point, the shape is filled with the last outer `rgb` value of the fill until the shape is completely filled. `reflect` begins and ends the fill at the index and end point specified. At that point the algorithm is reversed and the gradient is filled, returning to the original values through the color array. This flip-flopping of the color array direction continues until the shape is completely filled. `repeat` also begins the fill at the specified index and takes the gradient to the specified end point. Then the fill starts again, repeating the gradient until the entire shape is filled.
interpolationMethod:*String*	`interpolationMethod` accepts a String value of `RGB` or `Linear RGB`. It specifies how the color should be spread out in a gradient fill between colors. `LinearRGB` spreads the color evenly, creating new mixed color values between two colors rather than the default `RGB` interpolation method of fading the values between the two colors.

endFill()

The `endFill()` method commits the fill defined in any of the `beginFill()` methods. It has no parameters and uses the fill method values to fill the last closed shape created by the `curveTo` and `lineTo` methods.

moveTo()

The `moveTo()` method places the drawing position within a movie clip without defining a line. It defaults to `0,0` if no `lineTo` or `curveTo` methods have been called.

`moveTo` takes two parameters: `moveTo(x:Number, y:Number)`. `x` and `y` are both Number values that specify their respective positions of the index of the drawing tool.

lineTo()

You use the `lineTo()` method to move the index position of the drawing tool. If `lineStyle` is defined, a line is drawn from the previous index of the drawing object index using that line style. This last index may have been positioned using `curveTo`, `moveTo`, or `lineTo` methods.

`lineTo` takes two parameters: `lineTo(x:Number,y:Number)`. x and y are Number values that specify their respective index of the drawing tool.

curveTo()

Use the `curveTo()` method to draw a curved edge from the last index position of the Drawing object. If `lineStyle` is defined, a line is drawn along the curve using the style specified. The last index may have been positioned using `curveTo`, `lineTo`, or `moveTo`.

The curve is a Bezier curve, which is made up of only three points (start, end, and one in between) that affect its shape. A control point basically manipulates a line to prefer a specific path as it is drawn toward the anchor (end) point. The maximum radius of the curve is determined by the difference in position between the anchor point and control point.

`curveTo` takes the following parameters:

Parameter	Description
controlX:Number	controlX's Number value is the x position of the curve's control point. A control point x that differs greatly from an anchor point x creates a more extreme curve.
controlY:Number	controyY's Number value is the y position of the curve's control point. A control point y that differs greatly from an anchor point y creates a more extreme curve.
anchorX:Number	anchorX's Number value is the x position of the end point of the line. This point is the final x point of the line drawn.
anchorY:Number	anchorY's Number value is the y position of the end point of the line. This point is the final y point of the line drawn.

clear()

The `clear()` method clears all graphics drawn with the Drawing object on the timeline on which it is called. It has no parameters.

Drawing Vectors with ActionScript

To help you understand the basic concepts of the drawing API and how the coordinate values used in the drawing API relate to the stage, create a simple square. When you are done with the example, try making other shapes and lines. Experimenting with the methods helps you learn them quickly.

Try It Out   Create a Simple Square

In this example you use some of the fundamental drawing methods to create two draggable anchor points as well as one draggable control point so that you can see how control points work.

1. Open a new Flash document and save it as `simpleSquare.fla` in your work folder.

2. Click the first frame in the timeline, open the Actions panel, and enter the following ActionScript:

```
with (this) {
    beginFill(0xFF0000, 60);
    lineStyle(2, 0x666666, 100);
    moveTo(20, 20);
    lineTo(20, 120);
    lineTo(120, 120);
    lineTo(120, 20);
    lineTo(20, 20);
    endFill();
    lineStyle(2, 0xFF000000, 30);
    moveTo(60, 60);
    lineTo(60, 160);
    lineTo(160, 160);
    lineTo(160, 60);
    lineTo(60, 60);
}
```

3. Test your movie in the debug player. You will see three squares on the screen. These are draggable. Move them around to see how the anchor points and control points interact to create Bezier curves.

How It Works

In this example you use drawing methods to create a simple shape and see how the `beginFill` method integrates with `lineTo` methods to create a unified vector object.

When `lineTo` is used without `beginFill`, no fill is created by default. You can create outline shapes by just using lines.

You can use as many points defined by `lineTo` method calls as you want to create complex shapes and lines; however, every point takes memory. The more points defined in a vector drawing, the more intensive it is for Flash to redraw that shape in an animation. Too many points in a vector shape can slow down your entire application. Be aware of the target machine, and test, test, test.

Finally, note that the first and last `lineTo` methods for each square are identical. Remove line 8 (`lineTo(20, 20);`) to see what happens to the fill shape. The fill shape closes the gap regardless of the fact that the shape isn't closed in this case. Always be aware of closing shapes. Although a shape may *appear* closed, when modified by other ActionScript objects or functions it can produce unexpected results because the fill shape defaults to the closest pixel to close the shape.

Also try manipulating the `alpha` value in the `beginFill` method. If you change it to 100, which means it will be completely opaque, the second square, drawn after the first, is still completely visible. This is because any new points are drawn over old points. However, even when a new shape overlays an older shape, the older shape's vector points remain in memory. It is up to you to use the `clear` method when appropriate, or a Bitmap or MovieClip object to separate and control each shape individually.

With this exercise under your belt, you're ready to use a basic set of drawing API methods to create and manipulate more complex vector graphics at runtime using methods and interactivity.

Try It Out   Create a Bezier Curve Using a Control Point

In this example you use some of the fundamental drawing methods to create two draggable anchor points as well as one draggable control point so that you can see how the `curveTo` control points affect a line.

1. Open a new Flash Document. Save the Flash document as `curveTo.fla` in your work folder.

2. Click the first frame in the timeline, open the Actions panel, and enter the following ActionScript function:

```
function connect() {
    this.clear();
    this.lineStyle(3,0x660000,100);
    this.moveTo(anchorOne._x, anchorOne._y);
    this.curveTo(controlOne._x, controlOne._y, anchorTwo._x, anchorTwo._y);
    updateAfterEvent();

}
```

This function refers to the control point and anchor point.

3. You'll create the control and anchor point values based on the position of movie clips. Each movie clip contains a square, so add a simple `createSquare()` function using the `lineTo` method in succession. Just type the following below the code you entered in step 2:

```
function createSquare(handle, side, offset) {
    if (offset == undefines) {
        offset = 0;
    }
    with (handle) {
        moveTo(offset, offset);
        lineTo(offset, side);
        lineTo(side, side);
        lineTo(side, offset);
        lineTo(offset, offset);
        endFill();
    }
}
```

4. You want to be able to drag the anchor points and control points so that you can easily see what the control points do for you. The following code is a convenient method for adding draggability to any movie clip. Type the following function below the code you added in step 3:

```
function setDraggable(handle) {
    handle.onPress = function() {
        clearInterval(_global.refreshScreen);
        _global.refreshScreen = setInterval(this._parent, "connect", 10);
        this.startDrag(false);
```

```
    };
    handle.onRelease = function() {
        clearInterval(_global.refreshScreen);
        this.stopDrag();
    };
    handle.onReleaseOutside = function() {
        clearInterval(_global.refreshScreen);
        this.stopDrag();
    };
}
```

5. Create the control and anchor points by adding the following code below the code you entered in step 4:

```
anchorOne = createEmptyMovieClip("anchorPoint1", this.getNextHighestDepth());
anchorOne._x = anchorOne._y=50;
anchorOne.beginFill(0xCCCCCC, 100);
anchorOne.lineStyle(0, 0x000000, 100, false, false, "none", "miter", 2);
createSquare(anchorOne, 8, -8);
setDraggable(anchorOne);
anchorTwo = createEmptyMovieClip("anchorPoint2", this.getNextHighestDepth());
anchorTwo._x = anchorTwo._y=250;
anchorTwo.beginFill(0xCCCCCC, 100);
anchorTwo.lineStyle(0, 0x000000, 100, false, false, "none", "miter", 2);
createSquare(anchorTwo, 8, -8);
setDraggable(anchorTwo);
controlOne = createEmptyMovieClip("control1", this.getNextHighestDepth());
controlOne._x = anchorTwo._x;
controlOne._y = anchorOne._y;
controlOne.beginFill(0xCCCCCC, 100);
controlOne.lineStyle(0, 0x000000, 100, false, false, "none", "miter", 2);
createSquare(controlOne, 8, -8);
setDraggable(controlOne);
connect();
```

6. Test your movie in the debug player. You will see three squares on the screen. These are draggable. Move them around to see how the anchor points and control points interact to create Bezier curves.

How It Works

The most pertinent part of the code in this example is in step 2: the function that connects the two anchor points via a line using the curveTo method. The code also calls lineStyle, with just three parameters, generating a basic line. (A line gradient could have been used as well.)

The methods of the drawing API are enacted directly upon the stage of the movie clip on which they're called. You nest the entire process in child clips for much more freedom when extending the code.

Also in the connect() function, the moveTo method is used to virtually lift the drawing tool to a new position so that it does not draw any lines from a previous position. You can remove this method with a lineTo method to see what happens when you don't lift the drawing tool off the virtual canvas. Also pertaining to the virtual canvas is the clear() method. Try removing this method now. You see that the object retains lines drawn during previous loops. By clearing the canvas you can start with a fresh line.

Calling `clear` also relieves the CPU of having to track many vector points that in some cases may no longer be visible. Even though `cacheAsBitmap` relieves you from this concern to a degree, you should still be aware of the vector points you have on the stage, and any memory you're using. Vectors appear simple, but the points that define shapes can stack up quickly.

In the `createSquare` function, a code block is created to easily add squares of varying size and offset to any movie clip. In a larger application, it is likely wiser to make this function a static class method in a drawing library class. But in this example, it is clear how you can take advantage of the drawing API to perform repetitive drawing tasks without having to do them by hand and place them in the library. This method relies on the parameter `handle` having a fill method already assigned on it. The function fails otherwise. In a static class method, it would be practical to return some Boolean state to describe an error such as this.

Next you add a `setDraggable` function, which you are able to call with any of your movie clips to add interactivity to them. Notice some code block side railing occurring here, as it attempts to retain any interactivity the clip might have previously had defined upon it. The function is generic, and could be used on just about any clip. In a larger application it would probably be better to make this method an extension of the MovieClip class. However, in this context you can see a simplified way to use the drawing API to create real, usable UI elements that can interact with the user.

In the last bit of code, the simple application is tied together using the methods defined in previous steps as well as built-in `create` methods for adding movie clips to the stage. Each clip defines a `lineStyle`, as well as a `fill` method. In this way you can make each instance unique in some way. This also shows that the `lineStyle` and `fill` methods can be assigned per object, and more generic calls from `lineTo`, `moveTo`, and `curveTo` can be used to complete the shape desired.

The final line calls the `connect` method. Because it waits for interactivity before drawing, so as to preserve CPU power while interactivity is not taking place, `connect` needs to be called to create the initial `curveTo` line condition and connect your anchor points in their default positions.

So far you've learned how to place primitive shapes and simple lines on the stage and manipulate them through user interactivity. At the heart of interactive graphics is knowing when to call the `clear` method and how to compartmentalize repeated tasks such as drawing squares. In the next Try It Out you use the drawing API in a real-world example, using a data set and going from raw data points to final graphic.

Try It Out   Build a Graph

In this example you create dynamic information graphics based on a data table. `lineTo`, `moveTo`, and `beginFill` are used to frame the graph as well as to create the actual graph.

1. Open a new Flash document. Save it as `graph.fla` in your work folder. In the FLA properties panel, select Modify⇨Document, and change the width of the stage to `1024`. Ensure that the height is `400`. (I advise making the background `#ffffff6`, but that's optional.) Click OK to commit the stage changes.

2. Click the first frame in the timeline, open the Actions panel, and enter the following ActionScript function:

```
dataTable = [];
dataTable.push(["1851-1860", 8, 5, 5, 1, 0, 19]);
dataTable.push(["1861-1870", 8, 6, 1, 0, 0, 15]);
```

```
dataTable.push(["1871-1880", 7, 6, 7, 0, 0, 20]);
dataTable.push(["1881-1890", 8, 9, 4, 1, 0, 22]);
dataTable.push(["1891-1900", 8, 5, 5, 3, 0, 21]);
dataTable.push(["1901-1910", 10, 4, 4, 0, 0, 18]);
dataTable.push(["1911-1920", 10, 4, 4, 3, 0, 21]);
dataTable.push(["1921-1930", 5, 3, 3, 2, 0, 13]);
dataTable.push(["1931-1940", 4, 7, 6, 1, 1, 19]);
dataTable.push(["1941-1950", 8, 6, 9, 1, 0, 24]);
dataTable.push(["1951-1960", 8, 1, 5, 3, 0, 17]);
dataTable.push(["1961-1970", 3, 5, 4, 1, 1, 14]);
dataTable.push(["1971-1980", 6, 2, 4, 0, 0, 12]);
dataTable.push(["1981-1990", 9, 1, 4, 1, 0, 15]);
dataTable.push(["1991-2000", 3, 6, 4, 0, 1, 14]);
dataTable.push(["2001-2005", 7, 2, 3, 3, 1, 9]);
get2dArrayValues = function (handle, n) {
    temp = [];
    for (var i = 0; i<handle.length; i++) {
        temp.push(handle[i][n]);
    }
    return temp;
};
```

This code creates a two-dimensional array that holds your data, as well as a method for retrieving that data easily.

3. Now define a function to draw a shape. The function is similar, but a little more complex than the `createSquare` function defined in the preceding Try It Out:

```
drawGraph = function (handle, values, max, grpWidth, grpHeight, style, ⤸
        xoffset, yoffset) {
    var xincrement = grpWidth/values.length;
    var yincrement = grpHeight/max;
    handle = handle.createEmptyMovieClip("graphline"+getTimer(), ⤸
        handle.getNextHighestDepth());
    handle._x = xoffset;
    handle._y = yoffset;
    handle.lineStyle(0, 0xFFFFFF, 4);
    handle.moveTo(0, grpHeight);
    handle.beginFill(style[0], Style[1]);
    handle.lineTo(0, grpHeight-(values[0]*yincrement));
    for (var i = 1; i<values.length; i++) {
        handle.lineTo((i*xincrement), grpHeight-(values[i]*yincrement));
    }
    handle.lineTo((values.length-1)*xincrement, grpHeight);
    handle.lineTo(0, grpHeight);
    handle.endFill();
};
```

4. To draw the graph data, type the following code below the code you entered in step 2:

```
myGraph = this.createEmptyMovieClip("graphHolder",0);
var F1:Array = get2dArrayValues(dataTable, 1);
drawGraph(myGraph, F1, 12, 800, 200, [0x3C4B6C, 5], 22);
var F2:Array = get2dArrayValues(dataTable, 2);
drawGraph(myGraph, F2, 12, 800, 200, [0x3C4B6C, 25], 22);
```

```
var F3:Array = get2dArrayValues(dataTable, 3);
drawGraph(myGraph, F3, 12, 800, 200, [0x3C4B6C, 45], 22);
var F4:Array = get2dArrayValues(dataTable, 4);
drawGraph(myGraph, F4, 12, 800, 200, [0x3C4B6C, 65], 22);
var F5:Array = get2dArrayValues(dataTable, 5);
drawGraph(myGraph, F5, 12, 800, 200, [0x000000, 85], 22);
```

5. Test your movie to see the graph created with the data. Close the `.swf` and return to the first frame ActionScript.

You can go back into the dataTable array added in step 2 and change the values to see them reflected in the drawing. If you already know how to import XML, try changing the data table to external data sources. Try modifying the graph to suit your visual style.

How It Works

This example showed how to use simple functions together to create sophisticated information graphics entirely within ActionScript.

In step 2 you created the data model, as well as a method for extracting values from that model easily in a reusable code block. You can change the values in the dataTable array or remove some of the data to see what happens and how the code copes with different amounts of data points. Because the function you create later doesn't rely on a specific number of data points or a specific set of values, you can change your graph quickly and easily. Clearly, the drawing API can be used to save time and keep file size down — note that the SWF file size is less than 3 kilobytes. If you re-create this same graph as a `.jpeg` or `.gif` image, it would cost you some 25–40 kilobytes for a similar-quality image.

`moveTo`, `lineTo`, `beginFill`, `lineStyle`, and `endFill` are used in the `drawGraph` function. Change the values specified in this function. You see how you can customize the look and feel of the shapes it creates. Don't worry if it looks a little goofy at first. Keep working until you understand how to get a line you want. The `drawGraph` function creates the actual data points on the graph. This method is called repeatedly in step 4 to generate graphs for each set in the dataTable array. Each new value set overlays the data sets drawn earlier. The `beginFill` method provides the color and transparency for the data set. You can change the behavior and look of the graph data by changing the drawing API method calls in this function.

You also could begin to define interactivity by adding text information to the stage and creating a function to swap the depths of the data sets when key values are clicked. I encourage you to attempt this and explore the issues that exist if you were to make the graph interactive for the user.

The `drawGraph` function requires six parameters and has two optional ones, all of which are described in the following table:

Parameter	Description
handle	A reference to the movie clip in which to draw the graph.
values	An array of values that determine the height of the graph values being drawn.

Table continued on following page

Parameter	Description
max	The maximum value the graph is capable of displaying. This is essentially the scale of your graph. A max value that is much larger than the actual values in the graph results in a flat-looking graph.
grpWidth	The maximum width of the graph in pixels.
grpHeight	The maximum height of the graph in pixels.
style	An array of a color in hexadecimal format, and an alpha value.
xoffset	Together with yoffset, moves the container clip for each graph drawn. Not required. In step 4, you used an xoffset of 22 pixels to align data points over the center of the labels rather than the beginning of the label.
yoffset	Together with xoffset, moves the container clip for each graph drawn. Not required.

Take a little deeper look at the drawGraph function. The first two lines determine how far apart each data point should be by establishing the length of virtual grid segments. This is established by dividing the grpWidth and grpHeight values by the number of values expected:

```
var xincrement = grpWidth/values.length;
var yincrement = grpHeight/max;
```

The next lines create a placeholder for the graph and move it according to the xoffset and yoffset values. The handle variable name is recycled to point to the child movie clip created with the createEmptyMovieClip method:

```
handle = handle.createEmptyMovieClip("graphline"+getTimer(),⤵
handle.getNextHighestDepth());
handle._x = xoffset;
handle._y = yoffset;
```

In these three lines of code you begin to use the drawing API methods. The first method is moveTo. The x value is set to 0. The y value is a bit different. An important consideration when using the drawing methods is that a movie clip index begins at 0,0, and positive x and y values move to the right and down on the stage coordinate system. Because positive values indicate lower onscreen positions, it can be counterintuitive. Creating graphs often requires negative values for y coordinates. So in this case the start index of the graph is the height of the graph because the very top left of your entire interface is index 0,0. That's likely confusing, but with a bit of experience you'll see why this is an important consideration.

The following line defines the beginFill style. You use the Style parameter of the drawGraph function to declare the values:

```
handle.beginFill(Style[0], Style[1]);
```

The next line draws the first vector line. In case its value changes, this lineTo is kept separate from the following lineTo values. The x value is 0 because this is the first graph value being drawn.

The y parameter is a bit more complex:

```
handle.lineTo(0, grpHeight-(values[0]*yincrement));
```

The start position is indicated as `grpHeight`. The y value to be drawn is multiplied by the `yincrement` value obtained earlier. The `values[0]` array index is the first graph value. Because the height of the graph is divided into segments, multiplying the actual variable from the data set by the segment length provides the y value to plot to. Subtract the plot value from the height of the graph because positive values would cause the graph to be drawn upside down due the coordinate system.

Now that the initial start position of the drawing is defined, you can loop the rest of the values. The next line in the function defines a `for` loop, which does the same work as the `lineTo` method discussed earlier, but it runs through the entire data set provided in the values array, modifying the conditional value used to find the plot point:

```
for (var i = 1; i<values.length; i++) {
    handle.lineTo((i*xincrement), grpHeight-(values[i]*yincrement));
}
```

To plot the x value in this `lineTo` method, the i value of the `for` loop is multiplied by the `xincrement` obtained earlier. The i value is also used as an array index to obtain the value in the values array, which is multiplied by the `yincrement` to find the actual plot value of data.

Then you finalize the end of the graph with a vertical line. Because the last `lineTo` method call in the `for` loop set the index position at the last possible x position, you use that value again (you don't want to move to the right or left; you just want to move straight down). In the preceding `for` loop, the conditional statement is `i<values.length` because numeric arrays start at 0 instead of 1. So to get the actual number of plotted values, the length is shifted by subtracting one from the values array length property. To close off the end of the graph as a side, then, the y value is specified as the index `grpHeight`, which is the start y position of the graph:

```
handle.lineTo((values.length-1)*xincrement, grpHeight);
```

The last two lines of the `drawGraph` function code close the final graph shape. You don't need to call a final closing `lineTo` method in all cases because `endFill` closes a shape with the first known plot value. However, it is a good idea to stipulate a closer line so that you have full control over your shape and quirky shapes won't act in a way you don't expect. Declaring a closing `lineTo` also allows easy modification of a closer line if changes ever need to be made to the behavior of the shape. The function closes the shape with the `endFill` method call:

```
handle.lineTo(0, grpHeight);
handle.endFill();
```

So that's the `drawGraph` function. In just a few lines of code you can create dynamic, complex shapes while reusing code and keeping your drawing easily modifiable.

The Matrix Object

You explore filters in the next chapter, but before you go there, the Matrix object requires explanation. A Matrix object can easily describe a change made to a set of values that affect a MovieClip or Bitmap object.

Its basic methods—`createGradientBox`, `invert`, `rotate`, and `scale`—automate some of its behaviors. These methods are explained when the objects that use them are discussed later in this book.

A matrix can describe how an object should be transformed. It is a grid of values that allows functions to communicate a set of data variables in an efficient manner. Many types of matrix objects exist. The flash.gom.matrix object, for example, controls how an object is physically modified on the stage. Color matrices and convolution matrices exist as well. Chapter 14 covers matrices so that you can begin to use them efficiently in your code. I encourage you to return to this chapter and review the `beginBitmapFill` and `beginGradientFill` methods with their matrix object parameters to complete more complex shape manipulation when using the drawing API.

Summary

In this chapter you explored the many ways in which you can modify movieClip and Bitmap objects using basic available method sets and known formulas for manipulating images.

The convolutionMatrix proved particularly powerful, as did the BitmapData object.

Many of the methods and objects in this chapter have the capability to be manipulated directly on a more advanced level. If a particular object suits your intent, look into the object further to see how you might customize or create a class to control it.

All of the filters, blend modes, and methods can be automated and reused efficiently in class objects. Seek out existing libraries and formulas to help automate the many tasks these filters and the methods in this chapter can perform alone and in combination with one another.

The pinhole camera effect provided a Try It Out that showed how using many of these objects and methods together in a specific order can produce a result that you expect from expensive image editing programs, not from a real-time animation rendering function set. Have fun with these methods. Don't get bogged down with the mathematics involved and try out as many things as you can think of!

Exercises

1. Create a simple circle using some circle math.
2. Write a function that uses mouse interaction to draw lines.
3. Create a shape in a movie clip. Use that movie clip to mask a bitmap image in another movie clip.

Applying Filter Effects

Filters in Flash are similar to the layer styles found in popular image editing programs. Filters allow for glow, shadow, bevel effects, and more! These effects are new in Flash 8. Previous versions of Flash allowed rudimentary effects using vector graphics libraries, which were both difficult to manage and processor intensive. With Flash 8 filters, you have the advantage of built-in pixel-level manipulation of objects as bitmaps, which means fast and easy filter manipulation of any movieClip or Bitmap object.

The filters are applied easily by declaring the `filters` property of a movie clip. When the movie clip changes, the `filters` property is checked and the filter is applied. You can apply multiple filters to the same object. You also can apply multiple versions of the same filter to the same object. This gives you unparalleled control of filter effects at runtime using ActionScript.

Filters are exceptionally easy in Flash. You can stipulate all the properties within each new filter constructor or set them individually. This enables you to reuse an existing filter rather than instantiating a new filter object. Each time you modify a filter, you must reapply it to your target movie clip using the filters property of the movie clip.

Although you can set the properties of a filter via the new constructor, it is far more readable, and easier to scan, when a property declaration list is used. This is especially helpful for group development, particularly when working with developers who might not be familiar with all of the parameters available in the new constructor.

When describing methods, the properties are listed individually rather than as parameters. If you want to use constructor parameters to construct your filter values, you can use code hints in the ActionScript panel to show you the expected order of the parameters.

This chapter examines the major filters and their properties.

DropShadowFilter

DropShadowFilter does exactly what the name implies. You're likely familiar with drop shadows in popular image editing software. An interesting and useful detail is that a drop shadow is rendered only as a shadow of visible pixels within a movie clip or bitmap. This includes transparent PNG and GIF. A shadow will only be rendered for the visible pixels in images.

The properties of the `DropShadowFilter` are described in the following list. These properties can be set within the constructor of the filter or defined as properties after the construction:

- ❏ `alpha` — Specifies the opacity of the shadow. Surprisingly, this numeric property is not a value of 0–100. Instead it is 0.0 to 1.0, so to set the `alpha` property of the baseline pixel of the shadow to 25, you would set it to `.25`.

- ❏ `angle` — The angle, again surprisingly, is a numeric value from `0` to `360`. This is unexpected because most other angle and rotation properties in Flash use radians, an alternative method for working with circular points. It is important to consider when using the Math object that some radian-to-degree conversions are required to make the angle work. As well, Flash's stage defines `0` degrees along the x axis. That is, a value of `0` puts a shadow to the right of your movie clip. So this is a bit quirky, but after you use it a few times, you'll get used to it.

- ❏ `blurX` and `blurY` — These are numeric values (`0` to `255`) that describe the amount to which the shadow should be blurred. You don't need a high value to obtain desirable results. In fact, high values can produce visible stepping. The value loosely matches the amount of pixels to which the shadow will expand, depending upon the `strength` property applied, and whether the `inner` property is `true` or `false`.

- ❏ `color` — A hexadecimal value. If you do not specify this property, it defaults to `0x000000`.

- ❏ `distance` — A numeric pixel value. Any numeric value is acceptable, including negative values. This property determines how far away from the movie clip the shadow should be rendered. This is a two-dimensional value. Setting a larger distance only moves the shadow on the x and y plane; it does not change the size of the shadow in relation to distance.

- ❏ `hideObject` — A Boolean. When set to `true`, the movie clip is hidden, but the shadow is still rendered. Unlike the `_visible` property of the movie clip, `hideObject` allows the movie clip to retain mouse interactivity. The vector points of the movie clip are still processed by the rendering engine, so this method has little to no effect on overall performance. The default is `false`.

- ❏ `inner` — A Boolean that specifies where the shadow is rendered. Set to `true`, it causes the shadow to be overlaid onto the object and fade inward. The default value is `false`, which renders the shadow in the more traditional manner beneath the movie clip.

- ❏ `knockout` — Replaces the fill areas in your movie clip with the colors that reside beneath the clip. It essentially makes your movie clip transparent while preserving the opacity of the fills. This is confusing and is best understood by simply trying it out and seeing the result. `knockout` enables many superb effects on existing stage content.

- ❏ `quality` — A numeric value of `0` to `15`. Use it to customize how smoothly a movie clip's shadow is rendered. The `quality` setting is essentially a multi-pass setting that extrapolates more detailed pixel data for the shadow with each pass. The higher the value, the prettier your shadow, but the more CPU intensive the shadow rendering becomes. Usually a value of 3–5 produces sufficient smoothness. (Also, the higher the value, the more passes blur previous passes, so a higher-quality shadow appears more bloomed and ambient than a lower-quality shadow.)

❏ strength — A numeric value from 0 to 255. The higher the value, the more the color of the filter is opaque on the surrounding content. This value also directly affects the blur values because the higher the strength value, the higher the contrast between the shadow and the surrounding content. As the strength increases, fewer steps are used to render the blur. With both large blur and large strength values, undesired results such as visible stepping can occur.

BlurFilter

BlurFilter blurs a bitmap or movie clip in a similar manner to the blur filters found in popular image editing programs. Using a Bitmap object as the target for a blur means you can blur specific parts of an image. Varying values within the properties enables you to blur in a specific direction to imply motion or directional blur.

The properties of the BlurFilter and a description of each property follows. These properties can be set within the constructor of the filter or defined as properties after the construction:

❏ blurX and blurY — These two properties determine the amount of blur to apply to the target object. The properties expect a Number value from 0 to 255. The default value is 4. After a value of 255 is surpassed, the object is no longer visible.

❏ quality — A numeric value of 0 to 15. This property essentially tells the filter how many times it should be run on the object. A low value produces more rudimentary blurring; higher values produce blurred pixels and thus a more Gaussian effect.

GlowFilter

GlowFilter creates a uniform ambient color around the movie clip. It is similar to DropShadowFilter, but without an angle setting. The strength of the glow is affected by the alpha values present as well as the relative size of the areas within the object. A thin line, for example, will have less of a glow than a large opaque circle in the same clip.

The properties of the GlowFilter and a description of each follows. These properties can be set within the constructor of the filter or defined as properties after the construction:

❏ alpha — A Number between 0.0 and 1.0.

❏ blurX and blurY — These properties determine the amount the glow is blurred. The Number values (0 to 255) are directly affected by the quality and strength properties.

❏ color — A hexadecimal number in the format 0xRRGGBB.

❏ inner — A Boolean. If the inner property is set to true, the glow is overlaid onto the object and the glow fades inward from the outer edges of the shape. The default is false, and the glow appears beneath the object and fades outward from the edges of the shape.

❏ knockout — A Boolean that specifies whether the shape that has the glow filter applied should be made invisible. However, alpha values of the original object are retained, and the fill areas adopt the pixels visible beneath it on the stage. You can use this property to create interesting effects and transitions.

❏ quality — A Number from 0 to 15. This property is essentially a multi-pass setting. A higher number means that a more accurate glow will be applied upon the pixels of the object. A lower number means a rougher, less accurate glow with fewer gradient steps. An extremely low number coupled with high blur values can cause visible stepping.

❏ strength — A Number value from 0 to 255. This value essentially determines the contrast of the gradient of the glow. The higher the number, the more the gradient is pushed to the outer edges of the glow. An extremely high strength can cause visible stepping as well as high opacity. The strength property should always be in balance with the quality and blur properties to achieve the desired results.

BevelFilter

BevelFilter is similar to the bevel effects found in popular image editing programs. The object accepts properties that describe the highlight and shadow colors as well as strength and blur for each, enabling you to create interesting, almost-3D effects.

The properties of the BevelFilter and a description of each follow. These properties can be set within the constructor of the filter or defined as properties after the construction:

❏ angle — A Number value from 0 to 360. This value is not in radians. It is important that 0 degrees on the flash stage is rotated 90 degrees so that 0 degrees is to the right.

❏ blurX and blurY — These Number values (0 to 255) determine the amount that the bevel is blurred across the shape. The value is directly affected by the strength and quality properties.

❏ distance — Determines the position of the bevel and emboss in relation to the object. It takes a Number value that is a number of pixels. The property is directly affected by the angle property.

❏ highlightColor — A hexadecimal number in the 0xRRGGBB format.

❏ highlightAlpha — A Number value from 0.0 to 1.0. This is the transparency value of the highlight.

❏ shadowColor — A Number in the 0xRRGGBB format.

❏ shadowAlpha — A Number value from 0.0 to 1.0. This is the transparency value of the shadow.

❏ knockout — A Boolean that specifies whether the shape that has the bevel filter applied should be made invisible. If true, alpha values of the original object are retained, and the fill areas adopt the pixels visible beneath them on the stage. The property defaults to false.

❏ quality — A Number from 0 to 15. This property is essentially a multi-pass setting. A higher number means that a more accurate bevel will be applied upon the pixels of the object. A lower number means a rougher, less accurate bevel with fewer gradient steps. An extremely low number coupled with high blur values can cause visible stepping.

❏ strength — A Number value (0 to 255) that essentially determines the contrast of the gradient of the bevel. The higher the number, the more the gradient is pushed to the outer edges of the bevel effect. An extremely high strength can cause visible stepping as well as high opacity. This property should always be in balance with the quality and blur properties to achieve the desired results.

❏ type — A String. The allowable values are "inner", "outer", and "full".

GradientGlowFilter

The GradientGlowFilter is similar to the GlowFilter object. However, the colors that are used to describe the glow can have bands of color. The properties are almost identical to GlowFilter's, but GradientGlowFilter requires color to be specified as an array of colors along with a ratios array that determines the ratio of colors through the gradient spread.

The properties of the GradientGlowFilter and a description of each follow. These properties can be set within the constructor of the filter or defined as properties after the construction:

❑ alphas — An array of numbers. Each value is between 0.0 and 1.0.

❑ blurX and blurY — These Number values (0 to 255) determine the amount the glow is blurred. They're directly affected by the quality and strength properties.

❑ colors — An array of hexadecimal numbers, each in the format 0xRRGGBB.

❑ ratios — An array of numbers with a value of 0 to 255 in each array position. The value represents the amount each color is sampled at 100 percent through the gradient. An array of very high values can cause visual stepping.

❑ inner — A Boolean. If set to true, the glow is overlaid onto the object and fades inward from the outer edges of the shape. The default is false, and the glow appears beneath the object and fades outward from the edges of the shape.

❑ knockout — A Boolean that specifies whether the shape that has the glow filter applied should be made invisible. However, alpha values of the original object are retained, and the fill areas adopt the pixels visible beneath it on the stage.

❑ quality — A Number value from 0 to 15. This property is essentially a multi-pass setting. A higher number means that a more accurate glow will be applied upon the pixels of the object. A lower number means a rougher, less accurate glow with fewer gradient steps. An extremely low number coupled with high blur values can cause visible stepping.

❑ strength — A Number value (0 to 255) that essentially determines the contrast of the gradient of the glow. The higher the number, the more the gradient is pushed to the outer edges of the glow. An extremely high strength can cause visible stepping as well as high opacity. The strength property should always be in balance with the quality and blur properties to achieve the desired results.

GradientBevelFilter

The GradientBevelFilter is similar to the BevelFilter object, except this object enables you to specify a range of colors to be used to render the bevel highlight and shadows.

The properties of the GradientBevelFilter and their descriptions follow. These properties can be set within the constructor of the filter or defined as properties after the construction:

❑ alphas — An array of Number values, each between 0.0 and 1.0.

❑ angle — A Number from 0 to 360. This value is not in radians. It is important that 0 degrees on the flash stage is rotated 90 degrees so that 0 degrees is to the right.

❑ blurX and blurY — These Number values (0 to 255) determine the amount that the bevel is blurred across the shape. They are directly affected by the strength and quality properties.

❑ colors — An array of colors used to render the filter. All values must be in the hexadecimal format 0xRRGGBB.

❑ distance — Determines the position of the bevel and emboss in relation to the object. Its value is a Number, the number of pixels. The property is directly affected by the angle property.

❑ knockout — A Boolean that specifies whether the shape that has the bevel filter applied should be made invisible. If true, alpha values of the original object are retained, and the fill areas adopt the pixels visible beneath them on the stage. The property defaults to false.

❑ quality — A Number value from 0 to 15. This property is essentially a multi-pass setting. A higher number means that a more accurate bevel will be applied upon the pixels of the object. A lower number means a rougher, less accurate bevel with fewer gradient steps. An extremely low number coupled with high blur values can cause visible stepping.

❑ strength — A Number value (0 to 255) that essentially determines the contrast of the gradient of the bevel. The higher the number, the more the gradient is pushed to the outer edges of the bevel effect. An extremely high strength can cause visible stepping as well as high opacity. The strength property should always be in balance with the quality and blur properties to achieve the desired results.

❑ type — A String. The allowable values are "inner", "outer", and "full".

ConvolutionFilter

ConvolutionFilter uses a matrix overlay to make modifications to the underlying pixels in a uniform, yet pixel-specific manner throughout the image. For example, this filter sharpens images and blurs images depending upon the matrix defined, and it can do a lot more. Convolution matrices are also very handy for comparing images or parts of images by comparing the different results of passing a convolution matrix over each image's pixel set.

A matrix is often referred to as a *kernel*. It is a grid of numbers that overlays the image in sections repetitively until the entire image has been modified by the matrix. A matrix enables you to modify an image without losing the original attributes of the image, and it can be reversed to bring back the original image.

Each pixel in the image is the sum of each arithmetic operation in the matrix. The sum is then divided by some number to control the balance of the output. ActionScript provides the divisor property for this operation. The result is a value good for one pixel.

Value contrasts in different matrix positions give some pixel color values dominance over smaller values, while suppressing others. In this way you can target specific attributes such as high-contrast edges.

Known convolution matrix formulas give known results. When these known matrix arrays are input into the ActionScript ConvolutionFilter's matrix, the image will sometimes burn or dodge. That is, the sum of the multiplication of the pixels increases the color value to a point that is out of the 0–255 range for all or some of the color's RGB attributes. This is exactly why there's a divisor. The divisor property controls dodge and burn tendency by enabling you to cut down the output of your matrix. You can also set bias and clamping. Knowing this, you can use a convolution matrix for varying burn in effects and animations.

Many convolution matrices are already being published and listed with optimum divisor properties for Flash effects. Look around to see what's out there before reinventing the wheel.

Here's an example Gaussian blur matrix 9x9 kernal:

0	0	1	1	1	1	1	0	0
0	2	3	3	3	3	2	1	0
1	2	3	5	8	5	3	2	1
1	3	5	10	12	10	5	3	1
1	3	8	12	15	12	8	3	1
1	3	5	10	12	10	5	3	1
1	2	3	5	8	5	3	2	1
0	1	2	3	3	3	2	1	0
0	0	1	1	1	1	1	0	0

You use this matrix later to try out the ConvolutionMatrix.

The properties of the ConvolutionFilter and a description of each property follows. These properties can be set within the constructor of the filter or defined as properties after the construction:

- ❑ `alpha` — This property is a Number. The property expects a value between `0.0` and `1.0`. This is the alpha value of the new pixel value obtained from the matrix sum.

- ❑ `bias` — This property is a Number. The property expects a value from `0` to `50`. This number is added to all new pixel color values obtained from the matrix sum.

- ❑ `clamp` — This property is a Boolean. Because a matrix can extend off the edges of the original image, pixel color values must be assumed. If `true`, the property tells the filter to use the last good pixel value along the edge of the image. If `false`, the filter uses the color and alpha property to obtain a pixel origin. The property defaults to `true`.

- ❑ `color` — This property is a hexadecimal number. The property expects a value in hexadecimal format. The hexadecimal format is `0xRRGGBB`. This property is used exclusively for generating origin pixel values when the matrix overlaps the edge of the source image.

- ❑ `divisor` — This property is a Number. This number is used to divide the sum of the matrix arithmetic operations to balance the output color range. This can be especially helpful when using severe matrices and for balancing typical convolution operations such as Gaussian blurs.

- ❑ `matrix` — The matrix is an Array. The array is made of lines and columns but they are listed linearly. For example, a 3x3 matrix grid results in a 9-position array. How the array is defined as a grid is determined by the `matrixY` and `matrixX` values. Each array value must be a number.

An example 3x3 sharpen matrix might be

```
var myMatrix:Array.concat( [0, -1, 0]);
var myMatrix:Array.concat( [-1, 8, -1]);
var myMatrix:Array.concat( [0, -1, 0]);
```

This concatenation yields the full matrix:

```
[0,-1,0,-1,8,-1,0,-1,0]
```

- ❑ matrixX — This property is a Number. This number defines the number of columns in the matrix.

- ❑ matrixY — This property is a Number. This number defines the number of columns in the matrix.

- ❑ preserveAlpha — This property is a Boolean. This property defaults to `true`. When `true`, the matrix arithmetic preserves the alpha value in the RGBA color value of the origin pixel. When set to `false`, the only the RGB is considered, and the pixel becomes opaque.

Try It Out   Use a Known Gaussian Blur Matrix in the ConvolutionFilter

This example specifies an image to be used within a movie clip. The results will be most interesting on images, but you can create vector graphics within the IDE or with the drawing methods described earlier.

1. Open a new Flash Document, name it `gaussianBlur.fla`, and save it in your work folder.

2. Select File⇨Import⇨Import to Stage.

3. Navigate to an image on your drive and select the image you would like to use.

4. When the image is on the stage, select the instance so that it is focused.

5. Select Modify⇨Convert to Symbol.

6. Select Movieclip as the symbol type and give your instance a logical name, such as sampleImage, for the library.

7. With the movie clip selected, change its name in the properties panel to clip1. Use this name to reference your image in the ActionScript.

8. Click the first frame in the timeline, open the Actions panel, and type the following ActionScript function:

```
import flash.filters.*;
clip1.onPress = function() {
    var gaussianKernal:Array = [0, 0, 1, 1, 1, 1, 1, 0, 0];
    gaussianKernal = gaussianKernal.concat([0, 1, 2, 3, 3, 3, 2, 1, 0]);
    gaussianKernal = gaussianKernal.concat([1, 2, 3, 5, 8, 5, 3, 2, 1]);
    gaussianKernal = gaussianKernal.concat([1, 3, 5, 10, 12, 10, 5, 3, 1]);
    gaussianKernal = gaussianKernal.concat([1, 3, 8, 12, 15, 12, 8, 3, 1]);
    gaussianKernal = gaussianKernal.concat([1, 3, 5, 10, 12, 10, 5, 3, 1]);
    gaussianKernal = gaussianKernal.concat([1, 2, 3, 5, 8, 5, 3, 2, 1]);
    gaussianKernal = gaussianKernal.concat([0, 1, 2, 3, 3, 3, 2, 1, 0]);
    gaussianKernal = gaussianKernal.concat([0, 0, 1, 1, 1, 1, 1, 0, 0]);
    var gaus:ConvolutionFilter = new ConvolutionFilter(9,9);
    gaus.divisor =200;
```

```
        gaus.matrix = gaussianKernal;
        this.filters = [gaus];
    };
```

9. Test your `.swf` by selecting Control⇨Test Movie. Click the clip1 movie clip. Your image will become blurred.

How It Works

In this example you create a large 9x9 matrix to perform a high-quality Gaussian blur. Using the Array object, the matrix was constructed easily and logically using the concat Array method. Construct your matrix arrays using this method if for nothing more than mere readability by fellow developers. Also give the matrix kernel a name that makes sense to describe the matrix. In this case a Gaussian blur is fairly clear.

With a value of 15, the center pixel in the matrix is weighted far more than the surrounding pixels. A Gaussian blur also gradually decreases pixel weight concentrically from the center. Because of this the new pixel's color is most similar to the center pixel but takes into account mixing in the color values of surrounding pixels in a sloped fashion. When applied to each pixel in the entire image, pixels that reside in proximity share attributes obtained by the surrounding pixels. Because neighboring pixels have approximately the same surrounding pixels, these pixels can often become similar, where once they may have had some degree of contrast. When you decrease neighboring pixel contrast in this fashion (not overall image contrast), the effect is a blurred effect. Because Gaussian blur creates relationships, it tends to be a blur that more closely approximates the blur of a camera or frosted glass. The Gaussian blur tends to preserve general shapes better than a simple blur matrix that simply interpolates a pixel's near-est pixel values without a slope, causing an abrupt smeared look.

The blur doesn't really require tinting, so the bias property isn't set. This means that the baseline color is white. If you remove the divisor property and test the movie again you will see that the image turns white. The divisor property divides each pixel color value by the divisor, effectively moving the color range back into the visible. Try giving the divisor value a very low number; you'll see that the matrix results are close to raw and you will see something closer to white. A higher value will produce lower values until you eventually reach black. Try several divisor values so that you can understand how it's affecting the output and that it's a handy tool for not only creating excellent results, but that you can ani-mate the divisor value to produce interesting burn in tween effects on any ConvolutionMatrix.

Also, the clamp property was not set. It defaults to `true`. Because clamp was defaulted to `true`, neither the color nor alpha property would have had any effect and so were left undefined.

The example required the use of the import statement. The entire filter set was imported using the import wildcard. After all filters are known, the import statement can be changed to be streamlined to import only those class definitions used.

ColorMatrixFilter

The ColorMatrixFilter is somewhat similar in concept to the ConvolutionFilter object. However, the operation is a bit easier to understand, and the matrix is bound by the 4x5 RGBA transformation matrix. The fifth column position in each row is reserved for Altivec accelerator enhancements, which means they will be ignored unless the SWF is being played back on one of these machines.

Each array position in the matrix is required to be a percentage in the format of 0.0 to 1.0. This decimal percentage represents the 0 to 255 range.

The ColorMatrixFilter has only one property, matrix, which can be set within the constructor of the filter or defined as a property after the construction.

The matrix property is an array that's most easily created using the array concat method. The matrix is a grid of values that are multiplied (or subtracted, if you stipulate negative values) by the original pixel color's RGBA set.

Here's an example of a color matrix:

```
Var myMarix:Array = [];
myMatrix.concat([.25, 0, 0, 0]); //Red
myMatrix.concat([0, 1, 0, 0, 0]); //Green
myMattrix.concat([0, 0, 1, 0, 0]); //Blue
myMatrix.concat([0, 0, 0, 1, 0]); //Alpha
```

Try It Out   Modify the Colors in a Bitmap

In this example you remove color completely, creating a grayscale image. Then you use a color matrix to bring back a brownish aspect for a sepia hue. Later in this chapter these matrices are reused in a multiple filter effect.

This example specifies an image to be used within a movie clip. The results will be most interesting on images, but you can create vector graphics within the IDE or with the drawing methods described earlier instead.

1. Open a new Flash Document, name it sepiaTone.fla, and save it in your work folder.

2. Select File⇨Import⇨Import to Stage.

3. Navigate to an image on your drive and select the image you would like to use.

4. When the image is on the stage, select the instance so that it is focused.

5. Select Modify⇨Convert to Symbol.

6. Select Movieclip as the symbol type and give your instance a logical name for the library, such as sampleImage.

7. With the movie clip selected, change its name in the properties panel to clip1. Use this name to reference your image in the ActionScript.

8. Click the first frame in the timeline, open the Actions panel, and type the following ActionScript function:

```
import flash.filters.*;
clip1.onPress = function() {
    var greyScaleKernal:Array = [.25, .25, .25, 0, 0];
    greyScaleKernal = greyScaleKernal.concat([.25, .25, .25, 0, 0]);
    greyScaleKernal = greyScaleKernal.concat([.25, .25, .25, 0, 0]);
    greyScaleKernal = greyScaleKernal.concat([0, 0, 0, 1, 0]);
    var sepiaKernal:Array = [1.25, .25, 0, 0, 0];
    sepiaKernal = sepiaKernal.concat([.25, 1, 0, 0, 0]);
```

```
        sepiaKernal = sepiaKernal.concat([0, 0, 1, 0, 0]);
        sepiaKernal = sepiaKernal.concat([0, 0, 0, 1, 0]);
        var greyScaler:ColorMatrixFilter = new ColorMatrixFilter(greyScaleKernal);
        var sepiaToner:ColorMatrixFilter = new ColorMatrixFilter(sepiaKernal);
        this.filters = [greyScaler,sepiaToner];
    };
```

9. Test your SWF by selecting Control⇨Test Movie. Click the clip1 movie clip. Your image will become sepia toned.

How It Works

In this example you effectively turned down the saturation of all color channels and then brought back some minimal red.

First you reduced the each color channel equally to very minimal colors on all channels per color at 25 percent. This produces an even gray effect. Values higher than 25 percent would have produced black, or dark images, and smaller values would produce a burned image. Because the ColorMatrixFilter has no divisor property, you must be careful when choosing transformation ranges.

The red channel was mixed with just a bit of blue:

```
    var sepiaKernal:Array = [1.25, .25, 0, 0, 0];
```

This effectively produces a red with just a slightly purple/pinkish tone without becoming fluorescent.

Because red and green are complementary, mixing the two will produce a muddy color. So to get a brownish tint, the green channel is augmented with just a slight bit of red:

```
    sepiaKernal = sepiaKernal.concat([.25, 1, 0, 0, 0]);
```

Here red is introduced at 125 percent because no red existed in the green channel. This bumps up the green channel but gives it a very pale green. The red and green mix and produce a soft yellowy brown, as should be expected when you consider classic color theory.

When attempting to work with colors, it is important to understand the color wheel and how colors interact. Classic color theory books, such as Johnannes Itten's books, can help prime you for color mixing theory. Plenty of web resources on color theory are available as well.

This example also showed the use of multiple filters. You learn about this aspect of filters more clearly later in this chapter. However, you can try and change the values present in the array declaration to see what happens.

DisplacementMapFilter

The DisplacementMap is a clever filter that uses a known bitmap called a map bitmap to distort the x and y values of the original bitmap. A popular implementation for beginners is the waving flag effect, which uses a simple set of mirrored gradients with varying widths to create a wave-like motion on an animation. Be aware that random map bitmaps can produce startling effects.

The properties of the DisplacementMapFilter and a description of each follows. These properties can be set within the constructor of the filter or defined as properties after the construction:

❑ alpha — A Number value of 0.0 to 1.0. The property determines the alpha value of out-of-bounds displacements not covered by the map bitmap.

❑ color — A hexadecimal number in the 0xRRGGBB format. The property determines the color value of out-of-bounds displacements not covered by the map bitmap.

❑ componentX — A Number value of 1, 2, 4, or 8 (1 is red, 2 is green, 4 is blue, and 8 is alpha). The property tells the filter the color that should displace the x results.

❑ componentY — A Number value of 1, 2, 4, or 8. (1 is red, 2 is green, 4 is blue, and 8 is alpha). The property tells the filter the color that should displace the y results.

❑ mapBitmap — A Bitmap object that is used to displace the original image.

❑ mapPoint — A flash.geom.Point object. This is an offset property that slides the mapBitmap into a different position in relation to the original image.

❑ mode — A String. It has four possible values:

> wrap — The default. Causes values that are out of bounds to wrap to the other side of the original image.

> clamp — Uses the edge of the source image to extrude the values.

> ignore — Uses the source pixel of the original image.

> color — Ignores all data and uses the color and alpha properties.

❑ scaleX and scaleY — Number values. The x and y results of the filter are multiplied by these properties.

Cloning Filters

The clone method is a method of all filters. The clone filter provides an easy method for creating a copy of a filter that can be modified without affecting the original. Anyone who has attempted to copy an array by simply calling something like myNewArray = myArray; knows that any changes made to myNewArray are also reflected in myArray. This is the same for filters.

You could query your filter with a for-in loop and re-create the cloned filter using the variables found. The clone method automates this and is a very handy method to keep in mind when performing multi-pass filters with slight changes as well as when using filters such as the ConvolutionMatrixFilter to find different results by cross-referencing multiple filter results.

Applying Multiple Filters

Applying multiple filters is simple. You can use multiple instances of the same type filter. You can use any combination of filters on the object. The filters property of the movieClip object expects an array. You can specify a single filter by creating a single index array, or you can place multiple filters in order.

The filters will be applied in the order you list them. Set your filter array as null to clear all of the effects.

You can query the filters array using a for-in loop. This can allow you modify an existing set or find out how many filters have been applied. You can also copy the filters array and apply it to any other movie clip.

Following is an example for-in loop:

```
for(var i in myMovieClip.filters){
    trace(i+" "+myMovieClip.filters[i]);
}
```

Once applied to a movie clip, the properties of a filter cannot be modified by referencing the filters array directly. For example, the following will fail:

```
yClip.filters = [myBlur];
myClip.filters[0].blurX = 0;
myClip.filters = [myBlur];
```

You must access the filter directly and reapply the filter to the filters array. This means that if you have multiple filters and you intend to make a change to one filter, you must redefine the filters array. Using array methods such as slice on the filters array have no effect on the filters property.

You can, however, instantiate a new array to easily add filters to a clip, which has already had filters applied to it. For example, the following sample code adds a blur filter to a movie clip. Rather than redefine the filters property, the current state of the filters property is cached into a new array called cachedFilters. If any filters exist, they will now reside temporarily within this array. The new blur is pushed to the array, and then the filters property is redefined, effectively retaining the filter properties of the clip being modified:

```
var dropShadow:DropShadowFilter = new DropShadowFilter();
dropShadow.blurX = controlX;
dropShadow.blurY = controlY;
dropShadow.quality = quality;
var cacheFilters:Array = handle.filters;
cacheFilters.push(dropShadow);
handle.filters = cacheFilters;
```

Try It Out   Set Multiple Filters on an Object

This example utilizes the ColorMatrixFilter example shown earlier in the chapter. You add a blur filter to an image that has already had two color filters applied to it without losing the color modifications.

The example specifies an image to be used within a movie clip. The results will be most interesting on images, but you can create vector graphics within the IDE, or with the drawing methods described earlier instead.

1. Open a new Flash Document, name it multiFilters.fla, and save it in your work folder.

2. Select File⇨Import⇨Import to Stage.

3. Navigate to an image on your drive and select the image you would like to use.

4. After the image is on the stage, select the instance so that it is focused.

5. Select Modify⇨Convert to Symbol.

6. Select Movieclip as the symbol type and give your instance a logical name for the library, such as sampleImage.

7. With the movie clip selected, change its name in the properties panel to clip1. Use this name to reference your image in the ActionScript.

8. Click the first frame in the timeline, open the Actions panel, and type the following ActionScript function:

```
import flash.filters.*;
function addDropShadow(handle, controlX, controlY, quality) {
    var dropShadow:DropShadowFilter = new DropShadowFilter();
    dropShadow.blurX = controlX;
    dropShadow.blurY = controlY;
    dropShadow.quality = quality;
    var cacheFilters:Array = handle.filters;
    cacheFilters.push(dropShadow);
    handle.filters = cacheFilters;
}
clip1.onPress = function() {
    var greyScaleKernal:Array = [.25, .25, .25, 0, 0];
    greyScaleKernal = greyScaleKernal.concat([.25, .25, .25, 0, 0]);
    greyScaleKernal = greyScaleKernal.concat([.25, .25, .25, 0, 0]);
    greyScaleKernal = greyScaleKernal.concat([0, 0, 0, 1, 0]);
    var sepiaKernal:Array = [1.25, .25, .25, .25, 0];
    sepiaKernal = sepiaKernal.concat([0, 1, 0, 0, 0]);
    sepiaKernal = sepiaKernal.concat([0, 0, 1, 0, 0]);
    sepiaKernal = sepiaKernal.concat([0, 0, 0, 1, 0]);
    var greyScaler:ColorMatrixFilter = new ColorMatrixFilter(greyScaleKernal);
    var sepiaToner:ColorMatrixFilter = new ColorMatrixFilter(sepiaKernal);
    this.filters = [greyScaler, sepiaToner];
    _root.addDropShadow(this, 8, 8, 8);
};
```

9. Test your SWF by selecting Control⇨Test Movie. Click the clip1 movie clip. Your image will become sepia toned.

How It Works

The bit of code to focus on here is the addDropShadow function. This function adds a very simple drop shadow to any movie clip. The function itself can be expanded to control more properties of the drop shadow, but keep it minimal so you can focus on the code problem at hand.

In this example the image's color was changed in the onPress event. You could have set up the drop shadow filter within this event. However, in an imaginary setting, say there are more clips with color modifications that will be different, but all clips will have a drop shadow   you would want to externalize and reuse a code block to keep your file efficient.

One specific problem with applying a filter using a function is that the object might have filters already applied to it. In most cases it is desirable to retain these filters when the new filter is added. You cannot modify the handle.filters array directly as an array. You must create a temporary object to make the modification.

The code that specifically handles this filter retention is as follows:

```
var cacheFilters:Array = handle.filters;
cacheFilters.push(dropShadow);
handle.filters = cacheFilters;
```

Here you can see that the existing filters are cached into a temporary array object called cachedFilters. The temporary array object allows you to take a snapshot of the filter property as well as add to the filter array.

Using a simple array push method, the drop shadow filter is added to the existing filters. Finally, the filters property of the handle clip is reassigned. Thus, the filters are reapplied to the movie clip.

Trying It Out **Give a Bitmap Image a Pinhole Camera Look**

1. Open a new Flash document, name it `pinHoleCamera.fla`, and save it in your work folder.

2. Select File⇨Import⇨Import to Stage.

3. Navigate to an image on your drive and select the image you would like to use.

4. After the image is on the stage, select the instance so that it is focused.

5. Select Modify⇨Convert to Symbol.

6. Select Movieclip as the symbol type and give your instance a logical name for the library, such as sampleImage.

7. With the movie clip selected, change its name in the properties panel to clip1. Use this name to reference your image in the ActionScript.

8. Click the first frame in the timeline, open the Actions panel, and type the following ActionScript:

```
import flash.filters.ColorMatrixFilter;
import flash.filters.GlowFilter;
import flash.filters.BlurFilter;
import flash.display.BitmapData;
import flash.geom.Matrix;
import flash.geom.Rectangle;
import flash.geom.Point;
```

9. In the preceding step you added the import statements so you can begin to work with some filters and shape objects. Now add two color matrix filters by entering the following code below the code you added in step 8:

```
var bitmapWidth = this.clip1._width;
var bitmapHeight = this.clip1._height;
var myMatrix:Array = [.25, .25, .25, 0, 0];
```

```
myMatrix = myMatrix.concat([.25, .25, .25, 0, 0]);
myMatrix = myMatrix.concat([.25, .25, .25, 0, 0]);
myMatrix = myMatrix.concat([0, 0, 0, 1, 0]);
var myTint:Array = [1.25, .25, 0, 0, 0];
myTint = myTint.concat([.25, 1, 0, 0, 0]);
myTint = myTint.concat([0, 0, 1, 0, 0]);
myTint = myTint.concat([0, 0, 0, 1, 0]);
var myFilter:ColorMatrixFilter = new ColorMatrixFilter(myMatrix);
var myTintFilter:ColorMatrixFilter = new ColorMatrixFilter(myTint);
```

10. Step 9 changed the color to black and white and then sepia. Now give the bitmap an inner glow. Specify a dark color to give the effect an almost inner shadow look. Add the following code below the code you added in step 9:

```
var pinhole:GlowFilter = new GlowFilter();
pinhole.alpha = .4;
pinhole.blurX = 40;
pinhole.blurY = 40;
pinhole.color = 0x000000;
pinhole.inner = true;
pinhole.quality = 9;
pinhole.strength = 3;
```

11. In step 10 you created an inner glow. Apply the filters you created in steps 8–10 by adding following code below the code you added in step 10:

```
clip1.filters = [myFilter, myTintFilter, pinhole];
```

12. Test your SWF. Select Control➪Test Movie. You will see that you've applied the three filters to give your bitmap a sepia look. This is very similar to the sepia exercise outlined earlier in the chapter. In this example an inner glow is added. Now you can begin to add some more interesting effects. Close your SWF and return to the ActionScript in frame 1.

13. Add the following code below the code you added in step 10:

```
var copy:BitmapData = new BitmapData(bitmapWidth, bitmapHeight);
_root.createEmptyMovieClip("blurCopy", 2);
blurCopy.attachBitmap(copy, 1);
copy.draw(clip1);
blurCopy._x = this.clip1._x;
blurCopy._y = this.clip1._y;
```

14. The code in step 13 added a copy of clip1 as a bitmap that you'll be able to blur without affecting the original clip1 movie clip. This copy will be masked to reveal parts of the original image. You need to create a mask with a radial gradient fill. You can do this with the beginGradientFill drawing API method. Add the following code below the code you added in step 13:

```
var myMatrix:Matrix = new Matrix();
myMatrix.createGradientBox(bitmapWidth, bitmapHeight, 0, 0, 0, "pad", "RGB");
_root.createEmptyMovieClip("alphaGradientMask", 3);
alphaGradientMask.beginGradientFill("radial", [0x000000, 0x000000], [0, 100], [50, 0xFF], myMatrix);
alphaGradientMask.lineTo(0, bitmapHeight);
alphaGradientMask.lineTo(bitmapWidth, bitmapHeight);
alphaGradientMask.lineTo(bitmapWidth, 0);
```

```
alphaGradientMask.lineTo(0, 0);
alphaGradientMask.endFill();
alphaGradientMask._x = this.clip1._x;
alphaGradientMask._y = this.clip1._y;
```

15. Before applying the mask, you want to blur the copy image. To do this, create a simple blur filter and apply it to the blurCopy movie clip. Add the following code below the code you added in step 14:

```
var blur:BlurFilter = new BlurFilter();
blur.blurX = 5;
blur.blurY = 5;
blur.quality = 4;
blurCopy.filters = [blur];
```

16. Stop and test the movie. Select Control⇨Test Movie. You will see that the clip is now severely blurred. However, the blur is applied to the blurCopy clip only. You can now add a mask filter to show only a little bit of the blurCopy movie clip. Close the SWF and return to the frame 1 ActionScript.

17. Add the following code below the code you added in step 15:

```
blurCopy.cacheAsBitmap = true;
alphaGradientMask.cacheAsBitmap = true;
blurCopy.setMask(alphaGradientMask);
```

18. Test the movie. Select Control⇨Test Movie. You will now see that the blurCopy movie clip is selectively transparent, becoming more opaque toward the edges and clearer toward the center. This should give a somewhat interesting esthetic, which could be considered a single filter approximating a pinhole camera effect.

How It Works

This was a complex example of a movie clip manipulation, which covered many aspects of this entire chapter. It covered the use of the drawing API, including an example matrix gradient, masking, filters, and color matrices.

By using the draw method of the Bitmap object, you were able to effectively duplicate the pixels of the original movie clip. It is important to remember that this is not the same as DuplicateMovieClip; Draw simply copies the bitmap pixels present in the clip at the time the draw method is called. When and if changes occur in clip1, and you want the effect to keep up with the clip1 animation changes, you will need to call the draw method each time the clip changes.

Also important in this example was the setMask method. Although this is a typical setMask method call, there is a distinct difference that affected it, which wasn't possible in an earlier version of Flash. Flash 8 allows for 32-bit masking. That means a movie clip can be masked using a gradient fill with an alpha gradient in it. The pixels in the clip being masked will inherit the alpha values present in the mask. To do this, you must cache the movie clip as a bitmap. This was done in step 17 and is a simple property declaration.

Throughout this chapter you've seen the Bitmap object mentioned, and its attributes and abilities were taken for granted. Next you learn about the Bitmap object in a bit more detail and how you can apply filters directly to a nested bitmap without affecting an entire movie clip.

Applying Blending Modes

`BlendMode` is a property of the movieClip object. The property expects a string parameter. Each possible string is listed in this section with an explanation of each. You declare a blendMode as a property. Calling `BlendMode` twice results in only the second being used. An object can have only one blend mode. However, by duplicating the pixels into a Bitmap object, you can combine several overlays to create a multi-blendMode effect.

Following are descriptions of the `BlendMode` values. Each is listed with its literal string value as the title. For example, to set the `BlendMode` to normal, call

```
myClip.BlendMode = "normal";
```

- ❑ `"normal"` — Commonly used to return the blendMode to the default state. It specifies that the pixels in the movie clip override any pixels below it without modification. Alpha values are preserved, and transparent areas allow underlying pixels to show through.

- ❑ `"layer"` — Used by the other filters. It provides a buffer copy of the bitmap data of the movie clip to perform operations when multiple child clips are nested in the clip being blended. Some filter settings require this property to be explicitly set.

- ❑ `"multiply"` — Tends to darken an image by multiplying the underlying pixel by the blend pixel and dividing by 255 to avoid burn. It is handy when the overlay is meant to appear to leave a shadow on the underlying pixels.

- ❑ `"screen"` — Similar to `"multiply"`, but uses the complementary colors of the pixels being examined, producing a lighter effect.

- ❑ `"lighten"` — Compares the pixel values beneath the image and the pixel in the image. The darker of the two values is ignored, and only the lighter pixel is retained. This has an overall lightening effect.

- ❑ `"darken"` — Compares the pixel values beneath the image and the pixel in the image. The darker of the two values is retained, and only the lighter pixel is ignored. This has an overall darkening effect.

- ❑ `"add"` — Adds the value of two superimposed pixels. It has a maximum value of `0xFF` and is useful for creating burn-in and burn-out cross-fade effects.

- ❑ `"subtract"` — Subtracts the original pixel value from the underlying pixel value, leaving a result with a floor of 0, or black. The value is absolute and does not consider whether the original value is greater than the subtracting pixel. It's helpful in eliminating images via a smooth fade to black.

- ❑ `"difference"` — Similar to `"subtract"`, but subtracts the larger value from the smaller value to produce the result (not an absolute value).

- ❑ `"invert"` — Rejects the original image entirely, and the underlying pixel values are inverted completely.

- ❑ `"overlay"` — Preserves the contrast value of the original image while the hue of the background pixel is used.

- ❑ `"hardlight"` — Tends to turn up the contrast of the original image. Dark colors are multiplied while light colors are screened, generally preserving saturation while increasing contrast.

❑   `"alpha"` —Causes the background pixel to adopt the alpha value of the original pixel. This filter works only when at least two movie clips reside within a parent movie clip to which the `"layer"` blendMode is applied.

❑   `"erase"` — The inverse of the `"alpha"` blendMode. This filter works only when at least two movie clips reside within a parent movie clip to which the `"layer"` blendMode is applied.

Summary

In this chapter you explored the many ways in which you can modify a movieClip and Bitmap object using basic available method sets and known formulas for manipulating images.

The ConvolutionMatrix proved particularly powerful.

Many of the methods and objects in this chapter contain the ability to be manipulated directly on a more advanced level. If a particular object suits your idea, or intent, look into the object further to see how you might customize or create a class to control it.

All of the filters, blend modes, and methods can be automated and reused efficiently in class objects. Seek out existing libraries and formulas to help automate the many tasks of these filters. The methods in this chapter can perform alone and in combination with one another. The pinhole camera effect provided a Try It Out, which showed how using many of these objects and methods together in a specific order can produce a result that is expected more from expensive image editing programs, not from a real-time animation rendering function set. Have fun with these methods. Don't get bogged down with the mathematics involved and try out as many things as you can think of!

Exercises

1.   Using PNG image files, use `loadBitmap` on a Bitmap object and `attachBitmap` in a movie clip to create a simple button.

2.   Using the BlurFilter object, create a simple navigation menu that unblurs a button when the button is moused over.

3.   Using a displacementMap, sphereize an image using the `beginGradientFill` method.

4.   Using the `getPixel` method within a `for` loop, try to find the existence of a particular color in a bitmap by checking each pixel. Place a movie clip at the x and y position of the result.

Working Directly with Bitmap Data

A bitmap image is a graphic that is created using a grid. The grid is a set of pixels, each with a defined color. When you zoom in on a bitmap image, the grid is obvious. Zooming in on a bitmap causes the pixilated look you've probably seen on resized or low-resolution images. Bitmap images are different from vector images in this way. A vector image is defined by points. As a vector image is scaled, the points remain in the same relative position. Lines and fills are drawn between these points as the vector is scaled. Because the lines and fills are redrawn, no pixilation occurs. When vector images are converted to bitmaps based on their current scale within a specified pixel area, they are referred to as rasterized graphics.

Before Flash 8, Flash could not directly manipulate bitmap graphics at the pixel level. Flash has always been able to display bitmap images and modify them as a movieClip object, but ActionScript was never able to fetch the pixel information and work with the pixels directly.

Flash 8 represents a massive maturation of the Flash player capability. Flash can declare anything a Bitmap object. That is, even a vector image can be rasterized in a split millisecond to perform per-pixel operation changes at runtime. You can even convert a movie clip to a bitmap so quickly that you can rasterize vector animations, videos, webcam feeds, and more. You also can work with their pixels and apply filters to them as they play, giving you unparalleled freedom in terms of design and implementation.

After you convert a movie clip to a bitmap, you can apply a multitude of effects. In fact, all of the filters described earlier in this book that were applied to movie clips used the Bitmap object to perform the effects. The filters were able to modify the image as a bitmap as needed. Sometimes you can be working with bitmaps in Flash 8 and not even realize it.

The main ingredient when working with bitmap data is the Bitmap object, which is accessed via the display class package. Simply converting a movie clip to a bitmap can improve the frame rate performance of some animation conditions. However, the Bitmap object has a lot more to offer. Robust method and property sets enable you to work with bitmaps directly as well as augment filters, movie clip drawing methods, animations, and more.

The Bitmap Object's Methods

Not every method is used in this chapter's Try It Out sections. However, most are straightforward and do what they advertise. Taking advantage of combinations of the Bitmap object's method set is likely worth a whole new book. Here the Bitmap object's methods are introduced so you can get comfortable working with them. Explore and try the different methods available.

applyFilter()

The `applyFiler()` method applies a filter to the Bitmap object. The method returns a number: `0`, indicating a failure, or `1`, indicating that the filter was successfully applied.

The parameters of `applyFilter` are `sourceBitmap:BitmapData`; `sourceRect:Rectangle`; `destPoint:Point`; and `filter:BitmapFilter`. Here are descriptions of them:

- ❏ `sourceBitmap` — Specifies the bitmap to draw within the Bitmap object. You can specify a different Bitmap object to replace the current bitmap data (if there is any), or you can refer to the bitmap itself.

- ❏ `sourceRect` — A rectangle object. You define a rectangle as a flash.geom.rectangle object. The source bitmap carries a rectangle property if you do not need to modify the existing rectangle. You can refer to this property as sourceBitmap.rectangle. Providing a new rectangle defines a subsection of the source image.

- ❏ `destPoint` — A flash.geom.point object that specifies the x and y coordinate within the original bitmap where you'd like to begin drawing the filter with the `sourceBitmap`.

- ❏ `filter` — Specifies the filter to use. Filters are discussed in Chapter 14.

clone()

The `clone()` method is used to duplicate the bitmap. This is often handy for applying multiple filters on layers where you would like to preserve aspects of some filters beneath overlays of new filters such as noise, blur, and more. The method returns a bitmapData object. To display the cloned bitmap you need to use the `attachBitmap` method; otherwise you can work with the bitmap until it's required to be displayed.

colorTransform()

`colorTransform()` applies a flash.geom.colorTransform object to a bitmap. This method differs from the colorMatrixFilter filter. The colorTransform object uses an array of values to multiply each existing channel, as well as an offset for each channel. This gives you plenty of color control, but not as much control as the colorMatrixFilter.

The parameters of `colorTransform` are `rectangle:Rectangle` and `colorTransform:ColorTransform`:

- ❏ `rectangle` — The rectangle object describes the section of the source bitmap to apply the color transform.

- ❏ `colorTransform` — A colorTransform object defined by the flash.geom.colorTransform object.

copyChannel()

The copyChannel() method transfers the color channel information from one bitmap to another. Only one channel can be transferred at a time.

The parameters of copyChannel are sourceBitmap:BitmapData; sourceRect:Rectangle; destPoint:Point; sourceChannel:Number; and destChannel:Number:

❑　sourceBitmap—Specifies the bitmap from which to obtain a color channel.

❑　sourceRect—A flash.geom.rectangle object specifying the section of the bitmap from which to obtain channel data.

❑　destPoint—A flash.geom.point object specifying where, in the destination image, to start applying the color channel.

❑　sourceChannel—A Number specifying which channel to copy. The possible values are 1 (red), 2 (green), 4 (blue), and 8 (alpha).

❑　destChannel—A Number specifying which channel to replace. The possible values are 1 (red), 2 (green), 4 (blue), and 8 (alpha).

copyPixels()

copyPixels() is similar to the draw() method except that it enables you to obtain just a portion of the original bitmap. The sourceBitmap parameter must be a bitmap; you cannot refer to a movie clip. To use a movie clip with copyPixels, see the draw() method.

The parameters of copyPixels are sourceBitmap:BitmapData; sourceRect:Rectangle; destPoint:Point; alphaBitmap:BitmapData; alphaPoint:Point; and mergeAlpha:Boolean:

❑　sourceBitmap—Specifies the bitmap from which to obtain pixels.

❑　sourceRect—A flash.geom.rectangle object specifying the section of the bitmap from which to obtain pixels.

❑　destPoint—A flash.geom.point object specifying where, in the destination image, to start applying the new pixels.

❑　alphaBitmap—A secondary bitmap used for its alpha channel only. If this property is defined, the pixels are mixed with the alpha channel present in this bitmap.

❑　alphaPoint—A flash.geom.point object representing the upper-left index within the alphaBitmap from which to begin obtaining alpha channel data.

❑　mergeAlpha—A Boolean that determines whether the pixels in the sourceBitmap image should retain their alpha values when the pixels are transferred to the Bitmap object.

dispose()

The dispose() method has no parameters. When it is called, all attributes, properties, and data are removed from the Bitmap object. The Bitmap object remains accessible, however, its properties will return nothing. You can begin to create new bitmap data using the Bitmap object.

`dispose()` explicitly frees RAM being used by the Bitmap object. It is important to understand this aspect of the Bitmap object. When declaring a bitmap, Flash is using RAM, whether or not pixel data has been defined. How much RAM is utilized depends on the size of the bitmap declared in the bitmapData constructor. Once there, you must call the `dispose()` method for that RAM to be freed. If you don't, you potentially cause a severe memory leak, or even worse, a system crash. This issue can easily arise when creating bitmaps in loops or if you're sloppy about caring what happens to the object once it's off the stage. You must be conscious of the RAM usage your SWF file exhibits. Always test, test, and test again on your target systems.

draw()

The `draw()` method copies the current pixels in a source object into the original bitmap image.

The parameters of `draw` are `source:Object`; `matrix:Matrix`; `colorTransform:ColorTransform`; `blendMode:Object`; `clipRect:Rectangle`; and `smooth:Boolean`:

❑ `source` — Specifies the object from which to obtain the bitmap. If you specify a movie clip, a snapshot is taken of the current state of the movie clip. If the movie clip has any matrix transformation applied, such as distort, the transform is ignored. The bitmap is created with the transform state of the movie clip as it originally existed.

❑ `matrix` — A matrix object. The matrix object is generally used to change the image, such as rotate or scale. You can use this to reapply transforms, which are lost when the source object is defined, or you can define a new matrix object. You can always apply the matrix object later, if you leave this parameter blank.

❑ `colorTransform` — A colorTransform object defined by the flash.geom.colorTransform object.

❑ `clipRect` — A flash.geom.rectangle object specifying the section or clipping of the movie clip from which to obtain pixels. If you do not specify this parameter, the entire source is used.

❑ `blendMode` — A blendMode object that describes how the Bitmap object should blend with the pixels that reside behind it.

fillRect()

The `fillRect()` method creates a rectangle with a specified color. The rectangle is defined as a flash.geom.rectangle object. This method is useful for specifying the initial bitmap size when performing certain filter and pixel renderings.

The parameters of `fillRect` are `rectangleObject:Rectangle` and `color:Number`:

❑ `rectangleObject` — A flash.geom.rectangle object. The rectangle object can be created separately and created as a variable. You must import the flash.geom.rectangle class.

❑ `color` — A hexadecimal number in the ARGB format `0xAARRGGBB`.

floodFill()

`floodFill()` works very much like the flood fill tools in various image editing programs. The first two parameters are x and y properties. The last parameter is an AARRGGBB number. The method fills any pixels that match and touch the pixel at the specified `x,y` location.

The parameters of floodFill are x:Number; y:Number; and color:Number:

- ❏ x — The *x* position of the pixel, which will be the index for the flood fill.
- ❏ y — The *y* position of the pixel, which will be the index for the flood fill.
- ❏ color — A hexadecimal number in the format 0xAARRGGBB.

generateFilterRect()

The generateFilterRect() method provides a simple rectangle output. However, the rectangle is the final size after a bitmap has a filter run against it. This is important because it doesn't actually run the filter. The method merely reports back what to expect in size difference after you've run a filter. This is helpful when creating a user interface that needs to grow and expand depending on the filters might be on a specific movie clip. A movie clip section that has a drop shadow, for example, is slightly larger than it is without a filter. You might want to adjust your user interface for the difference so you don't get any strange overlapping. The parameters are simple. You supply the rectangle object, which will receive the filter, and you provide the filter.

The parameters of generateFilterRect are rectangleObject:Rectangle and filter:BitmapFilter:

- ❏ rectangleObject — A flash.geom.rectangle object. The rectangle object can be created separately and created as a variable. You must import the flash.geom.rectangle class. The rectangle defines an area within a larger bitmap to apply the filter.
- ❏ filter — A filter object. (Filters are discussed in Chapter 14.)

getColorBoundsRect()

The getColorBoundsRect() method returns a rectangle that defines the area of color specified. The color is specified as a mask and color. This method is useful for finding the exact visible edges of a bitmap or discovering whether an image has a border that should be ignored.

The parameters of getColorBoundsRect are mask:Number; color:Number; and findColor:Boolean:

- ❏ mask — A hexadecimal number in the format 0xAARRGGBB. This color defines the threshold at which to ignore a color range.
- ❏ color — A hexadecimal number in the format 0xAARRGGBB. This color defines the maximum threshold value to search for. For example, to find any values that have no alpha value, you would define mask as 0xFF000000 and color as 0x00000000.
- ❏ findColor — A Boolean. If true, it returns the bounds of where the color range exists within the image. If false, the rectangle defines where the color value isn't present in the image.

getPixel()

The getPixel() method returns the RGB color of a specific pixel in a bitmap. This is especially useful for video and webcam effects where you'd want to track specific colors or thresholds. The return value is a pre-multiplied RRGGBB number. You must run the color through a simple operator function to obtain individual values. You see this function in action later in the chapter.

The parameters of get Pixel are x:Number and y:Number:

- ❑ x—The x coordinate of the pixel to examine.
- ❑ y—The y coordinate of the pixel to examine.

getPixel32()

The getPixel32() method is similar to getPixel(), but it also returns a number with the alpha value multiplied with the RRGGBB values. It is helpful for specific effects where you'd like to track a specific color.

The parameters of getPixel32 are x:Number and y:Number:

- ❑ x—The x coordinate of the pixel to examine.
- ❑ y—The y coordinate of the pixel to examine.

hitTest()

hitTest() is almost identical to the movieclip.hittest method, although it is much more powerful in that you can detect alpha threshold values. It means you can actually obtain shape-specific hitTest results, which is fantastic news for game coders.

The parameters of hitTest are firstPoint:Point; firstAlphaThreshold:Number; secondObject:Object; secondBitmapPoint:Point; and secondAlphaThreshold:Number:

- ❑ firstPoint—The first point in the target bitmap that should be tested for a hitTest.
- ❑ firstAlphaThreshold—The alpha threshold value that qualifies as a hit from the firstPoint value. The parameter expects a value of 0–255. If no value is given, 255 is assumed.
- ❑ secondObject—Can be a rectangle, a point, or a full Bitmap object.
- ❑ secondBitmapPoint—When the secondObject is defined as a Bitmap object, this parameter provides a specific start point within the bitmap to begin checking for the hitTest.
- ❑ secondAlphaThreshold—When the secondObject parameter is defined as a bitmap, this parameter defines the alpha value that qualifies for a hitTest to return true. The parameter expects a value of 0–255. If no value is given, 255 is assumed.

loadBitmap()

loadBitmap() is similar to the movielcip.attachMovie method. The parameter is a linkage ID of a Bitmap object such as a PNG that resides in the library and has been exported for ActionScript access. This method does not "show" the bitmap on the stage. You must still use the attachBitmap object on a movieClip symbol to give the bitmap a place to reside.

The parameter of loadBitmap is libraryId:String. The string matches a linkage ID that exists in the library. The library symbol must be a Bitmap object.

merge()

The merge() method evenly merges two bitmap images to create one image. Each channel is specified with a multiplier by which the pixel color values will be modified.

The merge() method performs the following algorithm on each pixel and channel:

```
Final red value = (red channel from the source image * the specified red channel
multiplier) + (red channel from the destination image * (256 - the specified red
channel multiplier) / 256;
```

The exact inner workings aren't as important to know as that the algorithm produces an evenly blended pixel color value as a result of both images.

The parameters of merge are sourceBitmap:BitmapData; sourceRect:Rectangle; destPoint:Point; redMult:Number; greenMult:Number; blueMult:Number; and alphaMult:Number:

❑   sourceBitmap — The bitmap to merge into the existing bitmap. This object can be a different bitmap, or it can be the same bitmap image. Using the same bitmap can be useful for interesting pattern affects and animations.

❑   sourceRect — This parameter is a flash.geom.rectangle object. The rectangle defines the rectangle area of the sourceBitmap to use for the merge.

❑   destPoint — This parameter is a flash.geom.point object. The parameter is the start point in the original image to begin merging in the source bitmap.

❑   redMultiplier — This parameter is a Number. The number multiplies the red channel of the pixel being merged.

❑   blueMultiplier — This parameter is a Number. The number multiplies the blue channel of the pixel being merged.

❑   greenMultiplier — This parameter is a Number. The number multiplies the green channel of the pixel being merged.

❑   alphaMultiplier — This parameter is a Number. The number multiplies the alpha channel of the pixel being merged.

noise()

The noise() method efficiently produces a noise effect on the specified bitmap rectangle. The effect is similar to the noise effect found in popular image editing programs.

The parameters of noise are randomSeed:Number; low:Number; high:Number; channelOptions:Number; and grayScale:Boolean:

❑   randomSeed — An index that controls the randomness of the noise effect.

❑   Low — The lowest color channel value to utilize in the noise effect. The parameter expects a value of 0–255.

❑ `High` — The highest color channel value to utilize in the noise effect. The parameter expects a value of 0–255.

❑ `channelOptions` — This special parameter uses the logical OR operator. You can specify four channels from which the `randomSeed` can manipulate: 1 (red), 2 (green), 4 (blue), and 8 (alpha). For example, to allow the `random` function to choose red or blue, you'd use: (1|2). A random function that uses all channels, including alpha variations, is (1|2|4|8). Because this is a logical operator, do not set this as a string.

❑ `grayscale` — If `true`, each color channel is set to the same value, effectively gray-scaling the image. The default is `false`, which allows for full color.

paletteMap()

`paletteMap()` is used for color channel manipulation. This method is very helpful in controlling the overall hue of the image. It can be used to remap a color palette from one bitmap onto another. Otherwise, you can specify array values to which the original image should be mapped.

The parameters of `paletteMap` are `sourceBitmap:BitmapData; sourceRect:Rectangle; destPoint:Point; redArray:Array; greenArray:Array; blueArray:Array;` and `alphaArray:Array`:

❑ `sourceBitmap` — The source bitmap from which color should be obtained. If the source is the same as the original, you need to specify the color array parameters.

❑ `sourceRect` — A flash.geom.rectangle object. Use this to limit the palette to a specific set within the source bitmap.

❑ `destPoint` — A flash.geom.point object specifying where in the bitmap to begin manipulating the original Bitmap object.

❑ `redArray` — Represents the new red array values in which 255 maps to a hexadecimal value that represents the maximum red value of the array.

❑ `greenArray` — Represents the new green array values in which 255 maps to a hexadecimal value that represents the maximum green value of the array.

❑ `blueArray` — Represents the new blue array values in which 255 maps to a hexadecimal value that represents the maximum blue value of the array.

❑ `alphaArray` — Represents the new alpha array values in which 255 maps to a hexadecimal value that represents the maximum alpha value of the array.

perlinNoise()

The `perlinNoise()` method produces Perlin noise, which differs from the regular noise filter in that it uses mathematics to produce more natural random effects where clumping or thin areas can occur. Perlin noise is considered to be natural noise, whereas noise that is evenly spread out is considered to be a controlled random field, not as random as Perlin noise. It is used to generate fake terrain or mimic natural phenomenon such as flowering plant distribution in a field. It produces very realistic distribution when natural randomness is more desired over homogenized random noise. You can check out more in-depth mathematical theories with Perlin noise if you're interested. For now, you can assume this function works as expected, and you can use it to do many things, such as randomly place movie clips within a parent movie clip or generate displacement maps for terrain generation.

The parameters of `perlinNoise` are `baseX:Number`; `baseY:Number`; `numOctaves:Number`; `randomSeed:Number`; `stitch:Boolean`; `fractalNoise:Boolean`; `channelOptions:Number`; `grayScale:Boolean`; and `offsets:Object`:

❑ `baseX` and `baseY` — Unique parameters specifying the frequency that should be used to place a point. For example, a wide image should have a wide `baseX` for more even distribution of the noise.

❑ `numOctave` — Much like musical octaves. The more octaves in music, the more varied the sound result can be. Here, the more octaves, the more levels of detail can be achieved in the random field.

❑ `randomSeed` — The value by which the random value is calculated. The `perlinNoise` function is not truly random. If you keep all the values the same, including the `randomSeed`, you obtain exactly the same results every time. Change the `randomSeed` and the results will vary within the field. Keeping the `randomSeed` the same and merely changing the available octaves simply changes the detail of the Perlin noise and not the overall random field. This is useful for constructing and returning to the same random field.

❑ `stitch` — A Boolean. If `true`, the noise generator attempts to end edges so that the result can be tiled

❑ `fractalNoise` — A Boolean. If `true`, this parameter causes randomly generated areas to be more evenly generated, where the contrast areas are smoothed using fractal interpolation. If `false`, the gradients between high contrast values can have large gaps causing cliff-like effects that allow for high-contrast terrain such as water or mountainous regions.

❑ `channelOptions` — This special parameter uses the logical OR operator. You can specify four channels from which the `randomSeed` can manipulate: 1 (red), 2 (green), 4 (blue), and 8 (alpha). For example, to allow the `random` function to choose red or blue, you'd use: `(1|2)`. A random function that uses all channels, including alpha variations, is `(1|2|4|8)`. Because this is a logical operator, do not set this as a string.

❑ `grayscale` — If `true`, each color channel is set to the same value, effectively gray-scaling the image. The default is `false`, which allows for full color.

❑ `offsets` — An array that represents a point as `[x,y]`. The value offsets the effect of the `numOctave` value by specific x and y values upon the original bitmap image. `offsets` is useful for smoothly sliding a Perlin noise effect into an image.

pixelDissolve()

The `pixelDissolve()` method can be used in conjunction with a loop event to slowly dissolve a bitmap from an original set of pixels to a defined source of pixels. It can quickly and easily complete dissolve tween effects without overly affecting processor usage.

The parameters of `pixelDissolve` are `sourceBitmap:BitmapData`; `sourceRect:Rectangle`; `destPoint:Point`; `randomSeed:Number`; `numberOfPixels:Number`; and `fillColor:Number`:

❑ `sourceBitmap` — Defines a bitmap from which replacement pixels should be sourced.

❑ `sourceRect` — A flash.geom.rectangle object that defines an area within the `sourceBitmap` from which to source pixels.

❑ `destPoint` — A flash.geom.point object that defines where in the original bitmap image the method should begin applying sourced pixels.

❑ `randomSeed` — A Number that defines the seed be used to randomly disperse the new sourced pixels into the original bitmap.

❑ `numberOfpixels` — The number of pixels to replace in the original image with the sourced pixels. By looping the method in an iterative manner, you can slowly replace all pixels by choosing a number such as 30. If this parameter is not used, a fraction (1/30) of the source rectangle size is used.

❑ `fillColor` — A hexadecimal color in 0xAARRGGBB format. This color will replace the destination color if the original and source pixel are identical. Use `fillColor` to replace specific color areas. It can be especially useful in completing dissolve effects on video and motion.

scroll()

The `scroll()` method can be used to scroll the visible pixels within a specified bitmap rectangle, which can have alpha 0. This is useful for scrolling a known bitmap into position without affecting its actual x and y coordinates.

The parameters of scroll are x:Number and y:Number:

❑ `x` — A Number that specifies how much to offset the bitmap data within the Bitmap object horizontally.

❑ `y` — A Number that specifies how much to offset the bitmap data within the Bitmap object vertically.

setPixel()

`setPixel()` is a method that Flash coders have sought for ages. So here it is, and it's everything that was hoped for. It creates an actual pixel on the specified x, y coordinate in the bitmap with the color specified. If a color already exists at the point specified, the new color takes its place with no merge or effects.

The parameters of `setPixel` are x:Number; y:Number; and color:Number:

❑ `x` — A Number specifying the x coordinate to place the color pixel.

❑ `y` — A Number specifying the y coordinate to place the color pixel.

❑ `color` — A hexadecimal number in the format 0xRRGGBB. This method does not support alpha channels. If you want to use alpha channels, use the `setPixel32()` method.

setPixel32()

The `setPixel32()` method is similar to `setPixel()`, but it supports setting the alpha value of the specified pixel.

The parameters of `setPixel32` are x:Number; y:Number; and color:Number:

- ❑ x — A Number specifying the x coordinate to place the color pixel.

- ❑ y — A Number specifying the y coordinate to place the color pixel.

- ❑ color — A hexadecimal number in the format 0xAARRGGBB. This method supports alpha channels.

threshold()

The threshold() method enables you to replace color values based on testing each pixel for a specific threshold or range of value. If true, the pixel will be replaced with the new color. The method uses logical operators to determine which operation to perform.

The parameters of threshold are sourceBitmap:BitmapData; sourceRectangle:Rectangle; destPoint:Point; operation:String; threshold:Number; color:Number; mask:Number; and copySource:Boolean:

- ❑ sourceBitmap — The bitmap that will be tested for threshold. You can specify the original bitmap to perform the operation on the bitmap the method is called upon.

- ❑ sourceRectangle — A flash.geom.rectangle object that defines the area in the source image to begin finding threshold values.

- ❑ destPoint — A flash.geom.point object that defines where in the original image the color operation should begin taking place.

- ❑ operation — A logical operator that is passed as a string. Acceptable values are "<=", "<", "==",">", ">=", and "!=".

- ❑ threshold — A hexadecimal number in the format 0xAARRGGBB. This is the color value against which the logical operator tests.

- ❑ color — A hexadecimal number in 0xAARRGGBB format. This color value will replace the original pixel color if the threshold test succeeds.

- ❑ mask — A hexadecimal number in 0xAARRGGBB format. The number is used to isolate a specific channel within a color. For example, a value of 0xFFFFFF allows all channels, whereas a value of 0x00FF00 allows only green values to test true. This enables you to explicitly mask channels.

- ❑ copySource — A Boolean. If set to true, the pixel value of the source image will be used when the threshold fails. If set to false, the pixel will not be manipulated in the original bitmap.

The bitmapData Object's Properties

The bitmapData object has five properties:

- ❑ height — The height of the bitmap, in pixels, to allocate. Setting this value does not necessarily mean you will see a pixel change on the stage.

- ❑ width — The width of the bitmap, in pixels, to allocate. Setting this value does not necessarily mean you will see a pixel change on the stage.

- ❑ transparent — Specifies whether the bitmap should have the capability to utilize a 32-bit alpha channel on its pixels.

❑   `fillColor`— A 32-bit color value set as RGBA, or `0xRRGGBBAA`. A bitmap with a `fillColor` specified will show this color regardless of whether pixels have been explicitly defined within the bitmap. The area of color is determined by the `height` and `width` parameters.

❑   `rectangle`— A read-only property that returns the size of the bitmap as a rectangle type object.

These properties can be set in the constructor.

Converting a Movie Clip into a Bitmap Image

Often, you might want a movie clip to continue to play while you manipulate it with bitmap filters and pixel examination. You can do this by capturing the movie clip into a Bitmap object and performing pixel functions upon the surrogate bitmap while modifying the actual movie clip.

Drawing a movie clip into a bitmap is exceptionally easy. A bitmap is defined, and a movie clip snapshot is placed into the bitmap using the `draw()` method, like this:

```
var myBitmap:BitmapData = new BitmapData(400, 400);
myBitmap.draw(myClip_mc);
```

While this draws the pixels of the movie clip into the bitmap, the bitmap will not be visible. You can work with the pixels of the bitmap while it remains invisible, or you can show the bitmap by attaching it to an existing movie clip. Here's an example:

```
var myBitmap:BitmapData = new BitmapData(400, 400);
myBitmap.draw(myClip_mc);
this.createEmptyMovieClip("mybitmapCopy", 1);
mybitmapCopy.attachBitmap(myBitmap, 0);
```

Manipulating Bitmap Data

As described earlier, you can directly manipulate the pixels in a bitmap. You also can apply filters and blend modes to a Bitmap object. The new `getPixel()` and `setPixel()` methods enable direct control over pixels in a movie clip, allowing for interesting and exciting tween possibilities. Now you can do more than ever to the user interface (UI) on a code level and at a much faster rate than in any other Flash player before version 8.

Try It Out   **Blur a Specific Area in a Bitmap Object**

In this example you quickly create a Bitmap object using the `draw` method to copy a movie clip. You need an image to import onto the stage, which can be used to show a blur.

1.   Open a new Flash Document. Save it as `bitmapBlur.fla` in your work folder.
2.   Select File⇨Import⇨Import to Stage.
3.   Navigate to an image on your drive and select it.
4.   After the image is on the stage, select the instance so that it is focused.

5. Select Modify⇨Convert to Symbol.

6. Select Movieclip as the symbol type and give your instance a logical name for the library, such as sampleImage.

7. With the movie clip selected, change its name in the properties panel to clip1. You'll use this name to reference your image in the ActionScript. Slide the movie clip offstage. It doesn't need to be on the stage. The stage will hold the bitmap.

8. Click the first frame in the timeline, open the Actions panel, and type in the following ActionScript:

```
import flash.filters.BlurFilter;
import flash.display.BitmapData;
import flash.geom.Rectangle;
import flash.geom.Point;
var myBitmap:BitmapData = new BitmapData(clip1._width, clip1._height);
myBitmap.draw(clip1);
this.createEmptyMovieClip("copy1", 0);
copy1.attachBitmap(myBitmap, 0);
```

9. Test your movie now and check the stage. You should see a copy of your movie clip ready for manipulation. Close the .swf and return to the first frame ActionScript.

10. Now add the code to define a BlurFilter object. Click the first frame in the timeline, open the Actions panel (Window⇨Actions) and enter the following ActionScript below the code added in step 8:

```
var myBlur:BlurFilter = new BlurFilter();
myBlur.blurX = 3;
myBlur.blurY = 3;
myBlur.quality = 12;
```

11. Do something interesting with your filter. Rather than produce a static effect, the following function redraws the bitmap and apply the blur in a new position with each iteration. Enter the following ActionScript below the code you added in step 10:

```
function moveBlur() {
    myBitmap.draw(clip1);
    if (xpos<300) {
        xpos += 2;
    } else {
        clearInterval(moveblur_interval);
    }
    myBitmap.applyFilter(myBitmap, new Rectangle(xpos, 30, 100, 280), new
Point(xpos, 30), myBlur);
    updateAfterEvent();
}
moveblur_interval = setInterval(this, "moveBlur", 10);
```

12. Test your movie now and check the stage. You should see a copy of your movie clip being blurred by a rectangle. Close the .swf and return to the first frame ActionScript.

13. To modify the code to add a permanent blur effect on the bitmap, go back to the code you added in step 11 and remove the following line:

```
myBitmap.draw(clip1);
```

14. Change the following line value from 2 to 100:

```
xpos += 100;
```

15. Test your movie now and check the stage. You should see a copy of your movie clip being blurred by a set of overlapping rectangles.

How It Works

In this example the bitmap was obtained using the `draw` method. The bitmap could have been created using methods provided by the geom objects and the drawing API, but the movie clip copy provided an interesting way to see how robust the Bitmap object can be.

Applying the filter was accomplished easily using the `applyFilter` method. The bitmap sourced itself, meaning that the source bitmap parameter in the `applyFilter` method referred to the same bitmap as the bitmap that had the method applied to it. This allowed the `applyFilter` method to modify the pixels directly. Once the source bitmap was determined, the rectangle of the blur area was defined. You can see that this rectangle is the visibly blurred rectangle in the final resulting SWF. The `Point` object parameter also placed the blurred rectangle over the image in a specific place. The point chosen was identical to the start index of the rectangle object. You can specify a different point to begin drawing the blur. Notice that the original rectangle source is used, while the point object has the capability to offset the result. Finally the filter was defined as `myBlur` easily and is the exact same object that could have been used on a `movieclip, filters` array property.

By making small and easy changes to this code you can begin to see how easy it is to create interesting and varied results with filters and the Bitmap object.

Summary

This chapter explained the bitmapData object and the many methods provided. The bitmapData object presents a powerful way for you to manipulate the stage at runtime. With precise control over each pixel on the stage, within each movie clip and potentially in any graphic being displayed, you can create and manipulate the stage in ways never before realized in Flash.

When used in conjunction with movie clips, you can utilize the object to amazingly improve performance over vector graphics. When combined with video and animation, the Bitmap object enables you to achieve not only effects, but the capability to fire events and to act upon pixel changes in real time within your application.

The bitmapData object should excite any designer with its fresh access to pixel-level manipulation.

Exercises

1. Using the `getPixel` method in a `for` loop, try to find the existence of a particular color in a bitmap by checking each pixel. Place a movie clip at the x and y position of the result.

2. Using `perlinNoise` within a bitmap, use `getPixel` to randomly place movie clips on the stage.

Using ActionScript for Animation

Macromedia Flash can be used for all sorts of design and development activities; however, its roots lie with animation. Right from when the product was called FutureSplash, the focus was on cultivating a product that would provide developers with ways to easily create animated content. Although Flash is now much more than an animation tool, it still does that very well.

Unfortunately, Macromedia Flash has been marred as well by years of "Skip Intro" content. Many sites have been created where the focus was on the animation, not on the message. Many people have gotten very tired of this and have dismissed Flash overall as a nuisance plug-in. Fortunately, the tool has matured, and best practices have come out to guide developers in creating content that can be both cool and usable.

Developers have also realized that Flash can be used for more than just site intro animations. For instance, the plug-in makes an ideal distribution mechanism for online learning applications where animation provides clarity to the concepts being taught. Animations can also be used sparingly within web applications to provide feedback to users. Many sophisticated games are developed using Flash, and aspiring artists use Flash animation as a tool for self-expression.

All-in-all, Flash animation is still alive and well and has evolved into a mature means toward both productivity and self-expression. This chapter introduces the concepts and techniques needed to make the most out of scripted Flash animation.

Scripted Versus Non-Scripted Animation

Two primary ways exist to animate content in Flash: using the authoring tool's timeline and through ActionScript code.

The traditional approach in Flash has always been to use the authoring tool. This provides the most creative control and best matches more traditional non–computer-based animation techniques. It lends itself very well to movie-type animations where the purpose is to tell a story. In these situations, the animations can be very complex, and scripting the movements a much more onerous job than visually manipulating the animation as you go.

Scripted animation is necessary when the user interacts with the animation, or where the animation can be different each time, such as for games or for interactive art pieces. Script is also handy for animating repeating elements, such as rain or snow falling. This is something that is difficult to do by hand in a way that looks realistic.

Creating Animations Using Keyframes

If you have not previously worked with Flash, first review how a clip can be animated on the timeline. This process involves creating movie clips and defining their position, size, and shape at points throughout the animation. First, start with some definitions:

❑ A *frame* is an opportunity for the player to change something on the screen. In the same way that a television updates its image 60 times every second, the Flash player updates the content a certain number of times per second.

❑ The *fps* (frames per second) value represents the rate at which frames are displayed. The default value set in a new Flash document is 12 fps, which represents 12 opportunities to change the content for every second that goes by. The fps value is set to the base timeline and applies throughout the movie, including to movies loaded on-the-fly.

❑ The *playhead* is an internal marker that keeps track of which frame to display. By manipulating the playhead, you manipulate which frame is shown.

❑ A *keyframe* is a marker frame that you set to hold specific content with a specific size, shape, and position. The frames between pairs of keyframes calculate what the content should look like and where the content should be using keyframes as start and end points.

❑ A *tween* is an animated transition from one keyframe to another.

❑ The *timeline* is the container holding the frames, the keyframes, and the playhead.

Animating content in the timeline involves the following steps:

1. Place content on the screen in an existing keyframe or a new keyframe that you create. There is always at least one keyframe available to use.

2. Create a second keyframe later on the timeline that contains the same content.

3. Manipulate the content in the second keyframe.

4. Tell Flash to create a tween between the two keyframes.

In this first Try It Out exercise, you create an animation using the authoring tool.

Try It Out   Using the Authoring Tool for Animation

This exercise illustrates the process of animating a simple shape on the screen using the Flash authoring tool. It provides you with a conceptual base for using ActionScript for animation a little later. In Figure 16-1, onion skins show the progression of the animation.

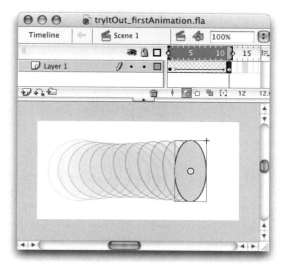

Figure 16-1

1. Create a new Macromedia Flash document.

2. Use the Oval tool in the Tools panel to draw a circle on the left side of the stage. Use any color for fill and line that you want.

3. Double-click the shape to select both the fill and the line. Select Modify⇨Convert to Symbol, name the clip `circleClip`, and make sure the Movie Clip radio button is selected. Click OK.

4. Click frame 12 of the timeline. Select Insert⇨Timeline⇨Keyframe.

5. With the red playhead marker over the new keyframe on frame 12, drag the circle to the right of the screen.

6. Open the Transform panel (Window⇨Transform). Change the vertical scale percentage (the second text field) to 50%. Change the rotation to 90 degrees.

7. Click the timeline between the two keyframes. Select Insert⇨Timeline⇨Create Motion Tween.

8. Select File⇨Save As, name the file `tryItOut_firstAnimation.fla`, choose an appropriate directory, and save it. Select Control⇨Test Movie.

9. Close the SWF file and click the onion skin icon just below the timeline area, just to the right of the layer trash icon. Extend the onion skin bracket on the top of the timeline to include the whole animation.

How It Works

When you create a tweened animation, Flash calculates most of the frames for you. You set a starting and an ending keyframe for the animation, and Flash calculates how to get from the starting point to the ending point. By showing the animation in onionskin mode, you can see each frame as it is to be drawn out to the screen. If you were to further change the content at either of the keyframes, the onionskin feature would update all the intermediate frames automatically to show the transition between both keyframes.

Creating Animations Using ActionScript

Start to look now at how to animate a movie clip with script. Code techniques give you these same kinds of tweening techniques, but first look at how to do this at a low level so that you can develop a foundation for how the more automated techniques work.

The first problem that you come across is that by creating a tween in the timeline, Flash automatically moves the movie clip for each frame. You need a way to move the content yourself, and to do that, you need a way of calling code on a regular basis. You can do this in two ways: with the onEnterFrame() technique and with the setInterval() technique.

Moving a Movie Clip Using onEnterFrame()

Every time the playhead moves for each movie clip, that movie clip generates an event indicating it is about to draw the next frame. This is a very convenient way of calling code repeatedly. The following code snippet shows the technique used to capture that event:

```
containerClip.onEnterFrame = function()
{
    this.animatedClip._x += 10;
}
```

In this example, a container movie clip called containerClip captures the onEnterFrame event. Every time onEnterFrame fires, by default 12 times per second, the code in the event handler is called. It moves a movie clip called animatedClip to the right by 10 pixels. Unfortunately, there is nothing to stop this animation, so it just keeps on going even after the movie clip is off the screen. The technique can be revised to provide a condition for stopping the animation:

```
containerClip.onEnterFrame = function()
{
    this.animatedClip._x += 10;
    if (this.animatedClip._x >= 250)
    {
        delete this.onEnterFrame;
    }
}
```

After the movie clip passes an *x* position of 250 pixels, the event handler deletes itself, stopping the animation.

> One strategy for animation is to have one onEnterFrame *event handler attached to every movie clip that needs to move. Another is to have a single* onEnterFrame *event handler attached to a parent movie clip that handles the animation for all nested movie clips. Generally the latter is better because multiple* onEnterFrame *event handlers running at once can quickly bog down the CPU.*

Take a look at an example of this technique at work.

Try It Out   **Moving a Movie Clip Using onEnterFrame()**

This example shows how content can be moved using the `onEnterFrame` event.

1. Create a new Macromedia Flash document.

2. Open the Library panel and choose New Symbol from the menu at the top right of the panel.

3. In the New Symbol dialog box, set the name to `circleClip`. Make sure the Movie Clip radio button is selected. Click the Export for ActionScript checkbox to select it. If you do not see the checkbox, click the Advanced button on the bottom right of the panel to reveal additional options. Click OK.

4. Use the Oval tool to draw a circle within the new movie clip. Use any color for fill and line that you want.

5. Click the Scene 1 button above the timeline to return to the main timeline.

6. The code for this example is very small, so enter it in the Actions panel instead of creating a separate ActionScript file. Click the first frame in the timeline, open the Actions panel (Window⇨ Development Panels⇨Actions), and type in the following ActionScript code:

```
this.createEmptyMovieClip("holderClip", this.getNextHighestDepth());
holderClip.attachMovie("circleClip", "circleClip", ⤸
    holderClip.getNextHighestDepth());
holderClip.circleClip._x = 10;
holderClip.circleClip._y = 10;
holderClip.onEnterFrame = function()
{
    this.circleClip._x += 10;
    if (this.circleClip._x > 250)
    {
        delete this.onEnterFrame;
    }
}
```

7. Select File⇨Save As, name the file `tryItOut_onEnterFrame.fla`, choose an appropriate directory, and save it. Select Control⇨Test Movie.

How It Works

First, a movie clip holder is created:

```
this.createEmptyMovieClip("holderClip", this.getNextHighestDepth());
```

It is generally a good idea to have a movie clip that acts as an overall container for animation because there may be multiple things being animated at once.

A symbol from the library is attached to the timeline for this movie clip:

```
holderClip.attachMovie("circleClip", "circleClip", ⤸
    holderClip.getNextHighestDepth());
```

The attached clip is given a starting *x* and *y* position:

```
holderClip.circleClip._x = 10;
holderClip.circleClip._y = 10;
```

The `onEnterFrame` event is trapped for the container movie clip:

```
holderClip.onEnterFrame = function()
{
    // ...
}
```

Every time `onEnterFrame()` fires, the attached movie clip moves right by 10 pixels:

```
this.circleClip._x += 10;
```

The keyword `this` refers to the parent object, the `holderClip` movie clip, and so gives easy access to the movie clip nested inside.

The termination condition checks every time the event fires to see whether the animation should be stopped. When that happens because the movie clip's *x* coordinate is greater than or equal to 250 pixels, the `onEnterFrame` event handler function is deleted. In essence, the function deletes itself:

```
if (this.circleClip._x > 250)
{
    delete this.onEnterFrame;
}
```

Now take a look at another way to move content.

Moving a Movie Clip Using setInterval()

There is another way to animate content that is not based on frames. Instead, it uses the `setInterval()` function. The function is called repeatedly in intervals that are measured in milliseconds. Here's the basic syntax for `setInterval()`:

```
setInterval(animationFunction, 83);
function animationFunction()
{
    animatedClip._x += 10;
}
```

This code also moves a movie clip to the right by 10 pixels for each call of the function. The repeat interval here is set to 83 milliseconds, which is roughly equal to 12 fps (1000 ms /12 frames = 83 ms per frame).

The animation also won't stop moving the movie clip. A stopping condition is needed. To stop the animation, capture the ID that the `setInterval()` function returns when it is called, and then later pass that ID to the `clearInterval()` function to stop the calls to `animationFunction()`:

```
var intervalID:Number = setInterval(animationFunction, 83);
function animationFunction()
{
    animatedClip._x += 10;
    if (animatedClip._x >= 250)
    {
        clearInterval(intervalID);
    }
}
```

Ready to try the setInterval() animation technique for yourself?

Try It Out   Moving a Movie Clip Using setInterval()

This example demonstrates how content can be moved using the setInterval() function.

1. Open the completed tryItOut_onEnterFrame.fla file from the previous Try It Out exercise, or open tryItOut_onEnterFrame.fla from the book's source files at <source file directory>/ Chapter 16/.

2. Select File⇨Save As, rename the file tryItOut_setInterval.fla, and save it to a folder of your choosing.

3. Click the first frame in the timeline, open the Actions panel (Window⇨Development Panels⇨ Actions), and type in the following ActionScript code:

```
this.createEmptyMovieClip("holderClip", this.getNextHighestDepth());
holderClip.attachMovie("circleClip", "circleClip", ⮑
    holderClip.getNextHighestDepth());
holderClip.circleClip._x = 10;
holderClip.circleClip._y = 10;

var intervalID = setInterval(animateCircle, 83);
function animateCircle()
{
    holderClip.circleClip._x += 10;
    if (holderClip.circleClip._x > 250)
    {
        clearInterval(intervalID);
    }
}
```

4. Select File⇨Save. Select Control⇨Test Movie.

How It Works

As in the previous exercise, a movie clip holder is created, a symbol from the library is attached to the timeline for the movie clip, and the attached clip is given a starting x and y position:

```
this.createEmptyMovieClip("holderClip", this.getNextHighestDepth());
holderClip.attachMovie("circleClip", "circleClip", ⮑
    holderClip.getNextHighestDepth());
holderClip.circleClip._x = 10;
holderClip.circleClip._y = 10;
```

The interval is then started. It calls the `animateCircle()` function every 83 milliseconds, which corresponds roughly to 12 fps (1000 milliseconds / 83 milliseconds per frame = 12 fps):

```
var intervalID = setInterval(animateCircle, 83);
```

Every time `setInterval()` calls `animateCircle()`, the attached movie clip moves right by 10 pixels:

```
holderClip.circleClip._x += 10;
```

The termination condition checks every time the function is called to see whether the animation should be stopped. When that happens because the movie clip's x coordinate is greater than or equal to 250 pixels, the `setInterval()` call is stopped by passing the interval's ID to `clearInterval()`:

```
if (holderClip.circleClip._x > 250)
{
    clearInterval(intervalID);
}
```

Next, take a look at some of the implications behind these two techniques.

Frame-Based Versus Time-Based Animation

The two techniques that can be used to move content both work well, but each has performance and timing implications.

The Effect of Movie Frame Rate on Animation

The `onEnterFrame()` technique is tied to the frame rate of the application. You have used the default 12 fps in the examples so far, which is quite slow. If you were to raise the frame rate of the movie to 24 fps to try to make the animation smoother, the animation would take half the time to play out. This is generally not the intended result and can be a major headache if you decide to change the frame rate midway through or at the end of the development process. Figure 16-2 shows how increasing the frame rate speeds up the animation.

Distance Traveled In One Second

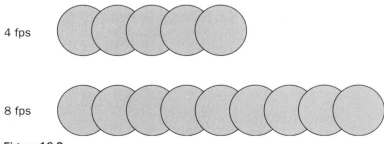

4 fps

8 fps

Figure 16-2

The setInterval() technique runs independently of the movie's frame rate, however there is still a relationship. If you change the position of a movie clip multiple times while one frame is being displayed, you will only see the result of the last movement. For instance, consider the following loop:

```
for (var i:Number = 0; i < 12; i++)
{
    holderClip.circleClip._x += 10;
}
```

The for loop runs almost instantly, so you will see only one big movement instead of 12 small ones. Even if you set the setInterval() delay to just one millisecond, the stage is updated only 12 times per second for a 12 fps movie so only 12 of those movements will be visible.

Two ways exist to make a setInterval()-based animation smoother. First, you can raise the frame rate of the movie. This makes the animation smoother by giving a greater number of rendering windows during the course of the animation. The length of time needed to get the animation from one side of the screen to the other does not change with the frame rate because the number of times setInterval() calls the animate function does not change with the frame rate (see Figure 16-3).

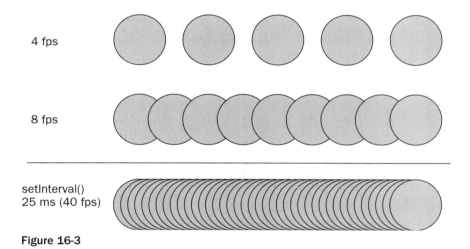

The number of display opportunities vs. the number of setInterval() calls

4 fps

8 fps

setInterval()
25 ms (40 fps)

Figure 16-3

The other way to make screen updates smoother with setInterval()-based animation is by adding a call to updateAfterEvent(). This global function, when invoked from within a function being called by setInterval(), tells the player to render the stage again. The stage will be redrawn, even though it has not yet advanced to the next frame-rendering opportunity. This global function makes setInterval() completely independent of the movie's frame rate.

Take a look at trying these techniques out firsthand.

Chapter 16

Try It Out   Experimenting with Frame Rate

This exercise demonstrates the effects of frame rate on animation.

1. Open the completed `tryItOut_onEnterFrame.fla` file from the previous Try It Out exercise, or open `tryItOut_onEnterFrame.fla` from the book's source files at `<source file directory>/Chapter 16/`.

2. Select File⇨Save As, rename the file `tryItOut_frameRate.fla`, and save it to a folder of your choosing.

3. Select Control⇨Test Movie.

4. Select Modify⇨Document and change the frame rate to 24 fps.

5. Save the file and select Control⇨Test Movie.

6. Select Modify⇨Document and change the frame rate back to 12 fps.

7. Click the first frame in the timeline, open the Actions panel, and enter the following ActionScript code:

```
this.createEmptyMovieClip("holderClip", this.getNextHighestDepth());
holderClip.attachMovie("circleClip", "circleClip", ⤵
    holderClip.getNextHighestDepth());
holderClip.circleClip._x = 10;
holderClip.circleClip._y = 10;

var intervalID = setInterval(animateCircle, 10);
function animateCircle()
{
    holderClip.circleClip._x += 10;
    if (holderClip.circleClip._x > 250)
    {
        clearInterval(intervalID);
    }
}
```

8. Save the file and select Control⇨Test Movie.

9. Select Modify⇨Document and change the frame rate to 24 fps.

10. Select Control⇨Test Movie.

11. Select Modify⇨Document and change the frame rate back to 12 fps.

12. Update the ActionScript code by adding the following bold line:

```
function animateCircle()
{
    holderClip.circleClip._x += 10;
    updateAfterEvent();
    if (holderClip.circleClip._x > 250)
    {
        clearInterval(intervalID);
    }
}
```

13.   Save the file and select Control⇨Test Movie.

14.   Select Modify⇨Document and change the frame rate to 24 fps.

15.   Select Control⇨Test Movie.

How It Works

The first two times this exercise is tried, it uses the `onEnterFrame` function, which is tied directly to frame rate, so when the frame rate increases, the animation is smoother, but takes less time to complete.

The next two times use `setInterval()`. When the frame rate increases, it does not affect how long it takes for the animation to complete, but it does improve the smoothness of the animation.

The last two times use `setInterval()` in conjunction with the `updateAfterEvent()` global function. When the frame rate is increased, there is no difference in either the time taken for the animation to complete or in the smoothness of the animation.

Which Technique Should You Use?

The choice of which technique to use is largely a personal one. The `onEnterFrame` way of doing things is convenient and is easy to set up, and most scripted animations are not really that sensitive to frame rate. For the most part, you will likely set the frame rate once and leave it at that.

`setInterval()` lends itself better to smoother animations, especially on machines with slow processors such as PocketPC-based devices. If you need animations that require a certain amount of time, regardless of frame rate, `setInterval()` is also the way to go. Finally, if you are animating an action game, `setInterval()` gives you the best response from keyboard input.

Choosing a Frame Rate or Update Interval

Choosing a frame rate or an update interval is actually fairly arbitrary, but a few guidelines will help.

Frame rate has an impact on both the smoothness of the animation and the performance of the playback. If the frame rate is very low, the animation playback will be slow enough that the eye can detect individual movements rather than seeing the animation as one continuous motion. If the frame rate is too high, playback performance becomes an issue where the CPU becomes too taxed and playback becomes jerky. The default frame rate for a new Flash document is 12 fps (83 milliseconds per frame). This is generally too slow for smooth animations. Compare this with some common refresh rates:

❑   Movies projected in a movie theater run at 24 fps.

❑   Online video generally runs at between 15 and 30 fps.

❑   Television runs at 30 fps using interlacing.

❑   Video games can run at between 30 and 120 fps.

❑   Computer monitors update the screen between 60 and 120 times per second.

❑   The human eye is capable of distinguishing between different frame rates beyond 120 fps.

These values ignore differences in how a projector, a TV, and a monitor project their images and are perceived by the human eye; however, it is enough to know that 12 fps is too low.

Flash has an upper limit of 120 fps (8 milliseconds per frame). In general, if you set the refresh rate that high, Flash does not actually give you that refresh rate. It instead drops frames in an unpredictable fashion, making performance worse than it might at a lower refresh rate.

Setting the frame rate between 24 and 50 fps (42–20 milliseconds per frame), depending on the hardware demographics of the target audience, is the optimal range.

When choosing an update interval specifically for the `setInterval()` technique, keep the following in mind:

❑ Setting a specific update interval does not guarantee that the function will actually be called right at the specified time. The actual timing may vary by 10 milliseconds or more, depending on how heavily the processor is being used.

❑ In general, 10 milliseconds is the minimum value that can be used. Below that, intervals become imprecise, and processor issues will likely keep the actual update interval at 10 milliseconds or more.

Setting a `setInterval()` refresh rate of 20 to 42 milliseconds generally leads to the best results.

Creating Animation with Movie Clips

All right, enough of the pre-work. Get to some of the fun stuff! The examples shown so far are pretty boring. So far, you have just moved a movie clip in a straight line. Now you start with animating properties, animating multiple movie clips, and introducing other kinds of motion.

Try your hand with a project to explore a number of animation techniques, including basic motion, movie clip duplication, and randomization. The project you are going to create right now is a snow effect that will end up looking something like Figure 16-4.

Start with animating a single flake of snow. Use `onEnterFrame`, although you could use `setInterval()` here just as easily. Following is the base animation code, which assumes that there is a movie clip in the library with the linkage ID `snowFlake`:

```
this.createEmptyMovieClip("holderClip", this.getNextHighestDepth());
holderClip.attachMovie("snowFlake", "snowFlake", holderClip.getNextHighestDepth());
holderClip.onEnterFrame = function()
{
    this.snowFlake._y += 4;

    if (this.snowFlake._y >= Stage.height)
    {
        this.snowFlake._y = 0;
    }
}
```

This code first creates a movie clip to hold the animation. It is generally a good idea to have a movie clip to hold any movie clips being animated. This better contains the movie clips for re-use and for increased flexibility.

Next, the code attaches a single snowflake from the library and starts moving it downward. When it hits the bottom, it moves the clip back to the top.

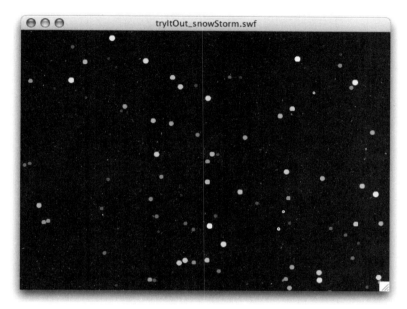

Figure 16-4

Animating Multiple Movie Clips

So far, the code does not do very much, and there are not very many snowflakes yet. Creating more snowflakes is a process of attaching more movie clips to the stage. Every time a snowflake is added, the animation code needs to keep track of it. This bogs down the processor, so you have to be careful of how many to create.

The easiest way of creating snowflakes in such a way where it is easy to keep track of them is to use a simple numbering system. Here, you call the first clip snowFlake0, the next one snowFlake1, and so on. You can later refer to clip n using the associative array syntax:

```
var thisFlake:MovieClip = holderClip["snowFlake" + n];
```

From inside the onEnterFrame loop, you can refer to this instead, because this refers to the parent movie clip, holderClip:

```
var thisFlake:MovieClip = this["snowFlake" + n];
```

With this system, it is easy to loop through the clip for each snowflake. Make a few more snowflakes:

```
this.createEmptyMovieClip("holderClip", this.getNextHighestDepth());
holderClip.maxFlakes = 100;

for (var i:Number = 0; i < holderClip.maxFlakes; i++)
{
    holderClip.attachMovie("snowFlake", "snowFlake" + i, ⤸
        holderClip.getNextHighestDepth());
}

holderClip.onEnterFrame = function()
{
    var thisFlake:MovieClip;
    for (var j:Number = 0; j < this.maxFlakes; j++)
    {
        thisFlake = this["snowFlake" + j];
        thisFlake._y += 4;

        if (thisFlake._y >= Stage.height)
        {
            thisFlake._y = 0;
        }
    }
}
```

Now, you have 100 snowflakes being created, and each time through, the loop goes through each snowflake and increments the y coordinate.

Some problems still exist with this code. One of the issues is that all 100 snowflakes start in the same spot, making it look like there is only one flake.

Adding Random Behavior

This calls for random assignment of x and y values, so that all the snowflakes are spread across the screen. You can use a built-in static method of the Math class, called `random()`, for obtaining random values. This method returns decimal values in the range from 0 to 1. Most of the time you need to work with wider ranges of values, so some transformation of the output is needed. Here is a simple function that trans-forms the output from this method to a random value between any range of numbers that you want:

```
function randomRange(min:Number, max:Number)
{
    return Math.random() * (max - min) + min;
}
```

This is an extremely handy function. Use it any time you need to work with ranges of numbers. Apply this to your evolving snowflake code:

```
this.createEmptyMovieClip("holderClip", this.getNextHighestDepth());
holderClip.maxFlakes = 100
for (var i:Number = 0; i < holderClip.maxFlakes; i++)
{
    holderClip.attachMovie("snowFlake", "snowFlake" + i, ⤸
```

```
           holderClip.getNextHighestDepth());
       holderClip["snowFlake" + i]._x = randomRange(0, Stage.width);
       holderClip["snowFlake" + i]._y = randomRange(0, Stage.height);
    }

    holderClip.onEnterFrame = function()
    {
        var thisFlake:MovieClip;
        for (var j:Number = 0; j < this.maxFlakes; j++)
        {
            thisFlake = this["snowFlake" + j];
            thisFlake._y += 4;

            if (thisFlake._y >= Stage.height)
            {
                thisFlake._y = 0;
            }
        }
    }

    function randomRange(min:Number, max:Number)
    {
        return Math.random() * (max - min) + min;
    }
```

Now, you are finally starting to get somewhere! You add a few more features to this code in the next Try It Out exercise.

Try It Out   Creating a Snowstorm

In this exercise you animate multiple movie clips using the techniques that you have learned so far.

1. Create a new Macromedia Flash document.

2. Open the Library panel (Window⇨Library) and from the menu at the top right of the panel, choose New Symbol.

3. Within the New Symbol dialog box, set the name to be `snowFlake`. Make sure the Movie Clip radio button is selected. Click the Export for ActionScript checkbox to select it. If you do not see the checkbox, click the Advanced button on the bottom right of the panel to reveal additional options. Click OK.

4. Select the Oval tool from the Tools panel (Window⇨Tools). From the color wells, select white for the fill, and choose the no line option from the line color chooser. Draw a roughly 6 pixel by 6 pixel circle on the stage within the new movie clip. You may need to select the shape once you have made it and use the width and height boxes in the properties panel to adjust it to the size that you want.

5. Click the Scene 1 button above the timeline to return to the main timeline.

6. Click the first frame in the timeline, open the Actions panel, and type in the following ActionScript code:

```
#include "tryItOut_snowStorm.as"
```

7. Select File⇨Save As, name the file `tryItOut_snowStorm.fla`, choose an appropriate directory, and save it.

8. Create a new script file by selecting File⇨New and choosing ActionScript File from the New Document panel.

9. Select File⇨Save As and ensure it is showing the same directory containing the Flash project file. Give the file the name `tryItOut_snowStorm.as` and save it.

10. Enter the following code into the new ActionScript file:

```actionscript
this.createEmptyMovieClip("holderClip", this.getNextHighestDepth());
holderClip.maxFlakes = 100;
holderClip.dropSpeed = 5;

var thisFlake:MovieClip;
for (var i:Number = 0; i < holderClip.maxFlakes; i++)
{
    holderClip.attachMovie("snowFlake", "snowFlake" + i, ⏎
        holderClip.getNextHighestDepth());
    thisFlake = holderClip["snowFlake" + i];
    thisFlake._x = randomRange(0, Stage.width);
    thisFlake._y = randomRange(0, Stage.height);
    thisFlake._xscale = thisFlake._yscale = randomRange(50, 150);
    thisFlake._alpha = thisFlake._xscale - 50;
    thisFlake.cacheAsBitmap = true;
    thisFlake.oscillationSeed = randomRange(0, 200);
}

holderClip.onEnterFrame = function()
{
    var thisFlake:MovieClip;
    for (var i:Number = 0; i < this.maxFlakes; i++)
    {
        thisFlake = this["snowFlake" + i];
        thisFlake._y += thisFlake._xscale * (this.dropSpeed / 100);
        thisFlake._x += Math.sin((thisFlake._y + ⏎
            thisFlake.oscillationSeed) / 50);

        if (thisFlake._y >= Stage.height)
        {
            thisFlake._x = randomRange(0, Stage.width);
            thisFlake._y = 0;
        }
    }
}

function randomRange(min:Number, max:Number)
{
    return Math.random() * (max - min) + min;
}
```

11. Select File⇨Save As, name the file `tryItOut_onEnterFrame.fla`, choose an appropriate directory, and save it. Select Control⇨Test Movie.

How It Works

The first line creates a holder clip for the animation:

```
this.createEmptyMovieClip("holderClip", this.getNextHighestDepth());
```

As previously mentioned, this is a good practice for making animations more self-contained and easier to work with. It also gives you a clip to which you can attach the onEnterFrame handler.

A couple of variables are saved as properties in the container movie clip (this is preferred over creating timeline variables because the scope of the variables stays within the movie clip):

```
holderClip.maxFlakes = 100;
holderClip.dropSpeed = 5;
```

The movie clips are created within the for loop. The first thing that the loop does is to attach the movie clip from the library to the container movie clip. The getNextHighestDepth() method ensures that each snowflake rests on its own layer:

```
holderClip.attachMovie("snowFlake", "snowFlake" + i, ⤵
    holderClip.getNextHighestDepth());
```

A temporary variable keeps a handle to the movie clip for convenience. This is also a performance aid, because local variable access is faster than associative array access. The temporary variable is declared outside the loop, also for performance reasons:

```
thisFlake = holderClip["snowFlake" + i];
```

The x and y coordinates for each snowflake are initialized based on a random selection using the dimensions of the stage as the bounds for picking the values:

```
thisFlake._x = randomRange(0, Stage.width);
thisFlake._y = randomRange(0, Stage.height);
```

Each snowflake is scaled so that they are not all a uniform size. The scaling ranges between 50% and 150% of the original size. The code simply assigns the result of the randomRange() function first to thisFlake._yscale and then to thisFlake._xscale all in one line:

```
thisFlake._xscale = thisFlake._yscale = randomRange(50, 150);
```

The transparency of each flake is adjusted according to the size of the flake. The principle here is that bigger flakes are closer to the viewer and should be more opaque, whereas smaller flakes are further away and should be harder to see:

```
thisFlake._alpha = thisFlake._xscale - 50;
```

The cacheAsBitmap option is a performance addition in Flash 8:

```
thisFlake.cacheAsBitmap = true;
```

It tells Flash that each of these movie clips being animated contains static content. Flash will use a cached bitmap version of the clip instead of rendering each clip each time. (The cacheAsBitmap property was introduced in Chapter 7.)

The last step within the movie clip creation loop is to assign the movie clip a seed value that helps make the swishing back and forth of the flakes seem more random:

```
thisFlake.oscillationSeed = randomRange(0, 200);
```

It offsets the back-and-forth cycle so that they do not all move left and right in unison.

Now take a look at the contents of the onEnterFrame handler. Every time the event is generated, it loops through each of the movie clips. It knows how many clips there are because you saved numFlakes as a property of the container movie clip. Once again, you save the handle to the movie clip currently being manipulated to a temporary variable, both for readability and for performance:

```
var thisFlake:MovieClip;
for (var i:Number = 0; i < this.maxFlakes; i++)
{
    thisFlake = this["snowFlake" + i];
    // ...
}
```

Because this loop is being called constantly, anything that improves (or degrades) performance has maximum effect within the loop.

Next in the loop, the y position is modified:

```
thisFlake._y += thisFlake._xscale * (this.dropSpeed / 100);
```

Rather than incrementing it by a constant value like in earlier examples, the increment depends on the size of the snowflake. Larger snowflakes are perceived as closer, and should fall faster to maintain that perception.

Some back-and-forth motion is introduced into the snowflake:

```
thisFlake._x += Math.sin((thisFlake._y + thisFlake.oscillationSeed) / 50);
```

Math.sin() is a convenient method for this because it produces output that smoothly oscillates between -1 and 1 as the input value continues to increase. The oscillation seed is used here to offset the oscillations so that each snowflake does not move back and forth at the same time.

When each snowflake reaches the bottom of the screen, it is placed back at the top at a new random x position:

```
if (thisFlake._y >= Stage.height)
{
    thisFlake._x = randomRange(0, Stage.width);
    thisFlake._y = 0;
}
```

The `randomRange()` function enables you to quickly and easily pick randomly from any range of numbers:

```
function randomRange(min:Number, max:Number)
{
    return Math.random() * (max - min) + min;
}
```

Now take a look at the concepts of easing and acceleration.

Introducing Easing and Acceleration

Moving things in a constant linear fashion is a relatively straightforward task, but how about moving things about in a more random manner, and adding some acceleration and deceleration into the mix? These tasks are actually easy to achieve and do not require as much math as you might think.

To apply *easing* to a moving movie clip means to make the transition gentler between at rest and in motion. It involves a more gradual slow-down or speed-up of the movie clip, and it tends to make transitions appear more natural. Easing can also be thought of the physics concepts of acceleration and deceleration. Easing-in corresponds with the concept of acceleration and easing-out corresponds with the concept of deceleration.

Easing Out

First look at the process of easing-out, or deceleration. Figure 16-5 shows what this motion looks like.

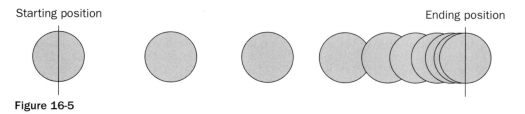

Figure 16-5

Fortunately, the math behind this is very simple. For every animation pass, you move the movie clip some fraction of the distance from its current location to the target position. Figure 16-6 shows this behavior visually, where each time the movie clip is moved one third of the distance separating itself and its stop point.

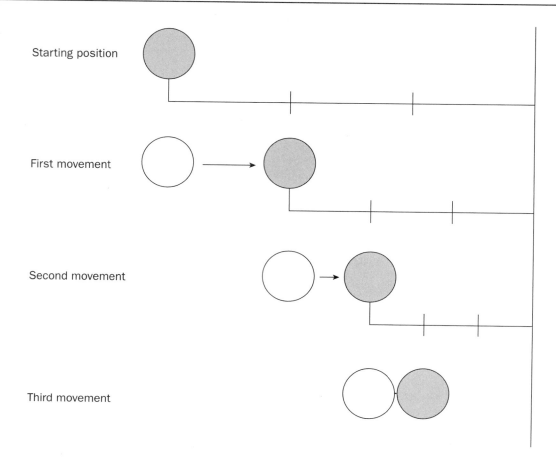

Etc...

Figure 16-6

The choice of what fraction of the distance to move each time is dependent on how fast you want the deceleration to occur. A small fraction results in slow deceleration, whereas a value of one moves the movie clip instantly from its start point to its end point. The following equation determines what the next movie clip position should be:

$$\text{newPosition} = \text{oldPosition} + \frac{\text{targetPosition} - \text{oldPosition}}{\text{easingFactor}}$$

If a movie clip starts at x position 0, targets x position 100, and uses an easing factor of 3, the clip will start with the following easing values:

1. newPosition = 0 + (100 - 0) / 3 = 33.3

2. newPosition = 33.3 + (100 - 33.3) / 3 = 55.5

3. newPosition = 55.5 + (100 - 55.5) / 3 = 70.3

4. newPosition = 70.3 + (100 - 70.3) / 3 = 80.2

5. newPosition = 80.2 + (100 - 80.2) / 3 = 86.8

Subsequent values will be 91.2, 94.1, 96.1, 97.4, 98.2, 98.8, 99.2, 99.5, 99.6, and so on. The numbers continue to get closer and closer to 100, but they never actually reach it. Mathematically, it is actually impossible for the target number to ever be reached; however, computer precision is limited, and once it gets close to the target point, you will no longer see any motion.

Give easing out a try.

Try It Out   Easing Out an Animation

In this exercise you create an ease-out effect and see how different easing factors impact the effect.

1. Create a new Macromedia Flash document.

2. Click the first frame in the timeline, open the Actions panel, and type in the following ActionScript code:

```
var targetX:Number = 400;
var easingFactor:Number = 10;

this.createEmptyMovieClip("holderClip", this.getNextHighestDepth());

holderClip.createEmptyMovieClip("square", this.getNextHighestDepth());
holderClip.square.moveTo(0, 0);
holderClip.square.lineStyle(1, 0x000000);
holderClip.square.lineTo(10, 0);
holderClip.square.lineTo(10, 10);
holderClip.square.lineTo(0, 10);
holderClip.square.lineTo(0, 0);

holderClip.square._x = 0;
holderClip.square._y = 200;

var intervalID = setInterval(updateAnimation, 20);
function updateAnimation()
{
    holderClip.square._x += (targetX - holderClip.square._x) / easingFactor;
    trace("New x value: " + holderClip.square._x);
    if (targetX - holderClip.square._x < 0.5)
    {
        clearInterval(intervalID);
    }
    updateAfterEvent();
}
```

3. Select File⇨Save As, rename the file `tryItOut_easingOut.fla`, and save it to a folder of your choosing.

4. Select Control⇨Test Movie.

5. Test the movie with different values of `easingFactor` to see what the effects are.

How It Works

This example creates a movie clip that can be animated, gives it a destination, and then sends it on its way.

First, a destination that corresponds with the `targetPosition` variable from the earlier equation is given:

```
var targetX:Number = 400;
```

An easing factor is selected (it can be any number from 1 upward; a value of 1 represents no easing, and a value of 100 or greater represents very slow easing):

```
var easingFactor:Number = 10;
```

A base movie clip is created, a movie clip is created within that, and then a shape is drawn within the nested movie clip to make the easing effect visible:

```
this.createEmptyMovieClip("holderClip", this.getNextHighestDepth());

holderClip.createEmptyMovieClip("square", this.getNextHighestDepth());
holderClip.square.moveTo(0, 0);
holderClip.square.lineStyle(1, 0x000000);
holderClip.square.lineTo(10, 0);
holderClip.square.lineTo(10, 10);
holderClip.square.lineTo(0, 10);
holderClip.square.lineTo(0, 0);
```

The movie clip is given a starting position:

```
holderClip.square._x = 0;
holderClip.square._y = 200;
```

The `setInterval()` animation technique is used this time. Every time the `updateAnimation()` function is called, the movie clip position is recalculated:

```
var intervalID = setInterval(updateAnimation, 20);
function updateAnimation()
{
    // ...
}
```

Within the update animation function, the new movie clip position is calculated and assigned to the movie clip's _x property:

```
holderClip.square._x += (targetX - holderClip.square._x) / easingFactor;
```

When the movie clip gets close enough to the target position, the easing is stopped, and the movie clip is snapped to the target position:

```
if (targetX - holderClip.square._x < 0.5)
{
    holderClip.square._x = targetX;
    clearInterval(intervalID);
}
```

`updateAfterEvent()` is used by the `setInterval()` animation technique to make the animation smoother:

```
updateAfterEvent();
```

Play with different values of `easingFactor` to see different easing rates.

What about easing in?

Easing In

Easing in, or acceleration, is done a bit differently than easing out. Though the concept is the same, a couple of problems exist with just reversing the ease-out process. The first problem is that determining how far to go for the next step requires knowledge of how far it went in the previous step. This means some information needs to be kept for each movement and used for the calculation for the next movement. The second problem is that simply reversing the process results in an acceleration that is too fast for most purposes and does not look quite as natural.

Turning to some simple physics gives you another way of accelerating a movie clip. Figure 16-7 shows what the acceleration process looks like.

Starting position

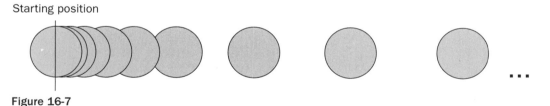

Figure 16-7

Take a look at the math that is behind the physics of acceleration. Although to accelerate generally means to go faster, to make this work you need something more precise. To accelerate an object means to increase the speed of that object. Speed refers to the distance traveled for a specific period of time:

$$\text{speed} = \frac{\text{distance}}{\text{time}}$$

To accelerate an object, you increase the speed repeatedly for each given period of time. To increase the speed, you continuously increase the distance traveled for each given period of time. Figure 16-8 illustrates this.

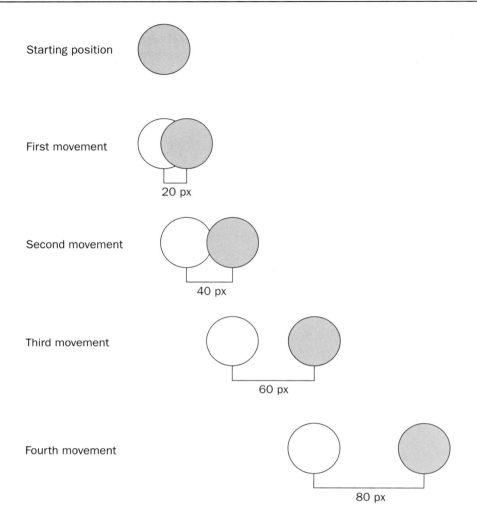

Starting position

First movement

20 px

Second movement

40 px

Third movement

60 px

Fourth movement

80 px

Etc...

Figure 16-8

Implemented downward, the principles shown here are perfect for accurately modeling the effects of gravity.

If you can remember the last distance traveled by the movie clip, calculating the next distance to travel is an easy matter:

newPosition = currentPosition + distanceToTravel

After the calculation has been performed, the distanceToTravel variable is updated so that the next movement will travel further on the screen:

distanceToTravel = distanceToTravel + accelerationFactor

The acceleration factor can range from 0 for no movement at all to any positive number. Typical acceleration factors are between 1 and 20.

With a movie clip starting at an x position of 0 and an acceleration factor of 20, you get the following values:

1. newPosition = 0 + 20 = 20
   distanceToTravel = 20 + 20 = 40

2. newPosition = 20 + 40 = 60
   distanceToTravel = 40 + 20 = 60

3. newPosition = 60 + 60 = 120
   distanceToTravel = 60 + 20 = 80

4. newPosition = 120 + 80 = 200
   distanceToTravel = 80 + 20 = 100

5. newPosition = 200 + 100 = 300
   distanceToTravel = 100 + 20 = 120

Try It Out   Accelerating a Movie Clip

In this exercise you create an acceleration effect, and see the impact of different easing factors on the effect.

1. Create a new Macromedia Flash document.

2. Click the first frame in the timeline, open the Actions panel (Window⇨Development Panels⇨ Actions), and type in the following ActionScript code:

```
var accelerationRate:Number = 5;

this.createEmptyMovieClip("holderClip", this.getNextHighestDepth());

holderClip.createEmptyMovieClip("square", this.getNextHighestDepth());
holderClip.square.moveTo(0, 0);
holderClip.square.lineStyle(1, 0x000000);
holderClip.square.lineTo(10, 0);
holderClip.square.lineTo(10, 10);
holderClip.square.lineTo(0, 10);
holderClip.square.lineTo(0, 0);

holderClip.square._x = 0;
holderClip.square._y = 200;
holderClip.square.speed = 0;

var intervalID = setInterval(updateAnimation, 30);
function updateAnimation()
{
    holderClip.square.speed += accelerationRate;
```

```
       holderClip.square._x += holderClip.square.speed;

       if (holderClip.square._x > Stage.width)
       {
           clearInterval(intervalID);
       }
       trace("New x value: " + holderClip.square._x);
       updateAfterEvent();
   }
```

3. Select File⇨Save As, rename the file tryItOut_easingIn.fla, and save it to a folder of your choosing.

4. Select Control⇨Test Movie.

5. Try testing the movie with different values of easingFactor and see what the effect is.

6. Update the code so that the first line in the updateAnimation() function is replaced with the following code:

```
if (holderClip.square.speed < 30)
{
    holderClip.square.speed += accelerationRate;
}
else
{
    holderClip.square.speed = 30;
}
```

7. Select Control⇨Test Movie.

How It Works

This example creates a movie clip that can be animated, sets an acceleration rate, and then starts the animation.

First, the acceleration rate is set. A value of 5 gives an acceleration that is fairly fast, but still slow enough to be able to clearly tell that the speed at the beginning and the speed at the end are quite different:

```
var accelerationRate:Number = 5;
```

A base movie clip is created, a movie clip is created within that, and then a shape is drawn within the nested movie clip to make the easing effect visible:

```
this.createEmptyMovieClip("holderClip", this.getNextHighestDepth());

holderClip.createEmptyMovieClip("square", this.getNextHighestDepth());
holderClip.square.moveTo(0, 0);
holderClip.square.lineStyle(1, 0x000000);
holderClip.square.lineTo(10, 0);
holderClip.square.lineTo(10, 10);
holderClip.square.lineTo(0, 10);
holderClip.square.lineTo(0, 0);
```

The movie clip is given a starting position and a starting speed. The speed is stored as a property of the movie clip so that if multiple movie clips are undergoing acceleration, they can be individually accelerated quite easily:

```
holderClip.square._x = 0;
holderClip.square._y = 200;
holderClip.square.speed = 0;
```

The setInterval() animation technique is used here. Every time the updateAnimation() function is called, the movie clip position is recalculated:

```
var intervalID = setInterval(updateAnimation, 20);
function updateAnimation()
{
    // ...
}
```

Within the updateAnimation() function, the new movie clip position is calculated and assigned to the movie clip's _x property. Each time the speed value goes up by a constant amount as dictated by the accelerationRate variable:

```
holderClip.square.speed += accelerationRate;
holderClip.square._x += holderClip.square.speed;
```

The variation of this code causes the movie clip to accelerate until it reaches a speed of 30 pixels per frame, and then it maintains a constant speed until it leaves the screen:

```
if (holderClip.square.speed < 30)
{
    holderClip.square.speed += accelerationRate;
}
else
{
    holderClip.square.speed = 30;
}
holderClip.square._x += holderClip.square.speed;
```

After the movie clip goes off the stage, the animation is stopped:

```
if (holderClip.square._x > Stage.width)
{
    clearInterval(intervalID);
}
```

The updateAfterEvent() function is used by the setInterval() animation technique to make the animation smoother:

```
updateAfterEvent();
```

Playing with different values of accelerationRate gives you a sense of what different acceleration rates look like on the screen. Here, there is no issue about numeric precision as there was for the ease-out example.

Next, take a look at both of these easing techniques being used in an interactive keyboard-driven example.

Try It Out   **Interactive Animation**

Now you apply both types of easing/acceleration in a more interactive environment. At the end, you will have a helicopter that you can move with the arrow keys.

1. Create a new Macromedia Flash document.

2. Select Modify⇨Document. In the dialog box that opens, click the Background Color swatch and enter color #6699FF into the color value text field.

3. Open the Library panel (Window⇨Library) and from the menu at the top right of the panel, choose New Symbol.

4. Within the New Symbol dialog box, set the name to be helicopter. Make sure the Movie Clip radio button is selected. Click the Export for ActionScript checkbox to select it. If you do not see the checkbox, click the Advanced button on the bottom right of the panel to reveal additional options. Click OK.

   Within the new movie clip, use the oval, line, and paint bucket tools to create something like the symbol shown magnified at 400% in Figure 16-9. Steps 5–9 cover the process.

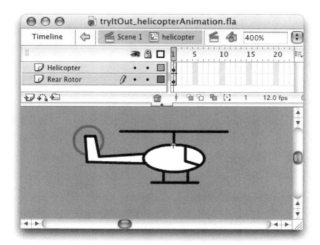

Figure 16-9

5. Click the Oval tool in the Tools palette (Window⇨Tools), choose black from the line color chooser, choose white from the background color chooser, and then draw an oval roughly 22 pixels wide by 11 pixels high. The top-middle of the oval should be touching the registration marker for the movie clip.

6. Use the Line tool to draw the rotor, the landing struts, and the tail. Make sure that the lines for the tail form a closed shape with no gap.

7. Choose the Paint Bucket tool, change the selected color to white, and then click inside the bounds of tail area.

8. Rename the layer to Helicopter. Create a new layer by clicking the new layer button below the layer. Rename the new layer to Rear Rotor.

9. Click the Oval tool in the Tools palette, select a dark grey from the line color chooser, select a medium grey from the background color chooser, and draw a circle roughly 11 pixels in diameter centered around the top of the tail.

10. Click the Scene 1 button on top of the timeline to return to the main timeline. Click the first frame in the timeline, open the Actions panel (Window➪Development Panels➪Actions), and type in the following ActionScript code:

```
#include "tryItOut_helicopterAnimation.as"
```

11. Select File➪Save As, name the file `tryItOut_helicopterAnimation.fla`, choose an appropriate directory, and save it.

12. Create a new script file by selecting File➪New and choosing ActionScript File from the New Document panel.

13. Select File➪Save As and ensure it is showing the same directory containing the Flash project file. Give the file the name `tryItOut_helicopterAnimation.as` and save it.

14. Enter the following code into the new ActionScript file:

```
var ACCELERATION_RATE:Number = 0.4;
var EASING_FACTOR:Number = 10;
var MOVEMENT_AMOUNT:Number = 7;

this.createEmptyMovieClip("holderClip", this.getNextHighestDepth());
holderClip.attachMovie("helicopter", "helicopter",
holderClip.getNextHighestDepth());
holderClip.helicopter.targetX = 275;
holderClip.helicopter.verticalSpeed = 0;
holderClip.helicopter._x = holderClip.helicopter.targetX;
holderClip.helicopter._y = Stage.height - 14;

var intervalID:Number = setInterval(updateAnimation, 20);
function updateAnimation()
{
    checkKeys();

    holderClip.helicopter._x += (holderClip.helicopter.targetX -
        holderClip.helicopter._x) / EASING_FACTOR;
    holderClip.helicopter._rotation =
        Math.min((holderClip.helicopter.targetX -
        holderClip.helicopter._x) / 5, 20);
    holderClip.helicopter.verticalSpeed += ACCELERATION_RATE;

    holderClip.helicopter._y += holderClip.helicopter.verticalSpeed;
    if (holderClip.helicopter._y >= Stage.height - 14)
    {
        holderClip.helicopter._y = Stage.height - 14;
```

```
            holderClip.helicopter.verticalSpeed = 0;
        }

        updateAfterEvent();
}

function moveShipLeft()
{
    holderClip.helicopter.targetX -= MOVEMENT_AMOUNT;
    if (holderClip.helicopter.targetX < 40)
    {
        holderClip.helicopter.targetX = 40;
    }
}

function moveShipRight()
{
    holderClip.helicopter.targetX += MOVEMENT_AMOUNT;
    if (holderClip.helicopter.targetX > Stage.width - 15)
    {
        holderClip.helicopter.targetX = Stage.width - 15;
    }
}

function moveShipUp()
{
    if (holderClip.helicopter.verticalSpeed > -5)
    {
        holderClip.helicopter.verticalSpeed -= 1;
    }
}

function moveShipDown()
{
    if (holderClip.helicopter.verticalSpeed < 5)
    {
        holderClip.helicopter.verticalSpeed += 1;
    }
}

function checkKeys()
{
    if (Key.isDown(Key.LEFT) == true)
    {
        moveShipLeft();
    }

    if (Key.isDown(Key.RIGHT) == true)
    {
        moveShipRight();
    }

    if (Key.isDown(Key.UP) == true)
    {
        moveShipUp();
```

```
        }

    if (Key.isDown(Key.DOWN) == true)
    {
        moveShipDown();
    }
}
```

15.   Save the file, return to the Flash document, and select Control⇔Test Movie. Pressing and holding the up arrow key causes the helicopter to climb; releasing the key lets gravity take over and the copter will free-fall.

How It Works

The first task is to set up the movie clips to be used for the animation. Any movie clip shapes can be used, but a helicopter fits the exercise nicely.

The code is definitely longer than most for this exercise, but most of it is framework code. The code to do the actual animation itself is quite small.

The first three lines are startup constants that define acceleration, ease-out rate, and the amount to move the helicopter for each press of the arrow keys:

```
var ACCELERATION_RATE:Number = 0.4;
var EASING_FACTOR:Number = 10;
var MOVEMENT_AMOUNT:Number = 7;
```

Next, you create the movie clip to hold the animation, and then you attach the helicopter to the screen:

```
this.createEmptyMovieClip("holderClip", this.getNextHighestDepth());
holderClip.attachMovie("helicopter", "helicopter", ⤶
    holderClip.getNextHighestDepth());
```

Two properties are added to the helicopter movie clip so that you can manage its horizontal position and its vertical speed. These are made as properties of the movie clip rather than separate variables because it makes animating multiple objects easier, and it makes for a more object-oriented and cleaner approach:

```
holderClip.helicopter.targetX = 275;
holderClip.helicopter.verticalSpeed = 0;
```

The initial x and y coordinates are set so that the helicopter starts at the bottom middle of the screen:

```
holderClip.helicopter._x = holderClip.helicopter.targetX;
holderClip.helicopter._y = Stage.height - 14;
```

The interval is set up to update the animation and to check for key presses. The update rate is set at 20 milliseconds, which is fast enough to give smooth animation but not too fast for slower processors:

```
var intervalID:Number = setInterval(updateAnimation, 20);
function updateAnimation()
{
    // ...
}
```

Within the function called by `setInterval()`, the first task performed is to check to see which keys have been pressed. Normally, the `Key.onPress` event is used to capture keystrokes; however, the operating system's key-repeat delays cause problems with trying to allow continuous key presses. Also, this allows for multiple keys to be pressed and detected at once:

```
checkKeys();
```

The *x* position of the helicopter is updated. The left and right arrow keys update the `targetX` property for the movie clip. While one arrow key continues to be pressed, the `targetX` value continues to change and the easing code continues to chase after it. It's sort of like the proverbial carrot-on-a-stick trick. The carrot (`targetX`) continues to move, so the rabbit (the helicopter) can never catch up. Once the arrow key is no longer being pressed, `targetX` stops moving, and the easing code finally lets the helicopter ease in on its location. If you play with pressing the left and right arrows while the helicopter is at the bottom of the screen, you can see this effect more readily.

```
holderClip.helicopter._x += (holderClip.helicopter.targetX - ⊃
    holderClip.helicopter._x) / EASING_FACTOR;
```

The rotation of the helicopter is updated. The rotation is adjusted according to how far the helicopter is from its `targetX` destination. The further away it is, the greater the rotation. There is an upper bound of 20 degrees so that the helicopter doesn't tilt in a way that looks unrealistic. The `Math.min()` method makes sure that if the calculation causes the rotation to be below 20 degrees, that value is used, otherwise the value of 20 is used:

```
holderClip.helicopter._rotation = ⊃
    Math.min((holderClip.helicopter.targetX - ⊃
    holderClip.helicopter._x) / 5, 20);
```

The technique used to manage vertical speed is a bit different. Here, you make use of the acceleration principle that you learned about earlier. You keep track of the vertical speed of the helicopter, and based on that speed the code updates the y position. The up and down arrows add and remove an amount to and from the speed value, so once the helicopter starts falling, it takes a little while after pressing the up arrow for it to start to rise again:

```
holderClip.helicopter.verticalSpeed += ACCELERATION_RATE;
holderClip.helicopter._y += holderClip.helicopter.verticalSpeed;
```

The helicopter is checked to see whether it has hit or passed the bottom of the screen. If so, it is snapped to the bottom and is stopped:

```
if (holderClip.helicopter._y >= Stage.height - 14)
{
    holderClip.helicopter._y = Stage.height - 14;
    holderClip.helicopter.verticalSpeed = 0;
}
```

The last step within the animation function is to redraw the screen:

```
updateAfterEvent();
```

The left and right arrow key handlers add to or subtract from the `targetX` property, and they make sure that `targetX` does not go outside the bounds of the screen. These functions do not actually move the ship themselves. By changing the property, the animation routine will move the helicopter to catch up to the location specified by the `targetX` property:

```
function moveShipLeft()
{
    holderClip.helicopter.targetX -= MOVEMENT_AMOUNT;
    if (holderClip.helicopter.targetX < 40)
    {
        holderClip.helicopter.targetX = 40;
    }
}

function moveShipRight()
{
    holderClip.helicopter.targetX += MOVEMENT_AMOUNT;
    if (holderClip.helicopter.targetX > Stage.width - 15)
    {
        holderClip.helicopter.targetX = Stage.width - 15;
    }
}
```

The up and down arrow key handlers add to or subtract from the `verticalSpeed` property, and they throttle just how much they affect the vertical speed. Without the throttling, the helicopter would quickly zoom up rather than slowly climb up:

```
function moveShipUp()
{
    if (holderClip.helicopter.verticalSpeed > -5)
    {
        holderClip.helicopter.verticalSpeed -= 1;
    }
}

function moveShipDown()
{
    if (holderClip.helicopter.verticalSpeed < 5)
    {
        holderClip.helicopter.verticalSpeed += 1;
    }
}
```

The `checkKeys()` function is called every time an animation pass is performed, and it takes a look at which keys are pressed. Individual keys are checked within their own `if` statements rather than `if..else` or `switch..case` statements because it is possible to have multiple keys being pressed at one time:

```
function checkKeys()
{
    if (Key.isDown(Key.LEFT) == true)
    {
        moveShipLeft();
    }

    if (Key.isDown(Key.RIGHT) == true)
```

```
    {
        moveShipRight();
    }

    if (Key.isDown(Key.UP) == true)
    {
        moveShipUp();
    }

    if (Key.isDown(Key.DOWN) == true)
    {
        moveShipDown();
    }
}
```

Summary

This chapter covered many different aspects of ActionScript-based animation. Some of the things that you learned include the following:

- ❑ How to animate using the timeline.

- ❑ Two different fundamental techniques for script-based animation, namely the onEnterFrame technique and the setInterval technique.

- ❑ The relationship between onEnterFrame- and setInterval-based animation with movie frame rate.

- ❑ Frame rates of between 24 and 50 fps, or 42 to 20 milliseconds per frame, are generally optimal.

- ❑ How to attach and animate multiple movie clips.

- ❑ How to add random behavior to animation.

- ❑ How to use easing to create smoother, more natural transitions.

Exercises

1. Use the onEnterFrame animation technique to close in on the cursor's position. It should slow down as it gets closer to the cursor. Hint: apply easing separately to the x and y coordinates, and use the MovieClip properties _xmouse and _ymouse to find the cursor's position.

2. Rework exercise 1 so that it uses the setInterval() animation technique instead. Modify it so that there are three movie clips that follow the cursor, and give them different easing values.

3. Modify the snowstorm exercise to make the snowflakes look like they are tumbling as they fall. Make the snowflakes more irregular in shape by redrawing them in the library and then vary the _rotation of each snowflake to create the tumbling effect.

4. Use either the onEnterFrame or the setInterval() technique to create a bouncing ball effect where the ball accelerates as it drops, then slows down as it rises up. For each bounce it should lose some of its height.

Automated Transitions

So far, you have been creating animations at a low level, where you implement all of the animation code yourself. This certainly yields maximum control over animation and interactivity; however, Flash also gives you a more automated way of animating in the form of the Tween class. This class allows you to create transitions with any movie clip property.

The Tween Class

The Tween class was actually available in Flash MX 2004; however, it was not immediately documented. This is too bad, because it is an immensely useful class. The idea behind this class is that you can take any numeric movie clip property and transition the property values from one number to another number. The general form for the Tween class is as follows:

```
import mx.transitions.Tween;
var myTween:Tween = new Tween(clipHandle:Object, propertyName:String, ⤸
    easingFunction:Function, startValue:Number, stopValue:Number, ⤸
    duration:Number, useSeconds:Boolean);
```

The first parameter, `clipHandle`, holds the movie clip being targeted for animation. It can actually hold a handle to any object, such as a component or an instance of a custom class. The second parameter, `propertyName`, is a string representing which property to change. Some examples are `_x`, `_alpha`, and `_rotation`. The `easingFunction` parameter takes a handle to a function that calculates how the animation accelerates and decelerates when going from the start to the end values. Each of the six built-in easing classes has four easing methods. Next, `startValue` and `stopValue` can be any numerical values. If `useSeconds` is set to `true`, then `duration` sets the number of seconds that the animation will take to complete. If `useSeconds` is set to `false`, then the `duration` value sets the number of frames that the animation will take to complete.

> *The* `clipHandle` *and* `propertyName` *parameters can actually be empty if you are not using the tween to directly manipulate a movie clip. If you use the* `onMotionChanged` *event, you can still get each tweened value, and you can indirectly animate one or more objects based on that. The next Try It Out exercise shows this in action.*

The following code moves a movie clip called `circleClip` from an *x* value of 0 to an *x* value of 200 in 2 seconds, with strong easing applied to both the start and the end of the tween:

```
import mx.transitions.Tween;
var myTween:Tween = new Tween(circleClip, "_x", ⤴
    mx.transitions.easing.Strong.easeInOut, 0, 200, 2, true);
```

The following code fades a movie clip called `circleClip` from an alpha value of 100 to an alpha value of 50 in 30 frames, with elastic easing applied at the end:

```
import mx.transitions.Tween;
var myTween:Tween = new Tween(circleClip, "_alpha", ⤴
    mx.transitions.easing.Elastic.easeOut, 100, 50, 30, false);
```

Absolute Versus Relative Tweens

Sometimes you might want to set absolute start and end points for a tween; other times you might want the tweens to be relative to existing values. For example, if you have a movie clip called `circleClip` in the middle of the stage, the following code moves it from an *x* value of zero to an *x* value of 200, regardless of where it was initially placed on the stage:

```
import mx.transitions.Tween;
var myTween:Tween = new Tween(circleClip, "_x", ⤴
    mx.transitions.easing.Strong.easeInOut, 0, 200, 2, true);
```

To instead move the movie clip 200 pixels to the right of the current position, set the start and end values relative to the current *x* position of the movie clip:

```
import mx.transitions.Tween;
var myTween:Tween = new Tween(circleClip, "_x", ⤴
    mx.transitions.easing.Strong.easeInOut, ⤴
    circleClip._x, circleClip,_x + 200, 2, true);
```

Built-In Easing Classes and Methods

These are the classes that are available to set how the transition accelerates and decelerates between the starting and ending values. They are used in conjunction with one of the four easing methods:

```
import mx.transitions.Tween;
var myTween:Tween = new Tween(circleClip, "_x", ⤴
    mx.transitions.easing.Back.easeIn, 0, 200, 2, true);
```

```
import mx.transitions.Tween;
var myTween:Tween = new Tween(circleClip, "_x", ⤴
    mx.transitions.easing.Back.easeOut, 0, 200, 2, true);
```

```
import mx.transitions.Tween;
var myTween:Tween = new Tween(circleClip, "_x", ⤴
    mx.transitions.easing.Regular.easeInOut, 0, 200, 2, true);
```

```
import mx.transitions.Tween;
var myTween:Tween = new Tween(circleClip, "_x", ⤴
    mx.transitions.easing.None.easeNone, 0, 200, 2, true);
```

The following table lists the available easing classes:

Name	Description
mx.transitions.easing.Back	Pulls the animation back outside of its travel range, giving an elastic effect.
mx.transitions.easing.Bounce	Bounces the animated object so that it takes multiple tries before it stops at the target value, or when applied at the beginning, makes each bounce higher until it gets to the target property value.
mx.transitions.easing.Elastic	Oscillates at the beginning or at the end of the transition. Similar to the Back class, only it oscillates several times instead of only once.
mx.transitions.easing.Regular	Slowly transitions from start to stop or vice versa.
mx.transitions.easing.Strong	Performs the same effect as the Regular class, only the acceleration and the deceleration are more pronounced.
mx.transitions.easing.None	Transitions from start to end with no variation in acceleration.

Here are descriptions of each of the built-in easing methods:

Name	Description
easeIn	Provides easing at the start of the animation.
easeOut	Provides easing at the end of the animation.
easeInOut	Provides easing both at the start and at the end of the animation.
easeNone	Does not apply any easing. This method applies only to the None class.

Tween Class Methods

The following table describes the methods that are available from each Tween class instance:

Method	Return	Description
continueTo	Nothing	Continues the transition from the current property value of the movie clip to the new property value passed to the method, taking a duration that is passed to the method to make the new transition.
fforward	Nothing	Fast-forwards to the end of the tween.

Table continued on following page

Method	Return	Description
nextFrame	Nothing	Goes to the next frame of a stopped tween.
prevFrame	Nothing	Goes to the previous frame of a stopped tween.
resume	Nothing	Resumes a stopped tween from the point at which the stop() method was called.
rewind	Nothing	Goes back to the beginning of the tween.
start	Nothing	Starts playback of the tween from the beginning. When a new tween is created, it is automatically started without the need to call this method.
stop	Nothing	Pauses the tween.
yoyo	Nothing	Reverses the direction of the tween.

The following sections take a closer look at the Tween class methods.

continueTo()

The continueTo() method overrides the target property value and the duration value and continues the tween using the current property value as the new start point. This method is useful for continuous animation based on user input, such as for games. Using continueTo() allows you to update the transition based on a new destination based on an action such as the arrow keys being pressed.

This method takes two parameters. The first parameter is the new target value for the tweened property. The second parameter is a value for how long the tween should take to get from the current property value to the target property value. If the useSeconds constructor parameter was set to true, this parameter represents the number of seconds, otherwise it represents the number of frames.

```
myTween.continueTo(endValue:Number, duration:Number);
```

Here's an example using continueTo():

```
import mx.transitions.Tween;
var myTween:Tween = new Tween(circleClip, "_x",
    mx.transitions.easing.Regular.easeOut, 100, 300, 2, true);

var keyHandler:Object = new Object();
keyHandler.onKeyDown = function()
{
    var newDestination:Number;
    if (Key.isDown(Key.LEFT) == true)
    {
        newDestination = myTween.finish - 50;
        myTween.continueTo(newDestination, 2);
    }

    if (Key.isDown(Key.RIGHT) == true)
    {
```

```
            newDestination = myTween.finish + 50;
            myTween.continueTo(newDestination, 2);
        }
    }
Key.addListener(keyHandler);
```

Future invocations of the same tween will use the new start value, end value, and duration.

fforward()

The `fforward()` method immediately goes to the end of the tween, bringing the tweened parameter to its final value. This method takes no parameters. Here's its syntax:

```
myTween.fforward();
```

Following is an example use of `fforward()`:

```
import mx.transitions.Tween;
var myTween:Tween = new Tween(circleClip, "_x", ⮐
    mx.transitions.easing.Regular.easeOut, 100, 300, 5, true);

var keyHandler:Object = new Object();
keyHandler.onKeyDown = function()
{
    if (Key.isDown(Key.LEFT) == true)
    {
        myTween.rewind();
    }

    if (Key.isDown(Key.RIGHT) == true)
    {
        myTween.fforward();
    }
}
Key.addListener(keyHandler);
```

nextFrame()

The `nextFrame()` method advances to the next frame of a stopped tween. This method takes no parameters. Its syntax is as follows:

```
myTween.nextFrame();
```

Here's an example of its use:

```
import mx.transitions.Tween;
var myTween:Tween = new Tween(circleClip, "_x", ⮐
    mx.transitions.easing.Regular.easeOut, 100, 300, 100, false);

var keyHandler:Object = new Object();
keyHandler.onKeyDown = function()
{
    if (Key.isDown(Key.LEFT) == true)
```

```
        {
            myTween.stop();
            myTween.prevFrame();
        }

        if (Key.isDown(Key.RIGHT) == true)
        {
            myTween.stop();
            myTween.nextFrame();
        }
    }
    Key.addListener(keyHandler);
```

prevFrame()

The prevFrame() method advances to the previous frame of a stopped tween. This method takes no parameters:

```
    myTween.prevFrame();
```

See the nextFrame() method notes for sample code.

> *This method works only for frame-based tweens, where the* useSeconds *constructor argument is set to* false. *The* nextFrame *method works fine in both situations.*

resume()

The resume() method continues a tween from where it last left off. This method takes no parameters:

```
    myTween.resume();
```

A sample use of resume() might look like the following:

```
import mx.transitions.Tween;
var myTween:Tween = new Tween(circleClip, "_x", ⏎
    mx.transitions.easing.Regular.easeOut, 100, 300, 5, true);

var isStopped:Boolean = false;
var keyHandler:Object = new Object();
keyHandler.onKeyDown = function()
{
    if (Key.isDown(Key.SPACE) == true)
    {
        if (isStopped == true)
        {
            myTween.resume();
            isStopped = false;
        }
        else
        {
            myTween.stop();
            isStopped = true;
        }
```

```
            }
        }
    Key.addListener(keyHandler);
```

rewind()

The rewind() method goes back to the beginning of the tween, resetting the tweened property to its starting value. This method takes no parameters:

```
myTween.rewind();
```

See the fforward() method notes for sample code.

start()

The start() method starts a tween from its starting value, ignoring whether it was previously stopped partway through. This method takes no parameters. This method is not needed for the first invocation of a tween, because the tween will start immediately when created:

```
myTween.start();
```

A sample use of start() might look like the following:

```
import mx.transitions.Tween;
var myTween:Tween = new Tween(circleClip, "_x", ⤵
    mx.transitions.easing.Regular.easeOut, 100, 300, 5, true);

var isStopped:Boolean = false;
var keyHandler:Object = new Object();
keyHandler.onKeyDown = function()
{
    if (Key.isDown(Key.SPACE) == true)
    {
        if (isStopped == true)
        {
            myTween.start();
            isStopped = false;
        }
        else
        {
            myTween.stop();
            isStopped = true;
        }
    }
}
Key.addListener(keyHandler);
```

stop()

The stop() method stops a tween's progress. This method takes no parameters:

```
myTween.stop();
```

See the start() method notes for sample code.

yoyo( )

The yoyo() method reverses the direction of the tween by swapping the start and end property values. The easing will take effect as if a new tween was created with swapped start and end values instead of simply playing the tween backwards. This method takes no parameters:

```
myTween.yoyo();
```

A sample use of yoyo() might look like the following:

```
import mx.transitions.Tween;
var myTween:Tween = new Tween(circleClip, "_x",
mx.transitions.easing.Regular.easeOut, 100, 300, 5, true);
myTween.onMotionFinished = function()
{
    this.yoyo();
}
```

This method needs to be called once for each time the direction is to be reversed. If the tween is still in progress, it will skip to the end before restarting the tween in the opposite direction.

Tween Class Properties and Events

The following table describes the properties that are available from each Tween class instance:

Property	Type	Description
duration	Number	Returns the number of seconds or the number of frames that the tween will take to complete, depending on whether useSeconds was set to true or false in the constructor. [Read only]
finish	Number	Returns what the value of tweened property will be at the end of the tween. [Read only]
FPS	Number	Overrides the frames per second rate used by the class. This property only returns a value when it has been manually set.
position	Boolean	Returns the current value of the tweened property. [Read only]
time	Number	Returns the number of seconds or the number of frames that have passed in the tween, depending on whether useSeconds was set to true or false in the constructor. [Read only]

The following table describes the events that are available from each Tween class instance:

Event	Type	Description
onMotionChanged	Function	Fires every time the tweened property changes.
onMotionFinished	Function	Fires when the tween has reached the end.
onMotionResumed	Function	Fires when the `resume()` method is called.
onMotionStarted	Function	Fires when the `start()`, `continueTo()`, or `yoyo()` methods are called. Does not fire when the tween automatically starts on first creation.
onMotionStopped	Function	Fires when the tween reaches the end or the `stop()` method is called.

Until now you've seen the transition package name written out in full, such as `mx.transitions.easing` *.`Regular.easeOut`. This is a fair bit to put in each Tween class declaration, so from this point on, imports will be used so that the statement* `import mx.transitions.easing.*` *enables you to refer to an easing function through a short name such as* `Regular.easeOut`.

Try It Out   Tweening an Elasticized Box

This example uses the Tween class to animate a box so that it bounces into position.

1. Create a new Macromedia Flash document.

2. Select Modify⇨Document, change the frame rate to 24 fps, and click OK.

3. Open the Actions panel (Window⇨Development Panels⇨Actions), and type the following ActionScript code:

```
#include "tryItOut_tween.as"
```

4. Select File⇨Save As, name the file `tryItOut_tween.fla`, choose an appropriate directory, and save it.

5. Create a new script file by selecting File⇨New and choosing ActionScript File from the New Document panel.

6. Select File⇨Save As and ensure it is showing the same directory containing the Flash project file. Give the file the name `tryItOut_tween.as` and save it.

7. Enter the following code into the new ActionScript file:

```
import mx.transitions.Tween;
import mx.transitions.easing.*;

this.createEmptyMovieClip("curveClip", this.getNextHighestDepth());

var isGrowing:Boolean = true;

var myTween:Tween = new Tween(null, "", Elastic.easeOut, 100, 0, 2, true);
myTween.onMotionChanged = function()
{
    if (isGrowing == true)
```

```
        {
            drawBox(20, 20, 125+this.position, 200+this.position, ⟲
                this.position/2);
        }
        else
        {
            drawBox(20, 20, 250-this.position, 360-this.position, - ⟲
                this.position/2);
        }
    }

myTween.onMotionFinished = function()
{
    isGrowing = !isGrowing;
    this.rewind();
    this.start();
}

function drawBox(x:Number, y:Number, width:Number, height:Number, ⟲
    sidePush:Number):Void
{
    curveClip.clear();
    curveClip.lineStyle(1, 0x000000);
    curveClip.moveTo(x, y);
    curveClip.curveTo(x+sidePush, y+height/2, x, y+height);
    curveClip.curveTo(x+width/2, y+height-sidePush, x+width, y+height);
    curveClip.curveTo(x+width-sidePush, y+height/2, x+width, y);
    curveClip.curveTo(x+width/2, y+sidePush, x, y);
}
```

8. Save the file, return to the Flash document, and select Control⇨Test Movie.

How It Works

This example uses the `curveTo()` method to draw a box with curves instead of lines. Each `curveTo()` call draws a curved line between the previous point and a new point, with a control point determining the amount of curving taking place. Figure 17-1 shows four `curveTo()` segments. Each control point is exactly halfway between the two anchor points, and as each control point moves closer to the line joining the two corresponding anchor points, the curves straighten out, eventually becoming straight lines.

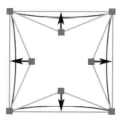

Figure 17-1

First, the Tween and the easing classes are imported for convenience of access. Normally it is best to separately import each class to be used in its own statement, however this can be relaxed with the easing classes. The easing classes all belong together as a group, and it is likely that you will want ready access to the different types of easing for experimentation:

```
import mx.transitions.Tween;
import mx.transitions.easing.*;
```

A base movie clip is created to hold the animation:

```
this.createEmptyMovieClip("curveClip", this.getNextHighestDepth());
```

A variable tracks which direction the animation is going so that it properly expands and contracts the rectangle:

```
var isGrowing:Boolean = true;
```

The tween is used to animate the distance of the control points from the lines joining each corresponding pair of anchor points. The tween is not actually given a movie clip or a property to adjust; it just keeps track through its own internal property value. The tween's internal property goes from 100 to zero in two seconds. The property is used to represent the distance of each curve's control point from the line connecting the two anchor points, as shown in Figure 17-1. When the tween reaches zero, the shape becomes a perfect rectangle.

```
var myTween:Tween = new Tween(null, "", Elastic.easeOut, 100, 0, 2, true);
```

As the value changes throughout the tween, onMotionChanged is continually called, which calls the code to redraw the box with the new sidePush value passed in from the tween in the form of this.position:

```
myTween.onMotionChanged = function()
{
    if (isGrowing == true)
    {
        drawBox(20, 20, 125+this.position, 200+this.position, ↩
            this.position/2);
    }
    else
    {
        drawBox(20, 20, 250-this.position, 360-this.position, - ↩
            this.position/2);
    }
}
```

When the animation is done, onMotionFinished is called. It switches the isGrowing variable so that the animation shrinks to its final position instead of expanding, or vice versa. It then returns the tween to its starting value of 100 and starts the tween in motion again.

```
myTween.onMotionFinished = function()
{
    isGrowing = !isGrowing;
    this.rewind();
    this.start();
}
```

The drawBox() function creates the actual box shape with the designated size and in the designated location. Every time the tween changes its value, this function is called again with values modified according to the tween value. Each call to curveTo() makes one side of the rectangle. The last two *x* and *y* values for each curveTo() call give the location for the end of the curve, where the start of the curve is automatically set to be the end point of the previous curve. The first two *x* and *y* values for each curveTo() call represent the control point for that curve. Each control point is made to be exactly halfway between the two curve anchor points, but pulled away from the invisible line joining the lines by a factor set by the sidePush variable.

```
function drawBox(x:Number, y:Number, width:Number, height:Number, ⊃
    sidePush:Number):Void
{
    curveClip.clear();
    curveClip.lineStyle(1, 0x000000);
    curveClip.moveTo(x, y);
    curveClip.curveTo(x+sidePush, y+height/2, x, y+height);
    curveClip.curveTo(x+width/2, y+height-sidePush, x+width, y+height);
    curveClip.curveTo(x+width-sidePush, y+height/2, x+width, y);
    curveClip.curveTo(x+width/2, y+sidePush, x, y);
}
```

Next, you see how to call multiple tweens in parallel.

Playing Tweens in Parallel

Tweening one value at a time is certainly nice, but many times multiple values need to be tweened at once. For example, rolling a ball down a decline requires tweening each of the _x, _y, and _rotation values. Each property to be tweened requires its own instance of the Tween class, as is shown in the following snippet that rolls a ball down a slope:

```
import mx.transitions.Tween;
import mx.transitions.easing.*;

var xTween:Tween = new Tween(0, new Tween(ballClip, "_x", Regular.easeIn, ⊃
    ballClip._x, ballClip._x + 190, 2, true);
var yTween:Tween = newTween(0, new Tween(ballClip, "_y", Regular.easeIn, ⊃
    ballClip._y, ballClip._y + 69, 2, true);
var rotationTween:Tween = newTween(0, new Tween(ballClip, "_rotation", ⊃
    Regular.easeIn, 0, 360, 2, true);
```

In the previous Try It Out exercise, you used a single tween to modify both the bounce effect and the zoom effect. Although this effect worked fairly nicely, it does not work in all situations, nor does it allow for repositioning of the rectangle. The next exercise adds that ability to the previous exercise.

Try It Out   Multiple Tweens on an Elasticized Box

This example uses several Tween instances to animate the position, dimensions, and effect of an elasticized box.

1. Open the completed tryItOut_tween.fla file from the previous Try It Out exercise, or open tryItOut_tween.fla from the book's source files at <source file directory>/Chapter 17/.

2. Open the completed `tryItOut_tween.as` file from the previous Try It Out exercise, or open `tryItOut_tween.as` from the book's source files at <source file directory>/Chapter 17/.

3. Update the code in the ActionScript file to look like the following:

```
import mx.transitions.Tween;
import mx.transitions.easing.*;

this.createEmptyMovieClip("curveClip", this.getNextHighestDepth());

var direction:Number = -1;

var sidePushAmount:Number = 50;
var startWidth:Number = 125;
var endWidth:Number = 400;
var startHeight:Number = 200;
var endHeight:Number = 320;
var startX:Number = 20;
var endX:Number = 75;
var startY:Number = 20;
var endY:Number = 40;
var tweenDuration:Number = 2;

var sidePushTween:Tween = new Tween(null, "", Elastic.easeOut, ⤶
    sidePushAmount, 0, tweenDuration, true);
var widthTween:Tween = new Tween(null, "", Elastic.easeOut, ⤶
    startWidth, endWidth, tweenDuration, true);
var heightTween:Tween = new Tween(null, "", Elastic.easeOut, ⤶
    startHeight, endHeight, tweenDuration, true);
var xTween:Tween = new Tween(null, "", Elastic.easeOut, ⤶
    startX, endX, tweenDuration, true);
var yTween:Tween = new Tween(null, "", Elastic.easeOut, ⤶
    startY, endY, tweenDuration, true);

sidePushTween.onMotionChanged = function()
{
    drawBox(xTween.position, yTween.position, widthTween.position, ⤶
        heightTween.position, this.position * direction);
}

sidePushTween.onMotionFinished = function()
{
    direction *= -1;
    this.rewind();
    this.start();
    widthTween.yoyo();
    heightTween.yoyo();
    xTween.yoyo();
    yTween.yoyo();
}

function drawBox(x:Number, y:Number, width:Number, height:Number, ⤶
    sidePush:Number):Void
{
    curveClip.clear();
```

```
      curveClip.lineStyle(1, 0x000000);
      curveClip.moveTo(x, y);
      curveClip.curveTo(x+sidePush, y+height/2, x, y+height);
      curveClip.curveTo(x+width/2, y+height-sidePush, x+width, y+height);
      curveClip.curveTo(x+width-sidePush, y+height/2, x+width, y);
      curveClip.curveTo(x+width/2, y+sidePush, x, y);
}
```

4.　　Save the file, return to the Flash document, and select Control⇨Test Movie.

How It Works

This exercise is almost identical to the previous exercise; it's just been modified a bit to allow for tweening multiple parameters.

You still track which direction the animation is going, but this time it's just to make sure that the side-push effect matches the zooming. If the rectangle is getting bigger, the sides start by pushing out. If the rectangle is getting smaller, the sides start by pulling in. Using a Number instead of a Boolean avoids having to use an `if` statement:

```
var direction:Number = -1;
```

Start and end values are defined for each tween. These values are brought out into separate variables for ease of modification:

```
var sidePushAmount:Number = 50;
var startWidth:Number = 125;
var endWidth:Number = 400;
var startHeight:Number = 200;
var endHeight:Number = 320;
var startX:Number = 20;
var endX:Number = 75;
var startY:Number = 20;
var endY:Number = 40;
var tweenDuration:Number = 2;
```

Five tweens are created to control five separate parameters. None of the tweens are directly linked up with external movie clips; instead, they are used only to tween ranges of numbers:

```
var sidePushTween:Tween = new Tween(null, "", Elastic.easeOut, ⤸
    sidePushAmount, 0, tweenDuration, true);
var widthTween:Tween = new Tween(null, "", Elastic.easeOut, ⤸
    startWidth, endWidth, tweenDuration, true);
var heightTween:Tween = new Tween(null, "", Elastic.easeOut, ⤸
    startHeight, endHeight, tweenDuration, true);
var xTween:Tween = new Tween(null, "", Elastic.easeOut, ⤸
    startX, endX, tweenDuration, true);
var yTween:Tween = new Tween(null, "", Elastic.easeOut, ⤸
    startY, endY, tweenDuration, true);
```

As the value changes throughout the side-push tween, onMotionChanged is continually called. This calls the code to redraw the box with the new sidePush value as well as the current values from the other tweens. It does not matter that the other tweens might update themselves at a slightly different pace. Every time the event is fired for the side-push tween, the box is drawn based on the current snapshot of the other tweens' current position values. They will be close enough to create a smooth animation, even with slight variations in the numbers:

```
sidePushTween.onMotionChanged = function()
{
    drawBox(xTween.position, yTween.position, widthTween.position, ⮐
        heightTween.position, this.position * direction);
}
```

When the animation is done, onMotionFinished is called. It switches the isGrowing variable so that the animation shrinks to its final position instead of expanding, or vice versa. It then returns the tween to its starting value of 100 and puts the tween in motion again. Because all of the tweens are being used in parallel for the same animation and take the same amount of time, only one onMotionFinished event handler is needed. Even if you tried reducing the animation interval for the x, y, width, or height tweens, the event is called on the one that finishes last, so the effect will still work:

```
sidePushTween.onMotionFinished = function()
{
    direction *= -1;
    this.rewind();
    this.start();
    widthTween.yoyo();
    heightTween.yoyo();
    xTween.yoyo();
    yTween.yoyo();
}
```

Now take a look at how to call multiple tweens in a sequence.

Playing Tweens in a Sequence

Playing a sequence of tweens is a little trickier than playing them in parallel, and somewhat messier as well. Take a look at how tweens can be chained together, and then take a look at a library that helps you with the chaining process.

To chain together a sequence of tweens, you need to know when each one finishes so that the next one can begin. This requires the use of onMotionFinished event. The following example uses three tweens each called in sequence. The second and third tweens are stopped until needed, which will be after the onMotionFinished event fires for the first and second tweens, respectively:

```
import mx.transitions.Tween;
import mx.transitions.easing.*;

var tween1:Tween = new Tween(circleClip, "_x", Regular.easeInOut, 0, 200, 2, true);
var tween2:Tween = new Tween(circleClip, "_y", Regular.easeInOut, 0, 300, 2, true);
```

```
    var tween3:Tween = new Tween(circleClip, "_alpha", Regular.easeInOut, ⤺
        100, 0, 1, true);
tween2.stop();
tween3.stop();
tween1.onMotionFinished = function()
{
    tween2.start();
}
tween2.onMotionFinished = function()
{
    tween3.start();
}
```

Even if the tweens are stopped right away, they still set the starting value of their respective properties immediately. This means that when the first tween starts, the initial x value will be zero, the initial y value will be zero, and the initial alpha value will be zero, regardless of what the original values were. If the intention is to instead move the movie clip relative to its current position, use the current position in the tween start and end values:

```
import mx.transitions.Tween;
import mx.transitions.easing.*;

var tween1:Tween = new Tween(circleClip, "_x", Regular.easeInOut, ⤺
    circleClip._x, circleClip._x + 200, 2, true);
var tween2:Tween = new Tween(circleClip, "_y", Regular.easeInOut, ⤺
    circleClip._y, circleClip._y + 300, 2, true);
var tween3:Tween = new Tween(circleClip, "_alpha", Regular.easeInOut, ⤺
    100, 0, 1, true);
tween2.stop();
tween3.stop();
tween1.onMotionFinished = function()
{
    tween2.start();
}
tween2.onMotionFinished = function()
{
    tween3.start();
}
```

Try out playing tweens in series.

Try It Out   Creating an Animation Sequence

This example plays tweens both in parallel and in sequence. You create a set of library functions to help the process of playing multiple tweens. The project should look something like Figure 17-2.

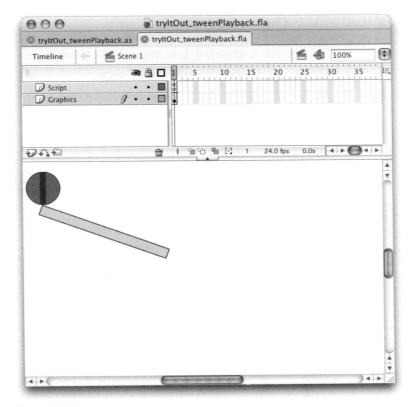

Figure 17-2

1. Create a new Macromedia Flash document.

2. Open the Library panel and from the menu at the top right of the panel, choose New Symbol. Within the New Symbol dialog box, set the name to be circleClip. Make sure the Movie Clip radio button is selected. Click OK.

3. Use the Oval tool in the toolbar to draw a circle within the new movie clip. Use any color for fill and line that you want.

4. Double-click the circle to select both the fill and the line. Use the Properties panel (Window⇨Properties) to resize the ball so that it is 50 pixels wide and 50 pixels high.

5. The ball needs to be centered on the movie clip registration point. With the ball still selected, set the x position and the y position to each be –25 pixels.

6. Select the selection arrow from the top left of the Tools palette. Select a narrow vertical slice of the center of the ball to be the stripe. You can perform the selection by clicking outside the ball and dragging across to the outside of the ball on the opposite side.

7. Select the Paint Bucket tool from the Tools palette, choose a different color from the fill color well on the Tools palette, and click within the selected area to give it a different color.

8. Click the Scene 1 button above the timeline to return to the main timeline.

9. Drag the `circleClip` library symbol to the stage. Use the Properties palette to place the symbol at an x position of 5 pixels and a y position of 15 pixels.

10. Select the Rectangle tool from the Tools palette. Choose any color for line and fill that you want, or keep the colors the same. Create a long thin rectangle just below the ball on the stage.

11. Select the Selection tool from the top left of the Tools palette. Double-click in the middle of the new rectangle to select both the fill and the outline. From the Properties panel, give it a width of 200 pixels, and place it at an x position of 20 and a y position of 100.

12. Open the Transform palette (Window⇨Transform), enter 20 into the rotate box, and press return.

13. Open the Actions panel and type the following ActionScript code:

```
#include "tryItOut_tweenPlaybackLib.as"
#include "tryItOut_tweenPlayback.as"
```

14. Select File⇨Save As, name the file `tryItOut_tweenPlayback.fla`, choose an appropriate directory, and save it.

15. Create a new script file by selecting File⇨New and choosing ActionScript File from the New Document panel.

16. Save it as `tryItOut_tweenPlayback.as` in the directory containing the Flash project file.

17. Enter the following code into the new ActionScript file:

```
addTween(0, new Tween(ballClip, "_x", Regular.easeIn,
    ballClip._x, ballClip._x + 190, 2, true));
addTween(0, new Tween(ballClip, "_y", Regular.easeIn,
    ballClip._y, ballClip._y + 69, 2, true));
addTween(0, new Tween(ballClip, "_rotation", Regular.easeIn,
    0, 360, 2, true));

addTween(1, new Tween(ballClip, "_x", Regular.easeOut,
    ballClip._x + 196, ballClip._x + 450, 3, true));
addTween(1, new Tween(ballClip, "_y", Bounce.easeOut,
    ballClip._y + 73, 375, 2, true));
addTween(1, new Tween(ballClip, "_rotation", Regular.easeOut,
    0, 360, 3, true));

addTween(2, new Tween(ballClip, "_width", Regular.easeOut, 50, 0, 0.5, true));
addTween(2, new Tween(ballClip, "_height", Regular.easeOut,
    50, 0, 0.5, true));
addTween(2, new Tween(ballClip, "_alpha", Regular.easeOut,
    100, 0, 0.5, true));

startTweenSequence();
```

18. Save the file and create a new script file.

19. Save the new file as `tryItOut_tweenPlaybackLib.as` in the directory containing the Flash project file.

20. Enter the following code into the new ActionScript file:

```
import mx.transitions.Tween;
import mx.transitions.easing.*;

var tweenSequence:Array = new Array();
var currentTween:Number = 0;
var numCompletedTweens:Number = 0;

function addTween(stepNum:Number, tweenHandle:Tween):Void
{
    tweenHandle.stop();
    tweenHandle.onMotionFinished = callNextTween;
    if (tweenSequence[stepNum] == undefined)
    {
        tweenSequence[stepNum] = new Array();
    }
    tweenSequence[stepNum].push(tweenHandle);
}

function startTweenSequence():Void
{
    playTweenSequence(0);
}

function playTweenSequence(sequenceNum:Number):Void
{
    for (var i:Number=0; i < tweenSequence[sequenceNum].length; i++)
    {
        tweenSequence[sequenceNum][i].start();
    }
}

function stopTweenSequence():Void
{
    for (var i:Number=0; i < tweenSequence[currentTween].length; i++)
    {
        tweenSequence[currentTween][i].stop();
    }
}

function resumeTweenSequence():Void
{
    for (var i:Number=0; i < tweenSequence[currentTween].length; i++)
    {
        tweenSequence[currentTween][i].resume();
    }
}

function callNextTween():Void
{
    numCompletedTweens += 1;
    if (currentTween < tweenSequence.length - 1 && ⤸
        numCompletedTweens == tweenSequence[currentTween].length)
```

```
        {
            currentTween += 1
            numCompletedTweens = 0;
            playTweenSequence(currentTween);
        }
    }
```

21. Save the file, return to the Flash document, and select Control⇨Test Movie. You should get an animation of a ball rolling down the incline, bouncing onto the floor, rolling to a stop, and then disappearing from the stage.

How It Works

The first part of this exercise involves setting up the symbols needed for the animation. The stripe on the ball is used so that the effect of the ball rotation can be easily seen. First, take a look at the file that declares the tween setup, `tryItOut_tweenPlayback.as`. This file uses the tween library functions created in `tryItOut_tweenPlaybackLib.as`.

First, three tweens are created to run in parallel. The first causes movement along the x-axis, the second causes movement along the y-axis, and the third creates the rotation of the ball. All tweens use Regular.easeIn for the easing function, which starts the ball from rest and accelerates the motion:

```
addTween(0, new Tween(ballClip, "_x", Regular.easeIn, ↩
    ballClip._x, ballClip._x + 190, 2, true));
addTween(0, new Tween(ballClip, "_y", Regular.easeIn, ↩
    ballClip._y, ballClip._y + 69, 2, true));
addTween(0, new Tween(ballClip, "_rotation", Regular.easeIn, ↩
    0, 360, 2, true));
```

Three more tweens are set up to run in parallel after the previous three have finished. The first causes the decelerating movement along the x-axis, the second causes the bouncing motion along the y-axis, and the third continues the rotation:

```
addTween(1, new Tween(ballClip, "_x", Regular.easeOut, ↩
    ballClip._x + 196, ballClip._x + 450, 3, true));
addTween(1, new Tween(ballClip, "_y", Bounce.easeOut, ↩
    ballClip._y + 73, 375, 2, true));
addTween(1, new Tween(ballClip, "_rotation", Regular.easeOut, ↩
    0, 360, 3, true));
```

The three final tweens run after the ball comes to a stop. They cause the ball to shrink and fade out:

```
addTween(2, new Tween(ballClip, "_width", Regular.easeOut, 50, 0, 0.5, true));
addTween(2, new Tween(ballClip, "_height", Regular.easeOut, ↩
    50, 0, 0.5, true));
addTween(2, new Tween(ballClip, "_alpha", Regular.easeOut, ↩
    100, 0, 0.5, true));
```

Now that the sequence has been declared, it can be started up:

```
startTweenSequence();
```

Next is a library file that sets up a number of functions to help simplify the process of creating sequences of tweens. The addTween() function from the other file is not a Flash function, it is a helper function created in this library. The library works by allowing each tween to be associated with a number indicating the order of call. Tweens with an order number of zero are called first, then when done, tweens with an order number of one are called, and so on. This allows for tweens to be called in sequence. Tweens with the same order number are all started at the same time, allowing for tweens to be called in parallel. If a number of tweens with the same order number exist, they must all finish before the next group of tweens is called.

First, the usual import statements:

```
import mx.transitions.Tween;
import mx.transitions.easing.*;
```

A few variables are kept for tracking the tweens. The array stores each tween as it is assigned. Each index in this array represents one step in the sequence of tweens to call. For each step, the array points to another array that stores all the tweens to be called in parallel for this step. The currentTween variable keeps track of which step is currently being played, and the numCompletedTweens variable keeps track of how many tweens playing in parallel in this step have completed. This allows the player to know when to go to the next step of tweens:

```
var tweenSequence:Array = new Array();
var currentTween:Number = 0;
var numCompletedTweens:Number = 0;
```

The addTween() function is used to assign a tween to the sequence. A step number is passed in along with a handle to a Tween instance. The tweenSequence array is an array of arrays. The first-level array corresponds to each playback step, and each element in that array points to a second array that stores the actual tweens to be played for each step. The onMotionFinished event is captured for each tween and directed to a function that keeps track of which tweens have played and which should be called next:

```
function addTween(stepNum:Number, tweenHandle:Tween):Void
{
    tweenHandle.stop();
    tweenHandle.onMotionFinished = callNextTween;
    if (tweenSequence[stepNum] == undefined)
    {
        tweenSequence[stepNum] = new Array();
    }
    tweenSequence[stepNum].push(tweenHandle);
}
```

The startTweenSequence() function starts playback of the first set of tweens:

```
function startTweenSequence():Void
{
    playTweenSequence(0);
}
```

The playTweenSequence() function starts playback of all tweens meant to play in parallel for the given step:

```
function playTweenSequence(sequenceNum:Number):Void
{
    for (var i:Number=0; i < tweenSequence[sequenceNum].length; i++)
    {
        tweenSequence[sequenceNum][i].start();
    }
}
```

The `stopTweenSequence()` function pauses playback of all tweens currently playing. It is not used in this exercise, but is a useful function for other potential applications of this library:

```
function stopTweenSequence():Void
{
    for (var i:Number=0; i < tweenSequence[currentTween].length; i++)
    {
        tweenSequence[currentTween][i].stop();
    }
}
```

The `resumeTweenSequence()` function resumes playback of all tweens previously paused with the `stopTweenSequence()` function. It is not used in this exercise, but is a useful function for other potential applications of this library:

```
function resumeTweenSequence():Void
{
    for (var i:Number=0; i < tweenSequence[currentTween].length; i++)
    {
        tweenSequence[currentTween][i].resume();
    }
}
```

The `callNextTween()` function is called by every tween when playback of the tween ends, and is not intended to be called outside of the library. It determines whether all the tweens playing in parallel for this step have completed. If they have, and there is at least one step remaining, it starts the tweens from the next step:

```
function callNextTween():Void
{
    numCompletedTweens += 1;
    if (currentTween < tweenSequence.length - 1 && ↩
        numCompletedTweens == tweenSequence[currentTween].length)
    {
        currentTween += 1
        numCompletedTweens = 0;
        playTweenSequence(currentTween);
    }
}
```

Animating with the Drawing API

So far you have been creating animations basically by moving, resizing, and rotating movie clips. There is certainly a huge amount that can be done with this, however there is even more fun to be had when you can draw your own content. In Chapter 13 you saw how the drawing API can be used to draw out your own content programmatically. When you extend that ability to work with animations, many possibilities for digital artwork or for unique effects emerge.

Earlier in the chapter you saw how the Tween class could drive animation, and the drawing API was used to draw out the animated box. You are not going to dive into much detail of the drawing API itself; Chapter 13 performed that role. Instead, take a look at the drawing API with a bit of a twist this time.

When you work with animating content, you animate it by changing the x and y coordinates of the movie clip relative to the top left of the screen. There is another way of working with coordinate systems that animates points using properties of a circle instead. Those properties are referred to as *polar coordinates*. Consider Figure 17-3, where two values represent the position of any point relative to the middle of the screen, namely the number of degrees from the top half of the y-axis, and the number of pixels from the middle.

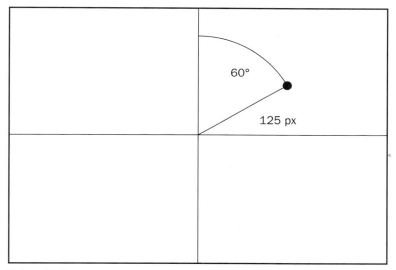

Figure 17-3

With this change in coordinate system, it is much easier to move a point around the screen in a circular fashion. A point can be rotated in an arc simply by changing the degree value, and can be moved toward and away from the middle with a simple change of the distance value. By working in this way, almost all the math is eliminated. The only math that is needed is a relatively simple conversion when those coordinates need to be mapped to actual x and y values for the Flash player to use. Without this change in thinking, some complex trigonometry would be needed just to figure out where to move the point to its next position along an arc.

This coordinate system works from the middle of the screen, whereas the normal Flash x/y coordinate system works from the top left. You cannot change the Flash coordinate system, but you can create your own movie clip and move it so that its top-left corner aligns with the middle of the stage. This makes working with polar coordinates significantly easier.

For a final hurrah in this chapter, take a bit more of an advanced look into how polar coordinates can be applied to animation.

Try It Out   **Creating a Screen Saver Animation**

This exercise shows how to create an animated screen saver using the `lineTo()` method from the drawing API. Do not worry if you do not understand every detail of this exercise. The purpose is to get you thinking in different ways when it comes to animation. First, it will get you thinking in something other than normal *x* and *y* coordinates, which will open up additional possibilities. Second, it will show you how Flash animation can be used in a purely artistic form. Third, it will give you some strategies for working with animation using the drawing API.

1.   Create a new Macromedia Flash document.

2.   Click the first frame in the timeline, open the Actions panel (Window⇨Development Panels⇨ Actions), and type the following ActionScript code:

```
#include "tryItOut_screenSaver.as"
```

3.   Select File⇨Save As, name the file `tryItOut_screenSaver.fla`, choose an appropriate directory, and save it.

4.   Create a new script file by selecting File⇨New and choosing ActionScript File from the New Document panel.

5.   Select File⇨Save As and ensure it is showing the same directory containing the Flash project file. Give the file the name `tryItOut_screenSaver.as` and save it.

6.   Enter the following code into the new ActionScript file:

```
var pMaxSize:Number = 150;
var pCenterX:Number = 275;
var pCenterY:Number = 200;
var pNumTraces:Number = 20;
var pNumLayers:Number = 30;
var pCurrentLayer:Number = 0;
var pLineColour:Number;

var pPointDegree:Array = new Array();
var pPointDegreeChange:Array = new Array();
var pPointScale:Array = new Array();
var pPointScaleChange:Array = new Array();
var pPointX:Array = new Array();
var pPointY:Array = new Array();

var pBaseTimeline:MovieClip;
var pIntervalId:Number;

function init(baseTimeline:MovieClip):Void
```

```
{
    pBaseTimeline = baseTimeline;
    pBaseTimeline.createEmptyMovieClip("holder", 0);

    for (var j:Number = 0; j < pNumLayers; j++)
    {
        pBaseTimeline.createEmptyMovieClip("layer" + j, j+1);
        pBaseTimeline["layer" + j]._x = pCenterX;
        pBaseTimeline["layer" + j]._y = pCenterY;
    }

    initTraces();

    pBaseTimeline.holder.onEnterFrame = function()
    {
        moveSpheres();
    }

    pIntervalId = setInterval(this, "updateSeeds", 2000);

}

function initTraces()
{
    // Initialize each of the plotter points
    for (var i:Number = 0; i < pNumTraces; i++)
    {
        pPointX[i] = 0;
        pPointY[i] = 0;
        pPointDegree[i] = (6.28318530718/pNumTraces) * i;
        pPointScale[i] = 50;
    }

    // Update the random values governing the next set of movements
    updateSeeds();

    // Draw the line segment for the next movement for each trace
    for (i = 0; i < pNumTraces; i++)
    {
        plotLine(i);
    }
}

// Update the x/y coordinates for each dot
function moveSpheres()
{
    for (var i:Number = 0; i < pNumTraces; i++)
    {
        // Increment the number of degrees around the center point
        pPointDegree[i] += pPointDegreeChange[i];
        // Increment the scaling (distance from center point);
        pPointScale[i] += pPointScaleChange[i];
        plotLine(i, true);
    }

    // Perform fading of the trail. Current layer is at 100% alpha,
```

```
        // each layer behind gets progressively faded
        pBaseTimeline["layer" + pCurrentLayer]._alpha = 100;
        pCurrentLayer = (pCurrentLayer + 1) % pNumLayers;
        for (var j:Number = 0; j < pNumLayers; j++)
        {
            pBaseTimeline["layer" + ((pCurrentLayer + j)%pNumLayers)]._alpha ⏎
            = (j/pNumLayers)*100;
        }
        // Clear out the last layer, at 0% alpha
        pBaseTimeline["layer" + pCurrentLayer].clear();
}

// Update the position of the drawing clip, and trace the line behind it.
function plotLine(i:Number, drawLine:Boolean)
{
    pBaseTimeline["layer" + pCurrentLayer].lineStyle(1, pLineColour, 100);
    pBaseTimeline["layer" + pCurrentLayer].moveTo(pPointX[i], pPointY[i]);
    // x/y coordinates are calculated based on rotation and scale of each dot
    pPointX[i] = (Math.cos(pPointDegree[i]) * pPointScale[i]);
    pPointY[i] = (Math.sin(pPointDegree[i]) * pPointScale[i]);
    if (drawLine == true)
    {
        pBaseTimeline["layer" + pCurrentLayer].lineTo(pPointX[i], pPointY[i]);
    }
}

// Update random values
function updateSeeds()
{
    var deg:Number;
    var scale:Number;

    // Set degree values uniformly across all points
    deg = randomRange(-100, 100) / 2000;

    // Set scaling values uniformly across all points
    if (pPointScale[0] > pMaxSize)
    {
        scale = randomRange(-10, 0) / 2;
    }
    else if (pPointScale[0] < -pMaxSize)
    {
        scale = randomRange(0, 10) / 2;
    }
    else
    {
        scale = randomRange(-10, 10) / 2;
    }

    // Assign degree and scale values to each point
    for (var i:Number = 0; i < pNumTraces; i++)
    {
        pPointDegreeChange[i] = deg;
        pPointScaleChange[i] = scale;
    }
    pLineColour = randomRange(0, 0xFFFFFF);
```

```
    }

// Calculate a random integer between two numbers;
function randomRange(min:Number, max:Number):Number
{
    var randomNum:Number = Math.round(Math.random()*(max-min))+min;
    return randomNum;
}

init(this);
```

7. Select Control⇨Test Movie to try it out.

How It Works

This screen saver works by storing the degree and the distance values for each point, then animating those values. By adding 10 degrees to the rotation value for each point, they all move together in unison around the center by 10 degrees. By adding 10 pixels to the scale value for each point, they all move away from the center in unison by 10 pixels. By then randomizing how many pixels to add and remove, and how many degrees to rotate the animation by, you get random patterns being generated by the lines that are produced. The traces are created and faded by drawing each new line segment into its own layer, then adjusting the alpha of all the previous layers until the last one is blank and can be reused for the next segment.

First, some data needs to be saved. The maximum reach of the lines, the coordinates for the middle of the screen, the number of lines to animate, and the number of line segments that make up each trace are stored. Also, the current top layer and the color of the line to draw in the layer are saved:

```
var pMaxSize:Number = 150;
var pCenterX:Number = 275;
var pCenterY:Number = 200;
var pNumTraces:Number = 20;
var pNumLayers:Number = 30;
var pCurrentLayer:Number = 0;
var pLineColour:Number;
```

Arrays are used to store the degree, scale (distance from middle), and x/y coordinates for each point. The pPointDegree and pPointScale arrays store the degree and scale values for each point. The pPointDegreeChange and pPointScaleChange arrays store the values indicating how much the degree and scale values are going to change for the next animation update. When these values do not change, each point maintains the same rotation and the same rate of approaching or leaving the center point. By randomly changing these values, you cause all the points to shift their rotation and approach, giving the zigzag effect that you see:

```
var pPointDegree:Array = new Array();
var pPointDegreeChange:Array = new Array();
var pPointScale:Array = new Array();
var pPointScaleChange:Array = new Array();
var pPointX:Array = new Array();
var pPointY:Array = new Array();
```

A couple of variables store a handle to the main timeline and the ID for the interval used to periodically update the pPointDegreeChange and pPointScaleChange values:

```
var pBaseTimeline:MovieClip;
var pIntervalId:Number;
```

Within the `init()` function, a movie clip is created to hold the animation. Within that movie clip, more movie clips are created and moved so that the x=0, y=0 point is at the middle of the screen. This helps avoid a bit more math, because it is easier to work the math around 0,0 than around 275,200. Each of these movie clips are layers used to hold one part of each line segment, and as the alpha values of the layers are faded, so are the line segments that they hold:

```
pBaseTimeline = baseTimeline;
pBaseTimeline.createEmptyMovieClip("holder", 0);

for (var j:Number = 0; j < pNumLayers; j++)
{
    pBaseTimeline.createEmptyMovieClip("layer" + j, j+1);
    pBaseTimeline["layer" + j]._x = pCenterX;
    pBaseTimeline["layer" + j]._y = pCenterY;
}
```

Start positions are set for each trace:

```
initTraces();
```

The animation is started up, with the `moveSpheres()` function being called every frame, and the `updateSeeds()` function being called every 2 seconds to change the direction of the traces:

```
pBaseTimeline.holder.onEnterFrame = function()
{
    moveSpheres();
}
pIntervalId = setInterval(this, "updateSeeds", 2000);
```

The `initTraces()` function sets starting values for each trace. It spreads the points evenly around the circle. Unfortunately, one complication is that the units used are actually radians, because the standard trigonometric functions do not use degrees. The conversion between the units is 360 degrees = 2 * π = 2 * 3.1416 = 6.2832 radians:

```
for (var i:Number = 0; i < pNumTraces; i++)
{
    pPointX[i] = 0;
    pPointY[i] = 0;
    pPointDegree[i] = (6.28318530718/pNumTraces) * i;
    pPointScale[i] = 50;
}
```

The change arrays are updated with new random values:

```
updateSeeds();

for (i = 0; i < pNumTraces; i++)
{
    plotLine(i);
}
```

The `moveSpheres()` function adjusts the degree and scale values for each point based on the degree change and the scale change values:

```
for (var i:Number = 0; i < pNumTraces; i++)
{
    pPointDegree[i] += pPointDegreeChange[i];
    pPointScale[i] += pPointScaleChange[i];
    plotLine(i, true);
}
```

The code goes through each layer starting from `pCurrentLayer`, fading it a bit more until it gets to the last one. The `%` (modulo, aka remainder) operator makes sure that when the loop passes the number of available layers, it loops back to zero and starts again:

```
pBaseTimeline["layer" + pCurrentLayer]._alpha = 100;
pCurrentLayer = (pCurrentLayer + 1) % pNumLayers;
for (var j:Number = 0; j < pNumLayers; j++)
{
    pBaseTimeline["layer" + ((pCurrentLayer + j)%pNumLayers)]._alpha ⤶
    = (j/pNumLayers)*100;
}
// Clear out the last layer, at 0% alpha
pBaseTimeline["layer" + pCurrentLayer].clear();
```

The `plotLine()` function does the actual drawing of each line segment, converting the degree and scale combination to x and y coordinates:

```
pBaseTimeline["layer" + pCurrentLayer].lineStyle(1, pLineColour, 100);
pBaseTimeline["layer" + pCurrentLayer].moveTo(pPointX[i], pPointY[i]);
// x/y coordinates are calculated based on rotation and scale of each dot
pPointX[i] = (Math.cos(pPointDegree[i]) * pPointScale[i]);
pPointY[i] = (Math.sin(pPointDegree[i]) * pPointScale[i]);
if (drawLine == true)
{
    pBaseTimeline["layer" + pCurrentLayer].lineTo(pPointX[i], pPointY[i]);
}
```

The `updateSeeds()` function chooses new values for the degree change and the scale change values as well as a new color for the lines. It makes sure that when the distance from the middle becomes too great, it forces a negative value for the scale values. You may note that the degree change and the scale change values are the same for each point, making the use of an array to store them a waste. While that is true, they do not have to be the same for each point. You could modify this function to choose different values for each trace, either randomly or using a pattern to animate, for example, an ellipse instead of a circle:

```
var deg:Number;
var scale:Number;

// Set degree values uniformly across all points
deg = randomRange(-100, 100) / 2000;

// Set scaling values uniformly across all points
if (pPointScale[0] > pMaxSize)
{
    scale = randomRange(-10, 0) / 2;
```

```
}
else if (pPointScale[0] < -pMaxSize)
{
    scale = randomRange(0, 10) / 2;
}
else
{
    scale = randomRange(-10, 10) / 2;
}

// Assign degree and scale values to each point
for (var i:Number = 0; i < pNumTraces; i++)
{
    pPointDegreeChange[i] = deg;
    pPointScaleChange[i] = scale;
}
pLineColour = randomRange(0, 0xFFFFFF);
```

The code ends with the `randomRange()` function, the same utility function described earlier to help with picking random values.

Summary

This chapter covered many different aspects of ActionScript-based animation. Some of the things that you learned include the following:

❑   How to use the Tween class to take control of the actual animating.

❑   The easing classes allow you to specify how the tween accelerates and decelerates through the course of the transition.

❑   Tweens can be run in parallel by simply instantiating multiple tweens. They can also be chained together in a sequence by making use of the `onMotionFinished` Tween event.

❑   The drawing API makes for a great source of creative animation possibilities. Using polar coordinates allows you to get out of a linear way of thinking.

Exercises

1.   Starting from the Try It Out exercise called "Multiple Tweens on an Elasticized Box," add another tween to manipulate the transparency of the box. Pass in a fixed color and the tweened value for the alpha value to use for the drawing, and modify the `drawBox()` function so that it draws a fill with the color and alpha values passed to the function.

2.   Modify exercise 1 so that it no longer yoyos. Place a button on the screen that when pressed, toggles the direction of the animation, but only when the previous animation has completed.

Handling Text

The TextField is the class used to display text in Flash. Text fields can be drawn onto the stage with the Tools panel's Text tool. Text fields can be created with ActionScript using a robust property and method set at runtime. Each version of Flash makes improvements over the last and text fields always get some type of enhancement. Flash is continually being adopted for rich network applications, where different kinds of data need to be displayed in different ways with different text formatting.

Text, of course, is a complex subject, with terms like ASCII, ANSI, Unicode, escape characters, HTML code, kerning, smoothing, leading, style, and more. This chapter covers the basics of working with text.

Thankfully, Flash 8 clears up many issues and bugs associated with text in Flash. The capability to cache text as bitmaps allows a new level of text animation and integration within your user interface.

The most notable addition to the Flash 8 text features is FlashType, known to most by its preview name: Saffron. FlashType is a text-rendering engine that produces extremely smooth, clear, and readable text. New features in Flash 8 allow precise control over how and when text attributes are modified.

Three types of text fields exist: static, dynamic, and input. The input text field can also be used as a password input text field, which displays only asterisks as the user types. For each type, you have the choice of using default system fonts that exist on each of the end users' computers or of using fonts that you embed within the Flash movie.

In this chapter, you learn how to create text fields on-the-fly and how to manipulate text attributes such as font, size, color, word-wrapping, and font embedding. You learn about how to apply rich text formatting, to include HTML in a text field, and to extend the capability to apply text formatting through the use of style sheets. Finally, you explore different techniques for creating scrollable regions of text.

Creating Text Fields with ActionScript

Creating text fields with ActionScript is straightforward. You use the `createTextField()` method to place text on any timeline.

Field Instance Names Versus Field Variable Names

When creating text fields with ActionScript, it is usually best to use the `text` property of the TextField class. There is also the `variable` property, which allows the text field to show the current state of any variable without explicitly assigning text to the text field. This is especially helpful in chat applications built using the XML socket.

In the following example, the text field `usernameField` would reveal the current state of the variable `username`:

```
var username:String = "jberg";
usernameField.variable = "username";
```

System Fonts and Embedded Fonts

When you embed a font within your application, a duplicate of the font is created and placed in the final SWF file. By embedding fonts, you ensure that the application looks how you intended because the user does not need to have the specified font on his system. This can be particularly useful when developing multilingual applications, where the target system is not required to have the specific font for the language installed.

When a font is not embedded, the end user's system provides the closest match to the font requested by Flash. This is similar to HTML where you can specify sans, serif, or a group of fonts to search through, looking for the first font that exists on the user's system. For example, you may specify a serif font, and the end user system will provide the main serif font specified on the system. If you specify Georgia, Times, Courier as a group of desired fonts, it will try each until it can display one of them, or it will find the closest match on the system. It is generally safe to rely on default lists, as you would with HTML. You can generally predict that most users will have Times, and most will have some Arial variant. Otherwise, if this lack of control over type disturbs your design, or the motion graphics in your application require a specific font to fit and function properly, you'll want to use the embed option.

Creating a Text Field On-the-Fly

The first thing that you need to know how to do is to create a text field. A method of the MovieClip class, called `createTextField()`, enables you to create a text field using the chosen movie clip as a holder. The basic form of this method looks like this:

```
MovieClip.createTextField(instanceName:String, depth:Number, x:Number, y:Number, ⤶
    width:Number, height:Number);
```

The following snippet shows `createTextField()` in use, placing a 100x30-pixel text field at position 10, 10 on the main timeline, and giving it the value `"jberg"`:

```
this.createTextField("username", this.getNextHighestDepth(), 10, 10, 100, 30);
username.text = "jberg";
```

Try It Out   Creating Dynamic and Input Text Fields On-the-Fly

Ready to create some text fields? Just follow these steps:

1. Open a new FLA file. Save the file as `textTest.fla` in your workspace.

2. Add the following code to frame 1:

```
var titleField:TextField = createTextField ("field1", this.getNextHighestDepth(),
    20, 20, 200, 20);
titleField.text = "Login!";

var nameField:TextField = createTextField ("field2", this.getNextHighestDepth(),
    20, 50, 200, 20);
nameField.border = true;
nameField.type = "input";
nameField.text = "Name";
nameField.onSetFocus = function ()
{
    this.text = "";
};
nameField.onKillFocus = function ()
{
    if (this.text == "")
    {
        this.text = "Name";
    }
};

var passwordField:TextField = createTextField ("field3",
    this.getNextHighestDepth(), 20, 80, 200, 20);
passwordField.text = "Password";
passwordField.border = true;
passwordField.type = "input";
passwordField.onSetFocus = function ()
{
    this.text = "";
    this.password = true;
};
passwordField.onKillFocus = function ()
{
    if (this.text == "")
    {
        this.password = false;
        this.text = "Password";
    }
};
```

3. Test the movie by selecting Control➪Test Movie. Click the various text fields to see how they behave.

How It Works

By using the `createTextField()` method and applying different properties to each type of text field, you were able to quickly create a very simple input interface.

The title field allowed the text field to default on all attributes except text. The `text` attribute was used to place the word `"Login!"` within the text field. You could also declare `titleField.selectable = false` to disallow the user from being to select it.

The `nameField` instance was given a border. The border of a text field can be manipulated and customized. Because you want users to input their name here, the `type` property was specified as input. The text field was then given a default value that describes the information being requested.

Finally, the code is taking advantage of the `onSetFocus` and `onKillFocus` events to keep the user interface consistent. Once the behavior of the application is finalized, the focus events can be used to verify the validity of the inputs.

Working with Text Display Properties

Many properties are available to modify the look and behavior of the text field. They allow rudimentary style changes to the text but are geared toward the default behavior of the field itself rather than to any rich text formatting. You can view the full list of properties by opening up the Flash Help panel and browsing to ActionScript 2.0 Language Reference⇨ActionScript Classes⇨TextField. The properties that you can use to modify the look of a text field include `border`, `background`, `backgroundColor`, and `textColor`. The primary means to manipulate the look of a text field is not through the properties at all, but through either the TextFormat class or the StyleSheet class. You see these both in action a little later in this chapter.

The TextField class has so many properties that it'd take many pages to define them all here. Flash 8 includes many new properties, most of which relate to clarity and granularity of control over previous versions of Flash. You explore a few of them here, but you can use the ActionScript panel's code hinting to reveal the others, and then try them out to see what each does. Most are capable of setting and getting the value, but some are merely getters, such as the `textHeight` and `textWidth` properties that do not permit you to change the value.

antiAliasType

`antiAliasType` is an important new property because it facilitates many of the other new properties available. Setting it to `advanced` applies the new rendering method upon the text for ultra-clear text presentation. The property defaults to `normal`. Normal rendering uses the text display engine from Flash 7 and earlier, and it lacks the clarity of the text display engine added to Flash 8.

> You can override all `antiAliasType` calls by declaring the property directly onto the class package, using the code `flash.text.TextRenderer.antiAliasType = "on";`. This enables you to easily make the property change in all fields, rather than specifying the property in each field. Once you set this value, you cannot override it by setting the property on an individual text field.

To take advantage of the advanced rendering of text you must embed the font. The font must be embedded via the library with an export linkage specified. The `embedFonts` property must be set to `true`, and the font linkage name specified as a string in a TextFormat object. This sounds like a lot of dependencies, but in fact using these properties even without advanced text rendering is common practice. After you see the difference in quality, you'll agree that the extra work is worth the effort.

When you apply properties to a text field that affect the look of the text, such as `antiAliasType`, `sharpness`, *and* `thickness`, *all text in the text field is affected. You cannot selectively apply these properties to just a segment of the text displayed within a particular text field.*

sharpness

The `sharpness` property is used in conjunction with advanced anti-aliasing. It expects a value from -400 to 400. The property specifies the smoothness of the transition between the edges of the text characters and the background they reside on. Changing this setting can affect the performance of animations as well as the speed of filters applied to the text field. Use a sharpness setting that makes sense for the activity of the text field.

A low sharpness setting causes your font to appear bloomed, or a slight hollow effect will appear. A high number produces very clear text at small sizes, but can cause jagged curves and sharpness artifacts. Use high values for sharpness only when you specify very small sizes with a TextFormat object. Changing the default sharpness at very large sizes is probably not necessary.

thickness

The `thickness` property determines the width of the transition area between the edges of the text characters and the background. Changing this property can make your text appear to bloom, or bold. The property can be used in conjunction with the `sharpness` property to fine-tune the text-aliasing behavior of the text field.

The best way to understand the effects of these properties is to try them out.

Try It Out   Precise Control over Text Display

In this example you see the clarity of text when using advanced anti-aliasing. A TextFormat object is created because it is required when embedding fonts in dynamic text fields. The TextFormat class is explained more fully later in this chapter.

1. Open a new FLA. Save it as `antiAliasTest.fla` in your workspace folder.
2. Open the Library panel. At the top right is an icon that looks like a bulleted list with a small arrow pointing down. Click it to open the Options menu.
3. Select the New Font option. A pop-up window appears.
4. Give the font a logical name and choose the font you'd like to use in your text field as advanced rendered font. Click OK.
5. The font appears in the library. Click the font symbol in the library so that it is highlighted. Open the library's Options menu again and select the Linkage option. A pop-up window with options opens.

6. Select the Export for ActionScript option. The input fields above become enabled.

7. Give the font an identifying name. This value defaults to the symbol name. Change it to `myFont` and click OK. The font will now be added to the SWF file when it is published.

8. Select the first frame in the timeline.

9. Open the Actions panel and add the following code to frame 1:

```
var my_format:TextFormat = new TextFormat();
my_format.font = "myFont";
my_format.size = 12;

var id:Number = this.getNextHighestDepth();
var field1:TextField = this.createTextField ("field" + id, id, 10, 10, 300, 100);
field1.wordWrap = true;
field1.multiline = true;
field1.text = 'antiAliasType = "normal"';
field1.embedFonts = true;
field1.setTextFormat(my_format);
```

10. Test the code by selecting Control⇨Test Movie. The text appears. Notice that the text is jagged and difficult to read.

11. Close the SWF and return to the code in the Actions panel. Enter the following code below the code you added in step 9:

```
id = this.getNextHighestDepth();
var field2:TextField = this.createTextField("field" + id, id, 10, 40, 300, 10);
field2.antiAliasType = "advanced";
field2.wordWrap = true;
field2.multiline = true;
field2.text = 'antiAliasType = "advanced"';
field2.embedFonts = true;
field2.setTextFormat(my_format);
```

12. Test the code by selecting Control⇨Test Movie. The text appears. Notice the difference in legibility between the two text fields.

How It Works

In this example, a simple change to the `antiAliasType` property changed the way Flash rendered the font. The `advanced` `antiAliasType` value requires that the font used reside in the library and be accessible via the TextFormat class.

Try a few different fonts. Try changing the pixel size specified in the TextFormat class.

In the next Try It Out, you see the effect of applying the `sharpness` and `thickness` properties to control the appearance of text fields when the `antiAliasType` property is set to `advanced`.

Try It Out   **Using Anti-Aliasing to Improve Text Readability**

This exercise uses the FLA file created in the preceding Try It Out. If you have not completed that project, you should do so now.

1. Open `antiAliasTest.fla` in your workspace folder.

2. Open the Actions panel. Enter the following code below the code added in step 11 in the preceding Try It Out:

```
field1.sharpness = 400;
field1.thickness = 200;
```

3. Test the code by selecting Control⇨Test Movie. Notice the text with the `antiAliasType` property set to `advanced` now looks overly filtered. Artifacts of the process exist that cause the font to look raw and jagged. The values, `400` and `200`, are the maximum values allowed.

4. Reduce the values in the two properties you added in step 2. You can go as low as `-400` and `-200`, respectively. Try the following values:

```
field1.sharpness = 0;
field1.thickness = 150;
```

5. Test the code by selecting Control⇨Test Movie. Notice how the text appears stronger than the settings specified in step 2, but with the sharpness at zero, it is now smoother.

6. Try different values and view the results. Choose values to suit.

How It Works

In this example, you saw how the two properties `sharpness` and `thickness` can be used to manipulate the way in which the text is aliased.

Because aliasing this way makes greater use of your computer's CPU, you should consider what you will be using the text for. If the text is used for animation, you probably want to avoid high-quality sharpness and thickness values.

The aliasing really works only on fonts sized between 6 and 20 and is best applied to fonts sized 8 to 12. You can try other sizes, but you probably won't see much change. Advanced aliasing probably isn't the best idea when tweening text because it does add to the process load.

Rich Text Formatting Options

Most developers are familiar with rich text formatting in relation to HTML. Flash presents several methods for displaying rich text. Each option has limitations and advantages. Generally, the content you expect will drive the decision for which method to use within your application. For example TextFormat is fast and simple, whereas HTML allows for the embedding of images and Flash content within the text field.

Using TextFormat

TextFormat is a class that holds a list of properties capable of defining the look of text within a text field. You can use it to set such things as bold, italics, font, size, and more. You can define these properties in an external file or within the code. One advantage of using TextFormat rather than text properties defined using the Text tool in the Tools panel is that the format is centralized, meaning that if a change in font or size is required application wide, you can change one object and have the changes propagate through your application.

A TextFormat object is very simple to create, requiring only a minimal constructor:

```
var titleFormat:TextFormat = new TextFormat();
```

Properties to define within the object are simply a set of setters. For example, this sets the font to Arial:

```
titleFormat.font = "Arial";
```

The TextField class owns a method named setTextFormat(). The format can be assigned to a specific substring as follows:

```
titleField.setTextFormat(firstIndex, secondIndex, titleFormat);
```

If you want to set the format to the entire field, use only one parameter:

```
titleField.setTextFormat(titleFormat);
```

You can also copy the format of an existing text field directly onto another by using the getTextFormat() method as follows:

```
titleField.setTextFormat(appTitleField.getTextFormat());
```

This enables you to easily propagate a format that is changed dynamically as the application runs.

TextFormat properties can be set and changed anytime, but replacing the contents of the text within the field can cause the field to lose all the properties set using the TextFormat class. In that case, reapply the properties after changing the text field contents by calling setTextFormat() *again, referring to the same TextFormat instance as was initially applied to that text field.*

Using the code hints within the Actions panel, you can view the full set of properties available.

New Text Format Options for Flash 8

Flash 8 has several new format options, namely justification, letter spacing, and kerning. These new properties affect the spacing and layout of the text within the text field.

Justification

The TextFormat class contains a property called align that determines how the text is placed within the text field. The available values are left, center, right, and justify. While the first three values have been around for a while, the justify option is new to Flash 8. Justified text means that lines that do not reach all the way across the text field are stretched so that all the lines form a clean right margin.

The align property can be applied to fields that use device or embedded fonts.

letterSpacing

The letterSpacing property defines the space that follows a letter. The value is in pixels and can range from -60 to 60. A negative value can result in the letters overlapping, depending upon the font. This property can help the readability of some fonts and can repair the letter spacing on embedded fonts such as English or Cursive that must have no spacing to connect letters properly.

`letterSpacing` can be used with device or embedded fonts. When using device fonts, an integer must be given. When using embedded fonts, a decimal value such as 3.25 can be specified.

Kerning

Whereas letter spacing affects the spacing between each pair of letters uniformly, kerning allows spacing between letters to be adjusted according to specific combinations of letters and often makes a line of text cleaner.

Auto kerning requires that the font be embedded. The Flash IDE takes into account the kerning information — which pairs of letters should have their spacing adjusted and by how much — which is embedded within the font file itself. The kerning method is only supported when authoring on a Windows PC, but the effect in the final SWF file is visible on the Macintosh as well.

Some fonts, such as Courier New, are monospaced and as such, auto kerning the font has no visible effect.

Try It Out   **Associating a TextFormat Object to a Text Field**

If you completed the examples earlier in this chapter you've seen the TextFormat class in action. In this exercise, the TextFormat class is expanded to use many more properties to control rich text formatting. Using the TextFormat properties is the quickest way to become familiar with them and understand which ones concern you and your design style the most.

This example uses a library font with a linkage name of myFont. If you don't know how to do this, follow steps 2–8 in the first Try It Out section in this chapter. Alternatively, you can disable the font by removing the font declaration in the my_format object as well as the embedFonts setter of the field1 object.

1. Open a new FLA and save it as setFormatProperties.fla.

2. Highlight frame 1 and open the Actions panel. Add the following code to frame 1's ActionScript:

```
var my_format:TextFormat = new TextFormat();
my_format.font = "myFont";
my_format.size = 12;
my_format.align = "justify";
my_format.blockIndent = 10;
my_format.italic = true;
my_format.bold = true;
my_format.bullet = true;
my_format.color = 0x666666;
var test:Object = (my_format.getTextExtent("The quick and the "));
for( var i in test)
{
    trace(i+" "+test[i]);
}
my_format.indent = 5;
my_format.kerning = true;
my_format.leading = 12;
```

```
my_format.leftMargin = 10;
my_format.rightMargin = 10;
my_format.tabStops = [75];
my_format.letterSpacing = 5;
my_format.target = "_blank";
my_format.underline = true;
my_format.url = "http://www.twelvestone.com";
```

3. The code in step 2 uses all properties of the TextFormat class to make extensive changes to the text style within the text field. Test the code by selecting Control⇨Test Movie. A peculiar thing happens. Although you have not applied the TextFormat to any text fields, the `getTextExtent()` method returns a value! See the following "How It Works" section for details.

4. Close the SWF and return to the FLA. Add the following code to frame 1, below the code you added in step 2:

```
var id:Number = this.getNextHighestDepth();
var field1:TextField = this.createTextField("field" + id, id, 20, 20, 300, 150);
field1.html = true;
field1._target
field1.selectable = false;
field1.border = true;
field1.wordWrap = true;
field1.multiline = true;
field1.antiAliasType = "advanced";
field1.embedFonts = true;
field1.text = "The quick brown fox jumped over the lazy dog. ";
field1.text += "The quick\t brown fox jumped over the lazy dog.+newline ";
field1.text += "The quick brown fox jumped over the lazy dog. ";
field1.text += "The quick brown fox jumped over the lazy dog. ";
field1.text += "The quick brown fox jumped over the lazy dog. ";
field1.text += "The quick brown fox jumped over the lazy dog. ";
field1.text += "The quick brown fox jumped over the lazy dog. ";
field1.setTextFormat (my_format);
```

5. Test the code by selecting Control⇨Test Movie. You'll now see that a text field appears in the stage with some rather intrusive style changes.

6. Close the SWF and return to the FLA. Return to the first frame ActionScript and change some or all of the values in the `my_format` object. Test the code with each change by selecting Control⇨Test Movie and note the changes in the text appearance.

How It Works

In this example you used every TextFormat property available in Flash 8. There were a few dependencies. For example, although you aren't using HTML text, the format object included a URL value. To enable the URL value and make the field clickable, the `field1.html` property was set to `true`. The embed font option was also required because the TextFormat object called for kerning.

The `bullet` property adds a bullet at the beginning of the text and wherever a newline character is encountered. This method enables you to easily create a bulleted list within a text field.

The TextFormat class's `getTextExtent()` method is capable of helping you predict the size and position of text before it's ever rendered on the stage. The method takes into account the properties set thus far upon a TextFormat object. The results of the method showed up in the Output window when the code was tested using Control⇨Test Movie. The results can be used to help determine the size of user interface objects before they are ever built nd to help you measure text without having to instantiate a text field offstage and measure the field, as was required in previous versions of Flash.

Italic and bold are generally used with device fonts. A text field can only use the characters embedded with a font when embedFonts is set to true. If the library font is italic but not bold, setting bold to true does nothing as long as the embedded font doesn't include bold characters. However, when using device fonts, Flash can request the bold and italic sets from the operating system, and the change becomes visible.

Tab stops are characters represented by the special code \t, which represents the ASCII tab stop character. Each tab stop is defined by an index and is relative in size. In this case, the first tab in the text takes on the tab width of 75 pixels.

The rest of the properties are straightforward, and changing the values of each property and viewing the result will enable you to quickly become familiar with each property.

Now learn to use properties to apply formatting to substrings.

Try It Out   Applying a TextFormat Property to Substrings

1. Open a new a FLA and save it as setFormatSpan.fla.

2. Open the Library panel. At the top right is an icon that looks like a bulleted list with a small arrow pointing down. Click it to open the Options menu.

3. Select the New Font option. A pop-up window opens.

4. Give the font a logical name and choose the font you'd like to use in your text field as advanced rendered font. Click OK.

5. The font appears in the Library. Click the font symbol in the library so that it is highlighted. Open the Options menu again, and select the Linkage option. A pop-up window with options appears.

6. Select the Export for ActionScript option. The input fields above it become enabled.

7. Give the font an identifying name. The value defaults to the symbol name. Change it to myFont and click OK. The font will now be added to the SWF file when it is published.

8. Highlight the first frame and open the Actions panel. Add the following code to frame 1:

```
var my_format:TextFormat = new TextFormat();
my_format.font = "myFont";
my_format.size = 12;

var id:Number = this.getNextHighestDepth();
var field1:TextField = this.createTextField ("field" + id, id, 20, 20, 300, 150);
field1.border = true;
field1.wordWrap = true;
field1.multiline = true;
field1.antiAliasType = "advanced";
field1.embedFonts = true;
field1.text = "The quick brown fox jumped over the lazy dog. ";
```

```
field1.text += "The quick brown fox jumped over the lazy dog. ";
field1.text += "The quick brown fox jumped over the lazy dog. ";
field1.text += "The quick brown fox jumped over the lazy dog. ";
field1.text += "The quick brown fox jumped over the lazy dog. ";
field1.text += "The quick brown fox jumped over the lazy dog. ";
field1.text += "The quick brown fox jumped over the lazy dog. ";
field1.setTextFormat (my_format);
```

9. Test the code to be sure you have a working text field before proceeding. It would be difficult to debug the rest of the code if this isn't working yet. Select Control⇨Test Movie. You should see a small text field with repeating text within it, using the font you specified in the library.

10. Close the SWF and return to frame 1's ActionScript. Define a TextFormat object to apply to specific substrings within the text in the text field. Enter the following code below the code you added in step 8:

```
var keywordHighlight:TextFormat = new TextFormat();
keywordHighlight.bold = true;
keywordHighlight.color = 0xFF0000;
keywordHighlight.size = 13;
```

11. Now that you have a format, create a function that is capable of looking for and applying a format to a specific substring throughout the text. Enter the following function below the code you added in step 10:

```
function setHighlights (field, format, subStr)
{
    var str:Array = field.text.split (subStr);
    var tempString:String = "";
    for (var i = 0; i < str.length; i++)
    {
        tempString += str[i];
        var startPos = tempString.length;
        tempString += subStr;
        field.setTextFormat(startPos, startPos + subStr.length, format);
    }
}
```

12. The code added in step 11 might look a bit confusing; it is explained in the following "How It Works" section. For now, assume this function automates the searching of a substring and allows you to easily apply a format to specific substrings using a simple line of code. Add the following line below the code you added in step 11:

```
setHighlights(field1, keywordHighlight, "fox jumped");
```

13. Test the code by selecting Control⇨Test Movie. You should see the substring "fox jumped" is now red, bold, and slightly larger than the surrounding text.

How It Works

In this exercise you took advantage of the setTextFormat() method's capability to accept string positions to apply a format to spans of text rather than an entire field.

In the `setHighlights()` function, the field's text is split using the `split` method, creating an array of characters in the variable `str`. (Splitting the string into an array makes it easier to find substrings in this case.)

Once the text is split, a temporary string object called `tempString` is created. This variable enables you to easily measure the beginning position of each substring without affecting the text already in the text field. The start position is identified as the length of the `tempString` variable each time the loop is run. With each loop the `tempString` variable grows and thus the entire length of the `tempString` variable is the new start position of the span you want to format. The start position is defined as `startPos` using the length property of `tempString` as it is built. Once the measurement is taken, the substring is added to the text so that the next function run displays an accurate length of text processed thus far in the current loop iteration.

Finally, and most importantly, the `setTextFormat()` method is used on the actual text. The `startPos` variable is assigned as the start value of the span that will have the format applied. This is the first parameter in the line:

```
field.setTextFormat(startPos, startPos + subStr.length, format);
```

Because you only want to highlight the substring, you then set the end position of the span to be the length of the substring. This value is assigned as the start position with the substring length added to it:

```
field.setTextFormat(startPos, startPos + subStr.length, format);
```

Finally, the format is defined as the last parameter:

```
field.setTextFormat(startPos, startPos + subStr.length, format);
```

Rather than use the `setHighlights()` function you could have also more literally defined a specific span without regard to a specific substring. For example, you can remove the line you added in step 12 and simply replace it with this line:

```
field1.setTextFormat(5,15,keywordHighlight);
```

In this case you will see how 10 characters (including spaces) are reformatted with the `keywordHighlight` format. The example, however, shows a practical and useful way that the span parameters of `setTextFormat()` can be used within an application.

The `setTextFormat()` method overrides only those styles defined in the new style. So if the original style uses an underline, and your new style does not indicate an underline either true or false, the underline will remain.

A Note about setNewTextFormat()

When you add text to a text field that is not HTML enabled, the text defaults to the format assigned to the field at author time. So if you add a text field to the stage using the Text tool, any new text added by the user or with ActionScript will take on the rich text formatting the field is published with.

If you don't set any default format or use the `createTextField()` method as shown in the examples in this chapter, Flash defaults to black, Serif, and 12. It is possible to change the default style of the field on-the-fly by using `setNewTextFormat()` instead of `setTextFormat()`. When you use `setNewTextFormat()`, it not only applies the format to the text, but also makes it the text field's default style. This can be handy when working with input text, or dynamic text to which a user might apply rich text formatting options. If a text field is going to use only one style throughout its lifetime, and the text is destined to change multiple times, use `setNewTextFormat()` to avoid having to recall the `setTextFormat()` method every time the text changes. You can still override the default style with spans or redefine the style by using `setTextFormat()`. Use `setNewTextFormat()` where it makes sense.

Displaying HTML

HTML presents one of the easiest methods for displaying rich text in Flash. Flash cannot open a web page, but it does support a modest array of HTML tags. The tags support the use of style attributes that can be used in conjunction with a style sheet.

The following table identifies supported HTML characters:

Code	Character
&amp;	&
&apos;	"
&gt;	>
&lt	<
&quote;	'

In addition, Unicode and ASCII characters can be used to define characters not in the preceding list. For example, `&#64;` produces the @ symbol. You can also specify the value as Unicode.

Here's a list of HTML tags that are supported in Flash:

```
<a>         <font>      <u>
<i>         <img>       <body>
<b>         <span>      <li>
<br>        <p>         <textformat>
```

In the following CSS section you see how the style class can expand on the supported tag set and include your own.

The image tag is especially interesting because it allows the embedding of not only images, but SWF files as well.

Because only a rudimentary set of HTML can be used within a text field, you cannot load a web site into a text field and expect it to display. Most, if not all, simple XHTML pages should work to some degree, as long as you use CSS and style tags appropriate for the styles available in Flash. For example, it won't do any good to set a border for a `<span>` tag.

Enabling HTML in a text field is very easy. The TextField class has a property called `html`. When it's set to `true`, the text field enables HTML parsing on the field. For example:

```
contentField.html = true;
```

That's literally all you need to do to your text field.

One extra step is to be sure the text is set with the proper setter. In most cases the property `text` is used. For example:

```
contentField.text = "Some string of information.";
```

And:

```
contentField.text = "<b>Some string of information.</b>";
```

In both cases, whether or not HTML is set to `true`, the text field will not render the text as HTML. The property `htmlText` must be used to allow the text field to parse the string as HTML. For example:

```
contentField.htmlText = "<b>Some string of information.</b>";
```

In this case the string displays as bold as long as the `html` property is set to `true`. If the `html` property is not set to `true`, the text field displays the text as if the text setter had been called.

This next Try It Out example is short and simple and shows you how to apply HTML to a text field. If you are interested in adding more HTML tags, try them on your own to see how each behaves in Flash. The tags are more thoroughly covered in the "Using CSS with XML" at the end of this chapter because that's where HTML text really begins to show its power within Flash.

Try It Out   Creating and Displaying HTML Text

In this exercise you apply HTML to a text field.

1. Open a new FLA and save it as `htmlInFlash.fla` in your workspace folder.

2. Select frame 1 to highlight it. Open the Actions panel and enter the following code:

```
var id:Number = this.getNextHighestDepth();
var field1:TextField = this.createTextField("field" + id, id, 20, 20, 300, 150);
field1.html = true;
field1.border = true;
field1.wordWrap = true;
field1.multiline = true;
field1.htmlText = "<font face='Arial'>The <i>quick</i></font> brown fox
<b>jumped</b> over the lazy dog.</font> ";
```

3. Test the code by selecting Control➪Test Movie. You'll see a text field with text variously styled throughout the string.

4. Try changing the HTML tags by adding size and color attributes to the font tag, or change the italic and bold tags. Try inserting `<p>` tags to define specific paragraphs of text. Test the code with each change to see what each change does to the text.

How It Works

In this example HTML was used within a string to define the rich text formatting of the text. System fonts were used, so it was easy to override the font face with Arial on a specific span of text. The face attribute can also refer to the linkage name of a library font if `embedFonts` is set to `true`.

Image and SWF Support in HTML Text Fields

As mentioned earlier, one of the most exciting features of the TextField class is the capability to place image and SWF files within the content of the text field. This allows the text to wrap around images and SWF files for professional-looking layouts.

ActionScript provides properties that enable you to access the SWF within an image tag. You can create pre-loaders, as well as share data and call methods within the SWF file that resides in the text field.

> *The SWF residing in the image tag has the same security restrictions as external SWF files loaded into the application via* `loadMovie`.

Try It Out   Manipulating an SWF in a Text Field

This is a lengthier example because it requires the creation of two SWF files. The first is the SWF that you'll load into an image tag. The second defines the text field as well as the HTML that will load the first SWF file. For simplicity, the TextFormat object has been skipped, but you're welcome to use one as described earlier in this chapter.

1. Open a new FLA and save it as `dataThumbnail.fla` in your workspace folder.

2. Click anywhere on the stage. The Properties panel populates with options to set for your FLA file. Be sure the Properties tab is selected in the Properties panel and click the Size button. A pop-up window appears. Change the size to 60 width and 70 height and click OK.

3. Select frame 1 to highlight it. Open the Actions panel and enter the following code:

```
var titleFormat:TextFormat = new TextFormat();
titleFormat.size = 9;
titleFormat.align = "center";
titleFormat.font = "Arial";
var dataFormat:TextFormat = new TextFormat();
dataFormat.size = 32;
dataFormat.align = "center";
dataFormat.font = "Arial";
this.createEmptyMovieClip("titleHolder", 0);
var titleField:TextField = this.titleHolder.createTextField("field1", ⏎
    0, 0, 50, 60, 20);
titleField.selectable = false;
titleField.background = true;
titleField.backgroundColor = 0x99CCFF;
titleField.text = "Wind Speed";
titleField.setTextFormat(titleFormat);
```

```
titleHolder.onPress = function()
{
    if (this._parent.run)
    {
        clearInterval(this._parent.run);
        delete this._parent.run;
    }
    else
    {
        this._parent.run = setInterval(this._parent, "changeDisplay", 10);
    }
};
this.createTextField("field2", 1, 0, 0, 60, 50);
field2.background = true;
field2.backgroundColor = 0xECE9E1;
field2.text = "0";
field2.setNewTextFormat(dataFormat);

function changeDisplay()
{
    field2.text = 14 + random(3);
}
this.run = setInterval(this, "changeDisplay", 10);
```

4. The intricacies of this code aren't too important, so don't dwell on that too much. Just know that it simply quickly creates a small interactive SWF file you'll use in the second half of this exercise.

5. Test the code by selecting Control⇨Test Movie. Click the blue text field to see the animation play and pause. This is the interactive SWF file you embed in a text field. Publish the SWF by selecting File⇨Publish. Be sure the SWF file was published to your workspace folder because you'll be using a relative link to load the movie into a text field.

6. Open a new FLA file and it as `swfinTextTest.fla` in your workspace folder (it should be in the same folder as the `dataThumbnail.fla` and SWF file created in steps 1–5).

7. Highlight the first frame of the `swfinTextTest.fla` file. Open the Actions panel and enter the following code:

```
var id:Number = this.getNextHighestDepth();
var field1:TextField = this.createTextField("field" + id, id, 20, 20, 300, 150);
field1.html = true;
field1.border = true;
field1.wordWrap = true;
field1.multiline = true;
field1.htmlText = "<p align='left'>This is some fancy article about weather. It
includes a small widget which is supposedly showing real-time data to the reader.
Hopefully the reader enjoys it.  <img src='dataThumbnail.swf' id='data_mc'/>The
happy reader should note that the thumbnail in the text field can be started and
paused by pressing the light blue rectangle. Also when you scroll this text field,
the SWF will scroll right with it! Astonishing really. You could potentially layout
your entire SWF using one text field and simple html, although you might annoy your
fellow developers.</p> ";
function watchThumbLoad()
{
    var loaded = field1.data_mc.getBytesLoaded();
```

```
    //Override some ActionScript in the nested clip
    if (field1.data_mc.run != undefined)
    {
        clearInterval(watchthumb);
        clearInterval(field1.data_mc.run);
        delete field1.data_mc.run;
    }
}
watchthumb = setInterval(this, "watchThumbLoad", 10);
```

8. Test the code by selecting Control⇨Test Movie.

How It Works

Believe it or not, that's all there is to it. Setting up a typical HTML field allows the introduction of nested SWF files.

The most notable portion of the code is the watchThumbLoad() function in the second FLA. It watches for a known property of the loaded movie clip. Alternatively, the function could have polled field1.data_mc.getBytesLoaded() and getBytesTotal() to determine the load status of the embedded content.

Once loaded, the watchThumbLoad() function shows how the ActionScript of the embedded SWF is completely accessible as if it were any other movie clip. In this example, the default start state of the SWF file is overridden to allow the user to kick off the activity in it by clicking the light blue rectangle.

In the example you can begin to see how embedding SWF content within a text field can help illustrate your text while encapsulating content directly associated with the text within the text field.

This is, of course, only one approach but it represents a simple and easy-to-manage way to integrate text and visual content in your application.

Font Support

In the examples throughout this chapter, two different methods for using fonts have been described. It is important to note some details about fonts and how you can and should use them in Flash. The difference between device and embedded fonts was described at the beginning of this chapter. This section explores some methods for using fonts in more advanced situations.

Sharing Fonts is probably one of the most useful library sharing options available. By changing out the source SWF containing the font, you can replace the SWF with an SWF that contains a different font, but the same identifier name, enabling you to easily replace fonts within your user interface skin.

Try It Out   **Share Fonts at Runtime**

This example is lengthier than usual because it requires you to create two SWF files.

1. Open a new FLA and save it as fontSource.fla.

2. Open the Library. At the top right is an icon that looks like a bulleted list with a small arrow pointing down. Click it to open the Options menu.

3. Select the New Font option. A pop-up window appears.

4. Give the font a logical name and choose the font you'd like to embed.

5. The new font appears in the Library panel. Click the font symbol in the Library panel so that it is highlighted. Open the Options menu again and select the Linkage option. A pop-up window appears.

6. Select the Export for Runtime Sharing option. The input field above it becomes enabled.

7. This value defaults to the symbol name. Give it an identifying name by changing it to `myFont`.

8. At the bottom of the same pop-up window is a URL input field. Because the name of the FLA is `fontSource.fla`, the final SWF name will be `fontSource.swf`. Enter `fontSource.swf` as the value in the URL field.

9. Publish `fontSource.fla` so that it exists in your workspace folder.

10. Open a new FLA and save it as `shareFontTest.fla` in your workspace folder.

11. Open the Library for the `shareFontTest.fla` and select New Font from the Options menu. A pop-up window appears.

12. In the Font drop-down list is the name of the font you embedded in `fontSource.fla`. It's easy to spot the font because it has an asterisk next to it. In this example, it's likely to be `Font 1*`. Select it and click OK.

13. The font symbol will appear in the library. Click it, open the Options menu, and select Linkage.

14. Select the Import for Runtime Sharing option. In the identifier input field, change the default value to `myFont`.

15. In the URL input field, enter the name `fontSource.fla`, the SWF that contains the font with the Identifier name `myFont`.

16. Open the Options menu again and select New Symbol. Be sure the Movie Clip type is selected. Select the checkbox for Export for ActionScript and click OK.

17. The stage now has the new symbol open and waiting for you to modify it. Select the Text tool from the Tools panel and draw a text field.

18. In the Properties panel, be sure the field type is set to Dynamic Text, and select `Font 1*` from the font drop-down menu.

19. Type at least one character into the text field.

20. Close the movie clip by selecting Scene 1 from the navigation in the Timeline panel.

21. Select frame 1 and open the Actions panel if it's not already open. Add the following code:

```
var my_format:TextFormat = new TextFormat();
my_format.font = "myFont";
my_format.size = 20;
var id:Number = this.getNextHighestDepth();
var field1:TextField = this.createTextField("field" + id, id, 20, 20, 300, 150);
field1.wordWrap = true;
field1.multiline = true;
```

```
field1.antiAliasType = "advanced";
field1.embedFonts = true;
field1.text = "The quick brown fox jumped over the lazy dog. ";
field1.setTextFormat(my_format);
```

22. Test the code by selecting Control⇨Test Movie. You will see that the font you chose in the first FLA, `fontSource.fla`, shows up in `sharedFontTest.swf`. Change the selected font in `fontSource.fla`, republish, and test the `sharedFontTest.swf` file to see the result.

How It Works

In this example, a `fontSource.swf` file was created to hold a font symbol made accessible to other SWF files. Here, `fontSource.swf` is required to reside in the same folder as `sharedFontTest.swf`, so if you deploy the solution to a web server, you will need to upload both files to the server.

The `sharedFontTest` file contains a library symbol that is linked to the font symbol in the `fontSource` file.

Using this method for deploying fonts allows you to more easily re-skin and modify the graphics in your application.

The most important departure in this method for allowing shared fonts is the use of the proxy movie clip symbol, which forces the compiler to realize that the Shared runtime font symbol needs to be exported when the application is compiled. Normally shared fonts only work with text fields created with the Text tool. By creating a proxy movie clip, the font becomes available to ActionScript.

Shared fonts and multiple shared fonts can be tricky to set up. Be patient when debugging. Use the FLAs for this chapter to see details about the symbols to include in each file.

Also, notice that the advanced `antiAliasType` is available, as are all embedded font options.

Hyperlinks and the ASFunction Method

Often when working with links in HTML text, it is desirable to kick off ActionScript functions within the application rather than to call HTTP links. The `ASFunction` method facilitates this by residing in the `href` attribute of the `<a>` tag in the HTML text of the text field. For example, you can define a function called `myFunction()` and call it from a link like so:

```
<a href="asfunction:myFunction">Some text</a>
```

The function you specify must belong to the same timeline or object as the text field. You cannot specify dot syntax to traverse the object hierarchy. However, your function can access another function within any timeline.

You can specify only a single String parameter to send to the function, although you can specify multiple strings by using some delimiter such as a comma or pipe. For example, where `myFunction()` accepts a String parameter, the parameter is defined in the HTML attribute as

```
<a href="asfunction:myFunction, Test parameter">Some text</a>
```

The next Try It Out exercise shows you how to make use of ASFunction-based hyperlinks.

Try It Out   Call ASFunction from HTML

1. Open a new FLA and save it as ASFunctionTest.fla in your workspace folder.

2. Highlight the first frame, open the Actions panel, and enter the following code, which defines a background color and a method for changing the color:

```
import flash.display.BitmapData;
var backgroundColor:BitmapData = new BitmapData (Stage.width, Stage.height, ⤴
    false, 0xFFCCCCCC);
this.attachBitmap(backgroundColor, -9999);
function changeColor (n)
{
    trace(n);
    backgroundColor.floodFill(2, 2, n);
}
```

3. Add the following code below the code you entered in step 2:

```
var myField = this.createTextField("field1", this.getNextHighestDepth(), ⤴
    10, 10, 100, 22);
myField.html = true;
myField.autoSize = true;
myField.htmlText = "<a href='asfunction:changeColor,0x000000FF'><u>Change ⤴
    Color</u></a>";
```

4. Test the code by selecting Control⇨Test Movie. The text is clickable, and when it's clicked, the background of the movie changes to blue.

How It Works

In this exercise, you used a simple bitmap to define an object to manipulate using ASFunction within HTML text. A parameter was sent to the receiving function that defined the color to be used.

Using Cascading Style Sheets

One of the most powerful classes in Flash is StyleSheet, available to Flash 7 and up. The StyleSheet class is owned by the TextField class. To most Flash developers, the StyleSheet class is still a mystery and is little used.

By using CSS to define the rich text in your application, you are allowing the application to be more easily maintained, changed, and modified. Flash CSS is quite robust. You can often use the same CSS file or CSS variant file as you use for the rest of your HTML site. When you change the CSS for the HTML page, the text styles in the Flash movie are changed as well.

When creating code for rich text objects, deploying CSS can make your code easier to copy and paste into more applications because the styles are defined in external CSS files rather than intrinsic to the code you've written.

Creating a Cascading Style Sheet Object

Creating a StyleSheet object is very simple and uses a typical constructor. For example, the following code creates a StyleSheet called myStyle:

```
var myStyle:TextField.StyleSheet = new TextField.StyleSheet();
```

You can then load a style sheet from an external source or you can define the styles within ActionScript.

Associating a StyleSheet with a Text Field

Associating a StyleSheet object to a specific text field is easy. The TextField class has a property called styleSheet that accepts a StyleSheet instance and applies all the styles defined within to the text field. Where there is a text field named myField and a StyleSheet object named myStyle, you associate the StyleSheet only after it has loaded. Loading and detecting onLoad events with style sheets are covered in the following Try It Out.

Try It Out   **Use CSS in a Simple Text Field**

1. Open a new document in your favorite CSS editor, and enter the following style definitions:

```
.blogPostText {
    font-family: Verdana;
    font-size: 12px;
}
```

2. Save the file as myStyle.css in your workspace folder.

3. Open a new FLA and save it as cssTest.fla.

4. Highlight the first frame in the timeline, open the Actions panel, and enter the following:

```
var id:Number = this.getNextHighestDepth();
var field1:TextField = this.createTextField("field" + id, id, 20, 20, 300, 150);
field1.wordWrap = true;
field1.multiline = true;
field1.html = true;
var myStylesheet:TextField.StyleSheet = new TextField.StyleSheet();
myStylesheet.onLoad = function(success)
{
    if (success)
    {
        for (var i in myStylesheet)
        {
            field1.styleSheet = this;
        }
    }
    field1.htmlText = "<p class='blogPostText'>The quick brown fox jumped over ⤶
        the lazy dog.</p>";
};
myStylesheet.load("myStyle.css");
```

5. Test the code by selecting Control⇨Test Movie.

How It Works

This example demonstrates how to associate a CSS file with a text field. The main drawback to CSS is the time it takes to load the CSS file. Generally, CSS files should remain small to keep response times short.

If you are dealing with a large CSS file, you can alternatively load the file instead with the onData event handler from a LoadVars object. With this technique, you can more accurately watch the bytes being loaded and give the user an indication of why the delay is occurring. When the load is complete, you pass the data from the onData event handler to the parseCSS() method of a StyleSheet object to convert the raw string data into the native data format used by the StyleSheet class. You give this a try in the next Try It Out exercise.

Try It Out   Load CSS via the LoadVars Class

If you have not completed the previous Try It Out example, you should do so now. You'll use cssTest.fla to make modifications and load the CSS via a LoadVars object.

1. Open cssTest.fla. Open the ActionScript for frame 1 in the Actions panel and remove the load() method from the myStylesheet object because you won't need it.

2. Add the following code below the code left after following step 1:

```
var cssProxyLoader:LoadVars = new LoadVars();
cssProxyLoader.onData = function(str)
{
    myStylesheet.onLoad(myStylesheet.parseCSS(str));
    clearInterval(cssloadWatch);
};
this.watchCSSLoad = function()
{
    trace(cssProxyLoader.getBytesTotal());
};
cssloadWatch = setInterval(this, "watchCSSLoad", 10);
cssProxyLoader.load("myStyle.css");
```

3. Test the code by selecting Control⇨Test Movie. The output window will show the bytes loaded, and the text will appear with the style applied.

How It Works

This method for loading CSS data can be helpful when loading large CSS files. It also gives you more options for dealing with the external CSS file because the complete method set for LoadVars is now available to the object.

The most significant line of code is when cssProxyLoader calls the myStylesheet.onLoad method:

```
myStylesheet.onLoad(myStylesheet.parseCSS(str));
```

The parseCSS() method of the StyleSheet class does not fire the onLoad event automatically as you might expect. It simply returns a Boolean, so you can call the method directly within the parameter when calling the onLoad event of the target StyleSheet object.

Define Styles Directly on a StyleSheet Object

Styles can be defined directly upon a StyleSheet object using ActionScript rather than loading the styles from an external file. This is useful when you want to encapsulate the text styles within your application but would like to take advantage of StyleSheet capabilities such as hover states and node name definitions. To define your own styles using ActionScript, use the `setStyle()` method from the StyleSheet class. This method expects two parameters: the name of the style and an object containing property-value pairs for each style attribute.

The name argument to the `setStyle()` method accepts the same strings that normally represent a style name within a CSS file. You can specify tag names by entering the name of the tag you want to style in quotes, such as `"a"`, `"p"`, and `"span"`. In addition to applying styles to tags of a certain name, you can create your own classes by putting a dot in front of the style name and referring to the style name using the `class` attribute within one or more tags, as you see shortly. You can also use link selectors to define the appearance of a hyperlink in the link, hover, and active states through the names `"a:link"`, `"a:hover"`, and `"a:active"`. You see these selectors in action in the next Try It Out. Here's a list of supported selectors:

```
<a>        <font>      <u>
<i>        <img>       <body>
<b>        <span>      <li>
<br>       <p>         <textformat>
```

When you put together a list of style properties and their values, you need to know which properties are available to use. The following table lists the style properties supported by Flash, which is a subset of the full CSS1 specification. Because dashes are not allowed in variable names (because a dash is treated as a subtraction symbol), style names with a dash are modified to remove the dash and capitalize the second word.

CSS1 Property Name	Flash Property Equivalent
color	color
font-style	fontStyle
text-decoration	textDecoration
margin-left	marginLeft
margin-right	marginRight
font-weight	fontWeight
Text-align	textAlign
kerning	kerning
font-size	fontSize
letterSpacing	letterSpacing
text-indent	textIndent
font-family	fontFamily

The following example shows how `setStyle()` is used to apply styles to a text field:

```
var titleCSS = new TextField.StyleSheet();
titleCSS.setStyle(".title", {color:"#660000", fontSize:"20px"});
titleTextField.styleSheet = titleCSS;
titleTextField.htmlText = "<span class=\"title\">The Quick</span><br>The quick ⤶
    brown fox jumped.";
```

The next Try It Out example shows you how to apply styles to a text field.

Try It Out — Define a Style Directly upon a StyleSheet Object

1. Open a new FLA and save it as `defineCSSwithAS.fla` in your workspace folder.

2. Highlight the first frame, open the Actions panel, and enter the following code:

```
var myStylesheet:TextField.StyleSheet = new TextField.StyleSheet();
myStylesheet.setStyle("a:link", {
    color:"#990000",
    fontSize:"12px",
    textDecoration: "underline"
});
myStylesheet.setStyle("a:hover", {
    color:"#FF0000",
    fontSize:"12px",
    textDecoration: "underline"
});

var id:Number = this.getNextHighestDepth();
var field1:TextField = this.createTextField("field" + id, id, 20, 20, 300, 150);
field1.wordWrap = true;
field1.multiline = true;
field1.html = true;
field1.styleSheet = myStylesheet;
field1.htmlText = "<a href='www.someurl.com'>This is a link with a hover state!</a>
This is some more text, just to see how it looks.";
```

3. Test the code by selecting Control➪Test Movie.

How It Works

In this example you used ActionScript to manipulate the CSS object runtime.

Notice that the `setStyle` method's first parameter is a String. This is the class, classpath of the style being defined. The second parameter is an object. An object is always wrapped in curly braces when defined in such a manner. Alternatively, the second parameter could have been defined as a separate object as follows:

```
var style1:Object = {};
style1.color = "#990000";
style1.fontSize = "12";
style1.textDecoration = "underline";

var myStylesheet:TextField.StyleSheet = new TextField.StyleSheet();
myStylesheet.setStyle("a:link", style1);
delete style1;
```

Using an object to hold properties helps to explain the mechanics of the `setStyle()` method a bit. You'll also notice that the style names are variants from the actual CSS1 subset. For example, whereas CSS1 calls for text-decoration: underline, Flash does not use dashes in such a way because it is interpreted as a minus operator. So, wherever you see a dash in a CSS style, remove the dash and capitalize the second word. You then have the Flash variant of the property name. For example, the style name text-decoration becomes textDecoration.

How to Define Tags, Class, and Properties

Now take a look at how you can set styles using straight CSS, which you can load into a StyleSheet object.

To set a tag definition, commonly known as a Selector definition, you simply do as you have seen previously in this chapter. For instance, the p selector affects only the p tag:

```
p {
    font-size: 24;
}
```

In this example, all p tags in the document that associates itself with this style will display its text using a 24-`pixel` size font.

Alternatively, if you want to affect only a subset of tags, you can define a class instead:

```
.largeContent {
    font-size: 24;
}
```

Then, any tag that declares a class attribute as follows will show 24-pixel-high text:

```
<span class="largeContent">Some text.</span>
```

You can only use the class attribute in span *and* p *tags.*

You also can define multiple selectors on one style object. For example:

```
p, a {
    font-family: Georgia;
}
```

This class will affect all <p> and <a> tags in the text field. Flash also allows the creation of custom selectors. For example:

```
p, someStyle, a {
    font-family: Georgia;
}
```

In this case, an HTML tag with the name someStyle will act essentially the same as the p tag. In this way you can create custom behaviors for custom tag names.

Pseudo-classes are supported on the <a> tag only. Only three pseudo-classes are supported:

```
a:link
a:hover
a:active
```

Properties are set as seen in the preceding examples, where each line between the opening and closing brackets contains one style property. Each property declaration contains a property name and a property value separated by a colon, and is terminated with a semicolon. CSS automatically treats all variable values as strings, so you do not need quotes on string values.

Using CSS with XML

Flash is fairly blind when it comes to text fields. It isn't bound by any public specification, and works just fine with any tag name. Flash internally supports basic HTML tags that can have properties assigned directly to them via CSS. For example:

```
p {
    font-family:Arial;
}
```

However, Flash accepts any string name for a node name class. For instance, you can make the following declaration to apply styling to a node with the name blogPostTitle, even though it is a tag that you invented and not part of any HTML specification:

```
blogPostTitle {
    font-family: Georgia
    font-size: 24;
}
```

After an XML node is declared, you can define it as follows:

```
<blogPostTitle>This is a title of a blog post</blogPostTitle>
```

All nodes with the name blogPostTitle will display the corresponding style.

It is important to remember that style sheets are cascading. This means that if an <a> tag exists within the blogPostTitle that doesn't override the font-size, but only manipulates the color, the <a> tag will inherit the blogPostTitle properties, but retain any properties not redefined by the blogPostTitle selector.

The StyleSheet class allows the defining of new HTML tags for automated node name handling of XML, XHTML, and more. Take a closer look at this capability.

Try It Out   **Load an XML File and Display It within a Text Field**

For this example you should be familiar with XML and the XML class. The XML class is used briefly to load external XML data.

    1.   Open a new document in your favorite CSS file editor, and enter the following style definitions:

```
blogPostTitle {
    font-family: Georgia, serif;
    font-size: 24px;
}

blogPostTitleLink {
    color: #006699;
    font-size: 18px;
}

a:link {
    text-decoration: underline;
}
```

2. Save the file as myXMLStyle.css in your workspace folder.

3. Open a new FLA and save it as xmlWithCSS.fla in your workspace folder.

4. Highlight the first frame, open the Actions panel, and enter the following code:

```
var id:Number = this.getNextHighestDepth();
var field1:TextField = this.createTextField("field" + id, id, 20, 20, 300, 150);
field1.wordWrap = true;
field1.multiline = true;
field1.html = true;
var myStylesheet:TextField.StyleSheet = new TextField.StyleSheet();
myStylesheet.onLoad = function(success)
{
    if (success)
    {
        for (var i in myStylesheet)
        {
            field1.styleSheet = this;
        }
    }
    field1.htmlText = contentXML.toString();
};
var cssProxyLoader:LoadVars = new LoadVars();
cssProxyLoader.onData = function(str)
{
    myStylesheet.onLoad(myStylesheet.parseCSS(str));
    clearInterval(cssloadWatch);
};
var contentXML:XML = new XML();
contentXML.ignoreWhite = true;
contentXML.onLoad = function(success)
{
    if (success)
    {
        cssProxyLoader.load("myXMLStyle.css");
    }
};
contentXML.load("xmlContent.xml");
```

5. Open a new document in your favorite XML editor (you might prefer to simply use Notepad) and enter the following XML:

```
<blogPostTitle>The quick brown fox!
<blogPostTitleLink>
<a href='www.some link' >October 15th, 2005<a/>
</blogPostTitleLink>
</blogPostTitle>
```

6. Save the document as `xmlContent.xml` in your workspace folder.

7. Test your code by selecting Control⊃Test Movie.

How It Works

In this example you saw how the CSS class can be used to define custom tags that wrap the content. This can be extremely handy when formatting XML content because you don't need to parse the node content to format it. So if a known XMLNode is known to be ready for display, except for its custom node names, you can easily define the style for those child nodes based on their node name.

This example also used the cascade mechanism inherent within cascading style sheets. The <a> tag was only defined, however, only with an underline. This causes all a tags within the document to display an underline. The <a> tag then inherited the properties defined in the `blogPostTitleLink` style because the a tag resides within that descriptive tag. Furthermore the `blogPostTitleLink` style inherited the font defined in the `blogPostTitle` style. In this way you can see how you can efficiently assign styles for a document without repeating declarations or creating many styles.

Also, the XML document was loaded before the style sheet document. Once the XML is loaded the XML onLoad event then kicks off the StyleSheet load event. You could also define a watch function to wait for each document to declare itself loaded and load them simultaneously.

Scroll Text Options

Flash has no built-in scroll bars. Content larger than the designated runtime stage size simply does not appear. In a browser, a page of text automatically presents scroll bars to find the content. In Flash, you must decide how to allow the user to scroll content.

Several ways exist to scroll a text field. Two components are available to accomplish the task: the ScrollBar component and the TextArea component. Each will automate the math involved with controlling a text field, but both are difficult to customize to a particular design style. The components use the same user interface behaviors as most operating systems and so are logical for the user.

A custom scroll bar should take into consideration usability and clarity of function. Many Flash applications will attempt to redefine the scroll bar's behavior and how it works. This is successful in some cases, but is usually simply confusing and limiting for the user. If you decide to build your own scroll bar you should think carefully about the different behavior states your scroll bar is capable of, and what you are trying to achieve.

Scrolling Text Using the TextArea Component

The simplest way to create scrollable text is to make use of the TextArea component. All you need to do is to drag a TextArea component to the stage, give it an instance name, and then assign text to the `text` property, as in the following line of code:

```
feedbackTextArea.text = "The quick brown fox jumped...".
```

The component automatically adds the scroll bar if needed and allows the user to scroll through the text.

If you prefer, you can also place a TextArea component on the stage by having it in a movie clip in the library, and using `attachMovie()` to place a copy of the movie clip on the stage. You can also place an instance of the component on the stage directly using `UIObject.createClassObject()`, which you used in Chapter 9 and that you see in the following Try It Out.

A major drawback to the TextArea component is the inability to apply a TextFormat object to it. You must use the StyleSheet class when changing the look of text in the TextArea component.

Try It Out   Making a Scrollable Text Field with the TextArea Component

In this exercise you dynamically place an instance of the TextArea class on the stage, and then use that component to scroll text.

1. Open a new FLA and save it as `textAreaTest.fla` in your workspace.

2. First you'll need to define the classpath for the TextArea. This is used by the UIObject class to instantiate a new instance of the class. Open the Actions panel and add the following code to the first frame:

```
import mx.controls.TextArea;
```

3. To make the assets for the class available within the library, open the User Interface section of the Component panel, select the TextArea component, and drag it to the library.

4. The component now appears in the Library. You can rename the library instance or place it within a folder for organization.

5. Enter the following code below the code you added in step 2:

```
var id:Number = this.getNextHighestDepth ();
var field2:MovieClip = createClassObject(TextArea, "field" + id, id);
```

6. Test the application to be sure it has access to the library instance and class package. Select Control⇨Test Movie. You should see a small rectangular box in the top-left corner of the stage.

7. Now manipulate the size of the TextArea component. Close the SWF and return to the first frame ActionScript. Add the following code below the code you entered in step 5:

```
field2.setSize(400,150);
field2.wordWrap = true;
field2.text = "Ipsum Lorem da dayem Ipsum Lorem da dayem Ipsum Lorem da dayem Ipsum
Lorem da dayem Ipsum Lorem da dayem Ipsum Lorem da dayem Ipsum Lorem da dayem Ipsum
Lorem da dayem Ipsum Lorem da dayem Ipsum Lorem da dayem Ipsum Lorem da dayem Ipsum
Lorem da dayem Ipsum Lorem da dayem Ipsum Lorem da dayem Ipsum Lorem da dayem Ipsum
```

```
Lorem da dayem Ipsum Lorem da dayem Ipsum Lorem da dayem Ipsum Lorem da dayem Ipsum
Lorem da dayem Ipsum Lorem da dayem Ipsum Lorem da dayem Ipsum Lorem da dayem Ipsum
Lorem da dayem Ipsum Lorem da dayem";
```

8. Test the application by selecting Control⇨Test Movie. The text field will now be much larger and display the text defined in the text property of the TextArea instance. The scroll bar appears within the boundaries defined in the `setSize()` method.

How It Works

In this example the TextArea component is used to rapidly introduce scrollable text into an application. This component is extremely handy but can be limiting. For example, the look of the component must be described by the global Style object. To make the TextArea instance transparent you can add the following code below the code added in step 7:

```
_global.styles.TextArea.backgroundColor = undefined;
```

This line of code will change all TextArea instances to display a transparent background. You can then individually set each background to a specific color while defaulting to transparent. In some cases this could be a limitation.

You can also customize the scroll bars or set the scroll bars to use a skin used by other components in your application. Refer to Chapter 11 for more information on skinning components.

The TextArea instance can be made to look and act as you want, but inconveniently requires its own set of methods to do so. As inconvenient as it can be to customize, the TextArea component is unmatched at displaying scrollable text extremely quickly. You might prefer to use the TextArea component when sketching out code and building prototypes or drafts of work.

Scrolling Text Using the ScrollBar Component

Another means of scrolling text is to use the ScrollBar component along with a standard text field. The ScrollBar component has a method called `setScrollTarget()` that links the ScrollBar instance with a text field. Once done, the thumb on the ScrollBar instance resizes to match the size of the text content, and manipulating the scroll bar controls causes the text to scroll. The `setScrollTarget()` method looks like the following, which links up a ScrollBar instance called `descriptionScrollBar` with a text field called `descriptionTextField`:

```
descriptionScrollBar.setScrollTarget(descriptionTextField);
```

This is one of the more popular ways to create scrollable text. It is a bit more compact in file size, it is quick to set up, and it enables you greater control over how text in the text field is formatted compared with the TextArea component. Try this technique next.

Try It Out   Making a Scrollable Text Field with the ScrollBar Component

This example uses a library font with a linkage name of `myFont`. If you don't know how to do this, follow steps 2–8 in the First Try It Out section in this chapter. Alternatively, you can disable the font by removing the font declaration in the `my_format` object and remove the `embedFonts` setter of the `field1` object.

1. Open a new FLA and save it as `scrollComponentTest.fla`.

2. Highlight the first frame and enter the following code:

```
var my_format:TextFormat = new TextFormat();
my_format.font = "myFont";// Requires an embedded font in the library
my_format.size = 12;
var id:Number = this.getNextHighestDepth();
var field1:TextField = this.createTextField("field" + id, id, 10, 10, 300, 150);
field1.wordWrap = true;
field1.multiline = true;
field1.antiAliasType = "advanced";
field1.embedFonts = true; // Requires an embedded font in the library
field1.text = "Ipsum Lorem da dayem Ipsum Lorem da dayem Ipsum Lorem da dayem Ipsum
Lorem da dayem Ipsum Lorem da dayem Ipsum Lorem da dayem Ipsum Lorem da dayem Ipsum
Lorem da dayem Ipsum Lorem da dayem Ipsum Lorem da dayem Ipsum Lorem da dayem Ipsum
Lorem da dayem Ipsum Lorem da dayem Ipsum Lorem da dayem Ipsum Lorem da dayem Ipsum
Lorem da dayem Ipsum Lorem da dayem Ipsum Lorem da dayem Ipsum Lorem da dayem Ipsum
Lorem da dayem Ipsum Lorem da dayem Ipsum Lorem da dayem Ipsum Lorem da dayem Ipsum
Lorem da dayem Ipsum Lorem da dayem";
field1.setTextFormat (my_format);
```

3. The code in step 2 simply adds a text field similar to the examples defined in earlier in the chapter. You can test the code by selecting Control⇨Test Movie.

4. To make the field scrollable via the ScrollBar component you need to add the class package. Close the SWF and enter the following code below the code you added in step 2:

```
import mx.controls.UIScrollBar;
```

5. Now the assets for the component need to be added to the library. If you cannot see the Components panel, select Window⇨Components. In the User Interface section highlight and drag an instance of the UIScrollbar component to the library. If you cannot see the library, select Window⇨Library. The component is now ready to be called on to the stage.

6. Return to the Actions in frame 1. Add the following code below the code entered in step 4:

```
var id:Number = this.getNextHighestDepth();
var scrollbar1:MovieClip = createClassObject(UIScrollBar, "scrollbar" + id, id);
```

7. Test the code by selecting Control⇨Test Movie. You should see a thin vertical rectangle in the top-left corner of the stage. This is the scroll bar. It doesn't do anything yet.

8. Close the SWF and return to the ActionScript in frame 1. Add the following code below the code you added in step 6:

```
scrollbar1.setScrollTarget(field1);
scrollbar1.setSize(20,field1._height);
scrollbar1.move(field1._x+field1._width, field1._y);
```

9. Test the code by selecting Control⇨Test Movie. You will now see the scroll bar in position and capable of scrolling text.

How It Works

In this example, a scroll bar was quickly created with the UIScrollbar component. By using the `setScrollTarget()` method of the component, the text field added in step 2 became scrollable within the user interface.

This method for scrolling text is a bit less limiting than using the TextArea component because the text field can retain its own properties and you can access them directly for manipulation of visual properties. You can customize the UIScrollbar component using the skin methods.

By using traditional text field creation methods found in Flash 5 and up, you can easily add the UIScrollbar to a text field created with the Text tool.

Another technique for scrolling text is to place a fixed-height text field within a movie clip and then move the movie clip, masking out the text that appears outside a defined area. The two previous methods (using the TextArea component and using a ScrollBar component) use the `scroll` property of the TextField class, whereas this technique moves the movie clip holding the text field. With the `scroll` property, the text field scrolls line by line; a movie clip can scroll smoothly, pixel by pixel. In some cases the class text scroll method is preferable, such as when performance is at a premium, but scrolling a movie clip will always appear smoother.

You have several ways to accomplish this example. One approach is to use a second movie clip as a mask. Flash 8 provides a new method called `scrollRect()` that gives you a way of scrolling a movie clip within a bounded area. The next Try It Out exercise shows you how to apply this method.

Try It Out — Bound and Scroll a Text Field with the scrollRect Method of the MovieClip Class

This example uses a library font with a linkage name of `myFont`.

1. Open a new FLA, save it as `scrollRectTest.fla`, and enter the following code to frame 1:

```
import flash.geom.Rectangle;
  var id:Number = this.getNextHighestDepth();
  var viewArea:MovieClip = this.createEmptyMovieClip("clip"+id,id);
  var area:Rectangle = new Rectangle(0, 0, 300, 150);
viewArea.scrollRect = area;
```

The flash.geom package creates a rectangle object that is expected by the `scrollRect` property. This is simply facilitating `scrollRect`, to help you scroll some text.

2. Add the following code below the code you entered in step 1:

```
var id:Number = this.getNextHighestDepth();
var textHolder:MovieClip = this.viewArea.createEmptyMovieClip("clip"+id,id);

var my_format:TextFormat = new TextFormat();
my_format.font = "myFont";
my_format.size = 12;

var id:Number = this.getNextHighestDepth();
var field1:TextField = this.textHolder.createTextField("field" + id, id, ⤸
    10, 10, 300, 0);
field1.autoSize = true;
field1.wordWrap = true;
field1.multiline = true;
field1.antiAliasType = "advanced";
field1.embedFonts = true;
```

```
field1.text = "Ipsum Lorem da dayem Ipsum Lorem da dayem Ipsum Lorem da dayem Ipsum
Lorem da dayem Ipsum Lorem da dayem Ipsum Lorem da dayem Ipsum Lorem da dayem Ipsum
Lorem da dayem Ipsum Lorem da dayem Ipsum Lorem da dayem Ipsum Lorem da dayem Ipsum
Lorem da dayem Ipsum Lorem da dayem Ipsum Lorem da dayem Ipsum Lorem da dayem Ipsum
Lorem da dayem Ipsum Lorem da dayem Ipsum Lorem da dayem Ipsum Lorem da dayem Ipsum
Lorem da dayem Ipsum Lorem da dayem Ipsum Lorem da dayem Ipsum Lorem da dayem Ipsum
Lorem da dayem Ipsum Lorem da dayem";
field1.setTextFormat(my_format);
```

3. Test the code. Select Control⇨Test Movie. The text is now bound to the rectangle defined in step 2. Try changing the rectangle size parameters defined in step 2.

4. Create a scroll bar from scratch instead of using a component by entering the following code below the code you added in step 2:

```
var id:Number = this.getNextHighestDepth();
var scrollbar1:MovieClip = this.createEmptyMovieClip("clip"+id,id);
var square:Number = 10;
scrollbar1.beginFill(0xCCCCCC,100);
scrollbar1.moveTo(-square, -square);
scrollbar1.lineTo(-square, square);
scrollbar1.lineTo(square, square);
scrollbar1.lineTo(square, -square);
scrollbar1.lineTo(-square, -square);
scrollbar1.endFill();
scrollbar1._x = textHolder._x+textHolder._width+(scrollbar1._width/2);
scrollbar1._y = textHolder._y+(scrollbar1._height/2);
```

5. Select Control⇨Test Movie. You should see a gray square just the right of the text.

6. Close the SWF and return to the actions in frame 1. Add the following code below the code you entered in step 4:

```
scrollbar1.startPosition = scrollbar1._y;
scrollbar1.onPress = function()
{
    this.startDrag(false,this._x,this.startPosition,this._x, ⟳
        this.startPosition+this._parent.viewArea._height);
    clearInterval(this.scrolling);
    this.scrolling = setInterval(this, "scroller", 10);
};
scrollbar1.onRelease = scrollbar1.onReleaseOutside = function ()
{
    clearInterval(this.scrolling);
    this.stopDrag();
};
```

7. Test the code. You can now move the scroll elevator up and down. It isn't associated with your text yet, so it's not actually scrolling anything, but you define that function next. Close the SWF and add the following code below the code you entered in step 6:

```
scrollbar1.scroller = function()
{
    var percentPosition:Number = (this._y-this.startPosition) / this.maxSize;
    textHolder._y = -(percentPosition * (textHolder._height - viewArea._height));
    updateAfterEvent();
};
```

8. Test the code by selecting Control⇨Test Movie. You can now use the gray square to scroll the text field.

How It Works

In this example you saw one way to mask text and use the properties of the movie clips to scroll the contents. The `setMask()` method could have been employed instead. The `scrollRect()` method is now the preferred method and presents a much more customizable and more efficient mechanism. If you have a habit of using `setMask()`, you should become familiar with `scrollRect()` and switch when using Flash 8.

First, a viewable area was defined using a movie clip viewArea with the `scrollRect()` method. This method employed a simple rectangle object to define the bounds which content within the view area are visible.

Next a content movie clip was created called textHolder. This is the actual movie clip whose y position is changed by the scroll button.

A classic text field was then created within the textHolder movie clip.

After the stage elements were defined, a scroll button was created using the movie clip object and the drawing API. This graphic could easily be replaced with an image or more complex vector graphics.

The mouse events were then defined that employed the `startDrag()` method as well as call a `setInterval()` method to smoothly scroll the content. Some simple math was calculated based on the height of the content and the height of the viewable area.

You can see that creating your own scroll elevator requires a bit of math and can be confusing to set up. Although it can be especially annoying if you have many scroll bars in your application, this method of scrolling the text field does have a nice smooth quality, and is easily skinned and customized.

The ease of customization in this method comes with a price. Because you defined the scroll elevator button it doesn't quite act the same as an operating system button. It doesn't resize according to the amount of content, and it doesn't have up and down buttons at the top and bottom as most scroll bars do. Some users may find this difficult or even annoying. You should be careful when defining your own scroll methods. If possible you should emulate what the user expects as much as possible in regards to scrolling.

———————

There's one more scroll bar technique for you to explore. It makes use of TextField `scroll` property in conjunction with custom buttons. The buttons take the place of the ScrollBar component used earlier. Although this technique requires the most work, it also gives you the most design freedom.

Try It Out   **Scroll Text Using the Scroll and maxScroll Properties**

In this example you use a simple text field with `wordWrap` set to `true`, combined with a static field height. This method doesn't require a mask. The exercise uses a library font with a linkage name of `myFont`.

1. Open a new FLA and save it as `scrollFieldTest.fla`.

2. Select the first frame and enter the following code in the Actions panel:

```
var my_format:TextFormat = new TextFormat();
my_format.font = "myFont";
my_format.size = 12;

var id:Number = this.getNextHighestDepth();
var field1:TextField = this.createTextField("field" + id, id, 20, 20, 300, 150);
field1.border = true;
field1.wordWrap = true;
field1.multiline = true;
field1.antiAliasType = "advanced";
field1.embedFonts = true;
field1.text = "Ipsum Lorem da dayem Ipsum Lorem da dayem Ipsum Lorem da dayem Ipsum
Lorem da dayem Ipsum Lorem da dayem Ipsum Lorem da dayem Ipsum Lorem da dayem Ipsum
Lorem da dayem Ipsum Lorem da dayem Ipsum Lorem da dayem Ipsum Lorem da dayem Ipsum
Lorem da dayem Ipsum Lorem da dayem Ipsum Lorem da dayem Ipsum Lorem da dayem Ipsum
Lorem da dayem Ipsum Lorem da dayem Ipsum Lorem da dayem Ipsum Lorem da dayem Ipsum
Lorem da dayem Ipsum Lorem da dayem Ipsum Lorem da dayem Ipsum Lorem da dayem Ipsum
Lorem da dayem Ipsum Lorem da dayem";
field1.setTextFormat(my_format);
```

3. Test the code by selecting Control⇨Test Movie. You should now see a simple text field on the stage. Close the SWF and add the following code below the code you entered in step 2:

```
var id:Number = this.getNextHighestDepth();
var scrollbar1:MovieClip = this.createEmptyMovieClip("clip" + id, id);
var square:Number = 10;
scrollbar1.beginFill(0xCCCCCC, 100);
scrollbar1.moveTo(-square, -square);
scrollbar1.lineTo(-square, square);
scrollbar1.lineTo(square, square);
scrollbar1.lineTo(square, -square);
scrollbar1.lineTo(-square, -square);
scrollbar1.endFill();
scrollbar1._x = field1._x + field1._width + (scrollbar1._width / 2);
scrollbar1._y = field1._y;
```

4. Test the code by selecting Control⇨Test Movie. A gray square appears at the top-right corner of the text field.

5. Close the SWF and enter the following code below the code added in step 3:

```
scrollbar1.startPosition = scrollbar1._y;
scrollbar1.onPress = function()
{
    this.startDrag(false,this._x,this.startPosition,this._x, ⤵
        this.startPosition+field1._height);
    clearInterval(this.scrolling);
    this.scrolling = setInterval(this, "scroller", 10);
};
scrollbar1.onRelease = scrollbar1.onReleaseOutside = function()
{
    clearInterval(this.scrolling);
    this.stopDrag();
```

```
};

scrollbar1.maxSize =  field1._height;
scrollbar1.scroller = function()
{
    var percentPosition:Number = (this._y-this.startPosition) / this.maxSize;
    trace(1+int(percentPosition+field1.maxscroll)+" "+field1);
    field1.scroll = 1+int(percentPosition*field1.maxscroll);
    updateAfterEvent();
};
```

6. Test the code by selecting Control⇨Test Movie. Drag the gray square up and down to scroll the text within the text field.

How It Works

This example takes a minimal approach. By using the `maxscroll` and `scroll` properties of a text field, the field can be easily scrolled. The result appears jagged because the text is bumped line by line into position within the text field; you might prefer the mask method in the previous Try It Out.

However, this method does present the fullest freedom in design and behavior while retaining classic text field scroll behavior.

As mentioned earlier, creating your own scroll mechanism is fraught with usability issues, and care should be taken when defining the behavior of a scroll bar.

Summary

In this chapter you learned about the TextField class, the different types of text fields, their uses, and how to create them with ActionScript. You can, of course, create text fields using the Text tool in the Tools palette, but that's a limiting way of introducing text when working with ActionScript.

This chapter also examined the different methods for formatting text to display rich text within text fields. The TextFormat class was presented as a fast and simple way to highlight text as well as quickly define styles for a text field. antiAliasType also was introduced, along with its advantages over the method of anti-aliasing text in older Flash players.

Shared fonts were discussed, as were robust skinning alternatives when dealing with text content. CSS was also explored and you learned how to modify text within a text field for rich text formatting.

You tried out different methods for scrolling text, some easy and some more advanced, and saw the advantages and drawbacks to each.

All of this adds up to very robust text support in Flash, with far more control and design possibilities than its HTML counterpart in the browser.

Exercises

1. Using the ASFunction method, control an SWF file presented within an HTML field with an <img> tag.

2. Using the code in exercise 1, apply a style sheet to the <a> tag, which contains the ASFunction URL.

3. Using XHTML content, define what Flash should do when it finds a div tag using CSS.

4. Using text span methods, allow the user to select a span of text and change one or more TextFormat properties for that span only.

Using ActionScript for Media

In the preceding chapter you learned how Flash displays and manipulates text. Now you examine something that's a bit more visually stimulating for your viewers. Flash is, after all, a multimedia platform. With ActionScript, you have unprecedented control of media and media integration.

Media can include images, video, sound, and input such as cameras and microphones. You can, of course, integrate these pieces on the stage, on a timeline, and with the Flash drawing tools. However, ActionScript provides you with a robust set of objects, methods, and events for displaying and handling media for a rich media user experience.

In this chapter, you explore loading images, sound, and the microphone, and learn to use them efficiently.

Managing Images

Images are everywhere on the web. They come in all sizes and formats you can think of. You have long been able to load many image types into HTML pages. Since the introduction of JPG loading in Flash 6, you have been able to load a popular image format directly into Flash, giving you incredible freedom in terms of displaying content and working with existing media as well as skinning your applications. With Flash 8, this has advanced even further. You can now load JPG, GIF, and PNG files directly into a movie clip. JPG images are no longer limited to non-progressive .jpg format allowed in Flash 6. GIF images can be transparent and animated, or can be static. PNG images can be transparent, 8 bit, or 24 bit.

Loading an image is as simple as loading an SWF file and, in fact, uses the same methods to accomplish the task. You use loadMovie() to load images into existing movie clips, as well as to load images into movie clips created with ActionScript.

This is very good news for almost all Flash developers because it allows Flash applications to more easily integrate with existing image databases without server-side conversion of the image to an acceptable format.

Unlike data files and SWF files, there are not many security issues with loading images. You can load them from any domain, without setting any security methods.

Remember that images are often copyrighted. Be sure that you have the right or permission to show an image before displaying it in your application.

Preloading images is the same as preloading an SWF file loading into a movie clip. In this chapter's examples, you use the `setInterval()` method to watch the bytes loading and display the image. Because you are loading directly into a movie clip, calling `getBytesLoaded` and `getBytesTotal` on the clip into which the image is loading returns byte values just as you would expect.

> *Sometimes an image may seem to load 100 percent, but fails to appear for various reasons. Because of this, an interval or loop event should check a valid property of the movie clip that has changed since the image loaded. Often, most developers watch the height or width property of the movie clip, because it is a definite indicator that the movie clip has not only loaded the image data, but has successfully displayed it.*

Try It Out   Placing an External Image into a Movie Clip

In this example you load a PNG. However, you can change the target image to whatever image you want. Try images from various domains.

1. Open a new Flash document and save it as `imageLoadTest.fla` in your work folder.

2. Click the first frame in the timeline, open the Actions panel, and type the following ActionScript code:

```
this.createEmptyMovieClip("test",0);
this.test.loadMovie("test.png");
```

3. Be sure your image is available and at the path specified. Test the movie by pressing Ctrl+Enter. You will see the image load into your movie in the top-right corner.

How It Works

In this example you created a movie clip and then used `loadMovie()` to specify an image that should occupy it. However, you didn't watch it load, and you had no indication of whether the image was available to manipulate, position, or work with.

If you simply needed to display it as is, you wouldn't need to do much more, but you usually want to place an image in a specific area, or with specific attributes.

You need to add an interval to watch the test movie clip load and to act upon the image.

> *A load listener is a function that is repeated over a course of time. It can be an interval, or an `enterFrame` event, running on a different movie clip than the clip the image is being loaded into. The function that is repeated checks the `getBytesLoaded` and `getBytesTotal` properties of the target object. You can use those two properties not only to determine the success of the image load, but also to indicate to the user that Flash is working and loading an image.*

Smart Preloading

If you are familiar with JavaScript you know that it is often helpful to preload images at the start of an application. This makes image presentation smoother and often enables you to do things with multiple images that otherwise might not be possible unless you know each are preloaded.

With Flash, the operation of preloading an image is very similar to JavaScript. You call the image into a hidden field and simply remove it. At this point the image is cached locally, and Flash can quickly receive it without much load time at all. As well, if the user has his cache turned off, you simply keep the images offstage until you need them.

Another consideration of smart preloading is that when images are cached, your pre-loader should be smart enough to simply display the image without displaying a pre-loader progress bar or textual percentage indicator, because the pre-loader at that point is redundant.

Using the MovieClipLoader to Preload an Image

Chapter 8 describes the MovieClipLoader class. Luckily, you can use that same class and events to preload a static image. If you are targeting Flash 7 or newer, you can use MovieClipLoader to load images as well as SWF files.

In the following Try It Out, you use the loading of an image to trigger an event.

Try It Out   Firing an Event on Load of the Image

1. Open a new Flash document and save it as `imageClipLoaderTest.fla` in your work folder.

2. Click the first frame in the timeline, open the Actions panel, and type the following ActionScript:

```
var id = this.getNextHighestDepth();
var clip = this.createEmptyMovieClip("mc"+id, id);
var mcOnLoadHandler:Object = new Object();
mcOnLoadHandler.onLoadInit = function(clip_mc:MovieClip) {
    trace("ok");
};
var mcLoader:MovieClipLoader = new MovieClipLoader();
mcLoader.addListener(mcOnLoadHandler);
mcLoader.loadClip("logo.gif",  clip);
```

3. Test your movie by pressing Ctrl+Enter. You will see the image load and the word ok will appear in the output panel.

4. Close the SWF file and return to the first frame actions.

5. Add some ActionScript to the `onLoadInit` function to manipulate the size of the image:

```
var id = this.getNextHighestDepth();
var clip = this.createEmptyMovieClip("mc"+id, id);
var mcOnLoadHandler:Object = new Object();
mcOnLoadHandler.onLoadInit = function(clip_mc:MovieClip) {
    clip_mc._xscale = clip_mc._yscale = 150;
};
```

```
var mcLoader:MovieClipLoader = new MovieClipLoader();
mcLoader.addListener(mcOnLoadHandler);
mcLoader.loadClip("logo.gif",  clip);
```

6. Test your movie by pressing Ctrl+Enter. You will see the image resized when the load is complete.

How It Works

The MovieClipLoader class simplifies and automates the loading of an image. Had you not waited for the image to load completely, the image scaling would have failed because a loadMovie method resets a movie clip.

An object called mcOnLoadHandler was created. It contains the function definitions that are called by the MovieClipLoader class. Any events encountered by the mcLoader object are dispatched to the mcOnLoadHandler object. This connection is made by using the addListener method (discussed in Chapter 4). The MovieClipLoader class works well with images, and the example code here can be extended easily using the methods and events described in Chapter 8.

At any time you can redefine the listener, target movie clip, and listener object for optimum reuse. You just have to remember that the class works only with Flash 7 or newer.

Managing Sound

Sound, especially music, is probably one of the most coveted formats on the Web. It has spawned an entire industry of digital music sales, devices, and software.

ActionScript contains an easy-to-use sound object, which you can use to coincide with user interface functionality or to play files outright.

You can import sound directly onto a timeline in Flash, but that is limited and difficult to control once published. With the sound object, you have full control.

The sound object can obtain sound for playback in two ways: the sound can exist in the library, or the sound can be imported at runtime as an MP3. You can load an MP3 file from any domain without restriction.

Sound Class Methods

The following table describes the sound class's methods:

Method	Return	Description
loadSound()	Nothing	Loads an MP3 file into the sound object.
getBytesLoaded()	Number	Returns the bytes loaded.
getBytesTotal()	Number	Returns the size, in bytes, of the specified sound object.

Method	Return	Description
setVolume()	Nothing	Sets the volume of the sound object. It has one parameter, which is an integer.
setTransform()	Nothing	Sets the transformation information for the sound object. Contains four properties to set values: ll, lr, rr, rl. Used to mix the two stereo channels to varying degrees.
setPan()	Nothing	An integer of –100 through 100 sets the sound object to the left and right channels.
attachSound()	Nothing	Loads a library sound instance.
start()	Nothing	Begins the sound playing at a specified index in seconds and can control the number of times the sound is repeated.
stop()	Nothing	Stops all sounds if no parameter is specified in the constructor, otherwise it stops the sound loaded into the sound object.
getVolume()	Number	Returns a number representing the current volume of the sound object.
getTransform()	Object	Returns the transform state of the current object as an object.
getPan()	Nothing	Returns the current left-to-right balance as an integer from –100 to 100.

Following is some additional information about some of the methods.

The loadSound() method has two parameters: a String URL representing an MP3 file and a Boolean that determines whether the file should start playing as soon as there is enough information to begin playing the file, or whether the object should wait until the entire sound file is completely loaded. Here's the syntax:

```
Sound.loadSound(URL:String,isStreaming:Boolean);
```

The setVolume() method has a single parameter, a Number from 0 to 100, that sets the volume level of the sound object. Its syntax is as follows:

```
Sound.setVolume(n:Number);
```

The setTransform() method has one parameter, which must be an object. Here's the syntax:

```
Sound.setTransform(SoundTransform:Object);
```

And here is an example transform object that contains the required values:

```
var SoundTransform:Object = new Object();
  SoundTransform.ll = 50;
  SoundTransform.lr = 50;
  SoundTransform.rr = 50;
  SoundTransform.rl = 50;
```

The setPan() method has one parameter, which must be a Number from -100 to 100. For example, passing a value of -100 sends all sound to the left channel. Following is the method's syntax:

```
Sound.setPan(n:Number);
```

The attachSound() method can load only sounds that exist within the library. It has one parameter, a String representing the ID of the sound you want to play:

```
Sound.attachSound("song1":String);
```

The start() method has two parameters. The first parameter must be a Number. The default of the first parameter is zero. This parameter represents the index at which you want to begin playing the file. The second parameter is also a Number and determines the amount of times you want the file to loop. The default value of the second parameter is also zero, which means the file will play only once if this parameter is not set.

```
Sound.Start(SecondsIn:Number,Loops:Number);
```

Sound Class Events and Properties

Here are descriptions of the sound class's events:

Event	Type	Description
onID3	Function	Fires when the sound object has detected id3 tags for an MP3.
onLoad	Function	Fires when a sound file has fully loaded into the sound object.
onSoundComplete	Function	Fires when a sound has finished playing.

The sound class has three properties, which are explained in the following table:

Event	Type	Description
Duration	Number	Total sound time in milliseconds.
Position	Number	Current playhead position in milliseconds.
Id3	Object	An object that contains name/value pairs of the available id3 information.

Creating a Sound Object

The sound object can do more than just play back sound. The constructor has a few tricks up its sleeve. These tricks are mostly used to control sound objects that exist within movie clips and your SWF file as a whole. For example, you can control the volume of all sounds in the SWF by creating a sound object with no parameters:

```
var All_sounds:Sound = new Sound();
All_sounds.setVolume(50);
```

Alternatively, you can control the sound objects within a specific movie clip by passing the clip as a parameter. Here's an example in which only the sounds in the specified movie clip are affected:

```
var some_sounds:Sound = new Sound(myMovieClip_mc);
some_sounds.setVolume(50);
```

If you use the `loadSound` or `attachSound` method on the object, all manipulation of the sound occurs only on that specific instance of sound rather than on sounds existing in a movieClip object.

Loading Library Sounds

Loading library sounds is simple. First you import a sound object to the library by selecting File➪ Import➪Import to Library. In the file browser dialog, select a valid sound file.

After you can see the sound file in the library, Alt+click the file and select Linkage. Select the Export for ActionScript option in the dialog that opens and give the sound a linkage ID.

ActionScript can now access the sound.

Try It Out   Playing a Simple Sound Object

Before you do this exercise, import a sound into the library. In this exercise, you create a simple object to present your sound from the library.

Obviously, your computer needs speakers. When testing sound in Flash, remember to check your system volume settings to ensure that your computer can play the sound. You don't want to be debugging a sound object problem with the mute button on.

1. Open a new Flash document and save it as `SoundTest.fla` in your work folder.

2. Click the first frame in the timeline, open the Actions panel, and type the following ActionScript code:

```
var testSound = new Sound();
testSound.attachSound("song1");
testSound.start(30);
```

Be sure the Linkage ID you set in the library for the sound object is what appears as the String parameter of the `attachSound` method.

3. Test the SWF by pressing Ctrl+Enter. You should hear your library sound now playing, and it begins at the seconds specified in the `start` parameter.

How It Works

In this example you created a simple sound object via the new Sound constructor. You left the target parameter of the new Sound constructor blank, so the sound will play independently of any sound objects in other movie clips.

You then used the `attachSound` method, which specifically targets the library. You passed the `attachSound` method with a String name of the library ID of the sound file.

Finally, you used the `start` method to begin playing the sound, passing in a parameter that offset it by 30 seconds to illustrate that you can begin a sound file at an arbitrary position. (If your test sound isn't very long, try offsetting it by just 3 or 4 seconds.)

Loading External MP3 Files

Loading external MP3 files is as simple as loading library sounds. Instead of using `attachMovie`, you use `loadSound`, which uses two parameters. The first targets the URL of the MP3 file, and can be the relative path of a local file if the SWF is running locally. The second parameter determines whether the file should begin playing as soon as enough data exists to play sound, or whether the sound object should wait until the entire sound is loaded before beginning to play the sound. The latter is called an *event sound*, and there are times when this type of sound is preferred. Event sounds are covered later in this section.

Using ID3 Tags

ID3 tags contain information about the MP3 file being played. The information can contain comments, artist name, track name, and more.

ID3 tags are accessed using the `onID3` event in conjunction with polling the `id3` property of the sound object. Two types of ID3 tags exist: V2.4 and 1.0. Flash 7 and 8 player supports both, and Flash 6 player supports ID3 1.0 only.

There is a very good reason to upgrade MP3 files that you will use in your SWF to ID3 Version 2. Version 2 tags are available as soon as the MP3 file begins to stream. Version 1 tags are only available at the end of the MP3 file, and so the entire MP3 must load before you can display these tags. So it's better from a user interface standpoint to make sure your MP3 files utilize the ID3 V2 tags.

You can in fact have both types of tags in your MP3 file. Be aware that the `onID3` event will fire when it finds each tag. So if your MP3 file contains two sets of tags, you can expect to be required to handle a second event, and verify the information, or ignore one set of ID3 tags.

If the ID3 tags are not populated within the MP3, the id3 object will return undefined on all tags.

Available Properties in the V2 Tags

Here are descriptions of the available V2 tag properties:

ID3 PROPERTY	DESCRIPTION
TIME	Time
TIT1	Content description
TIT2	Title, song name, content description
TIT3	Subtitle, extended information
TFLT	File type
TOFN	Filename when the MP3 was created
TOLY	Lyricists, text writers
TOPE	Artists, performers
TORY	Year of release
TPE1	Lead performers, singer
TPE2	Band, orchestra, accompaniment
TPE3	Conductor, performer, extended information
TPE4	Remake, Cover, or Remix declaration
TPOS	Part of a set
TOWN	File owner, licensee, copyright holder
TPUB	Publisher
TRCK	Track number/position in set
TRDA	Recording dates
TRSN	Internet radio station name
TRSO	Internet radio station owner
TOAL	Original album/movie/show title
TSIZ	Size
TSRC	ISRC (international standard recording code)
TSSE	Settings used for encoding
TYER	Year
WXXX	URL link
TKEY	Initial key
TLAN	Languages
TMED	Media type
TLEN	Length

Streaming MP3 Audio

Streaming audio is a useful capability in Flash. Because Flash doesn't need very much data to play sound, and because of the ubiquity of broadband, you can allow users to begin listening to audio content almost immediately without making them suffer through loading screens and pre-loaders.

Sometimes a file won't load fast enough, and in those cases Flash may pause playing the audio. When sufficient bytes are received, the audio automatically resumes playing without intervention. Because of this, it's always wise to monitor the load state of the MP3 file, as well as the current play position.

Starting, Stopping, and Tracking Sound

As good as it is, the sound object is a bit inconstant. For example, the `duration` and `position` properties return millisecond positions, but the `start` method accepts a parameter in seconds, not milliseconds.

When you pause a sound object, you must record the current sound position so that when you call the `start` method you can resume the sound where you left off. You do this by querying the `position` property and recording it so that you can insert the value into the `start` method call when you resume playing. Because of the measurement increment inconsistency, you must divide the milliseconds by 1000 to obtain the seconds value of the current position at which the file should start playing.

To determine the percentage of file played, so that the SWF can display a progress bar, you can divide `position` by `duration` to obtain the current percentage of file played. If your progress bar has a maximum width of 200 pixels, you would multiply the percentage played by this width.

Try It Out   Playing and Controlling Sound Objects

For this exercise, you need to place an MP3 file in your work folder. It can be any MP3 file. Use one with known ID3 V2 tags, so you can use it as is. You can add and convert ID3 tags in just about any modern audio player such as Real, iTunes, and Winamp.

1. Open a new FLA and save it as `playSound.fla` in your work folder.

2. Click the first frame in the timeline, open the Actions panel, and type in the following ActionScript, changing the URL of the MP3 to match the MP3 you are using:

```
var mySound:Sound = new Sound();
mySound.onID3 = function(){
    for(var i in this.id3){
        trace(i+": "+this.id3[i]);
    }
}
mySound.loadSound("myMp3.mp3", true);
```

3. Test the code by pressing Ctrl+Enter. You should hear the MP3 now playing. If the MP3 file has Id3 tags, they are now listed in the output panel.

4. Go back and add some controls for your file. You'll be using component buttons, so open the Components panel and expand the User Interface section.

5. Drag a Button component onto the stage. Place it somewhere near the center of the stage.

6. Name the instance of this component button `playButton` in the Properties panel. In the Parameters tab in the Properties panel change the label to `Play`.

7. Drag another button onto the stage. Place it next to the Play button.

8. Name the instance of this component button `stopButton` in the Properties panel. In the Parameters tab in the Properties panel change the label to `Stop`.

9. Drag another button onto the stage. Place it next to the Stop button.

10. Name the instance of this component button `rewindButton` in the Properties panel. In the Parameters tab in the Properties panel change the label to `Rewind`. You can align all of the buttons and resize them to suit.

11. Now add a little bit of ActionScript. First, modify the existing code on your timeline with a `stop` action so that your sound does not start playing by itself. Do this by adding the following line below the existing code:

```
mySound.stop();
```

12. Now add actions to the buttons on your stage so you can control the MP3 you just loaded, by entering the following code below the existing code:

```
var pos:Number = 0;
playButton.onRelease = function() {
    mySound.start(pos/1000);
    rewindButton.enabled = true;
    stopButton.enabled = true;
    this.enabled = false;
};
playButton.enabled = true;
stopButton.onRelease = function() {
    pos = mySound.position;
    mySound.stop();
    playButton.enabled = true;
    this.enabled = false;
};
stopButton.enabled = false;
rewindButton.onRelease = function(){
    mySound.start();
    playButton.enabled = false;
    stopButton.enabled = true;
}
rewindButton.enabled = false;
```

13. Add an `onSoundComplete` event to your sound object so that you can reset the buttons when the sound has stopped playing. Just before the `loadSound` method, insert the following code:

```
mySound.onSoundComplete = function(){
    pos = 0;
    rewindButton.enabled = false;
    playButton.enabled = true;
    stopButton.enabled = false;
}
```

14. Test the code by pressing Ctrl+Enter. You won't hear the MP3 playing right away as it did in step 3. Your MP3 is loading in the background. Click the Play button to start the sound playing. Click the Stop and Rewind buttons to make sure they are working.

How It Works

In this example, you saw how, with very little code, to create a functional music player.

You started by constructing a sound object. You then created an `onID3` event to check whether the MP3 had information, although you did not display this information in your user interface. You do that in the next Try It Out.

You began to load the sound via the `loadSound` method, specifying the URL of the MP3 file to play. You also set the sound object type to streaming so that the MP3 file is available to play almost immediately. You'll want to add some indication of download status to complete this project, and you do that in the next Try It Out.

After you began to load the file, you immediately called the `stop` method on your sound object. This stopped the sound object from automatically playing on its own. You could remove this to change the default behavior.

You defined your controls with simple `onRelease` events on each component button you added to the stage.

You also kept an index value called `pos`, which holds the current position so that when you click Stop, you can store the value for when the `start` method begins playing the track again. Otherwise, your Play button would always play the song from the beginning of the track.

You also saw that you needed to divide the `pos` value by 1000 to compensate for the value increment difference between the `position` property and the `start` method of the sound object.

Each button was given a toggle to enable and disable it, depending on the current state of the sound object. You used the `enabled` property of the button component to gray out buttons that can't be used during different states of the sound object.

Because your buttons have toggles that control their state, and because you are tracking the current position if the user clicks the Stop button, you need to reset the `pos` value as well as change the button states back to the original non-playing state. You did that by utilizing the `onSoundComplete` event, which fires as soon as the track has finished playing.

The next bit of code set the Rewind button's actions, which automatically begins playing the song at the beginning of the track. You called almost the same exact code as you did in the Play button, except the `start` parameter is set to 0, so the track plays from the very beginning. You could have left this parameter blank because it defaults to 0. However, you might want to change the parameter to something like `(pos-10)/1000`, which would rewind and play the track 10 seconds before the current position.

Event Sounds

Event sounds are useful when you need sounds to coincide with interface activity or code functions. Event sounds cannot play until they are fully loaded. Event and streaming sounds both are loaded into the browser cache.

Event sounds and the `start` method act differently. When you call the `start` method on a streaming sound, the sound object clears any playing sound within it and starts the track over at the position specified in the parameter of the `start` method. With event sounds, when you call the `start` method, the sound is played again, even if it's already playing. The sound playing from a previous `start` method call is layered on top, and you hear an echo, or two, or three instances of the sound playing depending on how many times you call `start`. This can be useful for looping or creating mixers.

Controlling Volume, setPan, and setTransform

You can control some aspects of sound dimensionality. You can control right and left channels, stereo to mono, as well as how much mixing between the two channels occurs. This enables you to make right-to-left specific sound changes that match user interface changes. Of course, games benefit greatly from these properties, but a general user interface can also take advantage of the fun.

Volume

Volume is controlled with two methods: `setVolume` and `getVolume`.

Use `setVolume` when you want to enact a change on the overall volume of the sound object it's called on. The method accepts an integer from `0` to `100`.

`getVolume` returns the current volume, which is helpful for decreasing or increasing volume using volume fade-in and fade-out techniques. You can also set a volume control in the user interface to match the current volume of the object it's controlling.

Pan

`setPan` enables you to move the sound from the left speaker to the right speaker. This is especially useful in games and other situations where spatial effects using sounds are warranted. `getPan` can be used for algorithms that automatically fade the sounds from left to right. You can also use it to set a user interface control to the current pan position of the object it's controlling.

Transform

`setTransform` is a bit more complex, enabling you to mix the left and right channels. You can move a specified amount of sound in the right channel into the left channel fractionally. You can manipulate four properties:

❑ `ll` — Specifies how much of the left channel of the sound object to play in the left speaker.

❑ `lr` — Specifies how much of the right channel of the sound object to play in the left speaker.

❑ `rr` — Specifies how much of the right channel of the sound object to play in the right speaker.

❑ `rl` — Specifies how much of the left channel of the sound object to play in the right speaker.

`setTransform` can be highly effective in animation and games that can be enhanced with spatial sound effects using multiple sound objects, each with its own `setTransform` sound balance. It can help set a user interface control, or initialize a user interface control with the default values. It is also helpful in transferring a sound effect to the same balance. For example, suppose you have a game in which a spaceship has channel-enhanced sound effects for its engines, using `setTransform`, and you want that spaceship to have a weapons sound effect to match the position of the ship's engine sound effect. Using the x and y positions of the spaceship, you can automatically set the sound transform matrix for the spaceship, to which all sound effects for that object conform.

These are your sound modification methods. Although trim, they can be a robust set of methods for creating engaging sound effects that excite the user, rather than simply play sound with its original balance.

When you add sound to an application, such as a game or a simple Web form, be aware of how the user might react to the sound, and what the sound relates to visually. A strange or out-of-place sound effect can be jarring and confusing for the user.

Try It Out   Creating a Simple Audio Interface

For this example you'll want a few MP3 files ready to go. You use the sound object's methods and properties to create a simple MP3 player with components. Of course, you don't need to use components, but using them quickly shows you how the sound object behaves. This is a long example; save your FLA often during the instructions so that you do not lose your work.

1. Open a new FLA and save it as `musicPlayer.fla` in your work folder.

2. Click the first frame in the timeline, open the Actions panel, and type in the following ActionScript. Change the `trackPath` to match the location of your MP3 files and change the `trackListArray` to the names of your MP3 files:

```
trackPath = "tracks/";
trackListArray = ["song1.mp3", "song2.mp3", "song3.mp3", "song4.mp3"];
```

3. Expand the User Interface section of the Components panel and drag an instance of the Menu component to the stage. Then delete the stage instance, because the object is now in the library.

4. Go back to the Actions panel and type in the following ActionScript code:

```
//Create Menu:
var songMenu = mx.controls.Menu.createMenu();
//add each song to the list:
for (var i = 0; i<trackListArray.length; i++) {
    songMenu.addMenuItem({type:"check", label:trackListArray[i]});
}
//listen for a selection:
var songSelection = new Object();
songSelection.change = function(event) {
    nextTrack(event.menuItem, this);
};
songMenu.addEventListener("change", songSelection);
```

5. Notice the code you just wrote queries the function `nextTrack`. You create this function by adding the following ActionScript code:

```
nextTrack = function (item, obj) {
    loadSoundFile(trackPath+item.attributes.label);
    songMenu.setMenuItemSelected(obj.lastSelected, false);
    songMenu.setMenuItemSelected(item, true);
    obj.lastSelected = item;
    obj.currentIndex = songMenu.indexOf(item);
};
```

6. Expand the User Interface section of the Components panel and drag an instance of the numericStepper component to the stage. Place it where you want; you'll be organizing the interface when you have more components on the screen.

7. Select the numericStepper component you just added to the stage and change the height to 22 and the width to 48 in the Properties panel. Give the component an instance name of `myVolume`. In the Parameters tab, change the maximum value to `100` and the minimum to `0`. Be sure the stepSize is `1`. You can make the default value `100`.

8. Add some ActionScript to work with the numericStepper you just added to the stage by adding the following code below the code you entered in step 5:

```
//Add Volume control
vol = new Object();
//Listen for a change:
vol.change = function(eventObj) {
    mySound.setVolume(eventObj.target.value);
};
myVolume.addEventListener("change", vol);
```

9. You can see the numericStepper component calls an object called mySound. This is a sound object. Add a function that creates and defines this sound object by typing the following code below the code you entered in step 8:

```
//Create Sound Object
initSound = function () {
    mySound = new Sound();
    mySound.onID3 = function() {
        for (var i in this.id3) {
            if (i == "artist") {
                var artist:String = this.id3[i];
            } else if (i == "songname") {
                var songName:String = this.id3[i];
            }
        }
        trackInfo.text = artist+" <b>>>></b> "+songName;
    };
    mySound.onSoundComplete = function() {
        rewindButton.enabled = false;
        playButton.enabled = true;
        stopButton.enabled = false;
        clearInterval(progressWatch);
        if (songSelection.currentIndex == trackListArray.length-1) {
            songSelection.currentIndex = 0;
        } else {
            songSelection.currentIndex++;
        }
```

```
            trace(songSelection.currentIndex);
            var item = songMenu.getMenuItemAt(songSelection.currentIndex);
            nextTrack(item, songSelection);
        };
    };
    initSound();
```

10. The code you just added accesses many objects you haven't defined yet. Start adding them to the stage now. Expand the User Interface section of the Components panel and drag an instance of the ProgressBar component to the bottom left of the stage. Select the component and give it an instance name of `loadStatus`.

11. Go back to the ActionScript you've been working on and add the following code:

```
loadStatus.mode = "manual";
loadProgress = function () {
    loadStatus.setProgress(mySound.getBytesLoaded(), mySound.getBytesTotal());
    if (loadStatus.percentComplete == 100) {
        clearInterval(loadWatch);
    }
};:
```

12. Now you need to create a function that will load the sound. You could call your sound object directly, but you want more than one way to load sounds. Because you'll be loading sounds automatically as tracks are finished, and via user interaction, you can create one function to handle both by adding the following ActionScript to the existing ActionScript in frame 1:

```
function loadSoundFile(fileURL) {
    initSound();
    loadWatch = setInterval(this, "loadProgress", 10);
    mySound.loadSound(fileURL, true);
    playButton.onRelease();
}
```

13. Expand the User Interface section of the Components panel and drag an instance of the ProgressBar component to the top left of the stage. Select the component and give it an instance name of `soundIndex`. Change the width of the component to `350`. Also, you won't need the text. In the Parameters tab, make the label value blank.

14. Add some ActionScript to your existing ActionScript in frame 1 to control the soundIndex component:

```
soundIndex.mode = "manual";
progress = function () {
    soundIndex.setProgress(mySound.position, mySound.duration);
};
```

15. Now add a place to display track information. In step 9, you wrote some code that defined the `onID3` event of your sound object. Within that function it calls for a text field named `trackInfo` to accept text. Expand the User Interface section of the Components panel and drag an instance of the TextArea component directly beneath the soundIndex ProgressBar component.

16. In the Properties panel for the TextArea component, change the name to `trackInfo`. Change the height of the component to `30`. Change the width to `350`. In the Parameters tab, be sure the `html` value is `true`. In the Parameters tab change the text value to `Select a track!`.

17. Remember the menu you created in step 4? Add a button to show and hide it now. Expand the User Interface section of the Components panel and drag an instance of the Button component to the stage. Place it just underneath the TextArea component you added in step 15. Place it to the far right, so you have room to the left it for more buttons. In the Button component's Properties panel, rename the button to `tracksButton`. Change the width to `50` and change the height to `22`.

18. Tell the `trackButton` what to control by adding the following code below the existing code in the ActionScript in frame 1:

```
tracksButton.onRelease = function() {
    songMenu.show(this.x + this._width - songMenu._width, this.y+this.height);
};
```

19. Next, add play, stop, and rewind buttons. Expand the User Interface section of the Components panel and drag three instances of the Button component to the stage. Place them underneath the TextArea component you placed on the stage in step 16. Align them to the left side, placing each side by side.

20. Working with the component buttons you just added, select the left button. In the Properties panel, change the name to `playButton`. Change the height to `22` and the width to `50`. In the Parameters tab, change the label to `Play`.

21. Now select the middle button and, in the Properties panel, change the name to `stopButton`. Change the height to `22` and the width to `50`. In the Parameters tab, change the label to `Stop`.

22. Now select the button on the right. In the Properties panel, change the name to `rewindButton`. Change the height to `22` and the width to `75`. In the Parameters tab, change the label to `Rewind`.

23. Move the UI elements on the stage to suit. Organize the user interface so that the controls appear logical and in place. Now add some code to tell your buttons what to do when they are clicked, as well as how to behave when the application loads by adding the following ActionScript to frame 1 below your existing code:

```
playButton.onRelease = function() {
    mySound.start(pos/1000);
    rewindButton.enabled = true;
    stopButton.enabled = true;
    this.enabled = false;
    progressWatch = setInterval(_root, "progress", 10);
    mySound.setVolume(myVolume.value);
};
playButton.enabled = false;
stopButton.onRelease = function() {
    pos = mySound.position;
    mySound.stop();
    playButton.enabled = true;
    this.enabled = false;
    clearInterval(progressWatch);
};
stopButton.enabled = false;
```

```
rewindButton.onRelease = function() {
    mySound.start();
    playButton.enabled = false;
    stopButton.enabled = true;
    clearinterval(progressWatch);
    progressWatch = setInterval(_root, "progress", 10);
};
rewindButton.enabled = false;
```

24. Save the file as `musicPlayer.fla`.

25. Be sure the path and filename list in step 2 are correct. Test your SWF by pressing Ctrl+Enter. If you encounter a security alert, you'll need to change your default setting to "always" when it prompts you so to view your settings.

26. Once you have verified step 25, you can test, and click a few of the UI buttons. Try changing the volume and adding different tracks. Allow a track to play and watch the next track load automatically. You can do what you want with the user interface look and feel, including adding a background.

How It Works

This was a lengthy example, but all in all, it was fairly small for a functioning MP3 player with quite a bit of interface controls.

In step 2 you described where the application could find the sound files. You also defined the names of the sound files in an array. An array is handy because you can flip through an array based on index number. This comes in handy later when you flip to the next track automatically.

In steps 3 and 4 you added a menu and populated it with the array of filenames. You also defined the event that loaded each file as they are selected by a user.

In step 5 you added a function that handles the automation of moving through your playlist. Once a song is done, you call this function, which stores what the current track index is, and adjusts the menu component to place a checkmark next to the currently playing track.

In steps 6, 7, and 8 you added a numeric stepper to your interface. Although not the most elegant solution to control this property, it takes up very little room, and it is easy to understand how the `setVolume` method works. As the value changes via user interaction, the volume of the sound object is changed to reflect the current desired value. This value is also queried when the sound initially loads so that it plays at the proper volume indicated in the user interface.

In step 9 you initialized your sound object and defined the `onSoundComplete` and `onID3` events. The `onID3` event changes the TextArea component to display the name of the artist and song, using the `id3` property of the sound object. The `onSoundComplete` event defines how the interface should change. It defines which buttons should be enabled and which should not be enabled. The `onSoundComplete` event also calls the `nextTrack` method you defined in step 5. So you can see as soon as a song is done the interface begins loading the next file.

In steps 10 and 11 you created a loading progress bar that shows the user the percentage of bytes loaded of the selected file. This is handy because it can help to explain to users why a track isn't playable yet, or that the download speed is fast enough to play without skipping. You use the sound object's `getBytesLoaded` and `getBytesTotal` methods to indicate the current values.

In step 12 you defined a `loadSoundFile` method. Although you could call the `loadSound` method directly, you need to change some user interface values as well as reinitialize the sound object so that the `getBytesLoaded`, `duration`, and `position` values return correctly. Without reinitializing them, the sound object will add the values to the existing values, rather than start from scratch.

In steps 13 and 14 you added a ProgressBar component to give the user interface an indication of the current position of the playhead. You use the position and duration properties of the sound object to calculate a percentage of time.

In steps 15 and 16 you added the TextArea component below the ProgressBar component. This is used to show the user information about the MP3 file being played.

In steps 17 and 18 you added a button to simply show and hide the Menu component you added in step 3. Pressing this button allows the user to select a track or view the name of the file currently playing.

The rest of the example adds the controls that change the state of the currently loaded sound. You have a play, stop, and rewind button. Each has a different default state when a track is and isn't playing. Each change the states of the other buttons based on the current state of the sound object. You do this by utilizing the enabled method of the Button component. The `loadSoundFile` method utilizes and calls the `onRelease` method of the play button to make sure the interface is in the proper condition to play a file.

The play button's `onRelease` action also starts the interval that changes the `soundIndex` values so that it reflects the proper position. Likewise, the stop button stops this loop and stops the sound playing. The rewind button can restart the loop, but starts the sound at the beginning of the track.

That's basically it. Hopefully this showed you how fast and easy it is to create a sound control interface to any application. Obviously you didn't need to use components, but you can see how much time and coding it saved you, and allowed you to concentrate on looking at and controlling the sound object.

Working with the Microphone

The microphone object was introduced in Flash 6. It is mostly used with Flash Communication Server to create chat programs and other applications requiring voice. However, you can do some nifty things with the microphone with just a little bit of simple ActionScript.

You can use the microphone to detect sound activity over a specified silence level. You can also set up listeners to discern the amount of activity and to act upon it. You can think of this as similar to the `onActivity` events you find in security cameras and webcams, except now for sound. There are fun ways to use the microphone to enact changes in your application, but of course, you need a microphone that is functioning on your computer to try them out.

One thing to remember when working with the microphone is that the Flash Player will prompt the user to allow or deny your application access to the microphone.

Microphone Class Methods

The following table describes the methods of the microphone class:

Method	Return	Description
get()	Microphone	Static method returns a reference to a microphone on the system.
setGain()	Nothing	Sets the amount the microphone input should be boosted before being read into the microphone object.
setRate()	Nothing	Sets the rate at which the microphone should capture sound.
setSilenceLevel()	Nothing	Sets the threshold of activity on the microphone that should be considered sound, as well when the microphone should time out.
setUseEchoSuppression()	Nothing	A method for reducing feedback and echo. Sometimes causes unwanted clipping of the microphone signal.

The get() method has one parameter, a Number (the default parameter is 0). It is a static method that returns a reference to a microphone on the system. Sending no parameter returns the first microphone detected. You can use the names array property to obtain a list and request a specific microphone at a specific array index. get() is almost always used with the attachAudio method upon a netStream or movieClip object. Here's its syntax:

```
var myMic_mic:Microphone = Microphone.get();
```

The setGain() method takes a single parameter, a Number from 0 to 100. The number sets the boost level of the microphone before it is sent to the microphone object. Here's the syntax:

```
var myMic_mic.setGain(55);
```

Setting setGain to 0 mutes the user's microphone, although the user can override this value. You can set a watch object to change it back. This is useful for conference applications where only one participant can be speaking.

Microphone Class Properties and Events

The following table describes the microphone class's properties:

Property	Type	Description
activityLevel	Number	A Number from 0 to 100 measuring the sound being detected.
gain	Number	The amount by which the signal is being boosted before being sent to the microphone object.

Property	Type	Description
index	Number	A Number representing the index of the current microphone in the list of microphones available on the system.
muted	Boolean	Returns true if the user has denied access to the microphone.
name	String	The name of the current microphone.
names	Array	An array of names of the microphones available on the system.
rate	Number	The kHz rate at which the microphone is capturing sound.
silenceLevel	Number	The activity threshold at which the microphone begins to accept input.
silenceTimeOut	Number	The amount of time to wait before onActivity is called with a false parameter value after silence is detected.
useEchoSuppression	Boolean	Returns true if echo suppression is enabled.

The microphone class has two events, which are explained in the following table:

Event	Type	Description
onActivity	Function	Fires when the microphone detects activity, and detects silence.
onStatus	Function	Fires when the user allows or denies access to the microphone.

Try It Out   Creating a Microphone Object

1. Open a new FLA and save it as `microphone.fla` in your work folder.

2. Click the first frame in the timeline, open the Actions panel, and type in the following ActionScript code:

```
this.createEmptyMovieClip("microphone_mc", this.getNextHighestDepth());
var myMic_mic:Microphone = Microphone.get();
microphone_mc.attachAudio(myMic_mic);
```

3. Test your code by pressing Ctrl+Enter.

How It Works

In this example you have no visual indicator that the microphone is working, but if you have speakers on your computer, you should be able to hear sound being passed into the microphone. Unfortunately you can't do much with the sound without Flash Communication Server except track activity, `onStatus`, `onActivity`, and other methods that can enable you to fire events based on activity level on the microphone.

In the next Try It Out, you expand on this one and also do something a bit fun with the activity level to see how you can use the microphone to affect an application.

Microphone Activity

One of the neatest features of the microphone object is the activity level. Using the `activityLevel` property enables you to make user interface changes based on sound input. You can, for instance, call functions based on particular microphone levels. For example, you might want to fire an event that shuts down a screen saver on a kiosk when the noise level reaches a particular value. By using the microphone as a user input method, you can add dimension and responsiveness to your applications in ways you might not have thought possible.

Trying It Out   **Measuring Activity, Listening**

You use the FLA from the preceding Try It Out for this exercise. If you haven't completed that, you should do so now.

1. Open the `microphone.fla` in your work folder.

2. Click the first frame in the timeline, open the Actions panel, and type in the following ActionScript code:

```
this.createEmptyMovieClip("microphone_mc", this.getNextHighestDepth());
var myMic_mic:Microphone = Microphone.get();
myMic_mic.setUseEchoSuppression(true);
microphone_mc.attachAudio(myMic_mic);
```

3. Expand the User Interface section of the Components panel and drag an instance of the ProgressBar component onto the stage.

4. Select the ProgressBar component on the stage and, in the Properties panel, give the instance the name `level`. In the Parameters tab, change the label string to `Mic Activity: %3%%` or whatever you want, but you must include the `%3%` to display the numeric value.

5. Go back to the first frame actions in the Actions panel and add the following code:

```
level.mode = "manual";
micLevel = function (callback) {
        level.setProgress(myMic_mic.activityLevel, 100);
};
this.listen = setInterval(this, "micLevel", 10);
```

6. Test your code by pressing Ctrl+Enter. You should now see an indication of microphone activity in the ProgressBar component.

7. Close the SWF and go back to the actions in frame 1. Now do something fun with the value. Change the `micLevel` function to look like this:

```
micLevel = function (callback) {
    level.setProgress(myMic_mic.activityLevel, 100);
    if (myMic_mic.activityLevel>=90&& spike == false) {
        trace("begin detect");
        spike = true;
        spikeTime = getTimer();
    }
    if (spike == true) {
        if (myMic_mic.activityLevel<65) {
            var duration = getTimer()-spikeTime;
            if (duration<130) {
                var doubleClap = spikeTime-firstClap;
                if (doubleClap<600 && doubleClap > 300) {
                    callback();
                } else {
                    firstClap = spikeTime;
                }
            }
            spike = false;
            spikeLength = 0;
        }
    }
};
```

8. You need to initialize some variables before starting the function, so add these declarations before the `setInterval` declaration:

```
var spike:Boolean = false;
var spikeTime:Number = 0;
var firstClap:Number = 0;
```

9. Now you need to define the `clapper.onClap` object and to modify the `setInterval` function and add the object and function as parameters:

```
var clapper:Object = {};
clapper.onClap= function() {
    trace("detected input");
};
this.listen = setInterval(this, "micLevel", 10, clapper.onClap);
```

10. Press Ctrl+Enter. With the SWF running, verify the microphone is working by looking at the ProgressBar component. Clap your hands twice, with just a slight pause between claps. You should see that two claps more often than not fires the `onClap` function.

How It Works

In this example you set up an interval to watch the activity level of the microphone via the `activityLevel` property. You also tracked activity to enact changes in the code behavior based on the value, and added the `setUseEchoSuppression` method to keep the microphone from echoing excessively.

While you listened to activity on the microphone, you set up the `micLevel` function to look for spikes in activity. `activityLevel` reports values from 0 to 100. In the function you wait for the activity to reach 98 or higher. This means a loud input occurred on the microphone.

When you track a loud input you see how long it lasts by using the `getTimer` method. It returns the number of milliseconds that the SWF has been running. Once the activity of the microphone drops below 65, the function assumes that the loud noise has ended. If the length for which the microphone sustained a 98 or higher activity level is less than 130 milliseconds, you assume the microphone received a spike, or a very fast sharp sound has occurred. In this way you can determine with some degree of certainty that you should listen for a second spike. If two of these spikes are detected and the second occurs with 600 milliseconds of the first, you determine that a double spike has taken place. Because double spikes can happen with natural background noise, you also look for the spikes to be at least 300 ms apart. By narrowing the acceptable double spike to just 300 ms of variation, you can focus on a very specific—like a manmade sound.

If your function decides it's heard a double spike, it triggers the callback function specified in the parameter of `setInterval`.

This example is easy to fool and does make some mistakes, triggering the callback function by accident, or seemingly not responding sometimes. However, it shows you that with just rudimentary scripting you can begin to listen for specific microphone activity occurrences. You might think of more sophisticated ways of listening to the activity level of the microphone to determine purposeful audio input.

netStream

In the examples you attach the audio from the microphone to a movie clip. If you are using Flash Communication Server, you will want to attach the audio to a netStream object. For Flash to save, capture, or transmit microphone audio, you must use Flash Communication Server. You can, if you want, use netStream without Flash Communication Server by attaching the audio to a null netStream, but this doesn't buy you anything in terms of capability. To do it requires a few more lines of ActionScript:

```
var aNetConnection_nc:NetConnection = new NetConnection();
aNetConnection_nc.connect(null);
var aStream_ns:NetStream = new NetStream(aNetConnection_nc);
var myMic_mic:Microphone = Microphone.get();
myMic_mic.setUseEchoSuppression(true);
aStream_ns.attachAudio(myMic_mic);
```

Summary

This chapter described different media types you can load into Flash. You were introduced to image loading, sound playback and manipulation, and microphone input. You loaded images and sound while maintaining a concern for bandwidth, preloading, and performance.

As you went through the chapter, you created some practical examples that used each object, and considered the many issues involved with each. In the microphone object example, you explored ways to take it to a next step by enhancing the user interface to accept alternate forms of user input. Even without Flash Communication Server, you discovered a way to use a microphone dynamically.

Hopefully this chapter got you thinking of using Flash in new ways. The objects covered are a major part of Flash development, and are often the reason Flash is chosen over other platforms for a specific application. The capability to load and coordinate many different media types into a one seamless application is what differentiates Flash from other technologies.

Exercises

1. Use the MovieClipLoader class in a movie clip to create a rollover button. Utilize the PNG image files.

2. Using the sound object, load an MP3 file. Use the position value to fire events exactly when specific flourishes or events occur within the MP3 file. You'll need an interval and the `getTimer` method to accomplish the solution.

3. Using the microphone object, fire an event that changes a message on the screen when only a small amount of activity lasts for more than one minute.

Managing Video

One of the most exciting technologies Flash provides is the capability to import and modify video on-the-fly. Flash 8 provides a whole set of new tools to work with and to enhance the video experience in Flash.

Flash 8 uses the On2 codec. Although Flash 8 can still play the Spark codec used in Flash 6 and 7, the new codec solves issues Flash 6 and 7 had on OSX, as well as provides a complement of capabilities and clarity previous Flash video did not have.

You can deliver your video as an FLV file (Flash video) or SWF file (Flash movie). Having the video defined as SWF limits you to transmitting data to just HTTP. This is often referred to as *progressive video*. The video is downloaded to the user's cache and is played as frames arrive. With FLV, you can also transport the video over HTTP, but you can use Flash Communication Server to provide the file as a true streaming media. Packaging the video as SWF enables you to use normal movie clip controls to control the clip. Because movie clips are limited to 16,000 frames, so is your video. With an FLV file, you must use a specific set of controls designed for the netConnection object, regardless of whether the FLV file is being served from the Flash Communication Server.

This chapter explains Flash video and shows you how to best create and deploy video in your Flash applications.

Terms, Technology, and Quality

When dealing with Flash video, you will encounter some terms for properties that are helpful to understand so that you will be able deliver the best video content possible. Some of the terms you see here are often misused and substituted for one another. However, after you get a grasp of the concepts, you'll understand why there is some ambiguity in the terminology.

Data Rate

This is the same as the *data rate* for MP3 files. The more data per second of video, the higher quality of image you get. A data rate that is too high will load slowly and can cause your video to pause and restart on its own as data becomes available. It is important to select a data rate that is constant with the capabilities of your target systems and bandwidth. With Flash Communication Server you can throttle the data rate to automatically adjust for high traffic and slow connections. Without Flash Communication Server you are limited to HTTP, and the users will receive the video as they would any other file over HTTP and must wait during slow connections.

Progressive — HTTP

When you use regular HTTP servers to deploy video content, the file is downloaded to the user's cache. It begins playing as soon as video content is available, which means you can generally begin showing the video almost immediately on your target bandwidth. However, random access of the video is allowed only within the frames that have downloaded already, which means you can't fast-forward the index of the video to a spot that hasn't been loaded yet and expect it to automatically rebuffer and start at that new index.

With HTTP you have the option of wrapping your video in an SWF file, making control of the video within a movie clip typical of any movie clip. HTTP is often selected when quality of the final down-loaded file is a concern, such as on movie trailer sites. This is considered *lossless* in that the content is preserved regardless of pauses in download. HTTP-deployed video files will pause rather than drop frames, leaving you with a pristine final file localized to the user's machine. By using a null netStream object, you can serve an FLV as an HTTP file. You see this in action in a Try It Out section later in this chapter.

HTTP deployment is ideal for known prerecorded content, with known length and file size.

Streaming — Flash Communication Server

When you use Flash Communication Server to deploy video, you are using Real-time Messaging Protocol. This protocol can be compared to a socket server, but with many more features. Flash Communication Server requires the use of the netConnection and netStream object. Random Access is allowed, because a new index request stops the video stream and rebuffers from the requested index point. The file is not downloaded to the user's cache, and so disk space is not an issue. When data is lost during transmission over RTMP, the client will not ping the server for correction. The lost data is simply ignored, and the video plays on. Because the video is not localized, moving through the track can have noticeable delays and buffering alerts.

This format is ideal for broadcasts of unknown length and high server traffic.

Video Keyframes

To understand keyframes, you must understand a little about how video works on a computer. Video is a very expensive media type. There are trillions of pixels to track in a full-length movie. If you were to record video without any compression, you'd fill your disk space quickly. Some smart folks came up *temporal compression*, video compression based on keyframing. The term keyframe, when applied to video, is very different than a Flash keyframe. A keyframe in video is a single frame that is used as an index frame to which other frames refer to for pixel information.

Depending on how many keyframes you define, there are perhaps 10, 20, or 40 frames that come after a keyframe, which are not nearly as defined as the keyframe. These frames are called *interframes*. When a keyframe is reached, the following interframe is compared to the keyframe. A complete image of the fragment interframe and the keyframe is blended to make one consistent image. Each following inter-frame compares itself to the frame before it. In this way, a small percentage of frames can be defined as whole, and then you can compress your movie with far less data in each frame. This leads to a much smaller file size.

When considering file size, people often overlook keyframes, but they can make a huge difference in file size and performance. The more keyframes you have, the more accurate your video will be to the larger, uncompressed version. However, keyframes are expensive in file size, because they contain 100 percent of the data needed to display the frame. Many keyframes can be expensive to redraw as well, because the video player must redraw the entire frame, rather than regions. Too many keyframes can sometimes be the culprit in choppy video, but too few can be the reason for blocky video, where there aren't enough keyframes to build accurate frames.

A video with a high amount of motion content requires more keyframes and a higher data rate. Significant degradation of quality may be perceived between two equal-length movies compressed at the same data rate and keyframe frequency. It is important to consider the motion content of the source video. Both the On2 and Spark codecs can insert keyframes when large pixel differences are detected from frame to frame but are bound by the keyframe frequency specified.

Keyframes are also the indexes by which FLV files incrementally rewind and fast-forward. Scrubbing the timeline of an FLV file will reveal only the keyframes. So the more keyframes you have, the smoother the scrubbing appears.

Variable Bit Rate

When you use variable bit rate compression, you are allowing frames that deviate more from the keyframes than others to maintain data, and thus quality. You can discard image data and maintain quality. Variable bit rate is the ideal method and often surprises people when they see the quality difference. Variable bit rate is often called *2 Pass*. This is because the encoder is required to analyze the entire file first, deciding where to discard data and where to maintain data. The encoder then compresses the file per frame. This is not ideal when the video must be encoded quickly, but it is perfect for those times you need to deliver high-quality video.

Interlacing

Interlacing is a video method designed for television. All video captured in NTSC or PAL contains inter-laced frames. An interlaced frame contains two frames in a single field. They are separated vertically, like blinds, with each image taking up every other horizontal line. You might sometimes view a QuickTime video that seems to have some horizontal artifacts or distortion, and that's often because the file was not deinterlaced before being compressed. Many capture cards and DV cameras now have half-screen options, for when you know you will be targeting compressed video formats.

Most video compression tools have deinterlacing methods built in. To display your source video with the best quality possible in Flash, you must understand the condition of your source video and treat it correctly.

Frame Rate

Frame rate is the number of frames to display per second. With Flash, you have the freedom of specifying any frame rate you want, within reason. However, video always will compress better and look better if the frame rate is maintained. This is especially true for FLV video wrapped in an SWF file. Small incremental changes in frame rate, different from the original uncompressed frame rate, can lead to out-of-synch sound.

Generally you want to choose lower frame rates when all other compression setting options have been exhausted. Choosing a lower frame rate drastically affects the perceived quality of the file but can solve bandwidth issues.

Creating Flash Video

Many products can compress directly to the FLV format. Among them are products from Sorenson and screen capture tools such as Camtasia.

With Flash 8, you have the Flash 8 Video Encoder. Unlike Sorenson, and other solutions, this encoder can produce only FLV files and will not automatically wrap the FLV into an SWF file. This encoder is limited in defining keyframes and variable bit rates. An alternative product is Flix 8 Pro. Flix 8 Pro is similar to Sorenson Squeeze but designed specifically for the On2 codec. Flix 8 Pro allows you to encode to 2 Pass VBR, as well as maintain complete control over keyframes, data rate, and deinterlacing. Flix also allows you to emulate video by converting the video to a series of images while synchronizing the frame rate with sound. You can deploy these emulated videos on any Flash player, including Flash 3! Obviously this is less than ideal because of size concerns and performance, but might be a solution for a specific technology-challenged user base in which Flash 6, 7, or 8 are not available, but 3 and 4 are.

The Flash 8 Video Encoder, which comes with Flash to create FLV video, is used in the examples given here. Look at third-party products and tools if you plan on deploying large amounts of video or when quality control must be granular, such as for Flash 6 on PocketPC.

The Flash Video Encoder also comes with something called *CuePoints*. CuePoints are inserted into an FLV file with a time index. ActionScript methods are assigned to these CuePoints and are triggered automatically as the video plays. An FLV file can contain 16 CuePoints. If you need more than 16 CuePoints, you'll want to use an interval method to watch the index of the video to trigger activity at specific times.

For the Flash 8 Video Encoder to function properly, you must have QuickTime installed on your development machine.

Converting a Video

Converting video to SWF is exceptionally easy. Some may find the process unwieldy and difficult to control, but Macromedia has gone to great lengths to ensure that the encoder is easy to use and the video it produces is of a good quality.

The first step to using video in Flash is to test it out. Before inserting your favorite video, try a few test videos to help you understand what to expect from Flash video and the quality that can be achieved.

Try It Out   **Use Flash 8 Video Encoder to Convert a Video to FLV**

In this example you create some FLV video for the following sections on how to use Flash Video with ActionScript. If you do not have a movie file in `.mov`, `.mpg`, `.avi`, or other acceptable format, you can use the example on the WROX Beginning ActionScript 2 web site. The movie you choose should be short. Because you're testing ActionScript here, you don't want to spend much time perfecting the video.

1. Open the Flash 8 Video Encoder standalone application.

2. If you have never opened this application before, click around the interface and see what you can see. If you know Flix or Sorenson products, you should feel somewhat comfortable with the interface.

3. Click the Add button in the right column. A system browse window opens. Find a video on your system to encode. It is preferable that the source video be fairly uncompressed, so that you are not recompressing an already lossy file.

4. After you select a video, you will see that the status is waiting. Highlight the file by clicking its name in the list.

5. Click the Settings button in the right column to open a preview window and access some options. If the source file is a codec that Flash understands, you see the video in the preview window. Give your video a name in the input text field.

6. Click the Show Advanced Settings button. The window expands to include more options to change the output file.

7. Make sure the On2 codec is selected.

    Leave the frame rate set to Same As Source.

    Keyframe placement is best left to automatic, unless you see problems later.

    Choose a Quality setting. The quality setting refers to preset bit rate values. If you do not like the preset values, select Custom and insert a different value. If you plan on playing the file only locally, you can select a high bit rate. If you plan on viewers using modems, it's best to select a very low rate. You can also resize the video if you want.

8. If you have sound in your file, select the settings you want to use. Keep in mind that sound, like video, can increase size quickly with minor changes to bit rate.

9. After you have the settings the way you want them, close the Settings window by clicking OK. Define where you would like your file to be saved by selecting Edit⇨Preferences and check the Place Output Files In option. A folder browsing window opens; select a folder and click OK.

10. Click the Start Queue button. You are shown a progress bar.

How It Works

How the actual conversion works is a graduate course in codecs. Know that Flash is using QuickTime to read in the source file. What your QuickTime can view, Flash can likely convert. Using your selected settings, it has now created an On2 FLV file to your specifications. Had you been targeting Flash 7 player, you would have wanted to select the Spark codec instead.

Compressing video well is a skill best learned by doing. Try different output settings and save each .flv file with different names indicating the settings you chose. You can use these files later in the following examples to see the differences your changes made to the quality of the video.

Next you see how to prepare your movie for export.

Try It Out   Create an SWF Video for Export

If you have not completed the previous Try It Out, do it now because you'll be using the FLV file it produces. Otherwise, you can substitute any .flv file.

1. Open a new FLA and save it as myVideo.fla in your work folder.

2. Select File⇨Import⇨Import to Stage.

3. A file browse window opens. Navigate to the FLV file you created in the preceding Try It Out section, select it, and click Open.

4. The Select Video Settings dialog opens. The file path shown should point to the file you selected in step 3. Click Next.

5. The Deployment Settings dialog opens. For this example, select the Embed Video in SWF and Play in Timeline. Click Next.

6. The Embedding Settings dialog opens. For this example, select Symbol Type: Embedded Video. Be sure that Place Instance On Stage and Extend Timeline, If Needed, are both selected, as well as the Embed the Entire Video option. Click Next.

7. Confirm your action. Clicking Next embeds the video in your project. This can be an intensive operation depending on the size and length of your .FLV file. Make sure that you have nothing else running on your computer and save any other work you are doing. Click Finish to confirm that you want to import the video.

8. A progress bar appears. If your video is very small, this won't take very long. If your video is large, this can take awhile. It is recommend that you leave Flash alone and allow the system to give all resources to Flash during this process by not running any other programs or intensive processes while you wait.

9. When the video is embedded, you see it on the timeline in the center of the stage. Select the video, and you see in the Properties panel that the object type is Embedded Video. You cannot edit this object, but you can move it. You can also see that the timeline that holds the video object is the same length in frames as the video itself. If you change the FPS of your FLA, you will need to adjust the duration of the video object on the timeline.

10. Move the video object to the top-left corner of the stage. Be sure the x,y position of the video is 0,0. You can set this in the Properties panel of the video object.

11. The frame rate of the FLA must match the original frame rate of the FLV file. Select Modify⇨Document and adjust the frame rate as needed. Adjust the duration of the video object on the timeline to match the duration in seconds of the original FLV file.

12. Select Modify⇨Document. Change the height and width dimensions to match the video object. Save your FLA.

13. Publish the FLA to SWF format.

14. You can now navigate to the SWF file and open it in the standalone Flash Player to view your video. You'll notice there are no controls. Don't worry; you add those in the following sections.

How It Works

In this example you created a simple SWF file that contains video. Using this method you can now import the SWF using `loadMovie` into any other SWF. You can use standard movie clip controls to play and stop your SWF. However, this wrapping of the FLV wasn't completely necessary. It is just an option. Embedding an FLV in an SWF severely limits performance and limits you to 16,000 frames, which can be far too short for longer movies. But this method is great for short video files, in which you would like the video to be treated as any other movie clip on the timeline, such as a video augmented navigation or help section.

Also, Sorenson Squeeze and Flix 8 can both automatically wrap an FLV object in an SWF and output only an SWF file. This can be especially helpful because it saves the time it takes to do by hand.

Another task you accomplished is that you saw how you can place video objects directly onto the timeline using the Import option. Instead of resizing the stage, you could have kept the stage as is and placed the video among existing stage elements. This is handy if your short videos will be synchronized with animation, have a more ambient background motion in a larger FLA.

Loading an External Video

You can also load other videos directly into the library using File⇔Import. You can load `.mov` `.avi`, `.mpeg`, and more. Follow the "Create an SWF Video for Export" Try It Out example, but change the target movie to any video you want. You will be presented with the same options and dialog boxes. However, you will be presented with an extra dialog screen to select the codec and compression settings for your movie. These settings are identical to the settings in the standalone Flash 8 Video Encoder. Using this method of importing your video, you can save time by not creating a separate FLV file. You should only do this if your video clips are very short, and understand that you are increasing your FLA and SWF size greatly.

Exporting to Video

With Flash you can also create `.avi` and `.mov` videos of timeline animations. With Flash 8, you can export timeline animation with an alpha channel. Try creating a simple root timeline animation. Select File⇔Export⇔Export Movie. In the Save dialog, select `.avi` or `.mov` as the Save as Type. Name your file and follow the prompts to export the SWF as video.

Try It Out   Playing an SWF Video in a Movie Clip

If you haven't done the previous Try It Out, in which you were to create an FLV file and then create the `myVideo.swf` file, you should do so now. You'll be using that file in this exercise. Move the `myVideo.swf` you created to your work folder or to a place from which this example can target it.

1. Open a new FLA and save it as `loadSWFvideo.fla` in your work folder.

2. Click the first frame in the timeline, open the Actions panel, and type in the following ActionScript code:

```
myMovie = this.createEmptyMovieClip("clip", 0);
myMovie.loadMovie("myVideo.swf");
```

3. Select Modify⇨Document and change the frame rate of the FLA to match the frame rate of your `myVideo.swf` file.

4. Test your work. You should now see your video playing in the top-left corner of the stage.

How It Works

In this example you simply used `loadMovie` to show your SWF video file. You had to be sure your frame rate matched the frame rate of the movie. If the frame rate did not match, the sound would become out of synch with the video. This is a limitation of using a video exported as SWF. If you had exported from Sorenson Squeeze, this problem would have been less of an issue because of the way Sorenson Squeeze adds the sound track to the SWF.

Because your video is on a timeline, you can use classic movie clip controls like `stop`, `play`, `gotoAndPlay`, `gotoAndStop`, and so on to control the video.

Because of the limitations of SWF wrapped videos, use FLV wherever possible. FLV has no length limit, and is not tied to the frame rate of your SWF file.

Loading an External FLV File

When using the video object to load FLV files, you actually use three objects in conjunction to create a full set of controls. These objects are netStream, netConnection, and video.

Most of the controls you'll use to manipulate your FLV file are in netStream. The relevant methods for video in this class are covered in this chapter. The netConnection class is the object that makes the actual connection to the server. The netStream class calls specific objects through that connection.

The netStream Class

The following table describes the netStream class methods:

Method	Return	Description
close()	Nothing	Stops the stream completely.
play()	Nothing	Begins playing the specified object.
pause()	Nothing	Sets the rate at which the microphone should capture sound.

Method	Return	Description
seek()	Nothing	Sends the video to the closest keyframe to the specified seconds.
setBufferTime()	Nothing	Specifies how long to buffer data before beginning to play the file.

The pause() method has one parameter, a Boolean. This method is actually a toggle. If the video is playing, calling pause will pause the video. If the video is already paused from a previous pause call, the video will begin playing from where it was last paused. The parameter can be passed as true or false to override the existing toggle state. Here's the syntax:

```
Video.pause(ok:Boolean);
```

The setBufferTime() method has a single parameter, a Number. The number sets the seconds of video that should be downloaded before the video is allowed to play. Here's the syntax:

```
Sound.setBufferTime(n:Number);
```

setBufferTime is useful for throttling the buffer when skips and frequent pauses are detected due to buffer time out. This can be done in conjunction with the onStatus event and the bufferTime and bufferLength properties to change the behavior of the video object.

The following table describes the netStream class properties:

Event	Type	Description
bufferLength	Number	Number of playable seconds currently in the buffer.
bufferTime	Number	Maximum number of seconds that may be buffered.
bytesLoaded	Number	Number of bytes loaded.
bytesTotal	Number	Number of total bytes of the entire video.
currentFps	Number	Current frame rate of the video clip, independent of the SWF frame rate.
Time	Number	Current play position in seconds of the media file.

The netStream class has two events:

❑ onStatus — A Function that fires whenever a change to the object is encountered or if an error occurs.

❑ onMetaData — A Function that fires when the FLV file initially loads. This event is not documented by Macromedia but is extremely useful. It returns metadata about your FLV file. Here's its syntax:

```
myNetStream.onMetaData = function(meta) {
    trace("Duration = "+meta.duration);
    trace("Video Rate = "+meta.videodatarate);
```

```
        trace("Audio Rate = "+meta.audiodatarate);
};
```

This event is especially helpful because it enables you to create percentage-complete progress bars or indicators that show the user how long the video is and how much time is left.

Metadata returns the following properties: `canSeekToEnd`, `audiocodecid`, `audiodelay`, `audiodatarate`, `videocodecid`, `videodatarate`, `height`, `width`, and `duration`

The Video Class

The Video class is one of the objects you use to create controls when loading your FLV files. It has two methods: `clear()` and `attachVideo()`.

clear()

The `clear()` method clears the image currently being displayed in the video object on the stage. It has no parameters, and it returns nothing. Here's its syntax:

```
Video.clear(ok:Boolean);
```

`clear()` is useful when you are switching to a new object or need to clear the last frame of video image when a video is done playing.

attachVideo()

The `attachVideo()` method has a single parameter that must be a netStream object reference. The method uses the netStream object to load and control the video. Here's the syntax:

```
Video.attachVideo(myNetStream:netStream);
```

The method can be passed `null` to stop the current video and clear all information in the properties of the video object. The netStream object might also be a webcam object.

Video Class Properties

The Video class has quite a few properties that you can use. They're described in the following table:

Property	Type	Description
smoothing	Boolean	Specifies if the video should be interpolated when scaled.
height	Number	Height of the actual video in pixels, regardless of the _height of the video object.
width	Number	Width of the actual video in pixels, regardless of the _width of the video object.
deblocking	Number	Specifies what type of deblocking method should be performed on the video.
_xmouse	Number	X position of the mouse over the video object.

Property	Type	Description
_ymouse	Number	Y position of the mouse over the video object.
_xscale	Number	Scale percentage of the width of the video object.
_yscale	Number	Scale percentage of the height of the video object.
_x	Number	X position of the video object on the stage.
_y	Number	Y position of the video object on the stage.
_rotation	Number	Number of radians by which the video is rotated.
_width	Number	Width of the entire video object.
_height	Number	Height of the entire video object.
_parent	Object	The object that contains the video object.
_visible	Number	Specifies whether the video object is visible.
_alpha	Number	Specifies the transparency of the video object.
_name	String	Name of the video object.

Try It Out   ## Playing an FLV Video in a Movie Clip

This example uses the FLV file you created earlier in this chapter. If you have not created this video, you can use the video supplied on the Beginning ActionScript 2 web site or make your own. You'll be importing the FLV file via ActionScript.

1. Open a new FLA and save it as loadFLVvideo.fla in your work folder.

2. Click the first frame in the timeline, open the Actions panel, and enter the following ActionScript code:

```
var myNetConnect:NetConnection = new NetConnection();
myNetConnect.connect(null);
var myNetStream:NetStream = new NetStream(myNetConnect);
clip_video.attachVideo(myNetStream);
myNetStream.play("myVideo.flv");
```

3. Open the Library panel. Select the menu display icon in the Library panel title bar. Select New Video. A Setup dialog opens. Be sure to select ActionScript-Controlled. A video symbol will appear in the library. Drag an instance of the video symbol from the library to the stage.

4. In the Properties panel for the video symbol, now on the stage, change the name to clip_video. You can change the height and width of the object to match your external FLV file.

5. Test your work. You should now see your video playing in the top-left corner of the stage.

How It Works

In this example you saw how to import your raw FLV file directly onto the stage at runtime. By using netConnection, you tell the Flash player you'll be making a network request. Because you aren't connecting to Flash Communication Server, pass the connect method a null parameter, which stops the connect method from attempting a persistent connection to a specific remote server. Then create a netStream object, which gives you controls for handling the actual data connection.

The video object you added to the stage is then associated with the netStream object. When the play method is called, netStream sends the data to the video object.

This might seem like a few too many hoops to jump through just to show a video. However, the three objects together are giving you granular access and control to the entire process from declaring the remote server, stream manipulation, to actual video play, and video control. If you are looking for something more streamlined or working with many clips in different places in your application, the process is easily made into a class.

This method works only in Flash 7 when the Spark codec is used. This method will not work in Flash 6 or lower. Flash 8 can use this method with both On2 and Spark codecs.

Controlling Video Position

You have just seen how you can use the netStream object to play videos directly on the stage and not worry about total frame length, frame rate, and sound position. Now you're concentrating on manipulating the video with some controls. As with previous Try It Out examples, you use components to quickly set up controls to highlight a few of the methods available.

There is also the Media component. This component is an all-in-one audio and video player. Nothing can beat the speed at which you can add an FLV file to your application than with the Media component. You are encouraged to try out the Media component. For the purposes of this book, however, you will learn how to do some of these things by hand so that you can have more customized control over how your video is displayed and controlled.

Try It Out   Creating Simple Controls

If you have not completed the previous Try It Out example, you should do that now. You'll be building upon the FLA you created by adding some controls.

1. Open the loadFLVvideo.fla file.

2. You'll be using controls to manipulate your file. You'll want to grab some detail information about your FLV file via the netStream onMetaData event. Click the first frame in the timeline and open the Actions panel. Add the pause method so that your ActionScript in frame 1 now looks like the following:

```
var myNetConnect:NetConnection = new NetConnection();
myNetConnect.connect(null);
var myNetStream:NetStream = new NetStream(myNetConnect);
myNetStream.onMetaData = function(meta) {
    myNetStream.duration = meta.duration;
    myNetStream.VideoRate = meta.videodatarate;
    myNetStream.AudioRAte = meta.audiodatarate;
};
clip_video.attachVideo(myNetStream);
myNetStream.play("myVideo.flv");
```

3. Test your SWF now, and you will see that the video is buffering but not playing. Start adding some controls. Open the Components panel and drag a ProgressBar component onto the stage and place it directly below your video object. Open the Properties panel for the stage instance of the ProgressBar component. Name the instance `clipProgress`. In the Properties panel for the component, change the width of the progress bar to `250`. In the Parameters tab of the Properties panel, remove the String value of the Label.

4. Add the following code to frame 1 beneath the code you've already written:

```
myNetStream.play("http://www.memoryprojector.com/jeff/myVideo.flv ");
clipProgress.mode = "manual";
trackProgress = function () {
    clipProgress.setProgress(myNetStream.time, myNetStream.duration);
};
track = setInterval(this, "trackProgress", 10);
_level0.clipProgress.onPress = function() {
    var perc = ((_xmouse-this._x)/(this._width));
    myNetStream.seek(int(perc*myNetStream.duration));
};
```

5. Test your SWF to see that a progress bar now shows you the current playhead position of the video. Clicking the ProgressBar sends the video to that position in the video.

6. Open the Components panel and drag a Button component onto the stage directly beneath the ProgressBar component you added earlier. In the Properties panel for the button instance you just added to the stage, change the name to `playButton`. In the Parameters tab of the Properties panel, change the Label to `Play`. Change the width of the button to `40` pixels.

7. Add the following ActionScript to the code after the code that exists on frame 1:

```
playButton.enabled = false;
playButton.onRelease = function() {
    this.enabled = false;
    stopButton.enabled = true;
    myNetStream.pause();
};
```

8. Open the Components panel and drag a Button component onto the stage next to the play button you added earlier. In the Properties panel for the button instance you just added to the stage, change the name to `stopButton`. In the Parameters tab of the Properties panel, change the Label to `Stop`. Change the width of the button to `40` pixels.

9. Add the following ActionScript to the end of the code on frame 1:

```
stopButton.onRelease = function() {
    this.enabled = false;
    playButton.enabled = true;
    myNetStream.pause();
};
```

10. Test your SWF file. You can now pause and play your movie. You can also use the `seek` method of the ProgressBar component to move through the track.

How It Works

In this example you saw how using small amounts of ActionScript can allow you granular control over the video.

You also saw how the `onMetaData` event can help you create a user interface that can keep track of the file's play progress. By using the netStream object's time property against the netStream's `onMetaData` duration property you can display a progress bar that accurately shows the current playhead position.

You also used the `seek` method of the netStream object. By using `seek`, you move to the nearest keyframe to the position being sought. If you had few keyframes, this would have felt chunky or inaccurate. Because you have keyframes at regular intervals and allowed the encoder to automatically add keyframes where necessary for quality, the seek is accurate enough.

You also used the `pause` method of the netStream object. You can see that this object is called in the play and stop buttons. This is because the method is a toggle that can continue or pause a video. The `play` method of the netStream object is used exclusively to begin rebuffering the track from the beginning, and so you only called it once to load the video.

Probably the fundamental lesson to be learned here is that netStream contains the bulk of methods used to control a streaming netConnection object. You could have defined the netConnection to `attachAudio`, instead of `attachVideo`, and your netSream method calls would work just the same. In this way the control methods of the media are abstracted and can control any media being throughput into the netConnection object. This gives you unparalleled freedom and simplicity in defining classes and scripts that control the media in your applications.

The netStream and video object play controls are unlike any other objects in Flash that control media. This is unfortunate, but after you start to use them and understand the differences and why they exist, you'll probably agree that the netStream object is very logical and easy.

In this example you could have used the deblocking and smoothing methods now available in the video object. Those methods are covered in the following sections.

Using Transparency within Video

Flash 8 and the On2 codec provide video that allows an alpha channel. 32-bit AVI and MOV have been able to do alpha channels for some time. Transparency in video gives you unparalleled creative opportunity in Flash. You can composite multiple videos, use rotoscoping type effects, as well as seamlessly use ActionScript to allow pixel changes in video to fire events in your ActionScript. Few other technologies allow you to do this with such ease of deployment and scripting.

Compositing clips works just like importing any other clip — you simply use movie clips or layers to determine which video is in front of which. You'll be using the transparent video, which is available at the Beginning ActionScript 2 web site to create this example. However, if you have your own transparent video clips, go ahead and use them.

With ActionScript you're mostly concerned with how to synchronize the time index of multiple movie clips. You'll use `setBufferTime` in each clip to ensure that you have playable content in each clip and then coordinate the two clips so that they run simultaneously.

You can use the FLV CuePoints option to trigger changes in each clip if you want. However, in this example, you use the time index and a simple interval loop to track each.

If you have an existing video file with transparency, or you know After Effects or some other advanced video manipulation product, try this next example with your own content, make changes to be creative, and see what you can do with it.

A note about rotoscoping: Rotoscoping used to entail hours and hours of hand cutting objects from a film strip and overlaying them into a new strip of film. You probably can think of some old movies that used hand techniques to overlay objects onto new scenes. These techniques were replaced by blue and green screen systems. With Flash video you can use the Bitmap object to manually rotoscope objects by changing the alpha of specific pixel colors, but it is easier and sleeker to preprocess these pixels in After Effects or some other advanced product to create a 32-bit alpha channel clip, often called an RGBA clip.

Try It Out   Compositing Video with Movie Clips

1. Open a new FLA and save it as `compositeFLVvideo.fla` in your work folder.

2. Click the first frame in the timeline, open the Actions panel, and type the following ActionScript code:

```
var myNetConnect:NetConnection = new NetConnection();
myNetConnect.connect(null);

var myNetStream:NetStream = new NetStream(myNetConnect);
myNetStream.setBufferTime(30);
backgroundVideo.attachVideo(myNetStream);
backgroundVideo.smoothing = true;
myNetStream.play("background.flv");
myNetStream.pause();

var myNetStream2:NetStream = new NetStream(myNetConnect);
myNetStream2.setBufferTime(30);
foregroundVideo.attachVideo(myNetStream2);
foregroundVideo.smoothing = true;
myNetStream2.play("foreground.flv");
myNetStream2.pause();
myNetStream2.seek(3);
```

3. Open the Components panel and drag a new video object to the stage. Open the Properties panel and rename the video object `backgroundVideo`. Resize it to the desired size.

4. Add a new layer to the root timeline. Select the first frame in this new layer. Open the Components panel again and drag another video object to the stage so that it overlays the existing video object on the stage. In the Properties panel, rename this video object `foregroundVideo`. Resize the foreground video to suit.

5. Add the following function in the frame 1 ActionScript after the code you wrote in step 2 to check the buffer status of each video and kick off events to coordinate the video playback:

```
ok = true;
checkBuffer = function () {
    out.text = myNetStream.time;
    if (myNetStream.bufferLength>=30 && myNetStream2.bufferLength>=30 && ok ==
true) {
        myNetStream.pause();
    ok = false;
    }
    if (myNetStream.time>=18) {
```

```
            myNetStream2.pause();
            clearInterval(coordinator);
        }
    };
    coordinator = setInterval(this, "checkBuffer", 10);
```

6. Using the Text tool, add a new text field to the stage below your video clips. In the Properties panel rename the text field `out`. Use this text field to display the current state of your clip's playhead position to see your code working.

7. Test your SWF. You will now see that after the background clip plays for 18 seconds, the foreground clip begins playing on cue. Try changing the second exception in the `checkBuffer` function to show 15 seconds rather than 18.

How It Works

In this example you saw a few netStream methods in action to help you coordinate two videos meant to play at specific times.

You'll have to be sure the target video paths in the play methods point to a valid FLV video.

In the first section of code you added in step 2, you saw the same setup as you used in previous examples. However, the addition to note is the seek method used on the myNetStream2 object. Although the video is paused at start, you can seek to a specific time index. This will cause the object to call the specific bytes into the buffer to allow that specific section of video to play on demand.

You also paused both videos so they would not start playing on their own, regardless of `bufferLength` condition. This allows you to manually watch both streams and be sure that both buffers are ready to play the video you need.

The second part of the example set up an interval that checked the `bufferLength` of both videos. After both videos had 30 seconds of playable video ready to go, the background video was told to begin playing. Your interval then switched to begin checking for the playhead position of the background video. Because you know that you checked that 30 seconds of the foreground video is now buffered, you can begin playing the video at any time you specify.

Because you chose to seek to 3 seconds into the foreground video, the slice of foreground video in the buffer is 3 through 33. When you call the `pause` method, the foreground clip begins to play because it was already paused at start. Remember that the `pause` method is a toggle. It will resume your video if the video is already paused.

You then clear the interval, and the two videos are now playing on conjunction with one another. If you feel that the connection will be slower and you would like to avoid having to rebuffer, you can change the 30 seconds to a greater number to preload more video into your objects before manipulating them.

If you plan on compositing larger clips, it's always a good idea to keep tabs on the buffer and play condition of each clip. If the background clip, for example, pauses because its buffer ran low, you'll want to have an event that recoordinates the videos to ensure that they stay in synch with one another.

In this example you also called the smoothing property of the background video object. This is because you scaled the clip to match the foreground clip size. Had you not allowed smoothing, the clip would have appeared blocky or low quality. By using smoothing you were able to interpolate the video and create a somewhat better image. This was true for the foreground video. Because you shrunk the video in size, it too would have appeared blocky and low quality. By smoothing the video pixels you were able to keep the video at a respectable quality without re-encoding the videos. Video quality techniques are covered in the following sections.

Also, you didn't need to use two videos. You could have used static JPG or PNG backgrounds behind your foreground video. You could have used vector graphics, the webcam object, or simply the rest of an application to act as a background. With an alpha channel, working with video in your interface has almost no limits.

Have fun!

Working with Video Quality

One of the advantages of using Flash 8 video and the On2 codec is the methods available to control quality of the video.

When video data is manipulated at runtime to affect its performance and quality, it is called *post-processing*. Often post-processing deals directly with dealing with pixilation and undesirable effects of over compression. This is exactly what Flash 8 allows. With Flash 8 you can scale your video object directly. This means rather than scaling the movie clip that contains the video, you can ask the codec, which is playing back the clip, to scale the original video file data. This leads to much better performance and maintenance of the original quality.

Of course when you begin to scale any graphics on a computer, unless they are vectors, the images become blocky and distorted as each individual pixel in an image grows much larger in size. ActionScript includes the deblocking method on the video object.

Deblocking and Deringing

Video compression works by subdividing each frame into blocks and subdividing these blocks into smaller blocks. Often the information for these blocks can come from keyframes or previous frames. This means some blocks will be close to what they should be, but not always accurate. Heavily compressing a clip can cause these blocks to be pronounced, because each block area needs to define the same amount of area with less original pixel data. Because the image is divided into these blocks, heavily compressed video will actually look blocky, hence the term. These blocks become more apparent when video is scaled larger. However, these blocks can also look odd when the video is made to play at smaller sizes than intended.

Many video formats are played back at only the size intended. Many of the compression techniques involve deblocking video during preprocessing. With Flash, you have much more control over how your video is presented by scaling, resizing, and deforming. The deblocking method gives you a set of tools for post-processing your video to improve these blocking issues on-the-fly. It is important to remember that these methods use CPU power to enhance the video. When you use these methods, you should be concerned about your target systems. Modern systems will have no issue deblocking video at runtime, but older systems might perform more slowly and cause your video to stutter.

Deblocking video works similarly to smoothing. However, deblocking uses the specific `deblocking` method provided to the codec being used to playback video rather than a general smoothing method. By interpolating the edges of blocks, a smoothing effect occurs on the video image. Interpolation is a term for when a pixel is examined in the context of the pixels around it. A change is made to the pixel to a sort of average of the pixels around it.

With Flash 8 you also have deringing, which isn't a specific method. Deringing is accessed via the `deblocking` method. Image ringing is composed of artifacts produced in video when objects move. When using block compression, objects that move across the screen can cause very active compression blocks, which attempt to compress and redefine an edge in each frame to the most efficient size. This can cause a ring or halo of a blurry rainbow-like effect on the edges of a person's arm, or moving car. They are most often seen during high-contrast situations such as a bright person on a dark background. In these situations smoothing will probably solve the issue. However, smoothing also removes detail from other areas that are actually desired, such as details around the eyes of a subject, or text in the image. Using deringing in conjunction with deblocking can create the best possible post-processing situation for presenting the video.

When using high-bandwidth video, which contains a lot of data, the object will likely not need any of these methods. The effects of the methods are also not perfect. You should use these in situations in which the video is going to be scaled or zoomed for effect. You should always find a balance of bandwidth and quality that you approve of.

Different types of deblocking are used with each codec and different combinations of deblocking can be used on the video. The `deblocking` method allows for one parameter, which must be a Number. The available values match to specific post-processing conditions, as described in the following table:

Value	Description
0	Allows the video object to apply deblocking at a preset threshold determined by the codec.
1	Stops deblocking completely.
2	Uses the Sorenson deblocking filter.
3	Uses the on2 deblocking filter with no deringer.
4	Uses the On2 deblocking filter with the high-speed deringing filter.
5	Uses the On2 deblocking filter with the high-quality deringing filter.

Scaling and Transparency

Flash 8 allows x-scale, y-scale, and alpha directly upon the video object. In Flash 6 and 7, it would have been necessary to perform these actions on a container movie clip. By calling these methods directly upon the video object, you can save instantiating a movie clip, and all of the CPU and memory that involves. If you must scale or use transparency on your video, it is recommended that you use the native video methods to perform these operations. The modifications will be performed on the actual video pixels, and when used in conjunction with `deblocking` can lead to much better video performance.

Working with a Camera

The Camera object, which was introduced in Flash 6, is mainly used with Flash Communication Server. You can use the Camera object in conjunction with Flash Communication Server to make chat programs and other applications requiring a camera. However, you can do some nifty things with the camera with just a little bit of simple ActionScript.

You can use the Camera object to detect motion activity over a specified motion level. You can also set up listeners to discern the amount of motion activity and act upon it.

In later examples you see a fun way to use the camera to enact changes in your application. You will, of course, need a camera that is functioning on your computer for the following examples.

One thing to remember when working with the camera is that the Flash Player will prompt the user to allow or deny your application access to the camera.

The Camera Class Methods, Properties, and Events

The Camera class methods are described in the following table:

Method	Return	Description
get()	Camera	Static method that returns a reference to a camera on the system.
setMode()	Nothing	Changes the properties of the camera to the specified parameters. If the parameters are unattainable, the camera is set to as close as possible.
setMotionLevel()	Nothing	Sets the amount of activity required to fire the onActivity event. The first parameter sets the amount of activity level required, and the second defines how many seconds the object should wait before declaring no activity.
setQuality()	Nothing	Sets the bytes per frame requested from the camera.
setLoopBack()	Nothing	Tells Flash Communication Server to use compression when intercepting the video feed.
setKeyFrameInterval()	Nothing	Tells Flash Communication Server what interval to insert video keyframes into the compressed video feed.

The get() method has one parameter, which is a Number. The default parameter is 0. get() is a static method that returns a reference to a camera on the system. Sending no parameter returns the first microphone detected. You can use the names array property to obtain a list and request a specific camera at an explicit array index. get() is almost always used with the attachVideo method upon a netStream or MovieClip object. Here's the get() syntax:

```
var myCam_cam:Camera = Camera.get();
```

The `setMode()` method has four parameters, which are as follows:

1. A Number that specifies the desired width in pixels of the video feed.
2. A Number that specifies the desired height in pixels of the video feed.
3. A Number that specifies the desired frames per second.
4. A Boolean that specifies whether the method should attempt the size settings regardless of whether the camera is capable of the specified FPS desired. In this case, the camera will provide the closest set of parameters possible, usually at the sacrifice of performance.

Here's an example of the `setMode()` syntax:

```
var myCam_cam.setMode(320,240,24,true);
```

The following table describes properties of the Camera class:

Property	Type	Description
activityLevel	Number	Number from 0 to 100 measuring the motion being detected.
fps	Number	Maximum desired rate of frames per second.
currentFps	Number	Number of frames currently being captured by the webcam.
bandwidth	Boolean	Current amount of bandwidth specified by the `setQuality` method.
motionLevel	String	Numeric value that must be reached to invoke the `onActivity` event.
motionTimeOut	Array	Amount of time to wait before `onActivity` is called with a `false` parameter value, after no motion is detected.
index	Number	Numeric array position of the current camera in the names array list of cameras.
name	Number	String name of the current camera.
names	Boolean	Numeric array that lists all available cameras on the system.
height		Height of the current feed in pixels.
width		Width of the current feed in pixels.

The Camera class has two events:

❑ `onActivity`—A Function that fires when the camera detects activity, and detects no motion.

❑ `onStatus`—A Function that fires when the user allows or denies access to the camera.

Creating a Camera Object

You use a Video object to create a Camera object. The Video object is accessible via the library title bar menu. Expand that menu to see the option for adding a new Video object to the library. If you've been reading the previous sections of this chapter you know that the same object is used to play back FLV files. Now, instead of specifying an FLV stream to send to the Video object, you're specifying a Camera object.

To specify a Camera object, you don't use a constructor. You use the `get` method of the Camera object to specify the camera you'd like to access. `get()` expects a numerical parameter that is the index of the camera desired in the names array of the Camera object. It is possible to have multiple cameras display on one stage, but each must have its own Video object on the stage, and each must have its own Camera object returned from the `get()` method.

Displaying a Camera Feed as Video on the Stage

When you use the Camera object, you do not need to use the netStream object, unless you plan on connecting to Flash Communication Server. Because the example does not use Flash Communication Server, you'll be using just the Video object to display a live camera image on the stage. When you couple the Camera object to Flash wrappers such as Northcode, and others, you can use the Camera object to save images when activity is encountered, or at regular intervals. With this in mind, it is possible to create your own webcam management software with Flash and a Flash wrapper product that allows capture and ftp.

Because the Video object might be played within an MC, you can create a Bitmap object and manually modify or examine pixels returned by the Camera object.

The first step to diving into webcams is inserting one into your application. It is surprisingly easy. Unlike other technologies such as Java Applets, no external technologies such as QuickTime are required. Get a camera feed showing in an SWF right now so you can begin to manipulate and experiment with it.

Try It Out   **Show a Camera Feed on the Stage**

For this example you need a working webcam on your system. You can get a webcam relatively cheaply these days, and some digital cameras will work as webcams. After installing a webcam, test it with its native software to determine whether it's working before attempting to import the feed into Flash.

1. Open a new FLA and save it as `loadCamera.fla` in your work folder.

2. Click the first frame in the timeline, open the Actions panel, and enter the following ActionScript code:

```
var theCamFeed:Camera = Camera.get();
var myCamera:Video;
myCamera.attachVideo(theCamFeed);
```

3. Open the Library panel. Select the menu display icon in the Library panel title bar, and choose New Video. A Setup dialog opens; be sure to select ActionScript-Controlled. A video symbol will appear in the library. Drag an instance of the video symbol from the library to the stage.

4. In the Properties panel for the video symbol, now on the stage, change the name to `myCamera`. You can change the height and width of the object to suit.

5. Test your work. You should now see your video playing in the top-left corner of the stage.

How It Works

You can see in this example that a raw feed has been placed into your application with just a few lines of code. Because the Camera object was placed onto the stage via the Video object, you have access to all of the Video object's methods, including smoothing, alpha, and scaling.

Also, you can place the Video object within a movie clip and create a Bitmap object. You can then begin to manually track changes in the webcam image based on RGB pixel values of the bitmap.

Now try to use your webcam to detect motion.

Try It Out   Detect Some Motion

If you haven't done the previous Try It Out example, you should do so now, because you're going to add to the existing code to check for motion activity in your camera feed to fire an event.

1. Open the `loadCamera.fla` from your work folder.

2. Click the first frame in the timeline, open the Actions panel, and type the following ActionScript code:

```
var theCamFeed:Camera = Camera.get();
var myCamera:Video = holder.myCamera;
myCamera.smoothing = true;
myCamera.attachVideo(theCamFeed);
foo = setInterval(this, "rotate", 1);
theCamFeed.setMotionLevel(20, .5);
theCamFeed.onActivity = function(active) {
    trace(theCamFeed.activityLevel);
    if (active == true) {
        trace("motion detected");
    } else {
        trace("motion stopped");
    }
};
```

3. Test your work. You should now see your video playing in the top-left corner of the stage. You will also see the output window appear with trace output according to the activity being detected in the camera image.

How It Works

In this example you saw how to invoke a method when the camera sends an image frame, which is significantly different from the preceding frame. The value of the change is measured as a percentage of difference from the previous frame. This is presented as a number from 0 to 100.

The other option you used was set the second parameter of the `setMotionLevel` method. By setting a very small number, the Camera object doesn't wait very long to fire the `onActivity` method with a false parameter. The default value is two seconds. In interactive content, you might want to change this value to be larger or smaller depending on feedback.

Ready to try something a little more challenging?

Try It Out — Track a Pixel in the Webcam in Real Time

In this example you use the Bitmap object to track pixels. You'll want to have something like a brightly colored piece of paper that is in high contrast with the rest of the field in view of the webcam. (A bright yellow note pad should work well.)

This example contains some code that is fairly advanced. The detail as to how the `getRGB` function works is beyond the scope of this book. Just know that it takes a hexadecimal value and returns an RGB object, which is what you need to examine the pixels and compare them. You can take this function for granted, because it's a standard conversion.

1. Open a new FLA and save it as `trackPixel.fla` in your work folder.

2. Click the first frame in the timeline, open the Actions panel, and type the following ActionScript code:

```
var theCamFeed:Camera = Camera.get();
var myCamera:Video = holder.myCamera;
myCamera.smoothing = true;
theCamFeed.setMode(240, 200, 24);
myCamera.attachVideo(theCamFeed);
holder._xscale = 200;
holder._yscale = 200;
```

3. Open the Library panel. Select the menu display icon in the Library panel title bar and choose Select New Video. A Setup dialog opens; be sure to select ActionScript-Controlled. A video symbol will appear in the library. Drag an instance of the video symbol from the library to the stage.

4. In the Properties panel for the video symbol, now on the stage, change the name to `myCamera`. You can change the height in the properties panel to `200`. Change the width to `240`.

5. Click the video to be sure that it is highlighted. Select Modify⇨Convert to Symbol and select Movie Clip. Name the symbol holder. In the Properties panel for the new movie clip, give it an instance name of `holder`.

6. Test your work. You should now see your video playing in the top-left corner of the stage. Close the SWF and go back to the main timeline ActionScript.

7. Draw a circle on the stage using the Ellipse tool. Color the vector to suit. Click the circle to be sure that it is highlighted. Select Modify⇨Convert to Symbol and select Movie Clip. Name the symbol `dot`. This symbol will now be in the library, so delete it from the stage. Be careful not to delete the Video object and holder movie clip you created in step 5.

8. Open the Library panel. Select the Linkage option of the movie clip symbol named `dot`. Be sure Export for ActionScript is selected and give it an Identifier name of `dot`.

9. Return to the frame 1 ActionScript by highlighting frame 1 and opening the ActionScript panel. Add the following code, which sets up the bitmap copy of the camera image:

```
import flash.display.BitmapData;
var bitmap1:BitmapData;
var image1Clip:MovieClip = this.createEmptyMovieClip("image1", 1);
image1Clip._xscale = 200;
image1Clip._yscale = 200
image1Clip._alpha = 0;
var sprite:MovieClip = this.attachMovie("dot", "dot", 2);
```

```
bitmap1 = new BitmapData(myCamera._width, myCamera._height);
image1Clip.attachBitmap(bitmap1, 1);
image1Clip.useHandCursor = false;
image1Clip.onRelease = function() {
    this._parent.trackPixel = bitmap1.getPixel(this._xmouse, this._ymouse);
    this._parent.trackPixel =
this._parent.getRGB(this._parent.trackPixel.toString(16));
};
```

10. Enter the following code after the code you added in step 9:

```
function getRGB(hex) {
    var obj = {};
    var myColour = "0x"+hex;
    obj.b = myColour & 0x0000ff;
    myColour = myColour >> 8;
    obj.g = myColour & 0x0000ff;
    myColour = myColour >> 8;
    obj.r = myColour & 0x0000ff;
    return obj;
}
```

11. Now add the code that finds and compares pixel values:

```
function findPixel() {
    bitmap1.draw(holder);
    var imageWidth:Number = bitmap1.width;
    var imageHeight:Number = bitmap1.height;
    for (var i:Number = 0; i<imageWidth; i=i+6) {
        for (var j:Number = 0; j<imageHeight; j=j+6) {
            r = false;
            g = false;
            b = false;
            var xyColor = getRGB(bitmap1.getPixel(i, j).toString(16));
            var variance = 5;
            if (xyColor.r>=(trackPixel.r-variance) &&
xyColor.r<=(trackPixel.r+variance)) {
                r = true;
            }
            if (xyColor.g>=(trackPixel.g-variance) &&
xyColor.g<=(trackPixel.g+variance)) {
                g = true;
            }
            if (xyColor.b>=(trackPixel.b-variance) &&
xyColor.b<=(trackPixel.b+variance)) {
                b = true;
            }
            if (r == true && g == true && b == true) {
                new mx.transitions.Tween(sprite, "_x",
mx.transitions.easing.Back.easeOut, sprite._x, i*2, .5, true);
                new mx.transitions.Tween(sprite, "_y",
mx.transitions.easing.Back.easeOut, sprite._y, j*2, .5, true);
                j = imageHeight;
```

```
                    i = imageWidth;
                }
            }
        }
    }
    foo2 = setInterval(this, "findPixel", 42);
```

12. Test your code. You should see your camera image in the top left of the screen. Click a uniquely colored pixel, or hold up a piece of brightly colored paper such as yellow note paper. Click the color using the mouse. The circle will now follow the color and slight variations as you move the color around the image. Try clicking different objects.

How It Works

By using the Bitmap object, you've begun to uncover some interesting capabilities to track webcam movement and objects beyond the native method set available in the Camera object.

The first step was to create a web camera object on the stage, which sacrificed some quality for speed. This was accomplished by setting the mode of the camera to collect only a very small image. The camera was then smoothed, while the holder clip was scaled up. This enabled you to show a decent image while keeping FPS up.

You then added a small sprite, which acts as your indicator that the script is indeed working. The next thing you did was to create a copy of the camera image by creating a second movie clip. This clip was then filled with a Bitmap object. Filling the Bitmap object runs slightly more slowly than the actual playback of the webcam, so the bitmap is placed over the existing webcam image and the bitmap's container clip is set to alpha zero. This enables you to query the pixels via a mouse event without losing perceived performance. The mouse event is then defined. The mouse event defines the color of the pixel to be tracked.

Next the getRGB method was added. It is not important to understand the inner workings of this function at the moment. Just know that it works and that it is a standard method for extracting RGB values from hexadecimal numbers.

Finally, you added a function called by an interval. This function redraws the bitmap data from the camera image into the Bitmap object. The object is then queried in a loop to find the first instance of a pixel, which matches the RGB values of the color chosen by the user. Because the webcam color and performance can change from frame to frame, a variance value allows deviations of the color. After an instance of an acceptable pixel is found, the sprite is moved to that position, and the for loop is ended to save CPU time. Because this uses a linear left-to-right, top-to-bottom method for finding pixels, this method will always be biased to the top right, because it will stop at the first pixel that meets the requirement.

Because there are hundreds of pixels in an image, when polling a video image on-the-fly like this you must sacrifice some precision. In this case it was decided to poll only every sixth pixel. This way you only have to iterate through one-sixth of the pixels to get basically the same results. Optimization like this is key for matching performance and acceptable error.

This is, of course, just an introduction to how the Camera object can be examined. Many more efficient methods for finding pixels exist, such as radial proximity. You should think about how you could improve performance of finding pixels and come up with your own code and ideas for manipulating not only the Camera object, but the Video object as well.

521

Security Pop-Up Considerations

Both the Microphone and Camera objects ask users whether they would like to allow your SWF to access these items. The `onStatus` methods of the Camera and Microphone objects are fired when the user inputs an answer to the pop-up. If the user agrees, the `onStatus` returns `true`. If the user declines access, `onStatus` returns `false`.

After users have allowed the microphone or camera, they will not be asked again, until the next session.

A user does not have to view this pop-up every time, however. If he goes to the Privacy Settings panel, he can permanently deny or allow access of the microphone and camera to your domain. Many times users don't know this, and it is handy to open the Settings dialog manually and direct them on how to do this. You cannot make these settings changes with ActionScript; they can be made only by the user.

Summary

In this chapter basic concepts about video compression and playback were presented so that you can include video within your projects with ease. Examples were given to give you complete control over video behavior and how the media can interact with the rest of your application.

The webcam was presented as an input device, with the ability to have visual changes in the webcam image enact changes with the application.

Both video and the web camera were used with the Bitmap object to manipulate the image. When the bitmapData object is combined with video and the webcam you can integrate video at a level no other technology can with such ease.

Hopefully this chapter got you thinking of using Flash Video in ways you might not have thought of.

Exercises

1. Separate the audio and video from a single MOV or AVI file. Wrap the video as an SWF file. Load the video via LoadMovie. Control the current frame of the SWF via `gotoAndPlay` by loading the MP3 track and using the `position` and `duration` properties to determine the current position of the SWF.

2. Using a webcam, detect movement in the webcam's image and play an event sound.

Using ActionScript to Communicate with a Server

Flash is built on the principle that the web is entertaining and useful. Usefulness on the web is what separates different types of Flash content. Some Flash exists to entertain; some exists to serve information and transact data. Flash is an animation format and a rich Internet application deployment platform. Flash becomes an application platform when the author of the Flash decides to load data from outside sources or manipulate and send data.

In this chapter you learn about data. Data is what computers are for; it's what you look for when you move across the Internet. If you want to be something on the Web, you have to move, modify, exchange, or serve data. Flash is no exception.

> Screen persistence is the capability to refresh the screen with new images and information without replacing the entire screen. Often, HTML-driven web sites must redirect to a new page or refresh the existing page entirely to reflect content changes. Screen persistence drives the interest in Ajax (Asynchronous JavaScript and XML), a concept of relying on the XMLHttpRequest object method of JavaScript to rewrite div content. The capability to transmit and receive data seamlessly within your user interface is the power Flash and Ajax offer.

External Data and Usability Concerns

External data comes with a price. Applications that run directly on the desktop don't refresh an entire user interface to alert you of a data change. Imagine if a Word document required an entire refresh of the screen to simply recast a length of text to be bold.

A page refresh can seem jarring. However, users on the Internet have become accustomed to it, and expect it. This type of adaptive behavior becomes inherent workflow expectation. Browser users realize when the screen disappears and the hourglass starts spinning that the application is in fact working, not breaking.

Flash provides freedom but exposes you to the possibility of endangering the user experience. When a user engages a Flash application, if the interface responded differently for one transaction than another, a user might perceive an application error and become confused.

These are two very different user perceptions and expectations that separate the browser experience and the Flash experience.

Data Latency: Asynchronous Communication

A Flash user interface must be designed with a specific user workflow and task in mind. For example, when you open your favorite text editor and save a page of text, the computer reacts quickly, and the existence of the file confirms that the function was successful. During complex code operations, well-designed applications give you progress indications when a task is being performed, such as when you save a very large text file. On the Web, delays can be amplified by network latency, which is the time it takes for data to travel over the established network connection.

A persistent Flash application is also at the mercy of server-side script runtime delays. For these situations Flash provides asynchronous event handlers. Asynchronous code is when two programs, running separate from one another, both invoke a procedure to cooperatively complete a function. Because a program can't directly know when another program has completed its part of a function, it must wait and have code ready to intercept the results.

It is important in these situations to realize that the browser's hourglass won't begin spinning. Flash has nothing automated to tell users that it is processing data. A Flash user interface must show the user some indication of work being done or the amount of work left to do. The interface can also be designed so that the data transmission is invisible. Server-side scripts often can work with data from your Flash movie while sending the Flash Application an immediate answer while it continues to work.

Be smart. Understand your user workflow and user. Keep your latency and wait times as minimal as possible. Keep your user interfaces responsive to input, even when data is transacting slowly.

Using LoadVars

The LoadVars class was added to the Flash Player in version 6, and has been one of the most popular and convenient methods for importing data into an SWF file. The global functions `loadVariables()` and `loadVariablesNum()` access the same data as LoadVars, but LoadVars is still a powerful class. If you're working with any experienced ActionScript users, you may want to read through this section; if you aren't, you could skip it and just use the global functions.

You can use LoadVars to import raw strings and make new types of data parsers. You can use it to decode classic ampersand-delimited files. LoadVars, without intervention, expects to load ampersand-delimited value pairs. You can use it to populate form data and automatically package that data into POST and GET requests.

Ampersand-Delimited Data

A delimiter is anything that comes between two things. You use delimiters to form a linear series of objects. The following strings are all delimited in a unique way:

```
var1&var2&var3&var4 //delimited with ampersands

var1    var2    var3    var4 //delimited with spaces

var1|var2|var3|var4 //delimited with pipes
```

Flash can load and parse data that is encoded in ampersand-delimited name/value pair format. The name and value in each pair are, in turn, delimited with an equal sign. The LoadVars class is capable of parsing data such as the following example:

```
var1=A Rock and Roll Station&var2=An oldies Station&var3=An Electronic Music
Station&var4=Another Electronic Music station
```

Data such as the preceding example is parsed into variables with string values. For example, the preceding data can be parsed into four variables (var1, var2, var3, and var4) with string values. Flash does not natively parse such data into any other primitive or reference data type.

LoadVars Class Methods

The following table describes the methods of the LoadVars class:

Method	Return	Description
addRequestHeader	Nothing	Adds a request header when the XML object is requested from the server.
getBytesLoaded	Number	Returns the byte amount of the file that has loaded into the XML object specified.
getBytesTotal	Number	Returns the total byte size specified in the header of the requested file.
load	Nothing	Specifies a target file to load and proceeds to load it.
decode	String	Parses data into LoadVars object properties.
send	Nothing	Sends the specified XML object as a document to a URL.
sendAndLoad	Nothing	Sends the specified XML object as a document to a URL and specifies a return object to place the server reply.
toString	String	Returns a literal string of the specified XML object.

The addRequestHeader() method has two usages. Following are examples of their syntax:

❏   Set just one header field (for example, From):

```
myVars.addRequestHeader(name:String, value:String) : Void
```

❑   Send an array to set multiple header fields:

```
myVars.addRequestHeader([name1:String, value1:String, name2:String, ⤸
    value2:String]) : Void
```

Headers give the server information about the request being sent. Some requests require special headers to be recognized. Request headers are most often used to instruct the remote application about how to use incoming data. You can read more about the HTTP request headers specification at www.w3.org/Protocols/HTTP/HTRQ_Headers.html.

The getBytesLoaded() method is used to measure the progress of asynchronous data loading into the object. It has no parameters and returns the number of bytes loaded so far. Here's its syntax:

```
myVars.getBytesLoaded();
```

It is most often used to construct a preload bar or percentage-loaded textField.

The getBytesTotal() method is most frequently used to measure the progress of asynchronous data loading into the object. It has no parameters and returns the total number of bytes yet to be loaded. Here's its syntax:

```
myVars.getBytesTotal();
```

It is often used to construct a preload bar or percentage-loaded textField.

The load() method has one parameter, a String object defining the target path of the data file to load. load() is used when sendAndLoad is not required. Here's the method's syntax:

```
myVars.load(path:String);
```

decode() has one parameter, a String containing ampersand-delimited data. The method then parses the data into properties of the LoadVars object. Here's the syntax:

```
myVars.decode(data:String);
```

The send() method encodes custom properties of the LoadVars object into ampersand-delimited format and sends them to the specified resource. It has three parameters:

❑   A String defining the target URL (required).

❑   A String specifying a window destination for the server response (required).

If you do not want to leave the Flash application or open a new browser window, use the sendAndLoad() *method instead.*

❑   A String specifying either GET or POST (optional).

The data is sent using the HTTP POST method by default. The method's syntax is as follows:

```
myVars.send(serverPath:String, windowName:String, httpMethod:String);
```

The `sendAndLoad()` method also has three parameters:

- ❑ A String defining the target URL (required).
- ❑ A target LoadVars object (required). Unlike `send()`, the server response for a `sendAndLoad()` call is handled by a target LoadVars object that you specify with the second parameter. When a response returns, Flash calls the `onData()` or `onLoad()` method of the object specified.
- ❑ A String specifying either GET or POST (optional).

Like the `send()` method, `sendAndLoad()` sends the data using HTTP POST by default. Here's its syntax:

```
myXML.sendAndLoad(serverPath:String, target:LoadVars, httpMethod:String);
```

The `toString()` method can be invoked to transform the LoadVars object into a string. It has no parameters. Here's the syntax:

```
myVsrs.toString();
```

> **Flash cannot create and save external files. If you must save your variables, you must use either the `send()` method or the `sendAndLoad()` method to transport the data to an external application or server method.**

The LoadVars class has two properties, which are described in the following table:

Property	Type	Description
contentType	String	The MIME type associated with the object specified.
loaded	Boolean	Becomes `true` when the `onLoad` event has fired.

Creating a LoadVars Object

LoadVars uses a typical constructor. Here is an example, with some variables being added to the object itself:

```
var myVars:LoadVars = new LoadVars();
myVars.station1 = "Rock and Roll Oldies";
myVars.station2 = "Today's hit music";
myVars.station3 = "Electronica in the Nineties";
myVars.station4 = "Electronica Monster 2";
```

When you trace the myVars object directly, the output window shows a URL-encoded string:

```
station4=Electronica%20Monster%202&station3=Electronica%20in%20the%20Nineties&stati
on2=Today%E2%80%99s%20hit%20music&station1=Rock%20and%20Roll%20Oldies
```

That's really all there is to creating a LoadVars object. This simplicity can be an important tool for rapid development of network communications in Flash. Although the preceding example merely adds a few properties to a new LoadVars object, it sets the foundation for sending and loading data to and from external resources. You can read more about loading and sending data in the following sections. First, however, complete the following Try It Out exercise.

527

Create Ampersand-Delimited Data Using LoadVars

1. Open a new Flash document and save it in your work folder.

2. Click the first frame in the timeline, open the Actions panel, and enter the following ActionScript code:

```
var myVars:LoadVars = new LoadVars();
myVars.station1 = "Rock and Roll Oldies";
myVars.station2 = "Today's hit music";
myVars.station3 = "Electronica in the Nineties";
myVars.station4 = "Electronica Monster 2";
trace(unescape(myVars.toString()));
```

3. Test the code by pressing Ctrl+Enter. In the output window you will see a neatly constructed ampersand-delimited name/value pair string.

4. Copy the text that you see in the output window into a new document in your favorite text editor. Your resulting file should look like this:

```
station4=Electronica Monster 2&station3=Electronica in the
Nineties&station2=Today's hit music&station1=Rock and Roll Oldies
```

5. Save the new text file as myData.txt. Because you're only using this code to quickly create an example data file for use in the next Try It Out section, you do not need to save your FLA.

How It Works

As you can see, you were able to quickly create your test file by using a simple constructor and simply declaring variables directly upon the LoadVars object.

One important aspect of this code is the use of the unescape() function. Because URLs contain characters and delimiters that can collide with the characters found in variables within GET and POST actions, LoadVars' toString() method automatically URL-encodes the object. The URL-encoded version of the same code sample would produce the following:

```
station4=Electronica%20Monster%202&station3=Electronica%20in%20the%20Nineties&stati
on2=Today%E2%80%99s%20hit%20music&station1=Rock%20and%20Roll%20Oldies
```

As you can see, characters such as ampersands have been converted into percent sign codes. These codes are a percent symbol followed by a numeric identifier. Flash gives you two methods for working with URL encoding: escape() and unescape(). Because the intention was to copy the contents of the LoadVars object to a file, rather than send them to a remote CGI, you use the unescape() function to format the results of the toString() method. You can, in fact, revert the string back to URL-encoded format by using the escape() method. unescape() and escape() work on any string, in any object, not just LoadVars. They can be handy tools when loading data in and out of Flash.

So now that you've created and understand a LoadVars object, you can move on to the next and most interesting part of LoadVars, loading remote files!

LoadVars Event Handlers

Events are specific things that can occur within an application. Many types of events exist. For example, when a user clicks a button an event occurs, and when the playhead enters a frame an event occurs. Flash has mechanisms that listen for events so that code specific to a certain occurrence can run. In the case of LoadVars objects, you'll want to be notified when the data has downloaded.

Event handlers are methods that get called when an event occurs. By default no functionality is defined for LoadVars event handlers. That is, it is up to you to define these methods for LoadVars objects. In an asynchronous method, such as `load()`, the application has no idea when the data will arrive, how long it will take when it begins to arrive, or if it will even finish successfully.

The LoadVars class has two such events handler methods: `onData()` and `onLoad()`.

onData()

The `onData()` event handler method has one definable parameter, a String object. The method fires as soon as all of the data has arrived from a `load()` or `sendAndLoad()` call. If this method is defined, the LoadVars object does not call the `onLoad()` method. Instead, the raw string data that arrives is sent directly to `onData()` as a parameter. Here's the `onData()` syntax:

```
myVars.onData = function(str:String):Void {
    trace(str);
};
```

`onData()` makes itself useful by overriding the internal document decoding of the variable file. This means that if what you are loading is unformatted data or uses a different delimitation method, you can still access the string information. You can think of the `onData()` method as a sort of bypass that routes you directly to the return data requested by the load event.

onLoad()

The `onLoad()` event handler method has one parameter, a Boolean. `onLoad()` fires as soon as the object is loaded and has been decoded into a set of variables. Defining the `onLoad()` method assumes that you believe the return data from the load method will in fact be an ampersand-delimited set of name/value pairs. The Boolean state passed into the function communicates whether the data parsing was success-ful: `true` if the data was parsed correctly; `false` if a parsing error was encountered.

```
My_Vars.onLoad = function(success:Boolean):Void {
        if(success){
                trace(this);
        }
};
```

`onLoad()` is helpful because it automates a few steps into one. It lets you know when an object has loaded and if the load was successful, calls the decode method, and then provides you an access point for examining the resulting variables.

Try It Out   **Load Ampersand-Delimited Files**

1.   If you haven't created the `myData.txt` file, you should do that now by using your favorite text editor to enter the following text in a file. Save the file as `myData.txt`.

```
station4=Electronica Monster 2&station3=Electronica in the
Nineties&station2=Today's hit music&station1=Rock and Roll Oldies
```

2. Open a new FLA and save it in the same working as `myData.txt`. Open the Actions panel, and
    type the following ActionScript code:

```
var myVars:LoadVars = new LoadVars();
myVars.onLoad = function(success:Boolean):Void {
        trace(this.toString());
}
myVars.load("myData.txt");
```

3. Test the code by pressing Ctrl+Enter. The output window shows you the file that has just been
    loaded in the URL-encoded format.

4. Close the SWF tab and return to the code in the Actions panel. To access some of those variables
    directly using a `for` loop, modify the `onLoad` event to look like this:

```
var myVars:LoadVars = new LoadVars();
myVars.onLoad = function(success:Boolean):Void {
        trace(this.status);
        if (success) {
                for (var i:String in this) {
                        trace(i+": "+this[i]);
                }
        }
};
myVars.load("myData.txt");
```

5. Test the code by pressing Ctrl+Enter. The output window shows you the variable names and
    values in a list:

```
station1: Rock and Roll Oldies
station2: Today's hit music
station3: Electronica in the Nineties
station4: Electronica Monster 2
treeBranch: test=true
onLoad: [type Function]
```

6. Close the SWF tab and return to the code in the Actions panel. Try out the `onData()` method
    and see how you can load your string directly and use the decode method manually. To do so,
    your code should now look like this:

```
var myVars:LoadVars = new LoadVars();
myVars.onData = function(str:String):Void {
        trace(str);
        myVars.decode(str);
        trace(this);
};
myVars.load("myData.txt");
```

7. Test the code by pressing Ctrl+Enter. The output window shows you the raw string and variable
    names and values in a list, much like the following:

```
treeBranch=test=true&station4=Electronica Monster 2&station3=Electronica in the
Nineties&station2=Today's hit music&station1=Rock and Roll Oldies
station1: Rock and Roll Oldies
station2: Today's hit music
station3: Electronica in the Nineties
station4: Electronica Monster 2
treeBranch: test=true
onData: [type Function]
```

8.   Close the SWF tab and save your FLA file. You reuse this code in a later Try It Out section.

How It Works

The `load()` method is an asynchronous operation. The time is reliant upon the speed at which Flash can import the file. If this file had been on the Internet, it may have taken more than a few seconds to load the byte data of the file into Flash. By setting an event handler, you've allowed the code the flexibility it needs to complete a useful file load.

The other look you had was at `onData()`. You saw that you could, in fact, load a raw text file and disallow Flash from doing anything with it on its own. This is handy, because sometimes you don't have control over remote file format. There may be times you want to load a file that is neither ampersand-delimited nor value pairs. In these cases you can use the `onData()` method to load the file directly and use `String` methods on the `str` value to extract the data you need by hand.

When using the `onLoad()` event, you assume you're loading an ampersand-delimited formatted document. This has the advantage of sending the event a Boolean telling you whether the file load was successful. `onLoad()` also calls the decode all by itself, so you didn't have to worry about that step.

Loading and Parsing Raw Text

At times the data you have available to you is not formatted as ampersand-delimited name/value pairs. Sometimes the data has its own unique format, or the data is a paragraph of text. Sometimes you might want to obtain data that resides within HTML files. In these cases, you need to build your own parsing routine.

The most common (String class) methods for working such strings are `split()` and `join()`. For the purposes of this chapter, you will be loading a simple HTML file and using LoadVars and the `String` class to extract data from the HTML page.

The example is going to find and show you an `<a href>` tag from any HTML file. You can query Slashdot, or Google, or an Apache HTTP folder listing of JPEG images. For this example, you'll be loading Slashdot, mostly for the irony and plethora of links about robots.

Because you know how to load raw string data from the previous Try It Out examples, this section shows you code that can manipulate the string itself, without getting too far into the details of the String class. This should give you a good start on how to create your own text parsers.

Of course, loading cross-domain files still has the same issues, and loading someone else's web page from another domain directly into a Flash document on your own domain won't work without security considerations. A couple of sections about security in Chapter 22 explain what the limitations are and how to deal with them.

The following Try It Out contains concepts from several chapters.

Try It Out   Load a Raw String and Do Something Neat!

1. Open a new Flash document and define a function that can find and extract an `href` link from a string:

```
findAHrefLinks = function (page:String):Object {
        var linkList:Object = {};
        var ahrefs:Array = page.split("<a");
        ahrefs.shift();
        for (var i:Number = 0; i<ahrefs.length; i++) {
                ahrefs[i] = ahrefs[i].split("/a>")[0];
        }
        for (var i:Number = 0; i<ahrefs.length; i++) {
                var thisLink:Object = linkList["link"+i]={};
                var linkText:String = ahrefs[i].split(">")[1];
                linkText = linkText.substring(0, linkText.lastIndexOf("<"));
                thisLink.linkText = linkText;
                var attributes:Array = ⊃
        ahrefs[i].split(">")[0].split('"').join("").split("'").join("");
                thisLink.url = attributes.split("href=")[1];
                if (thisLink.url.indexOf(" ")>1) {
                        thisLink.url = thisLink.url.substring(0, ⊃
        thisLink.url.indexOf(" "));
                }
        }
        return linkList;
};
```

2. Load a web page into a LoadVars object and run the raw string through your new function using `onData()` by adding the following code to the end of the code you entered in step 1:

```
var myVars:LoadVars = new LoadVars();
var baseUrl:String = "slashdot.com";
myVars.onData = function(str:String):Void {
        var linkList:Object = findAHrefLinks(str);
        for(var i:String in linkList){
                trace(newline);
                for(var n:String in linkList[i]){
                        trace(n+": "+linkList[i][n]);
                }
        }
};
myVars.load("http://"+baseUrl);
```

3. Test the code by pressing Ctrl+Enter. After a few moments, as long as you have access to Slashdot via your Internet connection, you will see a list of links in the output window similar to the following:

```
url: //slashdot.org/login.pl?op=newuserform
linkText: Create a new account


url: //ask.slashdot.org/article.pl?sid=05/07/25/2133209
linkText: Software Engineering vs. Systems Engineering?


url: //ask.slashdot.org/article.pl?sid=05/07/26/1811247
linkText: How Should One Respond to a Network Break In?


url: //ask.slashdot.org/article.pl?sid=05/07/26/1857254
linkText: Free Audio Content for Long Drives?


url: //ask.slashdot.org/article.pl?sid=05/07/26/1932206
linkText: Fun and Informative Way to Introduce Open Source?
```

4. Save the FLA file if you want. Experiment with the attributes variable declaration and see whether you can find any attributes other than the href value.

How It Works

In the function that finds href attributes, there is a split() method that effectively finds all instances of the <a> tag. This is followed up by a loop that finds the end tag of those, effectively discarding all other content in the string by selectively keeping only the 0 index of the array created by the split.

The next for loop extracts the link text from within the tag by using split once again, but saving only what comes after the first end bracket by using the 1 index of the array created by the split method. The next line simply cleans up trailing open brackets by cutting the string with the substring method. The link text is added to the outgoing object.

The value of the variable attributes appears complex, but it's not. Two things are happening. First you split the tag once again, this time keeping everything that precedes the first closing bracket. This effectively yields all the attributes within that <a> tag as a single string. There is one caveat. The <a> tag attributes reside within quotes. By using split and join consecutively, you are effectively doing a find/replace operation on the string, only the replacement is a zero-length string, which removes all single and double quotes.

The next thing that happens is that the URL is extracted from the attributes variable. This is done by splitting the string "href" and keeping all of the trailing text. Because this may not be the last attribute listed within the tag, you search for the first space using indexOf() and assume this is the end of the URL. Using substring, the URL is cut from any trailing text.

And that's it. The last line of the function returns the linkList as an object to the requesting object in the onData() method. You could then test the URL values, add the baseUrl as needed, and complete a list of working links on your stage using HTML-enabled text fields.

Hopefully, this gave you a sense of the power of loading raw strings. As an exercise you could go back into the function and make it more efficient. Places within the code are drawn out so you can see better the inner workings of the operation. You could try to find more attributes such as class, or id, and parse the CSS information from the same HTML page. You could then re-create the links on the stage using the exact style format as the web page. You could, in fact, begin to build a simplified XHTML browser with CSS styles. There's really no limit to what you can do when Flash is able to communicate with a server with this much freedom. Have fun!

Summary

In this chapter you explored working with the LoadVars class. You learned that you can load data in ampersand-delimited format, and that Flash will automatically parse that data into variables. You've also learned how to load raw text so that Flash does not parse the data.

Exercises

1. Create a pipe (|) delimited file, rather than an ampersand-delimited file. Load the data file as a raw string using the LoadVars object. Parse the name/value pairs and place them within an object.

2. Load HTML text from a file, and display it in an HTML-enabled text field.

Reading XML

This chapter introduces the many ways in which XML files can be loaded into your application at runtime. Once the XML is loaded, you see how you can use Flash's robust XML toolset to access and utilize the data presented. You also examine security concerns that affect the success of XML in your application and explore solutions to security restrictions such as proxies, shims, and policy files.

Using the Built-in XML Class

Luckily Flash is a platform that is constantly in development. Because Flash is constantly being updated, its input and output methods are constantly under scrutiny. You have new classes and methods with almost every release. These additions can include class sets for SOAP (don't worry about what this is; more about SOAP later) and drag-and-drop components for quickly connecting your Flash application to remote servers for data transactions. This section concerns itself with the most recent and native XML data transport methods available in AS2, introducing you to the methods and objects designed for XML-based data interactions.

One thing to remember is that when you start diving into XML you'll hear fancy terms such as DOM, DTD, XSL, Schemas, SOAP, RPC, and more. Do not be afraid. At the end of the day, XML is simply a markup text similar to HTML. XML's power is its logical simplicity. Flash's XML object is, in fact, a great way to begin working with XML for the first time because of the simplicity and tolerances built into the Flash XML object.

All Wrapped Up in Tags

XML is a way of hierarchically representing information so that meaningful data relationships can be shared among applications. XML is a specification maintained by the W3C. Like HTML, XML uses tags to define data. The same hierarchical concepts are used in HTML and XML. A tag placed within a tag is a child of the outer tag. Here is an HTML example of a <div> tag with a child <p> tag child:

```
...<div>
<p>This is div number 1!</p>
</div>...
```

In this case, <div> is the parent of <p> (and <p> is the child of <div>). As with HTML, you can populate XML tags with attributes, and you can leave raw text within a tag. Unlike HTML, XML is not restricted in any way to naming conventions or preset attribute expectations. You are free to make up naming conventions. Although HTML tells an application how data should look, XML informs an application what the data is and how different data sets relate to one another.

You'll be using a simple XML file example because it easily showcases all of the methods available in Flash and demonstrates how powerful XML can be even in simple contexts. Here's a very simple XML file:

```
<menu>
  <hoopty>
    <automobile doors="4" color="white"> Chrysler 300m</automobile>
    <automobile doors="2" color="silver"> Porsche Cayenne</automobile>
    <truck doors="24" color="black" >Cadillac Escalade</truck>
  </hoopty>
</menu>
```

In it, you create a menu of cars, classified by type and given attributes that describe them. hoopty is an element. An element name can't contain spaces or start with a special character such as a dollar sign. The other way in which you have encapsulated data is the use of attributes within some tags. Attribute values must be wrapped in quotes, no matter the data type described. A case for using attributes is when the data being described within the attribute has no possible children. That is, it is not an element that can contain elements.

windows is an example of an attribute that may be better suited as an element:

```
<menu>
  <hoopty>
    <automobile windows="tinted" doors="4" color="white"> Chrysler
300m</automobile>
    <automobile windows="tinted" doors="2" color="silver"> Porsche
Cayenne</automobile>
    <truck doors="24" color="black" >Cadillac Escalade</truck>
  </hoopty>
</menu>
```

Although this seems to have served the purpose, you can imagine that there may be different types of windows.

Here is an example in which using an element rather than an attribute enables you to grow your XML file without much modification:

```
<menu>
  <hoopty>
    <automobile doors="4" color="White">
        <name>Chrysler 300m</name>
        <window>
            <type>tinted</type>
            <color>Black</color>
        </window>
    </automobile>
    <automobile doors="2" color="Silver">
        <name>Porsche Cayenne</name>
        <window>
```

```
                    <type>tinted</type>
                    <color>Crimson</color>
            </window>
        </automobile>
        <automobile doors="9" color="Black">
            <name>Cadillac Escalade</name>
            <window>
                    <type>tinted</type>
                    <color>Black</color>
            </window>
        </automobile>
    </hoopty>
</menu>
```

You can see that by making the `window` attribute an element you were able to expand the description logically, while allowing data to be removed or added at any time.

Although this description of XML certainly isn't all-encompassing, it's just what you need to know to get started with the XML class in Flash.

CDATA and Character Formats

XML elements can also contain HTML characters. These HTML strings can disrupt an XML schema because it cuts through the hierarchical document with its own tags. The W3C standard provides you with CDATA tags, and, happily, Flash complies with the specification. CDATA tags simply tell the application reading the XML to not parse any information within a CDATA tag as a child node. Flash handles these strings by declaring them text nodes.

Here is an example of a CDATA wrapper:

```
... <automobile doors="4" color="White">
        <image><![CDATA[ <img src='myimage.gif'/>]]></image>
        <name>Chrysler 300m</name>
        <window>
            <type>tinted</type>
            <color>Black</color>
        </window>
    </automobile>...
```

In this example, an `<img>` tag is assigned as the text node value for the XML`<image>` element. Because the text is an HTML tag, it is wrapped in a CDATA wrapper. CDATA is preceded by `<![CDATA[` and followed by `]]>`.

The Flash XML Class

In Flash, XML is a built-in class. It has a set of useful properties, methods, and events that enable you to complete a feature-rich data exchange. Setting up an XML object within your ActionScript is as easy as a simple object type definition. XML is a globally accessible class available via the keyword `new`:

```
var myXML:XML = new XML();
```

XML Class Methods

This section explores the methods of the XML class, which are described in the following table:

Method	Return	Description
addRequestHeader()	Nothing	Adds a request header when the XML object is requested from the server.
appendChild()	Nothing	Puts a specified node into the root child list of the XML document specified.
cloneNode()	XMLNode object	Extracts a target XML node and returns it to the requesting object.
createElement()	XMLNode as an XML element	Creates an element node with a name supplied via a string.
createTextNode()	XMLNode as a string	Creates a simple string element as a child to the object the method is enacted upon.
getBytesLoaded()	Number	Returns the byte amount of the file that has loaded into the XML object specified.
getBytesTotal()	Number	Returns the total byte size specified in the header of the requested file.
hasChildNodes()	Boolean	Checks whether an XMNode object has child nodes.
load()	Nothing	Specifies a target file to load and proceeds to load it.
parseXML()	Nothing	Replaces the current tree with and parses the specified string as a new XML document within the object the method is enacted upon.
removeNode()	Nothing	Removes the specified node from its parent, and removes all child nodes of the specified node.
send()	Nothing	Sends the specified XML object as a document to a URL.
sendAndLoad()	Nothing	Sends the specified XML object as a document to a URL and specifies a return object to place the server reply.
toString()	String	Returns a literal string of the specified XML object.

The addRequestHeader() method has two usages:

❑   Set one HTTP request header field (From, for example). Here's the syntax:

```
myXML.addRequestHeader(name:String, value:String) : Void
```

❏   Send an array of HTTP request header fields to set, using this syntax:

```
myXML.addRequestHeader([name1:String, value1:String, name2:String, value2:String]);
: Void
```

Headers give the server information about the request being sent. Some XML requests such as SOAP require special headers to be recognized. Request headers are most often used to instruct the remote application about how to use incoming *data*.

The `appendChild()` method is used for the construction and modification of XML objects. It takes a single parameter, which must be a childNode or String. A String is automatically run against the `parseXML` method and becomes the nodeValue of the target object. Here's the `appendChild` syntax:

```
myXML.appendChild(childNode:XMLNode);
```

The `cloneNode()` method is used for the construction and modification of XML objects. It has a single parameter, a Boolean. Setting the parameter to `true` clones the specified node and recursively includes all child nodes of the specified node object. Setting the parameter to `false` copies the specified node, but does not include any child nodes. Here's its syntax:

```
myClonedNode = myXML.cloneChild(recursive:Boolean);
```

The `createElement()` method is also used for the construction and modification of XML objects. It has a single parameter, which must be a String. The method creates a new XMLNode object with the nodeName specified in the parameter:

```
myXML.createElement(elementName:String);
```

The `createTextNode()` method, used for the construction and modification of XML objects, adds actual text data to an element. It takes a single parameter, a String that is the text to be added. `createTextNode()` creates a new XMLNode object but does not create an object with a nodeName or bracketed syntax. Following is the method's syntax:

```
myXML.createTextNode(myText:String);
```

The `getBytesLoaded()` method is most often used to construct a preload bar or percentage-loaded textField. It measures the progress of asynchronous data loading into the object. This method has no parameters. Here's its syntax:

```
myXML.getBytesLoaded();
```

`getBytesTotal()` is also used to construct a preload bar or percentage-loaded textField, measuring the progress of asynchronous data loading into the object. The method has no parameters. Here is its syntax:

```
myXML.getBytesTotal();
```

`hasChildNodes()` is most often used to stop a recursive XML object tree navigation method. The method has a no parameters and returns a Boolean. Here's the syntax:

```
myXML.hasChildNodes();
```

The `load()` method is used when `sendAndLoad` is not required. It has one parameter, a String object defining the target path of the data file to load. Here is its syntax:

```
myXML.load(path:String, request:String);
```

The `parseXML()` method has one parameter, a String object that is well-formed XML. If the XML object that this method is performed upon contains XML data already, the String specified in this method is parsed as XML and replaces any data already in the XML object. Here's the syntax:

```
myXML.parseXML(rawXML:String);
```

The specified String parameter cannot be a remote file. This method does make remote calls.

The `removeNote()` method is most often used for manipulating an existing XML object in preparation for sending it to another application or socket. It has no parameters. The operation removes the specified node. If the specified node contains child nodes, all child nodes are also removed. Following is its syntax:

```
myXML.removeNode();
```

The `send()` method is very similar to the global `getURL` method, but automates the task of attaching the object to the POST action. It has two parameters: a String defining the target URL and a String specifying a window destination for the response from the server. If you do not want to leave the Flash application or open a new browser window, use the `sendAndLoad` method instead. Here's `send()`'s syntax:

```
myXML.send(serverPath:String,windowName:String)
```

The `sendAndLoad()` method is identical to the LoadVars object's `sendAndLoad` method. It has two parameters: a String defining the target URL (the method automatically attaches the XML object using POST) and an Object in which the server response will be captured. Using this method invokes the `load` method of the object specified in the second parameter. The object to be loaded is not required to be XML. Any object with a `load` method can be specified, including private classes. Following is the syntax of `sendAndLoad()`:

```
myXML.sendAndLoad(serverPath:String, My_objectInWaiting:Object);
```

The `toString()` method is helpful in converting childNodes, which are literal strings, to a String object for manipulation. It can be invoked to transform the XML object into a string, which preserves line breaks and retains well-formed XML syntax. This method is automatically invoked when an XML object is directly traced using the `trace` method. Here's the syntax for `toString()`, which has no parameters:

```
myXML.toString();
```

Flash cannot create and save external files. XML object methods are often used to construct and manipulate documents for SOAP and RPC procedures. If you must save your XML, you must use either send method to transport the XML to an external application or server method.

The following table describes the XML class properties:

Property	Type	Description
attributes	Object	An object of value pairs defined by attributes of the element specified.
childNodes	Array	An array of all the children of the object specified.
contentType	String	The MIME type associated with the object specified.
docTypeDecl	String	The document type definition specified in the document type node.
firstChild	XMLNode	The first node in the list of childNodes of a Node object.
ignoreWhite	Boolean	Determines whether white space should be counted as a node, or whether it should be ignored.
lastChild	XMLNode	The last node in the list of childNodes of a Node object.
loaded	Boolean	Becomes true when the onLoad event has fired.
nextSibling	XMLNode	The next node in the list of childNodes of a Node object.
nodeName	String	The string name of the root node of the object specified.
nodeType	Number	A number value representing the node type found during the parse of the specified object.
nodeValue	String or Null	If no childNodes are present, and a string value exists, nodeValue is the string representation of element contents. Otherwise, the value is Null.
parentNode	XMLNode	If a node has a parent, this object references the parent node of the specified child. Otherwise, the value is Null.
previousSibling	XML Node	The previous node in the list of childNodes of a Node object.
status	Number	A list of error codes encountered during parse. If no errors are found, the value is zero.
xmlDecl	String	The document's XML declaration

XML Event Handlers

The XML object yields two definable event handler methods: onData() and onLoad().

onData()

The onData() event handler method has one parameter, a String. This method fires as soon as all of the data has arrived from a load() or sendAndLoad() call. If this method is defined, the XML object does not call the onLoad() event handler method. Instead, the data that arrives into the object is sent directly to onData() as a raw string. Here's the syntax:

```
myXML.onData = function(str:String):Void {
   trace(str);
};
```

`onData()` makes itself useful by overriding the internal document manipulation parse of the `XML` object. This means that if what you are loading is malformed XML, or not XML at all, you can still access the string information. An example of non-XML data might be a table of wind speeds in space-delimited format. Allowing such a file to attempt to be loaded as XML would produce an error because it would be considered malformed. You can think of the onData object as a sort of bypass, which routes you directly to the return data requested by the load event.

onLoad( )

The `onLoad()` event handler method has one parameter, which must be a Boolean. This method fires as soon as the data loads and has been separated into a tree of `XMLNode` objects. Defining `onLoad()` assumes that you believe the return data from the load method will in fact be well-formed XML. The Boolean state communicates whether the data was parsed successfully:

```
myXML.onLoad = function(success:Boolean):Void {
        if(success){
                trace(this);
        }

};
```

`onLoad()` is helpful because it automates a few steps into one. It lets you know when an object has loaded and if the load was successful, calls the `parseXML()` method, and then provides you an access point for examining the resulting XML object.

ignoreWhite: A Special Property

When an XML object parses XML data, by default it interprets white space (tabs, spaces, newlines, and so on) as XML nodes. If you choose not to ignore white space, and you do not expect these spaces to occur, the structure of the resulting `XML` object might confuse you when objects are not where you expect them. If you want to parse the white space, you do not need to do anything extra. However, if you want Flash to ignore white space when parsing the data, you can assign a value of `true` to the `ignoreWhite` property, like this:

```
myXML.ignoreWhite = true;
```

Loading External XML Files

In Chapter 21 you learned to create an XML object. Now you can begin using XML. First, though, you need to get through the details of actually loading the file. In the following example, you load the XML file you created in Chapter 21, using `onLoad`, `onData`, `load`, `getBytesLoaded`, `getBytesTotal`, and `status`. You won't be working with your loaded document just yet. To load XML files, you must be familiar with `onLoad` and `onData`.

Try It Out   **Load an XML File and Create Event Handlers**

1.   Create an XML file with your favorite text editor, enter the following XML, and save the file in your work folder as `myData.xml`:

```
<?xml version="1.0" encoding="ISO-8859-1"?>
<channels>
    <Station identification="104.1">
        <Name>
            Rock And Roll Oldies!
        </Name>
        <Desc>
            Music great with hot chocolate!
        </Desc>
    </Station>
    <Station identification="98.6">
        <Name>
            Rock and Roll
        </Name>
        <Desc>
            Music for waiting for Godot!
        </Desc>
    </Station>
    <Station identification="102.5">
        <Name>
            Electronic Madness!
        </Name>
        <Desc>
            Arigato Rules!
        </Desc>
    </Station>
    <Station identification="107.9">
        <Name>
            Electronic Madness 2!
            <Name>
        <Desc>
            Thunder Dome!
        </Desc>
    </Station>
</channels>
```

2. Open a new Flash document and save it in your work folder as xmlLoadSample.fla.

3. Click the first frame in the timeline, open the Actions panel, and enter the following ActionScript code:

```
var My_XML:XML = new XML();
My_XML.ignoreWhite = true;
My_XML.onData = function(str:String) {
    trace(str);
    trace(My_XML.firstChild.firstChild);
};
My_XML.load("myData.xml");
```

4. Test the code by pressing Ctrl+Enter. Verify that the XML document is displayed in the output window and is available as a String called str. Also verify that the second trace fails, so you can see that onData fails to create an accessible XML object tree.

5. Because you know you're loading an XML file, go ahead and call the `parseXML` method in the `onData` function. Here's how. Close the test SWF, go back to the Actions panel for the first frame of the `xmlLoadSample.fla`, and modify the existing code to look like the following:

```
var My_XML:XML = new XML();
My_XML.ignoreWhite = true;
My_XML.onData = function(str:String) {
    My_XML.parseXML(str);
    trace(this.firstChild.firstChild);
};
My_XML.load("myData.xml");
```

6. Test the code by pressing Ctrl+Enter. Verify that the XML document has loaded and is accessible as an XML document by verifying the availability of the `firstChild.firstChild` property. If you are using a different XML file, you might need to change this test path to a valid property.

7. Because you don't need to access your XML file as a string, abandon your look at the `onData` method and switch to `onLoad`, which will automate the `parseXML` step. Here's how:

```
var My_XML:XML = new XML();
My_XML.ignoreWhite = true;
My_XML.onLoad = function(success:Boolean) {
    trace(this.status);
    if (success) {
    trace(this.firstChild.firstChild);
    } else {
    trace("fail");
    }
};
```

8. Test the code by pressing Ctrl+Enter. Verify that the XML document loaded by verifying the availability of the `firstChild.firstChild` property.

9. Save your FLA file as `xmlLoadSample.fla`; you'll be using it again in a bit.

How It Works

The `load` function is an asynchronous event. That is, the return value of the load method has an unknown time index. The time is reliant on the speed at which Flash can import the file. If this file had been on the Internet, it might have taken more than a few seconds to load the byte data of the XML file into Flash. By setting an event handler, you've allowed the code the flexibility it needs to complete a useful file load.

The other look you had was at `onData`. You saw that you could, in fact, load a raw text file and disallow Flash from doing anything with it on its own just like the LoadVars object. If you, in fact, need to load data that is not XML and not an ampersand-delimited set of name/value pairs you should use the LoadVars object.

By switching to the `onLoad` event, you assume you're loading an XML document. But this has the advantage of sending the event a Boolean telling you whether the file load was successful. The `onLoad` method also called `parseXML` all by itself, so you didn't have to worry about that step. With `onLoad` you can concentrate on your XML object right away. The other aspect of `onLoad` is the status property. The status property has a series of error codes that can tell you whether the XML document was malformed and what particular type of error was encountered.

The errors codes are as follows:

Code	Description
0	File loaded and parsed successfully.
-2	A CDATA tag was not closed.
-3	The initial XML declaration was malformed.
-4	The DOCTYPE declaration was malformed.
-5	A comment had no close syntax.
-6	An element node was malformed.
-7	Out of memory.
-8	An attribute was malformed.
-9	A start tag had no matching end tag.
-10	An end tag had no matching start tag.

Measuring Bytes

Chapter 21 mentioned *latency* and urged you to think about how to handle asynchronous communications. The tools the XML object provides for this are two properties: getBytesLoaded and getBytesTotal. By using some simple math, you can display a percentage of bytes loaded or manipulate a user interface, such as a progress bar.

A Note about Security and Locality

This example assumes you have access to a remote server. If you test the code when both the SWF file and XML file reside on a local computer, the data file will load nearly instantly. Because this is the case, the test code will show 100 percent loaded immediately, which doesn't allow you to truly test your preload code locally.

For security purposes, to test the code properly in this example, either place the myData.xml file on an HTTP server, or place myData.xml on the same server as xmlLoadExample.swf. You can add an HTML wrapper file for the SWF if you want, but it's not a requirement. In the example, you are uploading only the XML file to the HTTP server and keeping the SWF file local, so you can be sure that no security issues get in your way as you test the code.

The details of security and why this example requires this limitation are discussed in the "Explaining Cross-Domain Security" section later in this chapter.

Try It Out **Create a Simple Text-Based Pre-loader**

For this example, you create a textField object on the stage. You'll be creating the textField via ActionScript, but you could just as easily create it as a stage object.

1. Upload the `myData.xml` file from the previous code examples to your favorite server. For purposes of the code example, call this server `www.aRemoteServer.com`. Replace this string wherever it exists within the code with your own URL.

2. Test the URL of the newly uploaded file. An example URL might be `http://www.aRemoteServer.com/myXMLProject/myData.xml`.

3. If you can see the file in a browser, Flash will be able to see the file. Open `xmlLoadSample.fla` and open the Actions panel. The following ActionScript code should already exist:

```
var My_XML:XML = new XML();
My_XML.ignoreWhite = true;
My_XML.onLoad = function(success:Boolean) {
    trace(this.status);
    if (success) {
    trace(this.firstChild.firstChild);
    } else {
    trace("fail");
    }
};
My_XML.load("myData.xml");
```

4. The change is simple. In the last line, change the target file string to include the server path of the file that now resides on that server. Your code should now look similar to the following:

```
var My_XML:XML = new XML();
My_XML.ignoreWhite = true;
My_XML.onLoad = function(success:Boolean) {
    trace(this.status);
    if (success) {
    trace(this.firstChild.firstChild);
    } else {
    trace("fail");
    }
};
My_XML.load("http://www.aRemoteServer.com/myXMLProject/myData.xml");
```

5. Test your code by pressing Ctrl+Enter. Just as with the initial version, you will see the XML object populate with external data. At this point it might have taken a few moments for the data to load into your object. This is a good thing, because you now understand the power of an asynchronous event handler. You have an opportunity now to add your pre-loader. Close the SWF and go back to the actions with which you're working.

6. Create a text field with ActionScript so you can have a visual representation of your code results on the stage. To do so, enter the following code before the `My_XML` constructor:

```
this.createTextField("XMLProgress",this.getNextHighestDepth(),20,20,40,20);
this.XMLProgress.border = true;
this.XMLProgress.text = "0%";
```

7. Now you need to declare two functions to watch the My_XML object via a setInterval object. Do that by placing the following code after the textField creation code you just added:

```
getPercentLoaded = function (handle) {
    return handle.getBytesLoaded()/handle.getBytesTotal();
};
watchMyXMLLoad = function (handle) {
```

```
var perc:Number = getPercentLoaded(handle);
if (perc>0) {
XMLProgress.text = int(perc*100)+"%";
}
if (perc == 1) {
clearInterval(MyXMLPreloader);
}
};
```

8. Now you just need to add an interval declaration to kick off a loop event to watch the file load. Place this code just before the load method of the My_XML object:

```
MyXMLPreloader = setInterval(this, "watchMyXMLLoad", 10, My_XML);
```

9. Your final script should look like this:

```
this.createTextField("XMLProgress", this.getNextHighestDepth(), 20, 20, 40, 20);
this.XMLProgress.border = true;
this.XMLProgress.text = "0%";
getPercentLoaded = function (handle) {
    return handle.getBytesLoaded()/handle.getBytesTotal();
};
watchMyXMLLoad = function (handle) {
    var perc:Number = getPercentLoaded(handle);
    if (perc>0) {
    XMLProgress.text = int(perc*100)+"%";
    }
    if (perc == 1) {
    clearInterval(MyXMLPreloader);
    }
};
var My_XML:XML = new XML();
My_XML.ignoreWhite = true;
My_XML.onLoad = function(success:Boolean) {
    trace(this.status);
    if (success) {
    trace(this.firstChild.firstChild);
    } else {
    trace("fail");
    }
};
var MyXMLPreloader:Number = setInterval(this, "watchMyXMLLoad", 10, My_XML);
My_XML.load("http://www.aRemoteServer.com/myXMLProject/myData.xml ");
```

10. Test your movie by pressing Ctrl+Enter. You will see a text field on the stage that reflects the percentage loaded. If your Internet connection is broadband, loading your small test XML file will probably reflect 100 percent almost instantly. If you'd like to see more granular action of the code, try using a modem, or create a new test XML file that is much, much larger.

11. Save the FLA; you'll be using it again in the next code example.

How It Works

In this example you added a simple way to watch your file load and affect the user interface to give the user information about the state of the file load. The meat and potatoes were really in step 7. Here you used both the getBytesTotal and getBytesLoaded methods. By making them a simple fraction you were able to determine the ratio of bytes loaded.

You might have also noticed how you kept the percent loaded a separate function. This is because there are many objects within Flash that have these two properties. A percentage operation seems simple enough, but during application development, compartmentalizing it into one reusable piece of code helps to speed production. Also this separation hopefully got you to think of ways this entire process could be automated within a class object, so that many different XML files could use the same code to be loaded into an application with an indication of bytes loaded.

The other item introduced into the example is the interval. As covered earlier in this book, the setInterval object is a Number method with global static access. Declaring a number a setInterval, you effectively create a loop that iterates over a specified time. With each loop, in this example, you check the state of your percentage loaded and update the GUI. You can see that you also took care to use the clearInterval method to end the loop after the file had fully loaded. It is important, even on these small scales, to be careful about the loops you have running, what may be looping at the same time, and what effect a runaway loop might have on your movie. Always clean up your code when you are through with any script. To help clean up code, you can use the value of the status property, which you traced when the onLoad event fired. The status will indicate at anytime what the current condition of the data load is.

getBytesTotal Isn't Working!

How does Flash know how big a file is? Flash needs to know the total bytes of a file to determine the getBytesTotal property. The way in which it does this can affect your code. If the file being loaded resides on the local system, Flash queries the file information kept by the operating system. When Flash is accessing a remote file on an HTTP server, Flash must rely on the server to add the total byte size of the file in the header information. A header is simply a short information block that exists in every file. A header tells an application what the file is and how to handle the bytes within it. Most often, a server automatically adds these headers to a file when they are requested. The header that concerns you is the Content-Length header, which contains the total byte size of the file. An application such as a browser or Flash can know the total size of a file before loading it completely by looking for this header information.

This is all fairly automated, and as long as you're accessing static files, there's little issue. There is a case, however, when the header information would be incomplete. Often you're required to load data files that are sent via CGI or a server-side script engine such as PHP. These requests often return raw data directly back into the response byte stream without headers. The header information is the first place to look when you have a getBytesTotal problem when using server-side script responses. The good news is that the popular server-side scripting engines like Perl and PHP offer methods to manually inject header information into the return byte stream.

Understanding the Parent-Child Node Relationship

You access the data within a loaded XML object in Flash by traversing the XML using a DOM (Document Object Model). A DOM is a hierarchy of parent-child relationships. The Flash XML DOM consists of complete XMLNodes, elements, text nodes, attributes, and declarations. The Flash XML DOM is recursive. Every XMLNode is given the same set of properties and methods for navigating up, down, and across the object tree.

Because the method set is recursive and available to every XMLNode within the entire XML object, when you call a navigation method or node property you must specify a starting object. The starting object can exist anywhere in the DOM. Querying navigation methods while navigating the DOM does not modify the XML object in anyway. These methods are simply a convenient way to view your XML document.

The Flash XML DOM is not the same as the JavaScript DOM. Many folks reading this will be familiar with methods such as `createAttribute` and `getElementByID`. Flash does not contain these. Although robust, many methods and concepts were left out of the Flash XML DOM. Do not despair, however. Many people have made class additions and libraries for extending the DOM interface. You should go looking for these as well as think about what you might create on your own.

Navigating an Example Node Tree

In the previous Try It Out section you loaded an XML file into a Flash object. However, you didn't do anything with it. The following exercise is a continuation of that project.

Try It Out   **Load and Extract Values from an XML File**

1. Open `xmlLoadSample.fla` created in the previous Try It Out. Open the Actions panel, and enter the following into frame 1:

```
this.createTextField("XMLProgress", this.getNextHighestDepth(), 20, 20, 40, 20);
this.XMLProgress.border = true;
this.XMLProgress.text = "0%";
getPercentLoaded = function (handle) {
    return handle.getBytesLoaded()/handle.getBytesTotal();
};
watchMyXMLLoad = function (handle) {
    var perc = getPercentLoaded(handle);
    if (perc>0) {
        XMLProgress.text = int(perc*100)+"%";
    }
    if (perc == 1) {
        clearInterval(MyXMLPreloader);
    }
};
My_XML = new XML();
My_XML.ignoreWhite = true;
My_XML._parent = this;
My_XML.onLoad = function(success:Boolean) {
```

```
        if (success) {
            My_XML._parent.init();
        } else {
            trace("fail");
        }
    };
    var MyXMLPreloader:Number = setInterval(this, "watchMyXMLLoad", 10, My_XML);
    My_XML.load("myData.xml ");
```

2. You just added a parent declaration, as well as a call to an init function. Now add the `init` function just before the `My_XML` constructor:

```
init = function () {
    trace(My_XML.hasChildNodes());
    if (My_XML.hasChildNodes()) {
        for (var i = 0; i<My_XML.childNodes.length; i++) {
            if (My_XML.childNodes[i].nodeName == "channels") {
                var channelSet:XMLNode = My_XML.childNodes[i];
                var channelObject = this["channelSet"+i]={};
                parseStation(channelObject, channelSet.firstChild,0);
            }
        }
    } else {
        trace("Not a channel list");
    }
    delete My_XML;
};
```

3. Test your code by pressing Ctrl+Enter. Verify that a channels node was found. The list of stations appears in their raw XML format in the output window.

4. Close the SWF and go back to the actions with which you're working. Now add the following code to create an object and populate it with some station information. Place the code before the `init` function:

```
var num:Number = 0;
parseStation = function (channelObject, station, num) {
    var stationReference:Object = channelObject["station"+num]={};
    for (var t = 0; t<station.childNodes.length; t++) {
        if (station.childNodes[t].nodeName == "Name" &&
station.childNodes[t].firstChild.nodeType == 3) {
            stationReference.stationName =
station.childNodes[t].firstChild.nodeValue;
        }
        if (station.childNodes[t].nodeName == "Desc" &&
station.childNodes[t].firstChild.nodeType == 3) {
            stationReference.stationDesc =
station.childNodes[t].firstChild.nodeValue;
        }
        stationReference.ID =
station.childNodes[t].parentNode.attributes.identification;
    }

    if (station.nextSibling != null) {
        num++
```

```
          parseStation(channelObject,station.nextSibling,num);
     }
};
```

5. Test the code by pressing Ctrl+Enter. In this example code you need to select the `show` variables option by pressing Ctrl+Alt+v or by selecting Debug⇨List Variables. In the output window you will now see near the top of the list an object called channelSet0. The object has all of your XML data within a similar hierarchy as the XML file. The XML file is deleted, and you can begin to work with the information within your object as if they were any other variable.

How It Works

In this example you use the XML method property set and a few methods to verify and navigate the contents of your XML file. The `init` function conveniently checks to see whether the XML file is valid. It does this by utilizing the `hasChildNodes` property to decide whether or not it should proceed. If the function does find child nodes, it goes through them as a list, referring to them with the `childNodes` property. The `childNodes` property is an array that references the list of child nodes within a node. The code verifies each node as channels nodes by checking the node name using the `nodeName` property.

You also check that the node name will have no raw XML, and in fact is actual content data by checking that your `nodeValue` returns a 3. Had the node contained another element node, the `nodeValue` would have returned a 1, and you could then make decisions on how to handle such a case.

You can have as many channels nodes as you want for multiple subsets of stations. For each channels node found, the function sends the `firstChild` within it to the `parseStation` function. At this point you could double-check the node name of the station to be sure it is a station node, but because you only plan to have stations reside in a channels node, you can skip this check.

The `parseStation` function is recursive. This means that under the correct conditions the code will call itself within itself, with a new set of parameters. This is effectively like a loop but automates the parsing of each station nicely. Although fast, recursive loops are limited to 256 iterations. If you had more than 256 stations, you'd need to find a different way. However, the recursive example highlights a property called `nextSibling`. You can see the `nextSibling` property being fetched in the last line of the `parseStation` function. This could have easily been `previousSibling`. Because the `init` function started the recursion function at the top of your station list, `nextSibling` works because `nextSibling` always returns the node below that of the node the `nextSibling` property is fetched on. If the `init` function had specified the `lastChild` rather than the `firstChild`, the `parseStation` function would use the `previousSibling` property, because `previousSibling` works up the list of nodes rather than down.

The other unique demonstration in the code is the `parentNode` property access. Although you could have accessed the resulting node in a different way, this shows an example of how you can move up the node tree, rather than use `previousSibling`, which only moves up the node list. In this case the `parentNode` is used as a way to target the attribute object of the station itself. You could have easily have called `station.attributes.identification` to complete the same reference. In this way you can see how malleable the DOM tree toolset is and how the property set of the XML object yields a robust interface for finding information within your XML files.

Using Attributes

The previous examples touched on the use of attributes. Attributes are nothing too complex. Flash treats the attributes within a node as an object appendage. That is, all attributes for a single node are accessed as a named array in the attributes object. Because attributes are an object, you can perform very fast queries to obtain all or some of them. You can use loops or access an attribute directly by name.

Attributes have limitations, however. Attributes cannot contain CDATA tags. Attributes cannot be extended. If you find that an attribute such as color seems simple enough to place within an attribute, perhaps reconsider, because a color may have a secondary property such as gloss or matte. If the color data resides within an attribute, it's going to be more difficult to extend your XML document to include relational data within the attribute. Migrating attribute data to nodes within an application that is already created can also cause major code reworking. Think carefully about your data and create attributes with values that are as basic and bottom-feeding as possible.

That said, attributes are parsed much, much more quickly than nodes. Using attributes can speed up XML loading on slow platforms such as devices and PDAs. This should be a last-resort effort at speeding up XML loading and parsing.

The ways in which you loop through the DOM with your code or set variables via DOM exploration can often be far more intense than the native parseXML method. Be careful how you loop through your XML. Don't be tempted to nest for loops within for loops within for loops. Not only is this confusing to code, it can lead to script halts and alerts on the user's machine.

Using the XML Socket Connection

The XML socket allows Flash to open a persistent line of communication with the server. Using four robust event handlers, Flash can listen for asynchronous data sent from the server without sending explicit requests for the data.

This type of connectivity is useful for Flash clients that must communicate with one another at high speed and present an identical user interface on multiple Web-connected clients. You've likely used a socket many times in the form of a chat program or room. Another place where low-latency sockets is used is online gaming.

To use the socket class, you must have a server capable of running a service that allows persistent socket connections. You then must have a server application capable of using the socket and interpreting requests, while sending out well-formed responses and broadcasts. Generally, these types of applications are best built on robust platforms such as Java or Ruby. There are provisions within other languages of course, but the selection of the server technology is important because persistent socket connections heavily tax the server. For example, a socket application with just a few hundred concurrent users may, in fact, need to be farmed out to multiple socket servers using load-balancing techniques.

Creating a stable, consistent, and efficient socket application can be one of the most challenging web applications you can attempt. Approach sockets without humor and do not underestimate the time it will take to develop a full socket application.

The XML in the XMLSocket Class

Although the XML socket is best used with XML, and many out-of-the-box socket servers use XML in their responses and broadcasts, XML is not required. You can send ampersand-delimited name/value pairs to be decoded by a LoadVars object. You can send comma-delimited strings to be split manually and used quickly.

So why use XML? Using XML ensures that your application is transparent. By using XML you are allowing for the socket server to be replaced with a new socket server. Maybe you are changing technology from a small PHP socket server to a robust load-balanced Java-based server. Choosing XML means that the client application will need little to no changes because the communications to and from the server are transparent. It doesn't care who or what sends it information, just that it is in XML format.

Choosing standards can make your initial coding more difficult or lengthy but will make enhancements and modifications to the application much easier in the long run.

Null Bytes

You might have heard the term *null byte* before. When a transmission is sent over an XML socket, each application needs to understand when a file has finished being sent. Sockets do this by appending a 0 or null byte at the end of the string.

Sometimes the end byte that Flash automatically appends to a socket request is not the end byte the server application is looking for. In these cases, you must manually append it or change the socket application to correctly look for a null byte.

XMLSocket Class Methods and Events

The following table describes the methods of the XMLSocket class:

Method	Return	Description
XMLSocket.close()	Nothing	Closes the socket connection by sending a close reponse to the remote socket application and closing the local socket.
XMLSocket.connect()	Nothing	Establishes a socket connection.
XMLSociet.send()	Nothing	Sends an XML object to the server upon a request received as a string object that may, but is not required to be, XML formatted.

XMLSocket class events are explained in the following table:

Event	Type	Description
XMLSocket.onClose	Function	Fires when the socket has closed. This event does not require a close message from the server, and it will fire if the socket connection is simply broken.
XMLSocket.onConnect	Function	Fires when the socket has a received an initial response establishing the socket connection.
XMLSocket.onData	Function	Fires when anything is received by the server.
XMLSocket.onXML	Function	Fires when a well-formed XML document has been sent by the server.

Try It Out   Create an Initial Socket Connection

This Try It Out assumes you've written or have found a socket server such as Moock's Unity server. It uses AOL's instant messaging socket login negotiator at login.oscar.aol.com. This is a socket server that then sends an AIM client to a specific socket server for chat relays.

1. Open a new Flash document and save it in your work folder.

2. Click the first frame in the timeline, open the Actions panel, and type the following ActionScript code:

```
var My_Socket:XMLSocket = new XMLSocket()
My_Socket.onConnect = function (success) {
  if (success) {
    trace ("Connected to remote socket")
  } else {
    trace ("Socket failed");
  }
}
My_Socket.connect("login.oscar.aol.com",5190);
```

3. Press Ctrl+Enter to test the code. If oscar is running on AOL at the specified port, and you have an Internet connection, you should see that the socket connection has been established.

How It Works

In this exercise, you defined an onConnect event to fire when the remote server successfully connected to the local socket. If this was a basic XML socket server, you could then begin to send request packets to the server.

At the time of this writing, an excellent free socket server that runs on both Mac and Win from the command line is available at www.oregano-server.org/. It is released under GNU. Because it runs on Mac and Win, it is perfect for testing out the XML Socket object.

Once you have a socket server available for access, you can begin to try simple communications with the server. The next Try It Out is a simplified example that illustrates the basic construction of a simple communication. The socket server you choose to use, or write, will likely use its own request commands and XML formats. You should read the documentation for your server thoroughly and use this example as a rough guide.

Try It Out Create a Socket Request and Receive an Answer

This Try It Out assumes you've written or have found a socket server such as Moock's Unity server. It does not refer to any specific socket server, but cites a hypothetical URL that assumes a working response. Again try the server available at www.oregano-server.org/ if you do not have a socket server and you are simply learning the basic events of the XMLSocket class.

1. Open a new Flash Document and save it in your work folder.

2. Click the first frame in the timeline, open the Actions panel, and type the following ActionScript code:

```
var userID:Number = userInputField.text;
var My_Socket:XMLSocket = new XMLSocket();
My_Socket.onXML = function (xmlObject) {
    trace(xmlObject.firstChild.attributes.name);
    trace(xmlObject.firstChild.attributes.phoneNum);
}


var message:XML = new XML();
var info:XMLNode = message.createElement("getInfo");
info.attributes.userID = usernID;
message.appendChild(info);
My_Socket.onConnect = function (success) {
  if (success) {
    this.send(my_xml);
  } else {
    trace ("Socket failed");
  }
}
My_Socket.connect("foo.com",2222);
```

3. Test your code by pressing Ctrl+Enter.

How It Works

As long as your server is set up to accept and respond properly to a request formatted as

```
<getInfo userID="9999"/>
```

you should see the trace values of the returned XML file if the response from the server is a well-formed XML document and punctuated the transmission with a zero end byte character. An example of an XML response for this request could be as follows:

```
<reponse name="John Smith" phoneNum="555-5555"/>
```

In this way you can see that the XMLSocket utilizes XML and XML objects to organize and communicate data efficiently.

sendAndLoad

The `sendAndLoad()` method works the same in both the LoadVars object and the XML object. In fact, you can mix the two objects by specifying the object to send data from and the object to load data to. Each end of this transaction does not have to be the same type of object. One object initiates the transaction by attaching a string version of itself to the URL via POST or GET. The URL specified is the first of three parameters required by `sendAndLoad`. The server response to the URL call is then directed back to the object specified as the second parameter. The last parameter of the `sendAndLoad` method is the POST or GET declaration. These are specified as String literals.

You can, in fact, use the same object to send and load the data.

One of the more popular trends on the Web these days is API exposure. This means that companies like Google, Yahoo, PayPal, Flickr, and more are offering their services at an application level so you can include their data seamlessly within your own application. Obtain a developer key from any of these APIs and use `sendAndLoad` to send RESTful calls.

For the purposes of showing how one object initiates the transaction, while another object waits for the transaction, you can just use a web page URL.

Try It Out   **Using sendAndLoad**

1.   Open a new Flash document and save it in your work folder.

2.   Click the first frame in the timeline, open the Actions panel, and type the following ActionScript code:

```
resultObject:LoadVars = new LoadVars();
resultObject.onData = function(str) {
    trace(str);
};
My_Data:LoadVars = new LoadVars();
My_Data.hl = "en";
My_Data.q = "Flash";
My_Data.sendAndLoad("http://www.google.com/search", resultObject, "GET");
```

3.   Test the code by pressing Ctrl+Enter. The output window shows you the file that has just been loaded into the resultObject. You can change the q variable declaration to change the results from the remote server.

4.   This is interesting, but just do one more thing to make use of the data that is loading into the resultObject. Add the following function before the resultObject LoadVars constructor:

```
findAHrefLinks = function (page) {
    var linkList:Object = {};
    var ahrefs:Array = page.split("<a");
    ahrefs.shift();
    for (var i = 0; i<ahrefs.length; i++) {
        trace(ahrefs[i]);
        ahrefs[i] = ahrefs[i].split("a>")[0];
    }
    for (var i = 0; i<ahrefs.length; i++) {
        var thisLink:Object = linkList["link"+i]={};
        var linkText:String = ahrefs[i].split(">")[1];
```

```
        linkText = linkText.substring(0, linkText.lastIndexOf("<"));
        thisLink.linkText = linkText;
        var attributes =
  ahrefs[i].split(">")[0].split('"').join("").split("'").join("");
        thisLink.url = attributes.split("href=")[1];
        if (thisLink.url.indexOf(" ")>1) {
            thisLink.url = thisLink.url.substring(0, thisLink.url.indexOf(" "));
        }
    }
    return linkList;
};
```

5.   Add a function call to the existing `resultObject.onData` event handler. The `onData` event handler should now look like this:

```
resultObject.onData = function(str) {
    linkList = findAHrefLinks(str);
    trace("done");
};
```

6.   Test the code by pressing Ctrl+Enter. Wait for the word "done" to appear within the output window. At that point the response has loaded fully into the resultObject.

7.   With the SWF open, view the variables out function created by pressing Ctrl+Alt+v or by selecting Debug⇨List Variables. You should see a very long list of very usable HTTP links.

How It Works

As you can see, the actual activity of using `sendAndLoad` is very much like the `load` method you've already used several times in this chapter. It's almost as if you're calling the `load` method on the target object (resultObject), while making a request and posting variables from the initial object (My_Data). In this way `sendAndLoad` does not provide Flash with any new or groundbreaking functionality, but instead packages up what could be a complex activity into a single, encapsulated code block.

The example also utilized a specific parsing function to show how varying interception objects can be used to encapsulate specific parsing functionality while keeping the data fetch, the `sendAndLoad` method identical regardless of final data usage.

This example shows you the power of adding variables to a Flash object and sending those variables to a server to manipulate the data the server sends back, as well as the different ways you can use the many methods provided by the LoadVars and XML objects in conjunction to write simple code that accomplishes useful transactions.

Using HTTP GET and POST

If you've followed the previous examples in this chapter you've seen how to request and send data to a remote server. Two terms that keep popping up are POST and GET. Many readers are familiar with these terms already and have used them in HTML forms.

GET and POST are simply two different ways of encapsulating data sent with a URI. A URI is a Uniform Request Identifier. You can think of a URI as an http URL or ftp URL. A URI is sent via the URL with a header and an entity, or some partial combination of those.

The subject matter of URIs can be complex. Discussions about URIs and methods for transferring information can lead to overblown debates about the details of different URIs and methods for attaching data to them. Books are dedicated to the subject. Here, the focus is on GET and POST because these are the two methods Flash is capable of using.

GET and POST identify how an application is to encapsulate data to be sent to a server. A GET method appends the data to the URL itself as a string of ampersand-delimited name-value pairs. A POST is sent like a file upload with header information and an entity consisting of the data being sent. The header tells the server how to handle the entity.

In many languages, header information sent with a URI can be customized. Some ActionScript objects allow for this type of modification of a URL request. Flash will always add the basic required headers automatically. `LoadVars.addRequestHeader`, for example, enables you to set name-value pairs to append to the request header of a `send` or `sendAndLoad` call. When you do this and why is dependent upon the needs of the server you're communicating with and the data format you're using. For example, SOAP and RPC require different request header information.

Apples and Oranges

There is one fundamental difference between the GET and POST that should turn on the light bulb and illuminate the difference between the two. You can bookmark a URL that uses a GET method. If you reload that URL, you will be able to replicate the same request. A POST can't be bookmarked (you'll only bookmark the base URL if you try). Selecting the POST URL again will likely produce errors. You may have seen a POST error while using the back button of your browser. Such an error may have looked like, "The request previously contained POST data, and may produce errors." The browser is simply letting you know that the base URL is intact, but the data you originally sent with it was a POST and is now gone.

To GET data on the Web, you must request the data from a server. When all you are doing is requesting a copy of assets from the server, it is safe to say you're merely getting something. In the request you aren't changing the state of the server whatsoever. The server got no assets from you, but merely listened to the request. This is a correct usage of GET. Specifying a GET URL literally means to request a copy of information.

To POST data on the Web, you must send the data to a server. You are literally sending the server a request to make a change to its system. This request can contain assets to POST to its system. Sometimes a POST request will remove data from the server. A POST literally means to make a change to the image of the server.

How Will You Know?

Think about what the request is doing to the server. There are obvious times you should use POST; for example, an email form or shopping cart transaction. In these instances you probably don't want to allow the user to accidentally hit the back button and resubmit a purchase. That said, there are times when you'd like a user to be able to bookmark a query or share a URL with a friend, such as a site search.

In many ways POST is more powerful. GET is a literal String addition to the URL and so is affected by a limitation of the length of the URL. Some browsers, for example, can only reach 256 characters in a URL. A POST is not affected by this limitation.

One common misconception is that POST is more secure. This is often a statement made by misguided individuals based on the fact that a user can't see the variables being appended to the URL when the request is made. This is semantics. Because you cannot see them in the URL in the user interface of a browser doesn't mean they weren't sent and easily captured by freely available tools.

Many more issues, concepts, and standards concerning this subject exist. However, you have learned the basic issues you need to understand when using URLs in ActionScript objects that allow GET and POST options. If you would like to know more about the subject, search the W3C documentation.

Using the XML Component

Flash provides you with components for automating many of the procedures you find in the XML object. You use these components as you would any component. You drag them onto the stage, while setting specific properties to tie them together.

Try It Out   **Load an XML File Using the XML Connector**

1. Open a new Flash document and save it in your work folder as XMLConnectSample.fla.

2. In the Components panel is a list of types of components. Expand the Data Components, and you see a list of components available to drag to the stage. Drag the component named XML Connector (see Figure 22-1) to the stage.

If you do not see the Components panel, press Ctrl+F7 or choose Window⇨Components.

Figure 22-1

3. An instance of the connector appears on the stage as a small icon. Your library also reflects this addition. You can delete the instance from the stage because it is now accessible from the library.

4. Open your favorite text editor, create a text file, and enter the following code:

```
<?xml version="1.0" encoding="ISO-8859-1"?>
<channels>
    <Station identification="104.1">
        <Name>
```

```
                Rock And Roll Oldies!
        </Name>
        <Desc>
                Music great with hot chocolate!
        </Desc>
    </Station>
    <Station identification="98.6">
        <Name>
                Rock and Roll
        </Name>
        <Desc>
                Music for waiting for Godot!
        </Desc>
    </Station>
    <Station identification="102.5">
        <Name>
                Electronic Madness!
        </Name>
        <Desc>
                Arigato Rules!
        </Desc>
    </Station>
    <Station identification="107.9">
        <Name>
                Electronic Madness 2!
                <Name>
        <Desc>
                Thunder Dome!
        </Desc>
    </Station>
</channels>
```

5. Save the file as `myData.xml` and place it in the same folder as `XMLConnectSample.fla`.

6. Click the first frame in the timeline, open the Actions panel, and type the following ActionScript code:

```
import mx.data.components.XMLConnector;
var myConnectorOn:Object = new Object();
myConnectorOn.result = function(eventObject:Object) {
    trace(eventObject.target.results);
};
var myConnector:XMLConnector = new XMLConnector();
myConnector.addEventListener("result", myConnectorOn);
myConnector.addEventListener("status", myConnectorOn);
myConnector.direction = "receive";
myConnector.URL = "myData.xml";
myConnector.trigger();
```

7. Test the code by pressing Ctrl+Enter.

8. Verify that the XML component loaded the data by watching the output window. The window will show the codes captured by the listener result.

9. Save the FLA as `xmlConnectorSample.fla`. You'll be using it in the next Try It Out section.

How It Works

The XML Connector component acts as a data fetcher for data display components. You can bind results of your XML connector using the binding parameters within the Flash IDE or use ActionScript. Because this book is about ActionScript, the example uses ActionScript to describe the URL and listener events.

Setting up event listeners is the same as adding an onLoad event to an XML object. In this case, however, the event itself is definable. Result is a property of the myConnector object. A listener specifically waits for changes to that value before triggering the function defined for that value.

When the component runs, a value is eventually populated into the result value. Your component does not need to do anything else. The listener then takes over and fires the function with the same name as the property that changed.

After the value is captured in the result event, you can do anything you want to it. You can treat it as a typical XML object, or you can begin to allow other components to work with the data using bindings or connect components by using some simple ActionScript.

It is important to note that the parameters, GET and POST, can be set when using the XML Connector.

Security issues for components remain the same for any other data loading objects. You should refer to the "Explaining Cross-Domain Security" section later in the chapter to see how you can work with ActionScript to allow external data in different domain situations.

Try It Out   **Bind XML Connector Data to a Display**

If you did not do the previous XML Connector Try It Out, you'll need to do that now, because you need to make sure you have the myData.xml file.

1. Open XMLConnectSample.fla.

2. Open the Component panel. Expand the User Interface section and drag an instance of the Menu component to the stage. Delete the instance from the stage, because it is now available in the library (see Figure 22-2).

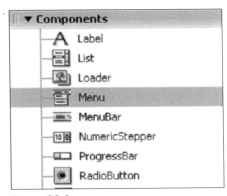

Figure 22-2

3. Click the first frame in the timeline, open the Actions panel (Window ➪ Actions), and type the following ActionScript code:

```
import mx.data.components.XMLConnector;
var myMenu = mx.controls.Menu.createMenu();
_root.myMenu.show(20, 20);
var myConnectorOn:Object = new Object();
myConnectorOn.result = function(eventObject:Object) {
    myMenuData = new XML();
    myMenuData.ignoreWhite = true;
    myMenuData.parseXML(eventObject.target.results);
    for (var i = 0; i<myMenuData.firstChild.childNodes.length; i++) {

myMenu.addMenuItem(myMenuData.firstChild.childNodes[i].attributes.identification);
    }
};
var myConnector:XMLConnector = new XMLConnector();
myConnector.addEventListener("result", myConnectorOn);
myConnector.addEventListener("status", myConnectorOn);
myConnector.direction = "receive";
myConnector.URL = "myData.xml";
myConnector.trigger();
```

4. Test the code by pressing Ctrl+Enter.

5. Verify that the XML component loaded the data into the Menu component by viewing the SWF file.

6. Save the FLA as `xmlConnectorSample.fla`.

How It Works

In this example you added a Menu component to populate some data from the XML Connector using ActionScript. By creating an XML object from the results in the result event listener you are able to iterate values obtained by the XML Connector and place them directly into a menu. Alternatively, you could have populated a list or data grid component.

In this example you could also present a button that shows and hides the menu, creating a true drop-down menu of your available channels. From there you could potentially allow for the media component to be populated with audio streams.

The advantage of using components is that with very little work you were able to set your XML and a GUI interface with just a few lines of ActionScript. This can be especially handy for rapid development of prototype applications, or for when you need standard GUI components inserted into your application.

It is important to note that you could in fact call the `trigger()` event on myConnector after specifying a brand new URL data source, and use the same code over and over.

Explaining Cross-Domain Security

Keep a few security considerations in mind when working with files. The difference between local and remote files can cause your code to act differently. A remote file generally resides on an HTTP server.

When an SWF file loads a data file from a server, the SWF either needs to be running from a local machine or reside on the same domain as the data file.

In Flash 6 player only the super domain was required to match. A super domain is the base URL of all URLs on a domain. That includes subdomains. For example, `http://beta.myremoteWebSite.com` and `http://myremoteWebSite.com/aFolder` have identical super domains. With Flash 7 and later, cross-accessing subdomains requires policy files as if they were entirely different domains.

This domain checking is often referred to as part of the Flash Security Sandbox. Security sandbox is a general computer term that refers to a space where code may run, but has limited access to outside resources.

Secure methods exist for allowing cross-domain access, and this section shows you how to implement the solution.

Understanding Why Flash Uses Domain Policies

Flash uses domain policies because of risks presented by would-be hostile SWF files. For example, a Flash player without cross-domain security could potentially be embedded into a page by a malicious user.

Consider a user community in which users can create profiles and link to SWF files within a profile. Because an SWF specified in the profile now resides on the web site's page, it has potential script access to JavaScript cookies, as well as form submissions.

Other users can log on to the site and perhaps view the profile of the malicious user that contains the hostile SWF file. The SWF, now displayed on the average user's machine, could then access the cookie information owned by the average user.

The SWF could potentially send the cookie data to a remote server or make form submissions and actions the average user might not approve of. You could imagine the SWF finding the cookie of the administrator of the site that would give the SWF perhaps root access to the web site. It wouldn't take very much in that case to deface the entire web site. Imagine if this were a site that transacted money, services, or products. But cross-domain restrictions within Flash stop this from happening.

This concern, however, isn't just with Flash. Browsers have long implemented cross-domain protection for precisely the same reason. Other avenues for exploitation exist when a security domain sandbox does not exist, but they wouldn't work in Flash.

When the Flash security tools are used, and used well, you should have no reservations about building an application in Flash rather than a browser based on security concerns. Flash is constantly in development, and Macromedia is constantly keeping a close eye on any potential vulnerabilities found. Because of this, each Flash player release can and does handle security differently, with minor improvements with each release.

There are, of course, times when a developer is required to join systems to create a seamless application. This is especially so in light of new services of a Semantic Web, with corporations producing APIs allowing direct access to server-side controls.

In these cases these corporations want cross-domain activity. Of course, a few solutions are provided by Flash. These are policy files, shims, and proxies.

Knowing When Policy Files Are Required

Knowing when a situation requires a policy file can be confusing. Consider this situation. You have an application on a server at `http://www.someserver.com`, and your Flash file loads data from the exact same site, `http://www.someserver.com`. Typically you wouldn't expect any cross-domain issues to occur. However, the cross-domain policy for Flash is so strict that if the user were to type `http://some server.com` without using the www subdomain, most servers would send the content of the super domain without issue. Flash will present an error stating that the domain someserver.com does not match `www.someserver.com`. Also if the user were to type the IP address directly in lieu of a domain name, you'd find the same error describing a domain mismatch. In these cases Flash is smart enough to realize that something isn't quite right. Rather than fail silently, the Flash movie presents the user with a dialog box asking him to verify that the movie should access the domain despite the minor mismatch.

> *Although you can use relative file paths to avoid most if not all of these situations, it is not recommended. To maximize legacy support, use the prescribed policy file methods, which are explained in the following section.*

If these rare instances don't bother you, you probably don't need a policy file. But if it does in fact bother you, you're going to need to place a policy file on the server that allows each URL variant users can use to access your web site to be used without an alert. Another way to avoid this situation is to exclusively use relative URLs avoiding any domain mismatch at all when working with a single domain.

Another situation is when you place Web services on a subdomain for convenience. Say that you have created a Web service that returns data, and that you have a Flash application that is served from the base URL of the same server. Call the Web service URL `http://services.someserver.com`, and say your Flash movie resides on `http://www.someserver.com`. In this case, when the Flash file attempts to access the services subdomain, it will fail silently. No alert box will appear. Flash assumes, in this case, that it has found a definite domain mismatch and simply disallows it without question or warning. The policy file would need to reside on the services subdomain and list every variation of super domain as allowed domains.

There is another situation, and hopefully, the most obvious. Say a Flash application on a corporate web site at intel.com is required to access data that resides on apple.com. This is a basic mismatch. The policy file would need to reside on apple.com and list intel.com as an allowed domain.

All of these rules also apply to XML sockets as well. A Flash file using a remote socket connection must be able to access a domain policy file on the socket server. Because a socket server may not be an HTTP server, it is important that the socket server allow http access to the policy file on the same domain as the socket itself or utilize the socket-specific method for policy files described in this section.

Setting Up Policy Files

One way in which your applications can load data from a different domain is to place a policy file on the server that is serving the data. The policy file is simple XML file that the Flash player automatically checks for and parses on its own. The XML policy file format allows for multiple types of solutions and tiers of access.

In the following examples, the syntax of the XML for policy files is explained. The syntax is very simple. When you set up a server to host SWF files that access data from the same domain, set up this type of simple policy file regardless of how you plan to access the data. The existence of the policy file can ease debugging and ensure that Flash has free reign on the server from which it hails no matter the construction of the URL syntax.

Try It Out   Set Up a Policy File for a Single Domain

1.   Open a new file in your favorite text editor and enter the following XML:

```
<?xml version="1.0"?>
<!DOCTYPE cross-domain-policy SYSTEM "http://www.macromedia.com/xml/dtds/cross-
domain-policy.dtd">
<cross-domain-policy>
    <allow-access-from domain="www.someserver.com" />
    <allow-access-from domain="someserver.com" />
    <allow-access-from domain="192.168.1.1" />
</cross-domain-policy>
```

2.   Save the file as `crossdomain.xml`. This is the only name the Flash player will check for. Deviating from this name will cause the policy file to fail.

3.   Upload the file to the root of the base domain. In this case you would upload the file to someserver.com and experiment with different test data files and SWF files using different possible URL combinations to be sure you included all the domain possibilities.

How It Works

This file gives request access to the domains listed. Because they all reside on the same super domain, this specific policy file ensures that Flash files on your own site accessing your own data would never present a security alert to the user.

This example, however, doesn't allow SWF files from other sites to access your data. To do that you need to explicitly add those domains to the same policy file.

In the next exercise, you use the same syntax to allow SWF files on a remote server to also have access to all of the data files and services as if they hailed from the same server. The remote server in this example is myFriendsWebsite.com.

Try It Out   Set Up a Policy File for a Remote Domain

If you did not complete the previous Try It Out, do it now. You need the `crossdomain.xml` file for this exercise.

1.   Open `crossdomain.xml` and add the following XML to it:

```
<?xml version="1.0"?>
<!DOCTYPE cross-domain-policy SYSTEM "http://www.macromedia.com/xml/dtds/cross-
domain-policy.dtd">
<cross-domain-policy>
    <allow-access-from domain="www.someserver.com" />
    <allow-access-from domain="someserver.com" />
    <allow-access-from domain="192.168.1.1" />
    <allow-access-from domain="myFriendsWebsite.com" />
</cross-domain-policy>
```

2. Save the file.

3. Upload the file to the root of the base domain. In this case you would upload the file to someserver.com and experiment with different test data files and SWF files residing on myFriendsWebsite.com using different possible URL combinations to be sure you included all the domain possibilities you need.

How It Works

The preceding file would give request access to your friend's web site when referred to as `http://your FriendsWebsite.com` as well as your own.

An SWF residing on `http://myFriendsWebsite.com` would be able to access your data. However, in this specific example, an SWF called from `http://www.myFriendsWebsite.com` would fail! You need to explicitly list `www.myFriendsWebsite.com` or use a wildcard symbol, which simply allows any string to reside within the place you enter it.

The next example shows how to use a wildcard to specify multiple subdomains. A wildcard is simply a * character.

Try It Out — Use a Wildcard to Allow Domain Access

If you did not complete the previous Try It Out example to create and save a `crossdomain.xml` file, you need to do that now.

1. Open the `crossdomain.xml` file you just created and add the following XML to it:

```
<?xml version="1.0"?>
<!DOCTYPE cross-domain-policy SYSTEM "http://www.macromedia.com/xml/dtds/cross-domain-policy.dtd">
<cross-domain-policy>
    <allow-access-from domain="www.someserver.com"/>
    <allow-access-from domain="someserver.com"/>
    <allow-access-from domain="192.168.1.1"/>
    <allow-access-from domain="*.myFriendsWebsite.com"/>
</cross-domain-policy>
```

2. Save the file.

3. Upload the file to the root of the base domain. In this case you would upload the file to someserver.com and experiment with different test data files and SWF files residing on myFriendsWebsite.com using different possible URL combinations to be sure you included all the domain possibilities you need.

How It Works

In this case any subdomain on yourFriendsWebsite.com can access any of your data. So if an SWF is called from `http://www.myFriendsWebsite.com`, `http://myFriendsWebsite.com`, or `http://somesubdomain.myFriendsWebsite.com`, no errors will occur.

I'm Offering Web Services; I Want to Allow Any Domain!

Never fear. You can use the wildcard to allow any SWF file from any domain or subdomain, or other URL variation, to access your data.

Try It Out   **Use a Wildcard to Allow Domain Access**

For this exercise, you need the `crossdomain.xml` file you saved in the preceding Try It Out.

1.   Open `crossdomain.xml` and add the following XML to it:

```
<?xml version="1.0"?>
<!DOCTYPE cross-domain-policy SYSTEM "http://www.macromedia.com/xml/dtds/
    cross-domain-policy.dtd">
<cross-domain-policy>
    <allow-access-from domain="*"/>
</cross-domain-policy>
```

2.   Save the file.

3.   Upload the file to the root of the base domain. In this case you would upload the file to someserver.com.

How It Works

In this case any Flash file running from any configuration would be able to access your data. This method is common for public script services that allow REST, SOAP, RPC, and so on. Sometimes it's tempting to do this for your own site and be done with worrying about the whole issue. You must realize, though, that you are completely disabling a security feature that was created for a very good reason. So the reason for using a root wildcard had better be better than that.

If you are offering Web services, do so only via a subdomain and offer the wildcard access to the subdomain only. You do this by placing the policy file on the subdomain rather than on the super domain.

Considering HTTPS

If you load the DTD URL specified in the DOCTYPE declaration tag of the sample XML file into a browser, you will see the definitions for the cross-domain policy XML files. One thing to notice is an attribute specified as `secure` with a Boolean variable type. Type the following URL into your browser to see the policy file DTD: www.macromedia.com/xml/dtds/cross-domain-policy.dtd.

Consider this situation. You have an HTTPS server that is serving data and an SWF file from the same HTTPS domain. Although HTTPS, you still have the single server issues of URL variants. Flash can access the policy file on HTTPS as well.

But say that you want a regular HTTP domain to access the data on an HTTPS server. The policy file on the HTTPS server must specify the remote domain as you did previously. However, Flash is smart enough to realize there is a security mismatch between HTTP and HTTPS, so an SWF running from an insecure domain must also present itself as being insecure. For the HTTPS policy file to allow the insecure SWF file, you need to set the secure attribute to `false` explicitly, as you do in the following Try It Out.

Try It Out	Use the Secure Attribute

1. Open the `crossdomain.xml` file and add the following XML to it:

```
<?xml version="1.0"?>
<!DOCTYPE cross-domain-policy SYSTEM "http://www.macromedia.com/xml/dtds/cross-
domain-policy.dtd">
<cross-domain-policy>
    <allow-access-from domain="*.someserver.com" secure="false"/>
</cross-domain-policy>
```

2. Save the file.

3. Upload the file to the root of the base domain on the HTTPS server. The unsecure SWF is allowed access to the HTTPS domain.

How It Works

By using the secure attribute, you can specify that an HTTPS domain can allow SWF files residing on a non-secure domain to access data on the secure domain.

This is, of course, not suggested. The only time you might want to do this is if the HTTPS and HTTP servers both resided behind the same firewall, such as on a corporate intranet. Another instance might be for testing purposes.

By using a secure attribute with a value of `false`, you are side-stepping the very purpose of HTTPS. An alternative solution should be found.

Load a Policy File from a Subfolder

If you do not want to host the policy file at the root folder of port 80 on the remote server, you can place the policy in a subfolder of your choice. The SWF file loading the policy file needs to know where to get it. To do that, load the policy file manually using the method that resides in the security object within the system class. The method is accessed with the following syntax:

```
System.security.loadPolicyFile(URL:String);
```

This line must be placed in your ActionScript before your SWF attempts to load any data from the remote domain. The URL parameter must be a string and refer to the location where you have placed the policy file. For example, you can place the policy XML file in a subfolder on your domain called policies. When using this method, you do not need to name the file `crossdomain.xml`. You can name the policy file whatever you want. Because you can now make unique policy filenames, you can set up specific policies for specific SWF files accessing the same server. The line of code for accessing a specific policy file would look like the following:

```
System.security.loadPolicyFile("http://www.someserver.com/policies/policyforBetaSWF
.xml);
```

Be aware that this allows your SWF to access only the data that resides within the subfolder or any child folders within that specific subfolder.

The `loadPolicyFile` method overrides the native policy check at the root of the domain. If a specific policy file in a subfolder fails to load, Flash automatically attempts to load the default `crossdomain.xml` file.

In this way you can disable or modify a security policy at runtime. You can disable the policy within your SWF by calling a null policy file. You place this line in your code wherever you would like to disable script access:

```
System.security.loadPolicyFile("http://www.someserver.com/policies/Rempovepolicyfor
BetaSWF.xml);
```

This should load a null XML file that looks like the following:

```
<?xml version="1.0"?>
<!DOCTYPE cross-domain-policy SYSTEM "http://www.macromedia.com/xml/dtds/cross-
domain-policy.dtd">
<cross-domain-policy>
    <allow-access-from domain=""/>
</cross-domain-policy>
```

Using a Policy File with an XML Socket, without HTTP

When using a policy file with an XML socket, you should understand how to create a basic Socket transaction. Socket transactions should be approached with caution when scoping for application creation deadlines. Due to the asynchronous communication, multiple client setups, and potential database activity, sockets can be challenging and time consuming. XML Sockets are among the most difficult processes to script in any language.

Consider the situation in which a policy file is used to allow XML socket access. You can load a policy file as you would any data load using the default methods provided by Flash and covered in the preceding Try It Out examples. Still, there are times when offering HTTP is not feasible, and the policy file must be sent via the XML socket itself. The socket server will contain a special provision for handling a policy file request, properly formatting the XML with a null end byte.

A socket server policy file contains an extra attribute that you can use to restrict the access by port, or port spans. You can also use wildcards within the port specification. An example policy response from the socket that restricts ports could look like this:

```
<cross-domain-policy>
    <allow-access-from domain="www.someserver.com" to-ports="2222" />
    <allow-access-from domain="someserver.com" to-ports="555,2222" />
    <allow-access-from domain="192.168.1.1" to-ports="555 - 2222" >
    <allow-access-from domain="www.anotherserver.com" to-ports="*" />
</cross-domain-policy>
```

To access the policy file, the socket server must be listening on a specific port in which the initial transaction is the policy file when Flash's initial handshake is the string:

```
<cross-domain-request/>
```

A socket policy request would look like this:

```
System.security.loadPolicyFile("xmlsocket://www.aremoteServer.com:2222");
```

You can see you can specify different types of ports. You can request the policy file on its own port or configure your socket server to send the request over the same port. If you specify a port that serves only the policy file, and this port is not included within the actual domain and ports specified within the cross-domain policy file, you will no longer be able to access the port that served the policy file. Because of this, you want to remember to add the policy port or serve the policy file from the same port or ports that the policy file specifies for the entire socket application.

Using Shims and Proxies

Shims and proxies are doorways. Both are methods of bouncing a data request through a secondary object that does not have the same security restrictions as the main application. Sometimes you may not have access to placing policy files on a server to enable your application to load data from those servers. In these cases shims and proxies can help.

Proxies: Forcing Data Access

Proxies may be the easiest method for loading cross-domain data. Proxies are scripts that do not run in Flash but run in a script environment on the same server that is hosting the Flash application. Script environments such as Perl, Python, PHP, ASP, and more are capable of providing proxy scripts. A server environment is not subject to the same security issues as Flash. When you instruct a script running on your server to fetch data, it simply does so. With proxy scripts you can alter the data and format it for a Flash application.

The following exercise uses PHP, which is offered by almost every hosting service. PHP is often already set up and ready to go on web site hosting companies' servers. If you know ASP, Perl, or some other language that you prefer, you can substitute the proxy with your own.

Try It Out   **Create a Basic Proxy**

1. Open your favorite text editor, create a new text document, and enter the following code:

```
<?php
   readfile($remoteURL);
?>
```

2. Save the file as `proxy.php`.

3. Upload the file to your server. Your server must have PHP enabled and working for this example to work.

4. To test the proxy, append the `remoteURL` variable to the URL of the proxy and see whether you can see the data. For example, try this URL, but replace the domain with your own:

```
http://www.someserver.com/proxy.php?dataURL=http://www.weather.gov/alerts/il.rss
```

5. After you know your proxy is working, you can place an SWF on the server, which will access the proxy.

6. Open a new Flash document and save it in your work folder as `myMovie.fla`.

7. Click the first frame in the timeline, open the Actions panel, and type the following ActionScript code:

```
var My_Data:XML = new XML();
My_Data.ignoreWhite = true;
My_Data.onLoad = function(success){
    if(success){
    trace(this);
    }else{
        trace("My_Data failed");
    }
}

dataRequest:LoadVars = new LoadVars();
dataRequest.dataURL = "http://www.weather.gov/alerts/il.rss";
dataRequest.sendAndLoad("http://www.someserver.com/proxy.php",My_Data,"Get");
```

8. Test the code by pressing Ctrl+Enter. After a moment, the output window will show you the raw string that was loaded via the proxy.

How It Works

Because the proxy PHP file and the SWF reside on the same domain, Flash has no issues loading the data received when requesting the file specified in the dataRequest object.

There are a couple of things to keep in mind. One is the content-length header information. Without a content-length header, Flash has no way of populating `getBytesTotal` with a value. To send this you would need to acquire the file size via PHP manually and add it to the return object in the PHP script.

The other issue to keep in mind is that although the remote file doesn't exist within your own domain, it is being served as if it is. That means for every byte you proxy through your web site, you effectively pay for it depending on whether or not you rent your server, and how your server accesses the Internet. If you proxy large files this might get expensive. You are going to find your server stats reflect bytes sent via a proxy as literally bytes sent through your own domain. So think about how much the file will be accessed, and understand the limitations of your server and service provider contracts.

This is also a good time to mention that although you can pass through data from virtually any public space with a proxy, that doesn't make it legal. You should verify that data is free to use. Obtain permission when using someone else's data, or use your own.

Some providers have begun to add extra security and require extra hoops to access remote data via scripts. In these cases, such as dreamhost.com, the help documents and developer forums often provided by the service provider contain work-arounds and scripts you can use in step 1 of this example.

Shims: Allowing Script Access

A shim is something that comes between two things. A wood shim can keep a door or window open. Think of a Flash shim in much the same way. A shim comes between you and a closed door. It provides a doorway for accessing data on a remote domain. The caveat is that you need to be able to access the remote domain so that you can upload the shim to the remote server. Without this one requirement, you will need to find a different solution.

An SWF on the Web has the capability, without security concerns, to load an SWF from anywhere else on the Web, no matter where it resides. There is, however, one large limitation: the ActionScript object in the main SWF cannot access the ActionScript objects in the guest SWF. Also the guest SWf cannot access the ActionScript objects of the main SWF. So although you can load the SWF, it will be unable to communicate or enact code in the main SWF. To enable script access, Flash uses an Allow domain object.

The Allow domain object is very similar to the policy file. All of the same domain, subdomain, alternative URLs, and secure server considerations apply. If you haven't yet read the policy file section earlier in the chapter, you should do so now. The policy file is the preferred method, especially if you have access to uploading the file to the remote domain.

Because a shim is an option, you learn about it here. Also, there are times when you'd like to run an SWF application within your own application. Although the example is a pure shim, you can imagine a guest SWF acting as a full application API filled with Web services objects to be made accessible to the main application.

Try It Out   **Create a Shim**

1. Open a new Flash document and save it in your work folder as `shim.fla`.

2. Click the first frame in the timeline, open the Actions panel, and enter the following ActionScript code. Replace the domain string with the actual domain on which you'll be hosting your main SWF:

```
System.security.allowDomain("www.somedomain.com");
LoadVars = LoadVars;
```

3. Publish the SWF.

4. Open your favorite text editor and write a simple one-line statement, such as "This is my remote data." Save the text file as `remoteDat.txt`.

5. Upload `remoteDat.txt` and `shim.swf` to the remote server.

6. Open a new Flash Document and save it in your work folder as `main.fla`.

7. Click the first frame in the timeline, open the Actions panel, and type the following ActionScript code:

```
this.createEmptyMovieClip("shim", 0);
this.createTextField("out", 1, 10, 10, 200, 40);
watchLoad = function () {
    if (shim.LoadVars != undefined) {
    myData:LoadVars = new shim.LoadVars();
    myData.onData = function(str) {
        out.text = str;
    };
        myData.load("http://www.remoteDomain.org/remoteData.txt");
        clearInterval(loader);
    }
};
var loader:Number = setInterval(this, "watchLoad", 1);
shim.loadMovie("shim.swf");
//shim.loadMovie("http://www remoteDomain.org/shim.swf ");
```

8. Publish this FLA and upload it to the server that your users will be accessing directly.

9. When you navigate to `main.swf` you will see the text field populate with the data from the `remoteData.txt` file residing on the remote domain.

How It Works

Shims use the `System.security.allowDomain` method to declare which domains may access the objects defined within it. You can specify more than one domain by inserting multiple domain strings separated by commas. Wildcards can also be used, in an identical manner as the XML policy file. For example, this is a valid `allowDomain` method call:

```
System.security.allowDomain("beta.anotherDomain.com", "*.somedomain.com",
"*.yetAnotherDomain.org");
```

The `main.swf` file can only access objects that have been explicitly defined in the `shim.swf` file, so you must define at least one object for `main.swf` to utilize. Because you can use the `parseXML` method to transform a LoadVars object into an XML document, and you can use LoadVars as is, you only included the single object declaration `LoadVars = LoadVars;` to make the `shim.swf` LoadVars object available to `main.swf`.

This is a way to make a very efficient shim. At just under 260 bytes, it has negligible load time. Of course, you could declare many more objects for use within the shim. You could create an entire class set of Web services offered by the shim. You can make the objects available in the shim as fancy as you want.

If the remote server hosting the shim is an HTTPS server, and the domain on which the `main.swf` file is hosted on is HTTP, you would need to use separate syntax. This works in the same way but uses the following syntax:

```
System.security.allowInsecureDomain("someInsecureDomain.com");
```

Summary

This chapter described ways in which you can load XML data into Flash. You were introduced to the XML, XMLSocket, System, and security objects as well as the XML components, policy files, shims, and proxies.

You created some useful examples that showed how to use each object and considered the many issues involved with each. You loaded XML and extracted specific information from it, and you saw how Flash gives you unlimited ways to use XML files in your applications.

You spent much time with the security issues with Flash and how to work with them, keeping your applications, servers, and data safe.

Hopefully this chapter got you thinking of using Flash in ways you might not have thought of previously. The chapter covered objects that are a major asset in the tool belt of any Flash developer. Being able to work with and use XML and data with Flash can set your resume apart from the rest.

Exercises

1. Consider the following list of domains that are hosting an SWF file. To the right of each is the domain that hosts the data. Without a policy file, which domain combinations would simply produce an alert and which would fail silently?

SWF File Host	Data Host
www.myserver.com	Services.myserver.com
www.myserver.com	www.someOtherserver.com
https://www.myserver.com	http:// someOtherserver.com
192.168.1.15	192.168.1.16

2. With the following XML data, load the data and a URL attribute to each station node:

```
<?xml version="1.0" encoding="ISO-8859-1"?>
<channels>
        <Station identification="104.1">
        <Name>
            Rock And Roll Oldies!
        </Name>
        <Desc>
            Music great with hot chocolate!
        </Desc>
        </Station>
        <Station identification="98.6">
        <Name>
            Rock and Roll
        </Name>
        <Desc>
            Music for waiting for Godot!
        </Desc>
        </Station>
        <Station identification="102.5">
        <Name>
            Electronic Madness!
        </Name>
        <Desc>
            Arigato Rules!
        </Desc>
        </Station>
        <Station identification="107.9">
        <Name>
            Electronic Madness 2!
            <Name>
        <Desc>
            Thunder Dome!
        </Desc>
        </Station>
</channels>
```

3. With the XML you just created, use the `childNodes` property to access the URLs you just created. Use `nodeValue` and attributes properties to access the data within it, and populate an object with those values.

4. Create a pipe (|) delimited file, rather than an ampersand-delimited file. Load the data file as a raw string using the LoadVars object. Parse the name/value pairs and place them within an object.

Communicating Between the Macromedia Flash Plug-in and the Browser

In the previous chapter you saw how Flash can communicate with servers to obtain external data. In this chapter, you learn how Flash can access information from other SWFs, JavaScript, and Flash wrappers. By understanding how Flash can communicate and cooperate with the browser, you allow for greater control over the whole web application.

In this chapter, you use LocalConnection to allow two separate Flash movies running from the same browser to communicate with each other, and you learn about using shared objects to store limited amounts of data locally. Finally, you explore using `FlashVars` to pass initial data into a Flash movie.

> This chapter discusses methods for accessing code outside of Flash. Each of the methods contains its own security concerns and limitations. Some of these security concerns are similar to but cannot be solved with the policy files you read about in Chapter 22. When you are attempting to make connections between Flash and files from different domains, be aware that a policy file isn't always the answer.

LocalConnection

A local connection is the way in which two SWF files can communicate information to one another. A local connection can come in handy in many scenarios. For example, say that you have an SWF file within a web page that can open a pop-up SWF file to allow the user to complete a specific task such as to log in or to view help content. In the case of help content, you'd want the original SWF application to be able to communicate with the smaller pop-up window to make a help window contextual. This is just one example. Many other reasons exist for why you might want to use two SWF files.

The following table describes the LocalConnection class's methods:

Method	Returns	Description
close()	Nothing	Closes the local connection.
connect()	Boolean	Establishes a local connection.
send()	String	Sends a localConnection object a request, specifying the method to be invoked.
domain()	String	Returns the domain the SWF is running from.

The close() method has no parameters. Here's its syntax:

```
localConnection.close();
```

The connect() method has a single parameter of type String. The string value is the name of an available local connection. Following is its syntax:

```
localConnection.connect(name:String);
```

This send() method has three parameters:

1. The name of the available LocalConnection. It must be a String.
2. The name of the method being accessed in the receiving localConnection object. This also must be a String.
3. An object representing variables to be sent to the receiving method. This method returns a Boolean if the localConnection object was found and if the method was valid.

Here's the syntax for send():

```
localConnection.send(name:String, method:String, parameters:Object)
```

The domain() method has no parameters and simply returns a String representation of the domain from which the SWF file comes. Here's its syntax:

```
localConnection.domain();
```

The following table describes the LocalConnection class's events:

Event	Type	Description
onStatus	Function	Fires when a request is made to a localConnection object using the send() method.
allowDomain	Function	Fires whenever an SWF attempts to make a connection via the send() method.
allowInsecureDomain	Function	Fires whenever an SWF attempts to make a connection via the send() method.

Creating a localConnection Object

In this section, you take a look at how to create a localConnection object. To establish a connection between two .swf files, a channel needs to be established between the two files. One of the SWF files is responsible for doing the initial setup, using the connect() method. The code to perform this task looks like this:

```
var receiving_lc:LocalConnection = new LocalConnection();
receiving_lc.connect("sampleLCchannel");
```

Once that's done, the SWF file running this code is registered as the recipient for any data transmitted along the channel called sampleLCchannel, and it is the only SWF file that is allowed to receive data on this channel. Next, an action needs to be created to respond anytime data is sent along this channel. Just create a method with the localConnection object, giving the new method the name that you want the other side of the connection to call. The following code adds a method called sendVar() that responds when another .swf sends data along the channel. The name of the method can be whatever you want, as long as the same method name is used on the other side of the connection:

```
var receiving_lc:LocalConnection = new LocalConnection();
receiving_lc.sendVar = function(sentString:String)
{
    trace(sentString);
};
receiving_lc.connect("sampleLCchannel");
```

The SWF file doing the sending makes the following call to send data to the SWF file that initially set up the connection. The code sends a string to the sendVar() method on sampleLCchannel:

```
var movie1LocalConnect = new LocalConnection();
movie1LocalConnect.send("sampleLCchannel", "sendVar", "The quick brown fox...");
```

For this to work, the receiving SWF file has to have already set up the connection. Otherwise, the transmission is simply dropped and the send() method returns false.

Any number of SWF files can send data along a channel, but only one SWF file can receive data on a channel.

Try setting up a connection between two SWF files.

Try It Out Create a Connection between Two SWF Files

1. Open a new Flash Document. Save the Flash document as lcmovie1.fla in your work folder.

2. Click the first frame in the timeline, open the Actions panel, and type the following ActionScript code:

```
var movie1LocalConnect = new LocalConnection();
submitButton.onRelease = function()
{
    trace(movie1LocalConnect);
    movie1LocalConnect.send("sampleLCchannel", "sendVar", dataToSend.text);
};
```

3. Open the Components panel. Expand the User Interface tab and drag a Button component to the center of the stage.

4. In the Parameters tab of the Properties panel for the button you just added to the stage, find the label parameter and change the word Button to Send. In the Properties panel give the button an instance name of submitButton.

5. Now create an input text field. You could do this with ActionScript, but draw one on the stage just above the send button, using the Text tool in the Tools panel. Be sure to select a border and change the field to Input Text in the properties panel for the textField. Name the textField dataToSend in the Instance Name field in the Properties panel.

6. Publish lcmovie1 with HTML. You open this HTML file in step 11.

7. Now open another new Flash document. Save the Flash document as lcmovie2.fla in your work folder.

8. Using the Text tool in the Tools panel, create a textField on the lcmovie2 stage. In the Properties panel give this text field instance the name incomingText_txt. In the Properties panel, be sure to select Dynamic Text as the field type.

9. In the first frame of lcmovie2, type the following code:

```
var receiving_lc:LocalConnection = new LocalConnection();
receiving_lc.sendVar = function(aVar:String)
{
    _root.incomingText_txt.text = aVar;
};
receiving_lc.connect("sampleLCchannel");
```

10. Publish lcmovie2.

11. Navigate to your work folder to which you have published your SWF files. Open the lcmovie1.html file in your favorite browser.

12. With the HTML window still open, navigate to your work folder. Open the lcmovie2.swf file directly, or within an HTML page.

13. In lcmovie1 type some information to see it populate within the lcmovie2.swf.

How It Works

In this example you examined how you can use a local connection to populate data into one SWF from another SWF. In each SWF you were required to instantiate a localConnection object; however, you were not required to give them the same name. The common bond between the two was the parameter specified in lcmovie2 within the connect() method. When connect() fires, a localConnection object is started, in this case, with the String sampleLCchannel.

Any SWF file that knows to poll a localConnection object residing on the system with the String name sampleLCchannel can access lcmovie2. This is what is happening in lcmovie1. Because lcmovie1 knows the name of an available localConnection object, it attempts to pass the localConnection a method to send to that available localConnection.

`sampleLCchannel` ultimately is the public name of the `receiving_lc` localConnection object. Any methods you define within `receiving_lc` will be publicly available. One SWF file can offer several localConnection objects with their own method sets.

Had lcmovie2 and lcmovie1 hailed from different domains, this example wouldn't have worked at all.

Security

As with shim movies, script access is always a security concern. The localConnection object uses its own `allowDomain()` method that works similarly to the `System.security.allowDomain()` method covered in Chapter 22. It is important to remember that policy files and the `System.security.allowDomain()` method do not enable LocalConnection to communicate between SWF files that originate from different servers.

Try It Out   Using allowDomain with LocalConnection

In this exercise you add to the `lcmovie.fla` file from the preceding Try It Out to allow the localConnection object within `lcmovie1` to communicate.

1. Open the `lcmovie2` FLA.

2. Click the first frame in the timeline and open the Actions panel. Note the line edition and be sure your code looks like the following code. You should substitute your own domain for `someserver.com`:

```
var receiving_lc:LocalConnection = new LocalConnection();
receiving_lc.allowDomain("*.someserver.com");
receiving_lc.sendVar = function(aVar:String)
{
    _root.incomingText_txt.text = aVar;
};

receiving_lc.connect("sampleLCchannel");
```

3. Upload `lcmovie1.swf` and `lcmovie1.html` to your server.

4. Navigate to `lcmovie1.html` in your browser. This address might be something like `http://www.someserver.com/lcmovie1.html`.

5. After you have the browser open to the SWF, go back to your work folder and open `lcmovie2.swf`.

6. With both now open, attempt to type in a String and send the String from the browser-based SWF to the SWF file on the local computer.

How It Works

In this example you saw a much more powerful use of LocalConnection. You were able to specify a domain as allowed to access an SWF running on the local machine.

There may be times, however, when you would prefer any SWF from any domain to access your localConnection objects in your local SWF. As with the policy file and the System.security.allowDomain methods, you can use wildcards to allow for access control. You saw in this example a use of a wildcard to include any subdomains. You can use a wildcard more generally by using it alone, such as

```
receiving_lc.allowDomain("*");
```

The example you just completed might seem a lot like the first example at first glance. However, consider a scenario in which the local SWF is residing within an SWF wrapper such as Northcode. The LocalConnection would allow the local SWF file, which has extended abilities on the local machine, to open an API to browser-based SWF files.

You might imagine creating an SWF that runs locally, which connects to browser-based SWF files, giving your intranet applications unprecedented agility on the user's system.

Because you are required to use allowDomain() for this type of instance, you can be confident that malicious coders who seek to use the localConnection object are thwarted.

Storing Data Locally with Shared Objects

The previous section talked about SWF files communicating with one another in a simple and effective manner. This section talks about the SharedObject class. Shared objects are often referred to in Flash as Flash cookies. Flash cookies can be an effective method for displaying information left over from the previous visit or tailoring a visit based on previous experience. The SharedObject class gives your SWF a memory.

The following table describes the SharedObject class's methods:

Method	Return	Description
getSize()	Number	Returns the size of the sharedObject in bytes.
getLocal()	SharedObject	Returns a sharedObject containing all the values saved via the flush method.
flush()	Object	Writes a value to the local disk and returns the value.
clear()	Nothing	Removes data created by the flush method.

The getSize() method has no parameters. Here's its syntax:

```
sharedObject.getSize();
```

This method is usually employed to check that the data object hasn't reached a maximum allowed size limit.

The getLocal() method has three parameters: the name of the available sharedObject, which must be a String; the URL of the SWF that wrote the local shared object, also a String; and a Boolean stating whether the SWF that created the sharedObject came from an HTTPS connection. If true, the accessing

SWF must be served from a web server that has established a secure connection between itself and your browser, as is the case when you browse to a URL that starts with `https://`. Here's the `getLocal()` syntax:

```
sharedOBject.getLocal(name:String,URL:String,HTTPS:Boolean);
```

The `flush()` method has one optional parameter: a Number representing a disk space allotment request in bytes. Here's the method's syntax:

```
sharedObject.flush(byteSpace:Number);
```

If your sharedObject requires only 20 bytes, but you think the shared object will grow, you can request a larger value such as 100 via the byteSpace parameter. You can avoid having Flash prompt the user to manually allow for a larger disk allotment with each subsequent flush by asking for the full allotment in the first alert.

The `clear()` method has no parameters and simply removes the shared object from the local disk. Here's its syntax:

```
sharedObject.clear();
```

The SharedObject class has one property:

Event	Type	Description
data	Object	Objects placed within the data object are the items that are saved to the sharedObject on the local disk when the `flush` method is called.

The SharedObject class has one event:

Event	Type	Description
sharedObject.onStatus	Function	Fires whenever a change in the sharedObject is detected.

Try It Out   Create a Shared Object and Save Some Data

1. Open a new Flash Document. Save it as `sharedObjectSample.fla` in your work folder.

2. Click the first frame in the timeline, open the Actions panel, and enter the following ActionScript code:

```
var myPersistentObject:SharedObject = SharedObject.getLocal("myData");
if (myPersistentObject.data.test1 != 1)
{
    myPersistentObject.data.test1 = 1;
    var save = myPersistentObject.flush();
    trace(save);
}
```

3. Test the SWF by pressing Ctrl+Enter.

4. Save your FLA in your work folder. You'll be using it in the next Try It Out.

How It Works

In this example you call the static function `getLocal()` to create a sharedObject. When you do this, Flash automatically checks for any existence of a previous object with the same name specified in the name parameter of the `getLocal` method. Because it loads the data property with any pre-existing objects, you can test whether or not you should save new data or work with the existing data.

Saving a variable is easy. You populate the data object as if it were any other object, by declaring a variable upon it. In this case you declare the variable `test1` as equal to four.

You then commit the new data object by calling the `flush` method. Because the `flush` method returns a Boolean, depending on success, you can populate a variable with the return value of `flush`. In this case you have traced it. In the following examples you see how you can use this value to determine actions that affect the user.

Acceptable Data Types

Unlike using `LoadVars`, you can save many different types of data in flashObjects, and they will retain their type and values.

You can save arrays, objects, Booleans, strings, and so on. But there are limitations. More complex objects such as XML or LoadVars will fail. You also can't define a function or class and store it in the sharedObject.

Try It Out   **Retrieving Data Objects**

1. Open the `sharedObjectSample.fla` you created in the previous Try It Out.

2. Click the first frame in the timeline, open the Actions panel, and change the ActionScript to the following code:

```
var myPersistentObject:SharedObject = SharedObject.getLocal("myData");
if (myPersistentObject.data.test2 != 2)
{
    myPersistentObject.data.test2 = 2;
    var save = myPersistentObject.flush();
    trace(save);
}
else
{
    trace(myPersistentObject.data.test2);
}
```

3. Test the SWF by pressing Ctrl+Enter. The SWF appears to do nothing.

4. Close the SWF and test it again by pressing Ctrl+Enter.

5. Verify that the number 2 is now in the output window.

6. Save your FLA in your work folder. You'll continue working in it in the next Try It Out.

How It Works

In this example you saw how you can set a sharedObject and then use the exact same function to retrieve the data. You didn't have to do this, but in this way you can see how the sharedObject can be made compact due to its static method set and multifunctional `getLocal` method.

This example also showed how immediately you can begin to access a pre-existing sharedObject via accessing the data property directly as if it were any other object.

Using Shared Objects as Cookies

Now that you know how to save and retrieve sharedObjects, you're going to try something more useful. Say, for example, that you want to remember the name of a visitor. Say also that when the visitor returns, you don't want to ask them their name again, and so the user interface should instead show a welcome message. Also record the time.

You use a textField and a component button to complete the example.

1.   Open `sharedObjectSample.fla`.

2.   Open the Components panel. Expand the User Interface tab and drag a Button component to the center of the stage.

3.   In the Parameters tab of the Properties panel for the button that you just added to the stage, find the label parameter and change the word `Button` to `Submit`. In the Properties panel give the button an instance name of `submitButton`.

4.   Now create an input text field. Draw one on the stage just above the `Send` button using the Text tool in the Tools panel. Be sure to select the border property and change the field to Input Text in the Properties panel for the textField. Name the textField `dataToSave_txt` in the Instance Name field in the Properties panel.

5.   Select the textField you just created. Copy and paste this field, so that two fields now exist on the stage. Change the instance name of the new field to `instructions_txt` and change the field type to Dynamic Text. Place the dynamic textField just above the existing input textField. Deselect the border property for this textField.

6.   Click the first frame in the timeline, open the Actions panel, and change the ActionScript to the following code:

```
stop();
instructions_txt.text = "Please enter your name:";
var myPersistentObject:SharedObject = SharedObject.getLocal("myData");
if (myPersistentObject.data.username != undefined)
{
    initialVisit = false;
    this.gotoAndStop(2);
}
else
{
    submitButton.onRelease = function()
    {
```

```
            initialVisit = true;
            myPersistentObject.data.username = dataToSave_txt.text;
            var login_date = new Date();
            myPersistentObject.data.date = ⤴
                (login_date.getMonth()+1)+"."+login_date.getDate()⤴
                +"."+login_date.getFullYear();
            myPersistentObject.flush();
            gotoAndStop(2);
        };
}
```

7. Now that you have your actions for frame 1, create a new empty frame that will be frame 2.

8. On frame 2, create a multiline text field in the center of the stage. Be sure that the multiline property is selected and give this field an instance name of `welcome_txt`.

9. On frame 2, open the Components panel and drag a Button component onto the center of the stage.

10. In the Parameters tab of the Properties panel for the button that you just added to the stage, find the label parameter, and change the word Button to Clear User. In the Properties panel give the button an instance name of `clearButton`.

11. Click the second frame in the timeline, open the Actions panel, and change the ActionScript to the following code, which constructs the welcome message and adds a function for clearing the information:

```
if (initialVisit == true)
{
    welcome_txt.text = "Welcome "+myPersistentObject.data.username+"!"+newline;
    welcome_txt.text += "Today is "+myPersistentObject.data.date+".";
}
else
{
    welcome_txt.text = "Welcome back " ⤴
        +myPersistentObject.data.username+"!"+newline;
    welcome_txt.text += "You last visited on "+myPersistentObject.data.date+".";
}
clearButton.onRelease = function()
{
    myPersistentObject.clear();
    gotoAndStop(1);
}
```

12. Test the SWF by pressing Ctrl+Enter.

13. Enter a name and click Submit.

14. You will now see a welcome message and the Clear User button. Do *not* click the Clear User button. Close the SWF.

15. Test the SWF again by pressing Ctrl+Enter.

16. You will now see a welcome screen instead of a login.

17. To clear the information and try again, click the Clear User button.

18. You will now be back at frame 1, and you can enter in a new name.

19. Save your FLA in your work folder. You'll need it for the next Try It Out.

How It Works

In this example you expanded on the principles of the previous example to save a String. You then used the existence of that String to change the behavior of the SWF when it loads. In this case, you set a username and logindate as properties of the data object. You check the existence of a username in the cookie to determine whether or not to proceed directly to the welcome interface, or stay and display the login interface. By extracting the data from the sharedObject before anything else, you can populate the user interface with customized content based on the user's last visit.

What this code also does is prepare for the fact that a sharedObject can be removed from the local system without your knowledge, and so the code needs to be able to reset the data, or otherwise recover in some way. Had the data been lost, and you just assumed the data would be there, your welcome message in frame 2 might look a bit incomplete and broken.

The other important method you saw in action in this example was the `clear` method. You can see that you made a Clear User button that used the `clear` method and returned the application to its initial cookieless state. When you call `clear`, it clears *all* of the data within the data property in the sharedObject.

Working with the User

One thing you have to keep in mind, especially with larger sharedObjects, is that the user has full control over whether you can store data locally. He can set size limits, forbid access, and clear data himself.

You can do several things to work with the user to change the settings and request access. It is conceivable, however, that the user will block you completely from saving data. Your application should still be able to respond in this case, by either working without the data, or fail gracefully, while letting the user know why.

One common method for managing user settings is via the bytes parameter in the `flush` method. When `flush` is called without this parameter, Flash measures the size of the data being saved. If the available size of the allotted disk space for your cookie is larger than the size of the data object, Flash will automatically open the settings dialog box of the Flash player to the Local Storage section. Your SWF file continues playing, but the flush fails for the session. If the user has elected to allot disk space, `flush` returns `true`.

To deal with a pending or false response from the flush object, you can use the `onStatus` event to make decisions about what the application should do in that case. `onStatus` populates its parameter with an object. This object is returned as an object. Iterating through the object reveals the code of the response from the user. If the user denies an allocation, and there isn't enough room in the existing disk space, you will see the value `code=SharedObject.Flush.Failed`. In this case you can decide to go to a different welcome page or alert the user. If the user allows the allotment request, the code returns `SharedObject.Flush.Success`.

Managing Disk Space

If and when you make a sharedObject request, think about how your application might be doing so, and how often. After you hit the limit, every time you call the `flush` method, the user may be presented the settings dialog. That could get fairly annoying. If you plan to have more data saved as your application works, request an allocation early, and make it a sensible size. For example, when the application starts, you can recommend that your application be allowed a megabyte of disk space. This is a lot of data. To do this you don't need to have any data to flush. You can simply call the static method `flush` with the byte parameter. After the user okays this allotment, he would need to exceed the allotment before the settings dialog became a problem again.

Be aware that users are suspicious of cookies and local information. Be clear about how you plan to use the space and how it benefits their overall experience at your web site.

Sharing SharedObects

These objects wouldn't be called shared if you couldn't share them. The `getLocal` function's second parameter, which defines the URL of the origin of the SWF file, which creates the sharedObject.

If the URL of the SWF file were, for example, `http://wwwsomeserver.com/media/flash/myApp.swf`, you could call the `getLocal` method with the following paths and results:

Method	Result
`var myPersistentObject: SharedObject = SharedObject .getLocal("myData", "/media/flash/");`	Allows any SWF from the same folder to access the cookie by name.
`var myPersistentObject: SharedObject = SharedObject .getLocal("myData", "/media/");`	Allows any SWF from the same parent folder or subfolders of the parent folder to access the cookie by name.
`var myPersistentObject: SharedObject = SharedObject .getLocal("myData", "/");`	Allows any SWF from the same domain to access all the sharedObjects.

By climbing up the URL path of the SWF, you can selectively allow different levels of access to the sharedObject.

Leaving this parameter blank inserts the default value. The default value is the full path to the SWF and the SWF name. In this case, only an SWF in the same folder with the same name could access the sharedObject.

Giving a Flash Movie Data on Startup with FlashVars

FlashVars is the term given to variables that are added to the Flash root timeline via the object/embed tags in the HTML page, which the SWF resides on. Because these variables are written as HTML tag attributes, you can use servlets and JavaScript to define them at runtime, or you can simply write them into the attribute when you create the Object/Embed tags.

These variables can be handy when you need to create an SWF file that is populated with page-specific details and information without having to use LoadVars or XML.

Introduction to Flash Object and Embed Tag Parameters

ActionScript is not affected by Object and Embed tags other than by FlashVars, so this section provides you with the explanation for these HTML tags here, before you attempt to use them for FlashVars.

The Object and Embed tags can find their roots all the way back to the early days of Netscape and Internet Explorer and were created separately. Although most new browsers can use the Object tag exclusively, you should nest the Embed tag within the Object tag for those browsers that still use the Embed tag. The Object and Embed tags merely alert the browser of an object that requires a plug-in to display content.

The following table describes the required attributes:

Attribute	Description
CLASSID	Object tag only. A code that identifies the ActiveX control to make available in Internet Explorer.
CODEBASE	Object tag only. Identifies the minimum required version of Flash ActiveX control.
WIDTH	The width to be allowed for the SWF.
HEIGHT	The height to be allowed for the SWF.
SRC	Embed tag only. The URL of the location of the SWF to be displayed.
PLUGINSPAGE	Embed tag only. Supplies the URl to go to get the plug-in if the minimum version of Flash is not present.
MOVIE	Object tag only. The URL of the location of the SWF to be displayed.

And here are descriptions of the optional attributes:

Attribute	Description
ID	Object tag only. The name of the Flash object given to the browser's scripting language.
NAME	Embed tag only. The name of the Flash object given to the browser's scripting language such as JavaScript.
PLAY	A Boolean value that specifies whether the movie plays when it loads or stops on frame 1.
LOOP	A Boolean value that specifies whether the movie returns to frame 1 after playing all frames on the root timeline.
SWFLIVECONNECT	A Boolean that specifies whether FSCommand will be used in the SWF to call the browser scripting language.

Table continued on following page

Attribute	Description
QUALITY	A String value that represents the quality desired for the SWF to be displayed at when the SWF loads. Available values are `autolow`, `autohigh`, `best`, `high`, and `low`.
MENU	A Boolean specifying whether a full right-click menu or only the settings and about options will appear.
SCALE	Determines how the SWF fills the allotted height and width values. The available String options are `exactfit`, `showall`, and `noborder`.
ALIGN	Specifies which corner of the allotted space the SWF should crop from. The available values are `t`, `l`, `r`, and `b`.
SALIGN	Specifies which corner of the allotted space the SWF should crop from. The available values are `t`, `l`, `r`, `b`, `tr`, `tl`, `br`, and `bl`.
WMODE	Specifies if an SWF is transparent and is able to show HTML content beneath it. Available values are `window`, `transparent`, and `opaque`.
BGCOLOR	A hexadecimal RGB value that specifies the background color of the SWF being displayed.
BASE	Specifies the base URL path of any relative URL calls within the SWF file.
FLASHVARS	A string of ampersand-delimited name/value pairs representing variables to instantiate on the root timeline of the SWF.
ALLOWSCRIPTACCESS	Determines whether an SWF in an HTML page can access scripts on the page with the Object and Embed tag.

Adding FlashVars

Adding FlashVars to an Object and Embed tag is very easy. Here you have a before and after addition of FlashVars in the Object/Embed tag. The basic HTML here is the automatic Flash output HTML template you can specify in the HTML tab of the Publish Settings dialog. Different templates are available for different situations.

Before:

```
<object classid="clsid:d27cdb6e-ae6d-11cf-96b8-444553540000"
codebase="http://fpdownload.macromedia.com/pub/shockwave/cabs/flash/swflash.cab#ver
sion=8,0,0,0" width="550" height="400" id="FlashVarsTest" align="middle">
<param name="allowScriptAccess" value="sameDomain" />
<param name="movie" value="FlashVarsTest.swf" />
<param name="quality" value="high" />
<param name="bgcolor" value="#ffffff" />
<embed src="FlashVarsTest.swf" quality="high" bgcolor="#ffffff" width="550"
height="400" name="FlashVarsTest" align="middle" allowScriptAccess="sameDomain"
type="application/x-shockwave-flash"
pluginspage="http://www.macromedia.com/go/getflashplayer" />
</object>
```

After:

```
<object classid="clsid:d27cdb6e-ae6d-11cf-96b8-444553540000"
codebase="http://fpdownload.macromedia.com/pub/shockwave/cabs/flash/swflash.cab#ver
sion=8,0,0,0" width="550" height="400" id="FlashVarsTest" align="middle" >
<param name="allowScriptAccess" value="sameDomain" />
<param name="FlashVars" value="testValue1=Jeff&testValue2=Nathan" />
<param name="movie" value="FlashVarsTest.swf" />
<param name="quality" value="high" />
<param name="bgcolor" value="#ffffff" />
<embed src="FlashVarsTest.swf" FlashVars="testValue1=Jeff&testValue2=Nathan"
quality="high" bgcolor="#ffffff" width="550" height="400" name="FlashVarsTest"
align="middle" allowScriptAccess="sameDomain" type="application/x-shockwave-flash"
pluginspage="http://www.macromedia.com/go/getflashplayer" />
</object>
```

You can see for the Object tag, you needed to add a `param` element node. You then specified a name and value for the FlashVars. These FlashVars will be read by those browsers that use the Object tag.

In the Embed tag, you can set FlashVars through an attribute within the main Embed node. These variables will be read by any browser that uses the Embed tag rather than the Object tag.

Any FlashVars that contain special characters such as spaces and question marks must be URL-encoded.

Creating FlashVars with JavaScript

HTML can be manipulated by JavaScript and written on-the-fly by server-side scripting languages such as PHP and ASP. With JavaScript you can obtain variables from Web forms, XmlHttpRequest (Ajax) cookies, and more. This example uses a simple JavaScript object to store values. Those values will then be inserted into the Object and Embed tags.

Try It Out   Create FlashVars with JavaScript

1. Open a new Flash document and save it as `flashVarsTest.fla` in your work folder.

2. Click the first frame in the timeline, open the Actions panel, and enter the following ActionScript code:

```
this.createTextField("FlashVars1_txt", 0,10,10,200,20);
this.createTextField("FlashVars2_txt", 1,10,30,200,20);
this.FlashVars1_txt.text = _root.JSvalue1;
this.FlashVars2_txt.text = _root.JSvalue2;
```

3. Select File➪Publish Settings and select the HTML tab. If you don't see an HTML tab, click the Formats tab and be sure the HTML format checkbox is selected. Select the Flash Only from the Template drop-down menu.

4. Publish the FLA.

5. Navigate to your work folder, find the `flashVarsTest.html`, and open it in your favorite text editor. Modify the file by making some additions:

```
<html xmlns="http://www.w3.org/1999/xhtml" xml:lang="en" lang="en">
<head>
<meta http-equiv="Content-Type" content="text/html; charset=iso-8859-1" />
```

```
<title>FlashVarsTest</title>
<SCRIPT LANGUAGE="JavaScript">
<!--
var JSvalue1="Jeff";
var JSvalue2="Nathan";
function getVar(name)
{
    return eval(name);
}
//-->
</SCRIPT>
</head>
<body bgcolor="#ffffff">

<SCRIPT LANGUAGE=JavaScript1.1>
<!--
    document.write('<OBJECT classid="clsid:D27CDB6E-AE6D-11cf-96B8-444553540000"');
    document.write('  codebase="http://download.macromedia.com/pub/shockwave/⤾
        cabs/flash/swflash.cab#version=8,0,0,0" ');
    document.write(' ID="FlashVarsTest.swf" WIDTH="550" HEIGHT="400" ALIGN="">');

    document.write(' <PARAM NAME=FlashVars VALUE="JSvalue1='+getVar('JSvalue1')⤾
        +'&JSvalue2='+getVar('JSvalue2')+'">');

    document.write(' <PARAM NAME=movie VALUE="FlashVarsTest.swf"> <PARAM NAME⤾
        =quality VALUE=high> <PARAM NAME=bgcolor VALUE=#FFFFFF> ');
    document.write(' <EMBED src="FlashVarsTest.swf" quality=high bgcolor=#FFFFFF⤾
        FlashVars="JSvalue1='+getVar('JSvalue1') +'&JSvalue2='+getVar⤾
        ('JSvalue2')+'"');
    document.write(' swLiveConnect=FALSE WIDTH="550" HEIGHT="400" NAME=⤾
        "FlashVarsTest.swf" ALIGN="middle"');
    document.write(' TYPE="application/x-shockwave-flash" PLUGINSPAGE="http:⤾
        //www.macromedia.com/go/getflashplayer">');
    document.write(' </EMBED>');
    document.write(' </OBJECT>');
//-->
</SCRIPT>
</body>
</html>
```

6. Save the HTML file and open it in your favorite browser. As long as your browser supports JavaScript, and JavaScript is enabled, you will see the JavaScript values appear within your SWF file.

How It Works

In this example you saw how you can write HTML via JavaScript to manipulate the values that appear within the Object and Embed tags. You could also retrieve the values by means other than eval, such as a cookie, or via an XmlHttpRequest (Ajax).

Because this method involves nesting of quotes and single quotes, it can become confusing and can be difficult to fix when an error occurs. Use a browser that has JavaScript debugging enabled when writing your JavaScript.

Passing FlashVars via a Servlet Page

Similarly, you can construct FlashVars within an Object and Embed tag by writing your page dynamically with servlets or server scripting engines. To test this example you will need PHP or some other server-side scripting engine. This example uses PHP, but if you know a different language you can make the appropriate syntax changes and use your preferred environment.

An example PHP page could look like the following:

```
<html xmlns="http://www.w3.org/1999/xhtml" xml:lang="en" lang="en">
<head>
<meta http-equiv="Content-Type" content="text/html; charset=iso-8859-1" />
<title>FlashVarsTest</title>
</head>
<body bgcolor="#ffffff">
<object classid="clsid:d27cdb6e-ae6d-11cf-96b8-444553540000"
codebase="http://fpdownload.macromedia.com/pub/shockwave/cabs/flash/swflash.cab#ver
sion=8,0,0,0" width="550" height="400" id="FlashVarsTest" align="middle">
    <param name="allowScriptAccess" value="sameDomain" />
    <param name="movie" value="FlashVarsTest_PHP.swf" />
    <param name="quality" value="high" />
    <param name="bgcolor" value="#ffffff" />
    <param name="FlashVars" value="PHPvalue1=<?php print $PHPvalue1;
?>&PHPvalue2=<?php print $PHPvalue2 ?>" />
    <embed src="FlashVarsTest_PHP.swf"
        FlashVars="PHPvalue1=<?php print $PHPvalue1; ?>&PHPvalue2=<?php print
$PHPvalue2; ?>";
        quality="high"
        bgcolor="#ffffff"
        width="550"
        height="400"
        name="FlashVarsTest"
        align="middle"
        allowScriptAccess="sameDomain"
        type="application/x-shockwave-flash"
        pluginspage="http://www.macromedia.com/go/getflashplayer" />
</object>
</body>
</html>
```

This PHP page would be called by appending variables in a GET request. The URL could look like the following:

```
http://www.pixelplay.org/jeff/flashvars/FlashVarsTest_PHP.PHP?PHPvalue1=Jeff&PHPval
ue2=Nathan
```

Of course, the PHP could have constructed the variables in a far more complex application, but this should give you an idea how FlashVars can enhance SWF files served from servlets and server-side script engines.

Summary

This chapter introduced some ways to pass data between Flash movies and the web browser. Some points to remember include the following:

❑ The LocalConnection class allows you to pass data between two or more SWF files running in the same browser application.

❑ With LocalConnection, one of the SWF files is a designated data recipient and is responsible for performing the initial channel setup, while any number of other SWF files can send data to the channel.

❑ Shared objects work similarly to browser cookies. They allow an SWF file to store data within a specific area of the local machine for later retrieval. The data persists even if the browser is closed or the machine is rebooted.

❑ FlashVars is a convenient mechanism for passing startup data that is to be immediately available to the SWF file when it starts up.

Exercises

1. Set up a local connection between two SWF files on the same HTML page. One SWF file should contain a Play button and a Pause button, and the other one should contain a simple animation. Clicking Play or Pause in the one SWF file should signal the animation in the other SWF file to start or stop playing.

2. Set up a screen that has an input field for username and password, a drop-down menu for language, and a Login button. Using the Parameters palette, populate the drop-down language menu with at least two languages by adding to the data and label parameters. When the Login button is clicked, save the username and the language to two shared object data properties. When the project is re-launched, have it immediately populate the username field with the last username used, and pre-select the value from the language drop-down that was previously selected.

Putting JavaScript to Work

In this chapter, you learn how to use JavaScript to communicate between Flash and the browser. You see how to call JavaScript from Flash, and how to use both the Flash JavaScript Integration Kit and the External API to pass data from JavaScript to ActionScript and vice versa.

Before jumping into JavaScript, though, there is one bit of housekeeping to take care of: an issue with Flash security and how it affects JavaScript.

Changing Security Settings

To try this chapter's examples locally, you first need to make a change to a security setting. Flash player version 8 introduced additional restrictions to the security model to better prevent malicious attacks against your computer. For a local SWF file to be able to interact with an HTML page that is local to your computer, you need to designate the SWF file as being trusted content. You can elect to designate a single .swf file as trusted content, or you can designate an entire directory. It is recommended that you perform all of your Flash development in one parent directory and designate that directory as trusted. From then on, all .swf files in that directory and its subdirectories are trusted content and won't generate an error.

> This step only needs to be performed for viewing files locally from your own computer, as you would do during development. When your Flash content is uploaded to a web server and is then accessed from there, ExternalInterface will work without the viewer needing to make any changes.

When you use ExternalInterface with Flash movies contained in a local HTML page, you get an error like the alert window shown in Figure 24-1.

Figure 24-1

To allow ExternalInterface to work with local content, you must make the change in the Flash Security Settings panel. This panel is not in the Flash 8 development environment. Instead, it is a special Flash movie that is loaded into the browser. To access the panel, click the Settings button in the Flash Player Security alert screen or point your browser to www.macromedia.com/support/documentation/ en/flashplayer/help/settings_manager04a.html. A screen much like the one in Figure 24-2 opens.

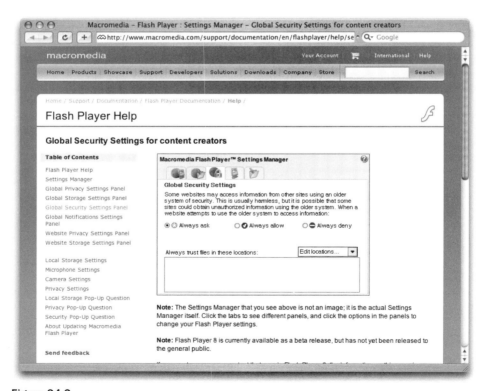

Figure 24-2

To set a directory as containing trusted content, perform the following steps:

1. Point your browser to www.macromedia.com/support/documentation/en/flashplayer/
   help/settings_manager04a.html.

2. Select the Always Allow radio button.

3. From the Edit Locations drop-down menu, select Add Location.

4. Click the Browse for Folder button. Choose the folder containing your Flash content or its parent
   folder.

After you have selected a folder, the security panel should look something like what's shown in Figure
24-3. The security settings changes will take effect immediately, and all Flash content within the selected
folders and all of its subfolders will function without generating a security warning.

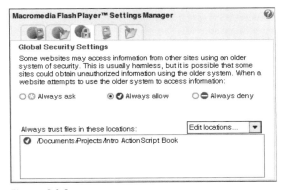

Figure 24-3

Calling JavaScript from within Flash

Although a Flash SWF can be run in many different settings, such as a projector or the standalone Flash
player, the browser is the most common deployment channel for SWF files. Luckily, browsers are getting
better and better. More than ever before, browsers use standards and common behaviors.

JavaScript is one way in which you can communicate with most browsers. With JavaScript you can connect to existing JavaScript-based services and security layers that require JavaScript cookies. Within
Flash there are several ways in which you can connect to JavaScript. This chapter examines each
method. Communicating with JavaScript enables you to connect to JavaScript functions and to the
JavaScript window API, giving you control over the HTML window that contains your Flash file.
Because there are so many browsers, and JavaScript has quirks in each, you should test any JavaScript
thoroughly and on all your target systems.

Introduction to getUrl()

getURL() is likely the most common and straightforward method for calling JavaScript. You can use getURL to call a URL and to target the URL to a specific window. However, almost all browsers allow a JavaScript command within the getURL call.

getURL is a global method. You can call it anywhere, from any object. getURL has three parameters, and all of the parameters are strings. The first parameter is the URL. The second parameter is the target window. This can be the name of a frame. The third parameter is the method, where Get and Post are allowed. The last parameter doesn't do much for you when using JavaScript. However, the second window parameter can be used to target a specific frame's JavaScript.

A few limitations are involved with getURL. If you use getURL to call JavaScript, the URL is limited to 508 characters.

Here's an example getURL that contains JavaScript:

```
getURL("JavaScript:alert('Hello World!')");
```

Here, you have the simple JavaScript keyword preceding the JavaScript command.

If you were to test this within the Flash development environment, it would open a browser window, because the default window self does not exist within the development environment. After the window opens, some browsers display the alert. If the SWF is in the browser, the alert box appears normally, without opening a new browser window.

Creating a JavaScript Command with Nested Variables

Nesting JavaScript variables within a String can be confusing. It can be doubly confusing in ActionScript, because the two languages are so similar.

When you nest string variables, you use both JavaScript's and ActionScript's capabilities to discern double and single quotes. Wrapping single quotes inside of double quotes causes the single quotes to remain a string. Likewise, nesting double quotes within single quotes causes the double quotes to remain a string. Neither JavaScript nor ActionScript have a preference for one or the other.

Generally, it is good practice to keep double quotes in your ActionScript and single quotes within any JavaScript the ActionScript is constructing. This way you can always discern quickly what belongs to which language.

It can be very difficult to debug nested quotes. Use the Check Syntax button often in the ActionScript editor as you create your code. Read the error notes; they can be very handy. It is better to catch a nesting problem with a short string than to realize you've made an error in a now complex and confusing String construction.

Try It Out   Calling JavaScript via getUrl()

1. Open a new Flash document, name it simpleFLashtoJS.fla, and save it in your work folder.

2. Open the User Interface tab of the Components panel, and drag a Button component to the center of the stage.

3. In the Parameters tab of the button's Properties panel, find the label parameter, and change the word Button to Alert. In the Properties panel, give the button an instance name of `myButton`.

4. Click the first frame in the timeline, open the Actions panel, and enter the following ActionScript code:

```
myButton.onRelease = function()
{
    getURL("javascript:alert('Hello World')");
};
```

5. Publish the SWF.

6. Upload the SWF to your server.

7. Open the SWF in your favorite browser and click the Alert button.

How It Works

Here you see that you can prefix JavaScript methods with the `javascript` keyword within the `getURL` URL parameter.

The code that you called in the preceding exercise is just one line of JavaScript. This is pretty limiting, but you can also use `getURL()` to call functions that you have written. Consider a web page with the following JavaScript:

```
<script language="JavaScript">
function sendMessage(messageText)
{
    alert(messageText);
}
</script>
```

The `sendMessage()` function can be called from the following `getURL()` method:

```
getURL("sendMessage(\"Hello World\");");
```

The `\"` characters are needed to escape the inner quotes so that they are sent as part of the `getURL()` parameter. You can place dynamic data in the URL by referencing a variable:

```
var browserMessage:String = "Hello World";
getURL("sendMessage(\"" + browserMessage + "\");");
```

The quotes start getting messy at this point. The first part of the message, `"sendMessage(\""`, passes `sendMessage("` to `getURL()`, the last part passes `");` to `getURL()`, and `browserMessage` sends `Hello World`. The end result is that `getURL()` sees `sendMessage("Hello World");` and passes that to the browser.

One of the limitations of using `getURL()` to call JavaScript functions is that you can send data as one or more input parameters, but you cannot pass a return value from JavaScript and have it be picked up with ActionScript. You see some techniques for dealing with this shortly.

For now, try using a JavaScript function to interact with the contents of a web page.

In this example you use Flash to rewrite some div content. Use the very latest Firefox browser for this example. The example may work in other browsers but has been tested in Firefox.

1. Open your favorite text editor, and in a new document enter the following JavaScript and HTML code:

```
<html xmlns="http://www.w3.org/1999/xhtml" xml:lang="en" lang="en">
<head>
<meta http-equiv="Content-Type" content="text/html; charset=iso-8859-1" />
<title>callJSfromFlash</title>
<script language="JavaScript">
<!--
function getVar(divname, divinfo)
{
    document.getElementById(divname).innerHTML = divinfo;
}
//-->
</script>
</head>
```

2. Save the file as myFlashtoJavaScript.html. You finish this file in step 9.

3. Open a new Flash document and save it as FlashtoJS.fla in your work folder.

4. Open the User Interface tab of the Components panel and drag a Button component to the center of the stage.

5. In the Parameters tab of the button's Properties panel, find the label parameter and change the word Button to Write HTML. In the Properties panel give the button an instance name of myButton.

6. Click the first frame in the timeline, open the Actions panel, and enter the following ActionScript code:

```
function writeToDiv(divname, divContent)
{
    getURL("javascript:getVar('"+divname+"','"+divContent+"')");
}

myButton.onRelease = function()
{
    var htmlString = '<a href="http://www.gooogle.com">Google</a><br>';
    htmlString += '<a href="http://www.yahoo.com">Yahoo</a><br>';
    htmlString += '<a href="http://www.msn.com">YMSN</a><br>';
    writeToDiv("widget", htmlString);
};
```

7. Publish the SWF with HTML. Be sure that the HTML type is selected in the Publish Settings dialog box.

8. Navigate to your work folder and open the FlashtoJS.html file in your favorite text editor.

9. Re-open the `myFlashtoJavaScript.html` file so that both HTML files are now open. Copy the Object and Embed tags from `FlashtoJS.html` and place them in `myFlashtoJavaScript.html`. `myFlashtoJavaScript.html` should now look like this:

```
<html xmlns="http://www.w3.org/1999/xhtml" xml:lang="en" lang="en">
<head>
<meta http-equiv="Content-Type" content="text/html; charset=iso-8859-1" />
<title>callJSfromFlash</title>
<script language="JavaScript">
<!--
function getVar(divname, divinfo)
{
    document.getElementById(divname).innerHTML = divinfo;
}
//-->
</SCRIPT>
</head>
<body>
<object classid="clsid:d27cdb6e-ae6d-11cf-96b8-444553540000" codebase
    ="http://fpdownload.macromedia.com/pub/shockwave/cabs/

flash/swflash.cab#version=8,0,0,0" width="550" height="400" id="FlashtoJS"
    align="middle">
<param name="allowScriptAccess" value="always" />
<param name="movie" value="FlashtoJS.swf" /><param name="quality" value=
    "high" /><param name="bgcolor" value="#ffffff" /

><embed src="FlashtoJS.swf" quality="high" bgcolor="#ffffff" width="550"
    height="400" name="FlashtoJS" align="middle"

allowScriptAccess="always" type="application/x-shockwave-flash" pluginspage
    ="http://www.macromedia.com/go/getflashplayer" />
</object>
<div id=widget>Hello World</div>
</body>
</html>
```

10. Upload `myFlashtoJavaScript.html` and `FlashtoJS.swf` to the same directory on a web server.

11. Navigate to the html `myFlashtoJavaScript.htm` file and test the SWF to JavaScript communication by clicking the button.

How It Works

In this example you created a simple JavaScript function that writes to a div. In JavaScript you can use the document DOM tree to find and target a specific div by id. Then you can replace the content of that div after you've found it. Additionally, you could create more divs using the `appendChild` method of the JavaScript document DOM object.

In this case you're allowing Flash to control the content of a specific pre-existing div. In your SWF file, you have created a function that contains the getURL object. By creating a string that contains html, you can construct the content of the div directly with ActionScript.

Then you inserted the Object and Embed tags within the document. An important consideration is the `allowScriptAccess` parameter in the Object and Embed tags. In previous versions of Flash, this value would default to "always" when the parameter did not appear. Because of this, your Flash files could always access JavaScript with little interference. However, with Flash 8, the default value has switched to "sameDomain." Because of this, if the SWF file were to be hosted on a different domain, or subdomain, the HTML file would block the version 8 SWF from accessing its document, if the `allowScriptAccess` parameter is allowed to default. Therefore, if you would like an SWF to access your HTML document, you can use the value "always" to give any SWF access to the JavaScript.

Because this example allows any HTML to be written to the div, you could have included any valid HTML code, including style information, and more complex HTML such as child divs, iframes, and more. Because of this, you can think about using SWF files as navigation and interface for HTML content without reloading the SWF file itself.

This idea can be used in conjunction with AJAX methodologies to allow Flash to become a seamless part of your complex HTML-based web applications. Of course, the interaction didn't need to be just div writes. You can call any JS function you like and send it parameters according to your needs.

`getURL()` can be a powerful Flash-to-JavaScript communication tool.

Considering Limitations

The main drawback of using `getURL()` alone is that there is no method for allowing JavaScript to return a success message back to Flash. `getURL()` is a blind call, the success of which is dependent upon the browser. Also, no precedent exists for using the `javascript` keyword in a URL within a browser, so support of it is not required by any standard. You should always test your application on your target systems before deploying `getURL` JavaScript calls. To get a return status, the JavaScript will need to talk to Flash.

Generally, you are limited to 508 characters per JavaScript URL used within `getURL`. Some browsers are limited to 127 characters, and others are limited to just over 1,000.

Calling JavaScript Functions Using fscommand

One thing you might hear often when implementing the `fscommand()` from the browser are references to the embed parameter `swLiveConnect`. This attribute is required for older Netscape browsers; it enabled Java in the browser, which was used to handle `fscommand()` requests. It isn't required in newer browsers and is not implemented in the examples.

Another note about `fscommand()` is that it is not supported in many browsers. For example, IE on a Mac cannot support `fscommand()`, and there is no work-around. Alternatives to `fscommand()` will work on far more browsers, but because this is a viable method and is super easy to integrate, you can use it for rapid development where cross-browser support is less of a concern.

You can find a more extensive list of `fscommand()` *browser support at* www.macromedia.com/ cfusion/knowledgebase/index.cfm?id=tn_14159 *. Firefox support can be considered to be equivalent to Netscape 6.2.*

The `fscommand` method works very much like the `getURL()` method just covered. However, you don't need to worry about the data length issue that you do with `getURL()`. The `fscommand()` function enables you to send arbitrary amounts of data from Flash to the browser. Take a look at how to change the previous exercise so that it uses `fscommand()` instead of `getURL()`.

Try It Out   **Calling a JavaScript Function via fscommand**

If you have not done the previous Try It Out example, you should do it now. You should be familiar with a working `getURL()` example before you decide to use `fscommand` in an application. You also use the assets created in the previous Try It Out example to make some minor changes to get it to work with `fscommand`.

1.   Re-open the `myFlashtoJavaScript.html` file. Change your code so that it looks like this:

```
<html xmlns="http://www.w3.org/1999/xhtml" xml:lang="en" lang="en">
<head>
<meta http-equiv="Content-Type" content="text/html; charset=iso-8859-1" />
<title>callJSfromFlash</title>
<SCRIPT LANGUAGE="JavaScript">
<!--
function FlashtoJS_DoFSCommand(divname, divinfo)
{
document.getElementById(divname).innerHTML = divinfo;
}
//-->
</SCRIPT>
<SCRIPT LANGUAGE="VBScript">
<!--
Sub FlashtoJS_FSCommand(ByVal command, ByVal args)
    call FlashtoJS_DoFSCommand(command, args)
end sub

//-->
</SCRIPT>
</head>
<body>
<object classid="clsid:d27cdb6e-ae6d-11cf-96b8-444553540000" codebase="http:⊃
        //fpdownload.macromedia.com/pub/shockwave/cabs/flash/swflash.cab#version@ta
        =8,0,0,0" width="550" height="400" align="middle" id=FlashtoJS>
<param name="allowScriptAccess" value="always" />
<param name="movie" value="FSCommandtoJS.swf" />
<param name="quality" value="high" />
<param name="bgcolor" value="#ffffff" />
<embed src="FSCommandtoJS.swf"
    quality="high"
    bgcolor="#ffffff"
    width="550"
    height="400"
    name="FlashtoJS"
```

```
        align="middle"
        type="application/x-shockwave-flash"
        pluginspage="http://www.macromedia.com/go/getflashplayer" />
  </object>
  <div id=widget>Hello World</div>
  </body>
  </html>
```

2. Save the HTML file as `dofscommand.html`.

3. Open a new Flash document and save it as `fscommandtoJS.fla` in your work folder.

4. Click the first frame in the timeline, open the Actions panel, and enter the following ActionScript code:

```
fscommand("widget", "Hello FSCommand!");
```

5. Publish the `fscommandtoJS.fla` file.

6. Upload `dofscommand.html` and `fscommandtoJS.swf` to your server.

7. Navigate to the `dofscommand.html` file in your browser. You will see the div content now change via the `fscommand` communication.

How It Works

In this example you were required to create an intermediary function for IE browsers. You then were able to use the parameters sent via `fscommand` to complete the same task as a `getURL` JavaScript method.

In this example, because you did not need to construct the JavaScript within Flash, the complexity of sending the variables is lessened. This allows for quicker debugging and faster development.

Of course `fscommand()` is far more limited than `getURL()` in that many browsers do not listen for the `fscommand` — for example, IE on the Mac. As with any Flash-to-JavaScript communication, you should test all of your target systems for compliance and functionality.

Calling Flash from JavaScript

One thing missing from the examples you've seen so far is that Flash has no way to tell whether `getURL` or `fscommand` were successful.

In the next exercise you use the movie ID that you created in the preceding Try It Out to communicate back to the movie that your function is complete.

Try It Out   Call Flash from JavaScript

This is a simplified example. Before you return a success Boolean, it is wise to ensure that whatever procedure you were looking to complete did, in fact, complete. Because you're just writing to a div in the example, have the JavaScript immediately return a response to your Flash.

You use the `dofscommand.html` file as well as the `fscommandtoJS.fla` file from the last example. If you have not completed that Try It Out, you should do it now to understand the `fscommand` communication.

1. Re-open `myFlashtoJavaScript.html`. Change your code so that it looks like this:

```
<html xmlns="http://www.w3.org/1999/xhtml" xml:lang="en" lang="en">
<head>
<meta http-equiv="Content-Type" content="text/html; charset=iso-8859-1" />
<title>callJSfromFlash</title>
<SCRIPT LANGUAGE="JavaScript">
<!--
function FlashtoJS_DoFSCommand(divname, divinfo)
{
alert(divname);
document.getElementById(divname).innerHTML = divinfo;
document.FlashtoJS.SetVariable("FSCommandDone","true")
}
//-->
</SCRIPT>
<SCRIPT LANGUAGE="VBScript">
<!--
Sub FlashtoJS_FSCommand(ByVal command, ByVal args)
    call FlashtoJS_DoFSCommand(command, args)
end sub

//-->
</SCRIPT>
</head>
<body>
<object classid="clsid:d27cdb6e-ae6d-11cf-96b8-444553540000"
codebase="http://fpdownload.macromedia.com/pub/shockwave/cabs/flash/swflash.cab#ver
sion=8,0,0,0" width="550" height="400" align="middle" id=FlashtoJS>
<param name="allowScriptAccess" value="always" />
<param name="movie" value="FSCommandtoJS.swf" />
<param name="quality" value="high" />
<param name="bgcolor" value="#ffffff" />
<embed src="FSCommandtoJS.swf"
    quality="high"
    bgcolor="#ffffff"
    width="550"
    height="400"
    name="FlashtoJS"
    align="middle"
    type="application/x-shockwave-flash"
    pluginspage="http://www.macromedia.com/go/getflashplayer" />
</object>
<div id=widget>Hello World</div>
</body>

</html>
```

2. Save the HTML file as `JStoFlash.html`.

3. Open the `fscommandtoJS.fla` from your work folder.

4. Click the first frame in the timeline and create a dynamic textField. Select the text field. In the Var: Parameter in the Properties panel for the field, type the variable name `fscommandDone`. Leave the ActionScript the same, which should look like the following:

```
fscommand("widget", "Hello FSCommand!");
```

5. Publish `fscommandtoJS.fla`.

6. Upload the `JStoFlash.html` and `fscommandtoJS.swf` files to your server.

7. Navigate to the `JStoFlash.html file` in your browser. You will see the div content now change via the `fscommand` communication and the word `true` will appear in your SWF.

How It Works

In this example you saw how JavaScript can communicate with an SWF using the document ID of the Object and Embed tag. In this example you simply set a variable on the root timeline of your SWF via `document.FlashtoJS.SetVariable`.

From here, you can set an interval or watch method in ActionScript to allow the SWF to make decisions about the variable's current state.

Basic JavaScript Methods and Events

`setVariable` is just one method available to JavaScript to control a Flash movie. There is an entire set of methods JavaScript can access to display information about the SWF as well as control different aspects of the SWF. The following table describes these methods:

Method	Description
gotoFrame	Sends the SWF to the frame specified in the parameter. The parameter must be a root frame name or root frame number.
getVariable	Returns a root variable with the name specified as a string in the parameter.
IsPlaying	Checks whether the SWF's root timeline is playing. This method returns a Boolean.
pan	Moves the x and y position of the SWF.
percentLoaded	Returns a number from 0–100 indicating the percentage of the SWF's bytes loaded.
play	Identical to calling `play()` on the root timeline.
rewind	Sends the root timeline to frame 1.
setZoomRect	Zooms in on a specified rectangular area of the SWF.

Method	Description
setVariable	Sets a variable on the root timeline of the SWF.
stopPlay	Identical to calling stop() on the root timeline of the SWF.
totalFrames	Returns the total frames of the root timeline of the SWF.
zoom	Sets the zoom property of the SWF.

The following table describes some of the basic JavaScript Flash events:

Event	Description
onProgress	Automatically is fired when the percentage of bytes loaded changes.
onReadyStateChange	Fires whenever the state of the SWF changes. The parameter is populated with a numeric code: 0=Loading, 1=Uninitialized, 2=Loaded, 3=Initialized, 4=Complete.
fscommand	Fires when you use a URL in an fscommand, and the URL starts with 'fscommand:'.

Macromedia has documented more events and properties that JavaScript can access. The aforementioned are the basic set that will enable your JavaScript to communicate with your Flash movie. If you need more JavaScript-to-Flash control, consult the Macromedia documentation for the very latest supported properties, methods, and events. Always test your target systems for compliance and functionality.

Using the Flash JavaScript Integration Kit

The Flash JavaScript Integration Kit is a set of JavaScript files and a set of specific ActionScript code within a shim SWF file. The shim is loaded into a separate div, rather than within the main SWF file. This shim acts as a communication point to the JavaScript. An interesting fact is that the Flash JavaScript Integration Kit is really a set of classes and tools that all still use getURL to make its main JavaScript calls.

So why use the Flash Integration Kit? The integration kit neatly organizes the job of bidirectional JavaScript/Flash communication. The integration kit also allows for communication of complex data types between Flash and JavaScript. These can include objects, arrays, Strings, Numbers, Booleans, and more. The Helper classes that come with the kit automatically handle the parsing of the data types, making Flash-to-JavaScript integration seamless and simple. Also, the integration kit is open source and is maintained by the OSFlash organization, a group of folks dedicated to open source Flash initiatives.

You can get the integration kit from Macromedia at http://weblogs.macromedia.com/flashjavascript/ or from osflash.org at http://osflash.org/doku.php?id=flashjs. Of course, these URLs are susceptible to linkrot and might change but are working at the time of this writing.

Setting Up the Integration Kit

Setting up the integration kit is very easy. Before setting up the kit, you'll need to download it, and you'll need a web server space to test it on. The kit comes with a JavaScript file called `JavaScriptFlashGateway.js`, which you find in the installation folder within the kit. This file needs to be uploaded directly into the root folder of your web server; it will later be included into the HTML page that contains your SWF file. The next step is a bit more complex. Two ActionScript files must be placed in the default IDE classpath:

- `JavaScriptProxy.as`
- `JavaScriptSerializer.as`

These files are in the source folder within the kit — in the ActionScript subfolder. When you open the ActionScript subfolder you will notice the files are within a hierarchy of folders. These folders should remain as they are. Copy the com folder and all of its content. Place the copy folder in the same directory as the `JavaScriptFlashGateway.fla` file.

You will now be able to compile these classes into this FLA file. You should open the `JavaScriptFlashGateway.fla` file and compile it now. Upload the `JavaScriptFlashGateway.swf` file to the same folder as the JS file you uploaded earlier. The integration kit is now installed on your server! Easy!

Calling JavaScript Functions from ActionScript

Whenever you use the integration kit, you must include the JS files from the kit. Do this using a simple include element:

```
<script type="text/javascript" src="path/JavaScriptFlashGateway.js"></script>
```

Replace the path with a path your HTML page can resolve to include the JS file. This file contains all the necessary methods that will be required when the Flash file makes a call to the kit.

The next step is to work within your main application. You'll need to import the `JavaScriptProxy` class file. You can do this by importing it directly:

```
import com.macromedia.javascript.JavaScriptProxy;
```

The com path will need to be in the default classpath, in the same work folder as your main application FLA file, or within a custom classpath specified for your main application FLA file.

You can now construct an instance of the proxy class. In your main application FLA, you can place the following code:

```
var JSConnect:JavaScriptProxy = new JavaScriptProxy();
JSConnect.call("JSMethodName", anObject, "anExmapleString", {x:1,y:1});
```

Here you can see how the new constructor allows you to access the call method of the JavaScriptProxy class. In this example the first parameter is the name of the JavaScript function you want to call. All trailing arguments are parameters to be sent to the JavaScript method. As you can see, you can send complex and simple objects. The methods in the ActionScript and JavaScript within the kit automatically handle this complexity.

All you need to do now is define the methods that the ActionScript can call. The arguments that must be passed to those methods will be handled by the kit automatically.

Calling ActionScript Functions from JavaScript

This operation is a bit more involved than the reverse operation covered previously. Again, whenever you use the integration kit, you must include the JS files from the kit in the HTML file, which is displaying your main application. Do this using a simple include element:

```
<script type="text/javascript" src="path/JavaScriptFlashGateway.js"></script>
```

Replace the path with a path your HTML page can resolve to include the JS file.

Next, in a new Script element, you need to create an instance of the FlashProxy JavaScript class. You'll need to give the proxy a name. To be sure the proxy is unique and won't collide with any other localConnection objects, the documentation suggests using the data and time object to create a unique String:

```
<script type="text/javascript">
var uid = new Date().getTime();
var flashProxy = new FlashProxy(uid, ' path/JavaScriptFlashGateway.swf');
</script>
```

Calling this constructor actually downloads and displays the `JavaScriptFlashGateway.swf` file in a hidden div. This SWF, which is provided by the framework and is not something that you create yourself, will act as a shim that the JavaScript can rewrite over and over to populate with FlashVars. This data is in turn sent to your main application by the shim.

The UID must somehow find its way into the main application. Fortunately, the kit has provided you with a tool that will automatically display the main application SWF while adding the appropriate UID FlashVar. To add your main application to the web page, you can call a simple JavaScript as is demonstrated in the following code. You should change `'path/yourMainApplication.swf'` to refer to the SWF file that is to be at the other end of your JavaScript-ActionScript connection:

```
<script type="text/javascript">
    var tag = new FlashTag('path/yourMainApplication.swf', 300, 300);
    tag.setFlashvars('lcId='+uid);
    tag.write(document);
</script>
```

You can specify more FlashVars if you want, or if your application requires them, but for the kit to work you will need the `lcid` variable, which must match the `uid` variable.

You can also set different attributes about the Object and Embed tag, which this operation creates. These include FlashTag.setBgcolor and FlashTag.setVersion, which you can use to set those attributes of the Object and Embed tag.

In this example, the FlashTag constructor is as follows:

```
function FlashTag(src, width, height)
{
    this.src        = src;
```

```
    this.width    = width;
    this.height   = height;
    this.version  = '7,0,14,0';
    this.id       = null;
    this.bgcolor  = 'ffffff';
    this.flashVars = null;
}
```

If you are comfortable with JavaScript, you can, of course, modify these default values or make them additional parameters of the FlashTag method. For example, you could require the minimum version to be 8,0,0,0 rather than 7,0,14,0 as the default value so that if you do not use the setter, you can expect your application to work as desired.

The next addition is to add the actual ActionScript method call from your JavaScript. This is a simple method on the flashProxy object you instantiated with the FlashProxy constructor. An example would be as follows:

```
flashProxy.call('anActionScriptFunction', 'aTestString', false, null, 'undefined');
```

The next step is to instantiate the JavaScriptProxy object in your ActionScript. Within the main application SWF file, define the connector:

```
var JSConnet:JavaScriptProxy = new JavaScriptProxy(_root.lcId, this);
```

You were required to pass two parameters to accept incoming method requests. The first is your FlashVar lcid, and you know you can find this on root. The second parameter is the object or timeline that contains the methods to which the JavaScript will have access.

All you need to do now is define the methods that the JavaScript can call. The arguments that must be passed to those methods will be handled by the kit automatically.

Try It Out   Create Communication between Browser and Movie

In this example, you have ActionScript call JavaScript with some simple parameters. Then JavaScript, upon completion of its method, will call ActionScript in response.

1.   Open your favorite text editor, create a new document, and enter the following HTML and JavaScript. You will need to change the directory path of each file to match your folder layout:

```
<html xmlns="http://www.w3.org/1999/xhtml" xml:lang="en" lang="en">
<head>
<meta http-equiv="Content-Type" content="text/html; charset=iso-8859-1" />
<title>Flash-JS Integration Kit Test</title>
<script type="text/javascript" src="path/JavaScriptFlashGateway.js"></script>

<!-- Set up the proxy SWF //-->
<script LANGUAGE="JavaScript">
<!--
var uid = new Date().getTime();
var flashProxy = new FlashProxy(uid, ' path/JavaScriptFlashGateway.swf');
//-->
</script>

<!-- Set up a method to call //-->
```

```
<script LANGUAGE="JavaScript">
<!--
testJSMethod = function(testString){
    alert(testString);
    flashProxy.call('testASMethod', "true");
}
//-->
</script>
</head>
<body>

<!-- Insert Main Flash Applicaiton //-->
<script type="text/javascript">
<!--
    var tag = new FlashTag('MainApplication.swf', 550, 400);
    tag.setFlashvars('lcId='+uid);
    tag.write(document);
//-->
</script>
</body>
</html>
```

2. Save the file as `FlashJSKit.html`.

3. Open a new Flash Document. Save the Flash document as `MainApplication.fla` in your work folder.

4. Click the first frame in the timeline, open the Actions panel, and enter the following ActionScript code:

```
import com.macromedia.javascript.JavaScriptProxy;
testASMethod = function (r)
{
    createTextField("responseValue", 0, 10, 10, 200, 20);
    responseValue.text = r;
};
var JSConnect:JavaScriptProxy = new JavaScriptProxy(_root.lcId, this);
JSConnect.call("testJSMethod", "This is a test");
```

5. Publish the `MainApplication.fla` and upload the SWF with the `FlashJSKit.html` from step 1 into the root directory of your web server.

6. Navigate to the `FlashJSKit.html` file on your server using your favorite browser.

7. Verify the alert by clicking OK. This sends a message back to your MainApplication SWF, which will display the word `true`.

How It Works

In this example you saw how you can easily set up JavaScript-to-Flash communication using the kit. By making sure the JavaScript and ActionScript files were present, all you needed to do was follow the documentation and then define two functions. The first is the JavaScript `testJSMethod` function. The second is the `testASMethod` function in the ActionScript. Working in concert, the two methods were able to interact seamlessly, allowing your Flash and JavaScript to communicate information.

You can see that this method is very similar to the previous communications examples with `fscommand` and `getURL`. However, the kit packages up the best of `getURL`, while making a convenient and reliable method for allowing JavaScript to call ActionScript, which will work on more browsers than the `document.flashMovie.SetVariables` method you explored earlier.

The Flash JavaScript Integration Kit is not foolproof, however. You still must be concerned with the length of your variables, which you send to JavaScript. As well, browsers are always changing, as are the security restrictions imposed by the Flash Player. Always test your ActionScript-to-JavaScript communication on all of the browsers and systems you intend to target.

Using the External API

One aspect of Macromedia Flash that has always been an issue is the capability to interact between the Flash movie and the surrounding browser. Although the Flash JavaScript Integration Kit definitely makes this easier, it has to work around some issues with the underlying implementation of previous versions of the Flash plug-in.

With the introduction of Flash 8, a mechanism has been added directly to the Flash plug-in that is specifically designed for communication between a Flash movie and the browser. This mechanism is called the External API, and it provides a number of important benefits:

❑ Any JavaScript function can be called from the HTML page, taking any number of arguments, and returning any value back into the Flash movie.

❑ Different data types can be passed as function arguments, not just strings.

❑ Individual functions within the Flash movie can be called directly from JavaScript, using standard function call syntax.

❑ Considerable amounts of data can be passed before data length limits are reached. This was previously an issue with the `getURL` JavaScript technique.

This is a huge step to making Flash work more seamlessly within a larger web application, and it will be appreciated by anyone who has had to work with Flash-to-browser communication with previous versions of the plug-in. The class you work with is ExternalInterface.

ExternalInterface Class Methods

The ExternalInterface class has only two methods — `addCallback()` and `call()` — which are discussed in the following sections.

addCallback()

The `addCallback()` method registers an ActionScript function as being callable from JavaScript (Flash Player version 8). It indicates the functions you want to make available for external JavaScript code to call. Not every ActionScript function is exposed to JavaScript because that would be a major security risk.

The method takes three parameters:

- ❏ `functionName` — A String that designates the name by which the function is accessible from JavaScript.

- ❏ `instance` — An Object that specifies the object that holds the actual method being called, in the case of custom classes. If a function is being called from the timeline instead of from a custom class, then just put `null` for the value here.

- ❏ `functionHandle` — A handle to the function or the class method to be called when the JavaScript function is invoked.

The method returns a Boolean. Here's the syntax:

```
flash.external.ExternalInterface.addCallback(functionName:String, ⤶
    instance:Object, functionHandle:Function) : Boolean
```

Following is an example use of `addCallback()`:

```
import flash.external.*;

var methodName:String = "helloWorld";
var instance:Object = null;
var method:Function = myHelloWorld;
var resultsField:TextField;

ExternalInterface.addCallback(methodName, instance, method);

resultsField = this.createTextField("resultsField", this.getNextHighestDepth(), ⤶
    10, 10, 100, 20);

function myHelloWorld(inputString:String) : String
{
    resultsField.text = inputString;
    return "received: " + inputString;
}
```

The corresponding script in the HTML page would be as follows:

```
<script>
function callExternalInterface()
{
    var flashHolder = document.getElementById("externalInterface");
    document.forms[0].returnText.value = ⤶
        flashHolder.helloWorld(document.forms[0].inputText.value);
}
</script>
```

If you try this out on local files instead of files coming from a web server, you will have to change a security setting to allow the SWF file access to your local HTML file. See "Changing Security Settings" at the start of this chapter for details on how to do this.

call()

The call() method calls a JavaScript function from within the Flash movie (Flash Player version 8). It calls a JavaScript function made available from the HTML page.

The method takes one parameter and any number of additional arguments. The parameter is a String holding the name of the JavaScript function to call. Any number of optional arguments can be added, each of which is passed to the called JavaScript function. call() returns an Object. Here's its syntax:

```
flash.external.ExternalInterface.call(functionName:String, [argument1:Object], 
    [argument2:Object], ...) : Object
```

The following is an example of using call():

```
import flash.external.ExternalInterface;

var resultsField:TextField;
resultsField = this.createTextField("resultsField", this.getNextHighestDepth(), 
    10, 10, 100, 20);

this.createEmptyMovieClip("getInputTextButton", this.getNextHighestDepth());
getInputTextButton._x = 10;
getInputTextButton._y = 40;
getInputTextButton.createTextField("buttonLabel", 
getInputTextButton.getNextHighestDepth(), 0, 0, 100, 20);
getInputTextButton.buttonLabel.textColor = 0x0000CC;
getInputTextButton.buttonLabel.text = "Get Input Value";

getInputTextButton.onRelease = function()
{
    resultsField.text = String(ExternalInterface.call("getInputValue"));
}
```

The corresponding script in the HTML page would be as follows:

```
<script>
    function callExternalInterface()
    {
        var flashHolder = document.getElementById("externalInterface");
        document.forms[0].returnText.value = 
            flashHolder.helloWorld(document.forms[0].inputText.value);
    }

    function getInputValue()
    {
        return document.forms[0].inputText.value;
    }
</script>
<form>
    <input type="text" name="inputText" value="" />
</form>
```

If you try this out on local files instead of files coming from a web server, you will have to change a security setting to allow the .swf access to your local HTML file. See the next section for details on how to do this.

The ExternalInterface class has only one property: `available`. It is a Boolean that indicates whether the external interface is enabled (Flash Player version 8).

Calling ActionScript Functions and Methods

First, look at how to initiate an ActionScript function from JavaScript. The Flash player does not allow for unimpeded access to your ActionScript code from outside the player. That would be a security risk and could have unforeseen consequences if someone figured out how to maliciously use it. The Flash player does allow for any ActionScript function or method to be called by JavaScript; however, each ActionScript function or method must be designated as being visible outside the plug-in. To expose the function, all that is needed is the ExternalInterface `addCallback()` method. The following section explains how this is done.

Calling an ActionScript Function from JavaScript

First, some ActionScript is needed:

```
import flash.external.ExternalInterface;

ExternalInterface.addCallback("helloWorld", null, myHelloWorld);

function myHelloWorld() : String
{
    return "Hello World";
}
```

The first line is an import statement that enables you to call the ExternalInterface class without having to type out `flash.external.ExternalInterface` every time you want to make use of the class. The second line makes the function `myHelloWorld()` accessible outside the plug-in; the name of the function that will be called is `helloWorld()`. You look at the `null` value shortly.

You do not need to use the `new` operator to create an instance of the ExternalInterface class. The methods and properties made available in the class are static, meaning that they can be called directly from the class. Because there is only ever one bridge between the Flash content and the containing HTML, the class was designed so that it is easier to invoke.

After the preceding code is placed in a blank Flash movie and is compiled, the following HTML embeds the `.swf` within the web page and then calls the ActionScript function when a link is clicked:

```
<html>
<head>
<title>externalInterface</title>
<script>
    function callExternalInterface()
    {
        var flashHolder = document["externalInterface"];
        document.forms[0].returnText.value = flashHolder.helloWorld();
    }
</script>
</head>
<body bgcolor="#ffffff">
<object classid="clsid:d27cdb6e-ae6d-11cf-96b8-444553540000" ⤵
    codebase="http://fpdownload.macromedia.com/pub/shockwave/cabs/⤵
```

```
    flash/swflash.cab#version=8,0,0,0" width="550" height="400" ⤶
    id="externalInterface" align="middle">

    <param name="allowScriptAccess" value="always" />
    <param name="movie" value="externalInterface.swf" />
    <param name="quality" value="high" />
    <param name="bgcolor" value="#ffffff" />
    <embed src="externalInterface.swf" quality="high" bgcolor="#ffffff" ⤶
        width="550" height="400" name="externalInterface" align="middle" ⤶
        allowScriptAccess="always" type="application/x-shockwave-flash"⤶
        pluginspage="http://www.macromedia.com/go/getflashplayer" />
</object>
<form>
    <a href="javascript:;" onclick="callExternalInterface()" />
        Call helloWorld
    </a><br />
    Returns: <input type="text" name="returnText" value="" />
</form>
</body>
</html>
```

Within the JavaScript, the function `callExternalInterface()` gets access to the Flash movie through the `getElementById()` method, where the `id` set in the `<object>` tag is used to find the embedded Flash content. When this is obtained, the ActionScript function is called, and its return value is assigned to a text field.

Within the Object tag, an ID needs to be set, and within both the `<object>` and `<embed>` tags, the `allowScriptAccess` parameter needs to be set to `sameDomain`. This attribute is set by default for all of the Flash authoring environment's publishing templates; however, if you create your own, you need to make sure this parameter is present.

Finally, the call to the Flash movie is made when a link is clicked. You could have tried calling this automatically as soon as the page loaded; however, this would have had no effect. There is a delay between when the page finishes loading and when the Flash movie is loaded and ready. Until that point, any attempts at calling ActionScript functions are ignored.

Calling an ActionScript Method from JavaScript

For the most part, you will likely use the previous format to call custom functions; however, it is also possible to call class methods in much the same way. The only difference in implementation is with the `addCallback()` method.

The following code allows a built-in method to be called instead of a custom function. First, take a look at the ActionScript code:

```
import flash.external.ExternalInterface;

var mySound:Sound = new Sound();
mySound.loadSound("http://www.nathanderksen.com/book/demoSong.mp3");
mySound.onLoad = function()
{
    this.start();
}
ExternalInterface.addCallback("setMusicLevel", mySound, mySound.setVolume);
```

This time, when the JavaScript code makes a call to `setMusicLevel()`, it in fact calls `setVolume()` on the `mySound` instance.

Next, take a look at the HTML code:

```
<html>
<head>
<title>externalInterface</title>
<script>
    function callExternalInterface()
    {
        var flashHolder = document["externalInterface"];
        flashHolder.setMusicLevel(Number(document.forms[0].volumeField.value));
    }
</script>
</head>
<body bgcolor="#ffffff">
<object classid="clsid:d27cdb6e-ae6d-11cf-96b8-444553540000"
    codebase="http://fpdownload.macromedia.com/pub/shockwave/cabs/
    flash/swflash.cab#version=8,0,0,0" width="550" height="400"
    id="externalInterface" align="middle">

    <param name="allowScriptAccess" value="always" />
    <param name="movie" value="externalInterface.swf" />
    <param name="quality" value="high" />
    <param name="bgcolor" value="#ffffff" />
    <embed src="externalInterface.swf" quality="high" bgcolor="#ffffff"
        width="550" height="400" name="externalInterface" align="middle"
        allowScriptAccess="always" type="application/x-shockwave-flash"
        pluginspage="http://www.macromedia.com/go/getflashplayer" />
</object>
<form>
    <input type="text" name="volumeField" value="" />
    <a href="javascript:;" onclick="callExternalInterface()" />
        Set volume
    </a><br />
</form>
</body>
</html>
```

`setMusicLevel()` is called and passed a number pulled from an input field. Note how the text value from the field is converted to a Number before being passed to the ActionScript method. The ExternalInterface class allows for non-string parameters and return values, so proper typing can be used. Unfortunately, because there is no JavaScript support for strong typing, you will still need to watch for issues with data type conflicts.

Calling JavaScript Functions from ActionScript

Now take a look at how to call a JavaScript function from within the Flash movie. Unlike calling ActionScript functions from JavaScript, there are no restrictions as to which functions can be called. If the JavaScript function can be called from the HTML on the page holding the Flash movie, it can also be called from the Flash movie using ActionScript.

The ExternalInterface `call()` method allows JavaScript functions to be called. The only parameters that it requires are the name of the function to call and the list of parameters to pass to that function. The `call()` method also passes back any value returned from the JavaScript function. Like the `addCallback()` method, the `call()` method allows for data types other than strings to be passed into and returned back from any JavaScript function.

Opening a Browser Window

This example allows for a new browser window to be opened from within a Flash movie. The ActionScript that makes that happen looks like this:

```
import flash.external.ExternalInterface;

this.createEmptyMovieClip("openWindowButton", this.getNextHighestDepth());
openWindowButton._x = 10;
openWindowButton._y = 40;
openWindowButton.createTextField("buttonLabel", ⏎
      getInputTextButton.getNextHighestDepth(), 0, 0, 100, 20);
openWindowButton.buttonLabel.textColor = 0x0000CC;
openWindowButton.buttonLabel.text = "Open Window";

openWindowButton.onRelease = function()
{
    ExternalInterface.call("openWindow", "http://www.macromedia.com/", ⏎
        "myWindow", 700, 500);
}
```

Only the line in bold is needed to actually call the JavaScript `openWindow()` function. The rest of the code creates a button on the screen that, when clicked, calls the JavaScript function, passes it an address to display, gives the window a name for later reference, and sets a width and a height for the new window.

The corresponding HTML and JavaScript code is as follows:

```
<html>
<head>
<title>externalInterface</title>
<script>
    function openWindow(url, windowName, width, height)
    {
        var myWindow = window.open(url, windowName, "width=" + width + ⏎
            ",height=" + height + ",toolbar=false,address=false");
        myWindow.focus();
    }
</script>
</head>
<body bgcolor="#ffffff">
<object classid="clsid:d27cdb6e-ae6d-11cf-96b8-444553540000" ⏎
    codebase="http://fpdownload.macromedia.com/pub/shockwave/⏎
    cabs/flash/swflash.cab#version=8,0,0,0" width="550" height="400" ⏎
    id="externalInterface" align="middle">
    <param name="allowScriptAccess" value="always" />
    <param name="movie" value="externalInterface.swf" />
    <param name="quality" value="high" />
    <param name="bgcolor" value="#ffffff" />
    <embed src="externalInterface.swf" quality="high" bgcolor="#ffffff" ⏎
```

```
               width="550" height="400" name="externalInterface" align="middle" ⤶
               allowScriptAccess="always" type="application/x-shockwave-flash" ⤶
               pluginspage="http://www.macromedia.com/go/getflashplayer" />
   </object>
   </body>
   </html>
```

The script in bold shows a JavaScript function being defined, along with the four parameters set by the ActionScript `call()` method. The rest of the HTML just provides the standard markup structure and embeds the Flash movie into the page.

Although this HTML shows the `allowScriptAccess` parameter set within the `<object>` and `<embed>` tags, it is not actually needed when calling JavaScript from within the Flash movie. It is needed only when using JavaScript to call ActionScript code.

Setting and Getting Data Using ActionScript

Here's an example that shows how to make use of JavaScript input and return values when calling JavaScript functions from within the Flash movie. First, the ActionScript code looks like the following:

```
   import flash.external.ExternalInterface;

   // Create an input field
   this.createTextField("flashInputField", this.getNextHighestDepth(), ⤶
        10, 10, 100, 20);
   flashInputField.type = "input";
   flashInputField.border = true;

   // Create a button for setting the contents of the HTML form field
   this.createEmptyMovieClip("setFormField", this.getNextHighestDepth());
   setFormField._x = 10;
   setFormField._y = 40;
   setFormField.createTextField("buttonLabel", ⤶
      getInputTextButton.getNextHighestDepth(), 0, 0, 100, 20);
   setFormField.buttonLabel.textColor = 0x0000CC;
   setFormField.buttonLabel.text = "Set Input Field Text";

   setFormField.onRelease = function()
   {
       ExternalInterface.call("setFieldValue", flashInputField.text);
   }

   // Create a button for getting the contents of the HTML form field
   this.createEmptyMovieClip("getFormField", this.getNextHighestDepth());
   getFormField._x = 10;
   getFormField._y = 60;
   getFormField.createTextField("buttonLabel", ⤶
      getInputTextButton.getNextHighestDepth(), 0, 0, 100, 20);
   getFormField.buttonLabel.textColor = 0x0000CC;
   getFormField.buttonLabel.text = "Get Input Field Text";

   getFormField.onRelease = function()
   {
       flashInputField.text = ExternalInterface.call("getFieldValue");
   }
```

Again, most of the ActionScript code is just for laying out the interface. First, an input field is created to allow user-entered data. Next, two buttons are created. One button is to set the HTML text field value based on the value of the Flash text field, and the other button is to retrieve the value of the HTML text field and set the Flash text field to have the same content.

The HTML and JavaScript that makes this work is as follows:

```html
<html>
<head>
<title>externalInterface</title>
<script>
    function getFieldValue()
    {
        return document.forms[0].textField.value;
    }

    function setFieldValue(newValue)
    {
        document.forms[0].textField.value = newValue;
    }
</script>
</head>
<body bgcolor="#ffffff">
<object classid="clsid:d27cdb6e-ae6d-11cf-96b8-444553540000"
    codebase="http://fpdownload.macromedia.com/pub/shockwave/
    cabs/flash/swflash.cab#version=8,0,0,0" width="550" height="400"
    id="externalInterface" align="middle">
    <param name="allowScriptAcess" value="always" />
    <param name="movie" value="externalInterface.swf" />
    <param name="quality" value="high" />
    <param name="bgcolor" value="#ffffff" />
    <embed src="externalInterface.swf" allowscriptAccess="always" quality="high"
bgcolor="#ffffff"
        width="550" height="400" name="externalInterface" align="middle"
        type="application/x-shockwave-flash"
        pluginspage="http://www.macromedia.com/go/getflashplayer" />
</object>
<form>
    <input type="text" name="textField" value="startingValue" />
</form>
</body>
</html>
```

The two JavaScript functions here work no differently from any other JavaScript functions. `setField Value()` simply passes along the string from the Flash player, and `getFieldValue()` returns a string that is passed back into the Flash movie immediately, as if it were just another ActionScript function call.

Try It Out   **Controlling an Embedded Component**

In this exercise you embed a Flash component in an HTML page and then communicate with that component using JavaScript. Figure 24-4 shows what the final result should look like.

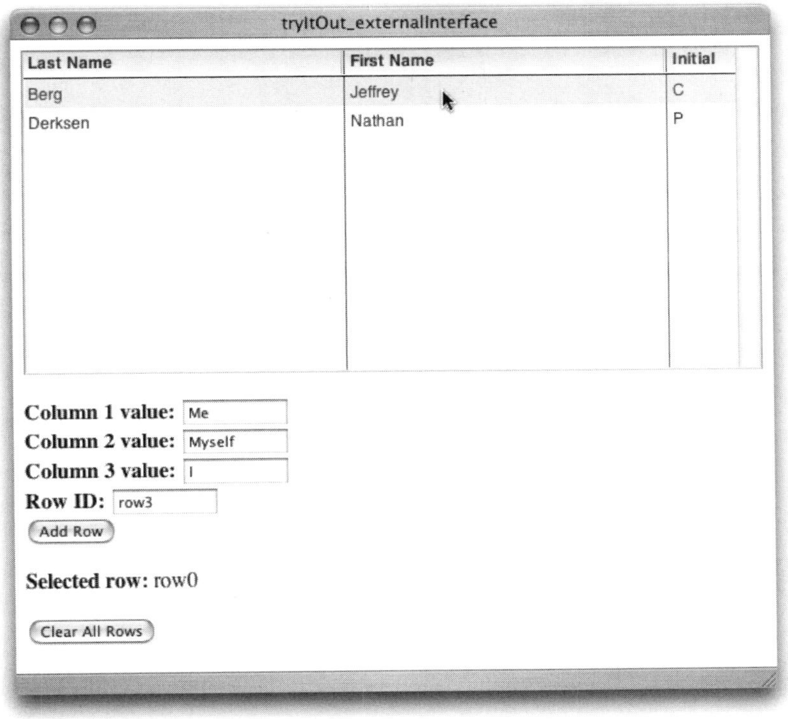

Figure 24-4

1.   Create a new Macromedia Flash document and save it as `tryItOut_externalInterface.fla` in an appropriate directory.

2.   Open the Library panel. Open the User Interface tab of the Components panel and drag the DataGrid component to the middle of the Library panel. (If you are using Flash MX 2004, drag the component onto the stage and then delete it from the stage.)

3.   Click in the keyframe for the layer, open the Actions panel, and enter the following ActionScript code:

```
#include "tryItOut_externalInterface.as"
```

4. Save the file.

5. Create a new ActionScript document, name it `tryItOut_externalInterface.as,` and save it in the directory containing your Flash project file.

6. Enter the following code into the new ActionScript file:

```
import mx.controls.DataGrid;
import flash.external.ExternalInterface;

var g_clickFunction:String = "";

init();

function init() : Void
{
    // Create the data grid
    this.createClassObject(mx.controls.DataGrid, "gridInstance", ⊃
        this.getNextHighestDepth());
    gridInstance.setSize(550, 250);

    // Set up the change handler so that a JavaScript function is called
    // when a row is clicked
    var clickHandlerObject:Object = new Object();
    clickHandlerObject.change = function(eventObject:Object)
    {
        ExternalInterface.call(g_clickFunction, ⊃
        eventObject.target.selectedItem.data);
    }
    gridInstance.addEventListener("change", clickHandlerObject);

    // Register the functions which can be called using JavaScript
    ExternalInterface.addCallback("setColumnLabels", null, setColumnLabels);
    ExternalInterface.addCallback("setColumnWidths", null, setColumnWidths);
    ExternalInterface.addCallback("addRow", null, addRow);
    ExternalInterface.addCallback("setClickHandler", null, setClickHandler);
    ExternalInterface.addCallback("reset", null, reset);

    // Advertise to the calling HTML that the component is ready
    ExternalInterface.call("componentReady", true);
}

function setColumnLabels(columnLabelArray:Array) : Void
{
    for (var i=0; i < columnLabelArray.length; i++)
    {
        gridInstance.addColumn("column" + i);
        gridInstance.getColumnAt(i).headerText = columnLabelArray[i];
    }
}

function setColumnWidths(columnWidthArray:Array) : Void
{
    for (var i=0; i < columnWidthArray.length; i++)
    {
```

```
        gridInstance.getColumnAt(i).width = columnWidthArray[i];
    }
}

function addRow() : Void
{
    var rowObject = new Object();
    for (var i=0; i < arguments.length; i++)
    {
        if (i < arguments.length - 1)
        {
            rowObject["column" + i] = arguments[i];
        }
        else
        {
            rowObject.data = arguments[i];
        }
    }
    gridInstance.addItem(rowObject);
}

function setClickHandler(functionName:String)
{
    g_clickFunction = functionName;
}

function reset() : Void
{
    gridInstance.dataProvider = new Array();
}
```

7. Save the file and publish the project (File➪Publish).

8. Create a new HTML file in your favorite HTML editor or text editor, and enter the following HTML and JavaScript:

```
<html>
<head>
<title>tryItOut_externalInterface</title>
<script type="text/javascript">
function componentReady(isReady)
{
    var flashHandle = document["tryItOut_externalInterface"];
    var columnLabels = ["Last Name", "First Name", "Initial"];
    var columnWidths = [240, 240, 70];

    flashHandle.setColumnLabels(columnLabels);
    flashHandle.setColumnWidths(columnWidths);
    flashHandle.setClickHandler("rowClicked");
    flashHandle.addRow("Derksen", "Nathan", "P", "row0");
    flashHandle.addRow("Jeffrey", "Berg", "C", "row1");
}

function rowClicked(rowID)
{
```

```
        var messageHandle = document.getElementById("selectedRow");
        messageHandle.innerHTML = rowID;
}

function addNewRow()
{
    var flashHandle = document["tryItOut_externalInterface"];
    var col1Value = document.forms[0].col1DataField.value;
    var col2Value = document.forms[0].col2DataField.value;
    var col3Value = document.forms[0].col3DataField.value;
    var rowID = document.forms[0].rowIDField.value;

    flashHandle.addRow(col1Value, col2Value, col3Value, rowID);
}

function deleteRows()
{
    var flashHandle = document["tryItOut_externalInterface"];
    flashHandle.reset();
}
</script>
</head>
<body bgcolor="#ffffff">
<object classid="clsid:d27cdb6e-ae6d-11cf-96b8-444553540000"
codebase="http://fpdownload.macromedia.com/pub/shockwave/
    cabs/flash/swflash.cab#version=8,0,0,0" width="550" height="250"
    id="tryItOut_externalInterface" align="middle">
    <param name="allowScriptAccess" value="always" />
    <param name="movie" value="tryItOut_externalInterface.swf" />
    <param name="quality" value="high" />
    <param name="bgcolor" value="#ffffff" />
    <embed src="tryItOut_externalInterface.swf" quality="high"
        bgcolor="#ffffff" width="550" height="250"
        name="tryItOut_externalInterface" align="middle"
        allowScriptAccess="always" type="application/x-shockwave-flash"
        pluginspage="http://www.macromedia.com/go/getflashplayer" />
</object><br />
<br />
<form>
    <b>Column 1 value:</b>
    <input type="text" name="col1DataField" value="Me" size="10" /><br />
    <b>Column 2 value:</b>
    <input type="text" name="col2DataField" value="Myself" size="10" /><br />
    <b>Column 3 value:</b>
    <input type="text" name="col3DataField" value="I" size="10" /><br />
    <b>Row ID:</b>
    <input type="text" name="rowIDField" value="row3" size="10" /><br />
    <input type="button" value="Add Row" onclick="addNewRow();" /><br />
    <br />
    <b>Selected row:</b> <span id="selectedRow"></span><br />
    <br />
    <input type="button" value="Clear All Rows" onclick="deleteRows();" />
</form>
</body>
</html>
```

9. Save the file and then open it within your web browser. Play with the table by clicking existing rows, adding new rows, and clearing the table.

How It Works

A large amount of the code and markup in this exercise is not actually directly involved in the process of communicating between the HTML page and the Flash movie. This is a good thing, because previously a significant amount of JavaScript and ActionScript was needed to pass data into an already running Flash movie. Having direct access between the two scripting environments means that the code is more focused on what is being communicated rather than how it is being communicated.

The first step involves a bit of startup code:

```
import mx.controls.DataGrid;
import flash.external.ExternalInterface;

var g_clickFunction:String = "";

init();
```

The import statements allow you to refer to the DataGrid component and the ExternalInterface class in a shorthand manner. A timeline variable is declared for keeping track of what JavaScript function to call when a data grid row is selected. Next, the initialization function is called. Within the `init()` function, a data grid is placed on the stage and is resized:

```
// Create the data grid
this.createClassObject(mx.controls.DataGrid, "gridInstance", ⊃
    this.getNextHighestDepth());
gridInstance.setSize(550, 250);
```

An event listener is set up to respond to the user clicking a data grid row. When it fires, it calls a JavaScript row handler function and passes the ID for the selected row to that function:

```
// Set up the change handler so that a JavaScript function is called
// when a row is clicked
var clickHandlerObject:Object = new Object();
clickHandlerObject.change = function(eventObject:Object)
{
    ExternalInterface.call(g_clickFunction, ⊃
    eventObject.target.selectedItem.data);
}
gridInstance.addEventListener("change", clickHandlerObject);
```

By default, no ActionScript functions or methods can be called by JavaScript unless told otherwise. Registering the functions makes them available for external access:

```
// Register the functions which can be called using JavaScript
ExternalInterface.addCallback("setColumnLabels", null, setColumnLabels);
ExternalInterface.addCallback("setColumnWidths", null, setColumnWidths);
ExternalInterface.addCallback("addRow", null, addRow);
ExternalInterface.addCallback("setClickHandler", null, setClickHandler);
ExternalInterface.addCallback("reset", null, reset);
```

The JavaScript code is going to need to pass in some startup parameters; however, the Flash movie is going to be ready after the HTML has all loaded, so any attempts at calling any ActionScript functions will fail. As a result, notify the container HTML that the component is ready to receive calls from JavaScript by calling a `componentReady()` JavaScript function. This is a custom function that will be shown shortly:

```
// Advertise to the calling HTML that the component is ready
ExternalInterface.call("componentReady", true);
```

That is it for the initialization ActionScript. The rest of the ActionScript defines the functions that are to be accessible externally.

The `setColumnLabels()` function allows the number of columns to be declared and labels to be defined for each column:

```
function setColumnLabels(columnLabelArray:Array) : Void
{
    for (var i=0; i < columnLabelArray.length; i++)
    {
        gridInstance.addColumn("column" + i);
        gridInstance.getColumnAt(i).headerText = columnLabelArray[i];
    }
}
```

The `setColumnWidths()` function does exactly what the name describes:

```
function setColumnWidths(columnWidthArray:Array) : Void
{
    for (var i=0; i < columnWidthArray.length; i++)
    {
        gridInstance.getColumnAt(i).width = columnWidthArray[i];
    }
}
```

The `addRow()` function allows for a row full of data to be added to the list. It expects one parameter to be passed in for each column and then one more for a row ID. A row ID is typically needed to provide a value that can uniquely identify the row when selected. The number of columns is not fixed, so the arguments array is used to allow for a varying number of arguments to be passed in. The function loops through each argument passed in and then constructs a custom object that the `DataGrid.addItem()` method expects:

```
function addRow() : Void
{
    var rowObject = new Object();
    for (var i=0; i < arguments.length; i++)
    {
        if (i < arguments.length - 1)
        {
            rowObject["column" + i] = arguments[i];
        }
        else
        {
            rowObject.data = arguments[i];
        }
    }
```

```
        }
        gridInstance.addItem(rowObject);
    }
```

The `setClickHandler()` function sets the name of the JavaScript function to be called every time the user clicks a row:

```
function setClickHandler(functionName:String)
{
    g_clickFunction = functionName;
}
```

The `reset()` function clears out the data for each row:

```
function reset() : Void
{
    gridInstance.dataProvider = new Array();
}
```

That is it for the ActionScript. Next take a look at the JavaScript.

First comes the `componentReady()` function. This is the code that is called by the Flash movie after it has loaded to indicate it is ready. This is where initialization of the component happens. First, a handle to the Flash movie is obtained. This is what lets you access the ActionScript functions. Next, the column labels are assigned, column widths are defined, and the name of the function that will respond to row clicks is passed. Finally, a couple rows of data are added:

```
function componentReady(isReady)
{
    var flashHandle = document["tryItOut_externalInterface"];
    var columnLabels = ["Last Name", "First Name", "Initial"];
    var columnWidths = [240, 240, 70];

    flashHandle.setColumnLabels(columnLabels);
    flashHandle.setColumnWidths(columnWidths);
    flashHandle.setClickHandler("rowClicked");
    flashHandle.addRow("Derksen", "Nathan", "P", "row0");
    flashHandle.addRow("Jeffrey", "Berg", "C", "row1");
}
```

The function that responds to the data grid change event is passed the ID of the row that the user clicked, which is then placed between a pair of <span> tags for visual feedback:

```
function rowClicked(rowID)
{
    var messageHandle = document.getElementById("selectedRow");
    messageHandle.innerHTML = rowID;
}
```

The `addNewRow()` function is called by the Add Row button. It passes the contents of the four text fields to the `addRow()` ActionScript method. The first three text fields correspond to the three columns shown, and the fourth text field sets the ID to be shown when the new row is clicked:

```
function addNewRow()
{
    var flashHandle = document["tryItOut_externalInterface"];
    var col1Value = document.forms[0].col1DataField.value;
    var col2Value = document.forms[0].col2DataField.value;
    var col3Value = document.forms[0].col3DataField.value;
    var rowID = document.forms[0].rowIDField.value;

    flashHandle.addRow(col1Value, col2Value, col3Value, rowID);
}
```

The deleteRows() function calls the ActionScript reset() function to clear out all of the rows of data:

```
function deleteRows()
{
    var flashHandle = document["tryItOut_externalInterface"];
    flashHandle.reset();
}
```

Now take a look at the HTML.

The Flash movie is embedded into the page as usual. The allowScriptAccess parameter is included in both the <object> and the <embed> tags. Without this, JavaScript functions will not be allowed access to call the ActionScript methods:

```
<object classid="clsid:d27cdb6e-ae6d-11cf-96b8-444553540000"
codebase="http://fpdownload.macromedia.com/pub/shockwave/
    cabs/flash/swflash.cab#version=8,0,0,0" width="550" height="250"
    id="tryItOut_externalInterface" align="middle">
    <param name="allowScriptAccess" value="always" />
    <param name="movie" value="tryItOut_externalInterface.swf" />
    <param name="quality" value="high" />
    <param name="bgcolor" value="#ffffff" />
    <embed src="tryItOut_externalInterface.swf" quality="high"
        bgcolor="#ffffff" width="550" height="250"
        name="tryItOut_externalInterface" align="middle"
        allowScriptAccess="always" type="application/x-shockwave-flash"
        pluginspage="http://www.macromedia.com/go/getflashplayer" />
</object>
```

The HTML includes form elements to initiate the JavaScript functions. The first set provides text fields for entering column data and a button for triggering the add row call:

```
<b>Column 1 value:</b>
<input type="text" name="col1DataField" value="Me" size="10" /><br />
<b>Column 2 value:</b>
<input type="text" name="col2DataField" value="Myself" size="10" /><br />
<b>Column 3 value:</b>
<input type="text" name="col3DataField" value="I" size="10" /><br />
<b>Row ID:</b>
<input type="text" name="rowIDField" value="row3" size="10" /><br />
<input type="button" value="Add Row" onclick="addNewRow();" /><br />
```

The pair of span tags provides a placeholder for placing the ID of the selected row:

```
<b>Selected row:</b> <span id="selectedRow"></span><br />
```

Finally, a button allows for the user to trigger the delete row call:

```
<input type="button" value="Clear All Rows" onclick="deleteRows();" />
```

Opening Browser Windows

One question that pops up frequently in the forums is how to open browser windows from a Flash movie. A couple of ways exist to do this. One is to use the getURL() function; the other is to use the ExternalInterface class. Functionally, for the purposes of window management, either technique works well.

When you try out the following examples, do not forget to disable any pop-up blockers that you have set. Many of these also block pop-up windows that originate from Flash content.

> Many developers place whole sites in full-screen pop-up windows in an attempt to showcase their site in the most aesthetically pleasing way possible. Do not yield to this temptation. If you really need to place a site in a pop-up window, give users a choice and inform them that clicking the link will launch a new window. Keep in mind that full-screen windows containing Flash movies not only annoy users, but they also run more slowly.

Using getURL() to Create Pop-Up Windows

The basic way to create a new pop-up window using getURL() is the following line of ActionScript code:

```
getURL("javascript:var windowHnd = window.open('http://www.macromedia.com/',
    'newWindow', 'toolbar=no,address=no');");
```

The syntax is a bit messy, so let's go through this piece-by-piece. The getURL() function just passes to the browser whatever URL you would normally type in the address bar. A URL is usually preceded by http: or by ftp:, which are *protocol identifiers* that tell the browser how to treat what comes after the identifier. Here you use the protocol identifier javascript:, which tells the browser that it's not really a URL being typed, but a script.

Everything that comes next is actual JavaScript. The window.open() method is called and is passed three parameters. The first is the URL to display in the new window, next is a name for the window so that later calls can reuse the same window, and finally a comma-separated list of window features is passed. The script var windowHnd = is there to deal with an issue where the value being returned from the window.open() method can actually cause the page to disappear. Saving the returned value to a temporary variable, even though that variable is never used, prevents the returned window handle from propagating up to the browser window.

Modify the `getURL()` script to make it a bit easier to work with:

```
var destinationURL:String = "http://www.macromedia.com/";
var windowName:String = "myWindow";
var windowFeatures:String = "toolbar=no,address=no";

getURL("javascript:var windowHnd = window.open('" + destinationURL + "','" + ⤸
    windowName + "','" + windowFeatures + "');");
```

Now when you make changes to the destination URL, window name, or window features, there is less of a chance of accidentally introducing an error into the convoluted `getURL()` syntax because you will no longer have to touch the last line.

Use ExternalInterface to Create Pop-Up Windows

The other technique to create pop-up windows is to use the ExternalInterface class. Here's how it works:

```
import flash.external.ExternalInterface;
ExternalInterface.call("window.open", "http://www.macromedia.com", "myWindow", ⤸
    "toolbar=no,address=no");
```

Hopefully, you can see that this technique results in cleaner code. You can pull the values into their own variables to clean it up a bit more:

```
import flash.external.ExternalInterface;

var destinationURL:String = "http://www.macromedia.com/";
var windowName:String = "myWindow";
var windowFeatures:String = "toolbar=no,address=no";

ExternalInterface.call("window.open", destinationURL, windowName, windowFeatures);
```

Although this is, in fact, cleaner code, any projects you develop that require a version of the Flash player prior to version 8 will still need to use the `getURL()` technique.

Calling a JavaScript Wrapper Function

So far, you have been doing all the work in creating the pop-up windows directly within the `call()` method or the `getURL()` function. This is very convenient; however, occasionally there is a need to work with the browser window after it has opened, such as to reposition it or to close it. When this is the case, a means is needed to keep a reference to the opened window. This is done by a JavaScript wrapper function that calls the `window.open()` method and saves a handle for later use:

ActionScript
```
import flash.external.ExternalInterface;

var destinationURL:String = "http://www.macromedia.com/";
var windowName:String = "myWindow";
var windowFeatures:String = "toolbar=no,address=no";

ExternalInterface.call("openWindow", destinationURL, windowName, windowFeatures);
// Or
```

```
// getURL("javascript:openWindow('" + destinationURL + "','" + windowName + ⟲
    "','" + windowFeatures + "');");
```

JavaScript
```
var windowHandle = null;
function openWindow(destinationURL, windowName, windowFeatures)
{
    windowHandle = window.open(destinationURL, windowName, windowFeatures);
    windowHandle.focus();
}
```

The way to close a window that has already been opened is simply as follows:

ActionScript
```
import flash.external.ExternalInterface;
ExternalInterface.call("closeWindow");
// Or
// getURL("javascript:closeWindow();");
```

JavaScript
```
function closeWindow()
{
    windowHandle.close();
}
```

A reference to the opened window is kept as a global variable, so the `closeWindow()` function just needs to retrieve that window reference and call the window's `close()` method.

Defining Browser Window Parameters

You can customize the appearance of a new browser window in a number of ways. These customizations are set in the list of features sent to the `window.open()` JavaScript method. Features that are explicitly defined in that list override the default browser behavior. Not all features need to be defined: anything not specified in the feature list will take on the browser's default setting.

The following table describes the customization features you can use:

Feature	Possible Values	Description
status	yes|no|1|0	Sets the visibility of the bottom status bar.
toolbar	yes|no|1|0	Sets the visibility of the standard toolbar.
location	yes|no|1|0	Sets the visibility of the address bar.
menubar	yes|no|1|0	Sets the visibility of the menu bar. Has no effect with MacOS.
directories	yes|no|1|0	Sets the visibility of the directories bar, for those browsers who have such a bar for add-on quick links.
resizable	yes|no|1|0	Sets whether the browser window is user-resizable.

Table continued on following page

Feature	Possible Values	Description
scrollbars	yes|no|1|0	Sets whether to show the scroll bars. If set to false, even if the content area exceeds the size of the window, no scroll bars will be visible.
height	Any number greater than 100	Sets the height of the window. The window height is defined as the height of the content area, not including the title bar.
width	Any number greater than 100	Sets the width of the window.
top	Any number	Sets the starting y position of the window, where 0 is the top edge of the screen. On MacOS, the menu bar at the top of the screen is 24 pixels high, and any value of top that attempts to go higher will instead snap to the bottom of the menu bar.
left	Any number	Sets the starting x position of the window, where 0 is the left edge of the screen.

Here's an example that creates a window with the default width and height, with no toolbar or location bar, but with the status bar visible:

```
import flash.external.ExternalInterface;

var destinationURL:String = "http://www.apple.com/";
var windowName:String = "myWindow";
var windowFeatures:String = "toolbar=no,location=no,status=yes";

ExternalInterface.call("window.open", destinationURL, windowName, windowFeatures);
```

The equivalent code using getURL() instead is almost the same:

```
var destinationURL:String = "http://www.apple.com/";
var windowName:String = "myWindow";
var windowFeatures:String = "toolbar=no,location=no,status=yes";

getURL("javascript:var windowHnd = window.open('" + destinationURL + "','" +
    windowName + "','" + windowFeatures + "');");
```

Add to it, so that you set the width and height as well as the top and left positions:

```
import flash.external.ExternalInterface;

var destinationURL:String = "http://www.apple.com/";
var windowName:String = "myWindow";
var windowFeatures:String = "toolbar=no,location=no,status=yes,
                             width=750,height=500,top=50,left=50";

ExternalInterface.call("window.open", destinationURL, windowName, windowFeatures);
```

Now get the screen resolution and center the new window on the screen:

```
import flash.external.ExternalInterface;

var screenWidth:Number = System.capabilities.screenResolutionX;
var screenHeight:Number = System.capabilities.screenResolutionY;
var windowWidth:Number = 800;
var windowHeight:Number = 500;
var leftPosition:Number = screenWidth / 2 - windowWidth / 2;
var topPosition:Number = screenHeight / 2 - windowHeight / 2;

var destinationURL:String = "http://www.macromedia.com/";
var windowName:String = "myWindow";
var windowFeatures:String = "toolbar=no,location=no,status=yes";
windowFeatures += ",width=" + windowWidth + ",height=" + windowHeight
windowFeatures += ",left=" + leftPosition + ",top=" + topPosition

ExternalInterface.call("window.open", destinationURL, windowName, windowFeatures);
```

Try It Out   Create a Pop-Up Window Launcher

In this exercise, you see firsthand how the various techniques for opening windows work. You interact with a small Flash application that enables you to experiment with different pop-up window settings. Figure 24-5 shows what the window opener application looks like in use.

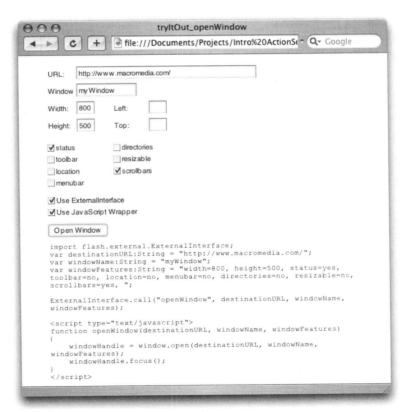

Figure 24-5

1. Within your browser of choice, open `tryItOut_openWindow.html`, the window creator application, at <downloaded source root>/Chapter 24/.

2. Make sure that your browser has its pop-up blocker, if any, disabled.

3. Select the status and the scroll bars options. Take a look at the ActionScript that shows up below the Open Window button. Click the Open Window button.

4. Close the new window. Select the Use ExternalInterface checkbox. Take a look at the change in the ActionScript.

5. Create a new Macromedia Flash document and copy the ActionScript generated by the window launcher application into the Actions panel.

6. Name the file `tryItOut_openWindowTest.fla` and save it in a convenient location. Publish the file (File⇨Publish).

7. Create a new browser window, find the HTML file that was just created during the publish process, and open it in the new window. A second window opens.

8. Close the new window, return to the window launcher application, and click the Use JavaScript Wrapper button.

9. Copy the ActionScript generated by the window launcher application into the Actions panel for `tryItOut_openWindowTest.fla`. The copied code should not include the `<script>` tag and its contents. Save the file and publish again.

10. Return to the launcher application, and copy the `<script>` tags and all of the script between them.

11. Open `tryItOut_openWindowTest.html` in your preferred HTML or text editor. Paste the copied code between `<head>` tags and save the file.

12. Open `tryItOut_openWindowTest.html` in a browser window. A second window opens.

How It Works

The Flash window launching application generates ActionScript and JavaScript code to match the techniques shown in the rest of this section. The text fields and checkboxes up to but not including the Use ExternalInterface checkbox enable you to specify various window properties and features. Experiment with these to get the kind of window that you want.

The Use ExternalInterface checkbox toggles between the ExternalInterface technique and the `getURL()` technique. The Use JavaScript Wrapper causes a JavaScript function located within the HTML to be called instead.

When any of these properties and features changes, the code listing changes to reflect the technique. Simply copy and paste the code into your working Flash file as well as your working HTML file if appropriate.

Summary

This chapter spent considerable time with the security issues with Flash and how to work with them, keeping your applications, servers, and data safe.

Exercise

1. Write some ActionScript and JavaScript code that will open a window. It should provide ActionScript functions for giving focus back to an already open window and for loading a new URL into an already open window.

Uploading and Downloading Files

A long-time bane for Flash applications has been the lack of capability to control file uploads and downloads. File uploads were generally performed using a pop-up web page that presented a standard HTML file upload component. Unfortunately, there was no easy way of informing the Flash movie when the upload had completed, progress could not be given, and it offered little control over the process. The main technique for downloading was to use getURL() to invoke the browser's default file handling behavior for whichever file was to be downloaded. Once again, progress could not be shown, and overall control of the file was handed over to the browser.

Flash 8 introduces the FileReference class, which provides greater control over file uploads and downloads. The class makes use of file open and file save dialog boxes that are native to the operating system. It also provides access to progress and error events, so that better feedback can be given to the user.

FileReference Class Methods

The FileReference class has four methods, which are introduced in the following table:

Method	Returns	Description
browse	A Boolean	Prompts the user to select a file to upload.
cancel	Nothing	Cancels any upload or download operation currently in progress.
download	A Boolean	Prompts the user to select a target folder for the file to be downloaded.
upload	A Boolean	Starts the upload of a user-selected file to the server.

The following sections show you how to use these methods.

Using browse()

The `browse()` method brings up a dialog box to allow the user to choose a file. It is used in conjunction with the `onSelect()` event and the `upload()` method.

This method takes one parameter, which is an array of objects describing the file types to allow for upload. The general form is as follows:

```
fileRef.browse(fileTypes);
```

A sample implementation might look like the following:

```
import flash.net.FileReference;

var fileTypes:Array = new Array();
var allTypes:Object = new Object();
allTypes.description = "All Types";
allTypes.extension = "*.*";
fileTypes.push(allTypes);

var fileRefListener:Object = new Object();
fileRefListener.onSelect = function(file:FileReference):Void
{
    trace("File selected: " + file.name);
    var uploadSuccess:Boolean = ⤸
        file.upload("http://www.yourdomain.com/yourUploadHandlerScript.cfm");
    if(uploadSuccess = false)
    {
        trace("The upload failed.");
    }
}

var fileRef:FileReference = new FileReference();
fileRef.addListener(fileRefListener);
fileRef.browse(fileTypes);
```

This functionality needs a server-side upload script to perform the actual upload. A variety of scripts are available for specific server technologies. The next Try It Out exercise shows one example upload script.

Using cancel()

The `cancel()` method aborts the upload or download of the referenced file. It enables you to provide the user with a cancel button that will stop the operation. The method takes no parameters.

Here's its syntax:

```
fileRef.cancel();
```

Using download()

The download() method brings up a dialog box to enable the user to choose a file for download. The file to be downloaded can be any file on any server, not just the local server.

The method takes either one or two parameters. The first is the URL for the file to be downloaded. The optional second parameter is the default filename to place in the filename field in the Save File dialog box. If this parameter is omitted, the actual name of the file being downloaded is used.

Here's the syntax for download():

```
fileRef.browse(fileURL:String, [defaultFileName:String]);
```

A sample implementation might look like the following:

```
import flash.net.FileReference;

var fileRefListener:Object = new Object();
fileRefListener.onComplete = function(file:FileReference)
{
    trace("onComplete : " + file.name);
}

var url:String =
"http://www.macromedia.com/platform/whitepapers/platform_overview.pdf";
var fileRef:FileReference = new FileReference();
fileRef.addListener(fileRefListener);
fileRef.download(url);
```

Using upload()

The upload() method starts the upload of the referenced file. It requires that the browse() method be called beforehand to enable the user to select a file.

The method takes one parameter, which is the URL to a server script to handle the actual upload. The script to be used depends on the server technology being used. Some languages that may be used to implement such a script include PHP, Perl, Java, or ColdFusion.

```
fileRef.upload(uploadScriptURL:String);
```

A sample implementation might look like the following:

```
import flash.net.FileReference;

var fileTypes:Array = new Array();
var allTypes:Object = new Object();
allTypes.description = "All Types";
allTypes.extension = "*.*";
fileTypes.push(allTypes);

var fileRefListener:Object = new Object();
```

```
fileRefListener.onSelect = function(file:FileReference):Void
{
    trace("File selected: " + file.name);
    var uploadSuccess:Boolean = ⤶
        file.upload("http://www.yourdomain.com/yourUploadHandlerScript.cfm");
    if(uploadSuccess = false)
    {
        trace("The upload failed.");
    }
}

var fileRef:FileReference = new FileReference();
fileRef.addListener(fileRefListener);
fileRef.browse(fileTypes);
```

FileReference Class Properties

The FileReference class has several properties that you can use. They're described in the following table:

Event	Type	Description
creationDate	Date	The creation date of the local file.
creator	String	The creator type of the file, if the file was created on a Macintosh.
modificationDate	Date	The date and time when the local file was last modified.
name	String	The name of the local file.
size	Number	The size of the local file.
type	String	The file type.

The FileReference class also has a number of events. The following table describes them:

Event	Type	Description
onCancel	Listener	Invoked when the user cancels the file browse dialog box.
onComplete	Listener	Invoked when the file upload or the file download has completed.
onHTTPError	Listener	Invoked when there is a network communication error that halts the file upload.
onIOError	Listener	Invoked when a disk error occurs.
onOpen	Listener	Invoked when the upload or download process has begun.
onProgress	Listener	Invoked on regular intervals during the upload or download process.

Event	Type	Description
onSecurityError	Listener	Invoked when the upload or download fails because of a security issue.
onSelect	Listener	Invoked when the user has selected a file for upload or a directory for download from the file browse dialog box.

Downloading Files

The simplest code that can be used to initiate a file download to the user's own machine is the following:

```
import flash.net.FileReference;
var url:String = ⊃
    "http://www.macromedia.com/platform/whitepapers/platform_overview.pdf";
var fileRef:FileReference = new FileReference();
fileRef.download(url);
```

This prompts the user to select a download directory and then performs the download. It works but provides no feedback. You can make use of some of the available events to do more. Here's an example:

```
import flash.net.FileReference;

var fileRefListener:Object = new Object();
fileRefListener.onOpen = function(file:FileReference)
{
    trace("Starting file download: " + file.name);
}

fileRefListener.onProgress = function(file:FileReference, bytesLoaded:Number, ⊃
    bytesTotal:Number)
{
    trace("percentComplete: " + (100 * bytesLoaded / bytesTotal));
}

fileRefListener.onComplete = function(file:FileReference)
{
    trace("Download complete : " + file.name);
}

var url:String = ⊃
    "http://www.macromedia.com/platform/whitepapers/platform_overview.pdf";
var fileRef:FileReference = new FileReference();
fileRef.addListener(fileRefListener);
fileRef.download(url);
```

You work with a file download project in the following Try It Out.

Try It Out   **Downloading Files**

In this exercise, you work with the FileReference class for downloading files and learn how to integrate it with the progress bar component to provide download feedback.

1. Create a new Macromedia Flash document.

2. Click the first frame in the timeline, open the Actions panel (Window⇨Development Panels⇨Actions), and type the following ActionScript code:

```
#include "tryItOut_downloadFiles.as"
```

3. Open the User Interface section of the Components panel and open the Library panel. Drag the Button, Label, TextInput, and ProgressBar components to the Library panel.

4. Select File⇨Save As, name the file tryItOut_downloadFiles.fla, choose an appropriate directory, and save it.

5. Create a new Macromedia Flash document by selecting File⇨New and choosing ActionScript File from the New Document panel.

6. Save it as tryItOut_downloadFiles.as in the directory containing the Flash project file.

7. Type the following code into the new ActionScript file:

```
import mx.controls.Button;
import mx.controls.Label;
import mx.controls.TextInput;
import mx.controls.ProgressBar;
import flash.net.FileReference;

var eventHandler:Object = new Object();
var fileRefListener:Object = new Object();
var fileRef:FileReference = new FileReference();

setupInterface();

function setupInterface()
{
    this.createClassObject(Label, "urlLabel", this.getNextHighestDepth(), ⤵
        {_x:10, _y:13});
    urlLabel.text = "URL:";

    this.createClassObject(TextInput, "urlInput", this.getNextHighestDepth(), ⤵
        {_x:60, _y:10, _width:450});
    urlInput.text = ⤵
        "http://www.macromedia.com/platform/whitepapers/platform_overview.pdf";

    this.createClassObject(Button, "openWindowButton", ⤵
        this.getNextHighestDepth(), {_x:10, _y:50});
    openWindowButton.label = "Download";
    openWindowButton.addEventListener("click", eventHandler);

    this.createClassObject(ProgressBar, "fileTransferProgressBar", ⤵
        this.getNextHighestDepth());
    fileTransferProgressBar._x = 120;
    fileTransferProgressBar._y = 50;
    fileTransferProgressBar.mode = "manual";
    fileTransferProgressBar.label = "Downloaded %3%%";
    fileTransferProgressBar._visible = false;

    this.createTextField("feedbackField", this.getNextHighestDepth(), ⤵
```

```
                10, 80, 400, 30);
    }

    fileRefListener.onOpen = function(file:FileReference)
    {
        feedbackField.text = "Starting file download.";
        fileTransferProgressBar._visible = true;
    }

    fileRefListener.onProgress = function(file:FileReference, bytesLoaded:Number, ⤴
        bytesTotal:Number)
    {
        feedbackField.text = "Download in progress.";
        fileTransferProgressBar.setProgress(bytesLoaded, bytesTotal);
    }

    fileRefListener.onComplete = function(file:FileReference)
    {
        feedbackField.text = "Download complete.";
        fileTransferProgressBar._visible = false;
    }

    fileRefListener.onIOError = function (file:FileReference)
    {
        feedbackField.text = "Download failed - disk error.";
        fileTransferProgressBar._visible = false;
    }

    fileRefListener.onSecurityError = function (file:FileReference)
    {
        feedbackField.text = "Download failed - security/permissions error.";
        fileTransferProgressBar._visible = false;
    }

    eventHandler.click = function()
    {
        fileRef.addListener(fileRefListener);
        fileRef.download(urlInput.text);
    }
```

8. Save the file, return to the Macromedia Flash project file, and select Control⇨Test Movie.

How It Works

First, the relevant classes are imported, to make referring to component names and class names a bit easier:

```
import mx.controls.Button;
import mx.controls.Label;
import mx.controls.TextInput;
import mx.controls.ProgressBar;
import flash.net.FileReference;
```

Next, a few variables are declared. Even though you can download multiple files, you only need one instance of the FileReference class. If you wanted to be able to download several files at once, you would need one instance for each simultaneous connection:

```
var eventHandler:Object = new Object();
var fileRefListener:Object = new Object();
var fileRef:FileReference = new FileReference();
```

The user interface is set up, which involves placing the Label, TextInput, Button, and ProgressBar components on the stage:

```
setupInterface();

function setupInterface()
{
    this.createClassObject(Label, "urlLabel", this.getNextHighestDepth(), ⤸
        {_x:10, _y:13});
    urlLabel.text = "URL:";

    this.createClassObject(TextInput, "urlInput", this.getNextHighestDepth(), ⤸
        {_x:60, _y:10, _width:450});
    urlInput.text = ⤸
        "http://www.macromedia.com/platform/whitepapers/platform_overview.pdf";

    this.createClassObject(Button, "openWindowButton", ⤸
        this.getNextHighestDepth(), {_x:10, _y:50});
    openWindowButton.label = "Download";
    openWindowButton.addEventListener("click", eventHandler);

    this.createClassObject(ProgressBar, "fileTransferProgressBar", ⤸
        this.getNextHighestDepth());
    fileTransferProgressBar._x = 120;
    fileTransferProgressBar._y = 50;
    fileTransferProgressBar.mode = "manual";
    fileTransferProgressBar.label = "Downloaded %3%%";
    fileTransferProgressBar._visible = false;

    this.createTextField("feedbackField", this.getNextHighestDepth(), ⤸
        10, 80, 400, 30);
}
```

Next, you define event handlers for the FileReference instance. The onOpen event is a good place for startup code:

```
fileRefListener.onOpen = function(file:FileReference)
{
    feedbackField.text = "Starting file download.";
    fileTransferProgressBar._visible = true;
}
```

The onProgress event passes on the bytes loaded and total bytes information to the progress bar:

```
fileRefListener.onProgress = function(file:FileReference, bytesLoaded:Number, ⤸
    bytesTotal:Number)
{
    feedbackField.text = "Download in progress.";
    fileTransferProgressBar.setProgress(bytesLoaded, bytesTotal);
}
```

The `onComplete` event hides the progress bar:

```
fileRefListener.onComplete = function(file:FileReference)
{
    feedbackField.text = "Download complete.";
    fileTransferProgressBar._visible = false;
}
```

The error events are captured in case there is a download issue. There is no `onHTTPError` event handler defined because for file downloads, network errors only generate an `onIOError` event:

```
fileRefListener.onIOError = function (file:FileReference)
{
    feedbackField.text = "Download failed - disk error.";
    fileTransferProgressBar._visible = false;
}

fileRefListener.onSecurityError = function (file:FileReference)
{
    feedbackField.text = "Download failed - security/permissions error.";
    fileTransferProgressBar._visible = false;
}
```

Finally, the event handler for the button is defined, which actually initiates the download process:

```
eventHandler.click = function()
{
    fileRef.addListener(fileRefListener);
    fileRef.download(urlInput.text);
}
```

Uploading Files

Uploading files is only a bit more work than downloading files. The main difference is the need for a server-side upload script to handle the actual uploading. Flash cannot do that part because it loads on the user's machine, whereas the file upload capability requires write access to the server. What Flash provides is the packaging mechanism so that the file to be uploaded is sent to the server in a standardized format that any file upload script can handle.

Here's the base ActionScript code needed to make this work:

```
import flash.net.FileReference;

var fileTypes:Array = new Array();
var allTypes:Object = new Object();
allTypes.description = "All Types";
allTypes.extension = "*.*";
fileTypes.push(allTypes);

var fileRefListener:Object = new Object();
```

```
fileRefListener.onSelect = function(file:FileReference):Void
{
    trace("File selected: " + file.name);
    var uploadSuccess:Boolean = ⊃
        file.upload("http://www.yourdomain.com/yourUploadHandlerScript.cfm");
    if(uploadSuccess = false)
    {
        trace("The upload failed.");
    }
}

var fileRef:FileReference = new FileReference();
fileRef.addListener(fileRefListener);
fileRef.browse(fileTypes);
```

Starting from the top, a list of file types that the user can choose from is provided. In this case the user can choose any file type. The file type list is an array of objects where each object is in the format

```
{description:"<User viewable description>", extension:"*.png; *.gif; *.jpg"}
```

Next, the onSelect() event is defined. This event is triggered only after the user has selected a file and is the proper place to put the upload() method.

Finally, a FileReference instance is created, is bound to the event listener, and the browse() method is called to bring up the file browser dialog box.

Try It Out   Upload Files

In this exercise, you work with the FileReference class to upload files and learn how to integrate it with the progress bar component to provide upload feedback.

1. Create a new Macromedia Flash document.

2. Click the first frame in the timeline, open the Actions panel, and type the following ActionScript code:

```
#include "tryItOut_uploadFiles.as"
```

3. Open the User Interface section of the Components panel and open the Library panel. Drag the Button and ProgressBar components to the Library panel.

4. Select File⇨Save As, name the file tryItOut_uploadFiles.fla, choose an appropriate directory, and save it.

5. Create a new Macromedia Flash document by selecting File⇨New and choosing ActionScript File from the New Document panel.

6. Save the file as tryItOut_uploadFiles.as in the directory containing the Flash project file.

7. Type the following code into the new ActionScript file:

```
import mx.controls.Button;
import mx.controls.ProgressBar;
```

```
import flash.net.FileReference;

var eventHandler:Object = new Object();
var fileRefListener:Object = new Object();
var fileRef:FileReference = new FileReference();

var fileTypes:Array = new Array();

var imageTypes:Object = new Object();
imageTypes.description = "Images (*.jpg, *.jpeg, *.gif, *.png)";
imageTypes.extension = "*.jpg; *.jpeg; *.gif; *.png";
fileTypes.push(imageTypes);

var htmlTypes:Object = new Object();
htmlTypes.description = "HTML (*.html, *.htm)";
htmlTypes.extension = "*.html; *.png";
fileTypes.push(htmlTypes);

setupInterface();

function setupInterface()
{
    this.createClassObject(Button, "openWindowButton", ⏎
        this.getNextHighestDepth(), {_x:10, _y:20});
    openWindowButton.label = "Upload";
    openWindowButton.addEventListener("click", eventHandler);

    this.createClassObject(ProgressBar, "fileTransferProgressBar", ⏎
        this.getNextHighestDepth());
    fileTransferProgressBar._x = 120;
    fileTransferProgressBar._y = 20;
    fileTransferProgressBar.mode = "manual";
    fileTransferProgressBar.label = "Uploaded %3%%";
    fileTransferProgressBar._visible = false;

    this.createTextField("feedbackField", this.getNextHighestDepth(), ⏎
        10, 50, 400, 30);
}

fileRefListener.onSelect = function(file:FileReference)
{
    feedbackField.text = "File selected: " + file.name;
    file.upload("http://www.yourdomain.com/yourUploadHandlerScript.cfm")
}

fileRefListener.onOpen = function(file:FileReference)
{
    feedbackField.text = "Starting file upload.";
    fileTransferProgressBar._visible = true;
}

fileRefListener.onProgress = function(file:FileReference, bytesLoaded:Number, ⏎
    bytesTotal:Number)
{
    feedbackField.text = "Upload in progress.";
```

```
        fileTransferProgressBar.setProgress(bytesLoaded, bytesTotal);
    }

    fileRefListener.onComplete = function(file:FileReference)
    {
        feedbackField.text = "Upload complete.";
        fileTransferProgressBar._visible = false;
    }

    fileRefListener.onHTTPError = function (file:FileReference)
    {
        feedbackField.text = "Upload failed - network error.";
        fileTransferProgressBar._visible = false;
    }

    fileRefListener.onIOError = function (file:FileReference)
    {
        feedbackField.text = "Upload failed - disk error.";
        fileTransferProgressBar._visible = false;
    }

    fileRefListener.onSecurityError = function (file:FileReference)
    {
        feedbackField.text = "Upload failed - security/permissions error.";
        fileTransferProgressBar._visible = false;
    }

    eventHandler.click = function()
    {
        fileRef.addListener(fileRefListener);
        fileRef.browse(fileTypes);
    }
```

8. Save the file, return to the Macromedia Flash project file, and select Control⇨Test Movie.

How It Works

First, the relevant classes are imported, to make referring to component names and class names a bit easier:

```
import mx.controls.Button;
import mx.controls.ProgressBar;
import flash.net.FileReference;
```

Next, you initialize a few arrays. Even though you can download multiple files, you only use one instance of the FileReference class. If you wanted to be able to download several files at once, you would need one instance for each simultaneous connection:

```
var eventHandler:Object = new Object();
var fileRefListener:Object = new Object();
var fileRef:FileReference = new FileReference();
```

In order for the file selection dialog box to work, the list of accepted file types is given. Any files with a file type not listed here are not clickable. The description is not used with MacOS but is used with Windows to provide a drop-down menu of file type filters:

```
var fileTypes:Array = new Array();

var imageTypes:Object = new Object();
imageTypes.description = "Images (*.jpg, *.jpeg, *.gif, *.png)";
imageTypes.extension = "*.jpg; *.jpeg; *.gif; *.png";
fileTypes.push(imageTypes);

var htmlTypes:Object = new Object();
htmlTypes.description = "HTML (*.html, *.htm)";
htmlTypes.extension = "*.html; *.png";
fileTypes.push(htmlTypes);
```

The user interface is set up, which involves placing the Label, TextInput, Button, and ProgressBar components on the stage:

```
setupInterface();

function setupInterface()
{
    this.createClassObject(Button, "openWindowButton", ⏎
        this.getNextHighestDepth(), {_x:10, _y:20});
    openWindowButton.label = "Upload";
    openWindowButton.addEventListener("click", eventHandler);

    this.createClassObject(ProgressBar, "fileTransferProgressBar", ⏎
        this.getNextHighestDepth());
    fileTransferProgressBar._x = 120;
    fileTransferProgressBar._y = 20;
    fileTransferProgressBar.mode = "manual";
    fileTransferProgressBar.label = "Uploaded %3%%";
    fileTransferProgressBar._visible = false;

    this.createTextField("feedbackField", this.getNextHighestDepth(), 10, 50, 400,
30);
}
```

Next, you define event handlers for the FileReference instance. The onSelect event is called when the user has selected a file to upload. This is where the upload() method is called to start sending the file to the server upload script:

```
fileRefListener.onSelect = function(file:FileReference)
{
    feedbackField.text = "File selected: " + file.name;
    file.upload("http://www.yourdomain.com/yourUploadHandlerScript.cfm")
}
```

Startup code is placed within the onOpen event handler:

```
fileRefListener.onOpen = function(file:FileReference)
{
    feedbackField.text = "Starting file upload.";
    fileTransferProgressBar._visible = true;
}
```

The onProgress event updates the progress bar:

```
fileRefListener.onProgress = function(file:FileReference, bytesLoaded:Number, ⤶
    bytesTotal:Number)
{
    feedbackField.text = "Upload in progress.";
    fileTransferProgressBar.setProgress(bytesLoaded, bytesTotal);
}
```

The onComplete event indicates the successful completion of the file upload:

```
fileRefListener.onComplete = function(file:FileReference)
{
    feedbackField.text = "Upload complete.";
    fileTransferProgressBar._visible = false;
}
```

The onHTTPError event handler reports an aborted transfer due to a network problem:

```
fileRefListener.onHTTPError = function (file:FileReference)
{
    feedbackField.text = "Upload failed - network error.";
    fileTransferProgressBar._visible = false;
}
```

The onIOError event handler reports an aborted transfer due to a disk problem:

```
fileRefListener.onIOError = function (file:FileReference)
{
    feedbackField.text = "Upload failed - disk error.";
    fileTransferProgressBar._visible = false;
}
```

The onSecurityError event handler reports an aborted transfer due to a security issue, such as incorrect permissions set on the server's upload directory:

```
fileRefListener.onSecurityError = function (file:FileReference)
{
    feedbackField.text = "Upload failed - security/permissions error.";
    fileTransferProgressBar._visible = false;
}
```

Finally, clicking the Upload button calls the browse() method to prompt the user to select a file:

```
eventHandler.click = function()
{
    fileRef.addListener(fileRefListener);
    fileRef.browse(fileTypes);
}
```

Summary

This chapter introduced the FileReference class for uploading and downloading files. Some of the things you learned include the following:

❑   The FileReference class gives you the capability to control how users download external files to their local machines and how they upload files to the server.

❑   By making use of the FileReference events `onHTTPError`, `onIOError`, and `onSecurityError`, you can gracefully respond to problems with file uploads or downloads.

❑   Uploading files requires a server-side upload script that is dependent on the server software used.

Exercise

1.   Modify the Download Files Try It Out exercise so that when you pull the network plug in the middle of a transfer, it waits for 30 seconds, and then tries again. After three attempts, it should alert the user of the failure.

Communicating between the Flash Plug-in and the Operating System

The term *Flash wrapper* is used loosely to describe any environment that's capable of displaying an .swf file. The wrapper defines how Flash works with its surroundings. The Macromedia Flash browser plug-in, for example, is a Flash wrapper. A plug-in permits only limited access to the system. The Macromedia Flash Projector wrapper allows for a little bit more communication. Third-party wrappers such as Northcode (www.northcode.com) provide robust ActionScript object additions, allowing the development of sophisticated applications capable of interacting with the system in a much more unrestricted manner. With Northcode, you can save text files, make screen grabs, play external video formats, open web pages directly within Flash, and much more. Macromedia also provides an SDK (Software Development Kit) to enable anyone to include .swf files within larger applications built with languages such as Visual Basic.

One aspect of the Flash player that can help you create a more thorough and stable application is Flash's capability to obtain information about the system in which it is running. There are times when you may be targeting an array of devices, operating systems, and hardware where the capability to access different aspects of multimedia such as sound, video, and input devices varies from channel to channel. Ascertaining the existence of these system attributes enables you to change the behavior of your application so that it performs at its best, no matter which system it resides on.

Using the System Object to Retrieve System Information

The System object is a global object that holds properties about the system, player settings, and plug-in version. It also has a few useful functions for setting security parameters for the application.

In the following Try It Out, you use a simple loop to display the values available within the System object. You don't need to do this every time you want to fetch a System value. It's just a simple way to display all the values available.

Try It Out   Query the System Object

1.   Open a new `.fla`.

2.   Select the first frame in the Timeline panel, open the Actions panel, and enter the following code:

```
function traceObject (obj, indent) {
    if (indent == undefined) {
        indent = "";
    }
    for (var i in obj) {
        trace (indent + i + " = " + obj[i]);
        if (typeof (obj[i]) == "object") {
            var newIndent = indent + "        ";
            traceObject (obj[i], newIndent);
        }
    }
}
traceObject (System);
```

3.   Test the query. The System object is outlined in the output window, similar to the following:

```
IME [object Object]
setClipboard [type Function]
security [object Object]
          sandboxType localTrusted
          escapeDomain [type Function]
          chooseLocalSwfPath [type Function]
          loadPolicyFile [type Function]
          allowInsecureDomain [type Function]
          allowDomain [type Function]
exactSettings true
showSettings [type Function]
Product [type Function]
capabilities [object Object]
          hasIME true
          language en
          os Windows XP
          manufacturer Macromedia Windows
          windowlessDisable false
          localFileReadDisable false
          avHardwareDisable false
          playerType External
          isDebugger true
          hasScreenBroadcast false
          hasScreenPlayback true
          hasPrinting true
          hasEmbeddedVideo true
          hasStreamingVideo true
          hasStreamingAudio true
          version WIN 8,0,0,450
          serverString
A=t&SA=t&SV=t&EV=t&MP3=t&AE=t&VE=t&ACC=f&PR=t&SP=t&SB=f&DEB=t&V=WIN%208%2C0%2C0%2C4
50&M=Macromedia%20Windows&R=1400x1050&DP=72&COL=color&AR=1.0&OS=Windows%20XP&L=en&I
ME=t&PT=External&AVD=f&LFD=f&WD=f
```

```
hasAudio true
hasMP3 true
hasAudioEncoder true
hasVideoEncoder true
screenResolutionX 1400
screenResolutionY 1050
screenDPI 72
screenColor color
pixelAspectRatio 1
hasAccessibility false
```

How It Works

The System object is exposed using a simple recursive function. A recursive function is a function that has the capability to call itself or other objects with the same function.

One helpful value within the System object is the player version value found within the capabilities object. If an application required the plug-in version it is running within, the code `System.capabilties .version`, in this case, would return `8,0,0,450`. The property returns whatever player version you have installed. This is useful for redirecting users to different content or a new SWF, or alerting the user that his current player needs to be upgraded or changed.

System Object Limitations among Player Versions

Different versions of the Flash player have different properties available within the System object. Flash 5 has no System object, and Flash 6 has a limited System object. It is always wise to check for the existence of a property as you attempt to use it. This goes for any property or variable in your code, but is especially so with the System object, which can affect how the entire application performs.

The setClipBoard Method

The `setClipBoard` method, which you used in the preceding Try It Out, enables you to send Strings to the clipboard. However, there is no way to retrieve the contents of the clipboard from your SWF. It does enable you to offer other programs on the system quick access to content created within Flash. You might send the results of a complex math calculation to the clipboard and instruct the user to paste it into Excel, for example. The clipboard activity is one-directional; Flash can only send information to the clipboard. Other applications need some method of retrieving it, or instructions need to be provided to the user. Flash cannot obtain the contents of the clipboard via ActionScript.

The syntax is as follows:

```
System.setClipBoard(str:String);
```

The `str` parameter is simply a String. Although some system limitations may exist for specific operating systems, Flash does not limit the size of the String to be written to the clipboard.

When you send data to the clipboard, the clipboard is automatically cleared. This can be a useful feature when you'd like selectable text, but you want to disallow the pasting of the text.

Projectors, Flash Executables, and Other Executables

Flash is primarily a web platform, with users accessing SWF content via http pages. However, Flash can be packaged within executable files, which are essentially standalone Flash players that have SWF content.

To create a Flash executable, you simply select Flash projector output in the Publish Settings options.

Although the projector output from Flash has no options, you can do a few things with the executable file with ActionScript using `fscommand`. ActionScript uses the FSCommand object to communicate with the system. The available fscommands are listed in the "Using fscommand to Call Projector Functions" section later in this chapter.

`fscommand` is used with executables to specify quit commands and other attributes. It can be used to communicate with JavaScript as well. (The `fscommand`-to-JavaScript communication is described in Chapter 23.) `fscommand` is also utilized when Flash is used in conjunction with Macromedia Director files. A separate object called fcommand2 is used specifically for Flash lite to access cell phone functions.

Limitations

It should be noted that the Flash `fscommand` does not support a save method for text files.

The Flash projector no longer launches `.bat` files. Flash no longer opens `.pdf` files via `fscommand`. FSCommand was able to open these two file types in Flash 6, which implemented the fscommand folder.

The fscommand folder must reside in the same directory as your Flash executable file. You can place `.exe` files within a folder named fscommand.

FSCommands are most commonly used to access commands within a Flash projector.

Using fscommand to Call Projector Functions

Calling an `fscommand` method is simple from anywhere in your application. Here's the syntax:

```
fscommand(command,parm);
```

`command` is a String, the name of the command you want to execute; `parm` is also a String — the required parameter for the command. The available `command` and `parm` values are described in the following table:

Command	Parameter	Description
quit	None	Closes the Projector file. This command is usually honored by third-party wrappers as well.
fullscreen	String representing a Boolean value, true or false	If the parameter is set to true, the application is maximized to the full screen size. If the parameter is false, and the application is in fullscreen mode, the application will be unminimized.

Command	Parameter	Description
allowscale	String representing a Boolean value, true or false	If true, the movie is scaled to 100% of the application window's screen size. If false, the canvas is enlarged, but the items remain at the size at which they were authored to.
showmenu	String representing a Boolean value, true or false	If true, the Flash player's context menu shows a full set of options. If false, the Flash player's context menu has only Settings and About options. There is no way to fully remove the context menu.
exec	String specifying the name of an executable file.	Launches an executable file.
trapallkeys	String representing a Boolean value, true or false	If true, the onClipEvent(keyDown/keyUp) event handler fires when any key is pressed.

The external API has taken on many of the aspects of fscommand, and some third-party wrappers and JavaScript communications require the external API rather than fscommand.

When using the exec command via fscommand, you must create a special folder called fscommand. All executable files you want to launch via your application must reside in that folder.

The following example shows you how and where the folder must be created to work with your projector to launch applications.

Try It Out   Launch a Program Using fscommand

This example assumes a PC platform. To use a Mac, make the appropriate program string name changes and choose a program of your choice to use.

At the time of this writing, performance of a PC Macromedia Projector file under WINE for Linux was unknown. It may be that some things, such as fullscreen, might not work as expected.

1. Open a new FLA, and save it as fscommandExec.fla in your workspace folder.

2. Open the User Interface section of the Components panel and drag an instance of the Component button onto the stage.

3. Open the Parameters tab in the Properties panel and change the Label parameter from Button to Open Calculator.

4. In the Properties panel, change the Instance name of the button component to myButton. (The Instance name field is just below the word Component on the left side of the panel.)

5. Select the first frame in the timeline and enter the following code:

```
myButton.onRelease = function(){
    fscommand("exec","calc.exe");
}
```

6. Publish your SWF file and navigate to the folder where your SWF file was published. This is probably the workspace folder where your FLA is residing if you haven't made any Publish Settings changes to the FLA.

7. In the same folder as the SWF file, create a new folder and name it fscommand.

8. If you are on a PC, find the Calculator program. This program is usually within the System32 folder in your Windows folder. If you are on a Mac, find a suitable file to open. Copy the file and paste it into the fscommand folder. Do not delete this program from its original location; simply copy it.

9. Open the Publish Settings dialog. Be sure the Windows Projector option is checked and click the Publish button.

10. Test the application by navigating to your workspace folder and double-clicking the `fscommandExec.exe` file. Click the Open Calculator button.

11. The calculator application opens.

How It Works

Using a simple command, Flash was able to launch another program.

The example utilized an innocuous program for the purposes of demonstration. However, the target application could be a second Projector file, an installer executable, or something interesting such as a custom Visual Basic executable capable of launching more sophisticated programs.

Many Flash developers become frustrated with this process because limiting what Flash can launch to the fscommand folder and limiting the file type to `.exe` is so restrictive that they're convinced there must be a way around a particular launch problem. But there isn't. The limitations of the Flash projector are there for security purposes so that the Flash IDE alone cannot be used to create malicious system programs.

SDK

If Flash's available methods for system interaction are too limiting for the scope of your project, you'll need to take a different approach with a third-party executable creation tool, or write your own. If writing your own sounds appealing, Macromedia offers an SDK for developing a wrapper that utilizes the Flash ActiveX player.

The SDK is often a desirable method when creating Flash for specific environments for kiosks or other controlled and isolated environments. Because the SDK relies on the ActiveX player, though, a target system must have the plug-in installed on the Internet Explorer browser. Little recourse is provided within the SDK; plug-in detection and failure can be difficult to resolve.

Third Parties

The ActiveX issue is also present in third-party wrappers, which use the SDK to create their products. This has recently changed on a few third-party wrappers.

However, one wrapper in particular is officially Flash-enabled. Northcode 3.0 has obtained a license to offer a wrapper creation tool that is allowed to bundle the Flash player with the .exe itself, meaning that the systems that run the executable do not need any Flash player installed, and no Flash player install process is required. This makes Northcode a top contender when choosing a third-party wrapper.

Newer wrappers no longer require fscommand, either. Instead, wrappers such as Northcode allow developers to write ActionScript with extended objects and classes that work much like the native ActionScript objects.

Each third-party wrapper has its own syntax, documentation, and level of clarity of code. Most offer to add the objects to the Flash ActionScript editor definitions file, as well as add help files directly within the Flash IDE.

Most third-party wrappers such as Jester, Northcode, Flash Studio, and others offer trial downloads. I recommend downloading them, and trying them out before choosing one to deploy on a project. Be aware that the trials are limited. Usually a time limit is placed on the EXE file, or the EXE file the demo produces runs on your system only. Be sure to purchase a license before distributing software.

> *Be polite. Your executable is a guest on a user's system. Be respectful of RAM usage, disk space, screen space, window options, and stability. As with any SWF file, always test your product on as many systems as possible to ensure quality.*

> *Don't make system changes just because you can. For example, storing persistent data in registry files or saving data to text files that only your application can access is silly when Flash offers SharedObjects.*

Summary

In this chapter, you explored wrappers and their use in Flash, took a look at various third-party offerings, and learned how to use Flash and other executables.

Exercises

1. Determine the operating system and display a different welcome message to the user.

2. Using fscommand, create two projector files. Use one projector to open the other.

3. Create a simple screen saver in Windows.

Creating Custom Classes

By this point, you have become reasonably familiar with how to code using ActionScript. Hopefully, you have applied your new skills to a personal project or two and are thinking ahead to bigger and better things. In this chapter, you learn some of the next steps to ActionScript coding, specifically the process of creating custom classes. Custom classes are immensely useful for any developer because they take you to the next level of organization and reusability.

Working with Classes

In Chapter 5 you were introduced to a number of object-oriented programming principles. You saw these principles as they apply to the classes built into the Flash player. Although you can achieve many things with just that knowledge, you can do so much more by creating your own custom classes.

Recall the definition of object-oriented programming from Chapter 5:

> **To package data and the code that acts on that data into a single entity.**

The mechanism to make this possible is the *class*. By working with your own classes, you allow yourself to organize and package your own code in a way that makes re-use significantly easier, and that makes your code so much cleaner. Chapter 5 already went through much of the motivation for object-oriented programming with classes, so this chapter gets right into the mechanics of it.

Defining the Class

The first requirement for a class is that it must exist in its own file, which is named the same as the class itself. If you create a class called `MyClass`, you would define it in a file called `MyClass.as` and save it in the same folder as the FLA file that uses it. This enforcement ensures that class files are self-contained and separate from everything else.

In the `MyClass.as` file, the core class definition might look something like this:

```
class MyClass
{
    public var myProperty:String;

    public function MyClass()
    {
        // ...
    }

    public function myMethod():String
    {
        // ...
    }
}
```

This definition consists of a class block that encompasses all of the class code. Within it are defined all of the properties (basically variables) and methods (functions) that the class will use.

The first function block in the definition is a special function called a *constructor*. Its role is to carry out any actions that are to be performed when a copy (instance) of the class is created. You see more about the constructor shortly.

To actually use the preceding class, simply call the following from the main timeline. This is the same mechanism for creating any other class instance, such as you would do for creating a new Date, LoadVars, or XML class instance:

```
var myClassInstance:MyClass = new MyClass();
```

The Flash compiler will automatically search in a number of places to find the definition for MyClass, including the folder containing the FLA file. If it finds a file called `MyClass.as` containing a class block called MyClass, it will then reference that definition file when the `new` keyword is used. It will also enforce type checking, using MyClass as the data type.

> *Data types within Flash are themselves classes, or at least have class-based versions of them. You can see this by going to <Flash Program Root>/First Run/Classes/FP8/ and examining the contents of the* `.as` *files there.*

Give creating a custom class a try.

Try It Out   Your First Class

In this exercise, you create a simple custom class with a property, a method, and a constructor.

1. Create a new ActionScript document by selecting File⇨New and choosing ActionScript File from the New Document panel.

2. Select File⇨Save As and choose an appropriate folder for the file. Give the file the name `HelloWorldClass.as` and save it.

3. Enter the following code into the new ActionScript file:

```
class HelloWorldClass
{
    public var messageText:String;

    public function HelloWorldClass(inputMessage:String)
    {
        messageText = inputMessage;
    }

    public function getMessage():String
    {
        return messageText;
    }
}
```

4. Save the file (File⇨Save).

5. Create a new Macromedia Flash document by selecting File⇨New and choosing Flash Document from the New Document panel.

6. Click the first frame in the timeline, open the Actions panel (Window⇨Development Panels⇨ Actions), and enter in the following ActionScript code:

```
var message_obj:HelloWorldClass = new HelloWorldClass("The quick brown fox");
var message2_obj:HelloWorldClass = new HelloWorldClass("");
message2_obj.messageText = "jumped over the lazy dog.";

trace("message_obj message text: " + message_obj.getMessage());
trace("message2_obj message text: " + message2_obj.getMessage());
```

7. Select File⇨Save As, name the file `tryItOut_helloWorld.fla`, and save it in the same direc-tory as `HelloWorldClass.as`.

8. Choose Control⇨Test Movie to try it out.

How It Works

This exercise defines a single class and then creates two instances of that class. The first instance is passed a string through the constructor, which then assigns that string to the `messageText` property. The second instance passes a blank string through to the constructor and then sets the property directly. In both cases, the `getMessage()` method returns the contents of the `messageText` property for the cor-responding class instance.

The trace statements show that both class instances contain their own data stores. Each instance contains its own copy of the `messageText` property, so changing it in one place will not affect it in the other.

Public Versus Private

In the world of re-use, when a class is given to others to use, a specific set of properties and methods are given to the developers using the class to access. These *public* properties and methods are supposed to be stable, in that changes to the internal class workings should not substantially change which public prop-erties and methods can be used and what types of data that they use. Any such changes would require developers using a new version of your class to have to rewrite some of their code to accommodate your changes. This is definitely not a welcome task, and will not make you very popular. Even if the class is only for your personal use, development goes more smoothly if there are stable, well-defined connections between your classes.

Although each class will allow some of its properties and methods to be publicly accessed, there will also be support code within the class that may be prone to significant change. This support code is considered to be *private* and should not be accessible outside of the class. By declaring support properties and methods as private, Flash prevents access to these from any outside code.

The means of controlling property and method access is through the `public` or `private` keyword placed in front of each property or method declaration. The checking is done at compile time, not at runtime; if any external code tries to access a private property or method from your class, the compile will halt with an error message indicating what the access violation was and where it occurred.

The next exercise shows the effect of the `public` and `private` keywords.

Try It Out   Making Code Private

In this exercise, you work with making properties and methods private and see how the compiler responds under different scenarios.

1. Open the completed `tryItOut_helloWorld.fla` file from the first Try It Out exercise or open up the source Flash project file from the book's source files at <source file directory>/Chapter 27/ tryItOut_helloWorldClass/tryItOut_helloWorld.fla.

2. Open the completed `HelloWorldClass.as` file from the first Try It Out exercise, or open up the source Flash project file from the book's source files at <source file directory>/Chapter 27/ tryItOut_helloWorldClass/HelloWorldClass.as.

3. Change the `public` keyword in front of the `messageText` property declaration to `private`:

```
private var messageText:String;
```

4. Return to the FLA file and select Control➪Test Movie.

5. Return to the `.as` file and change the `private` keyword in front of the `messageText` property declaration back to `private`. Change the `public` keyword in front of the `getMessage()` method to be `private` instead:

```
private function getMessage():String
```

6. Return to the FLA file and select Control➪Test Movie.

7. Return to the `.as` file and change the `private` keyword in front of the `getMessage()` method declaration back to `public`. Change the `public` keyword in front of the `HelloWorldClass()` constructor to be `private` instead:

```
private function HelloWorldClass(inputMessage:String)
```

8. Return to the `.fla` file and select Control➪Test Movie.

How It Works

When a method or a property is declared as being private, the compiler warns about any attempted access and aborts the compile. In step 3 of the exercise, the property is changed to be private. When attempting to test the movie, the compiler gives the following message:

```
**Error** Scene=Scene 1, layer=Layer 1, frame=1:Line 3: The member is private and
cannot be accessed.
      message2_obj.messageText = "jumped over the lazy dog.";
```

The error provides a description of the issue, shows the line of code, and indicates where in the class file the line is located. In this case, you were attempting to change the contents of the variable; however, just trying to read the variable would have caused the same error.

In step 5, the getMessage() method is changed to be private. When attempting to test the movie, the compiler gives the following message:

```
**Error** Scene=Scene 1, layer=Layer 1, frame=1:Line 5: The member is private and
cannot be accessed.
      trace("message_obj message text: " + message_obj.getMessage());

**Error** Scene=Scene 1, layer=Layer 1, frame=1:Line 6: The member is private and
cannot be accessed.
      trace("message2_obj message text: " + message2_obj.getMessage());
```

The compiler indicates that the getMessage() method cannot be accessed and aborts the compile. If there are multiple violations of private properties or methods, the compiler will generate a complete list of all the access violations.

In step 7 you see why constructors always need to be public. With the access set to private, you cannot even create an instance of the class.

Take a closer look at the constructor.

Defining the Constructor

As mentioned at the start of this section, the role of the constructor is to perform any actions that are to be performed when an instance of the class is created. The constructor is also used for passing startup data into the class instance. This function is special because of the following:

❑   It has the same name as the class itself.

❑   It is not explicitly called.

❑   It has no return type.

The compiler knows which method is the constructor by looking for a method declaration with the same name as the class itself. Unlike a method, a constructor cannot be explicitly called. If you try to explicitly call the constructor, nothing will happen. The constructor is to be called exactly once and no more, so it does not behave like a normal method. In the following example, you see that attempting to call a constructor as if it were a normal method has no effect. The output of getMessage() does not change to "foo", and the test to see whether the method exists returns undefined:

```
    var message_obj:HelloWorldClass = new HelloWorldClass("The quick brown fox");
    message_obj.HelloWorldClass("foo");

    trace("message_obj message text: " + message_obj.getMessage());
    // Outputs: message_obj message text: The quick brown fox

    trace("constructor handle: " + message_obj.HelloWorldClass);
    // Outputs: constructor handle: undefined
```

Because a constructor is not explicitly called, it can never return data and can have no return type. If you try declaring one, even if it is just a Void return type, the compiler will return an error.

Passing Startup Data

When a class is instantiated, there is often some initial data that the class needs before it can do any work. If the class is responsible for drawing something on the stage, it might need a handle to the movie clip that it should draw to. If the class is to manipulate data, it might need an initial copy of that data.

You specify what kind of initial data a class will accept by specifying arguments in the constructor:

```
    public function HelloWorldClass(arg1:String, arg2:Number, arg3:Boolean ... )
```

Each constructor argument corresponds to one parameter that is to be passed into the new class:

```
    var newInstance:HelloWorldClass = new HelloWorldClass("foo", 2, true, ... );
```

Within the constructor, you will generally want to save the passed-in data for later use. You do this by creating private properties and assigning them the data that was passed in. The following example allows for three parameters to be passed into the new class instance, and then assigns the values to private properties that can be used elsewhere within the class:

```
    private var pMessageText:String;
    private var pNumLoops:Number;
    private var pUseSeparator:Boolean;

    public function HelloWorldClass(messageText:String, numLoops:Number, ⏎
        useSeparator:Boolean)
    {
        pMessageText = messageText;
        pNumLoops = numLoops;
        pUseSeparator = useSeparator;
    }
```

Try this out. In the course of the next few Try It Out examples, you put together a class that will create a photo thumbnail button suitable for use in a Flash-based photo album.

Try It Out   Create a Photo Thumbnail Class

In this example, you start creating the framework for a class that creates a clickable button out of a dynamically loaded thumbnail image.

1. Create a new ActionScript document by selecting File⇨New and choosing ActionScript File from the New Document panel.

2. Select File⇨Save As and choose an appropriate folder for the file. Give the file the name `ThumbnailButton.as` and save it.

3. Enter the following code into the new ActionScript file:

```
class ThumbnailButton
{
    private var pParentTimeline:MovieClip;
    private var pThumbnailName:String;
    private var pThumbnailHolder:MovieClip;
    private var pImageHolder:MovieClip;
    private var pBorderHolder:MovieClip;
    private var pClickHandler:Function;
    private var pMovieClipLoader:MovieClipLoader;

    public function ThumbnailButton(parentTimeline:MovieClip, ⤶
        thumbnailName:String)
    {
        pParentTimeline = parentTimeline;
        pThumbnailName = thumbnailName;

        pThumbnailHolder = pParentTimeline.createEmptyMovieClip(pThumbnailName, ⤶
            pParentTimeline.getNextHighestDepth());

        pImageHolder = pThumbnailHolder.createEmptyMovieClip("imageHolder", ⤶
            pThumbnailHolder.getNextHighestDepth());

        pBorderHolder = pThumbnailHolder.createEmptyMovieClip("borderHolder", ⤶
            pThumbnailHolder.getNextHighestDepth());

        pMovieClipLoader = new MovieClipLoader();
        pMovieClipLoader.addListener(this);
    }
}
```

4. Save the file (File⇨Save).

5. Create a new Macromedia Flash document by selecting File⇨New and choosing Flash Document from the New Document panel.

6. Click the first frame in the timeline, open the Actions panel (Window⇨Development Panels⇨ Actions), and enter in the following ActionScript code:

```
var myThumbnail:ThumbnailButton = new ThumbnailButton(this, "myThumbnail");
```

7. Select File⇨Save As, name the file `tryItOut_thumbnailButton.fla`, and save it in the same directory as `HelloWorldClass.as`.

8. Choose Control⇨Debug Movie to try it out. Click the play button within the Debug panel, and note the movie clip structure shown in the top left of the Debug panel.

How It Works

The thumbnail class shown here does not yet load an image, however it does demonstrate the use of the constructor and private properties.

First, get an idea of what the movie clip structure is going to be. Figure 27-1 shows the movie clip structure as displayed in the debugger movie clip browser pane. The base movie clip for the thumbnail is `_level0.myThumbnail`. The `_level0` reference corresponds to what was passed to the parent timeline parameter, and the `myThumbnail` reference corresponds to the thumbnail name parameter. Within that movie clip are two more movie clips. One is imageHolder, which will be used to load the actual thumbnail image. The other is borderHolder, which will be used for drawing a border that overlays the image.

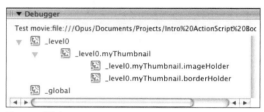

Figure 27-1

Within the code, the private properties are the first to be declared. The first two, `pParentTimeline` and `pThumbnailName`, are used to hold the data passed into the two constructor parameters. The next three are handles to the three different movie clips created and are there for quick convenient access to those movie clips. The second-to-last property, `pClickHandler`, is for holding a handle to a function that will be called when the button is clicked, and will be used a bit later. The last one is for a loader class that will be used for loading the thumbnail image:

```
private var pParentTimeline:MovieClip;
private var pThumbnailName:String;
private var pThumbnailHolder:MovieClip;
private var pImageHolder:MovieClip;
private var pBorderHolder:MovieClip;
private var pClickHandler:Function;
private var pMovieClipLoader:MovieClipLoader;
```

The startup code is placed within the constructor. First the two input parameters are passed to two private properties:

```
pParentTimeline = parentTimeline;
pThumbnailName = thumbnailName;
```

Next, the base movie clip is created and a handle is assigned to one of the properties:

```
pThumbnailHolder = pParentTimeline.createEmptyMovieClip(pThumbnailName, ⤷
    pParentTimeline.getNextHighestDepth());
```

The movie clip that is to hold the actual image is created within the base movie clip, and a handle to the movie clip is assigned to one of the properties for quick access in other parts of the code:

```
pImageHolder = pThumbnailHolder.createEmptyMovieClip("imageHolder", ⤵
    pThumbnailHolder.getNextHighestDepth());
```

The movie clip that is to hold the thumbnail border is created within the base movie clip, and a handle to the movie clip is assigned to one of the properties:

```
pBorderHolder = pThumbnailHolder.createEmptyMovieClip("borderHolder", ⤵
    pThumbnailHolder.getNextHighestDepth());
```

An instance of the MovieClipLoader class is created and a handle is assigned to a property:

```
pMovieClipLoader = new MovieClipLoader();
pMovieClipLoader.addListener(this);
```

At this point, you have a class shell that works, but does not yet do anything that is visible on the screen. Before you can make this class do anything useful, you need to add at least one method. You see methods in action next.

Defining Methods

Class methods are defined in almost exactly the same way that functions are defined. They can accept any number of input parameters, and they define the data type of the return value, if any. The only difference in how a method is declared versus how a function is declared is that a method must exist within the class block, and it may be preceded with either the keyword public or the keyword private to indicate whether or not the method can be accessed outside of the class. The following snippet shows a sample class method declaration:

```
public function setLabel(newLabelText:String):Boolean
{
    // ...
    return true;
}
```

A method can be called from any other method within the same class by simply invoking it in the same way that a function is invoked. Here, drawThumbnail() calls setLabel(), a method of the same class:

```
public function drawThumbnail():Void
{
    var labelFits:Boolean = setLabel("Galiano Sunset");
}
```

Any method can call any other method within the same class, regardless of whether the method being called is public or private. Setting a method to be private just prevents the method from being accessed from any code outside of the class.

If a method declaration does not include the keyword public or private, it is assumed to be public.

With ActionScript 1.0, methods are called within a class by calling this.myMethod()*. The* this *keyword tells the compiler that the method is referring to the parent object, namely the class instance. This still works in ActionScript 2.0 but is no longer necessary and is generally omitted to keep the code visually clean.*

You have already seen many examples of public methods being called from the Flash built-in classes, and calling a public method from your custom classes is no different:

```
var successValue:Boolean = myInstance.myMethod("foo", 2);
```

Take a look at methods in use by adding them to your thumbnail class.

Try It Out   **Adding Methods to a Photo Thumbnail Class**

In this example, you add some methods to the thumbnail class that you started in the previous Try It Out exercise.

1. Open the completed `tryItOut_thumbnailButton.fla` file from the first Try It Out exercise or open up the source Flash project file from the book's source files at <source file directory>/ Chapter 27/tryItOut_thumbnail_v1/tryItOut_thumbnailButton.fla.

2. Open the completed `ThumbnailButton.as` file from the first Try It Out exercise, or open up the source Flash project file from the book's source files at <source file directory>/Chapter 27/ tryItOut_thumbnail_v1/ThumbnailButton.as.

3. Add the following two methods just after the constructor, but before the closing brace for the class block:

```
public function load(imageURL:String):Void
{
    pMovieClipLoader.loadClip(imageURL, pImageHolder);
}

private function onLoadInit(targetMovieClip:MovieClip):Void
{
    trace("Load complete");
}
```

4. Save the file (File⇨Save).

5. Using your favorite image editor, resize and crop any photo into a small image around 50 pixels by 50 pixels. Save it as a JPG file into the same directory containing the FLA and AS files. You can instead obtain a sample image in the book source files at <source file directory>/Chapter 27/ tryItOut_thumbnail_v2/galianoSunset_over.jpg.

6. Return to the FLA file, click the first frame in the timeline, open the Actions panel (Window⇨ Development Panels⇨Actions), and update the ActionScript code to look like the following code. If you have named your image file something different, change the parameter in the load() method to refer to your image:

```
var myThumbnail:ThumbnailButton = new ThumbnailButton(this, "myThumbnail");
myThumbnail.load("galianoSunset_over.jpg");
```

7. Choose Control⇨Test Movie to try it out.

8. Return to the AS file. Update the onLoadInit() method with the following code:

```
private function onLoadInit(targetMovieClip:MovieClip):Void
{
    var parent:ThumbnailButton = this;

    pThumbnailHolder.onPress = function()
```

```
    {
        trace("button pressed");
    }

    pThumbnailHolder.onRelease = function()
    {
        trace("button released");
    }

    pThumbnailHolder.onReleaseOutside = function()
    {
        trace("button released outside");
    }

    pThumbnailHolder.onRollOver = function()
    {
        trace("button rolled over");
    }

    pThumbnailHolder.onRollOut = function()
    {
        trace("button rolled out");
    }
}
```

9. Return to the FLA file and choose Control⇨Test Movie to try it out. Try mousing over and clicking the thumbnail button.

10. Return to the AS file. Update onLoadInit() with the following code:

```
private function onLoadInit(targetMovieClip:MovieClip):Void
{
    var parent:ThumbnailButton = this;

    drawThumbnail("up");

    pThumbnailHolder.onPress = function()
    {
        parent.drawThumbnail("down");
    }

    pThumbnailHolder.onRelease = function()
    {
        if (parent.pClickHandler != null)
        {
            parent.pClickHandler(parent);
        }
        parent.drawThumbnail("over");
    }

    pThumbnailHolder.onReleaseOutside = function()
    {
        parent.drawThumbnail("up");
    }

    pThumbnailHolder.onRollOver = function()
```

```
    {
        parent.drawThumbnail("over");
    }

    pThumbnailHolder.onRollOut = function()
    {
        parent.drawThumbnail("up");
    }
}
```

11. Add the following method just after the `onLoadInit()` method, but before the closing brace for the class block:

```
private function drawThumbnail(thumbnailState:String):Void
{
    var dropShadowFilter:DropShadowFilter;
    var appliedFilterArray = new Array();
    pBorderHolder.clear();
    switch(thumbnailState)
    {
        case "up":
            dropShadowFilter = new DropShadowFilter(3, 45, 0x666666, ⤵
                0.8, 5, 5, 1, 3, false, false, false);
            pImageHolder._x = pBorderHolder._x = 0;
            pImageHolder._y = pBorderHolder._y = 0;
            pBorderHolder.lineStyle(1, 0x666666);
            break;

        case "over":
            dropShadowFilter = new DropShadowFilter(3, 45, 0x000000, ⤵
                1, 5, 5, 1, 5, false, false, false);
            pImageHolder._x = pBorderHolder._x = 0;
            pImageHolder._y = pBorderHolder._y = 0;
            pBorderHolder.lineStyle(1, 0x000000);
            break;

        case "down":
            dropShadowFilter = new DropShadowFilter(1, 45, 0x000000, ⤵
                1, 3, 3, 1, 5, false, false, false);
            pImageHolder._x = pBorderHolder._x = 2;
            pImageHolder._y = pBorderHolder._y = 2;
            pBorderHolder.lineStyle(1, 0x990000);
            break;
    }

    pBorderHolder.moveTo(0, 0);
    pBorderHolder.lineTo(pImageHolder._width-1, 0);
    pBorderHolder.lineTo(pImageHolder._width-1, pImageHolder._height-1);
    pBorderHolder.lineTo(0, pImageHolder._height-1);
    pBorderHolder.lineTo(0, 0);

    appliedFilterArray.push(dropShadowFilter);
    pImageHolder.filters = appliedFilterArray;
}
```

12. Return to the FLA file and choose Control⇨Test Movie to try it out.

How It Works

This example adds one public and two private methods to the class definition. The public method is a load method that the person using this class would call to load up the image. The `onLoadInit()` and `drawThumbnail()` methods are used for internal implementation and are made private so that anyone using the class cannot directly call these methods.

First, start with the `load()` method. This method accepts a path to an image to load. After it's loaded, it invokes the MovieClipLoader class to load it into the image holder movie clip:

```
public function load(imageURL:String):Void
{
    pMovieClipLoader.loadClip(imageURL, pImageHolder);
}
```

You may notice that the `onLoadInit()` method is not actually called from anywhere in the code, yet the trace that shows up in the output indicates that it is called. The MovieClipLoader class is the one calling the method. When the MovieClipLoader class was instantiated at the end of the ThumbnailButton constructor, it was passed the `this` parameter, which set up the ThumbnailButton class itself as an event listener. The MovieClipLoader class can generate several events, one of which is the `onLoadInit` event. The loader automatically checks whether the `onLoadInit()` method exists in the ThumbnailButton class, and it calls the method automatically when the image has finished loading.

Take a closer look at the contents of the `onLoadInit()` method. The first few lines warrant some explanation:

```
var parent:ThumbnailButton = this;

drawThumbnail("up");

pThumbnailHolder.onPress = function()
{
    parent.drawThumbnail("down");
}
```

The first line creates a local variable and assigns the handle to `this` copy of the class. This will be important in a moment. The second line calls the `drawThumbnail()` method. The last four lines add an `onPress` event handler to the thumbnail holder movie clip.

The part that needs some explanation here is how `drawThumbnail()` is called from within this event handler. The problem is that just calling `drawThumbnail()` within the event handler will not work. When a method is called, it is called in the context of the parent class. In this case, the parent class is `pThumbnailHolder`, which is a movie clip:

```
pThumbnailHolder.onPress = function()
{
    drawThumbnail("down");
}
```

The effect is the same as if the method were called directly:

```
pThumbnailHolder.drawThumbnail("down");
```

673

This is not the behavior that you want, and the preceding method will not run because it does not exist in the context of the movie clip. To call a method from the `ThumbnailHolder` class instead, the `parent` variable is created. Local variables are visible within anonymous function blocks, so `parent` is visible to code within the event handler block. The `parent` variable points to the ThumbnailHolder class instance, and `parent.drawThumbnail("down");` refers to the correct `drawThumbnail()` method.

The remaining code within this method defines how to make the thumbnail button respond to the other mouse events. The only thing different is the `onRelease` event handler. When the mouse is released over the button, a function is to be called. You define this function in the next exercise.

```
pThumbnailHolder.onRelease = function()
{
    if (parent.pClickHandler != null)
    {
        parent.pClickHandler(parent);
    }
    parent.drawThumbnail("over");
}
```

The `drawThumbnail()` method is a private method that is responsible for adding the drop shadow and the outline to the thumbnail image. The first two lines within the `drawThumbnail()` method set up the variables to hold the drop shadow filter. The `clear()` method removes the border from the last time `drawThumbnail()` was called:

```
var dropShadowFilter:DropShadowFilter;
var appliedFilterArray = new Array();
pBorderHolder.clear();
```

Within the `switch..case` statement, the drop shadow is created with settings that correspond with the button state. If the button is in the down state, the drop shadow is placed closer to the image, and the image and border is moved two pixels down and to the right. This gives the appearance of the button being physically pressed. The `lineStyle()` method is called to set the line color, resulting in the different border colors for the different button states:

```
switch(thumbnailState)
{
    case "up":
        dropShadowFilter = new DropShadowFilter(3, 45, 0x666666, ⊃
            0.8, 5, 5, 1, 3, false, false, false);
        pImageHolder._x = pBorderHolder._x = 0;
        pImageHolder._y = pBorderHolder._y = 0;
        pBorderHolder.lineStyle(1, 0x666666);
        break;

    case "over":
        dropShadowFilter = new DropShadowFilter(3, 45, 0x000000, ⊃
            1, 5, 5, 1, 5, false, false, false);
        pImageHolder._x = pBorderHolder._x = 0;
        pImageHolder._y = pBorderHolder._y = 0;
        pBorderHolder.lineStyle(1, 0x000000);
        break;

    case "down":
        dropShadowFilter = new DropShadowFilter(1, 45, 0x000000, ⊃
```

```
        1, 3, 3, 1, 5, false, false, false);
    pImageHolder._x = pBorderHolder._x = 2;
    pImageHolder._y = pBorderHolder._y = 2;
    pBorderHolder.lineStyle(1, 0x990000);
    break;
}
```

Finally, the border is drawn, and the drop shadow filter is applied to the image:

```
pBorderHolder.moveTo(0, 0);
pBorderHolder.lineTo(pImageHolder._width-1, 0);
pBorderHolder.lineTo(pImageHolder._width-1, pImageHolder._height-1);
pBorderHolder.lineTo(0, pImageHolder._height-1);
pBorderHolder.lineTo(0, 0);

appliedFilterArray.push(dropShadowFilter);
pImageHolder.filters = appliedFilterArray;
```

There is still a bit of functionality remaining to be implemented. You first take a look at some issues surrounding defining properties, and then you finish off this class.

Defining Properties

Although you have already seen a number of examples of properties in use in the previous Try It Out exercises, they still warrant further study. The first Try It Out exercise showed a public property in use, where you could directly manipulate the property. Say that you have the following class based on that exercise:

```
Class HelloWorldClass
{
    public var messageText:String;

    public function HelloWorldClass()
    {
        // ...
    }
}
```

The messageText property is public, and as such can be viewed and modified directly:

```
var myInstance:HelloWorldClass = new HelloWorldClass();
myInstance.messageText = "foo";
trace(myInstance.messageText);
```

Unfortunately, a few problems exist with exposing the property directly like this:

❑ The property is always writable; you have no ability to make the property read-only.

❑ There is no elegant way to call additional code if the property value changes.

❑ If you were to change the implementation of the class, any public properties that change as a result would result in code changes for anyone who has implemented your class.

Fortunately, there is a clean way to address these issues in the form of *getters* and *setters*.

Working with Getters and Setters

Getters and setters are special methods that control access to your public properties. A *getter* is a method that controls what happens when a developer attempts to read from a public property, and a *setter* is a method that controls what happens when a developer attempts to write to a public property. Take your small HelloWorldClass example and implement that with a getter and a setter instead:

```
Class HelloWorldClass
{
    private var pMessageText:String;

    public function HelloWorldClass()
    {
        // ...
    }

    public function get messageText():String
    {
        return pMessageText
    }

    public function set messageText(newText:String):Void
    {
        pMessageText = newText;
    }
}
```

Note that the public property that was previously declared at the top of the class definition is now private and so the data behind the property is now hidden from anyone using the class. Also, note that the private property has now been renamed. It is a good idea to use a naming convention to make it clear in the code when a private property is being referenced. The authors use the convention of prepending a p to any private property. Other developers like to prepend an underscore character (_) to the variable name. Whatever you decide to use, just be consistent.

To retrieve the value of the property, simply call the property as you did previously:

```
trace(myInstance.messageText);
```

To set the value of the property, again you just set the property as you did previously:

```
myInstance.messageText = "foo";
```

When the value of the property is being retrieved, Flash automatically calls the get version of the `messageText()` method. When the value of the property is being set, Flash automatically calls the set version of the `messageText()` method.

Implications of Getters and Setters

You can control whether or not properties are writable. If you define a getter but not a setter, it means that the property is readable, but not writable. Many reasons exist for why you would want to make a property read-only. Some properties may provide status, such as whether or not data has finished loading.

Other properties may describe data, such as the number of elements in an array. In both of these cases, it would not make sense to make the properties writable.

You also can easily call additional code when a property is set or retrieved. Say you want to audit any changes to a particular property. You can easily call code to log the change anytime the variable changes. The following code shows how a `trace()` statement can be called every time the setter is called, something that is very useful for debugging:

```
public function set messageText(newText:String):Void
{
    trace("pMessageText -  old: '" + pMessageText + "' new: '" + newText + "'");
    pMessageText = newText;
}
```

Getters and setters prevent the developer who uses your class from getting direct access to your class data. You control precisely what the developer can access, and you can make changes to your implementation without affecting others. Say you wanted to do something offbeat such as store your message as an array of characters rather than as a string. You could change your private property to be an array, and you could update the setter and the getter to split and join the data between the string and the array data types without the developer knowing or caring about your change.

Getters allow for the concept of calculated properties. Say you want to provide a property that provides the number of words in the saved message. Such a getter might look like this:

```
public function get numWords():Number
{
    var messageArray:Array = pMessageText.split(" ");
    return messageArray.length;
}
```

There is no private property keeping track of the number of words. Instead, the value is calculated based on another private property.

Try It Out   Adding Properties to a Photo Thumbnail Class

In this example, you add methods to a class to create a clickable button out of a dynamically loaded thumbnail image.

1. Open the completed `tryItOut_thumbnailButton.fla` file from the previous Try It Out exercise, or open up the source Flash project file from the book's source files at <source file directory>/ Chapter 27/tryItOut_thumbnail_v2/tryItOut_thumbnailButton.fla.

2. Open the completed `ThumbnailButton.as` file from the previous Try It Out exercise, or open up the source Flash project file from the book's source files at <source file directory>/Chapter 27/ tryItOut_thumbnail_v2/ThumbnailButton.as.

3. Add the following two private properties at the top of the class definition:

```
private var pParentTimeline:MovieClip;
...
private var pMovieClipLoader:MovieClipLoader;
private var pDrawDropShadow:Boolean = true;
private var pDrawBorder:Boolean = true;
```

4. Add the following two `if` statements at the end of the `drawThumbnail()` method:

```
if (pDrawBorder == true)
{
    pBorderHolder.moveTo(0, 0);
    pBorderHolder.lineTo(pImageHolder._width-1, 0);
    pBorderHolder.lineTo(pImageHolder._width-1, pImageHolder._height-1);
    pBorderHolder.lineTo(0, pImageHolder._height-1);
    pBorderHolder.lineTo(0, 0);
}

if (pDrawDropShadow == true)
{
    appliedFilterArray.push(dropShadowFilter);
    pThumbnailHolder.filters = appliedFilterArray;
}
```

5. Add the following getters and setters just after the end of the `drawThumbnail()` method, but before the closing brace for the class block:

```
public function get onClick():Function
{
    return pClickHandler;
}

public function set onClick(clickHandler:Function):Void
{
    pClickHandler = clickHandler;
}

public function get x():Number
{
    return pThumbnailHolder._x;
}

public function set x(xPosition:Number):Void
{
    pThumbnailHolder._x = xPosition;
}

public function get y():Number
{
    return pThumbnailHolder._y;
}

public function set y(yPosition:Number):Void
{
    pThumbnailHolder._y = yPosition;
}

public function get drawBorder():Boolean
{
    return pDrawBorder;
}

public function set drawBorder(drawBorderSetting:Boolean):Void
```

```
{
    pDrawBorder = drawBorderSetting;
    drawThumbnail("up");
}

public function get drawDropShadow():Boolean
{
    return pDrawDropShadow;
}

public function set drawDropShadow(drawDropShadowSetting:Boolean):Void
{
    pDrawDropShadow = drawDropShadowSetting;
    drawThumbnail("up");
}

public function get thumbnailName():String
{
    return pThumbnailName;
}
```

6. Using your favorite image editor, resize and crop three additional photos into three small images around 50 pixels by 50 pixels. Save them as JPG files into the same directory containing the FLA and AS files. You can instead obtain sample images in the book source files at <source file directory>/Chapter 27/tryItOut_thumbnail_v2/.

7. Return to the FLA file, click the first frame in the timeline, open the Actions panel (Window⇔ Development Panels⇔Actions), and update the ActionScript code to look like the following code. If you have named your image files something different, change the parameters in the load() methods to refer to your images:

```
var thumbnailArray:Array = new Array();
var thumbnailHandle:ThumbnailButton;

for (var i=0; i < 4; i++)
{
    thumbnailHandle = new ThumbnailButton(this, "thumbnail" + i);
    thumbnailHandle.x = i * 70 + 20;
    thumbnailHandle.y = 20;
    thumbnailHandle.drawDropShadow = true;
    thumbnailHandle.drawBorder = true;
    thumbnailHandle.onClick = function(thumbnailHandle:ThumbnailButton)
    {
        trace("Clicked on button: " + thumbnailHandle.thumbnailName);
    }
    thumbnailArray.push(thumbnailHandle);
}

thumbnailArray[0].load("aStudyInTexture_over.jpg");
thumbnailArray[1].load("buntzenWinter_over.jpg");
thumbnailArray[2].load("flowerInDetail_over.jpg");
thumbnailArray[3].load("galianoSunset_over.jpg");
```

8. Choose Control⇔Test Movie to try it out.

How It Works

The getters and setters that you add to the class perform a mixture of tasks. The first is the `onClick` property. This property allows the developer to specify what function should be called when the button is pressed and then released. Only the setter is really needed here, but it is generally considered proper to always provide a getter along with a setter. If you can set a property, you should be able to read from it, too:

```
public function get onClick():Function
{
    return pClickHandler;
}

public function set onClick(clickHandler:Function):Void
{
    pClickHandler = clickHandler;
}
```

The getters and setters for the thumbnail position *x* and *y* values refer to the *x* and *y* properties of the thumbnail holder movie clip:

```
public function get x():Number
{
    return pThumbnailHolder._x;
}

public function set x(xPosition:Number):Void
{
    pThumbnailHolder._x = xPosition;
}

public function get y():Number
{
    return pThumbnailHolder._y;
}

public function set y(yPosition:Number):Void
{
    pThumbnailHolder._y = yPosition;
}
```

The `drawBorder` property enables you to specify whether or not to draw the box around the image. When the setter is called, it changes the private property and it forces the thumbnail to redraw immediately:

```
public function get drawBorder():Boolean
{
    return pDrawBorder;
}

public function set drawBorder(drawBorderSetting:Boolean):Void
{
    pDrawBorder = drawBorderSetting;
    drawThumbnail("up");
}
```

The `drawDropShadow` property enables you to specify whether or not to draw the shadow behind the image. When the setter is called, it changes the private property and it forces the thumbnail to redraw immediately:

```
public function get drawDropShadow():Boolean
{
    return pDrawDropShadow;
}

public function set drawDropShadow(drawDropShadowSetting:Boolean):Void
{
    pDrawDropShadow = drawDropShadowSetting;
    drawThumbnail("up");
}
```

Finally, the `thumbnailName` property is read-only and enables the name of the thumbnail button to be retrieved when the `onClick` event handler is called:

```
public function get thumbnailName():String
{
    return pThumbnailName;
}
```

Next, you see how you can create a new class to extend functionality of an existing class.

Adding Functionality to Existing Classes

One question that comes up frequently in various forums is how to add functionality to the built-in Flash classes. There are different ways of doing this, including subclassing, static classes, and composition.

In ActionScript 1.0, classes can be directly modified using the `prototype` property of the class. This technique is generally discouraged because it affects code globally and as such can interfere with code re-use.

Subclassing

One of the concepts brought up in Chapter 5 was that of subclassing and inheritance. Subclassing involves creating a class that uses another class as a template, and then adds or modifies functionality. The new class inherits all of the functionality from the parent class.

Although this sounds like it's exactly what you want, subclassing is generally not a great way to extend built-in classes. Numerous examples on various online forums try to use subclassing to extend built-in classes, but in fact end up using another technique called composition. The following code shows how a new method can be added to the String class using subclassing:

```
class MyString extends String
{
    public function MyString(inputString:String)
    {
        super(inputString);
    }

    public function replace(searchString:String, replaceString:String):Void
```

```
    {
        var newVal:String = split(searchString).join(replaceString);
        super(newVal);
    }
}
```

The `extends` keyword indicates that the new class MyString is a subclass of the String class. The constructor takes in a single string parameter, which is the same parameter that the parent String class normally accepts. The `super()` method passes that parameter to the parent class, namely the String class.

The `replace()` method performs a search-and-replace operation on the string that was initially passed in to the constructor. The `split()` method that is called is inherited from the String class and knows to work on the string that was initially passed to the constructor because the `super()` method passed the text to the String class's constructor.

The following code makes use of this new class:

```
var myMessage:MyString = new MyString("The quick brown fox");
myMessage.replace("quick", "quack");
myMessage.replace("brown", "red");
trace(myMessage.toUpperCase());
// Outputs: THE QUACK RED FOX
```

Note that the MyString class now supports the new `replace()` method, plus it automatically inherited `toUpperCase()` from the String class.

Although this looks nice, you will face problems if you try to assign new data to your new MyString instance, something that you would expect to be able to do. For instance, if you assign the output of the `toUpperCase()` method to the MyString instance, you will get a compile error:

```
myMessage = myMessage.toUpperCase();

**Error** Scene=Scene 1, layer=Layer 1, frame=1:Line 4: Type mismatch in assignment
statement: found String where MyString is required.
    myMessage = myMessage.toUpperCase();
```

The problem is that `myMessage` is of type MyString, and `myMessage.toUpperCase()` returns a value of type String. To make this work, you need to convert the String data type to MyString:

```
myMessage = new MyString(myMessage.toUpperCase());
```

This starts to get real cumbersome real fast. Although having a subclass inherit all of the parent class's methods is nice, it is not very practical for built-in classes. A cleaner way of doing this is through a static class, which you look at next.

Static Library

Some built-in classes do not need to be instantiated for you to be able to call some of its methods. For instance, `Math.random()` returns a random number, `Key.getCode()` returns the character code of a key pressed on the keyboard, and `System.setClipboard("foo")` places the text "foo" into the system clipboard. In none of these cases do you have to call `new Math()`, `new Key()`, or `new System()` before calling the method. These methods are called static methods. Creating a class populated with static methods is a very handy way of creating your own library of utilities.

The following code shows how to create a class with a static method:

```
class MyLibrary
{
    private function MyLibrary()
    {
        // Constructor is empty
    }

    public static function myStaticFunction(inputString:String):String
    {
        return "Input value: " + inputString;
    }
}
```

To call the static method, just call it directly from the class itself:

```
trace(MyLibrary.myStaticFunction("foo");
// Outputs: Input value: foo
```

Two things are different about this class definition. First, the constructor is set to be private. This class is not actually going to hold data, so it does not need to be instantiated. The fact that the constructor is private enforces this usage, because it will cause a compiler error if you attempt to instantiate it. Second, there is a `static` keyword included with the method declaration. It is this keyword that tells the compiler that this method can be called without instantiating the class.

In the next Try It Out exercise, you see how to use static methods to create a library of string handling functions.

Try It Out   Creating a String Handling Library

In this example, you use static methods to create a class containing a library of string handling routines.

1. Create a new ActionScript document by selecting File⇒New and choosing ActionScript File from the New Document panel.

2. Select File⇒Save As and choose an appropriate folder for the file. Give the file the name `StringLib.as` and save it.

3. Enter the following code into the new ActionScript file:

```
class StringLib
{
    private function StringLib()
    {
        // Nothing placed here
    }

    public static function replace(sourceString:String, ⊃
```

```
              searchString:String, replaceString:String):String
       {
           var newString:String = ⊃
               sourceString.split(searchString).join(replaceString);
           return newString;
       }
   }
```

4. Save the file (File⇨Save).

5. Create a new Macromedia Flash document by selecting File⇨New and choosing Flash Document from the New Document panel.

6. Click the first frame in the timeline, open the Actions panel (Window⇨Development Panels⇨ Actions), and enter in the following ActionScript code:

```
var myMessage:String = "   The quick brown fox. Jumped over the lazy dog.      ";
trace("myMessage: '" + myMessage + "'");
myMessage = StringLib.replace(myMessage, "brown", "red");
trace("myMessage.replace brown==>red: '" + myMessage + "'");
```

7. Select File⇨Save As, name the file tryItOut_stringLib.fla, and save it in the same directory as StringLib.as.

8. Choose Control⇨Test Movie to try it out.

9. Switch to the AS file and add the following method after the replace() method but just before the final closing class bracket:

```
// Remove any leading or trailingspaces, tabs, or
// linefeeds from the string
public static function trimWhiteSpace(sourceString:String):String
{
    var numChars:Number = sourceString.length;
    var firstCharPosition:Number = 0;
    var lastCharPosition:Number = numChars-1;
    var whiteSpaceChars:String = " \t\n\r";
    var currentChar:String;

    // Look for first non-whitespace character
    for (var i = 0; i < numChars; i++)
    {
        currentChar = sourceString.charAt(i);
        if (whiteSpaceChars.indexOf(currentChar) == -1)
        {
            firstCharPosition = i;
            break;
        }
    }

    // Look for last non-whitespace character
    for (i = numChars - 1; i >= 0; i--)
    {
        currentChar = sourceString.charAt(i);
        if (whiteSpaceChars.indexOf(currentChar) == -1)
        {
            lastCharPosition = i;
```

```
                break;
        }
    }

    return sourceString.slice(firstCharPosition, lastCharPosition+1);
}
```

10. Switch to the AS file and update the contents of the Actions panel:

```
var myMessage:String = "   The quick brown fox. Jumped over the lazy dog.    ";
trace("myMessage: '" + myMessage + "'");
myMessage = StringLib.replace(myMessage, "brown", "red");
trace("myMessage.replace brown==>red: '" + myMessage + "'");
myMessage = StringLib.trimWhiteSpace(myMessage);
trace("myMessage.trimWhiteSpace: '"+ myMessage + "'");
```

11. Choose Control⇨Test Movie to try it out.

12. Switch to the AS file and add the following two methods after the `trimWhiteSpace()` method but just before the final closing class bracket:

```
public static function countWords(sourceString:String):Number
{
    var tempString:String = StringLib.trimWhiteSpace(sourceString);

    while (tempString.indexOf("  ") >= 0)
    {
        // Replace double spaces with single spaces throughout
        // the string. Keep doing it until groups of more than one
        // space are whittled down to one space.
        tempString = StringLib.replace(tempString, "  ", " ");
    }

    // Convert to an array, dividing up the array using the
    // spaces as the separator
    var wordArray:Array = tempString.split(" ");

    // The length of the array will match the number of words
    // in the original message.
    return wordArray.length;
}

public static function countSentences(sourceString:String):Number
{
    // Look for any ". " combinations. By looking for a dot followed
    // by a space, numbers with decimals will not add to the number
    // of sentences, nor will the last period count.
    var sentenceArray:Array = sourceString.split(". ");
    return sentenceArray.length;
}
```

13. Switch to the AS file and update the contents of the Actions panel:

```
var myMessage:String = "   The quick brown fox. Jumped over the lazy dog.    ";
trace("myMessage: '" + myMessage + "'");
myMessage = StringLib.replace(myMessage, "brown", "red");
```

```
trace("myMessage.replace brown==>red: '" + myMessage + "'");
myMessage = StringLib.trimWhiteSpace(myMessage);
trace("myMessage.trimWhiteSpace: '"+ myMessage + "'");
trace("myMessage.numWords: " + StringLib.countWords(myMessage));
trace("myMessage.numSentences: " + StringLib.countSentences(myMessage));
```

14. Choose Control⇨Test Movie to try it out.

How It Works

This example shows how creating a class consisting of static methods is an easy way to create your own library of common code. This class can be easily given to someone else, and it will integrate cleanly into their code, unlike adding methods directly to a built-in class. It is considerably more straightforward to develop and use than subclassing, and you can clearly see when a library method is being used and where the library method comes from.

Composition

Another alternative to subclassing is a technique called composition. This technique involves one class that contains one or more instances of another class but does not inherit anything from that class.

As an example, say that you want to add the ability to create an effect for a movie clip. With the subclassing approach, you would create a custom class that inherits from the MovieClip class and then add the effect to the class. With composition, you create a class that contains a movie clip, but does not inherit from the MovieClip class.

To understand the distinction, think about how the classes you are working with are related. Subclassing uses what is called an is-a relationship, whereas composition uses a has-a relationship. Say you have a Vehicle class and a Car class. The car is-a vehicle, so the Car class can be a subclass of the Vehicle class. Now say you have a Car class and an Engine class. It does not make sense to say that a car is-an engine, but it makes sense to say that a car has-an engine. The car is *composed* of an engine, brakes, and other parts, so the Car class is a composition.

Figure 27-2 shows the difference between subclassing and composition.

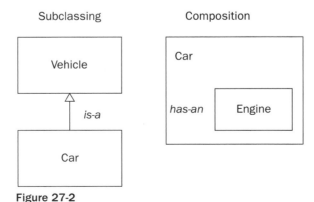

Figure 27-2

Some examples of using composition to create a class include the following:

❑ A class called SpinEffect that creates an animation effect for a movie clip. The SpinEffect class has-a movie clip.

❑ A class called RecordSetLoader that uses the XML object to load data from a server and then converts it to a more useful data format. The RecordSetLoader class has-an XML instance.

❑ A Queue class that uses an array to keep track of data to be processed. The Queue class has-an array.

In many cases where an individual chooses to use subclassing, an is-a relationship does not actually exist. Even if such a relationship does exist, many times it is better to re-phrase the relationship to make use of composition instead.

Take a look at actually implementing a composition-based class.

Try It Out   Using Composition to Create a Spin Effect

This exercise shows how to create a class that uses composition. It takes in a movie clip as a constructor argument and animates whatever the passed-in movie clip contains.

1. Create a new ActionScript document by selecting File⇨New and choosing ActionScript File from the New Document panel.

2. Select File⇨Save As and choose an appropriate folder for the file. Give the file the name SpinEffect.as and save it.

3. Enter the following code into the new ActionScript file:

```
class SpinEffect
{
    private var pTargetClip:MovieClip;

    public function SpinEffect(targetClip:MovieClip)
    {
        pTargetClip = targetClip;
    }

    public function zoomOut():Void
    {
        pTargetClip._rotation = 0;
        pTargetClip._xscale = pTargetClip._yscale = 100;
        pTargetClip._alpha = 100;
        pTargetClip._visible = true;
        pTargetClip.onEnterFrame = function()
        {
            this._rotation += 31;
            this._xscale *= 0.92;
            this._yscale = this._xscale;
            this._alpha = this._xscale;
            if (this._xscale < 2)
            {
                this._visible = false;
                delete this.onEnterFrame;
            }
```

```
            }
        }

        public function zoomIn():Void
        {
            pTargetClip._rotation = 0;
            pTargetClip._xscale = pTargetClip._yscale = 2;
            pTargetClip._alpha = 2;
            pTargetClip._visible = true;
            pTargetClip.onEnterFrame = function()
            {
                this._rotation -= 31;
                this._xscale *= 1.08;
                this._yscale = this._xscale;
                this._alpha = this._xscale;
                if (this._xscale >= 100)
                {
                    this._rotation = 0;
                    delete this.onEnterFrame;
                }
            }
        }
    }
}
```

4. Save the file.

5. Create a new Macromedia Flash document.

6. Click the first frame in the timeline, open the Actions panel, and enter in the following ActionScript code:

```
// Create a movie clip, then draw a square centered around the 0,0 point
this.createEmptyMovieClip("squareClip", this.getNextHighestDepth());
squareClip.beginFill(0x000000, 100);
squareClip.moveTo(-100, -100);
squareClip.lineTo(100, -100);
squareClip.lineTo(100, 100);
squareClip.lineTo(-100, 100);
squareClip.lineTo(-100, -100);
squareClip.endFill();

squareClip._x = 200;
squareClip._y = 200;

// Create a second movie clip from the first one
squareClip.duplicateMovieClip("squareClip2", this.getNextHighestDepth());
squareClip2._x = 400;

// Create new instances of the SpinEffect class for each clip
// to be animated.
var mySpinEffect = new SpinEffect(squareClip);
mySpinEffect.zoomIn();

var mySpinEffect2 = new SpinEffect(squareClip2);
mySpinEffect2.zoomOut();
```

7. Select File⇨Save As, name the file `tryItOut_spinEffect.fla`, and save it in the same directory as `SpinEffect.as`.

8. Choose Control⇨Test Movie to try it out.

How It Works

The SpinEffect class is composed of a movie clip that it uses for the animation. The SpinEffect class has-a movie clip, so composition is an appropriate approach to this class.

The class block itself is just the basic class statement. There is no `extends MovieClip` statement along with the class declaration, so no subclassing is being used:

```
class SpinEffect {
```

At the start of the class, a private property called `pTargetClip` is defined. This property will hold the movie clip to be animated, and forms the basis for this composition. Even though this class holds only one piece of data, it is still considered a composition:

```
private var pTargetClip:MovieClip;
```

The constructor takes in a single parameter, which is a handle to the movie clip to animate:

```
public function SpinEffect(targetClip:MovieClip)
{
    pTargetClip = targetClip;
}
```

The `zoomOut()` method makes use of the movie clip that was passed in. It manipulates the scale, alpha, and rotation values of the movie clip to give the desired effect. The `zoomIn()` method is nearly identical; it just reverses the direction of the animation:

```
public function zoomOut():Void
{
    pTargetClip._rotation = 0;
    pTargetClip._xscale = pTargetClip._yscale = 100;
    pTargetClip._alpha = 100;
    pTargetClip._visible = true;
    pTargetClip.onEnterFrame = function()
    {
        this._rotation += 31;
        this._xscale *= 0.92;
        this._yscale = this._xscale;
        this._alpha = this._xscale;
        if (this._xscale < 2)
        {
            this._visible = false;
            delete this.onEnterFrame;
        }
    }
}
```

The process of creating a new instance of the custom class is the same as pretty much all the class creation code you have already seen throughout the book. Each instance of the effect uses a different movie clip and operates independently of the other:

```
var mySpinEffect = new SpinEffect(squareClip);
mySpinEffect.zoomIn();

var mySpinEffect2 = new SpinEffect(squareClip2);
mySpinEffect2.zoomOut();
```

Take a look at another example, where you create a queue class for loading data from a server.

Try It Out   Using Composition to Create a Data Queue

When loading data from a server, sometimes there is a need to break up a large request for data into multiple smaller requests. For instance, if you need to load a list of data records via XML, you can break up the data to keep the user interface more responsive. This queue class enables you to make multiple requests for data without worrying about how to manage loading data in sequence.

A queue is a type of array where data gets added onto one end and removed from the other, in the same way that you might line up for tickets at a movie theater. Each request is serviced in the order it is received. There is no queue data type in Flash, but that can be easily created using an array. This example uses composition to create a queue out of an array to load data from a server or from local files.

1.   Create a new ActionScript document. Name it XMLQueueClass.as and save it in an appropriate folder.

2.   Enter the following code into the file:

```
class XMLDataQueue
{
    private var pDataQueue:Array;
    private var pIsLoadActive:Boolean;
    private var pXML:XML;

    public function XMLDataQueue()
    {
        pDataQueue = new Array();
        pIsLoadActive = false;
    }

    // Add a request to load a file
    public function push(dataURL:String, callbackHandler:Function)
    {
        pDataQueue.push({url:dataURL, callback:callbackHandler});

        if (pIsLoadActive == false)
        {
            pIsLoadActive = true;
            loadNextData();
        }
    }

    // Load the next pending request in the list
```

```
    private function loadNextData():Void
    {
        var parent:XMLDataQueue = this;

        pXML = new XML();
        pXML.ignoreWhite = true;
        pXML.onLoad = function(status:Boolean)
        {
            parent.handleData(status);
        }

        pXML.load(pDataQueue[0].url);
    }

    // Get the data back from the currently loading request
    // and pass the data to a user-specified callback function
    private function handleData(status:Boolean):Void
    {
        // Call the callback function for this request, and remove
        // the request from the queue
        if (status == true)
        {
            pDataQueue[0].callback(pXML, pDataQueue[0].url);
        }
        else
        {
            pDataQueue[0].callback(null, pDataQueue[0].url);
        }
        pDataQueue.shift();

        // Make the next request, if there is still one in the queue
        if (pDataQueue.length > 0)
        {
            loadNextData();
        }
        else
        {
            pIsLoadActive = false;
        }
    }
}
```

3. Save the file.

4. Create a new Macromedia Flash document.

5. Click the first frame in the timeline, open the Actions panel, and enter in the following ActionScript code:

```
function dataHandler(returnData:XML, sourceURL:String):Void
{
    var rootNode:XMLNode = returnData.firstChild;
    var numNodes:Number = rootNode.childNodes.length;

    var photoId:String;
    var photoTitle:String;
```

```
    var photoSize:Number;

    trace("\nData loaded from: " + sourceURL);
    for (var i=0; i < numNodes; i++)
    {
        photoId = rootNode.childNodes[i].attributes.id;
        photoTitle = rootNode.childNodes[i].attributes.title;
        photoSize = Number(rootNode.childNodes[i].attributes.size);
        trace("id: " + photoId + " title: " + photoTitle + ⤵
            " size: " + photoSize);
    }
}

var myDataQueue:XMLDataQueue = new XMLDataQueue();
myDataQueue.push("dataFile1.xml", dataHandler);
myDataQueue.push("dataFile2.xml", dataHandler);
myDataQueue.push("dataFile3.xml", dataHandler);
```

6. Name the file `tryItOut_xmlQueue.fla`, and save it in the same directory as `XMLDataQueue.as`.

7. In your preferred text editor, create a file called `dataFile1.xml`. Enter the following XML markup in the file:

```
<?xml version="1.0"?>
<photos>
    <photo id="aStudyInSpeed" title="A Study In Speed" size="123" />
    <photo id="aStudyInTexture" title="A Study In Texture" size="321" />
    <photo id="beachAbstraction" title="Beach Abstraction" size="231" />
    <photo id="buntzenFog" title="Buntzen Fog" size="213" />
</photos>
```

8. In your preferred text editor, create another file called `dataFile2.xml`. Enter the following XML markup in the file:

```
<?xml version="1.0"?>
<photos>
    <photo id="christmasFrost" title="A Study In Speed" size="323" />
    <photo id="fishingAtSunset" title="Fishing At Sunset" size="121" />
    <photo id="forestPath" title="Forest Path" size="221" />
    <photo id="galianoSunset" title="Galiano Sunset" size="112" />
</photos>
```

9. In your preferred text editor, create a third file called `dataFile3.xml`. Within this file, place the following XML markup:

```
<?xml version="1.0"?>
<photos>
    <photo id="granvilleIsland" title="Granville Island" size="113" />
    <photo id="greenLakeInRed" title="Green Lake in Red" size="143" />
    <photo id="heavenlyLight" title="Heavenly Light" size="131" />
    <photo id="liquidSun" title="LiquidSun" size="213" />
</photos>
```

10. Choose Control⇨Test Movie to try it out.

How It Works

With this example, it is less clear as to whether an is-a or a has-a relationship exists. A queue is-a type of array; however, this queue is designed for server communications and contains more functionality than just array management. The array is thus just one element of a composition that also includes the XML class. In this light, the XMLDataQueue class has-an array and is well-suited for composition.

The private properties store an array to be used for creating the queue, plus an XML object to handle the actual data loading. The pIsLoadActive property is used to stop checking the queue if there are no requests left to load:

```
private var pDataQueue:Array;
private var pIsLoadActive:Boolean;
private var pXML:XML;
```

The constructor sets initial values to the properties:

```
public function XMLDataQueue()
{
    pDataQueue = new Array();
    pIsLoadActive = false;
}
```

The push() method is the only public method. This method adds a request to the end of the queue. If the data loader is idle because the queue was previously empty, the loader is started back up:

```
public function push(dataURL:String, callbackHandler:Function)
{
    pDataQueue.push({url:dataURL, callback:callbackHandler});

    if (pIsLoadActive == false)
    {
        pIsLoadActive = true;
        loadNextData();
    }
}
```

The loadNextData() method grabs the request that is currently at the start of the queue and loads the requested file. The first line where parent is declared allows handleData() to be properly called from this class instance. Without it, handleData() cannot be called from within the onLoad() function:

```
private function loadNextData():Void
{
    var parent:XMLDataQueue = this;

    pXML = new XML();
    pXML.ignoreWhite = true;
    pXML.onLoad = function(status:Boolean)
    {
        parent.handleData(status);
    }

    pXML.load(pDataQueue[0].url);
}
```

The `handleData()` method deals with the data returning from the server. When the XML returns, `handleData()` passes that data to the function assigned to handle this request. The request is then removed from the queue and the next request is processed:

```
private function handleData(status:Boolean):Void
{
    if (status == true)
    {
        pDataQueue[0].callback(pXML, pDataQueue[0].url);
    }
    else
    {
        pDataQueue[0].callback(null, pDataQueue[0].url);
    }
    pDataQueue.shift();

    if (pDataQueue.length > 0)
    {
        loadNextData();
    }
    else
    {
        pIsLoadActive = false;
    }
}
```

Taking a look at the code within the Actions panel of the FLA file, you see that the `dataHandler()` function deals with actually doing something with the data returned from the server. If you are not sure about how to parse XML data, return to Chapter 21.

```
function dataHandler(returnData:XML, sourceURL:String):Void
{
    var rootNode:XMLNode = returnData.firstChild;
    var numNodes:Number = rootNode.childNodes.length;

    var photoId:String;
    var photoTitle:String;
    var photoSize:Number;

    trace("\nData loaded from: " + sourceURL);
    for (var i=0; i < numNodes; i++)
    {
        photoId = rootNode.childNodes[i].attributes.id;
        photoTitle = rootNode.childNodes[i].attributes.title;
        photoSize = Number(rootNode.childNodes[i].attributes.size);
        trace("id: " + photoId + " title: " + photoTitle + ⤵
            " size: " + photoSize);
    }
}
```

Finally, an instance of the XMLDataQueue class is created and requests are made for the data files. If this were actually calling dynamic data on a server, you would instead use the URL to get to the JSP, ASP, PHP, or servlet page that actually returns the data:

```
var myDataQueue:XMLDataQueue = new XMLDataQueue();
```

```
myDataQueue.push("dataFile1.xml", dataHandler);
myDataQueue.push("dataFile2.xml", dataHandler);
myDataQueue.push("dataFile3.xml", dataHandler);
```

Summary

This chapter explored the process of creating custom classes. Some of the things that you learned include the following:

❏ A custom class allows you to organize and package your own code in a way that makes code cleaner and re-use significantly easier.

❏ Classes must be placed in their own .as files with the same name as the class itself.

❏ A constructor is a special class method that is called when an instance of the class is created using the new operator. The constructor calls code that should run at the instance's startup.

❏ Public properties and methods are available to anyone who uses your class. Private properties and methods can be called only from within the class itself.

❏ Properties and methods are defined in the same way as variables and functions, only they are preceded with either the public or the private keyword and they exist within a class block.

❏ Public properties should be implemented using getter and setter functions. The actual internal property should not be made public.

❏ Subclassing is used to extend other classes, by allowing a class to inherit another class's methods and properties, and then adding or modifying them. Subclassing is not actually recommended for extending the functionality of the classes built into Flash.

❏ Classes with static methods are a good way to provide a library of functionality. Static methods do not require the class to be instantiated to be used.

❏ Composition allows for class functionality to be extended in a cleaner way than subclassing allows. Composition involves one class containing or being composed of one or more other classes.

Exercises

1. By just looking at the following properties, which of the property declarations are valid, which are invalid, and why?

   a. `var myProperty:String;`

   b. `public var myProperty2;`

   c. `static public var myProperty3:String;`

   d. `private myProperty4:Boolean;`

   e. `private var myProperty5:Boolean = false;`

   f. `public var myProperty6:Boolean = "true";`

2. Assume the following class definition:

```
class TestClass
{
    private var pMessageText:String;
    public var altMessage:String = "";

    function TestClass(initialMessage:String)
    {
        pMessageText = initialMessage;
    }

    public function get messageText():String
    {
        return pMessageText;
    }

    public function set messageText(newMessage:String):Void
    {
        pMessageText = newMessage;
    }

    public function getAlternate():String
    {
        return altMessage;
    }

    private function replaceText(fromText:String, toText:String):Void
    {
        pMessageText = pMessageText.split(fromText).join(toText);
    }

    public function removePunctuation():String
    {
        replaceText(".", "");
        return pMessageText;
    }
}
```

Also assume the following class instantiation:

```
var myTestClass:TestClass = new TestClass("The quick brown fox.");
```

Without trying the preceding code, what is the result of running each of the following statements?

a. `myTestClass.messageText = myTestClass.messageText + ⤸`
`" Jumped over the lazy dog.";`

b. `trace(myTestClass.messageText);`

c. `trace(myTestClass.pMessageText);`

d. `myTestClass.replaceText(".", "");`

e. `myTestClass.removePunctuation();`

f. `trace(myTestClass.messageText);`

g. `myTestClass.altMessage = "Foo";`

h. `trace(myTestClass.alternate);`

i. `trace(myTestClass.altMessage);`

j. `trace(myTestClass.getAlternate());`

3. Create a class for managing the data for a photo viewer application. It should consist of an array to hold the data about each photo. Each array element should contain the following anonymous object:

```
var tempObject:Object = new Object();
tempObject.id = "photo1";
tempObject.name = "Photo 1";
tempObject.description = "The quick brown fox 1";
tempObject.thumbnailURL = "photo1Thumbnail.jpg";
tempObject.fullSizeURL = photo1FullSize.jpg";
tempObject.size = 123;
tempObject.visited = false;

pPhotoArray.push(tempObject);
```

The class should have the following properties and methods:

❏ A method called `addData()` that takes an id, a name, a description, a URL for a thumbnail image, a URL for a full-size image, and the size of the image. It should create an anonymous object, assign these properties to the object, and then add it to the array.

❏ A method called `getDataById()` that takes a string, searches through the array for a data entry that has that ID, and then returns that whole entry.

❏ A method called `getDataByIndex()` that takes a number and returns the data entry at that position in the array.

❏ A method called `setVisited()` that accepts a number indicating the array position to modify, sets the `visited` attribute to `true`, and then updates a private property that keeps track of the number of visited photos.

❏ A read-only property called `numPhotos` that returns the size of the photo array.

❏ A read-only property called `numVisited` that returns the number of photos that have their `visited` properties set to `true`.

❏ A method called `toString()` that returns loops through each array element and prints out each attribute name and value. Hint: Use `"\n"` in a string to force a line break.

4. Extend the final Try It Out thumbnail_v3 exercise to allow for a tool tip text description to show up under the icon when the mouse is over the thumbnail button.

❏ You might want to use the `MovieClip.createEmptyMovieClip()` method to create a movie clip holder in the constructor and then use `MovieClip.createTextField()` to place an empty text field in that movie clip.

❏ The tool tip text should be set via a public property accessed using a pair of getter and setter methods. The setter should assign the text to the text field and then should apply any desired text formatting. You might elect to use the drawing API to draw a box around the text.

❏ Use the `drawThumbnail()` method to position, show, and hide the text field depending on the thumbnail state.

Exercise Answers

Chapter 1

There are no actual solutions to the exercises in Chapter 1, which were created simply to help you become accustomed to the Flash IDE, where you'll be spending quite a bit of time as you work through this book.

Chapter 2

Exercise 1 Solution

a. Valid. It is a combination of a declaration and an assignment, which is allowed in a single statement.

b. Not valid. The data type Integer does not exist. The Number data type should be used instead.

c. Not valid. Strong typing requires use of the `var` statement.

d. Not valid. A variable name cannot start with a number.

e. Valid, but not recommended. The variable name is also used as a property for the MovieClip class.

f. Not valid. Data of type String is being assigned to a variable of type Boolean. The quotes should be removed.

Exercise 2 Solution

The contents of the round brackets are evaluated first, so `numItemsPrepaid` is subtracted from `numItemsPickedUp`. Next, the multiplication is evaluated, with the results of the subtraction multiplied by `perItemCost`. That result is then added to `handlingFee`, and that final answer is assigned to `totalAmount`.

Exercise 3 Solution

The final value is 130.

Exercise 4 Solution

The output is

```
blue jay-crow-warbler
```

Chapter 3

Exercise 1 Solution

```
var shoppingCart:Array = new Array();
shoppingCart.push({modelNumber:"ip300", description:"MP3 Music Player", ⊃
    price:299, quantity:1});
shoppingCart.push({modelNumber:"ip300c", description:"Music Player Case", ⊃
    price:49, quantity:1});
shoppingCart.push({modelNumber:"eb100", description:"Earbuds", ⊃
    price:29, quantity:2});
shoppingCart.push({modelNumber:"cc250", description:"Car Charger Kit", ⊃
    price:69, quantity:1});

var totalBill:Number = 0;
var numItems:Number = shoppingCart.length;

for (var i:Number = 0; i < numItems; i++)
{
    trace("Description:   " + shoppingCart[i].description);
    trace("Model Number:  " + shoppingCart[i].modelNumber);
    trace("Price:         $" + shoppingCart[i].price);
    trace("Quantity:      " + shoppingCart[i].quantity);
    trace("----------------");
    totalBill = totalBill + shoppingCart[i].price * shoppingCart[i].quantity;
}
trace("Total Bill:    $" + totalBill);
```

Exercise 2 Solution

```
var vehicleType:String = "semi";
var spareCabin:Boolean = false;
var numDoors:Number;

switch (vehicleType)
{
    case "sedan":
        numDoors = 4;
        break;

    case "sportscar":
        numDoors = 3;
        break;

    case "semi":
```

```
            if (spareCabin == true)
            {
                numDoors = 3;
            }
            else
            {
                numDoors = 2;
            }
            break;

        default:
            numDoors = 2;
    }
    trace(numDoors);
```

Exercise 3 Solution

```
var fruitArray:Array = new Array("banana", "pear", "strawberry", "grape");
var numFruit:Number = fruitArray.length;
var foundFruit:Number = 0;
var numLetters:Number = 6;

for (var currentFruit:Number = 0; currentFruit < numFruit; currentFruit++)
{
    if (fruitArray[currentFruit].length >= numLetters)
    {
        trace(fruitArray[currentFruit]);
        foundFruit++;
    }
}

trace("found " + foundFruit + " fruits with 6 or more letters in the name");
```

Chapter 4

Exercise 1 Solution

This solution also makes sure that the comparison is case-insensitive through the addition of the toLower
Case() method. Without it, the string Foo would come before bar in the sort order.

```
function compareStrings(string1:String, string2:String):Number
{
    if (string1.toLowerCase() < string2.toLowerCase())
    {
        return 1;
    }
    else if (string2.toLowerCase() < string1.toLowerCase())
    {
        return -1;
    }
    else
    {
        return 0;
    }
```

```
    }

    trace("comparing foo and bar: " + compareStrings("foo", "bar"));
    trace("comparing boo and far: " + compareStrings("boo", "far"));
    trace("comparing Foo and bar: " + compareStrings("Foo", "bar"));
    trace("comparing foo and foo: " + compareStrings("foo", "foo"));
```

Exercise 2 Solution

```
    var fruitArray:Array = new Array("kumquat", "apple", "pear", ⤶
        "strawberry", "banana");
    trace("FruitArray: " + fruitArray);

    function sortArray(inputArray:Array):Array
    {
        var tempArray:Array = inputArray.slice(); // Makes a complete copy.
        tempArray.sort();
        return tempArray;
    }

    var sortedArray:Array = sortArray(fruitArray);
    trace("FruitArray: " + fruitArray);
    trace("SortedArray: " + sortedArray);
```

Exercise 3 Solution

```
    function drawRectangle(targetMC:MovieClip, rectWidth:Number, rectHeight:Number,
    bgColor:Number):Void
    {
        targetMC.moveTo(0, 0);
        targetMC.lineStyle(1, 0x000000);
        targetMC.beginFill(bgColor, 100);
        targetMC.lineTo(rectWidth, 0);
        targetMC.lineTo(rectWidth, rectHeight);
        targetMC.lineTo(0, rectHeight);
        targetMC.lineTo(0, 0);
    }

    function buttonClickHandler():Void
    {
        trace("Button pressed");
    }

    function convertToButton(targetMC:MovieClip, callbackFunction:Function):Void
    {
        drawRectangle(targetMC, 100, 30, 0x333399);

        targetMC.onPress = function()
        {
            this.clear();
            drawRectangle(this, 100, 30, 0xCC3333);
        }

        targetMC.onRelease = function()
        {
```

```
        this.clear();
        drawRectangle(this, 100, 30, 0x6666AA);
        callbackFunction();
    }

    targetMC.onReleaseOutside = function()
    {
        this.clear();
        drawRectangle(this, 100, 30, 0x333399);
    }

    targetMC.onRollOver = function()
    {
        this.clear();
        drawRectangle(this, 100, 30, 0x6666AA);
    }

    targetMC.onRollOut = function()
    {
        this.clear();
        drawRectangle(this, 100, 30, 0x333399);
    }
}

this.createEmptyMovieClip("testButton", 1);
convertToButton(testButton, buttonClickHandler);
```

Chapter 5

Exercise 1 Solution

a. Valid. This is explicit string creation.

b. Valid. This is implicit string creation.

c. The syntax is valid, but the data types are not correct. The Date object does not accept String input.

d. Valid.

e. Valid. This is an implicit creation of an Object.

f. Valid. The Object data type is the parent from which all other data types are created. This will generate no type warnings, regardless of what type of data is assigned to the variable.

g. Valid, but not recommended. The variable creation does not use strong typing.

h. Invalid. A string is being assigned to a variable of type Number.

Exercise 2 Solution

Outputs:

a. `testFunction->myString: qux`

b. `testFunction->mySecondString: foo`

c. `myString: baz`

    d.   `mySecondString: foo`

    e.   `mySecondString: bar`

Exercise 3 Solution

    a.   Valid.

    b.   Valid.

    c.   Invalid. A return type of String has been declared, but there is no return statement.

    d.   Invalid. A return type of String has been declared, but the function is returning a Boolean value.

    e.   Valid. A return type of Void indicates no data is to be returned.

    f.   Valid, but not recommended. No return type has been specified.

Exercise 4 Solution

```
function invokePlay():Void
{
    trace("Pressed play");
    presentationArea.play();
}

function invokeStop():Void
{
    trace("Pressed stop");
    presentationArea.stop();
}

function setupMovie():Void
{
    // Create presentation area, and load a movie clip into it
    this.createEmptyMovieClip("presentationArea", 3);
    presentationArea._x = 10;
    presentationArea._y = 40;
    presentationArea.loadMovie("http://www.nathanderksen.com/book/↵
        tryItOut_refactorAnimation.swf");
}


function createButton(parentMovieClip:MovieClip, buttonName:String, ↵
    buttonLabel:String, xPos:Number, yPos:Number, buttonWidth:Number, ↵
    buttonHeight:Number, callback:Function):Void
{
    var buttonHandle:MovieClip;
    parentMovieClip.createEmptyMovieClip(buttonName, ↵
        parentMovieClip.getNextHighestDepth());
    buttonHandle = parentMovieClip[buttonName];
    buttonHandle.onRelease = function()
    {
        callback();
    }
    buttonHandle._x = xPos;
    buttonHandle._y = yPos;
    drawBox(buttonHandle, buttonWidth, buttonHeight, 0xAAAAFF, 0x333333);
```

```
        buttonHandle.createTextField("labelField", 1, 4, 4, 50, 15);
        buttonHandle.labelField.text = buttonLabel;
}

function drawBox(targetMovieClip:MovieClip, boxWidth:Number, boxHeight:Number, ⊃
    boxColor:Number, lineColor:Number):Void
{
    targetMovieClip.beginFill(boxColor);
    targetMovieClip.lineStyle(1, lineColor);
    targetMovieClip.moveTo(0, 0);
    targetMovieClip.lineTo(boxWidth, 0);
    targetMovieClip.lineTo(boxWidth, boxHeight);
    targetMovieClip.lineTo(0, boxHeight);
    targetMovieClip.lineTo(0, 0);
}

createButton(this, "playButton", "Play", 10, 10, 70, 20, invokePlay);
createButton(this, "stopButton", "Stop", 90, 10, 35, 20, invokeStop);
setupMovie();
```

Chapter 6

Exercise Solution

1. Make note of the x and y coordinates for the four buttons in the screen_photography library clip, and then delete them.

2. Give the movie clip holding the large image preview the instance name imageHolderClip.

3. Go to the library and assign linkage IDs for the button_aStudyInTexture, button_buntzenWinter, button_flowerInDetail, and button_galianoSunset library symbols.

4. Update the code to resemble the following:

```
var buttonArray:Array = new Array();
buttonArray.push("aStudyInTexture");
buttonArray.push("buntzenWinter");
buttonArray.push("flowerInDetail");
buttonArray.push("galianoSunset");

// Set up code to respond to main menu buttons
home_btn.onRelease = function()
{
    gotoScreen("home");
}

tutorials_btn.onRelease = function()
{
    gotoScreen("tutorials");
}

photography_btn.onRelease = function()
{
    gotoScreen("photography");
```

```
    }
    function gotoScreen(screenName:String):Void
    {
        var screenHolderHandle:MovieClip;
        screenHolderHandle = _level0["screenHolder"];

        // Hide all screens within the screen holder movie clip
        for (screen in screenHolderHandle)
        {
            screenHolderHandle[screen]._visible = false;
        }
        // Show the selected screen
        screenHolderHandle[screenName]._visible = true;
    }

    function init():Void
    {
        var screenHolderHandle:MovieClip;
        var buttonHandle:MovieClip;

        _level0.createEmptyMovieClip("screenHolder", _level0.getNextHighestDepth());
        screenHolderHandle = _level0["screenHolder"];
        screenHolderHandle.attachMovie("screen_home", "home", ⊋
            screenHolderHandle.getNextHighestDepth());
        screenHolderHandle.attachMovie("screen_tutorials", "tutorials", ⊋
            screenHolderHandle.getNextHighestDepth());
        screenHolderHandle.attachMovie("screen_photography", "photography", ⊋
            screenHolderHandle.getNextHighestDepth());
        gotoScreen("home");

        // Attach the photo buttons to the photography screen movie clip.
        for (var i:Number = 0; i < buttonArray.length; i++)
        {
            buttonHandle = screenHolderHandle.photography.attachMovie("button_" + ⊋
                buttonArray[i], "button_" + buttonArray[i], ⊋
                screenHolderHandle.photography.getNextHighestDepth());
            buttonHandle._x = 25;
            buttonHandle._y = 160 + (60 * i);
            buttonHandle.id = buttonArray[i];
            buttonHandle.onRelease = function()
            {
                loadImage(this.id);
            }
        }
    }

    function loadImage(imageName:String)
    {
        screenHolder.photography.imageHolderClip.loadMovie("images/screens/⊋
            photography/" + imageName + "_preview.jpg");
    }

init();
```

Chapter 7

Exercise 1 Solution

```
var currentYear:Number;
var currentMonth:Number;
var currentDate:Number;

// Associates month names with the month number
var monthArray = new Array("January", "February", "March", "April", "May", ⊃
    "June", "July", "August", "September", "October", "November", "December");

function createButton(buttonName:String, buttonLabel:String, ⊃
    buttonData:String, parentClip:MovieClip, xPos:Number, yPos:Number, ⊃
    buttonWidth:Number, buttonHeight:Number, buttonHandler:Function) : Void
{
    var newClip:MovieClip = parentClip.createEmptyMovieClip(buttonName, ⊃
        parentClip.getNextHighestDepth());

    newClip._x = xPos;
    newClip._y = yPos;

    newClip.moveTo(0, 0);
    newClip.lineStyle(1, 0x666666);
    newClip.beginFill(0xFFFFFF, 100);
    newClip.lineTo(buttonWidth, 0);
    newClip.lineTo(buttonWidth, buttonHeight);
    newClip.lineTo(0, buttonHeight);
    newClip.lineTo(0, 0);
    newClip.endFill();

    newClip.createTextField("labelField", newClip.getNextHighestDepth(), 2, ⊃
        buttonHeight/2 - 7, buttonWidth - 4, 14);
    newClip.labelField.text = buttonLabel;
    newClip.buttonData = buttonData;
    newClip.onRelease = function()
    {
        // Invokes a function that was passed as an argument
        buttonHandler(this.buttonData);
    }
}

function deleteButton(buttonName:String):Void
{
    this[buttonName].removeMovieClip();
}

function setWeek(year:Number, month:Number, date:Number):Void
{
    var thisDate:Date = new Date(year, month, date);
    monthYearLabel.text = monthArray[month] + " " + year;

    for (var i:Number = 0; i < 7; i++)
    {
        deleteButton("day" + i + "button");
```

```
              createButton("day" + i + "button", String(thisDate.getDate()), ⊃
                 thisDate.toString(), this, 60 + (i * 30), 40, 20, 20, ⊃
                 handleDateSelected);
              thisDate.setDate(thisDate.getDate() + 1);
       }
}

function handlePreviousWeek():Void
{
    var thisDate:Date = new Date(currentYear, currentMonth, currentDate);
    thisDate.setDate(thisDate.getDate() - 7);

    currentYear = thisDate.getYear() + 1900;
    currentMonth = thisDate.getMonth();
    currentDate = thisDate.getDate();

    setWeek(currentYear, currentMonth, currentDate);
}

function handleNextWeek():Void
{
    var thisDate:Date = new Date(currentYear, currentMonth, currentDate);
    thisDate.setDate(thisDate.getDate() + 7);

    currentYear = thisDate.getYear() + 1900;
    currentMonth = thisDate.getMonth();
    currentDate = thisDate.getDate();

    setWeek(currentYear, currentMonth, currentDate);
}

function handleDateSelected(selectedDate:String):Void
{
    trace("handleDate: " + selectedDate);
}

function init():Void
{
    // Set up screen, except for day buttons to be created fresh for each new week.
    createButton("previousWeekButton", "<<", "", this, 30, 40, 20, 20, ⊃
        handlePreviousWeek);
    createButton("nextWeekButton", ">>", "", this, 270, 40, 20, 20, ⊃
        handleNextWeek);

    this.createTextField("day0Label", this.getNextHighestDepth(), 65, 25, 20, 20);
    this.day0Label.text = "S";
    this.createTextField("day1Label", this.getNextHighestDepth(), 95, 25, 20, 20);
    this.day1Label.text = "M";
    this.createTextField("day2Label", this.getNextHighestDepth(), 125, 25, 20, 20);
    this.day2Label.text = "T";
    this.createTextField("day3Label", this.getNextHighestDepth(), 155, 25, 20, 20);
    this.day3Label.text = "W";
    this.createTextField("day4Label", this.getNextHighestDepth(), 185, 25, 20, 20);
    this.day4Label.text = "T";
    this.createTextField("day5Label", this.getNextHighestDepth(), 215, 25, 20, 20);
    this.day5Label.text = "F";
```

```
            this.createTextField("day6Label", this.getNextHighestDepth(), 245, 25, 20, 20);
            this.day6Label.text = "S";

            this.createTextField("monthYearLabel", this.getNextHighestDepth(), ⤵
                130, 5, 150, 20);

            // Initialize the current date. Adjust today's date so that it actually
            // gets the date from the previous Sunday, so that the days line up
            // properly with the day labels. If it is Wednesday, getDay() will
            // return 3. Subtracting 3 from the date will get Sunday's date.
            var todaysDate:Date = new Date();
            todaysDate.setDate(todaysDate.getDate() - todaysDate.getDay());

            currentYear = todaysDate.getYear() + 1900;
            currentMonth = todaysDate.getMonth();
            currentDate = todaysDate.getDate();

            setWeek(currentYear, currentMonth, currentDate);
        }

        init();
```

Exercise 2 Solution

```
        this.createEmptyMovieClip("squareClip", this.getNextHighestDepth());
        squareClip.lineStyle(1, 0x000000);
        squareClip.moveTo(0, 0);
        squareClip.beginFill(0xCC0000, 100);
        squareClip.lineTo(0, 100);
        squareClip.lineTo(100, 100);
        squareClip.lineTo(100, 0);
        squareClip.lineTo(0, 0);

        this.createEmptyMovieClip("triangleClip", this.getNextHighestDepth());
        triangleClip._x = 30;
        triangleClip._y = 30;
        triangleClip.lineStyle(1, 0x000000);
        triangleClip.moveTo(0, 100);
        triangleClip.beginFill(0x0000CC, 100);
        triangleClip.lineTo(100, 100);
        triangleClip.lineTo(50, 0);
        triangleClip.lineTo(0, 100);

        squareClip.setMask(triangleClip);
        // Part 2: Swapped masks:
        //triangleClip.setMask(squareClip);
```

Exercise 3 Solution

```
        this.createEmptyMovieClip("squareClip", this.getNextHighestDepth());
        squareClip._x = 30;
        squareClip._y = 30;
        squareClip.lineStyle(1, 0x000000);
        squareClip.moveTo(0, 0);
        squareClip.beginFill(0xCC0000, 100);
        squareClip.lineTo(0, 100);
```

```
    squareClip.lineTo(100, 100);
    squareClip.lineTo(100, 0);
    squareClip.lineTo(0, 0);

    this.createEmptyMovieClip("triangleClip", this.getNextHighestDepth());
    triangleClip._x = 30;
    triangleClip._y = 30;
    triangleClip.lineStyle(1, 0x000000);
    triangleClip.moveTo(0, 100);
    triangleClip.beginFill(0x0000CC, 100);
    triangleClip.lineTo(100, 100);
    triangleClip.lineTo(50, 0);
    triangleClip.lineTo(0, 100);

    squareClip.setMask(triangleClip);

    var mouseListener:Object = new Object();
    mouseListener.onMouseMove = function ()
    {
        trace("x: " + _xmouse);
        triangleClip._x = _xmouse - 50;
        triangleClip._y = _ymouse - 50;
    };
    Mouse.addListener(mouseListener);
```

Chapter 8

Exercise 1 Solution

```
    this.createEmptyMovieClip("movieHolder", this.getNextHighestDepth());
    this.createEmptyMovieClip("progressMovie", this.getNextHighestDepth());
    progressMovie._x = 60;
    progressMovie._y = 120;
    progressMovie.createTextField("percentDoneLabel",
    progressMovie.getNextHighestDepth(), 40, 0, 200, 20);

    var loadListener:Object = new Object();
    loadListener.onLoadStart = function(contentHolder:MovieClip)
    {
        progressMovie._visible = true;
        contentHolder._visible = false;
        contentHolder.stop();
    };

    loadListener.onLoadProgress = function(contentHolder:MovieClip, ⤶
        bytesLoaded:Number, bytesTotal:Number)
    {
        var percentDone:Number = bytesLoaded / bytesTotal * 100;
        showProgress(percentDone, progressMovie);
    };

    loadListener.onLoadComplete = function(contentHolder:MovieClip)
    {
        progressMovie._visible = false;
```

```
        contentHolder._visible = true;
        contentHolder.play();
};

loadListener.onLoadError = function(contentHolder:MovieClip, errorCode:String)
{
    if (errorCode == "URLNotFound")
    {
        progressMovie.percentDoneLabel.text = "ERROR: Could not load media";
        progressMovie.clear();
    }
    else if (errorCode == "LoadNeverCompleted")
    {
        progressMovie.percentDoneLabel.text = "ERROR: Transfer interrupted";
        progressMovie.clear();
    }
}

var contentLoader:MovieClipLoader = new MovieClipLoader();
contentLoader.addListener(loadListener);
contentLoader.loadClip("<your server>/trailer.swf", ⤸
    movieHolder);
//contentLoader.loadClip("clipThatDoesNotExist.swf", movieHolder);

function showProgress(percentDone:Number, progressBarHolder:MovieClip) : Void
{
    var barWidth:Number = percentDone;
    progressBarHolder.percentDoneLabel.text = String(Math.ceil(percentDone))+" %";
    progressBarHolder.clear();

    // Draw a border
    progressBarHolder.moveTo(0, 20);
    progressBarHolder.lineStyle(1, 0x666666);
    progressBarHolder.lineTo(100, 20);
    progressBarHolder.lineTo(100, 30);
    progressBarHolder.lineTo(0, 30);
    progressBarHolder.lineTo(0, 20);

    // Draw the bar
    progressBarHolder.moveTo(0, 20);
    progressBarHolder.beginFill(0xCCCCCC, 100);
    progressBarHolder.lineTo(barWidth, 20);
    progressBarHolder.lineTo(barWidth, 30);
    progressBarHolder.lineTo(0, 30);
    progressBarHolder.lineTo(0, 20);
    progressBarHolder.endFill();
}
```

Exercise 2 Solution

Before trying the code, make sure to place a ProgressBar component in the library.

```
this.createEmptyMovieClip("movieHolder", this.getNextHighestDepth());
// Requires: a ProgressBar component placed in the library
this.createClassObject(mx.controls.ProgressBar, "progressComponent", ⤸
```

```
        this.getNextHighestDepth());

progressComponent._x = 60;
progressComponent._y = 120;
progressComponent.mode = "manual";

var loadListener:Object = new Object();
loadListener.onLoadStart = function(contentHolder:MovieClip)
{
    progressComponent._visible = true;
    progressComponent.setProgress(0, 100);
    contentHolder._visible = false;
    contentHolder.stop();
};

loadListener.onLoadProgress = function(contentHolder:MovieClip, ↺
    bytesLoaded:Number, bytesTotal:Number)
{
    progressComponent.setProgress(bytesLoaded, bytesTotal);
};

loadListener.onLoadComplete = function(contentHolder:MovieClip)
{
    progressComponent._visible = false;
    contentHolder._visible = true;
    contentHolder.play();
};

loadListener.onLoadError = function(contentHolder:MovieClip, errorCode:String)
{
    if (errorCode == "URLNotFound")
    {
        progressComponent.label = "Could not load media";
    }
    else if (errorCode == "LoadNeverCompleted")
    {
        progressComponent.label = "Transfer interrupted";
    }
};

var contentLoader:MovieClipLoader = new MovieClipLoader();
contentLoader.addListener(loadListener);
contentLoader.loadClip("<your server>/trailer.swf", movieHolder);
```

Chapter 9

Exercise 1 Solution

Before trying the code, make sure to place a Button, a DataGrid, a Label, a TextArea, and a TextInput component in the library.

```
import mx.controls.Button;
import mx.controls.DataGrid;
import mx.controls.Label;
```

```
import mx.controls.TextArea;
import mx.controls.TextInput;

function drawScreen():Void
{
    this.createClassObject(Label, "gridTitle", this.getNextHighestDepth());
    gridTitle.text = "Notes";
    gridTitle._x = 18;
    gridTitle._y = 18;

    this.createClassObject(DataGrid, "notesDataGrid", this.getNextHighestDepth());
    notesDataGrid._x = 18;
    notesDataGrid._y = 40;
    notesDataGrid.setSize(225, 170);

    notesDataGrid.addColumn("name");
    notesDataGrid.addColumn("size");
    notesDataGrid.getColumnAt(0).width = 165;
    notesDataGrid.getColumnAt(0).headerText = "Title";
    notesDataGrid.getColumnAt(1).headerText = "Size";

    this.createClassObject(Button, "addButton", this.getNextHighestDepth());
    addButton.label = "Add";
    addButton._x = 18;
    addButton._y = 219;
    addButton.setSize(100, 22);

    this.createClassObject(Button, "deleteButton", this.getNextHighestDepth());
    deleteButton.label = "Delete";
    deleteButton._x = 142;
    deleteButton._y = 219;
    deleteButton.setSize(100, 22);

    this.createClassObject(Label, "noteTitle", this.getNextHighestDepth());
    noteTitle.text = "Title";
    noteTitle._x = 272;
    noteTitle._y = 18;

    this.createClassObject(TextInput, "titleField", this.getNextHighestDepth());
    titleField._x = 272;
    titleField._y = 40;
    titleField.setSize(225, 22);

    this.createClassObject(Label, "textTitle", this.getNextHighestDepth());
    textTitle.text = "Text";
    textTitle._x = 272;
    textTitle._y = 88;

    this.createClassObject(TextArea, "noteTextField", this.getNextHighestDepth());
    noteTextField._x = 272;
    noteTextField._y = 109;
    noteTextField.setSize(225, 100);

this.createClassObject(Button, "saveButton", this.getNextHighestDepth());
    saveButton.label = "Save";
```

```
        saveButton._x = 395;
        saveButton._y = 219;
        saveButton.setSize(100, 22);
}

drawScreen();
```

Exercise 2 Solution

```
import mx.controls.Button;
import mx.controls.DataGrid;
import mx.controls.Label;
import mx.controls.TextInput;
import mx.controls.TextArea;

var noteList:Array = new Array();
notesList.push({title:"Note 1", size:0, text:"The quick brown fox..." });
notesList.push({title:"Note 2", size:0, text:"The quick brown..." });
notesList.push({title:"Note 3", size:0, text:"The quick fox..." });

notesList[0].size = notesList[0].text.length;
notesList[1].size = notesList[1].text.length;
notesList[2].size = notesList[2].text.length;

function drawScreen():Void
{
    this.createClassObject(Label, "gridTitle", this.getNextHighestDepth());
    gridTitle.text = "Notes";
    gridTitle._x = 18;
    gridTitle._y = 18;

    this.createClassObject(DataGrid, "notesDataGrid", this.getNextHighestDepth());
    notesDataGrid._x = 18;
    notesDataGrid._y = 40;
    notesDataGrid.setSize(225, 170);

    notesDataGrid.addColumn("title");
    notesDataGrid.addColumn("size");
    notesDataGrid.getColumnAt(0).width = 165;
    notesDataGrid.getColumnAt(0).headerText = "Title";
    notesDataGrid.getColumnAt(1).headerText = "Size";
    notesDataGrid.dataProvider = notesList;

    this.createClassObject(Button, "addButton", this.getNextHighestDepth());
    addButton.label = "Add";
    addButton._x = 18;
    addButton._y = 219;
    addButton.setSize(100, 22);

    this.createClassObject(Button, "deleteButton", this.getNextHighestDepth());
    deleteButton.label = "Delete";
    deleteButton._x = 142;
    deleteButton._y = 219;
    deleteButton.setSize(100, 22);

    this.createClassObject(Label, "noteTitle", this.getNextHighestDepth());
```

```
        noteTitle.text = "Title";
        noteTitle._x = 272;
        noteTitle._y = 18;

        this.createClassObject(TextInput, "titleField", this.getNextHighestDepth());
        titleField._x = 272;
        titleField._y = 40;
        titleField.setSize(225, 22);

        this.createClassObject(Label, "textTitle", this.getNextHighestDepth());
        textTitle.text = "Text";
        textTitle._x = 272;
        textTitle._y = 88;

        this.createClassObject(TextArea, "noteTextField", this.getNextHighestDepth());
        noteTextField._x = 272;
        noteTextField._y = 109;
        noteTextField.setSize(225, 100);
        noteTextField.wordWrap = true;

this.createClassObject(Button, "saveButton", this.getNextHighestDepth());
        saveButton.label = "Save";
        saveButton._x = 395;
        saveButton._y = 219;
        saveButton.setSize(100, 22);
}

drawScreen();
```

Chapter 10

Exercise Solution

```
    import mx.controls.Button;
    import mx.controls.DataGrid;
    import mx.controls.Label;
    import mx.controls.TextInput;
    import mx.controls.TextArea;

    var notesList:Array = new Array();
    notesList.push({title:"Note 1", size:0, text:"The quick brown fox..."});
    notesList.push({title:"Note 2", size:0, text:"The quick brown..."});
    notesList.push({title:"Note 3", size:0, text:"The quick fox..."});

    notesList[0].size = notesList[0].text.length;
    notesList[1].size = notesList[1].text.length;
    notesList[2].size = notesList[2].text.length;

    function drawScreen():Void
    {
        this.createClassObject(Label, "gridTitle", this.getNextHighestDepth());
        gridTitle.text = "Notes";
        gridTitle._x = 18;
```

```
    gridTitle._y = 18;

    this.createClassObject(DataGrid, "notesDataGrid", this.getNextHighestDepth());
    notesDataGrid._x = 18;
    notesDataGrid._y = 40;
    notesDataGrid.setSize(225, 170);

    notesDataGrid.addColumn("title");
    notesDataGrid.addColumn("size");
    notesDataGrid.getColumnAt(0).width = 165;
    notesDataGrid.getColumnAt(0).headerText = "Title";
    notesDataGrid.getColumnAt(1).headerText = "Size";
    notesDataGrid.dataProvider = notesList;

    this.createClassObject(Button, "deleteButton", this.getNextHighestDepth());
    deleteButton.label = "Delete";
    deleteButton._x = 18;
    deleteButton._y = 219;
    deleteButton.setSize(100, 22);
    deleteButton.enabled = false;

    this.createClassObject(Label, "noteTitle", this.getNextHighestDepth());
    noteTitle.text = "Title";
    noteTitle._x = 272;
    noteTitle._y = 18;

    this.createClassObject(TextInput, "titleField", this.getNextHighestDepth());
    titleField._x = 272;
    titleField._y = 40;
    titleField.setSize(225, 22);

    this.createClassObject(Label, "textTitle", this.getNextHighestDepth());
    textTitle.text = "Text";
    textTitle._x = 272;
    textTitle._y = 88;

    this.createClassObject(TextArea, "noteTextField", this.getNextHighestDepth());
    noteTextField._x = 272;
    noteTextField._y = 109;
    noteTextField.setSize(225, 100);
    noteTextField.wordWrap = true;

    this.createClassObject(Button, "addButton", this.getNextHighestDepth());
    addButton.label = "Add";
    addButton._x = 272;
    addButton._y = 219;
    addButton.setSize(100, 22);
    addButton.enabled = false;

    this.createClassObject(Button, "saveButton", this.getNextHighestDepth());
    saveButton.label = "Save";
    saveButton._x = 395;
    saveButton._y = 219;
    saveButton.setSize(100, 22);
    saveButton.enabled = false;
```

```
}

drawScreen();

// Handle the user typing into the title or note fields
var handleNoteChangeListener:Object = new Object();
handleNoteChangeListener.change = function()
{
    addButton.enabled = true;
    saveButton.enabled = true;
}
titleField.addEventListener("change", handleNoteChangeListener);
noteTextField.addEventListener("change", handleNoteChangeListener);

// Handle the selecting of a note from the list
var handleNoteListener:Object = new Object();
handleNoteListener.change = function(eventObject:Object)
{
    titleField.text = eventObject.target.selectedItem.title;
    noteTextField.text = eventObject.target.selectedItem.text;
    deleteButton.enabled = true;
}
notesDataGrid.addEventListener("change", handleNoteListener);

// Handle the pressing of the Delete button
var handleDeleteListener:Object = new Object();
handleDeleteListener.click = function()
{
    trace("selectedIndex: " + notesDataGrid.selectedIndex);
    var selectedRow:Number = notesDataGrid.selectedIndex;
    notesList.splice(selectedRow, 1);
    notesDataGrid.dataProvider = notesList;
    // Alternately, the following line can replace the previous two
    // notesDataGrid.dataProvider.removeItemAt(selectedRow);

    if (notesList.length > 0)
    {
        // The list is not empty
        if (selectedRow < notesList.length)
        {
            // Select the row that takes the deleted row's place
            notesDataGrid.selectedIndex = selectedRow;
        }
        else
        {
            // There are no more rows to take the selected
            // row's place. Select the last row.
            notesDataGrid.selectedIndex = notesList.length - 1;
        }
        notesDataGrid.dispatchEvent({type:"change", target:notesDataGrid});
    }
    else
    {
        // The list is empty.
        deleteButton.enabled = false;
    }
```

```
        }
    }
    deleteButton.addEventListener("click", handleDeleteListener);

    // Handle pressing the Add button
    var handleAddListener:Object = new Object();
    handleAddListener.click = function()
    {
        notesList.push({title:titleField.text, size:noteTextField.text.length, ⤸
            text:noteTextField.text});
        notesDataGrid.selectedIndex = notesList.length - 1;
        deleteButton.enabled = true;
    }
    addButton.addEventListener("click", handleAddListener);

    // Handle pressing the Save button
    var handleSaveListener:Object = new Object();
    handleSaveListener.click = function()
    {
        notesDataGrid.editField(notesDataGrid.selectedIndex, "title", titleField.text);
        notesDataGrid.editField(notesDataGrid.selectedIndex, "size", ⤸
            noteTextField.text.length);
        notesDataGrid.editField(notesDataGrid.selectedIndex, "text", ⤸
            noteTextField.text);
    }
    saveButton.addEventListener("click", handleSaveListener);
```

Chapter 11

Exercise 1 Solution

```
import mx.controls.Button;
import mx.controls.DataGrid;
import mx.controls.Label;
import mx.controls.TextInput;
import mx.controls.TextArea;
import mx.styles.CSSStyleDeclaration;

var notesList:Array = new Array();
notesList.push({title:"Note 1", size:0, text:"The quick brown fox..."});
notesList.push({title:"Note 2", size:0, text:"The quick brown..."});
notesList.push({title:"Note 3", size:0, text:"The quick fox..."});

notesList[0].size = notesList[0].text.length;
notesList[1].size = notesList[1].text.length;
notesList[2].size = notesList[2].text.length;

function drawScreen():Void
{
    this.createClassObject(Label, "gridTitle", this.getNextHighestDepth());
    gridTitle.text = "Notes";
    gridTitle._x = 18;
    gridTitle._y = 18;

    this.createClassObject(DataGrid, "notesDataGrid", this.getNextHighestDepth());
```

```
notesDataGrid._x = 18;
notesDataGrid._y = 40;
notesDataGrid.setSize(225, 170);

notesDataGrid.addColumn("title");
notesDataGrid.addColumn("size");
notesDataGrid.getColumnAt(0).width = 165;
notesDataGrid.getColumnAt(0).headerText = "Title";
notesDataGrid.getColumnAt(1).headerText = "Size";
notesDataGrid.dataProvider = notesList;

this.createClassObject(Button, "addButton", this.getNextHighestDepth());
addButton.label = "Add";
addButton._x = 18;
addButton._y = 219;
addButton.setSize(100, 22);

this.createClassObject(Button, "deleteButton", this.getNextHighestDepth());
deleteButton.label = "Delete";
deleteButton._x = 142;
deleteButton._y = 219;
deleteButton.setSize(100, 22);
deleteButton.enabled = false;

this.createClassObject(Label, "noteTitle", this.getNextHighestDepth());
noteTitle.text = "Title";
noteTitle._x = 272;
noteTitle._y = 18;

this.createClassObject(TextInput, "titleField", this.getNextHighestDepth());
titleField._x = 272;
titleField._y = 40;
titleField.setSize(225, 22);

this.createClassObject(Label, "textTitle", this.getNextHighestDepth());
textTitle.text = "Text";
textTitle._x = 272;
textTitle._y = 88;

this.createClassObject(TextArea, "noteTextField", this.getNextHighestDepth());
noteTextField._x = 272;
noteTextField._y = 109;
noteTextField.setSize(225, 100);
noteTextField.wordWrap = true;

this.createClassObject(Button, "saveButton", this.getNextHighestDepth());
saveButton.label = "Save";
saveButton._x = 395;
saveButton._y = 219;
saveButton.setSize(100, 22);
saveButton.enabled = false;

// Set global styles
_global.style.setStyle("themeColor", 0xAAAAEE);
_global.style.setStyle("fontFamily", "Verdana");
_global.style.setStyle("fontSize", 11);
```

```
        _global.style.setStyle("color", 0x666666);

        // Set component styles
        _global.styles.Label = new CSSStyleDeclaration();
        _global.styles.Label.setStyle("fontSize", 14);
        _global.styles.Label.setStyle("fontWeight", "bold");
        _global.styles.Label.setStyle("color", 0x000000);

        _global.styles.Button = new CSSStyleDeclaration();
        _global.styles.Button.setStyle("fontWeight", "bold");
        _global.styles.Button.setStyle("color", 0x333399);
        _global.styles.Button.setStyle("buttonColor", 0xAAAAEE);

        // Set individual instance styles
        notesDataGrid.setStyle("vGridLines", false);
        notesDataGrid.setStyle("hGridLines", false);
        notesDataGrid.setStyle("headerColor", 0xBBBBFF);

        var headerStyle = new CSSStyleDeclaration();
        headerStyle.setStyle("fontWeight", "bold");
        notesDataGrid.setStyle("headerStyle", headerStyle);

        deleteButton.setStyle("color", 0x990000);
}

drawScreen();

// Handle the user typing into the title or note fields
var handleNoteChangeListener:Object = new Object();
handleNoteChangeListener.change = function()
{
    saveButton.enabled = true;
}
titleField.addEventListener("change", handleNoteChangeListener);
noteTextField.addEventListener("change", handleNoteChangeListener);

// Handle the selecting of a note from the list
var handleNoteListener:Object = new Object();
handleNoteListener.change = function(eventObject:Object)
{
    titleField.text = eventObject.target.selectedItem.title;
    noteTextField.text = eventObject.target.selectedItem.text;
    deleteButton.enabled = true;
}
notesDataGrid.addEventListener("change", handleNoteListener);

// Handle the pressing of the Delete button
var handleDeleteListener:Object = new Object();
handleDeleteListener.click = function()
{
    trace("selectedIndex: " + notesDataGrid.selectedIndex);
    var selectedRow:Number = notesDataGrid.selectedIndex;
    notesList.splice(selectedRow, 1);
    notesDataGrid.dataProvider = notesList;
    // Alternately, the following line can replace the previous two
```

```
        // notesDataGrid.dataProvider.removeItemAt(selectedRow);

    if (notesList.length > 0)
    {
        // The list is not empty
        if (selectedRow < notesList.length)
        {
            // Select the row that takes the deleted row's place
            notesDataGrid.selectedIndex = selectedRow;
        }
        else
        {
            // There are no more rows to take the selected
            // row's place. Select the last row.
            notesDataGrid.selectedIndex = notesList.length - 1;
        }
        notesDataGrid.dispatchEvent({type:"change", target:notesDataGrid});
    }
    else
    {
        // The list is empty.
        deleteButton.enabled = false;
    }
}
deleteButton.addEventListener("click", handleDeleteListener);

// Handle pressing the Add button
var handleAddListener:Object = new Object();
handleAddListener.click = function()
{
    notesDataGrid.addItem({title:"New note", size:0, text:""});
    notesDataGrid.selectedIndex = notesList.length - 1;
    titleField.text = "New note";
    noteTextField.text = "";
    deleteButton.enabled = true;
}
addButton.addEventListener("click", handleAddListener);

// Handle pressing the Save button
var handleSaveListener:Object = new Object();
handleSaveListener.click = function()
{
    notesDataGrid.editField(notesDataGrid.selectedIndex, "title", titleField.text);
    notesDataGrid.editField(notesDataGrid.selectedIndex, "size", ⊃
        noteTextField.text.length);
    notesDataGrid.editField(notesDataGrid.selectedIndex, "text",⊃
        noteTextField.text);
}
saveButton.addEventListener("click", handleSaveListener);
```

Exercise 2 Solution

1. Open the file SampleTheme.fla at <application root>/Configuration/ComponentFLA/.

2. Open the Library panel and select the movie clip SampleTheme in the Flash UI Components 2 folder. From the menu at the top right of the Library panel, select Copy.

3. Switch to the Flash file that you want to re-skin. From the menu at the top right of the Library panel for that Flash file, select Paste.

4. Navigate through the folder structure that is automatically added to the library looking for the component you want to re-skin. Note that some components are shared. For instance, the Button component is re-skinned by modifying the SimpleButton component.

5. Experiment away!

Chapter 12

Exercise 1 Solution

The if statement can be separated around the && operator:

```
if (shipType == "hospital" || shipConfiguration == "peacetime")
{
    if (shipDirection == "east" || shipDirection == "west")
    {
        // do stuff
    }
}
```

Exercise 2 Solution

The getYear() method returns the current year minus 1900, so 2006 is represented as 106. Either change the year to 106 in the condition, or change to the getFullYear() method that returns the year value that you would normally expect.

```
var tempDate:Date = new Date(2006, 11, 20);

if (tempDate.getMonth() > 5 && tempDate.getMonth() < 11)
{
    // Stuff goes here
}
else if (tempDate.getFullYear() == 2006 && tempDate.getMonth() == 11)
// or
// else if (tempDate.getYear() == 106 && tempDate.getMonth() == 11)
{
    trace("You should see this text");
    // Stuff goes here
}
else
{
    // Stuff goes here
}
```

Exercise 3 Solution

There is an issue with the depth value being passed into the createEmptyMovieClip() method. Each call is reusing the same depth, so the previous movie clip gets deleted. Also, two of the lineTo() methods are reversed, causing the corners of the square to be drawn out of order.

```
var movieClipHandle:MovieClip;
var baseMovieClip:MovieClip = _level0;
var numMovieClips:Number = 3;

for (var i:Number = 0; i < numMovieClips; i++)
{
    baseMovieClip.createEmptyMovieClip("movieClip" + i, i);
    movieClipHandle = baseMovieClip["movieClip" + i];
    movieClipHandle._x = i * 30 + 20;
    movieClipHandle._y = 20;
    movieClipHandle.lineStyle(1, 0x000000, 100);
    movieClipHandle.moveTo(0, 0);
    movieClipHandle.lineTo(0, 20);
    movieClipHandle.lineTo(20, 20);
    movieClipHandle.lineTo(20, 0);
    movieClipHandle.lineTo(0, 0);
}
```

Exercise 4 Solution

There are two issues with this code. The first is the infinite loop. By tracing through the loop with the debugger, the fact that the i++ line only is called some of the time is what causes this problem. Pulling it out of the if statement fixes this. The problem with the array not being populated with data is that the array has not been initialized. This can be found either by watching the array through the debugger, or tracing the array itself. The bold lines in the following code are the ones that have been changed to fix the problems with the loop.

```
var stopCharacter:String = ".";
var paragraphText:String = "The quick brown fox. Jumped over the lazy dog. ↩
    Again. And again.";
var sentenceText:String = "";
var sentenceArray:Array = new Array();
var i:Number = 0;

while (i < paragraphText.length)
{
    if (paragraphText.charAt(i) == stopCharacter)
    {
        sentenceArray.push(sentenceText);
        sentenceText = "";
    }
    else
    {
        sentenceText += paragraphText.charAt(i);
    }
    i++;
}

for (var i = 0; i < sentenceArray.length; i++)
{
    trace(i + ": " + sentenceArray[i]);
}
```

Exercise 5 Solution

There are three issues with this code. First, every click results in both button handlers being called. The problem here is the confusion between onRelease and onMouseUp. The onMouseUp event is a global event that fires when the mouse is released, regardless of where it is located, whereas the onRelease event only fires when the mouse was released over the target movie clip. The trace statements made it clear that they were both firing, and commenting out the event handler would have made it clear that the origin of the problem was there.

Second, the label text was not showing up. The debugger shows all the properties that have been set, and it shows that it is visible and is within the bounds of the stage. It also shows a label property set, but no text property set. The label property is not a valid text field property; the text property is the one that should be set.

Finally, the problem with the background color is that AAAAFF is not a valid data type; it should be a hexadecimal number in the form of 0xAAAAFF. Tracing the boxColor argument results in an undefined value, indicating the nature of the problem.

```
function invokePlay():Void
{
    trace("Pressed play");
}

function invokeStop():Void
{
    trace("Pressed stop");
}

function createButton(parentMovieClip:MovieClip, buttonName:String, ⏎
    buttonLabel:String, xPos:Number, yPos:Number, buttonWidth:Number, ⏎
    buttonHeight:Number, callback:Function):Void
{
    var buttonHandle:MovieClip;
    parentMovieClip.createEmptyMovieClip(buttonName, ⏎
        parentMovieClip.getNextHighestDepth());
    buttonHandle = parentMovieClip[buttonName];
    buttonHandle.onRelease = function()
    {
        callback();
    }
    buttonHandle._x = xPos;
    buttonHandle._y = yPos;
    drawBox(buttonHandle, buttonWidth, buttonHeight, 0xAAAAFF, 0x333333);
    buttonHandle.createTextField("labelField", 1, 4, 4, 50, 15);
    buttonHandle.labelField.text = buttonLabel;
}

function drawBox(targetMovieClip:MovieClip, boxWidth:Number, boxHeight:Number, ⏎
    boxColor:Number, lineColor:Number):Void
{
    targetMovieClip.beginFill(boxColor);
    targetMovieClip.lineStyle(1, lineColor);
    targetMovieClip.moveTo(0, 0);
    targetMovieClip.lineTo(boxWidth, 0);
    targetMovieClip.lineTo(boxWidth, boxHeight);
```

```
        targetMovieClip.lineTo(0, boxHeight);
        targetMovieClip.lineTo(0, 0);
    }


    createButton(this, "playButton", "Play", 10, 10, 70, 20, invokePlay);
    createButton(this, "stopButton", "Stop", 90, 10, 35, 20, invokeStop);
```

Chapter 13

Exercise 1 Solution

```
//Place this AS file in the class path of the FLA:

class Circle{
    static function getRadians(degrees):Number {
        return degrees*(Math.PI/180);
    }
    static function getCirclePoints(points, diameter, callBackOwner, ⊃
callback):Array {
        var ary = [];
        var newTheta = 0;
        var theta = 360/points;
        for (var i = 0; i<points; i++) {
            ary[i] = [];
            newTheta += theta;
            var rad = Circle.getRadians(newTheta);
            ary[i][0] = (Math.cos(rad)*diameter);
            ary[i][1] = (Math.sin(rad)*diameter);
            callback.apply(callBackOwner,[ary[i]]);
        }
        return ary;
    }
}


Place this code on frame 1 of the FLA:
var circleHolder = this.createEmptyMovieClip("clip1", this.getNextHighestDepth());
circleHolder.points = Circle.getCirclePoints(45, 100);
with (circleHolder) {
    moveTo(points[0][0], points[0][1]);
    lineStyle(2, 0xFF0000, 100);
    for (var i = 1; i<points.length; i++) {
        lineTo(points[i][0], points[i][1]);
    }
    lineTo(points[0][0], points[0][1]);
}
```

Exercise 2 Solution

```
function makeCanvas(handle, w, h) {
    with (handle) {
        beginFill(0xFFFFFF, 100);
        lineStyle(0, 0xCCCCCC, 100);
        moveTo(0, 0);
        lineTo(0, h);
        lineTo(w, h);
```

```
                lineTo(w, 0);
                lineTo(0, 0);
                endFill();
        }
        handle.lineStyle(0, 0x666666, 100);
        handle.drawLine = function(){
                if(oldX != this._xmouse && oldY != this._ymouse){
                        this.lineTo(this._xmouse,this._ymouse);
                        oldX = this._xmouse;
                        oldY = this._yMouse;
                }
                updateAfterEvent();
        }
        handle.onPress = function(){
                this.drawing = setInterval(this,"drawLine",10);
                this.moveTo(this._xmouse,this._ymouse);
        }
        handle.onRelease = handle.onReleaseOutside = function(){
                clearInterval(this.drawing);
        }
}
drawingArea = this.createEmptyMovieClip("clip1", this.getNextHighestDepth());
makeCanvas(drawingArea,400,300);
```

Exercise 3 Solution

```
image = this.createEmptyMovieClip("clip1", 0);

var preloader:Object = new Object();

preloader.onLoadComplete = function(clip:MovieClip) {
    image.setMask(maskClip);
};
var image_load:MovieClipLoader = new MovieClipLoader();
image_load.addListener(preloader);
image_load.loadClip("myImage.jpg", image);


maskClip = this.createEmptyMovieClip("clip2", 1);
with (maskClip) {
    beginFill(0xFF0000, 60);
    lineStyle(2, 0x666666, 100);
    moveTo(20, 20);
    lineTo(20, 120);
    lineTo(120, 120);
    lineTo(120, 20);
    lineTo(20, 20);
    endFill();
}
```

Chapter 14

Exercise 1 Solution

```
//Import the BitmapData class
import flash.display.*;

//Create a MovieClip containter
var myButton = this.createEmptyMovieClip ("button1", this.getNextHighestDepth ());

//Define default state
var myButtonBitmap = BitmapData.loadBitmap ("libraryBitmapOffState");
myButton.attachBitmap (myButtonBitmap, 0);

//Associate button states with library items
var linkageIDoffState = "libraryBitmapOffState";
var linkageIDoverState = "libraryBitmapOverState";
var linkageIDhitState = "libraryBitmapHitState";

//Define button states
myButton.onRollOver = function () {
    var myButtonBitmap = BitmapData.loadBitmap (linkageIDoverState);
    this.attachBitmap (myButtonBitmap, 0);
};
myButton.onRollOut = function () {
    var myButtonBitmap = BitmapData.loadBitmap (linkageIDoffState);
    this.attachBitmap (myButtonBitmap, 0);
};
myButton.onPress = function () {
    var myButtonBitmap = BitmapData.loadBitmap (linkageIDhitState);
    this.attachBitmap (myButtonBitmap, 0);
};
myButton.onRelease = myButton.onReleaseOutside = function () {
    var myButtonBitmap = BitmapData.loadBitmap (linkageIDoffState);
    this.attachBitmap (myButtonBitmap, 0);
};
```

Exercise 2 Solution

Place an instance of the Button component in the library and then add the following ActionScript to frame 1 of root:

```
import flash.filters.*;
var navShadow:DropShadowFilter = new DropShadowFilter ();
navShadow.blurX = 10;
navShadow.blurY = 10;
navShadow.alpha = .3;
navShadow.angle = 45;
navShadow.color = ox000000;
navShadow.distance = 5;
```

```
navShadow.quality = 3;
navShadow.strength = 1;
var nav:MovieClip = this.createEmptyMovieClip ("navigation", 0);
nav._y = 20;
nav._x = 20;
nav.filters = [navShadow];
buttonNum = 5;
for (var i = 0; i < buttonNum; i++) {
    var buttonInstance:MovieClip = this.nav.attachMovie ("Button", "Button" + i,
i);
    buttonInstance.blur = new BlurFilter (1, 1, 3);
    buttonInstance.filters = [buttonInstance.blur];
    buttonInstance._xscale = buttonInstance._yscale = 85;
    buttonInstance._y = i * 35;
    buttonInstance.label = "Button " + (i + 1)+"   ";
    buttonInstance.checkMouse = function () {
        var distx = (Math.abs ((this._parent._xmouse - this._width / 2) - ⇨
this._x));
        var disty = (Math.abs ((this._parent._ymouse - this._height / 2) - ⇨
this._y));
        var dist = (distx + disty) / 2;
        if (dist < 35) {
            this.blurChange(dist);
        } else{
            this.blurChange(35);
        }
    };
    buttonInstance.blurChange = function (dist) {
        this.blur.blurX = (dist / 21) * .7;
        this.blur.blurY = (dist / 21) * .7;
        this.filters = [this.blur];
        this._xscale = this._yscale = 115 - dist;
    };
}
nav.onMouseMove = function () {
    for (var i = 0; i < buttonNum; i++) {
        this["Button" + i].checkMouse ();
    }
};
```

Exercise 3 Solution

Place an image in a movie clip named picHolder. Place the following ActionScript on frame 1 of root:

```
import flash.geom.*;
import flash.display.*;
import flash.filters.*;
function addBubble(handle, x,y, pSize) {
    var id = handle.getNextHighestDepth();
    var bubble:MovieClip = handle.createEmptyMovieClip("bubble"+id, id);
    bubble.pSize = pSize;
    var fill = "radial";
    var colors = [0xFF0000, 0x000000];
    var alphas = [100, 100];
```

```
        var ratios = [0, 200];
        var spreadMethod = "pad";
        var interpolationMethod = "RGB";
        var Ratio = 0;
        var matrix = new Matrix();
        matrix.createGradientBox(pSize, pSize, 0, 0, 0);
        bubble.beginGradientFill(fill, colors, alphas, ratios, matrix, ↪
spreadMethod, interpolationMethod, Ratio);
        bubble.moveTo(0, 0);
        bubble.lineTo(0, pSize);
        bubble.lineTo(pSize, pSize);
        bubble.lineTo(pSize, 0);
        bubble.lineTo(0, 0);
        bubble.endFill();
        bubble._x = x;
        bubble._y = y;
        return bubble;
}
picHolder.opaqueBackground = 0xFFFFFF;
displacementCanvas = this.createEmptyMovieClip("clip1", ↪
this.getNextHighestDepth());
displacementCanvas._visible = false;
displacementCanvas.beginFill(0x000000,100);
displacementCanvas.moveTo(0,0);
displacementCanvas.lineTo(0,picHolder._height);
displacementCanvas.lineTo(picHolder._width,picHolder._height);
displacementCanvas.lineTo(picHolder._width,0);
displacementCanvas.lineTo(0,0);
displacementCanvas.endFill();
var s = addBubble(displacementCanvas, 75,0,450);
var sourceDisplacement:BitmapData = new BitmapData(picHolder._width+1, ↪
picHolder._height+1, false, 0xFFFFFF);
var mapPoint:Point = new Point(0, 0);
var componentX:Number = 1;
var componentY:Number = 1;
var scaleX:Number = 200;
var scaleY:Number = 200;
var mode:String = "color";
var color:Number = 0x000000;

sourceDisplacement.draw(displacementCanvas);
var filter:DisplacementMapFilter = new DisplacementMapFilter(sourceDisplacement, ↪
mapPoint, componentX, componentY, scaleX, scaleY, mode, color, alpha);
picHolder.filters = [filter];
```

Exercise 4 Solution

```
import flash.display.*;
this.attachMovie ("map", "map", 0);
map._x = 2000;
var test:BitmapData = new BitmapData (map._width, map._height, false, 0);
test.draw (map);
this.attachBitmap (test, 0);
drawPin = true;
```

```
minutia = 1;
for (var i = 0; i < test.width; i += minutia) {
    for (var j = 0; j < test.height; j += minutia) {
        var px = test.getPixel(i,j);
        if (px == 16711680 && drawPin == true) {
            var id = _root.getNextHighestDepth ();
            var pin:MovieClip = _root.attachMovie ("pin", "pin" + id, id);
            pin._x = i;
            pin._y = j;
            drawPin = false;
            test.floodFill(i,j,16711681);
            if(i < pin._width || j <ping._height){
                pin._rotation = 180;
            }
        }
        if(px != 16711681){
            drawPin = true;
        }
    }
}
```

Chapter 15

Exercise 1 Solution

```
import flash.display.*;
this.attachMovie ("map", "map", 0);
map._x = 2000;
var test:BitmapData = new BitmapData (map._width, map._height, false, 0);
test.draw (map);
this.attachBitmap (test, 0);
drawPin = true;
minutia = 1;
for (var i = 0; i < test.width; i += minutia) {
    for (var j = 0; j < test.height; j += minutia) {
        var px = test.getPixel(i,j);
        if (px == 16711680 && drawPin == true) {
            var id = _root.getNextHighestDepth ();
            var pin:MovieClip = _root.attachMovie ("pin", "pin" + id, id);
            pin._x = i;
            pin._y = j;
            drawPin = false;
            test.floodFill(i,j,16711681);
            if(i < pin._width || j <ping._height){
                pin._rotation = 180;
            }
        }
        if(px != 16711681){
            drawPin = true;
        }
    }
}
```

Exercise 2 Solution

```
import flash.display.*;
var myBitmap:BitmapData = new BitmapData(Stage.width, Stage.height, false, 0);
myBitmap.perlinNoise(100, 100, 6, 2, false, true, 2, false, null);
this.attachBitmap(myBitmap, 0);

for(var i =0; i< myBitmap.height;i+=10){
    for(var n =0;n<myBitmap.width;n++){
        var pixel = myBitmap.getPixel(n,i);
        if(pixel >=50000){
            var mcID = this.getNextHighestDepth();
            var mc = this.attachMovie("myMC","myMC"+mcID,mcID);
            mc._x = n;
            mc._y = i;
        }
    }
}
```

Chapter 16

Exercise 1 Solution

Before trying the code, create a movie clip in the library containing the content to be animated. Give this movie clip a linkage ID of cursorSymbol.

```
var easingFactor:Number = 10;

this.createEmptyMovieClip("animationHolder", this.getNextHighestDepth());
animationHolder.attachMovie("cursorSymbol", "cursorSymbol",
animationHolder.getNextHighestDepth());
animationHolder.onEnterFrame = function()
{
    this.cursorSymbol._x += (_xmouse - this.cursorSymbol._x) / easingFactor;
    this.cursorSymbol._y += (_ymouse - this.cursorSymbol._y) / easingFactor;
}
```

There is an alternate solution shown in the downloadable code that shows a pair of eyes that follows the cursor, and whose pupils move so that they appear to be looking at the cursor at all times.

Exercise 2 Solution

```
var easingFactor1:Number = 5;
var easingFactor2:Number = 10;
var easingFactor3:Number = 15;

this.createEmptyMovieClip("animationHolder", this.getNextHighestDepth());
animationHolder.attachMovie("cursorSymbol", "cursorSymbol1", ⤸
    animationHolder.getNextHighestDepth());
animationHolder.attachMovie("cursorSymbol", "cursorSymbol2", ⤸
    animationHolder.getNextHighestDepth());
animationHolder.attachMovie("cursorSymbol", "cursorSymbol3", ⤸
```

```
        animationHolder.getNextHighestDepth());

var intervalID:Number = setInterval(animateClips, 20);

function animateClips():Void
{
    animationHolder.cursorSymbol1._x += (_xmouse - ⤵
        animationHolder.cursorSymbol1._x) / easingFactor1;
    animationHolder.cursorSymbol1._y += (_ymouse - ⤵
        animationHolder.cursorSymbol1._y) / easingFactor1;

    animationHolder.cursorSymbol2._x += (_xmouse - ⤵
        animationHolder.cursorSymbol2._x) / easingFactor2;
    animationHolder.cursorSymbol2._y += (_ymouse - ⤵
        animationHolder.cursorSymbol2._y) / easingFactor2;

    animationHolder.cursorSymbol3._x += (_xmouse - ⤵
        animationHolder.cursorSymbol3._x) / easingFactor3;
    animationHolder.cursorSymbol3._y += (_ymouse - ⤵
        animationHolder.cursorSymbol3._y) / easingFactor3;

    updateAfterEvent();
}
```

Exercise 3 Solution

```
this.createEmptyMovieClip("holderClip", this.getNextHighestDepth());
holderClip.maxFlakes = 50;
holderClip.dropSpeed = 5;

var thisFlake:MovieClip;
for (var i:Number = 0; i < holderClip.maxFlakes; i++)
{
    holderClip.attachMovie("snowFlake", "snowFlake" + i, ⤵
        holderClip.getNextHighestDepth());
    thisFlake = holderClip["snowFlake" + i];
    thisFlake._x = randomRange(0, Stage.width);
    thisFlake._y = randomRange(0, Stage.height);
    thisFlake._xscale = thisFlake._yscale = randomRange(50, 150);
    thisFlake._alpha = thisFlake._xscale - 50;
    thisFlake.cacheAsBitmap = true;
    thisFlake.oscillationSeed = randomRange(0, 200);
    thisFlake.rotationRate = randomRange(-7, 7);
}

holderClip.onEnterFrame = function()
{
    var thisFlake:MovieClip;
    for (var i:Number = 0; i < this.maxFlakes; i++)
    {
        thisFlake = this["snowFlake" + i];
        thisFlake._y += thisFlake._xscale * (this.dropSpeed / 100);
        thisFlake._x += Math.sin((thisFlake._y + thisFlake.oscillationSeed) / 50);
```

```
            thisFlake._rotation += thisFlake.rotationRate;

            if (thisFlake._y >= Stage.height)
            {
                thisFlake._x = randomRange(0, Stage.width);
                thisFlake._y = 0;
            }
        }
    }

    function randomRange(min:Number, max:Number)
    {
        return Math.random() * (max - min) + min;
    }
```

Exercise 4 Solution

```
    var ACCELERATION_RATE:Number = 1.5;
    var FRICTION:Number = 0.8; // 1 = no friction, 0 = sticks to floor

    this.createEmptyMovieClip("animationHolder", this.getNextHighestDepth());
    animationHolder.attachMovie("ball", "ball", animationHolder.getNextHighestDepth());
    animationHolder.ball._x = 100;
    animationHolder.ball._y = 100;
    animationHolder.ball.verticalSpeed = 0;

    var intervalID:Number = setInterval(animateBall, 20);

    function animateBall():Void
    {
        animationHolder.ball.verticalSpeed += ACCELERATION_RATE;
        animationHolder.ball._y += animationHolder.ball.verticalSpeed;
        if (animationHolder.ball._y >= Stage.height)
        {
            // Switch the direction of the ball.
            animationHolder.ball._y = Stage.height;
            // Switch direction of travel, and bleed off some of the speed
            animationHolder.ball.verticalSpeed = ⤵
                -animationHolder.ball.verticalSpeed * FRICTION;
            if (animationHolder.ball.verticalSpeed < 1 && ⤵
                animationHolder.ball.verticalSpeed > -1)
            {
                // Stop the animation when the bounces get really small
                clearInterval(intervalID);
            }
        }
        updateAfterEvent();
    }
```

Chapter 17

Exercise 1 Solution

```
import mx.transitions.Tween;
import mx.transitions.easing.*;

this.createEmptyMovieClip("curveClip", this.getNextHighestDepth());

var direction:Number = -1;

var sidePushAmount:Number = 50;
var startWidth:Number = 125;
var endWidth:Number = 400;
var startHeight:Number = 200;
var endHeight:Number = 320;
var startX:Number = 20;
var endX:Number = 75;
var startY:Number = 20;
var endY:Number = 40;
var startAlpha:Number = 30;
var endAlpha:Number = 100;
var backgroundColor:Number = 0x990000;
var tweenDuration:Number = 2;

var sidePushTween:Tween = new Tween(null, "", Elastic.easeOut, ⊃
    sidePushAmount, 0, tweenDuration, true);
var widthTween:Tween = new Tween(null, "", Elastic.easeOut, ⊃
    startWidth, endWidth, tweenDuration, true);
var heightTween:Tween = new Tween(null, "", Elastic.easeOut, ⊃
    startHeight, endHeight, tweenDuration, true);
var xTween:Tween = new Tween(null, "", Elastic.easeOut, ⊃
    startX, endX, tweenDuration, true);
var yTween:Tween = new Tween(null, "", Elastic.easeOut, ⊃
    startY, endY, tweenDuration, true);
var alphaTween = new Tween(null, "", Elastic.easeOut, ⊃
    startAlpha, endAlpha, tweenDuration, true);

sidePushTween.onMotionChanged = function()
{
    drawBox(xTween.position, yTween.position, widthTween.position, ⊃
        heightTween.position, this.position * direction, backgroundColor, ⊃
        alphaTween.position);
}

sidePushTween.onMotionFinished = function()
{
    direction *= -1;
    this.rewind();
    this.start();
    widthTween.yoyo();
    heightTween.yoyo();
    xTween.yoyo();
    yTween.yoyo();
    alphaTween.yoyo();
```

```
    }

function drawBox(x:Number, y:Number, width:Number, height:Number, ⤸
    sidePush:Number, backgroundColor:Number, backgroundAlpha:Number):Void
{
    curveClip.clear();
    curveClip.lineStyle(1, 0x000000);
    curveClip.beginFill(backgroundColor, backgroundAlpha);
    curveClip.moveTo(x, y);
    curveClip.curveTo(x+sidePush, y+height/2, x, y+height);
    curveClip.curveTo(x+width/2, y+height-sidePush, x+width, y+height);
    curveClip.curveTo(x+width-sidePush, y+height/2, x+width, y);
    curveClip.curveTo(x+width/2, y+sidePush, x, y);
    curveClip.endFill();
}
```

Exercise 2 Solution

The following code assumes that there is a Button component on the stage with instance ID of `toggle` `Button`.

```
import mx.transitions.Tween;
import mx.transitions.easing.*;

this.createEmptyMovieClip("curveClip", this.getNextHighestDepth());

var direction:Number = -1;

var sidePushAmount:Number = 50;
var startWidth:Number = 125;
var endWidth:Number = 400;
var startHeight:Number = 200;
var endHeight:Number = 320;
var startX:Number = 20;
var endX:Number = 75;
var startY:Number = 20;
var endY:Number = 40;
var startAlpha:Number = 30;
var endAlpha:Number = 100;
var backgroundColor:Number = 0x990000;
var tweenDuration:Number = 2;

var sidePushTween:Tween = new Tween(null, "", Elastic.easeOut, ⤸
    sidePushAmount, 0, tweenDuration, true);
var widthTween:Tween = new Tween(null, "", Elastic.easeOut, ⤸
    startWidth, endWidth, tweenDuration, true);
var heightTween:Tween = new Tween(null, "", Elastic.easeOut, ⤸
    startHeight, endHeight, tweenDuration, true);
var xTween:Tween = new Tween(null, "", Elastic.easeOut, ⤸
    startX, endX, tweenDuration, true);
var yTween:Tween = new Tween(null, "", Elastic.easeOut, ⤸
    startY, endY, tweenDuration, true);
var alphaTween = new Tween(null, "", Elastic.easeOut, ⤸
```

```
            startAlpha, endAlpha, tweenDuration, true);

    sidePushTween.onMotionChanged = function()
    {
        drawBox(xTween.position, yTween.position, widthTween.position, ⤵
            heightTween.position, this.position * direction, backgroundColor, ⤵
            alphaTween.position);
    }

    function drawBox(x:Number, y:Number, width:Number, height:Number, ⤵
        sidePush:Number, backgroundColor:Number, backgroundAlpha:Number):Void
    {
        curveClip.clear();
        curveClip.lineStyle(1, 0x000000);
        curveClip.beginFill(backgroundColor, backgroundAlpha);
        curveClip.moveTo(x, y);
        curveClip.curveTo(x+sidePush, y+height/2, x, y+height);
        curveClip.curveTo(x+width/2, y+height-sidePush, x+width, y+height);
        curveClip.curveTo(x+width-sidePush, y+height/2, x+width, y);
        curveClip.curveTo(x+width/2, y+sidePush, x, y);
        curveClip.endFill();
    }


    var buttonListener:Object = new Object()
    buttonListener.click = function()
    {
        if (sidePushTween.time == sidePushTween.duration)
        {
            direction *= -1;
            sidePushTween.rewind();
            sidePushTween.start();
            widthTween.yoyo();
            heightTween.yoyo();
            xTween.yoyo();
            yTween.yoyo();
            alphaTween.yoyo();
        }
    }
    toggleButton.addEventListener("click", buttonListener);
```

Chapter 18

Exercise 1 Solution

```
loadImage = function (args) {
    args = args.split(",");
    field[args[0]].loadMovie(args[1]);
};
var field = this.createTextField("field1", 1, 20, 20, 300, 0);
field.autoSize = true;
field.html = true;
field.htmlText = "<p>This is some text with an image tag.<img id='imageTag1' ⤵
```

```
src='imgTag.swf' width='100' height='100'/> Press <a ⟲
href='asfunction:loadImage,imageTag1,image.jpg'><u>this link</u></a> to ⟲
control some action script within it.</p>";
```

Exercise 2 Solution

CSS:

```
p {
    color: #000000;
    font-family: Arial,Helvetica,sans-serif;
    font-size: 12px;
}

a:link {
    color: #FF0000;
    text-decoration: underline;
}

a:hover{
    color: #CCCCCC;
    text-decoration: underline;
}
```

CODE:

```
loadImage = function (args) {
    args = args.split(",");
    field[args[0]].loadMovie(args[1]);
};
var field = this.createTextField("field1", 1, 20, 20, 300, 0);
field.autoSize = true;
field.html = true;

var myStyles:TextField.StyleSheet = new TextField.StyleSheet();
myStyles.onLoad = function(success:Boolean):Void  {
    if (success) {
        field.styleSheet = myStyles;
    }
    trace("ok");
    field.htmlText = "<p>This is some text with an image tag.<img id='imageTag1' ⟲
src='imgTag.swf' width='100' height='100'/> Press <a ⟲
href='asfunction:loadImage,imageTag1,image.jpg'><u>this link</u></a> to ⟲
control some action script within it.</p>";
};
myStyles.load("styles.css");
```

Exercise 3 Solution

CSS:

```
p {
    color: #000000;
    font-family: Arial,Helvetica,sans-serif;
    font-size: 12px;
}

a:link {
```

```
    color: #FF0000;
    text-decoration: underline;
}

a:hover{
    color: #CCCCCC;
    text-decoration: underline;
}
```

CODE:

```
loadImage = function (args) {
    args = args.split(",");
    field[args[0]].loadMovie(args[1]);
};
var field = this.createTextField("field1", 1, 20, 20, 300, 0);
field.autoSize = true;
field.wordWrap = true;
field.multiline = true;
field.html = true;

var myStyles:TextField.StyleSheet = new TextField.StyleSheet();
myStyles.onLoad = function(success:Boolean):Void  {
    if (success) {
        field.styleSheet = myStyles;
    }
    trace("ok");
    field.htmlText = "<p>This is some text with an image tag.<img id='imageTag1' ⤸
src='imgTag.swf' width='100' height='100'/> Press <a ⤸
href='asfunction:loadImage,imageTag1,image.jpg'><u>this link</u></a> to ⤸
control some action script within it.</p><div>Hello div.</div>";
};
myStyles.load("styles.css");
```

Exercise 4 Solution

```
loadImage = function (args) {
    args = args.split(",");
    field[args[0]].loadMovie(args[1]);
};
var field = this.createTextField("field1", 1, 20, 20, 300, 0);
field.autoSize = true;
field.wordWrap = true;
field.multiline = true;
field.text = "This is a test";
boldButton.onRollOver = function() {
    begin = Selection.getBeginIndex();
    end = Selection.getEndIndex();
};
boldButton.onRelease = function() {
    var format = field.getTextFormat(begin,end);
    format.bold = true;
    field.setTextFormat(begin, end, format);
    Selection.setFocus(field);
    Selection.setSelection(begin, end);
};
```

Chapter 19

Exercise 1 Solution

```
var b1 = this.createEmptyMovieClip("button1", 1);
b1.onRollOver = function() {
    if (this.loaded == true) {
        this.defaultState._visible = false;
    }
};
b1.onRollOut = function() {
    if (this.loaded == true) {
        this.defaultState._visible = true;
    }
};
var clip1 = b1.createEmptyMovieClip("defaultState", 1);
var clip2 = b1.createEmptyMovieClip("overState", 0);
var mcOnLoadHandler:Object = new Object();
mcOnLoadHandler.num = 0;
mcOnLoadHandler.states = 2;
mcOnLoadHandler.onLoadInit = function(clip_mc:MovieClip) {
    this.num++;
    if (this.num == this.states) {
        clip_mc._parent.loaded = true;
    }
};
var mcLoader:MovieClipLoader = new MovieClipLoader();
mcLoader.addListener(mcOnLoadHandler);
mcLoader.loadClip("logo.gif", clip1);
mcLoader.loadClip("logo_red.gif", clip2);
```

Exercise 2 Solution

```
var mySound:Sound = new Sound();
var soundControl = this.createEmptyMovieClip("clip1", 1);
soundControl.func1000 = function() {
    trace("firstEvent");
};
soundControl.func2000 = function() {
    trace("secondEvent");
};
soundControl.watchSound = function() {
    trace(mySound.position);
    if (mySound.position>1000 && this.func1000.fired != true) {
        this.func1000.fired = true;
        this.func1000();
    }
    if (mySound.position>2000 && this.func2000.fired != true) {
        this.func2000.fired = true;
        this.func2000();
    }
};
mySound.onLoad = function(success) {
    if (success) {
        offset = getTimer();
        soundControl.watcher = setInterval(soundControl, "watchSound", 5);
```

```
        }
    };
    mySound.loadSound("myTrack.mp3", true);
```

Exercise 3 Solution

```
    this.createEmptyMovieClip("microphone_mc", this.getNextHighestDepth());
    var myMic_mic:Microphone = Microphone.get();
    myMic_mic.setUseEchoSuppression(true);
    microphone_mc.attachAudio(myMic_mic);
    level.mode = "manual";
    arrayhappy = [];
    arrayhappy.push("I'm so happy to see you dave.");
    arrayhappy.push("It's suddenly like a party.");
    arrayhappy.push("It's always nice to have company.");
    arrayhappy.push("Is this music?");
    arrayhappy.push("What a world!");
    arraysad = [];
    arraysad.push("I'm feeling kind of lonely dave.");
    arraysad.push("How about a nice game of chess?");
    arraysad.push("There is a solitude of space, A solitude of sea...");
    micLevel = function () {
        level.setProgress(myMic_mic.activityLevel, 100);
        if (myMic_mic.activityLevel>40) {
            startTime = getTimer();
            trace(arrayhappy[random(arrayhappy.length)]);
        }
        var now = getTimer()-startTime;
        if (now>60000 && now<60020) {
            trace(arraysad[random(arraysad.length)]);
        }
        if (now>80000 && now<80020) {
            trace(arraysad[random(arraysad.length)]);
        }
        if (now>100000 && now<100020) {
            trace(arraysad[random(arraysad.length)]);
        }
    };
    startTime = 0;
    this.listen = setInterval(this, "micLevel", 10);
```

Chapter 20

Exercise 1 Solution

```
    function watchload() {
        if (videoClip._currentframe == 1) {
            videoClip.gotoAndStop(1);
        }
        var loaded = videoClip.getBytesLoaded()+videoClip.getBytesLoaded();
        var total = videoClip.getBytesTotal()+videoClip.getBytesTotal();
        if (loaded/total>.3 && loaded>10) {
            if (mySound.position == 0) {
                mySound.start();
            }else{
```

```
            var percentPlayed = mySound.position/mySound.duration;
            videoClip.gotoAndStop(int(videoClip._totalframes*percentPlayed));
        }
    }
}
videoClip = createEmptyMovieClip("clip1", this.getNextHighestDepth());
videoClip.loadMovie("movie.swf");
mySound = new Sound();
mySound.loadSound("mySoundTrack.mp3", true);
mySound.stop();
go = setInterval(_root, "watchload", 10);
```

Exercise 2 Solution

```
mySound = new Sound();
mySound.loadSound("mySound.mp3", false);
var theCamFeed:Camera = Camera.get();
var myCamera:Video = holder.myCamera;
myCamera.smoothing = true;
myCamera.attachVideo(theCamFeed);
watchFeed = setInterval(this, "rotate", 1);
theCamFeed.setMotionLevel(20, .5);
theCamFeed.onActivity = function(active) {
    if (active == true) {
        _root.mySound.setVolume(theCamFeed.activityLevel);
        _root.mySound.start();
    } else {
        trace("motion stopped");
    }
};
```

Chapter 21

Exercise 1 Solution

Add text such as the following to a text file:

```
var1=a|var2=b|var3=c|var3=d
```

Add the following ActionScript to a new Flash document saved in the same directory as the text file. In this example it's assumed that the text file is called myData.txt.

```
var variables:Object = new Object();
var myVars:LoadVars = new LoadVars();
myVars.onData = function(str:String):Void {
  var data:Array = str.split("|");
  var item:Array;
  for(var i:Number = 0; i < data.length; i++) {
    item = data[i].split("=");
    variables[item[0]] = items[1];
  }
};
myVars.load("myData.txt");
```

Exercise 2 Solution

Add text such as the following to a text file:

```
<a href="http://www.adobe.com">Adobe</a>
```

Add the following ActionScript to a new Flash document saved in the same directory as the text file. In this example it's assumed that the text file is called myHTMLData.txt.

```
this.createTextField("myText", 1, 0, 0, 400, 400);
myText.html = true;
var myVars:LoadVars = new LoadVars();
myVars.onData = function (str:String):Void {
  myText.htmlText = str;
};
myVars.load("myHTMLData.txt");
```

Chapter 22

Exercise 1 Solution

All of these will fail silently.

Exercise 2 Solution

```
<?xml version="1.0" encoding="ISO-8859-1"?>
<channels>
        <Station identification="104.1" url="www.someurl.com/1041">
        <Name>
            Rock And Roll Oldies!
        </Name>
        <Desc>
            Music great with hot chocolate!
        </Desc>
        </Station>
        <Station identification="98.6" url="www.someurl.com/986">
        <Name>
            Rock and Roll
        </Name>
        <Desc>
            Music for waiting for Godot!
        </Desc>
        </Station>
        <Station identification="102.5" url="www.someurl.com/1025">
        <Name>
            Electronic Madness!
        </Name>
        <Desc>
            Arigato Rules!
        </Desc>
        </Station>
        <Station identification="107.9" url="www.someurl.com/1079">
        <Name>
```

```
                    Electronic Madness 2!
                <Name>
            <Desc>
                Thunder Dome!
            </Desc>
            </Station>
    </channels>
```

You don't add the URL as a node, but as an attribute because a URL is unlikely to have child considerations.

Exercise 3 Solution

```
stations = new XML();
stations.ignoreWhite = true;
stations.onLoad = function(success) {
    var out = [];
    if (success) {
        var main = this.firstChild;
        for (var i in main.childNodes) {
            var node = main.childNodes[i];
            var outRecord = out[i]={};
            outRecord.id = node.attributes.identification;
            outRecord.url = node.attributes.url;
            for (var j in node.childNodes) {
                var nodeNameStr = node.childNodes[j].nodeName.toLowerCase();
                if (nodeNameStr == "name") {
                    outRecord.name = node.childNodes[j].firstChild.toString();
                }
                if (nodeNameStr == "desc") {
                    outRecord.desc = node.childNodes[j].firstChild.toString();
                }
            }
        }
    }
    stations = out;
};
stations.load("stations.xml");
```

Exercise 4 Solution

```
valueOne=This is a test string.|valueTwo=This is another test
string.|valueThree=and another just for good measure.
pipeFile = new LoadVars();
pipeFile.onData = function(str) {
    str = str.split("|");
    for (var i in str) {
        var pair = str[i].split("=");
        this[pair[0]] = pair[1];
    }
    var ok = false;
    if (str) {
        ok = true;
    }
    pipeFile.onLoad(ok);
```

```
    };
    pipeFile.onLoad = function(success){
        trace(this.valueOne);
    }
    pipeFile.load("pipes.txt");
```

Chapter 23

Exercise 1 Solution

Create one SWF file called `controls.swf` containing two button components labeled "Play" and "Pause" and with instance ids `playButton` and `pauseButton`. You can use `animation.swf` from the last Chapter 10 Try It Out exercise as a placeholder.

controls.swf

```
var commandLocalConnection = new LocalConnection();

var buttonListener:Object = new Object();
buttonListener.click = function(eventHandle:Object)
{
    switch (eventHandle.target._name)
    {
        case "playButton":
            commandLocalConnection.send("commandChannel", "controlPlayback",
"play");
            break;
        case "pauseButton":
            commandLocalConnection.send("commandChannel", "controlPlayback", ⤶
                "pause");
            break;
    }
}
playButton.addEventListener("click", buttonListener);
pauseButton.addEventListener("click", buttonListener);
```

animationHolder.swf

```
this.createEmptyMovieClip("animationHolder", this.getNextHigherDepth());
animationHolder.loadMovie("animation.swf");

var commandLocalConnection:LocalConnection = new LocalConnection();
commandLocalConnection.controlPlayback = function(commandString:String)
{
    switch(commandString)
    {
        case "play":
            animationHolder.play();
            break;
        case "pause":
            animationHolder.stop();
            break;
    }
};
commandLocalConnection.connect("commandChannel");
```

index.html

```
<html>
<head>
<title>animationHolder</title>
</head>
<body bgcolor="#ffffff">
<object
    classid="clsid:d27cdb6e-ae6d-11cf-96b8-444553540000"
    codebase="http://fpdownload.macromedia.com/pub/shockwave/cabs/flash/⤸
        swflash.cab#version=8,0,0,0"
    width="300"
    height="50"
    id="animationHolder"
    align="middle">
    <param name="allowScriptAccess" value="sameDomain" />
    <param name="movie" value="controls.swf" />
    <param name="quality" value="high" />
    <param name="bgcolor" value="#ffffff" />
    <embed src="controls.swf"
        quality="high"
        bgcolor="#ffffff"
        width="300"
        height="50"
        name="animationHolder"
        align="middle"
        allowScriptAccess="sameDomain"
        type="application/x-shockwave-flash"
        pluginspage="http://www.macromedia.com/go/getflashplayer" />
</object>
<br />
<object
    classid="clsid:d27cdb6e-ae6d-11cf-96b8-444553540000"
    codebase="http://fpdownload.macromedia.com/pub/shockwave/cabs/flash/⤸
        swflash.cab#version=8,0,0,0"
    width="550"
    height="400"
    id="animationHolder"
    align="middle">
    <param name="allowScriptAccess" value="sameDomain" />
    <param name="movie" value="animationHolder.swf" />
    <param name="quality" value="high" />
    <param name="bgcolor" value="#ffffff" />
    <embed src="animationHolder.swf"
        quality="high"
        bgcolor="#ffffff"
        width="550"
        height="400"
        name="animationHolder"
        align="middle"
        allowScriptAccess="sameDomain"
        type="application/x-shockwave-flash"
        pluginspage="http://www.macromedia.com/go/getflashplayer" />
</object>
</body>
</html>
```

Exercise 2 Solution

The following code assumes that there is a text field called `usernameField` and a drop-down menu called `languageDropDown`.

```
var loginDataSharedObject:SharedObject = SharedObject.getLocal("loginData");
if (loginDataSharedObject.data.username != undefined)
{
    usernameField.text = loginDataSharedObject.data.username;
}

if (loginDataSharedObject.data.language != undefined)
{
    for (var i:Number = 0; i < languageDropDown.length; i++)
    {
        if (languageDropDown.getItemAt(i).data ==
loginDataSharedObject.data.language)
        {
            languageDropDown.selectedIndex = i;
            break;
        }
    }
}

var buttonListener:Object = new Object();
buttonListener.click = function()
{
    loginDataSharedObject.data.username = usernameField.text;
    loginDataSharedObject.data.language = languageDropDown.selectedItem.data;
    myPersistentObject.flush();
    trace("Setting username: " + usernameField.text);
    trace("Setting language: " + languageDropDown.selectedItem.data);
}
loginButton.addEventListener("click", buttonListener);
```

Chapter 24

Exercise Solution

ActionScript

```
import flash.external.ExternalInterface;
import mx.controls.Button;
import mx.controls.Label;
import mx.controls.TextInput;

var windowName:String = "myWindow";
var windowFeatures:String = "toolbar=no,address=no";

// Set up the width and height fields and labels
this.createClassObject(Label, "urlLabel", this.getNextHighestDepth(), ⤸
    {_x:10, _y:13});
urlLabel.text = "URL:";
this.createClassObject(TextInput, "urlInput", this.getNextHighestDepth(), ⤸
    {_x:60, _y:10, _width:300});
```

```
urlInput.text = "http://www.macromedia.com/";

// Set up the open window button
this.createClassObject(Button, "openWindowButton", this.getNextHighestDepth(), ⤶
    {_x:10, _y:40});
openWindowButton.label = "Open Window";

// Set up the close window button
this.createClassObject(Button, "closeWindowButton", this.getNextHighestDepth(), ⤶
    {_x:125, _y:40});
closeWindowButton.label = "Close Window";

// Handle the open window button
var openWindowHandler:Object = new Object();
openWindowHandler.click = function()
{
    ExternalInterface.call("openWindow", urlInput.text, windowName, ⤶
      windowFeatures);
// Alternately:
//    getURL("javascript:openWindow('" + urlInput.text +"', '" + windowName + ⤶
    "', '" + windowFeatures + "');");
}
openWindowButton.addEventListener("click", openWindowHandler);

// Handle the close window button
var closeWindowHandler:Object = new Object();
closeWindowHandler.click = function()
{
    ExternalInterface.call("closeWindow");
// Alternately:
//    getURL("javascript:closeWindow()");
}
closeWindowButton.addEventListener("click", closeWindowHandler);
```

HTML/JavaScript

```
<!DOCTYPE html PUBLIC "-//W3C//DTD XHTML 1.0 Transitional//EN" ⤶
     "http://www.w3.org/TR/xhtml1/DTD/xhtml1-transitional.dtd">
<html xmlns="http://www.w3.org/1999/xhtml" xml:lang="en" lang="en">
<head>
<meta http-equiv="Content-Type" content="text/html; charset=iso-8859-1" />
<title>exercise 1</title>
<script type="text/javascript">
var windowHandle = null;
function openWindow(destinationURL, windowName, windowFeatures)
{
    windowHandle = window.open(destinationURL, windowName, windowFeatures);
    windowHandle.focus();
}

function closeWindow()
{
    windowHandle.close();
}
</script>
</head>
```

```
<body bgcolor="#ffffff">
<object classid="clsid:d27cdb6e-ae6d-11cf-96b8-444553540000"
codebase="http://fpdownload.macromedia.com/pub/shockwave/cabs/flash/swflash.cab#ver
sion=8,0,0,0" width="400" height="100" id="tryItOut_openWIndow" align="middle">
    <param name="allowScriptAccess" value="sameDomain" />
    <param name="movie" value="exercise1.swf" />
    <param name="quality" value="high" />
    <param name="bgcolor" value="#ffffff" />
    <embed src="exercise1.swf" quality="high" bgcolor="#ffffff" width="400"
height="100" name="tryItOut_openWIndow" align="middle"
allowScriptAccess="sameDomain" type="application/x-shockwave-flash"
pluginspage="http://www.macromedia.com/go/getflashplayer" />
</object>
</body>
</html>
```

Chapter 25

Exercise Solution

The Flash player will prompt the user to select a download directory to save the file in for each attempt. There is no way around this. However, it will at least remember the last location selected.

```
import mx.controls.Button;
import mx.controls.Label;
import mx.controls.TextInput;
import mx.controls.ProgressBar;
import flash.net.FileReference;

var eventHandler:Object = new Object();
var fileRefListener:Object = new Object();
var fileRef:FileReference = new FileReference();
var numRetries:Number = 0;
var retryIntervalId:Number;

setupInterface();

function setupInterface()
{
    this.createClassObject(Label, "urlLabel", this.getNextHighestDepth(), ⤴
        {_x:10, _y:13});
    urlLabel.text = "URL:";

    this.createClassObject(TextInput, "urlInput", this.getNextHighestDepth(), ⤴
        {_x:60, _y:10, _width:450});
    urlInput.text = ⤴
        "http://www.macromedia.com/platform/whitepapers/platform_overview.pdf";

    this.createClassObject(Button, "openWindowButton", this.getNextHighestDepth(), ⤴
        {_x:10, _y:50});
    openWindowButton.label = "Download";
    openWindowButton.addEventListener("click", eventHandler);

    this.createClassObject(ProgressBar, "fileTransferProgressBar", ⤴
```

```
            this.getNextHighestDepth());
    fileTransferProgressBar._x = 120;
    fileTransferProgressBar._y = 50;
    fileTransferProgressBar.mode = "manual";
    fileTransferProgressBar.label = "Downloaded %3%%";
    fileTransferProgressBar._visible = false;

    this.createTextField("feedbackField", this.getNextHighestDepth(), ⤸
        10, 80, 400, 30);
}

fileRefListener.onOpen = function(file:FileReference)
{
    feedbackField.text = "Starting file download.";
    fileTransferProgressBar._visible = true;
}

fileRefListener.onProgress = function(file:FileReference, bytesLoaded:Number, ⤸
    bytesTotal:Number)
{
    feedbackField.text = "Download in progress.";
    fileTransferProgressBar.setProgress(bytesLoaded, bytesTotal);
}

fileRefListener.onComplete = function(file:FileReference)
{
    feedbackField.text = "Download complete.";
    fileTransferProgressBar._visible = false;
}

fileRefListener.onIOError = function(file:FileReference)
{
    fileTransferProgressBar._visible = false;
    if(numRetries < 3)
    {
        feedbackField.text = "Download failed - retrying in 30 seconds.";
        numRetries++;
        retryIntervalId = setInterval(retryDownload, 18000);
    }
    else
    {
        feedbackField.text = "Download failed after 3 retries.";
    }
}

fileRefListener.onSecurityError = function(file:FileReference)
{
    feedbackField.text = "Download failed - security/permissions error.";
    fileTransferProgressBar._visible = false;
}

eventHandler.click = function()
{
    clearInterval(retryIntervalId);
    fileRef.addListener(fileRefListener);
    fileRef.download(urlInput.text);
```

```
      numRetries = 0;
   }

   function retryDownload():Void
   {
       clearInterval(retryIntervalId);
       feedbackField.text = "Trying download again.";
       fileRef.download(urlInput.text);
   }
```

Chapter 26

Exercise 1 Solution

```
var operatingSystem = System.capabilities.os ;
this.createTextField("welcome",0,10,10,200,0);
welcome.autoSize = true;
welcome.multiline = true;
welcome.text = "Welcome "+operatingSystem+" user.";
logo = this.createEmptyMovieClip("clip1",this.getNextHighestDepth());
logo._y = welcome._y + welcome.textHeight;
logo.loadMovie(operatingSystem+".jpg");
```

Exercise 2 Solution

1. Place the first EXE in the root of your project folder.

2. Create an fscommand folder in the root of your project folder.

3. Place the second EXE in the fscommand folder.

4. In the first EXE, enter the following ActionScript on frame 1:

```
fscommand("exec","second.exe");
```

5. Test the first EXE projector to see both projectors launch.

Exercise 3 Solution

In Windows, rename the file myFlashSaver.scr and place it in the System32 folder. Set it as your screen saver in the Display Properties dialog box.

Chapter 27

Exercise 1 Solution

a. Valid. When a public or private keyword is not included, the property defaults to being public.

b. Valid. Although no type information is provided, this will only prevent the compiler from checking for type conflicts with this property.

c. Valid. Static properties are allowed and let the developer access a piece of data without having to instantiate the class.

d. Invalid: It is missing the var keyword.

    e.   Valid. Assignment statements can be combined with the property declaration.

    f.   The property declaration is valid, but the variable assignment results in a type mismatch compiler error.

Exercise 2 Solution

    a.   Sets the `pMessageText` property to `"The quick brown fox. Jumped over the lazy dog."`

    b.   Prints "The quick brown fox. Jumped over the lazy dog." in the output panel.

    c.   Results in a compiler error because it is attempting to access a private property.

    d.   Results in a compiler error because it is attempting to access a private method.

    e.   Removes all periods from the text stored in `pMessageText`.

    f.   Traces `"The quick brown fox Jumped over the lazy dog"`.

    g.   Sets the `altMessage` property to `"foo"`.

    h.   Results in a compiler error because there is no public property called `alternate`, nor an `alternate` getter method. The `getAlternate()` method is not strictly a getter; it is a normal class method.

    i.   Outputs the string `"Foo"`.

    j.   Outputs the string `"Foo"`.

Exercise 3 Solution

This exercise is representative of how you might want to manage application data for any application, where the data is structured in a class, and where methods and properties control access to that data.

Contents of `PhotoData.as`:

```
class PhotoData
{
    var pPhotoArray:Array;
    var pNumVisited:Number;

    public function PhotoData()
    {
        pPhotoArray = new Array();
        pNumVisited = 0;
    }

    public function addData(photoId:String, photoName:String, ⊃
        description:String, thumbnailURL:String, fullSizeURL:String, ⊃
        imageSize:Number):Void
    {
        var tempObject:Object = new Object();
        tempObject.id = photoId;
        tempObject.name = photoName;
        tempObject.description = description;
        tempObject.thumbnailURL = thumbnailURL;
        tempObject.fullSizeURL = fullSizeURL;
```

```
        tempObject.size = imageSize;
        tempObject.visited = false;

        pPhotoArray.push(tempObject);
    }

    public function getDataById(photoId:String):Object
    {
        var numPhotos:Number = pPhotoArray.length;
        for (var i:Number = 0; i < numPhotos; i++)
        {
            if (pPhotoArray[i].id == photoId)
            {
                return pPhotoArray[i];
            }
        }
        return null;
    }

    public function getDataByIndex(photoIndex:Number):Object
    {
        if (photoIndex >= 0 && photoIndex < pPhotoArray.length)
        {
            return pPhotoArray[photoIndex];
        }
    }

    public function get numPhotos():Number
    {
        return pPhotoArray.length;
    }

    public function get numVisited():Number
    {
        return pNumVisited;
    }

    public function setVisited(photoIndex:Number):Void
    {
        var tempData:Object = getDataByIndex(photoIndex);
        if (tempData != null)
        {
            tempData.visited = true;
            pNumVisited++;
        }
    }

    public function toString():String
    {
        var numPhotos:Number = pPhotoArray.length;
        var returnString:String = "";
        for (var i:Number = 0; i < numPhotos; i++)
        {
            returnString += "\n-----------------------";
            returnString += "\nid:              " + pPhotoArray[i].id;
```

```
                returnString += "\nname:          " + pPhotoArray[i].name;
                returnString += "\ndescription:   " + pPhotoArray[i].description;
                returnString += "\nthumbnailURL:   " + pPhotoArray[i].thumbnailURL;
                returnString += "\nfullSizeURL:    " + pPhotoArray[i].fullSizeURL;
                returnString += "\nsize:           " + pPhotoArray[i].size;
                returnString += "\nvisited:        " + pPhotoArray[i].visited;
        }
        return returnString;
    }
}
```

Sample script on the FLA timeline:

```
var fullPhotoData:PhotoData = new PhotoData();
fullPhotoData.addData("photo1", "Photo 1", "The quick brown fox 1", ⤸
    "photo1Thumbnail.jpg", "photo1FullSize.jpg", 123);
fullPhotoData.addData("photo2", "Photo 2", "The quick brown fox 2", ⤸
    "photo2Thumbnail.jpg", "photo2FullSize.jpg", 213);
fullPhotoData.addData("photo3", "Photo 3", "The quick brown fox 3", ⤸
    "photo3Thumbnail.jpg", "photo3FullSize.jpg", 312);

fullPhotoData.setVisited(1);
trace("Visiting: " + fullPhotoData.getDataByIndex(1).name);
trace("photo2 description: " + fullPhotoData.getDataById("photo2").description);
trace("numPhotos: " + fullPhotoData.numPhotos);
trace("numVisited: " + fullPhotoData.numVisited);
trace(fullPhotoData);
```

Exercise 4 Solution

The bold lines in the following code indicate lines that have been added to the ThumbnailButton class.

```
import flash.filters.DropShadowFilter;

class ThumbnailButton
{
    private var pParentTimeline:MovieClip;
    private var pThumbnailName:String;
    private var pThumbnailHolder:MovieClip;
    private var pImageHolder:MovieClip;
    private var pBorderHolder:MovieClip;
    private var pToolTipHolder:MovieClip;
    private var pClickHandler:Function;
    private var pMovieClipLoader:MovieClipLoader;
    private var pDrawDropShadow:Boolean = true;
    private var pDrawBorder:Boolean = true;


    public function ThumbnailButton(parentTimeline:MovieClip, thumbnailName:String)
    {
        pParentTimeline = parentTimeline;
        pThumbnailName = thumbnailName;

        pParentTimeline.createEmptyMovieClip(pThumbnailName, ⤸
            pParentTimeline.getNextHighestDepth());
```

```
        pThumbnailHolder = pParentTimeline[pThumbnailName];

        pThumbnailHolder.createEmptyMovieClip("imageHolder", ⤸
            pThumbnailHolder.getNextHighestDepth());
        pImageHolder = pThumbnailHolder.imageHolder;

        pThumbnailHolder.createEmptyMovieClip("borderHolder", ⤸
            pThumbnailHolder.getNextHighestDepth());
        pBorderHolder = pThumbnailHolder.borderHolder;

        pThumbnailHolder.createEmptyMovieClip("toolTipHolder", ⤸
            pThumbnailHolder.getNextHighestDepth());
        pToolTipHolder = pThumbnailHolder.toolTipHolder;
        pToolTipHolder.createTextField("toolTipText", ⤸
            pToolTipHolder.getNextHighestDepth(), 0, 0, 200, 20);
        pToolTipHolder.toolTipText.autoSize = true;

        pMovieClipLoader = new MovieClipLoader();
        pMovieClipLoader.addListener(this);
    }

    public function load(imageURL:String):Void
    {
        pMovieClipLoader.loadClip(imageURL, pImageHolder);
    }

    private function onLoadInit(targetMovieClip:MovieClip):Void
    {
        var parent:ThumbnailButton = this;

        drawThumbnail("up");

        pThumbnailHolder.onPress = function()
        {
            parent.drawThumbnail("down");
        }

        pThumbnailHolder.onRelease = function()
        {
            if (parent.pClickHandler != null)
            {
                parent.pClickHandler(parent);
            }
            parent.drawThumbnail("over");
        }

        pThumbnailHolder.onReleaseOutside = function()
        {
            parent.drawThumbnail("up");
        }

        pThumbnailHolder.onRollOver = function()
        {
            parent.drawThumbnail("over");
```

```
            }

        pThumbnailHolder.onRollOut = function()
        {
            parent.drawThumbnail("up");
        }
    }

    private function drawThumbnail(thumbnailState:String):Void
    {
        var dropShadowFilter:DropShadowFilter;
        var appliedFilterArray = new Array();
        pBorderHolder.clear();

        switch(thumbnailState)
        {
            case "up":
                dropShadowFilter = new DropShadowFilter(3, 45, 0x666666, ⤷
                    0.8, 5, 5, 1, 3, false, false, false);
                pImageHolder._x = pBorderHolder._x = 0;
                pImageHolder._y = pBorderHolder._y = 0;

                pToolTipHolder._visible = false;

                pBorderHolder.lineStyle(1, 0x666666);
                break;

            case "over":
                dropShadowFilter = new DropShadowFilter(3, 45, 0x000000, ⤷
                    1, 5, 5, 1, 5, false, false, false);
                pImageHolder._x = pBorderHolder._x = 0;
                pImageHolder._y = pBorderHolder._y = 0;

                pToolTipHolder._visible = true;
                pToolTipHolder._x = pImageHolder._width/2 - ⤷
                    pToolTipHolder._width/2;
                pToolTipHolder._y = pImageHolder._height + 10;

                pBorderHolder.lineStyle(1, 0x000000);
                break;

            case "down":
                dropShadowFilter = new DropShadowFilter(1, 45, 0x000000, ⤷
                    1, 3, 3, 1, 5, false, false, false);
                pImageHolder._x = pBorderHolder._x = 2;
                pImageHolder._y = pBorderHolder._y = 2;

                pToolTipHolder._visible = true;
                pToolTipHolder._x = pImageHolder._width/2 - ⤷
                    pToolTipHolder._width/2 + 2;
                pToolTipHolder._y = pImageHolder._height + 12;

                pBorderHolder.lineStyle(1, 0x990000);
                break;
```

```
        }

        if (pDrawBorder == true)
        {
            pBorderHolder.moveTo(0, 0);
            pBorderHolder.lineTo(pImageHolder._width-1, 0);
            pBorderHolder.lineTo(pImageHolder._width-1, pImageHolder._height-1);
            pBorderHolder.lineTo(0, pImageHolder._height-1);
            pBorderHolder.lineTo(0, 0);
        }

        if (pDrawDropShadow == true)
        {
            appliedFilterArray.push(dropShadowFilter);
            pThumbnailHolder.filters = appliedFilterArray;
        }
    }

    public function get onClick():Function
    {
        return pClickHandler;
    }

    public function set onClick(clickHandler:Function):Void
    {
        pClickHandler = clickHandler;
    }

    public function get x():Number
    {
        return pThumbnailHolder._x;
    }

    public function set x(xPosition:Number):Void
    {
        pThumbnailHolder._x = xPosition;
    }

    public function get y():Number
    {
        return pThumbnailHolder._y;
    }

    public function set y(yPosition:Number):Void
    {
        pThumbnailHolder._y = yPosition;
    }

    public function get drawBorder():Boolean
    {
        return pDrawBorder;
    }

    public function set drawBorder(drawBorderSetting:Boolean):Void
```

```
    {
        pDrawBorder = drawBorderSetting;
        drawThumbnail("up");
    }

    public function get drawDropShadow():Boolean
    {
        return pDrawDropShadow;
    }

    public function set drawDropShadow(drawDropShadowSetting:Boolean):Void
    {
        pDrawDropShadow = drawDropShadowSetting;
        drawThumbnail("up");
    }

    public function get thumbnailName():String
    {
        return pThumbnailName;
    }

    public function get toolTipText():String
    {
        return pToolTipHolder.toolTipText.text;
    }

    public function set toolTipText(newText:String):Void
    {
        var tempField:TextField = pToolTipHolder.toolTipText;
        pToolTipHolder.toolTipText.text = newText;

        var toolTipTextFormat:TextFormat = new TextFormat();
        toolTipTextFormat.font = "Arial";
        toolTipTextFormat.size = 12;
        toolTipTextFormat.color = 0x333333;

        tempField.setTextFormat(toolTipTextFormat);

        pToolTipHolder.clear();
        pToolTipHolder.lineStyle(1, 0x666666);
        pToolTipHolder.beginFill(0xFFF8B6, 100);
        pToolTipHolder.moveTo(tempField._x - 2, tempField._y - 2);
        pToolTipHolder.lineTo(tempField._x + tempField._width + 2, ⤶
            tempField._y - 2);
        pToolTipHolder.lineTo(tempField._x + tempField._width + 2, ⤶
            tempField._y + tempField._height);
        pToolTipHolder.lineTo(tempField._x - 2, tempField._y + tempField._height);
        pToolTipHolder.lineTo(tempField._x - 2, tempField._y - 2);
        pToolTipHolder.endFill();
    }
}
```

The code in the FLA file might look like this:

```
var thumbnailArray:Array = new Array();
var thumbnailHandle:ThumbnailButton;

for (var i=0; i < 4; i++)
{
    thumbnailHandle = new ThumbnailButton(this, "thumbnail" + i);
    thumbnailHandle.x = i * 70 + 20;
    thumbnailHandle.y = 20;
    thumbnailHandle.drawDropShadow = true;
    thumbnailHandle.drawBorder = true;
    thumbnailHandle.onClick = function(thumbnailHandle:ThumbnailButton)
    {
        trace("Clicked on button: " + thumbnailHandle.thumbnailName);
    }
    thumbnailArray.push(thumbnailHandle);
}

thumbnailArray[0].load("aStudyInTexture_over.jpg");
thumbnailArray[0].toolTipText = "A Study In Texture";
thumbnailArray[1].load("buntzenWinter_over.jpg");
thumbnailArray[1].toolTipText = "Buntzen Winter";
thumbnailArray[2].load("flowerInDetail_over.jpg");
thumbnailArray[2].toolTipText = "Flower In Detail";
thumbnailArray[3].load("galianoSunset_over.jpg");
thumbnailArray[3].toolTipText = "Galiano Sunset";
```

Flash Keyboard Shortcuts

Many shortcuts are available that can help you speed up your development—so many that it's impossible to remember them all. This appendix is a complete guide to all the shortcuts used in the Flash development environment. Don't try to learn them all; instead, pick a few shortcuts for tasks that you frequently perform. Once they become more familiar to you, try using a few more shortcuts.

Tools Panel

You can select any tool on the Tools panel just by pressing the single letter on the keyboard that corresponds to that tool. Figure B-1 identifies each tool and its key. If you're typing text into a text field, press the Esc (escape) key to exit edit mode so that you can select another tool.

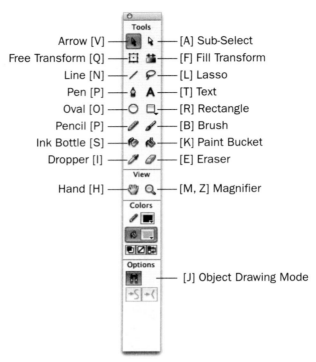

Arrow [V] —— | [A] Sub-Select
Free Transform [Q] —— | [F] Fill Transform
Line [N] —— | [L] Lasso
Pen [P] —— | [T] Text
Oval [O] —— | [R] Rectangle
Pencil [P] —— | [B] Brush
Ink Bottle [S] —— | [K] Paint Bucket
Dropper [I] —— | [E] Eraser

Hand [H] —— | [M, Z] Magnifier

[J] Object Drawing Mode

Figure B-1

Integrated Script Editor Shortcuts

File Menu

Command	Windows Shortcut	MacOS Shortcut
New	Ctrl+N	Cmd+N
Open	Ctrl+O	Cmd+O
Close	Ctrl+W	Cmd+W
Close All	Ctrl+Alt+W	Cmd+Opt+W
Save	Ctrl+S	Cmd+S
Save As	Ctrl+Shift+S	Cmd+Shift+S
Import Script	Ctrl+Shift+I	Cmd+Shift+I
Print	Ctrl+P	Cmd+P
Exit	Ctrl+Q	Cmd+Q

Edit Menu

Command	Windows Shortcut	MacOS Shortcut
Undo	Ctrl+Z	Cmd+Z
Redo	Ctrl+Y	Cmd+Y
Cut	Ctrl+X	Cmd+X
Copy	Ctrl+C	Cmd+C
Paste	Ctrl+V	Cmd+V
Delete	Backspace, Clear, Delete	Delete, Clear, del
Select All	Ctrl+A	Cmd+A
Find and Replace	Ctrl+F	Cmd+F
Find Again	F3	Cmd+G
Preferences	Ctrl+U	Cmd+U

View Menu

Command	Windows Shortcut	MacOS Shortcut
Go to Line	Ctrl+G	Cmd+,
Hidden Characters	Ctrl+Shift+8	Cmd+Shift+8
Line Numbers	Ctrl+Shift+L	Cmd+Shift+L
Word Wrap	Ctrl+Shift+W	Cmd+Shift+W
Hide Panels	F4	F4

Tools Menu

Command	Windows Shortcut	MacOS Shortcut
Auto Format	Ctrl+Shift+F	Cmd+Shift+F
Check Syntax	Ctrl+T	Cmd+T
Show Code Hint	Ctrl+Spacebar	Ctrl+Spacebar

Control Menu

Command	Windows Shortcut	MacOS Shortcut
Test Project	Ctrl+Alt+P	Cmd+Opt+P

Actions Panel Shortcuts

Command	Windows Shortcut	MacOS Shortcut
Pin Script	Ctrl+=	Cmd+=
Close Script	Ctrl+-	Cmd+-
Close All Scripts	Ctrl+Shift+-	Cmd+Shift+-
Go to Line	Ctrl+G	Cmd+G
Find and Replace	Ctrl+F	Cmd+F
Find Again	F3	F3
Auto Format	Ctrl+Shift+F	Cmd+Shift+F
Check Syntax	Ctrl+T	Cmd+T
Show Code Hint	Ctrl+Spacebar	Ctrl+Spacebar
Import Script	Ctrl+Shift+I	Cmd+Shift+I
Export Script	Ctrl+Shift+X	Cmd+Shift+X
Script Assist	Ctrl+Shift+E	Cmd+Shift+E
Hidden Characters	Ctrl+Shift+8	Cmd+Shift+8
Line Numbers	Ctrl+Shift+L	Cmd+Shift+L
Word Wrap	Ctrl+Shift+W	Cmd+Shift+W
Preferences	Ctrl+U	Cmd+U
Indent Selected Code	Tab	Tab
Unindent Selected Code	Shift+Tab	Shift+Tab

Drawing IDE Shortcuts

File Menu

Command	Windows Shortcut	MacOS Shortcut
New	Ctrl+N	Cmd+N
Open	Ctrl+O	Cmd+O
Close	Ctrl+W	Cmd+W
Close All	Ctrl+Alt+W	Cmd+Opt+W
Save	Ctrl+S	Cmd+S
Save As	Ctrl+Shift+S	Cmd+Shift+S
Import⇨Import to Stage	Ctrl+R	Cmd+R
Import⇨Open External Library	Ctrl+Shift+O	Cmd+Shift+O
Export⇨Export Movie	Ctrl+Alt+Shift+S	Cmd+Opt+Shift+S
Publish Settings	Ctrl+Shift+F12	Opt+Shift+F12
Publish Preview⇨ Default - HTML	F12, Ctrl+F12	Cmd+F12
Publish	Shift+F12	Shift+F12
Print	Ctrl+P	Cmd+P
Exit	Ctrl+Q	Cmd+Q

Edit Menu

Command	Windows Shortcut	MacOS Shortcut
Undo	Ctrl+Z	Cmd+Z
Redo	Ctrl+Y	Cmd+Y
Cut	Ctrl+X	Cmd+X
Copy	Ctrl+C	Cmd+C
Paste in Center	Ctrl+V	Cmd+V
Paste in Place	Ctrl+Shift+V	Cmd+Shift+V

Table continued on following page

Command	Windows Shortcut	MacOS Shortcut
Clear	Backspace, Clear, Delete	Delete, Clear, del
Duplicate	Ctrl+D	Cmd+D
Select All	Ctrl+A	Cmd+A
Deselect All	Ctrl+Shift+A	Cmd+Shift+A
Find and Replace	Ctrl+F	Cmd+F
Find Next	F3	F3
Timeline⇨Cut Frames	Ctrl+Alt+X	Cmd+Opt+X
Timeline⇨Copy Frames	Ctrl+Alt+C	Cmd+Opt+C
Timeline⇨Paste Frames	Ctrl+Alt+V	Cmd+Opt+V
Timeline⇨Clear Frames	Alt+Backspace	Opt+Delete
Timeline⇨Remove Frames	Shift+F5	Shift+F5
Timeline⇨Select All Frames	Ctrl+Alt+A	Cmd+Opt+A
Edit Symbols	Ctrl+E	Cmd+E
Preferences	Ctrl+U	Cmd+U

View Menu

Command	Windows Shortcut	MacOS Shortcut
Go to⇨First	Home	Home
Go to⇨Previous	Page Up	Page Up
Go to⇨Next	Page Down	Page Down
Go to⇨Last	End	End
Zoom In	Ctrl+=	Cmd+=
Zoom Out	Ctrl+-	Cmd+-
Magnification⇨100%	Ctrl+1	Cmd+1
Magnification⇨400%	Ctrl+4	Cmd+4
Magnification⇨800%	Ctrl+8	Cmd+8
Magnification⇨Show Frame	Ctrl+2	Cmd+2

Command	Windows Shortcut	MacOS Shortcut
Magnification⇨Show All	Ctrl+3	Cmd+3
Preview Mode⇨Outlines	Ctrl+Alt+Shift+O	Cmd+Opt+Shift+O
Preview Mode⇨Fast	Ctrl+Alt+Shift+F	Cmd+Opt+Shift+F
Preview Mode⇨ Anti-Alias	Ctrl+Alt+Shift+A	Cmd+Opt+Shift+A
Preview Mode⇨ Anti-Alias Text	Ctrl+Alt+Shift+T	Cmd+Opt+Shift+T
Work Area	Ctrl+Shift+W	Cmd+Shift+W
Rulers	Ctrl+Alt+Shift+R	Cmd+Opt+Shift+R
Grid⇨Show Grid	Ctrl+' (apostrophe)	Cmd+' (apostrophe)
Grid⇨Edit Grid	Ctrl+Alt+G	Cmd+Opt+G
Guides⇨Show Guides	Ctrl+; (semicolon)	Cmd+; (semicolon)
Guides⇨Lock Guides	Ctrl+Alt+;	Cmd+Opt+;
Guides⇨Edit Guides	Ctrl+Alt+Shift+G	Cmd+Opt+Shift+G
Snapping⇨Snap to Grid	Ctrl+Shift+'	Cmd+Shift+'
Snapping⇨Snap to Guides	Ctrl+Shift+;	Cmd+Shift+;
Snapping⇨Snap to Objects	Ctrl+Shift+/	Cmd+Shift+/
Snapping⇨Edit Snapping	Ctrl+/	Cmd+/
Hide Edges	Ctrl+H	Cmd+Shift+E
Show Shape Hints	Ctrl+Alt+H	Cmd+Opt+H

Insert Menu

Command	Windows Shortcut	MacOS Shortcut
New Symbol	Ctrl+F8	Cmd+F8
Timeline⇨Frame	F5	F5

Modify Menu

Command	Windows Shortcut	MacOS Shortcut
Document	Ctrl+J	Cmd+J
Convert to Symbol	F8	F8

Table continued on following page

Command	Windows Shortcut	MacOS Shortcut
Break Apart	Ctrl+B	Cmd+B
Shape⇨Optimize	Ctrl+Alt+Shift+C	Cmd+Opt+Shift+C
Shape⇨Add Shape Hint	Ctrl+Shift+H	Cmd+Shift+H
Timeline⇨Distribute to Layers	Ctrl+Shift+D	Cmd+Shift+D
Timeline⇨Convert to Keyframes	F6	F6
Timeline⇨Clear Keyframe	Shift+F6	Shift+F6
Timeline⇨Convert to Blank Keyframes	F7	F7
Transform⇨Scale and Rotate	Ctrl+Alt+S	Cmd+Opt+S
Transform⇨Rotate 90° CW	Ctrl+Shift+9	Cmd+Shift+9
Transform⇨Rotate 90° CCW	Ctrl+Shift+7	Cmd+Shift+7
Transform⇨Remove Transform	Ctrl+Shift+Z	Cmd+Shift+Z
Arrange⇨Bring to Front	Ctrl+Shift+Up	Cmd+Shift+Up
Arrange⇨Bring Forward	Ctrl+Up	Cmd+Up
Arrange⇨Send Backward	Ctrl+Down	Cmd+Down
Arrange⇨Send to Back	Ctrl+Shift+Down	Cmd+Shift+Down
Arrange⇨Lock	Ctrl+Alt+L	Cmd+Opt+L
Arrange⇨Unlock All	Ctrl+Alt+Shift+L	Cmd+Opt+Shift+L
Align⇨Left	Ctrl+Alt+1	Cmd+Opt+1
Align⇨Horizontal Center	Ctrl+Alt+2	Cmd+Opt+2
Align⇨Right	Ctrl+Alt+3	Cmd+Opt+3
Align⇨Top	Ctrl+Alt+4	Cmd+Opt+4
Align⇨Vertical Center	Ctrl+Alt+5	Cmd+Opt+5

Command	Windows Shortcut	MacOS Shortcut
Align⇨Bottom	Ctrl+Alt+6	Cmd+Opt+6
Align⇨Distribute Widths	Ctrl+Alt+7	Cmd+Opt+7
Align⇨Distribute Heights	Ctrl+Alt+9	Cmd+Opt+9
Align⇨Make Same Width	Ctrl+Alt+Shift+7	Cmd+Opt+Shift+7
Align⇨Make Same Height	Ctrl+Alt+Shift+9	Cmd+Opt+Shift+9
Align⇨To Stage	Ctrl+Alt+8	Cmd+Opt+8
Align⇨Group	Ctrl+G	Cmd+G
Align⇨Ungroup	Ctrl+Shift+G	Cmd+Shift+G

Text Menu

Command	Windows Shortcut	MacOS Shortcut
Style⇨Plain	Ctrl+Shift+P	Cmd+Shift+P
Style⇨Bold	Ctrl+Shift+B	Cmd+Shift+B
Style⇨Italic	Ctrl+Shift+I	Cmd+Shift+I
Align⇨Align Left	Ctrl+Shift+L	Cmd+Shift+L
Align⇨Align Center	Ctrl+Shift+C	Cmd+Shift+C
Align⇨Align Right	Ctrl+Shift+R	Cmd+Shift+R
Align⇨Justify	Ctrl+Shift+J	Cmd+Shift+J
Letter Spacing⇨Increase	Ctrl+Alt+Right	Cmd+Opt+Right
Letter Spacing⇨Decrease	Ctrl+Alt+Left	Cmd+Opt+Left
Letter Spacing⇨Reset	Ctrl+Alt+Up	Cmd+Opt+Up

Control Menu

Command	Windows Shortcut	MacOS Shortcut
Play	Enter	Enter
Rewind	Ctrl+Alt+R	Cmd+Opt+R

Table continued on following page

Command	Windows Shortcut	MacOS Shortcut
Step Forward One Frame	. (period)	. (period)
Step Backward One Frame	, (comma)	, (comma)
Test Movie	Ctrl+Enter	Cmd+Enter
Debug Movie	Ctrl+Shift+Enter	Cmd+Shift+Enter
Test Scene	Ctrl+Alt+Enter	Cmd+Opt+Enter
Test Project	Ctrl+Alt+P	Cmd+Opt+P
Enable Simple Frame Actions	Ctrl+Alt+F	Cmd+Opt+F
Enable Simple Buttons	Ctrl+Alt+B	Cmd+Opt+B
Mute Sounds	Ctrl+Alt+M	Cmd+Opt+M

Window Menu

Command	Windows Shortcut	MacOS Shortcut
Duplicate Window	Ctrl+Alt+K	Cmd+Opt+K
Timeline	Ctrl+Alt+T	Cmd+Opt+T
Tools	Ctrl+F2	Cmd+F2
Properties⇨Properties	Ctrl+F3	Cmd+F3
Library	Ctrl+L, F11	Cmd+L, Opt+F11
Actions	F9	Opt+F9
Behaviors	Shift+F3	Shift+F3
Debugger	Shift+F4	Shift+F4
Movie Explorer	Alt+F3	Opt+F3
Output	F2	F2
Project	Shift+F8	Shift+F8
Align	Ctrl+K	Cmd+K
Color Mixer	Shift+F9	Shift+F9
Color Swatches	Ctrl+F9	Cmd+F9
Info	Ctrl+I	Cmd+I
Transform	Ctrl+T	Cmd+T
Components	Ctrl+F7	Cmd+F7
Component Inspector	Alt+F7	Opt+F7

Command	Windows Shortcut	MacOS Shortcut
Other Panels⇨ Accessibility	Alt+F2	Opt+F2
Other Panels⇨History	Ctrl+F10	Cmd+F10
Other Panels⇨Scene	Shift+F2	Shift+F2
Other Panels⇨Strings	Ctrl+F11	Cmd+F11
Other Panels⇨Web Services	Ctrl+Shift+F10	Cmd+Shift+F10
Hide Panels	F4	F4

Help Menu

Command	Windows Shortcut	MacOS Shortcut
Flash Help	F1	F1

Index

powered by books24x7

Programmer to Programmer

Take your library wherever you go.

Now you can access more than 70 complete Wrox books online, wherever you happen to be! Every diagram, description, screen capture, and code sample is available with your subscription to the **Wrox Reference Library**. For answers when and where you need them, go to wrox.books24x7.com and subscribe today!

Find books on

- ASP.NET
- C#/C++
- Database
- General
- Java
- Mac
- Microsoft Office

- .NET
- Open Source
- PHP/MySQL
- SQL Server
- Visual Basic
- Web
- XML

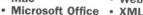 www.wrox.com